SECURITY+ TRAINING GUIDE OBJEC

Unit/Objective/Subobjective *Page*

continues

Security+

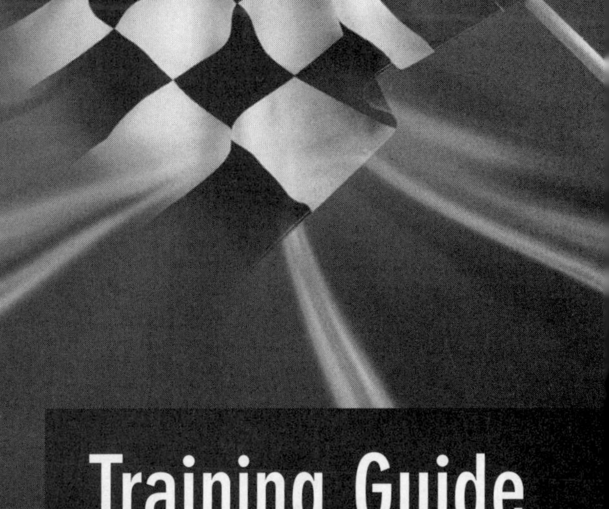

Todd King

Training Guide

SECURITY+ TRAINING GUIDE

International Standard Book Number: 0-7897-2836-2

Library of Congress Catalog Card Number: 2002108480

Printed in the United States of America

First Printing: April 2003

06 05 04 03 4 3 2 1

Trademarks

All terms mentioned in this book that are known to be trademarks or service marks have been appropriately capitalized. Que Certification cannot attest to the accuracy of this information. Use of a term in this book should not be regarded as affecting the validity of any trademark or service mark.

Warning and Disclaimer

Every effort has been made to make this book as complete and as accurate as possible, but no warranty or fitness is implied. The information provided is on an "as is" basis. The authors and the publisher shall have neither liability nor responsibility to any person or entity with respect to any loss or damages arising from the information contained in this book or from the use of the CD or programs accompanying it.

PUBLISHER
Paul Boger

EXECUTIVE EDITOR
Jeff Riley

DEVELOPMENT EDITOR
Steve Rowe

MANAGING EDITOR
Charlotte Clapp

PROJECT EDITOR
Tonya Simpson

PRODUCTION EDITOR
Megan Wade

INDEXER
Chris Barrick

PROOFREADER
Juli Cook

TECHNICAL EDITORS
Patrick Ramseier
Clement DuPuis

TEAM COORDINATOR
Pamalee Nelson

MULTIMEDIA DEVELOPER
Dan Scherf

INTERIOR DESIGNER
Louisa Klucznik

COVER DESIGNER
Charis Ann Santillie

PAGE LAYOUT
Cheryl Lynch

Que Certification • 201 West 103rd Street • Indianapolis, Indiana 46290

A Note from Series Editor Ed Tittel

Congratulations on your purchase of *Security+ Training Guide*, the finest exam preparation book in the marketplace!

As Series Editor of the highly regarded Training Guide series, I can assure you that you won't be disappointed. You've taken your first step toward passing the Security+ exam, and we value this opportunity to help you on your way!

As a "Favorite Study Guide Author" finalist in a 2002 poll of CertCities readers, I know the importance of delivering good books. You'll be impressed with Que Certification's stringent review process, which ensures the books are high-quality, relevant, and technically accurate. Rest assured that at least a dozen industry experts—including the panel of certification experts at CramSession—have reviewed this material, helping us deliver an excellent solution to your exam preparation needs.

We've also added a preview edition of PrepLogic's powerful, full-featured test engine, which is trusted by certification students throughout the world.

As a 20-year-plus veteran of the computing industry and the original creator and editor of the Exam Cram series, I've brought my IT experience to bear on these books. During my tenure at Novell from 1989 to 1994, I worked with and around its excellent education and certification department. At Novell, I witnessed the growth and development of the first really big, successful IT certification program—one that was to shape the industry forever afterward. This experience helped push my writing and teaching activities heavily in the certification direction. Since then, I've worked on more than 70 certification related books, and I write about certification topics for numerous Web sites and for *Certification* magazine.

In 1997 when Exam Cram was introduced, it quickly became the best-selling computer book series since "*...For Dummies*," and the best-selling certification book series ever. By maintaining an intense focus on the subject matter, tracking errata and updates quickly, and following the certification market closely, Exam Cram was able to establish the dominant position in cert prep books.

You will not be disappointed in your decision to purchase this book. If you are, please contact me at etittel@jump.net. All suggestions, ideas, input, or constructive criticism are welcome!

Ed Tittel

CONTENTS AT A GLANCE

TABLE OF CONTENTS

Part II: Final Review

Part III: Appendixes

About the Author

Todd King currently serves as Chief Executive Officer for SYS Consulting and Training, Inc., a Denver-based computer-consulting firm. He has specialized in several areas of networking, including network design, analysis, and security. Prior to starting SYS, Inc., Todd was in the United States Air Force as a survival instructor. He currently holds a B.S. in marketing from Florida State University and an A.A. Instructor of Technology and an A.A. in Survival and Rescue Operations from the Community College of the Air Force. His professional certifications include MCSE on Windows 2000, MCSE +Internet on NT 4, MCSA, MCT, CCNP, CCDP, CNX, A+, Net+, iNet+, CTT, and Security+.

Acknowledgments

I would like to extend my deepest thanks to Ed Tittel and the team at LANWrights for their efforts in coordinating this book and taking a chance on an unpublished author. Thanks especially to Mary Burmeister for helping keep me on track and putting up with me. Thanks to James Michael Stewart for his endorsement of me and also to Kim Lindros for her initial efforts to get me on board this project. I would also like to thank the numerous other authors who contributed to this project: Dennis Suhanovs, Shawn Porter, John Pironti, Michael Solomon, John Millican, and Ed Tittel. Special thanks also goes to the Que Certification team who made this book possible: Jeff Riley, Steve Rowe, Tonya Simpson, Megan Wade, and the tech editors, Clement DuPuis and Patrick Ramseier.

Thanks, too, to Luke, DocJelly, and CB for their inspiration and help when needed. Finally, I would like to thank my wife, Lisa, for putting up with the late nights and weekends lost while I put my efforts into this book.—Todd King

We Want to Hear from You!

As the reader of this book, *you* are our most important critic and commentator. We value your opinion and want to know what we're doing right, what we could do better, what areas you'd like to see us publish in, and any other words of wisdom you're willing to pass our way.

As an executive editor for Que, I welcome your comments. You can email or write me directly to let me know what you did or didn't like about this book—as well as what we can do to make our books better.

Please note that I cannot help you with technical problems related to the *topic* of this book. We do have a User Services group, however, where I will forward specific technical questions related to the book.

When you write, please be sure to include this book's title and author as well as your name, email address, and phone number. I will carefully review your comments and share them with the author and editors who worked on the book.

Email: `feedback@quepublishing.com`

Mail: Jeff Riley
Que Certification
201 West 103rd Street
Indianapolis, IN 46290 USA

For more information about this book or another Que title, visit our Web site at `www.quepublishing.com`. Type the ISBN (excluding hyphens) or the title of a book in the Search field to find the page you're looking for.

How to Use This Book

Que Certification has made an effort in its Training Guide series to make the information as accessible as possible for the purposes of learning the certification material. Here, you have an opportunity to view the many instructional features that have been incorporated into the books to achieve that goal.

Chapter Opener

Each chapter begins with a set of features designed to allow you to maximize study time for that material.

List of Objectives: Each chapter begins with a list of the objectives as stated by Microsoft.

Objective Explanations: Immediately following each objective is an explanation of it, providing context that defines it more meaningfully in relation to the exam. Because Microsoft can sometimes be vague in its objectives list, the objective explanations are designed to clarify any vagueness by relying on the authors' test-taking experience.

OBJECTIVES

This chapter covers the following CompTIA objectives for the Security+ exam:

Understand basic terminology.

- There are a large number of words and acronyms used in the security industry. It is important to understand the meaning and use of each of them.

Recognize, explain, and differentiate access control methods.

- **Mandatory Access Control (MAC)**
- **Discretionary Access Control (DAC)**
- **Role-Based Access Control (RBAC)**

- The primary purpose of this objective is to help you identify the different methods that can be used to control access to resources in your security environment.

Recognize, explain, and differentiate authentication methods.

- **Username/Password**
- **Kerberos**
- **Challenge Handshake Authentication Protocol (CHAP)**
- **Certificates**
- **Tokens**
- **Biometrics**
- **Multifactor**
- **Mutual authentication**

- This objective shows the differences between authentication methods and which methods are preferred in a given situation.

CHAPTER 1

General Security Concepts

OUTLINE

Chapter Outline: Learning always gets a boost when you can see both the forest and the trees. To give you a visual image of how the topics in a chapter fit together, you will find a chapter outline at the beginning of each chapter. You will also be able to use this for easy reference when looking for a particular topic.

OUTLINE

STUDY STRATEGIES

- Communications security is a topic both broad and deep. Therefore, some of its aspects might not lend themselves to practice or hands-on experience as well as others do. But to get the most out of this chapter, you will need access to an installation of Microsoft Internet Information Server (IIS) version 5 or newer, Microsoft Internet Explorer (version 5.x or 6.x), and either Microsoft Outlook or Outlook Express.
- Make sure that you are familiar with the basic operation and commands associated with the most commonly used TCP/IP application protocols, including the File Transfer Protocol (FTP), Simple Mail Transfer Protocol (SMTP), and Hypertext Transfer Protocol (HTTP).
- Take some time and effort to set up a Web server and bring it to an up-to-date patch level. Request a trial X.509 certificate from a public certificate authority (CA) for testing purposes and use it to configure HTTP Secure (HTTPS) on your Web server. Request a personal X.509 certificate and use it with your email software to explore Secure/Multipurpose Internet Mail Extensions (S/MIME) functionality and issues.
- Set up a few Windows 2000 servers and configure virtual private network (VPN) servers and clients.

Study Strategies: Each topic presents its own learning challenge. To support you through this, Que Certification has included strategies for how to best approach studying in order to retain the material in the chapter, particularly as it is addressed on the exam.

INSTRUCTIONAL FEATURES WITHIN THE CHAPTER

These books include a large amount and different kinds of information. The many different elements are designed to help you identify information by its purpose and importance to the exam and also to provide you with varied ways to learn the material. You will be able to determine how much attention to devote to certain elements, depending on what your goals are. By becoming familiar with the different presentations of information, you will know what information will be important to you as a test-taker and which information will be important to you as a practitioner.

EXAM TIP

As you work your way through the book, you will likely run across many of these words and acronyms. As you come across these new terms, try writing the definitions until you have them memorized.

Exam Tip: Exam Tips appear in the margins to provide specific exam-related advice. Such tips may address what material is covered (or not covered) on the exam, how it is covered, mnemonic devices, or particular quirks of that exam.

Note: Notes appear in the margins and contain various kinds of useful information, such as tips on the technology or administrative practices, historical background on terms and technologies, or side commentary on industry issues.

Chapter 1 GENERAL SECURITY CONCEPTS 37

Early access control policy was first defined by the military. In 1967, a group was assembled to review and address computer security issues. The government and military networks of the time stored sensitive and classified information on their systems. This information needed to be protected while being stored, as well as while in transit between newly connected sites. The task force group published a document called "Security Controls for Computer Systems," which eventually evolved into what we know today as the "Orange Book." The Orange Book, or Trusted Computer System Evaluation Criteria (TCSEC), sets the criteria for deployment, configuration, and evaluation of computer systems in a secure manner. In addition, the Orange Book defines a classification hierarchy for computer security in an effort to make deployment and maintenance of a required (or desired) security level easier.

NOTE

It should be noted that these policies are not mutually exclusive. An organization might choose to deploy one, two, or all three types of access control to achieve its security goals.

ACCESS CONTROL TECHNIQUES

Recognize, explain, and differentiate access control methods.

Access control is best described as the process by which use of resources and services is granted or denied. To be effective, access control is used in conjunction with authentication (which is covered in detail in the following section). After a user or device has identified itself to the network, controls can be put in place that grant or deny rights and privileges to that user's ID. The method for putting those controls in place is referred to as an *access control policy.*

Objective Coverage Text: In the text before an exam objective is specifically addressed, you will notice the objective is listed to help call your attention to that particular material.

WARNING

Pay Attention to How the Message Encryption Process Really Works
It is a fairly popular misconception to assume that messages get encrypted to the sender's private key and decrypted by the sender's public key. If this were the case, the attacker would be able to decrypt intercepted communication using a public key attached with the sender's X.509 certificate.

Warning: In using sophisticated information technology, there is always potential for mistakes or even catastrophes that can occur through improper application of the technology. Warnings appear in the margins to alert you to such potential problems.

STEP BY STEP

9.1 Assigning User-Based Privileges in Windows 2000 Professional

1. Create a user account by right-clicking My Computer and selecting Manage. This launches the Computer Management MMC interface.
2. Select the Local Users and Groups node in the left window pane, and select the Users folder (see Figure 9.1). Create a user named Bob.

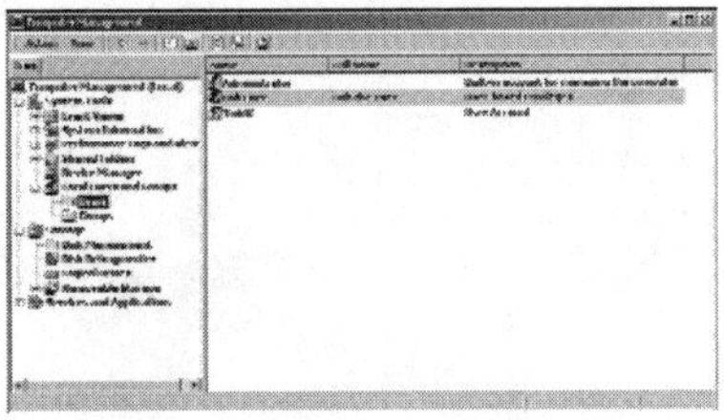

FIGURE 9.1
Creating a user in Windows 2000.

NOTE

Problems Viewing the Security Tab If the Security tab doesn't show, the volume is not formatted as an NTFS volume and this exercise won't work.

Remove Everyone To achieve true user-level privilege settings, you need to remove the default group Everyone.

3. Launch Windows Explorer and create a folder called Test, as shown in Figure 9.2.

Step by Step: Step by Steps are hands-on tutorial instructions that walk you through a particular task or function relevant to the exam objectives.

Figure: To improve readability, the figures have been placed in the margins wherever possible so they do not interrupt the main flow of text.

Chapter 1 GENERAL SECURITY CONCEPTS 27

As businesses adopted the use of computers, more and more proprietary data was stored on them. Information is still the single most important resource. Now, instead of managing business networks of 10–25 computers, we have networks of thousands and thousands of computers. Throw the Internet into the mix and the sheer number of systems becomes staggering. Businesses now store vital data on computers, and this information needs to be protected. Examples of common business information you might want to protect are as follows:

REVIEW BREAK

MAC, DAC, and RBAC

- MAC is an access control method centrally controlled and managed. Users have no influence on permissions and can't pass permissions on.
- DAC allows users to set permissions as they see the need to do so, within the guidelines of the broader MAC guidelines.
- RBAC is a more complete integration of MAC and DAC, focusing on group management instead of users. Security administrators group users and assign MAC permissions based on a role in the company. DAC is used by users in the groups to manage finer permissions control.

Review Break: Crucial information is summarized at various points in the book in lists or tables. At the end of a particularly long section, you might come across a Review Break that is there just to wrap up one long objective and reinforce the key points before you shift your focus to the next section.

IN THE FIELD

INTERNAL NETWORK SECURITY

How important is internal network security? We see people every year spend millions of dollars protecting their networks from the Internet. The Internet does pose an enormous threat to any company connected to it, but you can't forget to protect the network from the inside out.

We started a risk analysis for a widget manufacturing firm (they shall remain nameless to protect the innocent). We spent about four weeks interviewing employees, meeting with the executives, and planning with the people in the information technology (IT) department. This was an overhaul of their existing security policy, which had been in place for about two years. A lot had changed in two years.

continues

In the Field Sidebar: These more extensive discussions cover material that perhaps is not as directly relevant to the exam, but which is useful as reference material or in everyday practice. In the Field may also provide useful background or contextual information necessary for understanding the larger topic under consideration.

CASE STUDIES

Case Studies are presented throughout the book to provide you with another, more conceptual opportunity to apply the knowledge you are developing. They also reflect the "real-world" experiences of the authors in ways that prepare you not only for the exam but for actual network administration as well. In each Case Study, you will find similar elements: a description of a Scenario, the Essence of the Case, and an extended Analysis section.

CASE STUDY: TIMBER NETWORK, INC.

ESSENCE OF THE CASE

Here are the essential elements in this case:

- Identify the members of the security policy development committee.
- Identify each element of the security policy necessary for this organization.
- Incorporate any legal or regulatory requirements applicable to this industry.
- Establish strategies for security policy approval, implementation, and maintenance.
- Implement the security policy.

SCENARIO

Timber Network, Inc., is a provider of secure business-to-business communication services focusing on the timber industry. Timber Network's clients use its services to conduct business electronically, cutting down paperwork and delays in order processing. The generic interface enables many providers and consumers to pass transaction messages to and from each other without the requirement that each vendor support all other interface types.

Essence of the Case: A bulleted list of the key problems or issues that need to be addressed in the Scenario.

Scenario: A few paragraphs describing a situation that professional practitioners in the field might face. A Scenario will deal with an issue relating to the objectives covered in the chapter, and it includes the kinds of details that make a difference.

Analysis: This is a lengthy description of the best way to handle the problems listed in the Essence of the Case. In this section, you might find a table summarizing the solutions, a worded example, or both.

CASE STUDY: TIMBER NETWORK, INC.

Timber Network's security staff is developing an updated security policy to address potential concerns related to the growth of the business and integration of federally regulated transactions. The Environmental Protection Agency (EPA) regulates transactions involving federally protected timber and requires standards of operation and reporting. Instead of modifying the existing policy, Timber Network has decided to create a new security policy to address all the current business needs.

Consider the elements Timber Network should address as it develops a security strategy.

ANALYSIS

The most important step in creating a security policy is to establish a policy committee that includes as many representatives from management and organization executives as possible. The only way a policy will have sufficient momentum to be effective is through the support from the top of an organization. After the policy team is selected, it will meet to decide on the major elements of the security policy. Timber Network decides to create a simple policy consisting of the following sections:

- Acceptable use policy
- Privacy policy
- Separation of duties policy
- Password policy
- Human resource policy
- Incident response policy
- Regulatory compliance policy
- Code of ethics
- Implementation and maintenance policy

Policy owners are assigned for each element of the policy, and each owner develops a section. For example, the Security Director develops the password policy and incident response policy. After the initial drafts are completed, the policy team reviews and amends the policies until the policy is adopted. After all policies are adopted, the overall security policy is published and the implementation phase begins.

Remember that the development of a security policy is an iterative process in which standards, guidelines, and procedures are also included in each element.

EXTENSIVE REVIEW AND SELF-TEST OPTIONS

At the end of each chapter, along with some summary elements, you will find a section called "Apply Your Knowledge" that gives you several different methods with which to test your understanding of the material and review what you have learned.

CHAPTER SUMMARY

KEY TERMS

- Availability
- Chain of custody
- Code of ethics
- Confidentiality
- Due care
- Evidence
- Guideline
- Incident
- Integrity

In this chapter, we discussed the importance of a strong, cohesive security policy from a competitive business perspective and from the legal realities organizations find themselves dealing with in today's marketplace. The best first defense from security violations and related problems is a strong security policy. It documents the organization's vision and preparation in addressing various security threats.

A good security policy is really a collection of smaller, targeted policies. Each element of the overall security policy addresses concerns in a specific area. The following policy areas were covered in this chapter:

- Acceptable use policy
- Due care policy
- Privacy policy

Key Terms: A list of key terms appears at the end of each chapter. These are terms that you should be sure you know and are comfortable defining and understanding when you go in to take the exam.

Chapter Summary: Before the Apply Your Knowledge section, you will find a chapter summary that wraps up the chapter and reviews what you should have learned.

Chapter 8 SECURITY POLICY AND PROCEDURES 523

APPLY YOUR KNOWLEDGE

Exercises

8.1 Choosing Appropriate Security Policy Elements

In this exercise, you develop an awareness of the types of policies required for your own organization.

Estimated Time: 15 minutes

Think about the major operational groups of your organization. Create a short list of each of the groups (divisions, departments, and so on) that would need a specific security policy. One group we discussed in this chapter was the human resources group. See if you can identify any others.

Create a list of each group and the major features of a policy each might need when developing a comprehensive security policy. Remember, this is an exercise. It is not necessary for your list to be exhaustive. The point of the exercise is to begin the process of thinking about security needs from a high level.

8.2 Developing a Hiring Policy

In this exercise, you develop one of the policies discussed in the chapter. When a new employee is hired, certain tasks must be completed to ensure the overall security of your system.

Estimated Time: 10 minutes

Create a list of items that must be completed for each new employee. You can express this list as a set of guidelines (high-level tasks) or as a procedure (specific steps to take). Think of everything a new employee must have and know to access appropriate parts of your information system. Do not forget about any necessary training!

Review Questions

1. What is a security policy, and how does it affect the security of an organization?
2. Which element of a security policy (policies, guidelines, procedures, or standards) is the most detailed?
3. What are three methods used to implement separation of duties?
4. Are long passwords more secure than short passwords?
5. What is an incident?

Exam Questions

1. Who is responsible for security in an organization? (Choose the best answer.)

   A. Executives

   B. Everyone

   C. Management

   D. Staff

   E. Consultants

2. Which is the best definition of a procedure?

   A. Protection for unauthorized access

   B. Legally binding rules

   C. Step-by-step instructions

   D. Foundation for policies

   E. Shop standards

Review Questions: These open-ended, short-answer questions allow you to quickly assess your comprehension of what you just read in the chapter. Instead of asking you to choose from a list of options, these questions require you to state the correct answers in your own words. Although you will not experience these kinds of questions on the exam, these questions will indeed test your level of comprehension of key concepts.

Exam Questions: These questions reflect the kinds of multiple-choice questions that appear on the Microsoft exams. Use them to become familiar with the exam question formats and to help you determine what you know and what you need to review or study more.

Exercises: These activities provide an opportunity for you to master specific hands-on tasks. Our goal is to increase your proficiency with the product or technology. You must be able to conduct these tasks in order to pass the exam.

Chapter 8 SECURITY POLICY AND PROCEDURES 523

APPLY YOUR KNOWLEDGE

Exercises

8.1 Choosing Appropriate Security Policy Elements

In this exercise, you develop an awareness of the types of policies required for your own organization.

Estimated Time: 15 minutes

Think about the major operational groups of your organization. Create a short list of each of the groups (divisions, departments, and so on) that would need a specific security policy. One group we discussed in this chapter was the human resources group. See if you can identify any others.

Create a list of each group and the major features of a policy each might need when developing a comprehensive security policy. Remember, this is an exercise. It is not necessary for your list to be exhaustive. The point of the exercise is to begin the process of thinking about security needs from a high level.

8.2 Developing a Hiring Policy

In this exercise, you develop one of the policies discussed in the chapter. When a new employee is hired, certain tasks must be completed to ensure the overall security of your system.

Estimated Time: 10 minutes

Create a list of items that must be completed for each new employee. You can express this list as a set of guidelines (high-level tasks) or as a procedure (specific steps to take). Think of everything a new employee must have and know to access appropriate parts of your information system. Do not forget about any necessary training!

Review Questions

1. What is a security policy, and how does it affect the security of an organization?
2. Which element of a security policy (policies, guidelines, procedures, or standards) is the most detailed?
3. What are three methods used to implement separation of duties?
4. Are long passwords more secure than short passwords?
5. What is an incident?

Exam Questions

1. Who is responsible for security in an organization? (Choose the best answer.)

   A. Executives

   B. Everyone

Answers to Exam Questions

1. **B.** Although all answers are partially correct, the best answer is everyone because a chain is only as strong as its weakest link.
2. **C.** The answer is step-by-step instructions. The other answers address unrelated topics.
3. **C.** Many incidents are not identified as violations to the security policy. Although the other answers might indicate why a specific incident was not reported, the most common reason is lack of recognition.

Answers and Explanations: For each of the Review and Exam questions, you will find thorough explanations located at the end of the section.

Suggested Readings and Resources: The very last element in every chapter is a list of additional resources you can use if you want to go above and beyond certification-level material or if you need to spend more time on a particular subject that you are having trouble understanding.

526 Part I EXAM PREPARATION

APPLY YOUR KNOWLEDGE

Suggested Readings and Resources

Publications

1. Amoroso, Edward G. *Fundamentals of Computer Security Technology.* Upper Saddle River, NJ: Prentice Hall, 1994.
2. Department of Defense. *Department of Defense Trusted Computer System Evaluation Criteria.* Darby, PA: Diane Publishing Co., 1985.
3. Krause, Micki and Harold F. Tipton, eds. *Information Security Management Handbook, Fourth Edition Volume I.* Boca Raton, FL: Auerbach Publications, 1999.
4. Smith, Martin R. *Commonsense Computer Security: Your Practical Guide to Information Protection, Second Edition.* New York: McGraw-Hill Companies, 1994.
5. Russell, Deborah and G. T. Gangemi, Sr. *Computer Security Basics.* Sebastapol, CA: O'Reilly & Associates, Inc., 1991.
6. Weckert, John and Douglas Adeney. *Computer and Information Ethics.* Westport, CT: Greenwood Publishing Group, 1997.

Introduction

The *Security+ Training Guide* is designed for aspiring security professionals, system or network administrators, or other information technology professionals with the goal of obtaining the CompTIA Security+ certification. According to CompTIA, "There is an undeniable need for a mechanism that provides a knowledgeable and skilled IT security workforce with validated skills. Holding the Security+ certification verifies a job candidate's abilities and takes the guesswork out of hiring, while filling this important gap in the IT workforce."

This book is your one-stop shop. Everything you need to know to pass the exam is in here. You do not have to take a class in addition to buying this book to pass the exam. However, depending on your personal study habits or learning style, you might benefit from buying this book *and* taking a class.

Que Certification Training Guides are meticulously crafted to give you the best possible learning experience. The instructional design implemented in the Training Guides reflects the content and focus of the Security+ certification exam. This Training Guide provides you with the factual knowledge base you need for the exam and takes it to the next level with case studies, step by steps, exercises, and exam questions that require you to engage in the analytic thinking and problem solving necessary to successfully answering the questions found in the Security+ exam.

How This Book Helps You

This book takes you on a self-guided tour of all the areas covered by the Security+ exam and teaches you the specific skills you need to achieve that certification.

This book also includes helpful hints, tips, real-world examples, and exercises, as well as references to additional study materials. Specifically, this book is set up to help you in the following ways:

- **Organization**—The book is organized by individual exam objectives. Every objective you need to know for the Security+ exam is covered in this book. We have attempted to present the objectives in a way that matches how they're organized in the CompTIA exam objectives. However, we have not hesitated to reorganize those objectives where necessary to make the material as easy as possible for you to learn. We have also attempted to make the information accessible in the following ways:
  - The full list of exam units and objectives is included in the beginning of this book.
  - A Study and Exam Tips section is added at the beginning of your Training Guide. Read this section early on to help you develop effective study strategies for learning the content in the *Security+ Training Guide*. This section also provides valuable exam-day tips and information on adaptive tests.
  - Each chapter begins with a list of the objectives to be covered.
  - Each chapter also begins with an outline that provides an overview of the material and the page numbers where particular topics can be found.
  - The objectives are repeated where the material most directly relevant to it is covered (unless the whole chapter addresses a single objective).

- **Instructional features**—This book has been designed to provide you with multiple ways to learn and reinforce the exam material. Following are some of the helpful methods:
  - **Objective Explanations**—As mentioned previously, each chapter begins with a list of the objectives covered in the chapter. In addition, immediately following each objective is an explanation in a context that defines it more meaningfully.
  - **Study Strategies**—The beginning of the chapter also includes strategies for approaching the studying and retaining of the material in the chapter, not only particularly as it is addressed on the exam, but also in ways that will benefit you on the job.
  - **Exam Tips**—Exam tips appear in the margins to provide specific exam-related advice. Such tips address what material is covered (or not covered) on the exam, how it is covered, mnemonic devices, or particular quirks of that exam.
  - **Review Breaks and Summaries**—Crucial information is summarized at various points in the book in lists or tables. Each chapter also ends with a summary.
  - **Key Terms**—A list of key terms appears at the end of each chapter.
  - **Notes**—These appear in the margins and contain various types of useful or practical information, such as tips on technology or administrative practices, historical background on terms and technologies, or side commentary on industry issues.
  - **Warnings**—When designing, implementing, or applying security policy, practices, or procedures, the potential for mistakes or even catastrophes that occur because of improper designs or settings exists. Warnings appear in the margins to alert you to such potential problems.
  - **In the Field**—These discussions cover material that might not be directly relevant to the exam but that is useful as reference material or in everyday practice. In the Field sidebars also can provide useful background or contextual information necessary for understanding the larger topic under consideration.
  - **Case Studies**—Each chapter concludes with a case study. The cases are meant to help you understand the practical applications of the information covered in the chapter. They also help prepare you for the knowledge of terminology, concepts, and best security practices that is required when answering Security+ exam questions.
  - **Step By Steps**—These are hands-on, tutorial instructions that walk you through a particular task, analysis, or function relevant to the exam objectives.
  - **Exercises**—Found at the end of the chapter in the "Apply Your Knowledge" section, exercises are performance-based opportunities for you to learn and assess your knowledge.
- **Extensive practice test options**—This book provides numerous opportunities for you to assess your knowledge and practice for the exam. The practice options include the following:
  - **Review Questions**—These open-ended questions appear in the "Apply Your Knowledge" section at the end of each chapter.

They allow you to quickly assess your comprehension of what you just read in the chapter. Answers to the questions are provided later in a separate section titled "Answers to Review Questions."

- **Exam Questions**—These questions also appear in the "Apply Your Knowledge" section. Use them to help you determine what you know and what you need to review or study further. Answers and explanations for them are provided in a separate section titled "Answers to Exam Questions."
- **Practice Exam**—A practice exam is included in the "Final Review" section. The "Final Review" section and the "Practice Exam" are discussed shortly. There is also a Practice Exam on the CD:
    - **PrepLogic**—The *PrepLogic Practice Tests, Preview Edition* software included on the CD-ROM provides further practice questions.

> **NOTE** For a description of the PrepLogic software, please see Appendix F, "Using the *PrepLogic Practice Tests, Preview Edition* Software."

- **Final Review**—This part of the book provides you with two valuable tools for preparing for the exam:
    - **Fast Facts**—This condensed version of the information contained in the book will prove extremely useful for last-minute review.
    - **Practice Exam**—A practice test is included. Questions are written in a style similar to that used on the actual exam. Use it to assess your readiness for the real thing, and use the extensive answer explanations to improve your retention and understanding of the material.

The book includes several other features, such as a section titled "Suggested Reading and Resources" at the end of each chapter that directs you toward further information that could help you in your exam preparation or your actual work. There are valuable appendixes as well, including a glossary (Appendix B), an overview of the CompTIA certification program (Appendix D), and a description of what is on the CD-ROM (Appendix E).

CompTIA exams are provided by Vue and Thompson Prometric. For more information about the exam or the certification process in North America, contact Vue at

Vue Testing Services: 877-551-PLUS (7587)

`http://www.vue.com/comptia/`

Or, you can contact Thompson Prometric at

Thompson Prometric Security+: 800-977-3926

`http://www.2test.com/tcl/ZipCode.jsp`

What the Security+ Exam Covers

The Security+ Exam (SY0-101) covers the computer security associate topics represented by the test objectives. These objectives reflect knowledge about the following concepts, practices, procedures, processes, methodologies, and so forth:

- 1.0 General Security Concepts—30% of the exam
- 2.0 Communication Security—20% of the exam

- 3.0 Infrastructure Security—20% of the exam
- 4.0 Basics of Cryptography—15% of the exam
- 5.0 Operational/Organizational Security—15% of the exam

> **NOTE** The preceding objectives are quoted verbatim from the "CompTIA Security+" Web page at `http://www.comptia.com` with permission from CompTIA Corporation.

Before taking the exam, you should be proficient in the various topic areas just quoted in the following sections.

1.0 General Security Concepts

- Access Control
  - MAC/DAC/RBAC
- Authentication
  - Kerberos
  - CHAP
  - Certificates
  - Username/Password
  - Tokens
  - Multifactor
  - Mutual authentication
  - Biometrics
- Nonessential Services and Protocols—Disabling unnecessary systems/process/programs
- Attacks
  - DOS/DDOS
  - Back door
  - Spoofing
  - Man-in-the-middle
  - Replay
  - TCP/IP hijacking
  - Weak keys
  - Mathematical
  - Social engineering
  - Birthday
  - Password guessing
  - Brute-force
  - Dictionary
  - Software exploitation
- Malicious Code
  - Viruses
  - Trojan horses
  - Logic bombs
  - Worms
- Social Engineering
- Auditing—Logging and System Scanning

2.0 Communication Security

- Remote Access
  - 802.1x
  - VPN

- RADIUS
- TACACS/+
- L2TP/PPTP
- SSH
- IPSec
- Vulnerabilities

▶ Email

- S/MIME
- PGP
- Vulnerabilities
- Spam
- Hoaxes

▶ Web

- SSL/TLS
- HTTP/S
- Instant Messaging
- Vulnerabilities
- Naming conventions
- Packet sniffing
- Privacy
- Vulnerabilities
- JavaScript
- ActiveX
- Buffer overflows
- Cookies
- Signed applets
- CGI
- SMTP relay

▶ Directory—Recognition not Administration

- SSL/TLS
- LDAP

▶ File Transfer

- S/FTP
- Blind FTP/Anonymous
- File sharing
- Vulnerabilities
- Packet sniffing

▶ Wireless

- WTLS
- 802.11x
- WEP/WAP
- Vulnerabilities
- Site surveys

3.0 Infrastructure Security

▶ Devices

- Firewalls
- Routers
- Switches
- Wireless
- Modems
- RAS
- Telecom/PBX
- VPN
- IDS
- Network monitoring/diagnostic

- Workstations
- Servers
- Mobile devices

- Media
  - Coax
  - UTP/STP
  - Fiber
  - Removable media
  - Tape
  - CD-R
  - Hard drives
  - Disks
  - Flashcards
  - Smartcards
- Security Topologies
  - Security zones
  - DMZ
  - Intranet
  - Extranet
  - VLANs
  - NAT
  - Tunneling
- Intrusion Detection
  - Network-based
  - Active detection
  - Passive detection
  - Host-based
  - Honeypots
  - Incident response
- Security Baselines
  - OS/NOS hardening (concepts and processes)
  - File system
  - Updates (hotfixes, service packs, patches)
  - Network hardening
  - Updates (firmware)
  - Configuration
  - Enabling and disabling services and protocols
  - Access control lists
  - Application hardening
  - Updates (hotfixes, service packs, patches)
  - Web servers
  - Email servers
  - FTP servers
  - DNS servers
  - NNTP servers
  - File/print servers
  - DHCP servers
  - Data repositories
  - Directory services
  - Databases

4.0 Basics of Cryptography

- Algorithms
  - Hashing
  - Symmetric
  - Asymmetric

- Concepts of Using Cryptography
  - Confidentiality
  - Integrity
  - Digital signatures
  - Authentication
  - Nonrepudiation
  - Access control
- PKI
  - Certificates—make a distinction between which certificates are used for which purpose (basics only)
  - Certificate policies
  - Certificate practice statements
  - Revocation
  - Trust models
- Standards and Protocols
  - Key management/certificate lifecycle
  - Centralized versus decentralized
  - Storage
  - Hardware versus software
  - Private key protection
  - Escrow
  - Expiration
  - Revocation
  - Status checking
  - Suspension
  - Recovery
  - M of N control
  - Renewal
  - Destruction
  - Key usage
  - Multiple key pairs (single, dual)

5.0 Operational/Organizational Security

- Physical Security
  - Access control
  - Physical barriers
  - Biometrics
  - Social engineering
  - Environment
  - Wireless cells
  - Location
  - Shielding
  - Fire suppression
- Disaster Recovery
  - Backups
  - Offsite storage
  - Secure recovery
  - Alternative sites
  - Disaster recovery plan
- Business Continuity
  - Utilities
  - High availability/fault tolerance
  - Backups

- Policy and Procedures
  - Security policy
  - Acceptable use
  - Due care
  - Privacy
  - Separation of duties
  - Need to know
  - Password management
  - SLA
  - Disposal/destruction
  - HR policy
  - Termination—adding/revoking passwords, privileges, and so on
  - Hiring—adding/revoking passwords, privileges, and so on
  - Code of ethics
  - Incident response policy
- Privilege Management
  - User/Group/Role management
  - Single sign-on
  - Centralized versus decentralized
  - Auditing (privilege, usage, escalation)
  - MAC/DAC/RBAC
- Forensics (Awareness, Conceptual Knowledge, and Understanding—Know What Your Role Is)
  - Chain of custody
  - Preservation of evidence
  - Collection of evidence
- Risk Identification
  - Asset identification
  - Risk assessment
  - Threat identification
  - Vulnerabilities
- Education—Training of End Users, Executives, and HR
  - Communication
  - User awareness
  - Education
  - Online resources
- Documentation
  - Standards and guidelines
  - Systems architecture
  - Change documentation
  - Logs and inventories
  - Classification
  - Notification
  - Retention/Storage
  - Destruction

Hardware and Software You'll Need

As a self-paced study guide, *Security+ Training Guide* is meant to help you understand terms, concepts, and procedures that you can refine through hands-on experience. To make the most of your studying, you need to have as much background on and experience with system and network security as possible.

The best way to do this is to combine studying with work in the areas of system and network security. This section gives you a description of the minimum computer requirements you need to enjoy a solid practice environment.

Many of the concepts presented in this book explore the use of various security tools, utilities, commands, and applications. To fully practice some of the exam objectives, you will need access to two (or more) networked computers. Access to the Windows Server products might also be beneficial. The following presents a detailed list of hardware and software requirements:

- Windows XP Professional or Windows 2000 Professional (and optionally Windows 2000 Server or Windows Server 2003). Other operating systems, such as various versions of Unix, Linux, or the Macintosh OS might make a suitable substitute but often require the use of different, platform-specific security tools, utilities, commands, and applications.
- A server and a workstation computer on the Microsoft Hardware Compatibility List.
- Pentium 233MHz (or better) (Pentium 300 recommended).
- A minimum 1.5GB of free disk space.
- SuperVGA (800×600) or higher-resolution video adapter and monitor.
- Mouse or equivalent pointing device.
- CD-ROM or DVD drive.
- Network interface card (NIC) or modem connection to the Internet.
- Presence of an existing network or the use of a two-port (or more) miniport hub to create a test network.
- 128MB of RAM or higher (64MB minimum).

Obtaining access to the necessary computer hardware and software is easier in a corporate business environment. However, allocating enough time within the busy workday to complete a self-study program can be difficult. Most of your study time will occur after normal working hours, away from the everyday interruptions and pressures of your regular job.

Advice on Taking the Exam

More extensive tips are found in the Final Review section titled "Study and Exam Prep Tips," but keep this advice in mind as you study:

- **Read all the material**—CompTIA has been known to include material not expressly identified in the objectives. This book includes additional information not directly reflected in the objectives in an effort to give you the best possible preparation for the examination—and for real-world experiences to come.
- **Do the Step By Steps and complete the exercises in each chapter**—They will help you gain experience using the specified methodology or approach. As noted previously, good performance on the Security+ exam requires that you develop good analytical, troubleshooting, and problem-solving skills; completing these tasks will help you do so.
- **Use the questions to assess your knowledge**—Don't just read the chapter content; use the questions to find out what you know and what you don't. If you are struggling at all, study some more, review, and then assess your knowledge again.
- **Review the exam objectives**—Develop your own questions and examples for each topic listed. If you can develop and answer several questions for each topic, passing the exam should not be difficult.

NOTE

Exam-Taking Advice Although this book is designed to prepare you to take and pass the Security+ certification exam, there are no guarantees. Read this book, work through the questions and exercises, and when you feel confident take the Practice Exam and additional exams using the *PrepLogic Practice Tests, Preview Edition* software. This should tell you whether you are ready for the real thing.

When taking the actual certification exam, be sure you answer all the questions before your time limit expires. Do not spend too much time on any question. If you are unsure, answer it as best you can and then mark it for review when you have finished the rest of the questions. However, this advice will not apply if you are taking an adaptive exam. In that case, take your time on each question. There is no opportunity to go back to a question.

Remember, the primary object is not to pass the exam—it is to understand the material. After you understand the material, passing the exam should be simple. Knowledge is a pyramid; to build upward, you need a solid foundation. This book and the CompTIA certification programs are designed to ensure that you have that solid foundation.

Good luck!

QUE CERTIFICATION

The staff of Que Certification is committed to bringing you the very best in computer reference material. Each Que book is the result of months of work by authors and staff who research and refine the information contained within its covers.

As part of this commitment to you, the Que reader, Que invites your input. Please let us know whether you enjoy this book, whether you have trouble with the information or examples presented, or whether you have a suggestion for the next edition.

Please note, however, that the Que staff cannot serve as a technical resource during your preparation for the CompTIA certification exams or for questions about software- or hardware-related problems. Please refer instead to the email address, URLs, and phone numbers for CompTIA cited earlier in this Introduction.

If you have a question or comment about any Que book, there are several ways to contact Que Certification. We will respond to as many readers as we can. Your name, address, or phone number will never become part of a mailing list or be used for any purpose other than to help us continue to bring you the best books possible. You can write to us at the following address:

Que Certification
Attn: Jeff Riley
201 W. 103rd Street
Indianapolis, IN 46290

If you prefer, you can fax Que Certification at 317-817-7448.

You also can send email to Que at the following Internet address:

`feedback@quepublishing.com`

Que is an imprint of Pearson Education. To obtain a catalog or information, contact us at `quemedia@quepublishing.com`. To purchase a Que Certification book, call 800-428-5331.

Thank you for selecting *Security+ Training Guide*.

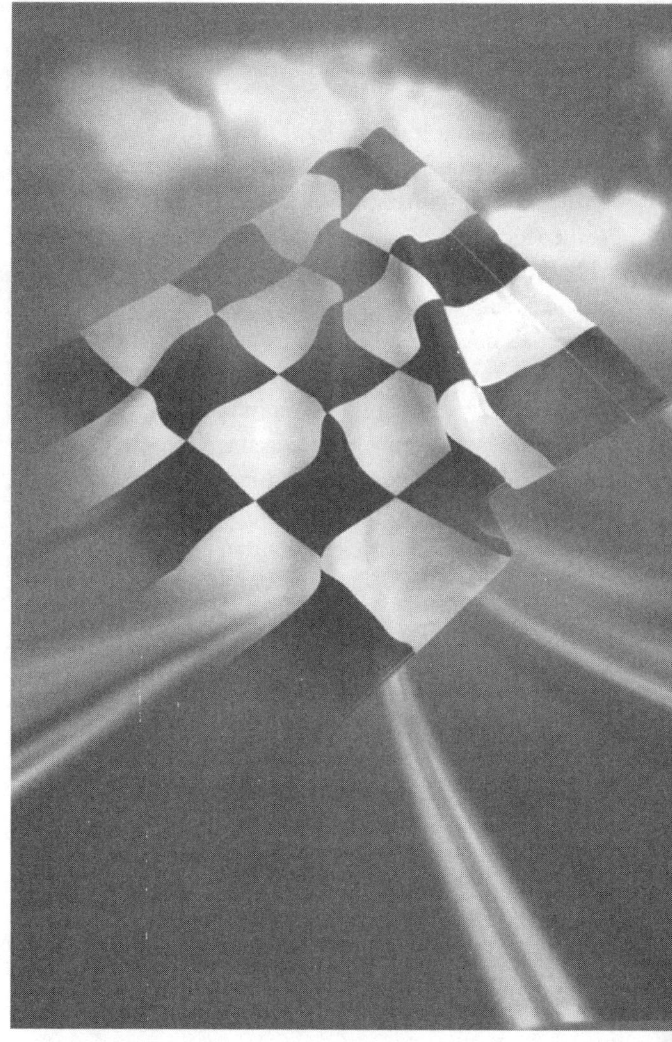

Study and Exam Prep Tips

This element of the book provides some general guidelines for preparing for the Security+ certification exam. It is organized into four sections. The first section addresses your learning style and how it affects your preparation for the exam. The second section covers your exam preparation activities and general study tips. This is followed by an extended look at the Security+ exam, including tips that apply to the Security+ exam format and question types. Finally, potential changes to the CompTIA testing policies, and how these might affect you, are discussed.

LEARNING STYLES

To better understand the nature of preparation for the test, you need to understand learning as a process. You are probably aware of how you best learn new material. You might find that outlining works best for you, or, if you are a visual learner, you might need to "see" things. Whatever your learning style, test preparation takes place over time. Obviously, you shouldn't start studying for an exam the night before you take it; it is essential to understand that learning is a developmental process. Understanding it as a process helps you focus on what you know and what you have yet to learn.

To help you recognize your preferred learning style, tackle any chapter in this book as an experiment and read through it. Try simply to read certain parts, skip diagrams and tables in other parts, read at least one part aloud to yourself, and take notes on one or more sections. Then, sit down and try to repeat as much of each section as you can remember. The section from which you remember the most—whether spoken, read, viewed, or noted—will help you identify which study techniques work best for you. Hence, it will also help you identify and make the most of your preferred learning style.

Thinking about how you learn should help you recognize that learning takes place when you are able to match new information to old. You have some previous experience with computers and networking, and general IT security. Now you are preparing for this certification exam. Using this book, software, and supplementary materials not only adds incrementally to what you know, but also, as you study, the organization of your knowledge actually restructures as you integrate new information into your existing knowledge base. This leads to a more comprehensive understanding of the tasks and concepts outlined in the objectives and of computing in general. Again, this happens as a result of a repetitive process rather than a singular event. Keep this model of learning in mind as you prepare for the exam, and you will make better decisions concerning what to study and how much more studying you need to do.

STUDY TIPS

There are many ways to approach studying, just as there are many types of material to study. However, the tips that follow should work well for the type of material covered on the certification exams.

Study Strategies

Although individuals vary in the ways they learn, some basic principles of learning apply to everyone. You should adopt some study strategies that take advantage of these principles. One of these principles is that learning can be broken into various depths. Recognition (of terms, for example) exemplifies a more surface level of learning in which you rely on a prompt of some sort to elicit recall. Comprehension or understanding (of the concepts behind the terms, for example) represents a deeper level of learning. The ability to analyze a concept and apply your understanding in a new way represents further depth of learning.

Your learning strategy should enable you to know the material at a level or two deeper than mere recognition. This helps you perform well on the exam. You will know the material so thoroughly that you can easily handle the recognition-level types of questions used in multiple-choice testing. You will also be able to apply your knowledge to solve new problems or synthesize concepts you might have dealt with only individually in the past.

Macro and Micro Study Strategies

One strategy that can lead to this deeper learning includes preparing an outline that covers all the objectives—and that breaks them into subobjectives—for the Security+ exam you are working on. You should delve a bit further into the material and include a level or two of detail beyond stated objectives and subobjectives for the exam. Then, expand your outline by coming up with a statement of definition or a summary for each point it holds.

An outline can offer two approaches to studying. First, you can study the outline by focusing on the organization of the material it covers. Work your way through the points and subpoints of your outline; make your goal to learn how they relate to one another. For example, be sure you understand how each one of the main objective areas is similar to and different from the other areas. Then, do the same thing with your subobjectives; be sure you know which subobjectives pertain to each objective area and how they relate to one another.

Next, you can work through the outline and focus on learning the details. Memorize and understand terms and their definitions, facts, rules and strategies, advantages and disadvantages, and so on. In this pass through the outline, attempt to learn detail rather than the big picture (the organizational information you worked on in the first pass through the outline).

Research has shown that attempting to assimilate both types of information at the same time seems to interfere with the overall learning process. Separate your studying into these two approaches, and you will perform better on the exam.

Active Study Strategies

The process of writing and defining objectives, subobjectives, terms, facts, and definitions promotes a more active learning strategy than merely reading the material. In human information-processing terms, writing information forces you to engage in more active encoding of the information. Simply reading it exemplifies more passive processing. Likewise, working through the various reviews and summaries in the materials and making notes on them also helps increase your knowledge of the details.

Next, determine whether you can apply the information you have learned by attempting to create examples and scenarios on your own. Think about how or where you could apply the concepts you are learning. Again, write down this information to process those facts and concepts actively.

The hands-on nature of the step-by-step tutorials and exercises at the end of each chapter provide further active learning opportunities and also reinforce concepts and skills.

Common-Sense Strategies

Finally, you should follow common-sense practices when studying. Study when you are alert, reduce or eliminate distractions, and take breaks when you become fatigued.

Give yourself sufficient time to absorb and master the material you are studying. Although life is full of deadlines, your test results are more likely to be positive if you give yourself enough time to read, learn, process, and integrate your new knowledge, rather than zoom forward to take the exam as soon as possible.

Pretesting Yourself

Pretesting allows you to assess how well you are learning. One of the most important aspects of learning is *meta-learning*. Meta-learning has to do with realizing when you know something well or when you need to study some more. In other words, you recognize how well or how poorly you have learned the material you are studying.

For most people, this can be difficult to assess objectively on their own. Practice tests are useful because they reveal more objectively what you have learned and what you have not learned. You should use this information—particularly for questions or topics you find difficult or for questions you cannot answer correctly—to guide review and further study. Developmental learning takes place as you cycle through studying, assessing how well you have learned, then reviewing, and then assessing again until you feel you are ready to take the exam.

You might have noticed a practice exam included in this book. Use it as part of the learning process. The *PrepLogic Practice Tests, Preview Edition* test simulation software included on the CD also provides an excellent opportunity to assess your knowledge. Together, these practice test banks give you three opportunities to perform a self-assessment.

You should seta goal for your pretesting. A reasonable goal would be to score consistently in the 90% range.

> **NOTE**
> See Appendix F, "Using the *PrepLogic Practice Tests, Preview Edition* Software," for more information on the test simulation software.

EXAM PREP TIPS

Having mastered the subject matter, the final preparatory step is to understand how the exam will be presented.

Make no mistake: The CompTIA Security+ exam will challenge your knowledge and test-taking skills. This section starts with the basics of exam design, reviews the primary exam format, talks about a future potential exam format, and concludes with hints targeted to each of the exam formats covered.

The Current Security+ Exam

At present, the Security+ exam is released in one basic format. What we call an exam format here is really little more than a combination of the overall exam structure and the presentation method for exam questions.

Understanding the exam format is key to good preparation because the format determines the number of questions presented, the difficulty of those questions, and the amount of time allowed to complete the exam.

When exam formats vary, each exam format uses the same types of questions. At present, the only types of questions used on the Security+ exam are variations on the standard multiple-choice question. In fact, you will encounter two basic types of multiple-choice questions on this exam: multiple-choice, single answer and multiple-choice, multiple answer (described in detail later).

It is important that you understand the types of questions you will be asked and the actions required to properly answer them.

The rest of this section addresses the current Security+ exam format, describes a potential new format the organization could introduce at any time, and then tackles the question types. Understanding these formats and question types will help you feel more comfortable when you take the exam.

Exam Format

The two basic formats for the CompTIA exams are the traditional *fixed-form exam* and the *adaptive form.* As its name implies, the fixed-form exam presents a fixed set of questions during the exam session. The adaptive form, however, uses only a subset of questions drawn from a larger pool based on your answers of previous questions. Although the same questions are used in an adaptive exam, there are likely to be fewer of them.

Fixed-Form

A fixed-form computerized exam is based on a fixed set of exam questions. Currently, this is the only form of the Security+ exam available. Here, individual questions are presented in random order during a test session. If you take the same exam more than once, you won't necessarily see the identical questions. This is because two or more final forms are typically assembled for every fixed-form exam CompTIA releases.

The final forms of a fixed-form exam are identical in terms of content coverage, number of questions, and allotted time, but the questions vary. You might notice, however, that some of the same questions appear on, or rather are shared among, different final forms. When questions are shared among multiple final forms of an exam, the percentage of sharing is generally small.

Fixed-form exams also have a fixed time limit in which you must complete the exam. The *PrepLogic Practice Tests, Preview Edition* software on the CD-ROM that accompanies this book provides fixed-form exams that match the characteristics of the current Security+ exam.

Finally, the score you achieve on a fixed-form exam, which is reported for the Security+ exams on a scale of 100 to 900, is based on the number of questions you answer correctly. The passing score for the Security+ exam is 764 (85% correct).

The typical format for a fixed-form exam is as follows:

- 100 questions.
- 90-minute maximum testing time (plus a 15-minute pre-exam practice session to learn how to use the testing software).
- Question review is allowed, including the opportunity to change your answers and move between questions.

Although CompTIA does not yet offer an adaptive form of the Security+ exam, they might choose to do so in the near future. That is why we describe this type of exam in the following section. (Because adaptive exams usually take much less time to complete than fixed-length ones, this allows testing centers to handle a greater number of test-takers; hence, the appeal of this offer.)

Adaptive Form

An adaptive-form exam has the same appearance as a fixed-form exam, but its questions differ in quantity and in their process of selection. Although the statistics of adaptive testing are fairly complex, this process determines your level of knowledge or understanding of the exam subject matter. This assessment begins with the presentation of questions of varying levels of difficulty and ascertaining at what difficulty level you can reliably answer them. Finally, the assessment determines whether that knowledge level is above or below the level required to pass the exam.

Examinees at different levels of knowledge see different sets of questions. Examinees who demonstrate little expertise with the subject matter continue to be presented with relatively easy questions. Examinees who demonstrate a high level of expertise are presented with progressively more difficult questions. Individuals whose knowledge falls into varying levels of expertise might answer the same number of questions correctly, but because the higher-expertise examinee can correctly answer more difficult questions, he receives a higher score and is more likely to pass the exam.

The typical design for the CompTIA adaptive form exam is as follows:

- 20–30 questions.
- 30-minute testing time.
- Question review is not allowed, providing no opportunity for you to change your answers or move between questions.

The Adaptive-Exam Process

Your first adaptive exam will be unlike any other testing experience you have had. In fact, many examinees have difficulty accepting the adaptive testing process because they feel that they were not provided the opportunity to adequately demonstrate their full expertise.

You can take consolation from the fact that adaptive exams are painstakingly put together after months of data gathering and analysis and that adaptive exams are every bit as valid as fixed-form exams. The rigor introduced through the adaptive testing methodology means that there is nothing arbitrary about the exam items you see. It is also a more efficient means of testing, requiring less time to conduct and complete than traditional fixed-form exams.

As the adaptive exam progresses, questions of varying difficulty are presented. Based on your pattern of responses to these questions, the knowledge assessment is recalculated. At the same time, the standard error estimate is refined from its initial estimated value of one toward some target value. When that standard error matches its target value (all this is handled in the background by the testing software), the exam is terminated. Thus, the more consistently you answer questions of the same degree of difficulty, the more quickly the standard error estimate drops, and the fewer questions you end up seeing during the exam session.

As you might suspect, one good piece of advice when taking an adaptive exam is to treat every exam question as if it were the most important one. The adaptive scoring algorithm attempts to discover a pattern of responses that reflects some level of proficiency with the subject matter. Incorrect responses almost guarantee that additional questions must be answered (unless, of course, you get every question wrong). This is because the scoring algorithm must adjust to information that is not consistent with the emerging pattern.

Question Types

Two basic question types appear on the Security+ exam. Examples of these two types appear in this book and the *PrepLogic Practice Tests, Preview Edition* software. We have attempted to cover all variations on these types that were known at the time of this writing. Most of the question types discussed in the following sections can appear in each of the two exam formats we've covered previously.

A typical Security+ exam question is based on the idea of measuring knowledge of important security terms and concepts and the ability to describe everyday security tasks. Therefore, most of the questions are written so as to present you with a statement of fact or a description of a set of circumstances or pose some kind of security problem. The answers indicate choices for proper names or terminology or descriptions of security tasks or regimens that you might apply to solve a problem. Keep this in mind as you read the questions on the exam. You will encounter many questions that call for you to recite various terms or facts, but you will also have to understand this information in context.

The following sections look at the two types of multiple-choice questions.

Multiple-Choice Questions

In the Security+ exam, the multiple-choice question is the sole type that appears. These multiple-choice questions come in two forms:

- **Regular multiple-choice**—Also called an alphabetic question, it asks you to choose one correct answer.
- **Multiple-answer multiple-choice**—Also called a multialphabetic question, this version of a multiple-choice question requires you to choose two or more answers as correct. Invariably, you are told precisely the number of correct answers to choose.

Examples of such questions appear at the end of each chapter.

Putting It All Together

Given all these pieces of information, the task now is to assemble a set of tips that will help you successfully tackle the various types of Security+ exams.

More Exam Preparation Tips

Generic exam-preparation advice is always useful. Tips include the following:

- Become familiar with the terms and concepts behind the exam material. Review the exercises and Step by Steps in the book.
- Review the current exam objectives on the CompTIA Web site. The documentation CompTIA makes available over the Web identifies the body of knowledge every exam is intended to test.

- Memorize foundational technical detail, and concentrate on mastering key terms, concepts, and (where appropriate) technologies.
- Take any of the available practice tests. We recommend the one included in this book and the ones you can create using the *PrepLogic Practice Tests, Preview Edition* software on the CD-ROM.
- Look on the CompTIA Web page for samples and demonstration items. These tend to be particularly valuable for one significant reason: They help you become familiar with new testing technologies before you encounter them on a real exam.

During the Exam Session

The following generic exam-taking advice that you've heard for years also applies when you're taking the Security+ exam:

- Take a deep breath and try to relax when you first sit down for your exam session. It is very important that you control the pressure you might (naturally) feel when taking exams.
- You will be provided scratch paper. Take a moment to write down any factual information and technical detail that you committed to short-term memory.
- Carefully read all information and instruction screens. These displays have been put together to give you information relevant to the exam you are taking.
- Accept the nondisclosure agreement and preliminary survey as part of the examination process. Complete them accurately and quickly move on.
- Read the exam questions carefully. Reread each question to identify all relevant detail. The Security+ exam has some questions that are purposely not clearly worded.
- Tackle the questions in the order in which they are presented. Skipping around won't build your confidence; the clock is always counting down.
- Don't rush, but also don't linger on difficult questions. The questions vary in degree of difficulty. Don't let yourself be flustered by a particularly difficult or wordy question—mark it and move on. You can later review marked items. Sometimes you will see questions, complimentary to the ones you could not answer earlier, which can inadvertently provide hints.

Fixed-Form Exams

Building from this basic preparation and test-taking advice, you also need to consider the challenges presented by the various exam designs. Because a fixed-form exam is composed of a fixed, finite set of questions, add these tips to your strategy for taking a fixed-form exam:

- Note the time allotted and the number of questions on the exam you are taking. Make a rough calculation of how many minutes you can spend on each question, and use this figure to pace yourself through the exam.
- Take advantage of the fact that you can return to and review skipped or previously answered questions. When you reach the end of the exam, return to the more difficult questions.
- If you have session time remaining after you complete all the questions (and if you aren't too fatigued), review your answers. Pay particular attention to questions that seem to have a lot of detail.
- As for changing your answers, the general rule here is *don't*! If you read the question carefully and completely and felt like you knew the correct answer, you probably did. Don't second-guess yourself.

If, as you check your answers, one clearly stands out as incorrect, however, of course you should change it. But if you are at all unsure, go with your first impression.

- Answer all the questions even if you are unsure of the correct answers. On a four-choice multiple-choice question there is a 25% chance that you will be right. To further increase your percentage in this category, use the "educated guess" approach, which involves eliminating all the choices that are obviously incorrect or silly. Choose the best answer, in your opinion, from the remaining choices. On a fixed exam, incorrect answers are better than incomplete ones.

Adaptive Exams

If you are planning to take an adaptive exam, keep these additional tips in mind:

- Read and answer every question with great care. When you're reading a question, identify every relevant detail, requirement, or task you must perform and double-check your answer to be sure you have addressed every one of them.
- If you cannot answer a question, use the process of elimination to reduce the set of potential answers, and then take your best guess. Stupid mistakes invariably mean that additional questions will be presented.
- You cannot review questions and change answers. When you leave a question, whether you've answered it or not, you cannot return to it. Do not skip any questions, either; if you do, they will be marked as incorrect.

FINAL CONSIDERATIONS

Here are some other requirements or factors you might need to consider as you plan to take (or retake) the Security+ exam:

- CompTIA puts no limit on the number or frequency of retakes, but you must pay another exam fee each time you take this exam. This fee depends on the price you paid for the initial exam. This can be a relatively heavy toll; therefore, you should study and prepare as thoroughly as possible in case you have to take this exam more than once. This will keep overall costs down. Better to wait and study a little longer and to spend less money than to rush to the next retake, only to fail again!
- New questions are likely to be seeded into the Security+ exam as time goes by. After performance data is gathered on new questions, examiners replace older questions on all exam forms. This means that the questions that appear on exams change regularly.
- The Security+ exam might be republished in adaptive form. In that case, follow our advice for that type of exam (which is why we included it here).

If you don't pass an exam on the first or second attempt, the exam's content (or form) could likely change significantly by the next time you take it. It could be updated from fixed-form to adaptive, or it could have a different set of questions or question types.

CompTIA's intention is not to make its exams more difficult by introducing unwanted change, but to create and maintain valid measures of the technical skills and knowledge associated with its credentials. Preparing for the Security+ exam means not only studying the subject matter, but also planning for the testing experience itself. With continuing changes likely, this is the only sane approach.

PART I

EXAM PREPARATION

OBJECTIVES

This chapter covers the following CompTIA objectives for the Security+ exam:

Understand basic terminology.

- ▶ There are a large number of words and acronyms used in the security industry. It is important to understand the meaning and use of each of them.

Recognize, explain, and differentiate access control methods.

- **Mandatory Access Control (MAC)**
- **Discretionary Access Control (DAC)**
- **Role-Based Access Control (RBAC)**

- ▶ The primary purpose of this objective is to help you identify the different methods that can be used to control access to resources in your security environment.

Recognize, explain, and differentiate authentication methods.

- **Username/Password**
- **Kerberos**
- **Challenge Handshake Authentication Protocol (CHAP)**
- **Certificates**
- **Tokens**
- **Biometrics**
- **Multifactor**
- **Mutual authentication**

- ▶ This objective shows the differences between authentication methods and which methods are preferred in a given situation.

CHAPTER 1

General Security Concepts

OBJECTIVES

Identify nonessential services and protocols and take the appropriate action.

- ▶ The complexity of modern operating systems becomes a factor when trying to secure your environment. This objective identifies common services that can be turned off or secured to help prevent unauthorized access.

Recognize attacks and take appropriate action.

- **DoS/DDoS**
- **Back door**
- **Spoofing**
- **Man-in-the-middle**
- **Replay**
- **Transmission Control Protocol/Internet Protocol (TCP/IP) hijacking**
- **Password guessing (brute force/dictionary)**
- **Software exploitation**

- ▶ This area is a crucial one. The objective here is to know your enemy. You need to know what types of attacks exist, to which attacks you might be vulnerable, and how to implement security to help prevent attacks against your network and its resources.

Recognize malicious code and take appropriate action.

- **Viruses**
- **Trojan horses**
- **Logic bombs**
- **Worms**

- ▶ Melissa, I Love You, Klez, Nimda, and Code Red are just a few of the more recent code attacks. Knowing how malicious code is used will help you protect your network and users from these and other common forms of attack.

Understand the concept of social engineering.

- ▶ Sometimes the most effective way to get what we want is to just ask. Social engineering exploits human nature and human behavior. This exam objective ensures that you are aware of this form of attack.

Understand the concepts of auditing.

- ▶ What files have changed? Who changed them? When was something last updated, modified, and by whom? All these questions can be answered using auditing. Tracking the use of resources and the attempted use of resources is an important feature of an ongoing security policy.

OUTLINE

Outline

Study Strategies

- Security is a broad subject. This chapter focuses on an overview and introduction to many security concepts. Consider this chapter as the topsoil of a football field—not deep, but very wide.
- When studying security, it is more important to understand the concepts than the mechanics. In other words, you should know what a given concept is in relation to security but not necessarily know how to deploy it in a particular operating system.

INTRODUCTION

Many certifications are worthy of pursuit in today's networking environment. However, security is probably one of the most interesting, dynamic, and challenging. The modern network is a complex mesh of different components with one purpose: to make resources available to legitimate users. Unfortunately, over the last decade, access to networks by unauthorized users has grown at an exponential rate. We develop and deploy equipment and applications so quickly to meet the demands of the computer consumer (both business and home consumers alike) that we do not have the time to properly test and secure these components. The result is that our networks are at risk.

The risk is not just from a professional hacker. (*Hacker* is a name commonly given to someone who gains unauthorized access to a network.) Enough Web sites, tools, and chat rooms are available to make even a curious home user a devastating threat to a corporate network.

This chapter introduces you to the concepts of network security and lays the groundwork for the rest of the book. You'll examine the methods for identifying users through authentication, controlling users through access control, and identifying potential attack postures that threaten the most modern of networks. Finally, you'll look at how to track the use and misuse of resources through auditing.

Whether you read this chapter as a prelude to taking your Security+ exam or read it simply to become better at your job, read on. The realm of security awaits!

A BRIEF HISTORY OF NETWORKS AND SECURITY

We've often found in teaching, as well as in consulting, that it helps to have an understanding of where a need or concept comes from. The history of networking security stems from information security, which dates back thousands of years. We can even look to Caesar and the great Roman army. Even then, knowledge was power and protecting that knowledge was crucial to the business of Rome.

Caesar employed a basic form of encryption to protect his messages sent to and from the battlefield.

This desire and need to protect information continues, but the methods by which data is protected have changed. In the early days of computing, little changed to affect the methods by which information was protected. This is primarily because early computers did not really store data; they processed it. The data was printed to paper for analysis and review rather than being stored on the computers.

The paper is what was protected because it held the important information. We set up security that reflected the method of storage and transfer of the data: We locked it in filing cabinets, put it behind locked office doors, and locked it inside our desks to protect sensitive information. When the data was needed outside a protected area, we would attempt to protect it in transit with guards and locked briefcases.

The true shift in protecting information came when computers began to be used to store data. We no longer had the worries of tracking and protecting paper; it was all neatly stored on magnetic media. Mainframes made security easy. Typically, they were used only by the largest of companies, universities, and governments and were housed in protected, climate-controlled areas. Additionally, you had to be at a terminal directly connected to the mainframe to gain access to the data stored on it, and you had to have a considerable amount of knowledge to be able to use a mainframe. Because these large computers were typically set up this way, breaking into them was difficult.

Personal computers (PCs), and later the Internet, revolutionized the way we produce, store, evaluate, and use information. Now you can store as much data on a home computer as a public library holds in all its books and periodicals. In the early days of the PC revolution, users typically helped each other out. People freely exchanged ideas and information, debugged each other's programs in an effort to understand systems better, and even hacked on the keyboard to try to break the system and then rewrote programs to try to make them better. The thought of somebody stealing data did not occur to users because it was freely shared. This attitude prevailed for much of the 1980s and early 1990s.

As businesses adopted the use of computers, more and more proprietary data was stored on them. Information is still the single most important resource. Now, instead of managing business networks of 10–25 computers, we have networks of thousands and thousands of computers. Throw the Internet into the mix and the sheer number of systems becomes staggering. Businesses now store vital data on computers, and this information needs to be protected. Examples of common business information you might want to protect are as follows:

- **Personnel data**—Such as home phone numbers, Social Security numbers (for our readers in the United States), salary information, and employee review data
- **Business plans**—Such as merger information, reorganization, division sell-offs, and stock buy-backs
- **Proprietary information**—Data concerning business products such as chemical formulas, recipes, designs, and research data
- **Information that gives you a business advantage**—Such as partnerships, business processes, and business methodologies

You have a job to do. You need to be able to share only the right information with the right individuals or companies when they need it. Whether that information is stored on a local computer or transmitted across the Internet, you need to be sure your data is secure, unaltered, and delivered to the intended recipient on demand. After all, a network is there to be used.

IN THE FIELD

INTERNAL NETWORK SECURITY

How important is internal network security? We see people every year spend millions of dollars protecting their networks from the Internet. The Internet does pose an enormous threat to any company connected to it, but you can't forget to protect the network from the inside out.

We started a risk analysis for a widget manufacturing firm (they shall remain nameless to protect the innocent). We spent about four weeks interviewing employees, meeting with the executives, and planning with the people in the information technology (IT) department. This was an overhaul of their existing security policy, which had been in place for about two years. A lot had changed in two years.

continues

continued

New operating systems had been deployed, the company had grown by about 200%, and it had deployed an intranet system to help manage company information flow. In addition, it boasted a revamped Internet site that included e-commerce. It also deployed a section of its Web site to allow only its partners access to some internal business information by way of the Internet (extranet).

The Web exposure was an area of obvious concern to the IT department and executives. The more serious area of concern for us, however, was a lack of internal security policies and procedures. Many new employees had no training on security issues and could not identify information and resources that were at risk. Many users had their passwords written down, and a majority of the new servers that had been deployed had only the default security settings (everyone had full control).

We wrote our report and gave our presentation highlighting issues we believed to be critical to the business. The Internet and related technology was number six on our list of fifteen major issues. Our top three problems had nothing to do with the outside exposure of the network.

We discussed, debated, and politely tried to win our argument for implementing new internal security policy, but we were overruled. The company chose to spend its security budget (around $35,000) on the Internet exposure and new extranet configuration.

A month after our report, a person posing as a college student gained access to the facility. The "student" claimed to be writing a report for a college thesis. He was shown the entire operation of the company, including the ability to sit down at a workstation and browse the intranet Web sites. One such internal Web site had research and development information on it that related to a new widget that was in the testing phase. The Web page the student looked at stated that the widget had failed every major test and would have to go back to formula (back to the drawing board).

The student was actually a reporter doing a story on the latest technology in the widget industry. The story written included the information from the development Web site. Prior to this incident, the company enjoyed a good reputation in the industry and a stock price that hovered around $90/share. Three days after the story was published, the stock was selling at $22/share. A special board meeting was called and numerous press releases were issued to try to calm the fears of the investors, corporate clients, and banking partners.

Looking at just the loss in share price, the incident cost the company $3.4 million. However, the incident cost the company considerably more than that in goodwill, reputation, and industry leverage. The company suffered for about a year and was finally purchased at a rumored price of $34/share.

How important is internal network security to you?

Basic Terminology

One of the first things required when tackling a new subject area is the vocabulary. Learning security is no different. In an effort to make learning the new terminology easier, we have grouped the terms into common areas. Please note that we only give basic definitions of these terms. As you read this book, you will learn more about them.

Users

The keystone of security is identifying users and processes. Once these are identified, control is possible. The terms that follow are commonly associated with discussions of users and the processes they create:

- **AAA**—Authentication, Authorization, and Accounting (or Auditing). See more on each of these later in this list.
- **Access control list (ACL)**—An access control list is associated with a given resource (file, folder, router interface, and so on) and describes groups, users, machines, applications, and their permissions associated with that particular resource (see Figure 1.1). The access control list is usually accessible only by users who have been given the right (authorization) to change or view permissions.
- **Accounting/Auditing**—This examines what you have been doing. Accounting, also referred to as *auditing*, is used to track what a user has done.

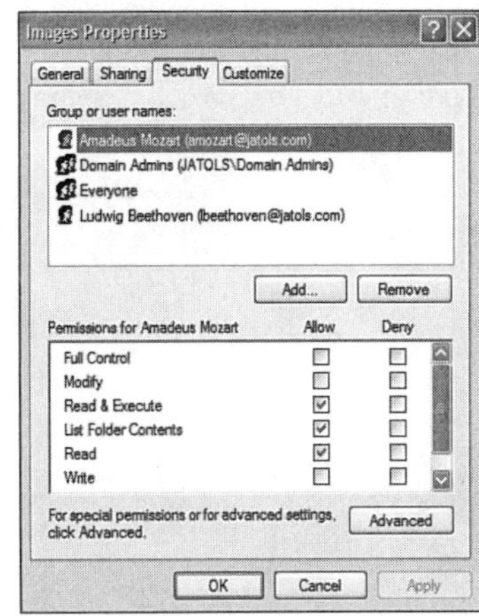

FIGURE 1.1
This is an ACL from a Windows XP folder called `images`.

- **Authentication**—The process by which a user is identified. Before being allowed to use resources, a secure network requires a user to be identified. One method of authentication is providing a username and password; other authentication methods exist and are explained in detail in the next section.
- **Authorization**—After a user is authenticated, authorization identifies what resources he's allowed to use, to which servers he can connect, and potentially whether he's allowed to access certain services (such as the Internet).
- **Biometric authentication**—An authentication process that utilizes some part of the user's body for the identification. Fingerprints, voice-print, and retinal scans are a few of the possible types of biometric authentication.
- **Multifactor authentication**—This describes a situation in which more than one authentication mechanism is used at the same time. For example, you might be required to type a username and password and place your thumb on a thumbprint scanner to properly identify yourself.
- **Mutual authentication**—The process of authenticating both parties in a network connection or process. An instance in which this might occur is on the Web. When attaching to a Web site, you might be required to log on. At the same time, the Web software on your computer requests the server certificate (see the following list) for positive ID of the server.

NOTE

Remember that a user does not necessarily have to be a human. A device, program, or server system can be controlled on your network just as a human would by making it authenticate.

Data

Data can be controlled and manipulated in many ways. The following terms deal with sending, receiving, and verifying receipt of data:

- **Asymmetric keys**—The use of public key cryptography based on key pairs. Each half of the key pair is different but tied together mathematically. Each key in the pair can encrypt data so only the other half of the key pair can decrypt it. The private key is held with the owner of the key pair, whereas the public key is freely distributed to anyone who wants to use it.

- **Certificate authority (CA)**—A system or entity trusted to generate and distribute digital certificates. A CA can be privately run within a company or publicly run as a third-party CA.
- **Certificate**—Also known as a digital certificate, this is an electronic form of identification commonly used for authentication and data encryption. Certificates are generated by certificate authorities (see the previous definition).
- **Confidentiality**—Sending data so it can be read only by the intended recipient. This process is usually achieved through encryption (defined later).
- **Digital signature**—A method of using a private key in a key pair to digitally sign data. The originator can be verified by using the public key of the key pair. In addition to signature verification, it can also be used to ensure a message was not tampered with.
- **Encryption**—An algorithm is used to scramble data. Most algorithms are based on complex mathematical formulas.
- **Integrity**—Data integrity is achieved when data is sent and received without alteration. This is often proven through the use of a checksum on the originating message.
- **Key/Keys/Key pairs**—A *key* is a set of steps or behaviors generally used to encrypt and decrypt data using a mathematical formula. Keys can be symmetric or asymmetric. If key formulas are connected, they are said to be a *key pair*.
- **Nonrepudiation**—The inability to deny a signature. This is usually in reference to the use of a digital signature or certificate. It allows users to send data such as email with a verified electronic signature.
- **Public key infrastructure (PKI)**—The policies and behaviors that surround the deployment and management of key pairs. This generally includes certificate authorities, registration authorities, and certificates.
- **Registration authority (RA)**—The RA verifies credentials supplied by an agent and then sends the CA an okay to issue a certificate. This software is usually integrated into the CA software; however, in large CA environments, it might be separated.

- **Repudiation**—The capability to deny a signature. In the context of security, this is denial of the receipt or transmission of data such as email.
- **Symmetric keys**—Key-based cryptography in which both the sender and the receiver have the same key. This can also be called *shared secret cryptography*.

Encryption

Encryption, as defined in the previous section, is the process of scrambling data so that it can't be read. There are different methods to do this and multiple strengths of encryption. The following are some fundamental terms associated with encryption:

- **Authentication header (AH)**—Deployed in IP Security (IPSec), an AH is used to ensure your data has not been altered. The AH does not encrypt the data itself.
- **Data Encryption Standard (DES)**—Developed by IBM in 1974, DES is a widely used form of encryption utilizing symmetric keys and a 64-bit key length. Triple DES is a more recent version of the method and runs the process three times.
- **Diffie-Hellman**—An encryption key algorithm developed in the mid-1970s and named after its two creators. It defines a secret key exchange system commonly used to scramble data between two networking entities.
- **Encapsulated secure payload (ESP)**—Deployed in IPSec, ESP is designed to make the contents of a data packet unreadable by any but the intended recipient.
- **IP Security (IPSec)**—A method of securing data integrity or confidentiality, or both. This technology is deployed at the Network layer, allowing application data to be encrypted whether the application supports encryption. IPSec is deployed as a tunneling technology. Data confidentiality is supported through encapsulated secured payload, and data integrity is achieved through an authentication header.

- **Pretty Good Privacy (PGP)**—A form of encryption commonly used in email. It uses a modified PKI configuration for its encryption routine. PGP encrypts selected data with a shorter, weaker key for fast processing and then encrypts the data key with a stronger, more complex key based on standard PKI. The term *pretty good privacy* comes from the fact that the data is encrypted with a weaker key than normally used in standard PKI.
- **Rivest-Shamir-Adleman (RSA)**—An encryption algorithm developed in 1978. It uses public/private key pairs to authenticate and encrypt between two network entities.
- **Secure Socket Layer (SSL)**—A common form of encryption used on Web-based systems. The client requests the encryption by typing in HTTPS (or selecting a hyperlink) in a browser instead of HTTP. SSL typically uses certificates as its encryption mechanism and is commonly used on e-commerce Web systems.
- **Transport Layer Security (TLS)**—Similar to SSL, TLS provides security mechanisms for protecting data when sent across a public network, such as the Internet. TLS is designed to prevent message forgery, tampering, and eavesdropping.

Network

A network represents a large collection of hardware, software, and resources. There is also a large collection of terms that help describe and identify it:

- **Bastion host**—A system used as a gateway for hosting internal applications or data on the public Internet. The host is typically the only point of contact available for outside users to get into the private network. It is highly secured because of its exposure and probability as a target of attack.
- **Demilitarized zone (DMZ)**—Also called the *free-trade-zone* or the *neutral zone*. This is an area in your network that allows a limited and controlled amount of access from the public Internet. The DMZ often hosts the corporation's Web and File Transfer Protocol (FTP) sites, email, external Domain Name Service (DNS), and the like. This network segment usually lies between the internal corporate network and the public Internet.

- **Firewall**—A software- or hardware-based system designed to protect one network from another. Although this system is most commonly associated with protecting a private network from the public Internet, it can also be used to segment and protect internal networks from each other.
- **Intrusion detection system (IDS)**—A software and hardware system designed to monitor traffic and system access.
- **Network address translation (NAT)**—This is the process of protecting internal hosts by obscuring the source or destination of a packet when communicating on the Internet. Several private classes of addresses will not route across the Internet (as defined by RFC 1918). If using these addresses, a NAT server is required to give hosts a routable source address.
- **Packet (versus frame)**—A *packet* is an encapsulated set of data with a source and destination network layer address embedded. A *frame* is an encapsulated set of data that is completely formed and ready for transmission on the wire. The difference is important in network sniffing, packet tracing, and troubleshooting.
- **Port address translation (PAT)**—This process changes source and destination ports as well as network address information to properly route packets from protected hosts to the Internet.
- **Point-to-Point Protocol (PPP)**—A standard protocol developed for dial-up users. It is flexible and widely supported in the industry.
- **Point-to-Point Tunneling Protocol (PPTP)**—An enhancement to PPP that allows users to use a local Internet connection to connect to a private network using an encrypted tunnel.
- **Remote Access Dial-in User Services (RADIUS)**—RADIUS is used by large companies and ISPs that support large RAS populations. Multiple RAS servers and certain types of network equipment can use a single RADIUS server for all authentication.
- **Remote Access Services (RAS)**—This is a service normally provided to end users that allows them to dial in to a private network from anywhere. The connection, once made, allows the user to access the network as if she were local.

- **Remote procedure calls (RPCs)**—Programming calls that applications make to remote services or servers. To the application end user, the application appears to run completely on the local system.
- **Screening router**—A router that is set up to throw away unwanted traffic before it hits a firewall or other more complex device. It serves to clean up as much traffic as possible, saving resources and processing time on other devices.
- **Snorting/Sniffing**—The process of looking at live network data traffic and packet contents. Many of the applications that accomplish this are used by administrators and hackers alike. After it is captured, the data can be viewed offline and even replayed.
- **Stateful packet inspection**—A form of firewall protection that works by inspecting the traffic flow or state. This is more secure than the classic packet filter mechanisms used on routers and servers.
- **Tunneling**—An additional layer of encapsulation used during data encryption. Tunneling can also be used to encapsulate one type of protocol in another (IPX in IP tunneling, for example).

Hacking/Attacks

Mostly slang, many of the following terms describe the act of attacking a network or attack methods or targets:

- **Bot**—Short for robot. This term is given to a computer that has been successfully attacked and infected with a small program that allows a hacker remote control capabilities or code that automates attacks.
- **Cracker**—A user who breaks into your network for profit or with intent to do damage.
- **Hacker**—A user who breaks into a network for the challenge of it. Similar to a cracker but is driven by curiosity.
- **Lamer**—A slang term used as a insult in the hacking community as in, "Your software sucks and you have no idea what you're doing; you're a complete lamer."

- **Luser**—A hacker insult (see lamer).
- **Script kiddie**—A term given to hackers who use prebuilt scripts or code to execute attacks. Generally considered an insult among hackers, it implies that a hacker is too stupid to write his own code.
- **Sniffing**—The process of electronically extracting data from the network, allowing a user to view the contents of unprotected packets.
- **Social engineering**—An attack form based on deceiving a user. This usually involves tricking an individual into revealing passwords, proprietary information, network security data, and so on.
- **Spam**—A term given to unsolicited emails commonly received from the Internet. Believed to have been taken from a *Monty Python* skit.
- **Spoofing**—The capability to electronically impersonate a network system. This impersonation is typically built around the use of another system's IP address. The attacker exploits a trust relationship that exists between a source and destination based on address information.
- **Trojan horse**—A compiled program that appears to run normally but contains hidden code designed to attack a system, the network, or information.
- **Zombie**—The same as a bot.

EXAM TIP

As you work your way through the book, you will likely run across many of these words and acronyms. As you come across these new terms, try writing the definitions until you have them memorized.

ACCESS CONTROL TECHNIQUES

Recognize, explain, and differentiate access control methods.

Access control is best described as the process by which use of resources and services is granted or denied. To be effective, access control is used in conjunction with authentication (which is covered in detail in the following section). After a user or device has identified itself to the network, controls can be put in place that grant or deny rights and privileges to that user's ID. The method for putting those controls in place is referred to as an *access control policy.*

Early access control policy was first defined by the military. In 1967, a group was assembled to review and address computer security issues. The government and military networks of the time stored sensitive and classified information on their systems. This information needed to be protected while being stored, as well as while in transit between newly connected sites. The task force group published a document called "Security Controls for Computer Systems," which eventually evolved into what we know today as the "Orange Book." The Orange Book, or Trusted Computer System Evaluation Criteria (TCSEC), sets the criteria for deployment, configuration, and evaluation of computer systems in a secure manner. In addition, the Orange Book defines a classification hierarchy for computer security in an effort to make deployment and maintenance of a required (or desired) security level easier.

Although private sector businesses and civilian consumers might not need the same security levels as described in the Orange Book, much can be gained by understanding the principles and procedures set forth in its pages. It identifies a common standard by which we can measure our business computer systems and the security implemented on them. By following the principles outlined in the Orange Book (and other books in the Rainbow series) you can also secure government contracts that require adherence to the standards identified.

The three common access control methods used today are

- Mandatory access control (MAC)
- Discretionary access control (DAC)
- Role-Based access control (RBAC)

MAC and DAC are well defined in the Orange book; however, the third access control policy, RBAC, is a relative newcomer. We look at each in more detail in the following sections.

NOTE It should be noted that these policies are not mutually exclusive. An organization might choose to deploy one, two, or all three types of access control to achieve its security goals.

Mandatory Access Control

According to the Orange Book, *Mandatory access control (MAC)* is defined as a policy used to control access to classified and sensitive information throughout its lifecycle. The rules are to be relative to the classification of the data being protected, with the most sensitive data being protected by the strongest policy and rules.

A MAC policy directly compares a user's clearance level with the current classification of the information and allows only authorized or cleared individuals an appropriate level of access (such as read and write). The Orange Book defines this configuration of permissions and protection as a mathematical lattice that first protects data from unwanted access by unknown users and then protects data while being accessed by authorized users from accidental or intentional misuse. The MAC policy also states that the system (not the users) is in charge of the permissions and those permissions should not be arbitrarily changed by any process or behavior. (For a complete discussion of the Orange Book policy, see `http://www.radium.ncsc.mil/`.)

Several things are learned from the Orange Book definitions on MAC. When deploying a MAC policy, users are not allowed to change permissions or rights associated with objects. In a MAC situation, setting or changing security rests with either a designated security officer or an information administrator, not the user of the information. The policy also informs us that information must be classified by sensitivity (as in classified, secret, and top-secret) and compared to a user's clearance. In other words, if you have a secret clearance, the access control system should not allow you to view top-secret data.

Problems arise when trying to deploy a pure MAC policy. Take as an example a user named Bob. Bob logs on to the network with top-secret clearance and accesses a top-secret document that he has permission to read and write to. The privilege to read in most major operating systems would also give Bob the ability to copy the document to a new location, assuming he has write privileges to the destination. So Bob mistakenly copies the file from his home directory to a public folder on the network that has read privileges assigned to all users and read/write privileges assigned to Bob. During the copy process to the public folder, Bob is not allowed to change the rights associated with the file (part of the MAC policy). The operating system, however, has a built-in default behavior when creating a new object in the public folder (the copy process creates a new object). This default behavior assigns the new object (the copied top-secret file) the same privileges as the public folder (all users have read permissions).

In a true MAC environment, the initial copy operation should fail. As Bob tries to copy the file from a top-secret location to a non-top-secret location, the operating system should be able to distinguish the disparity of security levels. Most operating systems are not built to do this, however. Despite almost two decades of work and hundreds of millions of dollars in research and development costs, we still have few operating systems that truly deploy a working MAC policy. These systems fail under less than optimum human control and suffer from the growing complexity of networks, operating systems, applications, and hardware advances. (For more information, see `http://www.all.net/CID/Defense/Defense7.html`.)

Given that pure MAC is virtually unattainable, some mixture of policy will occur. Current policies often reflect both mandatory and discretionary access control.

Discretionary Access Control

Discretionary access control (DAC) involves a more user-centric management view. The Orange Book defines discretionary access control as the principle type of access control used and available in modern operating systems. DAC security is based on the user controlling access to information. The user or an application in use on behalf of the user has the right to specify what access others get to the information under the managing user's control. This type of security control delegates or decentralizes the security policy away from the security team concept seen in MAC. The Orange Book also states that the DAC security policy is not a replacement for MAC, but rather a supplement allowing a finer amount of control. A DAC policy is still constrained by MAC guidelines, such as the classification of the data as secret or top-secret, but a user with an appropriate level of MAC access has, at her discretion, the ability to assign security to others deemed to have a need to know. (For a complete discussion of the Orange Book policy, see `http://www.radium.ncsc.mil/`.)

In this context, DACs are mixed with MACs to produce a desired access control policy. As stated, MAC is still in place, but some level of control is passed to the users. In large network environments, DAC is seen as a necessity because of scalability issues. As networks grow to thousands of users, the burden of mandatory control configuration for resources becomes too great. By mixing the two access control methods, administrators set up classifications for information, identify trusted users, and assign those trusted users an initial level of control. Trusted users then have some level of control on who (other than themselves) can view or have access to data.

The configuration of DAC requires an emphasis to be placed on training your trusted users. Unfortunately, training is an area that is often overlooked. Without proper training, there is a high degree of probability that users will incorrectly configure discretionary access and cause security breaches through misconfiguration of resource access.

Role-Based Access Control

Role-based access control (RBAC) takes the combination of mandatory and discretionary to the next level. Even in moderately sized networks, it is never advisable to manage access control on an individual user basis. Scalability is again the issue here. Rather than focusing on individual user access and privilege, RBAC seeks to group users by common behaviors and access needs.

When deploying RBAC, the first step is to focus on user roles in the company. Let's look at a medium-sized manufacturing company of 7,000 users. The roles users can have typically follow or parallel the corporate organizational structure. A sample of roles might include

- Network Administration
- Help Desk Operations
- Human Resources
- Production
- Research and Development
- Management
- Executives

Each of these roles would then be translated into groups in the network security policy. Rights, privileges, and access would then be assigned to the identified groups. For instance, as a help desk operator, Suzie needs to be able to view user accounts and reset passwords. In an RBAC environment, a specific group for help desk personnel would be created. Suzie's account would be put into the help desk group, and she would be indirectly granted the permissions and rights assigned to the group by virtue of her membership.

This approach to access control is a combination of mandatory and discretionary methods. The mandatory aspect of this model would be the identified needs of groups, as seen in the following small sample:

- **Help Desk Operations**—Users in this group need to be able to read users' account statuses, reset passwords, and modify account lockout statuses.
- **Human Resources**—Users in this group need the ability to create new user accounts, modify existing group memberships, create and maintain groups, and read or modify users' settings.
- **Executives**—Users in this group need the ability to access servers in the corporate network, access any printer, and access key files used for generating reports.

The discretionary aspect of this model is actually now in layers. The first layer of discretionary access is based on which users get placed into which groups. This is up to the discretion of the security team (or the network administrators). The second layer of discretionary access comes from the users after they're placed in a particular group. These group members can now pass on rights and privileges to other users at their discretion.

EXAM TIP

Remember to focus more on the concepts of and differences between MAC, DAC, and RBAC. The exam attempts to objectively measure your understanding of the concepts, not subjectively test you on the mechanics of how to implement a particular access control methodology.

REVIEW BREAK

MAC, DAC, and RBAC

- MAC is an access control method centrally controlled and managed. Users have no influence on permissions and can't pass permissions on.
- DAC allows users to set permissions as they see the need to do so, within the guidelines of the broader MAC guidelines.
- RBAC is a more complete integration of MAC and DAC, focusing on group management instead of users. Security administrators group users and assign MAC permissions based on a role in the company. DAC is used by users in the groups to manage finer permissions control.

Authentication Methods

Recognize, explain, and differentiate authentication methods.

Authentication is the process used to identify an agent requesting the use of resources. An authentication request can be presented by any of the following agents:

- Human
- Computer system
- Network device, such as a router or switch
- Software program

Authentication can take place locally on a single computer system or be passed over a network to a centralized authentication system. In each of these situations, the purpose of authentication is to associate a set of credentials (supplied by the agent) with an electronic ID. The electronic ID can then be granted (or denied) access to resources, group membership, and rights on the network and its computer systems.

Authentication generally involves the use of one of the following three methods:

- Something you know (a password or PIN)
- Something you have (a swipe card or token)
- Something you are (this would use fingerprints or some other physical characteristic)

We'll start by looking at username/password combinations and the variations associated with that form of authentication. This concentrates on the "something you know" approach.

Username/Password

Authentication based on straight username and password is probably the most recognized and best-supported authentication method currently deployed. Each of the following operating systems and their various versions support standard username- and password-based authentication:

- ▶ Microsoft Windows
- ▶ Unix
- ▶ Macintosh
- ▶ Linux
- ▶ Novell

> **NOTE** Many options exist for the creation of a username. Some common examples for John Smith might include `smithjo001`, `josmith001`, or `j_smith001`. Regardless of which option you choose, it should be defined by a policy and followed for consistency. Train your users that the usernames they use are half of the logon security and should be protected with as much vigilance as their passwords.

The method for creating usernames varies from company to company, but it generally includes the user's last name, a portion of his first name, and a numeric value to avoid duplicates. Using John Smith as an example, the username supplied during the authentication process might be `jsmith001`.

The method for creating passwords can vary widely among different companies and even among different users. Here are some basic guidelines to follow to ensure that your passwords are considered secure. Passwords should

- ▶ Be at least eight characters in length
- ▶ Contain uppercase letters
- ▶ Contain lowercase letters
- ▶ Contain numbers
- ▶ Contain special characters

An example of a secure or strong password is `iW@sjCA0202`. The trick to passwords and password complexity is to create a password that contains all the required elements and to make it a password you can remember. Too often, users create excellent complex passwords and find they forget them or, far worse, write them down.

As network and security professionals, we are constantly told to create strong passwords. We pass this requirement on to our users, but rarely have we been told *how* to create a strong, secure, memorable password. Here is a method you can use and pass on to your users:

1. Think of an event that has happened in your life.
2. Create a statement around the event. For example, I was in San Jose California in February 2002.

3. Take certain letters out of the statement and arrange them to create a password that is very complex and yet very easy to remember: i Was @ (in/at) san jose CAlifornia in 02, 2002, or `iW@sjCA0202`.

The password created by this method has a total of 269,561,249,468,963,000,000 possible combinations, as illustrated by Table 1.1.

TABLE 1.1

CALCULATING MATHEMATICAL COMBINATIONS FOR PASSWORDS

Password Component	*Possible Values*	*Mathematical Values*
Uppercase letters	A–Z	26
Lowercase letters	a–z	26
Numbers	0–9	10
Special characters	!, @, #, $, %, ^, and so on	10; conservative number of special characters

If you add the mathematical values, you get 72 (26 + 26 + 10 + 10) possible values for each character in a given password. Take 72 to the power of the total number of characters in your password, and you have the total possible password combinations. In our example, the password `iW@sjCA0202` is 11 characters long, so the formula is 72^11.

Any password, no matter how complex, is worthless if it can be viewed in clear text. The most common time for this to occur is during a network logon, file access, or service request. To protect your username and password during these processes, software mechanisms can be used. Most of these mechanisms are built into the operating systems. One of the most powerful is Kerberos.

Kerberos

In Greek mythology, Kerberos was the three-headed hound that guarded the entrance to Hades. It was impossible to get by the beast unless you presented the proper credentials for entry into the underworld. The same is said to be true of the Kerberos protocol used in modern operating systems.

In the networking world, Kerberos is a unique authentication method developed by the Massachusetts Institute of Technology (MIT). It is designed to do the following:

- Secure usernames and passwords during transmission over the network
- Allow mutual authentication
- Achieve Single-Sign-On (SSO) or the ability to log on once and access all necessary resources without having to log on again
- Decrease the time it takes to access resources
- Scale to huge network size

Building an understanding of Kerberos is best achieved by building an analogy. Let's say you work for a circuit board manufacturing company. You work on a campus that has six buildings, each with five floors. There are 6,000 workers on this campus, and the buildings and floors are subdivided into hundreds of offices.

When you come to work for the company, you're issued an ID card that has your picture on it. Encoded on the card is the following information:

- Your name
- The department you work in
- The password you use to gain access to all resources
- All rights and privileges you're assigned in the company
- Salary and personal information pertaining to employment

The card is made of gold, and if you lose it, you have to pay for its replacement (a little added incentive to make you take care of your card). If it gets stolen, the holder of your card can impersonate you completely until you notify the company and have the card deactivated (and you still get to pay to replace it).

Using older authentication methods, you would use this one card to gain access to any resources you need to do your job. If you need to get into one of the buildings, you would swipe your card at the front door and it would let you in (assuming you have been granted access).

After you were in the building, if you needed to get into your office, you would again swipe your card. In addition, you would use your card to get to your files in your filing cabinet or your desk, research papers out of the corporate library, and so on.

The problem with this method is the exposure of your swipe card. You constantly have to pull your card out to get to your resources, exposing it to theft or loss.

For our example, your username and password are the equivalent of the swipe card. The network and its services are representative of the buildings, offices, and files. In older authentication schemes, you constantly have to prove your identity through multiple logons. Even if not prompted to do so interactively, the operating system or application would present your credentials to servers on your behalf so that you could access resources, thus exposing your username and password multiple times throughout a normal workday.

Let's continue with the building example. The plant manager has decided to implement a new system for gaining access to the campus and its resources. Each morning as you arrive at your building, you stop at one of the local security desks (each building has its own security desk). At the security desk, you present your gold ID badge to the security officer. The security guard checks your ID and verifies that you are who you say you are. After ensuring your identity, the security guard issues you a blue plastic swipe card that has a special code on it and sets the card to expire at the end of the workday. If you need access to any resources throughout the day, you can use your blue card instead of the gold one. (You can leave the gold swipe card in your wallet or desk for safety.)

Let's say you need access to the research and development office. You go to the nearest security desk and present your blue swipe card and a request to get into the office. The security officer issues you another swipe card (maybe a green swipe card) that has two codes on it. One code is only for the research and development office door; the other code is your personal code (from the blue card). The final step is to go to the office door and swipe your green card. Assuming that the office administrator for that particular office has permitted you access in the security system, the door opens. The green swipe card is good only as long as you are in that office.

In Kerberos, the scenario would go something like this:

1. You log on in the morning by sending an authentication request to an authentication server (AS). The AS is the equivalent to the morning check-in at the security desk.
2. The AS issues you a ticket granting ticket (TGT) that allows you to request resources on the network from servers. The TGT is the blue swipe card.
3. Armed with your TGT, you submit a request to a ticket granting server (TGS) to access a particular network sever named FOO. This second request is the same as your request for getting into a specific office.
4. The TGS issues you a session ticket. This is the equivalent of the green swipe card good for just that one office door.
5. You go to server FOO and request a session.
6. The server replies by granting or denying your request for a session based on access control settings. As long as a session remains, your session ticket is good until it expires (usually eight hours).

The AS and TGS are typically co-located on the same server, integrated as part of the same service. This server is known as the Key Distribution Center (KDC), as noted in Figure 1.2.

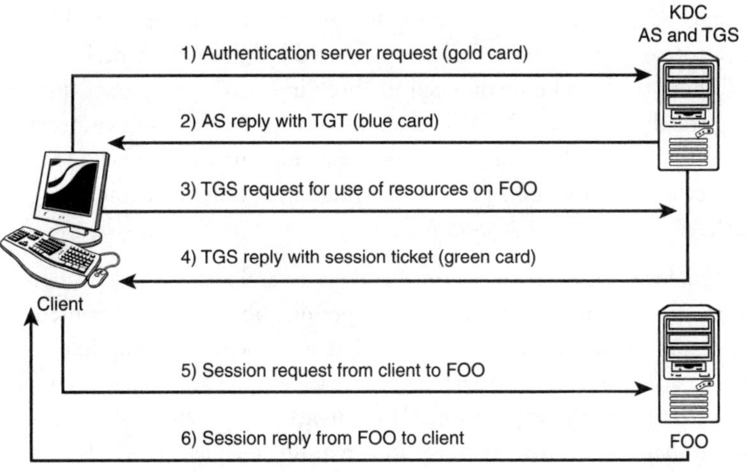

FIGURE 1.2
Kerberos server configuration.

Behind the scenes, there is another process that is an added security feature. When the security guard issued you your green card, your personal code (from the blue card) was embedded in it along with the door code. This allows the door swipe mechanism to identify you when you swipe the card (authentication of the user). A subtle feature is also in play with the green card: It is coded so you can open only the appropriate office door. This feature allows you to verify that you're entering the correct office. (You're authenticating the "door" at this point.) This is called *mutual authentication.*

In Kerberos, when you request services from a server, you go to a trusted third party (the KDC). Both you and the server trust the KDC to properly authenticate all possible clients (servers included). You authenticate yourself by typing a username and password. The server is an authenticated member of a domain or realm, and this membership behavior is encoded in the software of the operating system and managed by an administrator. Both the KDC and the servers are in the same domain (for this example anyway) and have established a relationship through a database entry (similar to your user account). This is necessary because the server doesn't have the opportunity to log on in the same way we do. With both the server and you (the client) authenticated, codes are embedded on the session tickets that allow each entity to authenticate the other during the session request.

When discussing Kerberos, KDCs, and this process as a whole, a common question we get is, "How far does the trust extend?" It depends on you as a security or system administrator. In our work example, each building is its own domain or realm and each building supports its own KDCs (as represented by the security desks). Within your building, you need to check in (log on) only once during the day and your TGT is valid. What if you need resources from one of the other buildings? You must extend your trust to include the other security desks in the other buildings. This is an emerging behavior called *single-sign-on (SSO).*

NOTE

On a recent project, we integrated Windows 2000, Unix, Linux, and an AS400 system with Kerberos components. By doing so, the company's users could log on one time in the morning and access resources on any of the systems. This procedure eliminated a large number of help desk calls, reduced security audit failures, simplified administration of the network, and increased user productivity and morale. (The increase in morale was attributed to all of the above.) All this was accomplished over a two-week period.

SSO allows a user to log on once and get to any resources in his network environment (assuming proper permissions have been granted and appropriate trusts are in place). The early belief that multiple logon accounts and different passwords were more secure has been disproved over the years. Multiple logon accounts increase the likelihood that users will write down information, such as passwords, to remember it, which leads to security breaches. System administrators find properly assigning security access more difficult because of the large number of user accounts that must be maintained.

As Kerberos gains in popularity as an authentication mechanism, more and more vendors are choosing to support it in the application and operating system software they produce. This support for SSO enables you to set up a more usable and secure network environment for your users.

There are additional dynamics going on in the architecture of Kerberos that are unnecessary for our discussion. If you would like more information, search the Web for Kerberos Authentication.

Challenge Handshake Authentication Protocol

Challenge Handshake Authentication Protocol (CHAP) is commonly used over dial-up links encapsulated in the Point-to-Point Protocol (PPP). CHAP was designed to replace the Password Authentication Protocol (PAP).

The problem with PAP is that the username and password were sent in clear text across the network during the authentication phase of the connection setup. As networks and dial-up services grew, clear text authentication was seen as a serious problem.

CHAP works at layer two in the PPP dial-up protocol and must be satisfied before a link is fully established. No data traffic is allowed to pass prior to the CHAP challenge and successful response. During the link negotiation sequence of PPP, the Link Control Program goes through the following steps:

1. It receives username and password input from the keyboard.
2. It uses a media digest (MD) routine to scramble the password into what is known as a *hashed password*, and then it sends the username and hash to the dial-up server.
3. The dial-up server receives the authentication request and looks up the username in the user database. It retrieves the password and sends it through the same MD5 hash routine. If the sent hash matches the local hash result, the password sent must be the password stored in the database and a successful logon is achieved.

This process is shown in Figure 1.3.

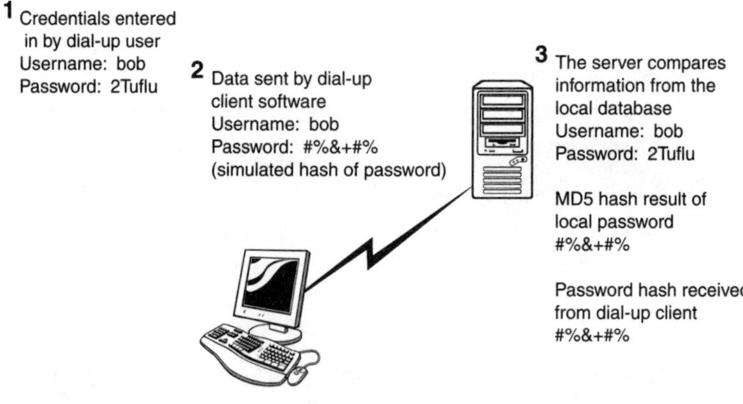
1 Credentials entered in by dial-up user
Username: bob
Password: 2Tuflu
2 Data sent by dial-up client software
Username: bob
Password: #%&+#%
(simulated hash of password)
3 The server compares information from the local database
Username: bob
Password: 2Tuflu
MD5 hash result of local password
#%&+#%
Password hash received from dial-up client
#%&+#%
Using Message Digest 5 (MD5) hashing algorithm, the dial-up software sends the password as garbled text.

FIGURE 1.3
CHAP authentication sequence.

After successful negotiation, CHAP can also send interim challenges to ensure that the link endpoints (client and server) are still the original systems. This helps deter a would-be hacker from stealing (hijacking) your session after a successful authentication sequence. Although CHAP is a fairly basic form of authentication, it is widely supported by software manufacturers, is well documented, and is easy to deploy. Certificates, on the other hand, are far more secure but need a bit more effort to deploy properly.

Certificates

We started this section by defining the concept of authentication: proving your identity or the identity of a server, piece of network equipment, service, or program. Now take that concept into the very open and very public Internet. The Internet is a playground with all the benefits and drawbacks of a real playground. There's a whole world you can have on the Internet, such as buying, selling, communicating with chat and email, researching, and even playing games. As with any playground, the Internet also has its dangers, such as bullies, thieves, and general miscreants, that lurk in its dark corners—waiting to take advantage of the unsuspecting or unprotected.

The difference on the Internet is that you don't see people face to face. You usually interact on the Internet through a browser and see exactly what they want you to see. This adds a dimension to the Internet playground that we never had to deal with as kids on the swings of our youth.

Another issue is that users and servers on the Internet are typically separated by numerous network devices, which are under the control of agents we don't see or know. Without some form of identification, we don't even know whether we are connected to the correct server. Our information passes across communications equipment that is subject to eavesdropping with no possible way for us to know whether someone is actually listening. A *digital certificate* is an electronic identification/encryption system developed for use in just such a playground. Certificates serve two main purposes: agent identification and data encryption.

Authentication

Our main focus in this chapter is identification. Encryption is covered in Chapter 5, "Cryptography Algorithms." A trusted authority, known as a certificate authority, issues certificates to individuals and companies for the purpose of electronic identification. Certificates can be used for identifying any of the following:

- Users
- Servers
- Other networking equipment, such as routers and firewalls
- Software programs

After a CA has verified the identity of the requesting agent, a certificate is issued and installed. The certificate can then be used to digitally sign transmissions and encrypt data streams.

Certificates work much the way a driver's license works. When you first get your driver's license, you go to the department of motor vehicles (DMV) with proof of your identity (usually a birth certificate) and are issued a license (after passing the test, of course). Once issued, your state driver's license can be used for much more than just proving you're allowed to drive. Most banks and stores will accept a driver's license as proof of your identity when you purchase goods with a check. You can even use your driver's license as proof of citizenship in certain situations. There is a trust implied when this happens: You trust the DMV to issue you an ID card that can be used to prove identity (and ability to drive), and the banks, stores, and border patrol trust the DMV to make sure it issues an ID to people only after they have proven their identity. This trust doesn't always occur—some stores will not accept an out-of-state license as proof of identity.

We learned in Kerberos that a trust must be developed between networking entities. We see this trust again in the use of certificates. The Kerberos trust is generally created between network agents under common administrative control. The trust built using certificates can be identical to this; however, it can also be very different. With certificates, a trust can be built between agents outside your administrative control. A trust of this nature is often referred to as a *third-party trust.*

Using Certificates

The following two situations will help you understand when certificates are very useful.

In our first scenario, you are shopping online and are about to purchase clothing from a vendor. As you enter privileged data, such as your name, home address, and credit card numbers, how do you know that you are on the vendor's Web site and not on a Web site that is set up to look like the vendor's?

In the second scenario, you just received an email from a client. The client is requesting an order of 5,000 widgets from you. How do you verify that the email came from a legitimate client and not an imposter before putting the order into the system?

In each of these situations, you can verify the information by picking up the phone and calling someone. But then why have a Web site? Why take orders through email? We have a need for an electronic ID similar to a driver's license. Standard username and password methodology would fail here because we can't possibly set up users for all customers participating in e-commerce. It doesn't make sense for email, either. Are you going to create an internal email account for an external client? How about 1,000 clients? How about all the users who might order widgets from you over the Internet? It is just not feasible.

Remember that authentication is

- Something you know (a password or PIN)
- Something you have (a swipe card or token)
- Something you are (this would use fingerprints or some other physical characteristic)

Generating a Certificate

We have illustrated in the examples that straight usernames/ passwords (something you know) are not secure, flexible, or scalable enough to be used to prove your identity. So, we turn to something you have—in this case, the certificate. Now let's look at the mechanics of how to get a certificate and how it works.

To get a certificate, you can follow these steps:

1. Using software, you create a certificate request file (see Figures 1.4 and 1.5).

FIGURE 1.4
Certificate request from Windows XP.

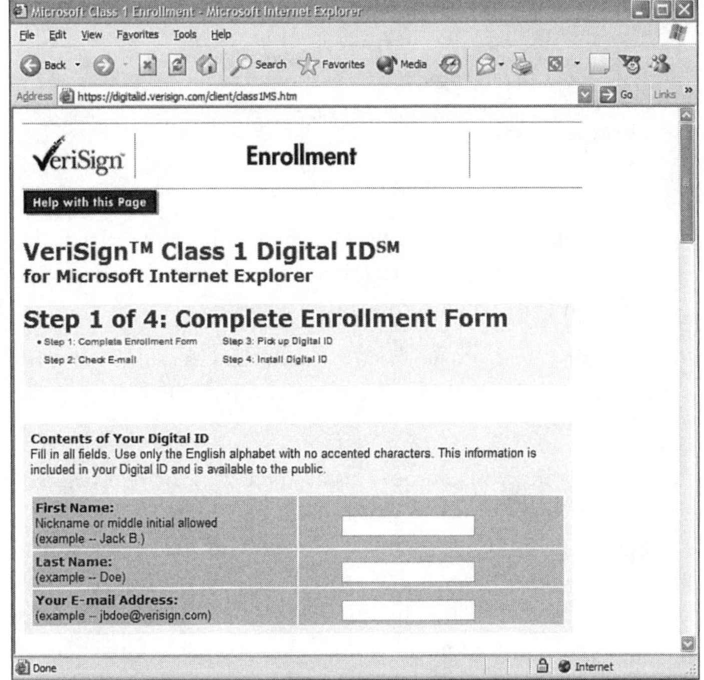

FIGURE 1.5
Web-based enrollment form from Verisign.com.

2. After a certificate request file has been created, you can email the file to a CA or submit the request directly online through a Web browser. The following is an example of an X.509 request file:

```
-----BEGIN NEW CERTIFICATE REQUEST-----
MIICdTCCAh8CAQAwZTEPMA0GA1UEAxMGZGNzdGFuMRUwEwYDVQQLEwx
➥XZWIgU2Vy
dmljZXMxEDAOBgNVBAoTB1dpZGdldHMxDzANBgNVBAcTBkRlbnZlcj
➥ELMAkGA1UE
```

```
CBMCQ08xCzAJBgNVBAYTAlVTMFwwDQYJKoZIhvcNAQEBBQADSwAw
➥SAJBANa/imvg
y7lRO0SWhAuLOJAsRxtPQDpURdGYfE8W2Cy41rDozBmnO8ruUiVV
➥zorKJ+IZbFMi
jL60KSY+z/7BUk0CAwEAAaCCAVMwGgYKKwYBBAGCNw0CAzEMFgo1Lj
➥AuMjE5NS4y
MDUGCisGAQQBgjcCAQ4xJzAlMA4GA1UdDwEB/wQEAwIE8DATBg
➥NVHSUEDDAKBggr
BgEFBQcDATCB/QYKKwYBBAGCNw0CAjGB7jCB6wIBAR5aAE0AaQBj
➥AHIAbwBzAG8A
ZgB0ACAAUgBTAEEAIABTAEMAaABhAG4AbgBlAGwAIABDAHIAeQBw
➥AHQAbwBnAHIA
YQBwAGgAaQBjACAAUAByAG8AdgBpAGQAZQByA4GJAF8TbgM+o
➥HAWmVHXn/FkNjwK
6CjFvLKa3Cr+0A9np3M+v1nLfQ2eQpBspyxstH/i33+1Ykgyas
➥WFmievHXaoF8gK
iIpRet5Irz04gussS2jV+ub93JyhceFK1Kxl2bbm+zO/zbsUoqTlt
➥Fb+8gh4Gp8q
cQ8kc6eiIbpRJy+ADxB+AAAAAAAAAAAwDQYJKoZIhvc
➥NAQEFBQADQQCYycoBsyM0
dooPBSWooKR7ubMWNrgmO2EBiAMnS+ox3QSA5SN7zVj/djvn
➥TU2dobBMoeNYxA5K
FvVkeOUhKpEf
-----END NEW CERTIFICATE REQUEST-----
```


3. Depending on the type of certificate you have requested, the CA will verify your identity to a certain level of confidence and then issue you a certificate.

4. After the certificate has been created, the CA will email it back to you or, if submitted online, you can retrieve it through the Web browser.

5. At this point, you can now install the certificate and begin using it. An example of a completed certificate is shown in Figure 1.6.

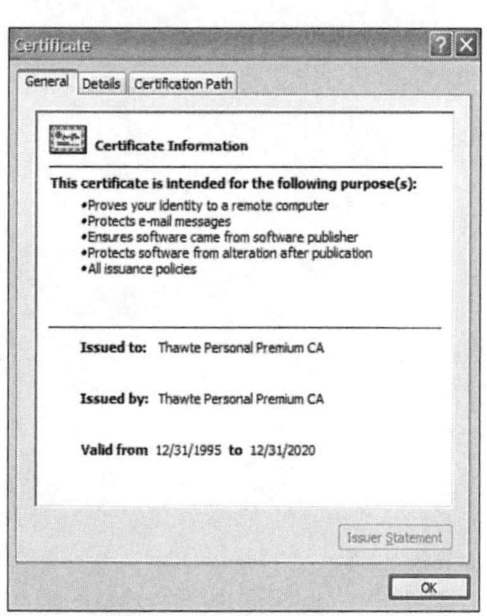

FIGURE 1.6
Information included in the final certificate (Thawte certificate shown).

Certificates generally follow the International Telecommunication Union-Telecommunication (ITU-T) X.509 standards for syntax and format. Information included in the certificate varies based on the purpose of the certificate (user ID, email, server ID, and so on), but it typically includes the following:

- Version
- Serial number
- Signature algorithm ID
- Issuer name
- Subject name

- Subject public key information
- Issuer unique ID

Generally, you can view the details of a given certificate as shown in Figure 1.7.

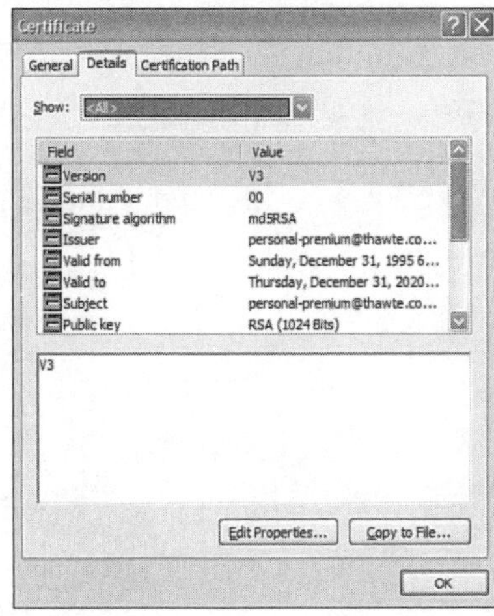

FIGURE 1.7
Certificate details (Thawte certificate shown).

Two types of certificate authorities can generate certificates: *self signed* and *third party.*

A *self-signed* CA is set up by you and run in your company. Similar to Kerberos, its primary purpose is protecting authentication of users *within* your network environment (this might include your partners and even special clients) and encrypting data during transmission. This type of CA is being deployed more and more in large companies to help them protect the data traversing their internal networks and to sign internal corporate emails.

The level of trust produced by a self-signed CA is fairly low for users outside your network environment. Going back to our original example, it is the equivalent of you producing and distributing your own driver's licenses. If no one else trusts you, your certificates are useless on the Internet.

A *third-party* CA is used to prove your identity to others on or across the Internet. Examples of third-party CAs include

- VeriSign
- Entrust
- Thawte

Different types of certificates are available with a varying price range depending on the purpose of the certificate. VeriSign uses a class system (class 1, class 2, class 3, and so on), and Thawte simply names the certificate for its purpose (Web, email, code signing, and so on). A higher level of trust is implied when using a third-party CA because your identity is being verified by a completely different agency.

The effort the third-party company uses to prove your identity is directly related to the cost and use of the certificate. This effort can be as minimal as checking to see whether your email account is valid (used for free message signing certificates) to a more vigorous effort including phone calls, faxes, emails, and calls to the state revenue department to ensure your business is legitimate (used for Web certificates).

The Mechanics of Authentication Using Certificates

So far, we've covered the general premise behind certificates, their format, how to generate them, and the types of CAs that can be deployed to support your certificate needs. The next step is to cover how certificates allow you to authenticate an agent.

The X.509 certificate technology is built on the premise of having two separate keys—a *public key* that can be freely distributed and a *private key* that is held by the owner of the key pair. Because the keys are different, they are called *asymmetric keys* (or *asymmetric cryptography*). It is critical that the private key reside only with the owner of the key pair. If the private key is copied or compromised, impersonation can take place. The keys are mated mathematically and can be used to prove identity in the following way:

1. Using one of the methods described earlier, Bob (a user) installs an email certificate into his email program. Bob is the owner of the certificate and has both the public and private keys installed.

2. When Bob sends email to Jim (another user), he can use a digest of the email (shortened version), encrypt it with his private key, and embed it in the email. This is known as a *digital signature.* This allows the receiver to verify the sender and has an added benefit of ensuring the message is not tampered with (see Figure 1.8).

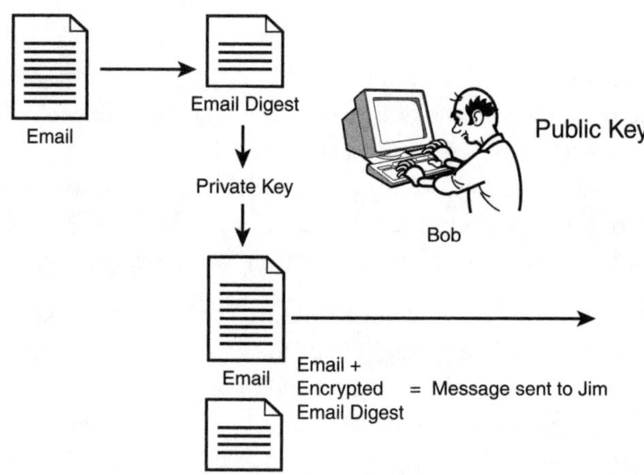

FIGURE 1.8
Signing email to prove identity.

> **NOTE**
> Keep in mind this example does not have Bob encrypting his email, only signing it. The email message itself is still in clear text.

3. To prove that the email came from Bob and was not tampered with, Jim can download Bob's public key. The public key can be retrieved from Bob's machine or some other published location, such as a Web site (see Figure 1.9).

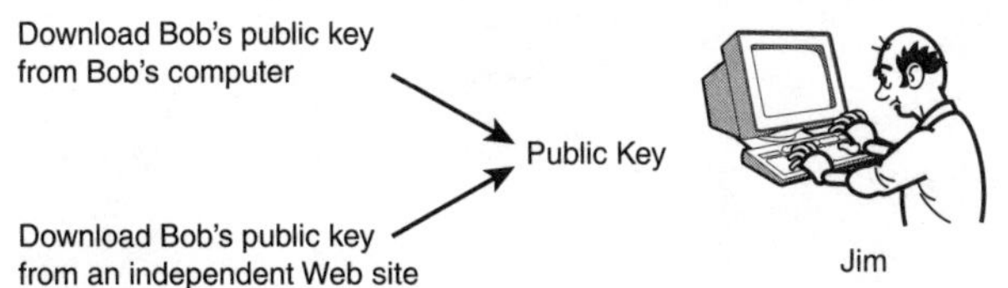

FIGURE 1.9
Retrieving a public key.

4 Jim can now process the embedded signature. The public and private keys are mated in such a way that only a signature of the private key holder will produce a valid result when processed through the public key (see Figure 1.10).

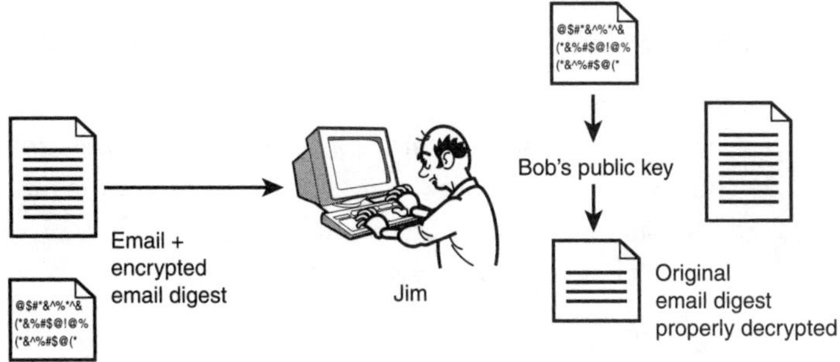

FIGURE 1.10
Processing the signature.

There are several ways to explain an improper decryption, as shown in Figure 1.11:

- Someone trying to impersonate Bob sent Jim a message signed with a different private key.
- The message has been tampered with or altered.
- The messaged was corrupted during the delivery process.

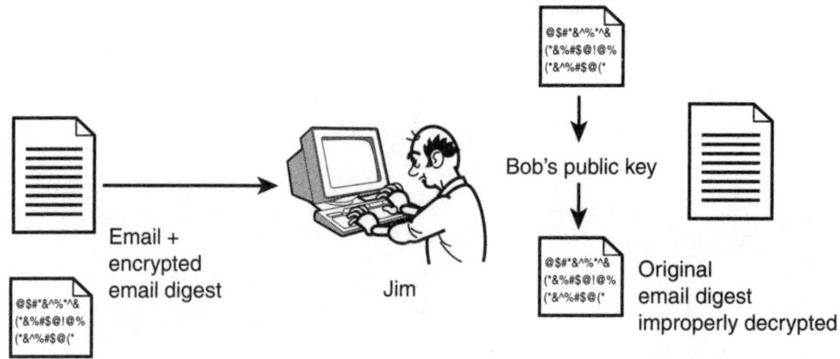

FIGURE 1.11
Incorrect digest produced.

Note that the authentication process in this example is unidirectional. Only Jim can authenticate Bob's email. If Bob needed to authenticate communications from Jim, Jim would also have to install a certificate key pair. This authentication process is not limited to emails; developers can sign their software code, and servers and clients can sign their data traffic and network connections.

There are a few weaknesses with certificates as with passwords and usernames:

- If your private key is stolen or copied, the thief can impersonate you and your digital signature. Because of the nature of the certificate and the method of authentication, it might be a long time before you realize someone has your private key.
- Someone sitting at the computer on which your private key is installed could gain access to any resource that allows certificate authentication.
- If the certificate authority that has issued your key is compromised or becomes untrustworthy, your key and its capability to sign on your behalf become worthless.
- Finally, the entire issue of certificates is based on two or more parties trusting a mutual third party. If this can't be agreed upon or if, for any reason, the third-party issuer is found to be negligent or inaccurate in its verification of identity, the entire certificate infrastructure can lose its value.

Each of the methods we have looked at so far involves a somewhat static behavior. Usernames/passwords, Kerberos, CHAP, and certificates all deal with static passwords or the installation of a static certificate. It is understood that passwords can be changed and certificates can be updated, but each is reusable over some defined period of time.

Our next authentication mechanism—tokens—generates a new password each time you request a logon.

Tokens

Companies are storing larger amounts of important data than ever on their networks. If the prize is valuable enough, people will come after it. In a majority of networks, all it takes is a stolen password. Passwords can be compromised by any of the following methods:

- Verbal transfer (intentional or not)
- Being written down and stored in an unsecured manner
- Dedicated and more technical attack form, such as network monitoring

It is a common vulnerability that many companies can no longer afford to expose themselves to. Using a token authentication method can help you reduce your network's exposure to this type of threat.

A *token* in the computing world is similar in function to a subway token. You use it once for entry, and it is gone. This dynamic, one-time password generation method can be one of the most secure if it is set up properly. If someone sees you type your password, overhears you say it, or manages to pull it off the network by means of a network-sniffing tool, it is worthless because it should never be used again.

Two types of token systems can be deployed: software and hardware. Software-based systems are easier to deploy than hardware systems and are generally easier to use as well. The trade-off is that software token systems are also easier to compromise. When deciding between software- or hardware-based deployment, reducing security costs is a typical reason for choosing a software-based system. This must be weighed carefully through risk analysis and possible recovery costs should the software system be compromised. A saying that rings true more often than not is, "Hardware is cheap; problems are expensive!"

Additional factors to consider when deciding between hardware or software token systems include the following:

- What type of data is at risk?
- What type of security environment is currently in place?

- What is the current technical level of the staff and users?
- What is the long-term goal of the company?

If the resources being protected are similar to email and day-to-day operations files, a software system is probably a good choice. If, however, the data is highly sensitive or highly valuable (such as bank transactions or corporate financial data), deploying a more secure hardware-based token system can be cheaper. Keep in mind another truism in security:

> A system that is moderately secure and correctly used by everyone is most likely better than a highly secure system that is used improperly or bypassed for the sake of getting work done.

Software Token System

The software-based token system is deployed in two software pieces. The first piece sits on a back-end system and is used to store usernames, PINs, and the access control software. The second piece is a client that is installed on any of the following:

- Desktop
- Laptop
- Handheld (Palm, iPAC, and so on)
- Integrated wireless systems (such as Nokia and Ericsson)

The two pieces of software (server and client) are synchronized to each other and tied into each user account. This configuration produces a unique password process for each user configured in the database. When a user attempts to access a resource protected by the token system, she is prompted for a PIN (stored in the user database) and password that is generated by the local token software. The combination is sent from the client's device (desktop, laptop, and so on) to the security server. If the PIN/password combination matches the server's calculated PIN/password combination, the user is allowed access.

Problems can arise if the system is not deployed in a secure enough environment. To illustrate, let's say Suzie gets up and leaves her computer unattended while she is still logged on. Bob can compromise the system by transferring (*cloning*) Suzie's software token configuration file (literally copying the file from her system to a different one).

This file is installed locally when the token software is installed. By copying her configuration file, Bob has acquired half of the necessary security information. Now he can either guess at Suzie's PIN or attempt to talk her into telling him what it is (social engineering). If this scenario is a possibility in your environment or you desire a higher level of security, you probably should deploy a hardware-based token system.

Hardware Token System

Hardware token systems are very similar to software token systems. The major difference is that the client software resides in a portable device such as a card or key fob. (A key fob is a small device that generally fits onto a key ring. It is smaller than a card but is used the same way.)

The expense is greater to deploy and maintain this technology. Each user needs her own card or key fob, and support must be implemented to handle the loss, theft, and replacement of these physical devices. The trade-off for the extra cost and work is that the system is far more difficult to break into and cloning a key device is next to impossible.

When a client accesses a protected resource, a request for a PIN is made and the code is currently displayed on her local device. On the server is a similar device that is synchronized with the card or key fob used by the client. If the PIN and number match what is currently expected by the server, the user is allowed access. These codes are built to change at an administrative interval (typically every 60 seconds).

If we go back to our example with Suzie and Bob, there's no way for Bob to clone Suzie's physical token, thus reducing the chance of a security compromise. Newer token systems are being built that require the token be inserted into a special port (USB or modified serial) on the system for logon to occur. If the token is removed (when going to a meeting, for instance), the PC system is automatically locked and can be unlocked only by reinserting the token into the port.

This technology is being expanded further to include building and office door lock systems as well. When Suzie arrives at work, for example, she can insert her token into the electronic door system and enter her PIN to unlock the door. At the same time, the accounting system can be notified of her arrival at work (no more time cards).

When she arrives at her office, she again can insert her token and be allowed access. Finally, she can sit at her desk, insert the token into the special port on her PC, and log on to the network. If she needs to get up and leave the office, she only needs to take her token with her and her system is automatically secured.

With either software or hardware token authentication, someone still could steal the token, acquire the PIN, and compromise the security system—although this risk is greatly reduced compared to simple passwords and certificates. A user can lose or forget her token, leaving her unable to log on and rendering her completely nonproductive until the token is replaced and the system updated. To overcome this last issue in authentication, you need to shift focus from something you know or something you have to something you are.

Biometrics

Biometric authentication is by far the most secure form of authentication and is one of the most convenient. Using this authentication method, a part of your physical characteristic is used for positive identification. This method ensures that authentication can't be lost, stolen, or borrowed, and impersonation is mathematically improbable. Using hardware (typically in the form of a scanner or camera) and software, biometrics measures and stores a particular characteristic and associates it with a user account in the network environment. The physical characteristic used can be any of the following:

- Fingerprints
- Hand/palm geometry
- Voiceprint
- Facial geometry
- Iris profile
- Retinal scan
- Signature

Fingerprints

A good biometric is one that is unaffected by age. Your fingerprints, for example, are formed between the first and second trimester and remain unchanged until death. Another trait of a good biometric is uniqueness. From the inception of fingerprint recording until today, no two people have been found to have exactly the same fingerprints. The hardware that supports fingerprint authentication methodology is small and nonintrusive, and over the last several years it has become quite affordable with many vendors from which to choose. Figure 1.12 shows a keyboard with an integrated fingerprint system and card reader.

FIGURE 1.12
Keyboard with integrated fingerprint system.

The only issues that might cause problems are damaging or scarring of your fingertips (the system can be updated easily) and the criminal stigma associated with fingerprints and fingerprinting as a form of ID.

Hand/Palm Geometry

Hand or palm geometry is based on measuring (also called *profiling*) and analyzing the shape of your hand. The devices used are larger and can be set to differing levels of precision. These devices are commonly integrated as part of access control systems for room or building entry. Figure 1.13 shows a hand-scanning device integrated with a door lock system.

The issue with this particular biometric device is its size. Hand scanners are more likely to be used to secure your office from unauthorized personnel than for logging on to the network.

FIGURE 1.13
Hand scanner.

Voiceprint

The method of voiceprint identification is also cheap and easy to use. The hardware used is just a microphone. Plus, it is not very intrusive in the work area and is simple to train people to use.

A significant drawback to voice identification is its susceptibility to error relative to other methods listed in this section. Colds, changes in humidity, and ambient/background noise can cause your voice (or the sound waves) to change, thus causing a failure to be properly identified. Aging and trauma can also cause your voice to change (remember a good biometric shouldn't change over time).

Facial Geometry

Similar to hand or palm geometry, this biometric measures the shape of your face and head. The required hardware is a simple digital camera, readily available and fairly cheap. Although this particular method of authentication is not yet very popular, it is easy to set up and maintain. Figure 1.14 shows a digital camera sold as a package with facial recognition software. The camera pictured is a door lock integrated system; desktop systems are smaller and just as easy to use.

FIGURE 1.14
Digital camera used in facial authentication.

The negative aspects of using facial geometry include poor recognition behavior in varying degrees of ambient light and the expense of having a camera mounted on all workstations. Fingerprint scanners are cheaper and typically more reliable.

Iris Profile

The iris is the colored part of the human eye. However, it's not the color that is used for authentication, but the pattern of the iris itself. Color would not be a guarantee of individuality, but the pattern of the iris is similar to a fingerprint. Cameras used to scan the eye are not particularly expensive, nor are they as intrusive as a retinal scan (covered next), making this form of identification quick and easy. Iris scans can even be done with glasses on and contact lenses in.

The biggest problems with this ID method are the expense of the software, the limited number of vendors, and difficult integration compared to fingerprint and facial geometry methods.

Retinal Scans

This form of authentication might be one of the best known because of movies and TV. The equipment used is the most invasive of the biometric technologies and involves a device that reads the pattern of blood vessels located at the back of the eye. The device is usually wall mounted and would be more appropriate for office or server room access control than logon authentication.

Multifactor

Any of the authentication methods described previously can be overcome if used by itself, as noted in Table 1.2.

TABLE 1.2

WEAKNESSES OF USING A SINGLE AUTHENTICATION METHOD

Authentication Method	*Defeated by*
Username/Password; Kerberos; CHAP	Theft; disclosure (written down); dissemination (given out); guessing

continues

TABLE 1.2 *continued*

WEAKNESSES OF USING A SINGLE AUTHENTICATION METHOD

Authentication Method	*Defeated by*
Certificates; software tokens	Cloning; unsecured PC
Hardware tokens	Theft of token
Biometrics	Depends on the method (see later in this section)

Multifactor authentication involves combining two or more authentication methods. In fact, in our discussion of software and hardware tokens, our examples included the use of a PIN during the authentication process. This is an excellent example of two-factor authentication. A user must possess both the token *and* the PIN to log on properly. If the system were built to use just the token, the security could easily be defeated through token cloning (software) or theft (hardware).

Even a biometric used by itself could potentially be compromised. As unpleasant as it might sound, someone could cut off a finger or hand in an attempt to bypass a biometric device. Digital imaging and voice recordings might also be used in an attempt to defeat security. Two- or even three-factor authentication mechanisms are commonly deployed where biometrics are used.

IN THE FIELD

MULTIFACTOR, INDEED!

How much is too much when it comes to security? Is there such a thing? While consulting on a government project, we ran across the following as entry requirements into a secured area: retinal scan, palm geometry, token card, and PIN (eight digits, no less). The information being secured was, as you have probably guessed, of an extremely sensitive nature. We can't tell you what was being protected, but we can tell you the measures taken to ensure its security (just knowing might be as much of a deterrent as anything else):

1. You and your partner (no getting into this area alone!) must insert your token cards into a card reader at the same time to activate the system (which looks like a bank ATM slot).

The card readers are approximately 15 feet apart (you can't insert both cards fast enough by yourself).

2. After the cards have been read and checked for access, the palm system activates. You both place your hands on a palm scanner. Your body temperature must be +/– 3° of normal (no cutting off of hands—the severed hand would be too cold).
3. If the palm read is successful, the system activates an iris profiler and you look at a spot on the wall while your iris is checked.
4. The final action is to input an eight-digit PIN. The keys on the keypad are LEDs. You must push a button to randomize the placement of the numeric values so that the numbers are never in the same place from one user to the next (no one could look over your shoulder to watch the pattern typed in and guess your PIN).

There are time constraints, too. You and your partner must complete a given step within 5 seconds of each other. The entire four-step process must be completed within 4 minutes to be successful, and after the palm scanner is active, your hand must remain in place to continue the authentication process (if you remove your hand, the whole system resets). Although this might represent an extreme example (seen by most only in the movies), it does illustrate multifactor authentication and the security it affords.

Mutual Authentication

Each of the previous sections so far has discussed a form of authentication that is one-way. *Mutual* authentication describes a behavior where a client process verifies its identity to a server (or service) and a server (or service) verifies its identity to the client. Mutual authentication is implemented in several authentication protocols (CHAP and Kerberos) and also in software (Web services, IPSec, and virtually anything you want to pay for).

In Kerberos, for example, authentication has a built-in mechanism for mutual authentication. Following the resource request process step by step, we can identify the flow of a connection request and see where the mutual authentication takes place:

1. Bob (or rather his system) sends a message to the AS requesting to talk to server Kirk.

2. Upon receipt of the request, the AS creates two identical session keys and encrypts them. Key one is encrypted with Bob's private code and is tagged with the server's name, Kirk. Key two is encrypted with Kirk's private code and tagged with the user's name, Bob. It sends both keys to Bob.

3. Bob decrypts key one that was encrypted using his code. The system identifies the key based on the Kirk tag included (this is the session key to talk to Kirk). Bob's machine might have many sessions open, and the key tag allows the system to keep the keys properly sorted. Bob can't open key two because it is encrypted with the server's code. Bob creates key three, which has a timestamp on it and encrypts it using his session key. Bob sends both key two and key three to Kirk.

4. Kirk opens key two (session key identical to Bob's) that was encrypted using the server's private code. Kirk identifies this key based on the tag Bob embedded in it. Again, it is likely that Kirk, as a server, will have many sessions with numerous clients and the tag helps keep the keys properly segmented. Kirk then uses the session key to unlock Bob's timestamp message. The timestamp is used to prevent replay attacks.

Through the use of the KDC and each of the private codes, the systems have been mutually authenticated. Only Bob could have unlocked key one (it was encrypted with Bob's code), and only the destination server, Kirk, could have unlocked key two.

Bob's code is known only to the KDC (it is built from his password), and Kirk's code is known only to the KDC (it was built when Kirk was first installed into the KDC's realm). This is the behavior that provides authentication for both systems through a third-party system (the KDC).

Certificates can also be used for mutual authentication and work in a similar fashion with one client verifying the digital signature of the other.

REVIEW BREAK

Authentication Review

- Authentication identifies users so that security can be set and enforced.

- Many forms of authentication exist, including username/password, Kerberos, CHAP, certificates, tokens, and biometrics.
- Some environments require the added security of using more than one form of authentication. Multifactor authentication can be deployed to overcome the weaknesses of a single form of user identity verification.
- Mutual authentication provides an authentication routine that allows verification of the users as well as the services and servers used.

Thus far, we've established terminology, access control, and authentication. Our next area of focus is services provided by servers.

Identifying Nonessential Services and Protocols

Identify nonessential services and protocols and take the appropriate action.

There it is, your shiny new server sitting in the rack, completely preconfigured by the manufacturer to your specifications. It has more RAM than the first 10,000 computers ever built put together. When the eight CPUs on its motherboard begin to process, you can feel the breeze from the cooling system. It is just waiting to be plugged in and brought online. It is tempting to do that, but there's a nagging voice telling you to go through and check it out (if you can't hear the voice yet, you will by the time we're done with you).

New computer systems (especially servers) come from the manufacturer loaded to the gills with services, software, and protocols that will never be used. No matter how well you describe your desired configuration, remember that most systems are preconfigured by the manufacturer for the most common of environments, not the most secure. This behavior leaves the new server exposed to hacking exploits and a myriad of security risks posed by having services and applications installed without proper protective measures taken.

It is up to you to

- Plan the desired function of the server. List services, protocols, and applications to be installed and supported.

- Evaluate the current state of the server relative to the plan.
- Configure the server to meet the plan's objectives.

Planning is your first goal. Unfortunately, it is also the goal that is most often overlooked. We have found over the years that it is ineffective to sit down at a server and try to configure it properly without a plan. Trying to remember all the different settings that need to be implemented and all the services that should be turned off (or on) is just too daunting a task given the complexity of the current operating systems. Evaluation and configuration of the systems is not broken out in the following details, as you'll see. Configuration and evaluation is a matter of mechanics after the plan is built. Because each operating system has its own set of tools, configuration scripts, and interfaces to accomplish the tasks set forth in the plan, it would be too consuming to try to cover all the possibilities here.

The easiest way to start this process is to start asking questions. Write the questions down along with the answers and you're halfway there. Questions to ask about the setup of a new or existing server include the following:

- What is the purpose or role of the server?
- Which services are required/critical for proper functioning of the operating system?
- Which services are required/critical to the role of the server?
- What networking (or service) protocols are required/critical for the server?
- Are any services or protocols installed that are not necessary for the current role of the server?

Server Role

The recommendations and discussions of this particular area are not specific to any operating system but are more of a general approach. You should take this information and further develop your security plan around the operating systems currently deployed in your environment.

You can ease security issues and develop a clear path to configuration of services by defining the role of the server up front. Common roles for servers include

- **File and print server**—Used for access to common user files, home directories, and print capabilities.
- **Web server**—Used to host internal or external Web sites and Web-based applications.
- **FTP server**—Used to store files for internal or external download (and possibly upload).
- **Email server**—It is used for email, but it can also be used to host custom messaging applications, public folders, group schedules, and other groupware applications.
- **News/Usenet (NNTP) server**—Similar to email but passive. Users can post and retrieve messages in a common location (unlike email, which is actively sent to you).
- **Application server**—Application servers host applications (other than those previously listed) such as database systems, custom accounting apps, point-of-sale systems, and so on.
- **Logon server (user authentication system)**—These servers are tasked with authenticating users when they log on to their workstations. These servers can act as any other type of server as well.
- **Network services server**—These servers host applications that are required for the network to function properly. These include hostname servers (Windows Internet Naming Service [WINS] and DNS), monitoring/performance applications (sniffing tools, management stations for SNMP), and configuration servers (Trivial File Transfer Protocol [TFTP] and Dynamic Host Configuration Protocol [DHCP]).

You should also identify the server as being on the public or private portion of your network. After this is accomplished, you can move to identifying required services for the operating system.

Required/Critical Services

Each operating system requires different services for proper operation. It is important to review these services, identify their proper configuration, and document policy concerning their deployment. Standardization through documentation will make new server deployments much easier and more secure.

The goal is to start with the bare minimum of services and turn on only those necessary for proper operation. The operating system manufacturer should have required services listed in the documentation, and additional recommendations can be found by searching the Web.

We have found that one of the easiest ways to achieve your goals is to do a clean installation. Regardless of how the computer system is shipped to you, wipe the disk and start from scratch. There is almost no way to tell what add-in software or additional configuration changes have been made by the manufacturer. The only way to be sure is to perform a clean installation, following your policies and checklists. Although this can be a time investment on your part up front, it is worth it. As a side benefit, it ensures that you have all the proper software available (and skills necessary) to rebuild the server should you ever need to. As pressure grows to get systems deployed, it is often stated that "we don't have time to do all that." Oddly enough, when it breaks or is hacked, everyone seems capable of finding the time to fix it.

Don't cut corners. If security is your goal, take the time to do it right the first time, every time.

Required Protocols

Protocols, like services, should be used only if required. Determine which protocols are required for your network environment, and document the proper configuration and deployment steps for each. Let's look at a decision process using a communications protocol first and ask these questions:

- Which protocols are required for the desktops and servers to communicate?
- Which protocols will be used for remote access services?

- How will the clients and servers be configured—manually or dynamically?
- Will the choice of protocol require additional services?
- Are there known security issues associated with the protocol(s) chosen?

Let's assume you have a network environment consisting of Unix and Windows operating systems, and you're going to use TCP/IP as your communications protocol. The next decision is whether to deploy TCP/IP statically or to allow your clients to be autoconfigured through DHCP.

Static host configuration is more time-consuming, is more secure, requires fewer services on the network, and takes up less bandwidth. Static configuration does not scale well as the network grows, however. DHCP configuration requires that you run a DHCP service on your network. This service is responsible for handing out host configuration, including TCP/IP address, subnet mask, and gateway at a minimum. Optional information can also be configured on the client, including domain name suffix, DNS server addresses, backup gateways, and other operating system-specific options. DHCP also takes up network bandwidth, requires you to run an additional service, and is considered less secure because unknown users can plug into your network and receive a proper TCP/IP configuration. The big benefit to DHCP is that it can scale easily to support networks of thousands of users.

The choice to configure your clients statically or dynamically is yours. Given the infinite number of possible network configurations and security desires, there's no one perfect recommendation that can be made here. You must weigh the factors, consider the implications on your security, and deploy as you see fit.

As we have discussed, if you choose to deploy TCP/IP dynamically in your network, it will require the use of an additional service, DHCP. TCP/IP also requires that you have a Domain Name System (DNS) server deployed for proper name resolution services. In our sample network, we run both Unix and Microsoft operating systems and therefore should deploy both DNS and the Windows Internet Naming Service (WINS) for NetBIOS name resolution. These services allow clients to use friendly names on the network instead of having to memorize IP address information.

Research should be done to identify the risks associated with running each choice of service and protocol. What problems might arise if you deploy DNS on Windows NT? What if you deploy DNS on Windows 2000 or Unix? Research and record your findings; also, identify possible solutions to reduce the risks associated with each service and protocol. As you will see next, the best solution is to remove services and protocols when possible, eliminating the associated risk all together.

Removing Protocols and Services

Each new service generally brings new protocols and new security risks with it. It is up to you to identify these risks and reduce your exposure to them as much as possible. Operating systems are constantly redeveloped, and new features are added on so quickly that it is almost impossible to keep up. (Does anyone remember when an OS fit on a floppy?) It is up to you to choose the features required and desired for your network and deploy them in a safe and reliable manner.

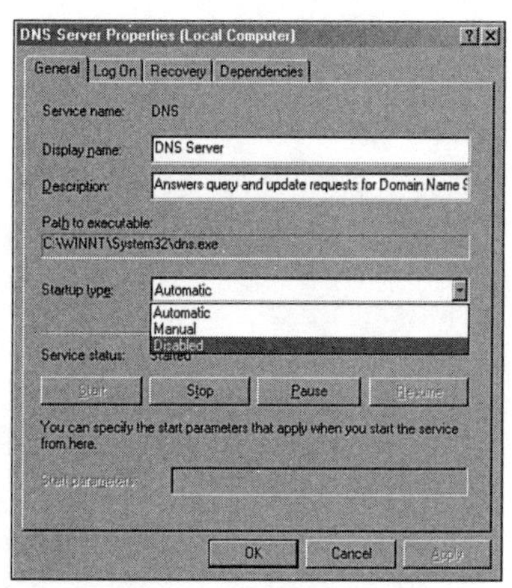

FIGURE 1.15
Windows 2000 Control Panel interface for disabling services.

If you accept a server out of the box, it might have services installed that not only take up resources and generally slow down the system, but that also can pose security risks. Find these services and uninstall them or turn them off. Why run Web services, remote shell, Terminal Services, and FTP applications if you aren't going to use them? If they are left installed and improperly configured, someone else might use them. As shown in Figure 1.15, Windows 2000 offers a graphic interface to disable services that cannot be removed.

Planning cannot be emphasized enough. Secure networks require planning time. One of the biggest issues you are likely to face is the pace at which networking technology (software and hardware) is deployed. The philosophy that seems to have developed over the last few years is "deploy first, configure later." Companies want to deploy new servers, services, and technology as fast as they can to take advantage of what each has to offer, and little consideration is given to the potential risks that invariably come with new technology.

Today's IT departments are doing more with less: less people, less time, and less money. This typically leads to less security as well. A network deployed without planning turns into a FrankenNetwork.

A *FrankenNetwork* is built of pieces and parts and connected with whatever resources are available at the time. This network rapidly turns into an uncontrollable monster that runs us, instead of us running it. Fight this trend and plan.

> **NOTE** The term *FrankenNetwork* is somewhat of an insult to Dr. Frankenstein, who had a plan and followed it very well.

The five "P" philosophy states that *proper planning prevents poor performance.* We've discussed the fact that the number of services and protocols offered in the newer operating systems is enormous. Identify those services that are required based on desired functionality, and remove everything else. This minimalist approach helps reduce complexity and the avenues of attacks that plague the modern network.

REVIEW BREAK

Reviewing Nonessential Services and Protocols

- Plan first and identify roles for your servers in your organization.
- Identify the services and protocols required for each role.
- When deploying new servers, identify their roles and use your plans and guidelines to set up the servers so they are secure.
- Remove unwanted services and protocols when possible.

ATTACKS

Recognize attacks and take appropriate action.

> **EXAM TIP** As you read the section on attacks, find the common attack methods and identify the preventative measures. The test is likely to concentrate on this area because it is important to understand your enemy to set up proper security.

In April 2002, the Computer Security Institute (CSI) released statistics from the 2002 computer crime survey. The seventh such annual survey of large companies illustrates a growing trend in attacks on corporate networks. The following are some statistics taken from this report that surveyed 503 companies:

- 90% of respondents (primarily large corporations and government agencies) detected computer security breaches within between April 2002 and April 2003.
- 80% acknowledged financial losses because of computer breaches.

- 44% (223 respondents) were willing and/or able to quantify their financial losses. These 223 respondents reported $455,848,000 in financial losses.
- As in previous years, the most serious financial losses occurred through theft of proprietary information (26 respondents reported $170,827,000) and financial fraud (25 respondents reported $115,753,000).
- For the fifth year in a row, more respondents (74%) cited their Internet connection as a frequent point of attack than cited their internal systems as a frequent point of attack (33%).
- 34% reported the intrusions to law enforcement. (In 1996, only 16% acknowledged reporting intrusions to law enforcement.)

The statistics outline the possibility of financial gain as one reason someone might attack your network. Almost half a billion dollars was lost just by the respondents of this one survey. How much more was lost by companies not included in the questionnaire? $285 million was lost from theft of proprietary information or financial fraud. It is safe to say that bored or curious teenagers at home are not the only threat to your network anymore. Attacks are increasing, as is their impact to the corporate bottom line. Understanding attacks involves understanding the following:

- Why might you be attacked?
- Who would execute the attack(s) against you?
- What types of attacks would be used?

Why You?

Behavior in the cyber-world is becoming a mirror of our behavior in the real world. The social community that has developed in networking and on the Internet carries with it all the same behaviors as the social communities in which we live. Differences do exist, however. The anonymity of the Internet (and to some degree in networking) and the lack of physical contact allow a greater sense of freedom. The checks and balances that govern our behavior in the physical world might not have the same influence in the cyber-world.

This freedom has played a part in the attitudes, behavior, and motivations that have developed in the Internet and networking communities. Understanding the "why" of an attack helps you protect your network and might even enable you to predict when an attack might occur. Common motivations for network attacks include

- **Monetary gain**—The need or desire to gain financially. This motivation can lead to attacks on systems that store financial data such as credit card numbers. Other attack targets might include banks and their transactions.
- **Information gain**—The desire to have more information than others. This can be used as a motivation to steal proprietary information, employee records, or data of a sensitive nature. The information can be used to help focus attention on the individual who has stolen it (if you want to know, come ask me), for monetary gain (inside stock information, selling of designs/ideas), for political insight (knowing who will be promoted), or for personal advancement (information that allows advancement through access to privileged information).
- **Revenge**—The age-old need to get back at someone for harm done, either real or perceived. This motivation can account for the purposeful destruction, alteration, or manipulation of data, equipment, and the network as a whole, or even attacks on intangible assets such as the corporate image.
- **Curiosity**—A desire to understand or know about systems more completely. This motivation explains why people break into computer systems and leave them unharmed. In fact, an electronic note might be left explaining how it was done to help the company close security holes.
- **Political, religious, and ideological differences**—The desire to express one's belief and be heard above the crowd. This motivation has received much more attention since the events of September 11, 2001. This motivation can result in the same goals as outlined in each of the previous motivations.
- **Malicious intent**—The need to attack for her own sake. This is probably the hardest of the motivations to understand. Driven by this motivation, an attacker might seek out the goals of any of the other previously mentioned motivations. The primary goal is "tonnage" (see the following note) or adding to the prestige of the attacker among her peers.

NOTE

The term *tonnage* was probably taken from naval terminology. After a naval battle, damage to the enemy was assessed not just by how many ships were sunk but also by how much each ship weighed (in tons). The heavier a ship was, the more important and the greater the prestige associated with sinking it. As a slang term in computer attacks, it is the same. Successfully attacking a highly visible Web site or network is more *tonnage* than attacking a smaller, less prominent one. In addition, the longer the network is affected (down or not fully functional), the more prestige that is earned.

This list of motivations is by no means complete. This is an attempt to list common motivations discovered in previous computer attacks, in which the perpetrator was either caught and questioned or communicated the motivation to the victim during or after the attack.

Who Would Attack?

Armed with what motivates an attacker, you can now profile who might possibly attack your company and its network(s). Attackers can generally be put into three groups:

- An individual or group with intimate knowledge of the network
- An individual or group with inside knowledge of the network
- An individual or group with no inside knowledge of the network

Someone with an intimate knowledge of the network poses the greatest risk to your network and its security. This user might be a current or former employee with administrative, root, or supervisory privileges on the network. Motivation for this user is typically monetary/informational gain or revenge. Other motivations such as curiosity can also play a role. Even if this user does not have a high level of privilege, considerable damage can still be done because of his level of knowledge and the wide availability of attack tools.

A user who has inside knowledge of the network can be a current or former employee, a partner, or a contractor. He generally does not have administrative privilege but does have a level of knowledge sufficient enough that, when combined with the tools available, can cause a lot of damage to the network and its resources. The motivation for this attacker is typically the same as for someone with an intimate knowledge of the network.

The final user has no inside knowledge of the network; the information used for the attack is gathered from information that is publicly available and developed into a company profile. This attacker generally attacks the company's Internet connection in an attempt to penetrate the corporate infrastructure. The real threat from this type of user is not the knowledge but the sheer number of possible attackers of this type. Although a majority of the Internet community does not have the programming knowledge to mount a successful attack, the number of prebuilt tools and scripts and the amount of information that can be found make the threat from this type of user real. The motivation for this attacker can be any of the previously listed motivations, from monetary gain to pure malicious intent.

Now that we have identified the common motivations that prompt users to attack and the user types you're likely to defend against, let's look at the tools of the trade.

What Types of Attacks?

The types of attacks have fallen into natural categories over the past few years based on the methods used in the attack. Another look at the CSI computer crime survey shows some current statistics associated with the various attack types and abuses:

- 40% detected system penetration from the outside.
- 40% detected denial-of-service attacks.
- 78% detected employee abuse of Internet access privileges (for example, downloading pornography or pirated software or inappropriate use of email systems).
- 85% detected computer viruses.
- 38% suffered unauthorized access or misuse on their Web sites within the last 12 months. 21% said they didn't know whether there had been unauthorized access or misuse.
- 25% of those acknowledging attacks reported from two to five incidents. 39% reported ten or more incidents.
- 70% of those attacked reported vandalism (only 64% in 2000).
- 55% reported a denial of service.
- 12% reported theft of transaction information.
- 6% reported financial fraud (only 3% in 2000).

Most of these numbers are steadily increasing. Some of these increases can be attributed to an increase in the number of networks on the public Internet and a growing population of computer-literate users.

In an effort to prevent your network from becoming part of the preceding statistics, you need to know which types of attacks are common and which methods can be deployed to prevent them or reduce the impact they can have. The attacks that we cover include

- Denial-of-service (DoS) and distributed denial-of-service (DDoS)
- Back door
- Spoofing
- Man-in-the-middle
- Replay
- TCP/IP hijacking
- Weak keys
- Mathematical
- Birthday
- Password guessing

This discussion strives to point out not only the description of the attack types, but also some examples of each and some prevention or protection methods. You will note that some of the attacks are combinations or modifications of several types.

Denial-of-Service and Distributed Denial-of-Service Attacks

As its name implies, the purpose for a denial-of-service attack is to deny use of resources or services to legitimate users. A particularly difficult aspect of this type of attack is that it can be executed without the need to identify yourself or present credentials of any kind to the network or its servers.

Utilities used by administrators to test network connectivity and host availability are widely available and commonly used to perform these forms of attacks. In the correct hands, these utilities help troubleshoot and diagnose problems on the network or host. In the wrong hands, they can cause valid network users to lose existing connections or be denied new connections or use of services such as DNS, Web, FTP, and email.

Examples of DoS attacks include the following:

- **Smurf/Smurfing**—This attack is based on ping and the Internet Control Message Protocol (ICMP) echo reply function. An attacker first finds networks that currently allow ICMP messages. Then he pings the broadcast address associated with the targeted network addresses found in step 1, causing all hosts on the targeted networks to respond with an echo reply. The attacker replaces the original source address in the ping packets with the source address of the victim (this is called *spoofing*; see later in this list), causing a flood of traffic (in the form of the replies) to be sent to the unsuspecting network device (which could be a server, client, router, and so on). This attack could affect the Internet service provider (ISP) hosting the victim's Internet connection, the network on which the host resides, and the host.
- **Fraggle**—This attack is based on the smurf attack; the difference is that it uses the User Datagram Protocol (UDP) instead of ICMP. The attacker sends spoofed UDP packets to broadcast addresses as in the smurf attack. These UDP packets are directed to port 7 (echo) or port 19 (chargen). The chargen port generates characters when queried, so the return traffic to the victim has the same effect as a smurf attack. The attacker can also be successful at looping traffic between the two ports, increasing the amount of traffic generated to the victim.
- **Ping floods**—This attack attempts to reduce service or block activity on a host by sending ping requests directly to the victim. The system CPU is overloaded as it attempts to respond to the ping requests. This attack generally degrades service, but it can cause older systems to crash.
- **Land**—This attack exploits a behavior in several operating systems and their respective TCP/IP stacks. The attacker spoofs a TCP/IP synchronization (SYN) packet to the victim system with the same source and destination IP address and the same source and destination ports. This causes the operating system to slow down (or *hang*) while it tries to respond to what it believes is its own packet. Some vulnerable operating systems include versions of Windows, Unix, Macintosh OS, and CISCO IOS. (See the references at the end of the chapter for additional sites where more details can be found.)

- **Teardrop**—This form of attack targets a known behavior of UDP in the TCP/IP stack of some operating systems. The teardrop attack sends fragmented UDP packets to the victim with an overlapping offset in the second and subsequent packets. When the operating system attempts to rebuild the original packets from the fragments, the fragments overwrite each other (because of the corrupted offset), generating an invalid UDP packet. If the operating system cannot gracefully handle the error, it most likely crashes or reboots.
- **Bonk**—This attack is aimed primarily at Windows machines and allows an attacker to crash a system by sending corrupt UDP packets to the DNS service port of 53.
- **Boink**—Similar to bonk, a boink targets multiple ports instead of just port 53.
- **SYN flooding**—The connection-oriented protocol TCP has a process called a *three-way handshake.* A source host requests a session with a destination system by sending a TCP SYN request. The destination system responds with an acknowledgement (ACK) and returns a SYN response. The source system is then supposed to send a final ACK packet. In this attack, the source system sends a flood of SYN requests and never sends the final ACK, creating a half-open TCP session. The successful attack fills up the destination computer's connection buffer, eliminating any new connection requests from valid users.

The preceding list is by no means complete—it is simply intended to give you some examples of attacks that have been used and the vulnerabilities that were exploited. Security holes are continually patched (or closed), and new problems are identified. You'll need to do your homework to ensure you keep up with the latest attacks and methods. One of the newer forms of attacks is a simple expansion of a DoS attack referred to as a distributed denial-of-service (DDoS) attack.

DDoS attacks are multicell attacks. The first step for an attacker is to distribute zombie or bot code, which allows the attacker partial or full control of the newly infected computer system. Because few of us are willing to give up control of our systems to an outsider for the purpose of attacking other systems on the Internet, the attacker typically hides the zombie code inside another application or in an email.

When the application is installed (or the email read), the zombie code is installed, activates, and calls its owner. This enables the zombie code to get through most, if not all, firewall configurations. Most firewalls are built to stop unknown traffic originating from the outside from getting to the inside network (outside-to-inside). Because the zombie is on the inside and originates (or sources the traffic) via the call back to its owner, the firewall sees this as acceptable (inside-to-outside) traffic.

After an attacker has enough systems compromised with installed zombie software, he can initiate an attack against a victim from a widely distributed number of hosts. The distribution of hosts makes isolating the zombies and stopping the attack difficult; it also obscures the true attacker completely. These attacks come in the form of standard DoS attacks, but the effects are multiplied by the total number of zombie machines under the control of the attacker. A recently published attack on Gibson Research illustrates this type of attack very well. The attack itself is well documented on the Gibson Research Web site at `www.grc.com`. The DDoS attack was executed over several days and was accomplished using more than 450 separate zombie machines. One of the individual attacks, documented over a weekend, identified more than 2.3 billion malicious packets being sent to a single IP address. Using filtering techniques and with the help of the local ISP, the company was finally able to block the attack and regain its Web presence. While doing forensics during and after the attacks, Steve Gibson was able to decode the zombie software and use programming techniques to find and communicate with his attacker.

The attack was executed against Gibson Research by a 13-year-old Internet user for an alleged insult made by Steve Gibson, who referred to the 13-year-old as a script kiddie (revenge). The story illustrates the amount of traffic that can be generated by a single user with the right tool, and thankfully it also identifies ways to help control these types of attacks or reduce their effects.

By using filters, DoS and DDoS attacks can be turned away. Many of the attacks outlined in this section exploit ICMP and UDP, which are both connectionless protocols. You can set up filters on your external routers to throw away packets involved in these types of attacks, but you will still suffer the effects of lost bandwidth as illustrated by the attack on Steve Gibson's Web site. An additional drawback to filtering is the loss of some services, ping, and other utilities used to test for network and host availability.

Another filter that should be set up is one that denies traffic originating from outside the network but that has an inside address. This filter helps prevent attacks such as the land attack. Applying the latest manufacturer's operating system patches or fixes also helps prevent other attacks.

Back Door

A back door is not an attack in its own right; it allows a user to enter a system from a different interface or with different credentials (much like the back door to a house allows entry). In the previous DDoS example, the zombie software is a back door. It allows remote control of the system and gives the owner of the zombie a way to attack others or infiltrate the infected computer's network. By itself, the zombie back door is harmless, but in the hands of an attacker, it represents an avenue for attack or entry into a secure system.

Software programmers can put back doors in place to give them the capability to debug and change code during test deployments of software. These useful behaviors should be removed after the software has been deployed in a production environment to prevent their misuse.

As illustrated, one type of back door can also be installed code on a current production system, allowing unregulated access to systems or services. Besides the zombie or bot software, other known software used as a back door includes

- Virtual Network Computing (VNC)
- Back Orifice
- NetBus
- Sub7 (or SubSeven)
- PC Anywhere
- Terminal Services

These applications are typically hidden inside silly games (Whack-a-mole, Pie Bill Gates, and so on) or software that is advertised as some sort of utility (screensavers, Windows Themes, or a disk or scanner/defragmenter). When harmful code is hidden inside another application, it is called a *Trojan horse* (discussed later).

Some of the applications, such as Terminal Services or PC Anywhere, can be purposefully installed by internal users to gain unregulated access to servers or PCs from the public Internet.

Another form of a back door is a privileged user account. An existing user who already has privileges often creates the back door account, which is set up to look like a normal user's account and given a high-level privilege that allows an attacker to come in under an alias.

Prevention of back door attacks comes with user education, proper access privileges, and deployment of software. Users should be instructed to download software off the Internet from only approved sites or only after checking with the security team. By educating users in the potential risks associated with not following this policy, you will achieve a buy-in from them.

If proper access privileges are set, users will not have the right or privilege to alter operating system files. In Windows NT, 2000, and XP, a normal user does not have this privilege to begin with and you shouldn't give it to her. Installation and use of software such as antivirus packages can catch many of these back door applications, including Back Orifice, NetBus, and Sub7. (Note that the preceding statement includes the terms *installation* and *use*.) Many companies install these types of packages and then neglect the update process. Make sure your antivirus software downloads (or checks for) the latest virus definition files daily. Auditing functions or auditing software can also be deployed to help track users and their behavior. Auditing, covered in the last section, can help prevent the creation and use of back door accounts by showing the creation of these user accounts and their subsequent use.

Spoofing

Spoofing involves modifying the source address of traffic or source of information. The idea behind spoofing is illustrated in the land attack, in which the attacker creates a packet with the source and destination IP addresses both set to the victim's address. The capability to create these packets (altering the source IP address) is not a behavior normally built into a network device. A special program or utility is required for a computer to generate traffic in this fashion. In the case of the land attack, the spoof is the attack itself. There are other motivations to spoof the source of traffic.

Many forms of network security are built on IP addressing filters. Spoofing seeks to circumvent this security by setting up a connection from a client and sourcing the packets with an IP address that is permitted through the filter.

Spoofing can also include impersonating entire services such as Web, FTP, and email (source of information). In this form of attack, a hacker can impersonate a valid service by sourcing traffic using the service's IP address or name. In extreme cases of spoofing, users on the Internet have been known to copy entire Web sites to their own Web servers and corrupt name resolution (DNS) entries to redirect clients to their Web server, in effect spoofing an entire Web site. This type of spoofing allows the attacker to place any information on the Web site that is desired, and users might never realize that the Web site is not the correct one.

Email is also a good example of a service that can be spoofed. Instructions are readily available on how to generate email that appears to come from a different user. This form of attack is often used to get additional information from network users to complete a more aggressive attack. A hacker sends an email using an administrator's name in the "from" line, telling a target user that she needs to change her password to a given string for troubleshooting or maintenance purposes. If the target user follows the directive, the attacker now has a known username and password that can be used to infiltrate a system.

Prevention techniques for spoofing begin by setting up address filters. IP filters should be built on all Internet connected routers to throw away packets originating from an outside (Internet) interface that has an inside source address (as shown in Figure 1.16).

Additional spoof protection comes from the use of certificates on servers and clients. By using certificates you allow Web and email services signing capabilities (see the section "The Mechanics of Authentication Using Certificates," earlier in this chapter). Securing network transmissions with IPSec can also be used between critical servers and clients to prevent these types of attacks from taking place.

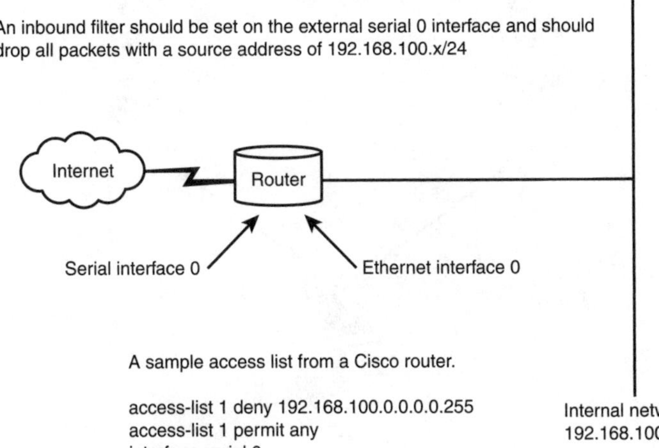
An inbound filter should be set on the external serial 0 interface and should drop all packets with a source address of 192.168.100.x/24
Internet
Router
Serial interface 0
Ethernet interface 0
A sample access list from a Cisco router.
access-list 1 deny 192.168.100.0.0.0.0.255
access-list 1 permit any
interface serial 0
ip access-group 1 in
Internal network
192.168.100.0/24

FIGURE 1.16
Using router access lists to block spoof attempts.

Man-in-the-Middle

A man-in-the-middle attack is commonly used to gather information in transit between two hosts. The information could be of any type, including credit card numbers, passwords, account information, or anything else of interest to the attacker. In this attack, a third system is placed between two hosts (electronically) already communicating or currently in the process of setting up a communication channel. The attacker establishes a session with each of the victims and represents what appears to be a valid end point of communication to each. This gives the attacker the ability to intercept the data and record (or read) it and then pass it on to the second victim. The attacker can also choose to alter the data instead of merely passing it along. In Figure 1.17, Bob is the attacker and is intercepting data transmissions from Suzie and John.

The attack requires almost real-time capabilities, but modern computers and applications can accomplish the task.

To protect your systems from man-in-the-middle attacks, you need to protect the services and resources necessary to insert a system into a session. Name resolution services, such as DNS, can be compromised and used to redirect the initial request for service providing an opportunity to execute a man-in-the-middle attack. Protect DNS by restricting access to its records and name-caching system—read-only access for all but the DNS administrators is appropriate.

FIGURE 1.17
Man-in-the-middle attack.

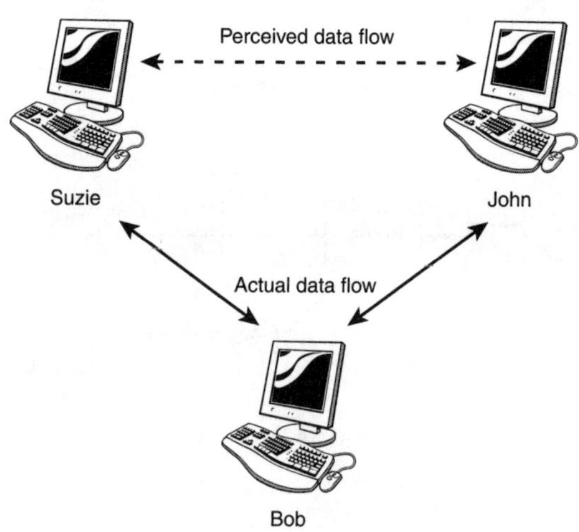

Physical access to the network between the two hosts is required if the attack is attempted on an internal network system. So, you must ensure that access to the wiring closets and switches is protected from unauthorized use.

Positive mutual authentication between the end points of a given session is probably the best way to prevent man-in-middle attacks. Certificates can be used for mutual authentication in these instances, but an attacker can possibly intercept the request for public keys and substitute her keys instead. To prevent this, a public key exchange can be accomplished using floppies. Installation of both public keys could then be accomplished on the respective machines without using the network, thus preventing the possibility of key substitution.

Replay

A replay attack is similar in part to a man-in-the-middle attack. In this instance, an attacker intercepts traffic between two end points and retransmits or replays it later. An attack of this type can be used to replay bank transactions or other similar types of data transfer in the hopes of replicating activities such as deposits or transfers. The data can also be replayed after being altered in the hopes of changing the original transactions. In some forms of this attack, an authentication sequence is replayed against a server or similar resource in an attempt to gain access with valid user credentials.

Protecting yourself against replay attacks involves some type of time value, nonrepeating serial number, or timestamp associated with the packets. In the Kerberos authentication process covered earlier in the chapter, the client sends a session request to a server with a timestamp embedded in the request. The server will, by default, accept the request only within a 5-minute time window (this value is adjustable). If an attempt is made to replay the authentication later, it is disregarded and can generate an alert depending on the operating system and the current Kerberos configuration. Timestamping can also be found in other forms of communication. IPSec, as an example, uses timestamps in the packets to prevent replays of data traffic and to provide authentication and data encryption.

TCP/IP Hijacking

Hijacking is a term given to an attack used to steal a session from a legitimate user. This is a simple step added to a man-in-the-middle attack. After authentication has taken place, the attacker sets up between the client and server in standard man-in-the-middle fashion. The attacker then sends a reset request to the client, more or less kicking him off the session. In the meantime, the session continues with the server now talking to the attacker.

After a session is hijacked, the attacker can then install a back door using the credentials of the victim, create a new back door account for herself, or view files and use services to which the victim would normally have access. This can be done fairly quickly, allowing the attacker to come back later and allowing the victim to reestablish the session with the server (wondering what happened).

Using a secured data stream can help prevent hijacking. When using IPSec, a user logs on to a server and establishes a secret session key, which can be used to encrypt all data being transmitted between the server and client. Because the encryption occurs as part of the authentication process, hijacking this type of session is very difficult. If a man-in-the-middle attack is successfully used prior to the authentication process, the session could still be hijacked with the attacker providing the encryption keys.

Another protection mechanism is the use of unique initial sequence numbers (ISNs). If an operating system uses the same starting sequence number in its TCP sessions, it can predictably be used to execute a hijack. The attacker would know the beginning sequence number of a given session, allowing her to produce packets with correct sequencing and enabling her to easily steal the session.

Using unique ISNs makes this process unpredictable, and guessing becomes a game of probabilities, with the odds heavily in your favor. Most operating systems have patches to ensure that they generate unique ISNs.

Password Guessing

NOTE: Keep in mind that a person at a console or keyboard can still attempt password guessing; it doesn't have to be done by a program. Programs are simply a more efficient and faster method to crack passwords.

Passwords often represent the main form of security in a network. User-generated passwords are often far too weak to represent good security. We covered the basic principles of difficult passwords earlier in the chapter, stating that they should consist of uppercase and lowercase letters, numbers, and special characters. If your users are left to choose passwords for themselves and no mechanism is in place to force difficult password selection, they will often choose passwords that are easy to guess or crack using software programs. Two basic categories are associated with trying to guess a password: brute-force and dictionary attacks.

Brute Force

Brute force describes a method of pure guessing. Every password combination is tried during the course of a brute-force attack, so password complexity plays an important role when dealing with brute-force routines. Let's say your password is a four-digit PIN. The total possible number of combinations is 10,000 (10^4). Simply by moving to a four-character password the combination jumps to 456,976 (26^4). If you combine the two and use characters and numbers, the number of possible passwords jumps to 1,679,616 (36^4).

As humans, it is hard for us to cycle through a million plus password combinations, but for a computer, it is all in a day's work (or 20 minutes' work). Special programs exist that try to guess passwords. L0phtcrack is one such program that is designed to crack passwords in network traffic streams or in password files. It works very quickly, taking only about 10 minutes on a four-character (number and lowercase) password (a dual processor Pentium 450 was used).

The following are some password characteristics that make brute-force attacks easier:

- **Weak keys**—Today's computers are far more powerful than systems from five years ago. If a weak key or math algorithm is used to encrypt data, brute-force attacks against the data are more likely to succeed. When given the choice, always use the strongest available encryption key strength.

- **Mathematical**—A brute-force attack can be more successful if the encryption algorithm is already known (MD5, SHA, RSA, and so on). If the cryptographic formula is known, the attack can concentrate on breaking the cipher used more efficiently than pure guessing.
- **Birthday**—This attack is based on statistics. The birthday paradox states that in a room full of 23 or more people, the probability of two or more sharing a birthday is better than 50/50. Given this understanding, the attack method seeks to find two messages with the same hash value (called a *collision*). Using this method, you could take the digital signature from one message and apply it to a generated message that produced the same hash. This process would effectively defeat the signature without having to break the cryptographic cipher.

Measures can be put in place to help reduce the use of brute-force password guessing tools, however. These include the following:

- **Enforce difficult passwords for you users**—Make the password length at least eight characters, and require the use of uppercase and lowercase letters, numbers, and special characters.
- **Implement an account lockout routine**—This will lock the account after three to five failed logon attempts, preventing an automated cracking routine from being able to cycle through passwords until the right one is found.
- **Monitor the network for excessive failed logon attempts**—This can indicate that someone is trying to brute-force attack your systems.
- **Monitor the network for the use of sniffing tools**—If passwords can be captured off the network, they can be cracked offline.

Dictionary

Brute-force attacks usually include a dictionary attack as a first step. Human behavior tells us that we like to choose passwords that relate to our everyday life. A dictionary attack cycles through known words in a dictionary file, testing the user's password to see whether a match is made. The dictionary files for the cracking programs can often be updated and even customized to further increase the likelihood of a positive guess.

To prevent dictionary attacks, follow the same steps as brute-force attack prevention.

Software Exploitation

Software exploitation is not a single attack but a method of searching for specific problems, weaknesses, or security holes in software code. Operating system software as well as application software is subject to the scrutiny of thousands of users. Many of the open-source code operating systems and applications are particularly vulnerable to this behavior. As the name implies, *open source* means the source code (that makes up the operating system or application) is freely viewable and, in most cases, can be downloaded from the Web for free or at very low cost. Some good examples of software of this nature include Linux and Unix (and their many flavors), Apache Web Server, Internet Protocol over Fibre Channel (IPFC, firewall management), and many others. Many companies have standing policies that forbid the use or distribution of open-source applications because of this very problem. A strong benefit to open-source code is the speed with which problems are found and fixed. Because anyone can view the code and make changes to it, problems that are discovered are often fixed within a day or so and, in some cases, in hours.

It is easy to play devil's advocate on the subject of open- or closed-source code and exploitation. Closed-source applications offer the benefit of source code that is normally well protected from public view, but the disadvantage is that many of these closed-source operating systems and application packages contain problematic code that can be fixed only by the manufacturer. Windows 2000, Macintosh OS X, Microsoft Office, Lotus Notes, and Oracle are some examples of closed-code systems. If a problem is found in any of these systems, the users of these applications are dependent on the manufacturer to properly patch the problem after it has been identified. Negative publicity is associated with problem code and because of this, some manufacturers are slow to admit a problem exists. This can cause delays in fixing an identified weakness or security problem in the closed-code software arena.

Preventing an attacker from exploiting software *bugs* (as they are commonly referred to) is a matter of keeping the latest manufacturer's patches applied and monitoring the Web for newly discovered problems.

REVIEW BREAK

Reviewing Attacks

- Knowing what motivates attackers can help you protect your network. We looked at greed, revenge, curiosity, and others.
- Attacks come in all shapes and sizes. Many use standard troubleshooting utilities, whereas others imbed code and allow attackers control over your system.
- Educating yourself and your users is one of the first steps in defense. Proper passwords, good software discipline, and protective software can help prevent attacks or reduce their impact on your network and its systems.

Malicious Code

Recognize malicious code and take appropriate action.

In today's network environment, malicious code has become a serious problem. Software labeled as malicious is designed to do something to the computer. The target is often the information stored on the local computer, but other resources or even other computers can be targeted, as you'll see in the following discussion. The categories of malicious code that we cover include the following:

- Viruses
- Trojan horses
- Logic bombs
- Worms

Viruses

One of the earliest known forms of malicious code is the virus. The name *virus* comes from the behavior of the code and its similarities to biological viruses. A biological virus is a small chunk of DNA, incapable of replication and damage on its own. It attaches to a cell and either takes over, using the cell's mechanics to replicate (almost like a parasite), or uses the cell's contents to replicate itself and destroy the cell in the process.

A *software virus*, in similar fashion, is a small chunk of code designed to attach to other code. It typically has a dual purpose: It needs to replicate, and it typically has some other purpose or action that it takes when triggered to do so. The replication process often occurs when an infected file is executed or launched. The virus attaches itself to other files, adding its code to the application's code, and continues to spread in this fashion. Some examples of software viruses include

- **Stoned**—When executed, this virus replaces the master boot record information with its own code. Several variants (also called *mutations*) produce different results. The stoned virus is transmitted via floppy from one computer system to another, and the most destructive variant of this virus renders the hard drive or floppy unbootable and possibly destroys files. The mildest form displays the message `This computer is stoned.`
- **Michelangelo**—A more destructive virus, the Michelangelo erases the contents of the infected drive on March 6 (the birth date of the virus's namesake) of the current year. The virus had more publicity than actual impact and is, by some accounts, credited more with raising virus awareness than causing any damage.
- **Form**—The odd behavior of the original version of this virus causes the keys on your keyboard to make a clicking noise when pressed. This behavior occurs on the 18th of each month on any computer infected with this virus.
- **Melissa**—This virus is representative of a whole new breed of email macro viruses. The Melissa virus is received by email and embedded in a Microsoft Word document. When the email recipient opens the document, the virus sends email to the first 50 addresses in the victim's address book and attaches itself to each email. This virus exploits the behavior of Microsoft's Visual Basic for Applications (VBA) scripting language, which is used to create macros. Although simple in design, its effects were felt worldwide, causing large companies to shut down their email systems until the virus could be contained.
- **I Love You**—A variant of the Melissa virus, this code exploits the same VBA code. Instead of the first 50 addresses in the victim's address book, however, this virus mails itself to all addresses in the address book. It also infects the Normal.dot template in Microsoft Word, causing all new documents created to be infected as well.

The viruses listed represent a very small number of the total population of computer viruses. As shown, some viruses simply use system resources and bandwidth, whereas others do actual damage to the information on the system. In all cases, the viruses cost you money, represented by the time it takes to clean the software and recover lost data (if any).

> NOTE
>
> A small number of viruses can actually damage physical hardware. One particular virus aimed at servers infects RAM and accesses the hard drive every 3 seconds. This causes the hard drive to spin indefinitely at full speed, wearing it out much more quickly than normal.

An entire industry has been built around protecting systems from virus infection. Installing and maintaining antivirus software is one of the best methods of avoiding problems caused by this type of code. Additionally, you should train your users not to download software from unknown sources and ensure that removable media (floppies, Zip drive disks, and the like) are scanned before being used.

Trojan Horses

Trojan horses were mentioned earlier in the chapter during the discussion of back door attacks. A *Trojan horse* appears to be useful software (and in fact may be), but code is hidden inside that will attack your system directly or allow the system to be infiltrated by the originator of the code (hence, the analogy to the famous horse). A common use of late for Trojan horses is the installation of zombie software used for remote control attacks (see the earlier discussion of DoS/DDoS and back door attacks).

Because the Trojan horse is typically hidden inside utility or game software, its capability to spread is reliant on the popularity of the software and users' ability and willingness to download and install the software. Many of the Trojan horse programs can be found by antivirus software; therefore, the steps to protect a computer from Trojan horse software are the same as protecting the system from virus code.

Logic Bombs

This particular form of malicious code is also known as *slag code.* It is really a virus or Trojan horse that is built to go off when a particular event occurs or a certain amount of time passes. As an example, a programmer might create a logic bomb to check the network system for her user account every day at 3 a.m. If, during the check, the user account is not present (in other words, the programmer has been fired), the code executes and deletes all the user accounts on the system or executes some other destructive action such as erasing files.

If a logic bomb is implemented as a virus or Trojan horse, antivirus software will probably do the trick. If the bomb is placed inside a custom application or code set, however, finding it and removing it can be far more difficult. During software development, it is often a good idea to bring in someone from outside the company (such as a programming consultant) to evaluate the code as a check-and-balance to keep logic bombs from being inserted.

Worms

The final form of malicious code that we will look at is called a worm. *Worms* are similar in function and behavior to viruses, Trojan horses, and logic bombs—with the exception that they are self-replicating. The previous forms of malicious code discussed thus far require a user to do something to infect additional systems. In the case of a boot sector virus, for instance, a user writes a file to a floppy, thus infecting the floppy. The floppy is then used in another machine, which then infects the master boot record on that machine, and then the process is repeated. A worm, on the other hand, is built to take advantage of a security hole in an existing application or operating system, find other systems running the same software, and then automatically replicate itself to the new host. This process repeats with no user intervention whatsoever.

EXAM TIP

As mentioned in the section "Attacks," earlier in the chapter, know what types of malicious code exist and how the code can be used against you. Viruses and worms are the black plague of the modern network. Don't focus too much on the specific names listed in this section; focus more on the behavior of those types of code attacks and the measures necessary to protect your network.

One of the more recent worms, Code Red, exploits a weakness in systems running Microsoft's Internet Information Servers (IIS versions 4 and 5). After an IIS server is infected, it searches the network (local and Internet) looking for other IIS servers to infect. The infection rates worms can achieve are astounding because of this automatic replication behavior. A minor change in the Code Red virus allowed it to infect more than 350,000 systems in 14 hours. In addition to its replication behavior, the worm attacked the `www.whitehouse.gov` site and altered its Web pages to state that the page had been "hacked by Chinese." Code Red II is a mutation of the original and has done little outward damage (other than using bandwidth in the replication of itself), but it did install a back door that allowed other code to be executed, effectively turning the system into a zombie that could be used for DDoS attacks.

SOCIAL ENGINEERING

Understand the concept of social engineering.

The last attack that needs to be addressed can often be one of the easiest and most productive attacks of all. It is called *social engineering*, and it plays on human behavior and how we interact with one another. The attack oftentimes doesn't feel like an attack at all. Some scenarios of social engineering attacks are shown in the following list:

- An administrator calls you at 4:55 p.m. and states that he's in real trouble. He's attempting to do a network backup operation, and it keeps failing. The failure happens because you're currently accessing a server, so he says that he can gracefully disconnect you from the server, get the backup routine running, and go home on time, if you could give him your username and password.

- Someone approaches you as you enter a secured building. She identifies herself as a contractor and tells you that she doesn't have a badge to get into the building, she's late for a meeting, and the person who was supposed to meet her hasn't shown up yet.

- You receive an email from an administrator stating that several of the user accounts have been modified. The administrator tells you that for you to access the Internet, you have to change your password to `corp123` and then log on using the newly configured password. Then, after 15 minutes, you can change your password to something different and reauthenticate.

In each of these situations, an attacker tries to manipulate corporate users to gain access or knowledge that will allow further discovery. In the first two scenarios, empathy and urgency work to convince users that it is okay to give out the information or allow access to the building. In the third scenario, use of the Internet will be taken away if you don't comply. Each attack plays on human behavior and our inherent willingness to trust others.

The best defense against social engineering is training. Teaching users what to do in these common situations and helping them understand the basics of how the network system works should be the first step. Teaching users that network administrators have the power to change passwords would let them know that scenarios 1 and 3 are likely attacks and that the behavior should be reported immediately.

In scenario 2, a user needs to understand that it is not okay, under any circumstances, to let an unknown individual onto company property. Areas that are secured in such a fashion will have a security desk, and the company user should attempt to escort the contractor to that location. If the contractor won't follow, the user should still go to the security desk and report the behavior.

AUDITING

Understand the concepts of auditing.

The final section of this chapter focuses on auditing. *Auditing,* or *accounting* as it is sometimes called, is the process of tracking users and their actions on the network. The types of activities that can be audited include users doing the following:

- Logging on or off the network
- Reading, writing, deleting, or modifying files
- Using printers
- Using network services such as DNS, WINS, Terminal Services, and so on
- Using remote access services (dial-in or VPN services)

When setting up auditing, we can give you only the basics in advice. Auditing is a very precise behavior that should be built around goals and policies developed by the security team. Plan, plan, plan! Without effective planning and well-defined structure to your audit policy, it is unlikely that we can help you do anything but fill up your log files and hard drives. Steps to take when initiating an audit policy include

1. **Identify potential resources at risk in your networking environment**—Rarely will all resources need to be audited, so a list of key resources that need to be protected should be developed. These resources typically include files, software, and services, each of which should be protected from unauthorized access. Accounting applications, accounting files, personnel files, corporate secrets, logon services, and remote access services are just a few to watch for. This option is very company-specific, so many other resources that are not discussed here will likely be on your list.

2. **After the resources are identified, set up the actual audit policy through the operating system tools**—Each operating system will have its own tools for tracking and logging access. If the policy incorporates auditing large amounts of data or popular activities (such as Web surfing), ensure that the hardware can handle the extra load. Auditing can easily add 20%–30% additional load on a standard server.
3. **Build time and resources to view the logs into your auditing plan**—After you have auditing turned on, log files will be generated. What use will it be if your systems are compromised and the intrusion is recorded in your logs, but it is six months before you read them? Many operating systems produce log files in text file format. You should import these files into a database system and either view the data graphically or use the database to query for anomalies. Visually sorting through log files should be a last resort.

Auditing can be as simple or complex as you want to make it. Be consistent regardless of the plan you come up with. As you begin to understand the patterns of your users and the network in general, it will be easier than you think to identify odd or suspicious behaviors.

CHAPTER SUMMARY

In this chapter, we covered many concepts that will take you through the rest of the book. By covering general concepts of computer security, we have given you a foundation upon which you can build a more detailed understanding of security and its many facets.

In the first section, you learned basic terminology. Like any new area or field of study, new words and concepts are a likely source of confusion and a block to better learning. In that section, you increased your vocabulary and added to the ever-growing list of acronyms that will be used in your discussions about security.

In the next section, we discussed the fundamentals of access control. You learned the differences between mandatory, discretionary, and role-based control mechanisms that can guide you to a more secure network configuration. These access methods are summarized in Table 1.3.

KEY TERMS

- Accounting
- Auditing
- Authentication
- Authorization
- Back door
- Biometrics
- Certificate
- Certificate authority
- CHAP

Chapter Summary

- Denial of service and distributed denial of service (DoS/DDoS)
- Discretionary access control (DAC)
- Kerberos
- Logic bomb
- Mandatory access control (MAC)
- Man-in-the-middle
- Multifactor authentication
- Mutual authentication
- Replay
- Role-based access control (RBAC)
- Social engineering
- Spoofing
- TCP/IP hijacking
- Token
- Trojan horse
- Virus
- Worm

TABLE 1.3

Access Control Methods

Method	*Characteristics*
Mandatory access control	A system of access control set up by security or information managers. Users cannot modify permissions or pass permissions to others.
Discretionary access control	A system of access control in which users have complete discretion to assign permissions to data they own or control.
Role-based access control	A system of access control that has both mandatory and discretionary access control characteristics. A base level of mandatory permissions is set and associated with a group or collection of users. Users in the group can, at their discretion, pass on rights and permissions to others.

Authentication mechanisms were covered in detail in the section that followed. Here you learned how a user proves his identity. From simple usernames and passwords to biometric retinal scans, identity is the key to controlling access to network resources. Table 1.4 summarizes the details of each of the authentication methods covered.

TABLE 1.4

Authentication Methods

Method	*Characteristics*
Username/password	A widely supported and very common form of authentication. It can be compromised if the username and password are written down, stolen, or given out.
Kerberos	A specific form of username/password authentication mechanism that makes stealing passwords from the network harder. It can be compromised in the same fashion as standard username/password method.
Challenge Handshake Authentication Protocol (CHAP)	A username/password method commonly used over dial-up connections or links encapsulated in PPP. It allows mutual authentication and encrypted password transfers. It can be compromised in the same fashion as the standard username/password method.

CHAPTER SUMMARY

Method	*Characteristics*
Certificates	A method of identification that uses public key cryptography. This authentication scheme supports mutual authentication and is commonly used on the Internet and in IPSec communications. It can be compromised through key cloning or physical access to the computer on which the certificate is installed.
Tokens	Uses software- or hardware-generated one-time passwords. Software provides lower security and is cheaper to implement. Hardware requires the use of a physical device and is more expensive to deploy, but it is much more secure. The software system can be compromised by cloning or the use of the computer on which the software is installed. The hardware system can be compromised if the hardware token is stolen.
Biometrics	Uses personal characteristics of the user for authentication. Common methods include fingerprints, voiceprints, iris profiling, facial profiling, and retinal scans. The system is open to compromise if the characteristic can be reproduced (voiceprint) or removed (fingerprint).

Because each of the authentication systems has a weakness, you also learned about multifactor authentication, or the use of more than one method to positively authenticate users.

You next learned how to identify and turn off nonessential services and protocols. We taught you to be cautious of systems that are preconfigured from the manufacturer. Although the services and protocols differ between operating systems, the result is the same: Have a minimalist approach to operating system services and remove (if possible) or turn off all nonessential services and protocols.

We covered attacks, malicious code, and social engineering in the next sections. You learned common attack categories and attack methods, which range from DoS/DDoS attacks to software exploitation, viruses, Trojan horses, logic bombs, and worms. In each section, you learned the basic behaviors of the attacks, read some examples, and then learned how to defend against them.

Finally, we covered how to keep an eye on things. Auditing is one of the hinge pins in your security door. Without it, you could have a problem and not be aware of it, so in this section you learned how to evaluate resources, implement auditing, and review your audit policy.

APPLY YOUR KNOWLEDGE

Review Questions

1. List the three access methodologies and describe the characteristics of each.
2. What is the purpose of multifactor / authentication?
3. What form of authentication uses human characteristics?
4. How does a man-in-the-middle attack work?
5. What is the difference between brute-force password guessing and dictionary password guessing?
6. How does a worm differ from a virus?
7. What is spoofing?
8. How does a Trojan horse work?
9. When setting up a new server how should services and protocols be configured?
10. What is the primary purpose of auditing?

Exam Questions

1. Which of the following best describes role-based access control?

   A. Users get to decide who has access to files used and the level of permissions that will be set.

   B. The security team sets up and controls all access to files and the level of privilege that each user will have.

   C. Users and administrators collectively decide which users get access to files and what privilege each user will have.

   D. Administrators set up groups and assign permissions and rights to the groups. Users are allowed to pass permissions and rights to other users only in the given level of control.

2. Your company is deciding on a new method for authentication. Your boss asks you for an explanation of the differences between hardware- and software-based tokens. Which of the following would best explain these differences?

   A. Hardware-based tokens are installed into the computer system and generate one-time passwords for users, whereas software-based tokens can be transported with the user regardless of the system and generate reusable passwords.

   B. Software-based tokens are installed onto a computer system and generate one-time passwords for users, whereas hardware-based tokens can be transported with the user and generate one-time passwords.

   C. Hardware-based tokens are installed into the computer system and generate one-time passwords for users, whereas software-based tokens can be transported with the user regardless of the system and generate one-time passwords.

   D. Software-based tokens are installed onto a computer system and generate one-time passwords for users, whereas hardware-based tokens can be transported with the user and generate reusable passwords.

3. You are the security administrator for a large network and have been tasked with installing and configuring a new authentication system.

APPLY YOUR KNOWLEDGE

Which of the following would be the most secure?

A. Biometrics using a retinal scanning device

B. Kerberos authentication

C. Biometrics using iris profiling and a software-based token system

D. A hardware-based token system

4. You're setting up a new Web server. You've finished configuring a new machine that was pre-installed with the following components:

Web server	NetBEUI
FTP server	IPX/SPX
Telnet server	NNTP server
TCP/IP	

Which components should you remove to make the server as secure as possible? (Choose all that apply.)

A. Web server

B. FTP server

C. Telnet server

D. TCP/IP

E. NetBEUI

F. IPX/SPX

G. NNTP server

5. You're the security administrator for a bank and have been capturing network traffic with a network-sniffing tool. You note that over the last 4 hours you have seen the exact same pattern of 150 packets repeated every 35 minutes. What type of attack is likely being executed against your network?

A. Spoofing

B. Man-in-the-middle

C. Worm

D. Replay

E. Virus

6. Which of the following accurately describes the difference between a worm and a virus?

A. A virus needs no user intervention to replicate.

B. A worm needs no user intervention to replicate.

C. A virus is open-source code and attacks only open-source software.

D. A worm buries itself in the operating system software and infects other systems only after a user executes the application in which the worm is buried.

7. You are checking your network to ensure users are conforming to the new password security policy that requires them to use difficult passwords. You plan on using a password-cracking program. You will first execute a __________ attack on the passwords and then execute a __________ attack to check the passwords for strength.

A. Dictionary/brute-force

B. Brute-force/dictionary

C. Brute-force/CHAP

D. CHAP/brute-force

E. Guessing/Trojan horse

Apply Your Knowledge

8. You have created a utility for defragmenting hard drives. You have hidden code inside the utility that will install itself and cause the infected system to erase the hard drive's contents after running the fourth time. Which of the following attacks have been implemented in your code? (Choose two.)

   A. Spoofing

   B. Man-in-the-middle

   C. Trojan horse

   D. Replay

   E. Virus

9. Which of the following weaknesses are shared by software tokens and certificates? (Choose all that apply.)

   A. Cloning

   B. Brute-force guessing

   C. Theft of the computer

   D. Password compromise

   E. Loss of the private key

10. Your network is under attack. Currently, traffic patterns and packet addresses indicate that the attack is being executed by several hundred systems on the Internet issuing ICMP echo requests. Which type of attack is being executed against you?

    A. Spoofing

    B. Man-in-the-middle

    C. Worm

    D. DoS

    E. DDoS

    F. Replay

11. A piece of malicious code has infected one of your servers. It is designed to check for the existence of an individual workstation by IP address. If the workstation doesn't respond to a ping seven days in a row, the code reformats the server's hard drive. Which type of code has infected your server?

    A. Trojan horse

    B. DDoS

    C. Worm

    D. Virus

    E. Logic bomb

12. The process in which a sever authenticates a client and a client authenticates the server is called __________.

    A. Multifactor authentication

    B. Dual-token authentication

    C. Mutual authentication

    D. Dual-factor authentication

    E. Reverse authentication

13. Which of the following actions will help defend against IP address spoofing attacks?

    A. Installing certificates on clients and servers

    B. Setting up IP address filters

    C. Deploying Kerberos authentication

    D. Installing fiber-optic cabling

    E. Installing antivirus software

14. What is the first step to accomplish when implementing auditing?

    A. Plan.

    B. Configure resources to be audited.

    C. Determine the method of log review.

    D. Create macros to dump audit logs into a database.

    E. Attack the network to see which resources are poorly protected.

15. Which of the following is the most common form of authentication in use today?

    A. Biometrics

    B. Username/password

    C. Kerberos

    D. Hardware token

    E. Certificates

Answers to Review Questions

1. Mandatory, discretionary, and role-based.

   Mandatory access control is set up by a central authority (security team), and users have no capability to change permissions or rights.

   Discretionary access control allows users to change rights and permissions at their discretion.

   Role-based is a mixture of mandatory and discretionary. A security team sets up groups and assigns permissions and rights to the groups. Users have discretionary control over the permissions and rights in the guidelines set by the group.

2. Multifactor authentication is designed to overcome weaknesses in any single form of authentication using two or more authentication methods.

3. Biometric authentication uses human characteristics such as fingerprint, voiceprint, iris profiling, facial profiling, and so on to establish identity.

4. A man-in-the-middle attack is designed to insert the hacker between communicating hosts in the hopes of capturing password or sensitive data.

5. Brute-force password attacks try every possible password combination, whereas a dictionary attack attempts to guess the password by comparing it to common words found in a dictionary file.

6. A worm can replicate without human interaction, whereas a virus requires a user to execute a program so that replication can occur.

7. Spoofing is the capability to alter the source address or source of information. IP address spoofing alters the source address; Web spoofing alters the source of information.

8. A Trojan horse is code hidden inside an apparently good/usable application or utility. After the utility is installed, the Trojan horse program installs as well.

9. Only required services and protocols should be installed; all other services and protocols should be removed or turned off.

10. Auditing allows you to track which resources users have been using (files, services, servers, and so on) and helps you track activity on your network.

APPLY YOUR KNOWLEDGE

Answers to Exam Questions

1. **D.** Role-based access control is best described as a hybrid between mandatory and discretionary. Administrators set up and manage permissions and rights based on groups. Users have a discretionary capability in the group permissions.
2. **B.** Both hardware- and software-based tokens generate one-time passwords. Software-based tokens are installed on the computer, whereas hardware-based tokens are portable devices such as token cards or key FOBs.
3. **C.** Multifactor authentication is the most secure method listed.
4. **A, D.** The Web server and TCP/IP are the only required components listed. All others should be turned off or removed as a best security practice.
5. **D.** The fact that the packets are exactly the same and repeat over time is a classic symptom of a replay attack.
6. **B.** A worm exploits a code-based weakness and can self-replicate.
7. **A.** A dictionary attack is accomplished before a brute-force attack to flush out very weak and easily cracked passwords.
8. **C, E.** The first attack is a Trojan horse (hidden code), and the second is a classic virus (erase hard drives).
9. **A, C.** Both certificates and software tokens are installed on a local computer. It is possible to copy (clone) the certificate or software token configuration file. If the computer is stolen (laptop), impersonation can take place.
10. **E.** The description fits a classic distributed denial-of-service attack (DDoS).
11. **E.** Logic bombs behave like viruses with the exception of built-in logic that checks a condition. If the condition is met (or not), the virus executes.
12. **C.** Whenever both parties (client and server) authenticate each other, it is called mutual authentication.
13. **B.** By setting up filters to throw away external packets with internal source addresses, you can help prevent spoofing. Each of the other listed actions addresses some other security weakness.
14. **A.** Plan first, then implement, and then review logs.
15. **B.** Most operating systems (even simple ones) support some level of basic username/password authentication.

APPLY YOUR KNOWLEDGE

Suggested Readings and Resources

Online Material

1. Barkley, John. "Aspects of Security Policies" (http://hissa.nist.gov).
2. Coar, Ken. "Security and Apache: An Essential Primer Mandatory Versus Discretionary Access Control" (http://www.linuxplanet.com).
3. Gerck, E. "Overview of Certification Systems: X.509, CA, PGP and SKIP" (http://www.mcg.org.br).
4. Gibson, Steve. "The Strange Tale of Denial of Service Attacks Against GRC.COM" (http://www.grc.com).
5. Grand, Joe. "Authentication Tokens: Balancing the Security Risks with Business Requirements" (http://www.atstake.com).
6. Lynch, Clifford. "A White Paper on Authentication and Access Management Issues in Cross-organizational Use of Networked Information Resources" (http://www.cni.org).
7. Suares, Stuart. "Biometric Security Systems" (http://www.biometricsecurity.com.au).
8. Tung, Brian. "The Moron's Guide to Kerberos" (http://www.isi.edu).
9. "What is a digital signature and what is authentication?" (http://www.rsasecurity.com).

Publications

1. *ALS Designing Microsoft Windows 2000 Network Security.* Redmond, WA: Microsoft Press, 2001.
2. Carter, Earl, and Rick Stiffler. *Cisco Secure Intrusion Detection System.* Indianapolis, IN: Cisco Press, 2002.
3. Feghhi, Jalal, and Peter Williams. *Digital Certificates Applied Internet Security.* Reading, MA: Addison-Wesley, 1999.
4. Harris, Shon. *All in One CISSP Certification Exam Guide.* New York, NY: McGraw-Hill, 2002.
5. Maiwald, Eric. *Network Security: A Beginner's Guide.* New York, NY: McGraw-Hill, 2001.
6. McClure, Stuart, Joel Scambray, and George Kurtz. *Hacking Exposed: Network Security Secrets and Solutions, Third Edition.* New York, NY: McGraw-Hill, 2001.
7. Northcutt, Stephen, Donald McLachlan, and Judy Novak. *Network Intrusion Detection An Analyst's Handbook, Second Edition.* Indianapolis, IN: New Riders, 2000.

OBJECTIVES

This chapter covers the following CompTIA-specified objectives for the Communications Security section of the Security+ exam.

Understand communication security in wireless, wired, and application-specific environments.

- **Know security controls available in different popular applications.**
- **Know and recognize security threats associated with electronic communications.**

▶ Communications security is a vital component in ensuring the continuity and survival of companies and organizations in a world overtaken by industrial espionage, cut-throat competition, and malefactors in search of sensitive information to which they have no rights. Because digital and electronic communications are both important and potentially vulnerable, they must be subject to proper security controls. This chapter introduces the threats to which communications can be subject and the security controls that should apply to them across a variety of platforms and application environments.

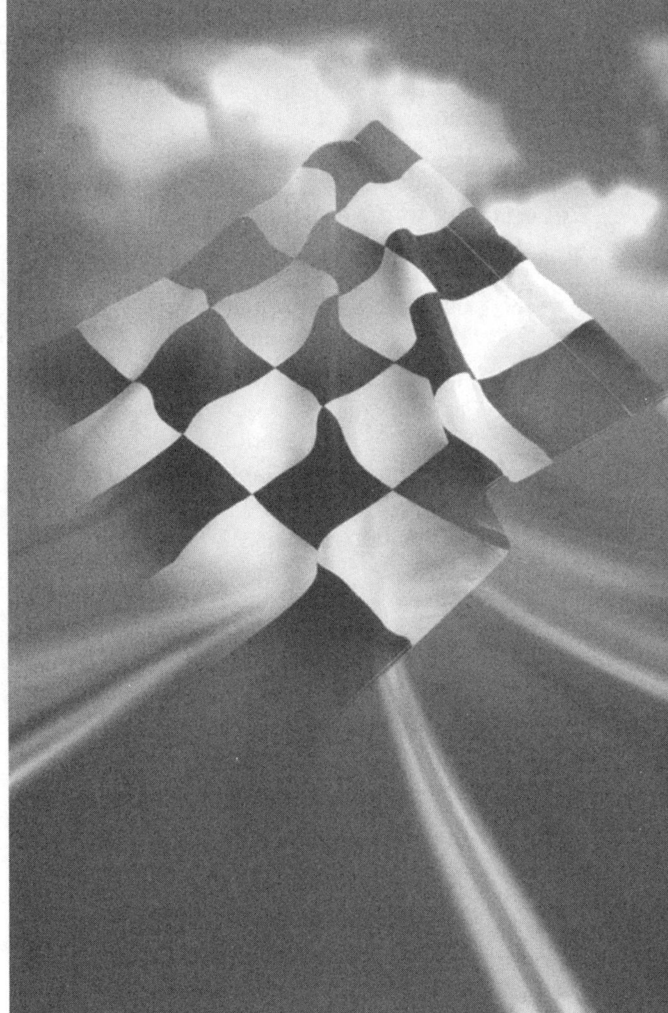

CHAPTER 2

Communication Security

Outline

Outline

Study Strategies

- Communications security is a topic both broad and deep. Therefore, some of its aspects might not lend themselves to practice or hands-on experience as well as others do. But to get the most out of this chapter, you will need access to an installation of Microsoft Internet Information Server (IIS) version 5 or newer, Microsoft Internet Explorer (version 5.x or 6.x), and either Microsoft Outlook or Outlook Express.
- Make sure that you are familiar with the basic operation and commands associated with the most commonly used TCP/IP application protocols, including the File Transfer Protocol (FTP), Simple Mail Transfer Protocol (SMTP), and Hypertext Transfer Protocol (HTTP).
- Take some time and effort to set up a Web server and bring it to an up-to-date patch level. Request a trial X.509 certificate from a public certificate authority (CA) for testing purposes and use it to configure HTTP Secure (HTTPS) on your Web server. Request a personal X.509 certificate and use it with your email software to explore Secure/Multipurpose Internet Mail Extensions (S/MIME) functionality and issues.
- Set up a few Windows 2000 servers and configure virtual private network (VPN) servers and clients.

INTRODUCTION

Securing your business and personal communications is crucial to survival in a world heavily reliant on communications technology. Many of the communications technologies used today can potentially expose important information to anyone savvy or motivated enough to break into your systems or eavesdrop on wireless communications. This is because an overwhelming percentage of threats and hazards come from connections to the outside world in the forms of email, Internet access, wireless devices, and so forth. These connections can expose your systems to harmful predators in pursuit of access to mission-critical business or personal information about products, services, business partners, clients, co-workers, friends, and more. Lax communications security can easily damage an otherwise successful business, or it can impact human relations and finances negatively.

This chapter reviews the issues and vulnerabilities that motivate an urgent need to secure communications media and common communications applications such as Web and email. It also reviews various technologies and mechanisms used for communications security.

RECOGNIZING AND ADMINISTERING REMOTE AND WIRELESS ACCESS

Understand communication security in wireless, wired, and application-specific environments.

Networks have been accessed using remote access tools and technologies for many years. In this context, *remote access* means that one or more users are granted authorized access from outside normal network boundaries to some proprietary system(s) for purposes agreeable to all parties involved. Common examples where remote access is deemed useful include employees who work from home, offshore consulting or programming companies, remote administration or troubleshooting, and so forth. The following sections describe protocols, standards, and technologies used to establish and secure remote administration and telecommuting scenarios.

Since the mid-1990s, wireless networking technologies have become quite popular and are in increasing use in the workplace and in small office, home office (SOHO) networks. Although wireless networking might not always involve remote access tools or techniques, it is similar enough to remote access to make it subject to many of the same types of vulnerabilities and exploits and to many of the same kinds of security measures and tools. Thus, we cover both topics under the same general heading.

Securing Wireless Networks

802.1x is a set of IEEE networking communications standards that describes various types of wireless networks. In particular, these standards include

- 802.11 Wireless Local Area Networks (Wireless LANs)
- 802.15 Wireless Personal Area Networks (WPANs; 802.15)
- 802.16 Wireless Metropolitan Area Networks (Wireless MANs)

As we write this chapter, there is even an advisory group around an emerging 802.18 standard that is focused on radio frequency networking (although it hasn't yet resulted in any product implementations that we know of). The other three wireless IEEE technologies—namely 802.11, 802.15, and 802.16—utilize port-based network access controls. These technologies permit devices such as cell phones, computers, and PDAs to access various types of secured systems and services at various bandwidths and frequencies.

> EXAM TIP
>
> **802.11 Wireless Networking**
> Although learning to recognize other 802.1x designations is a good idea, the Security+ exam concentrates its coverage on 802.11 wireless networking, which basically functions as a type of wireless Ethernet and integrates easily and directly with wired 802.3 Ethernet networks.

Wireless networks have several obvious advantages when compared to wired networks that make them attractive to organizations and individual users alike. They are easy to deploy; they can transmit data at LAN speeds; and they are inexpensive to install and maintain. Also, using wireless communication technologies to extend LANs keeps companies from extending their cabling (it is cheaper than running new category 5 twisted-pair or fiber cables). At the same time, wireless networking provides the significant convenience of mobility to LAN users. This is especially important for executives, technicians, and sales personnel who potentially have significant mobility needs.

On the other hand, because wireless networking perforce broadcasts signals into the atmosphere—which makes it absurdly easy to eavesdrop on such communications—it is also prey to significant security vulnerabilities and exposures. Simply put, neither well-run companies or organizations nor savvy individual users should employ wireless technologies without some understanding of the potential security exposures involved and how they can be remedied.

Wireless Networks and Security

Because they must broadcast signals into the atmosphere, wireless networks suffer from some serious security disadvantages. Compared to LANs, wireless networks have only a few physical security controls, or none at all. Anyone within 300 feet of wireless access points (the hubs that normally interconnect wireless and wired users and resources) can easily monitor all related network traffic.

Furthermore, if eavesdroppers obtain the correct access codes, they can gain undetected, unauthorized access to the network and all its contents and services. Thus, wireless networks must be capable of preventing traffic interception before or during the logon process, must provide controls for securing data transmission after the logon, and must guarantee availability and connectivity to users regardless of their physical locations (so long as they are within the reception range of whatever wireless technology might be in use).

Until recently, most wireless networks were based on the IEEE 802.11 standards, which according to many independent industry reviews have serious data transmission security shortcomings.

To eliminate existing 802.11 shortcomings, as well as improve the overall wireless posture on the market, the Institute of Electronic and Electric Engineers (IEEE) together with the Wireless Ethernet Compatibility Alliance (WECA) proposed an addition to the 802.11 standard: 802.11i, the Robust Security Network amendment to the 802.11 family of standards. This new standard significantly improves user authentication and media access control mechanisms found in 802.11b (the current prevailing Ethernet-based LAN wireless networking standard). But it is not expected to be complete (and related equipment available) until the end of 2003. Also, implementing 802.11i will require replacing (or upgrading) hardware; therefore, it will come at a significant cost. For many applications, however, the added security will make it worthwhile (and in some cases, absolutely necessary).

WHY IS 802.11I MORE SECURE THAN OTHER 802.11 VERSIONS?

Although the 802.11i standard is currently under development, it's proposed form is settled enough to describe here. Specifically, 802.11i is designed to overcome limitations in 802.11b that relate to the strength and type of encryption used and to the mechanics of key generation and exchange. The following new features are proposed:

- It addresses problems found in the Wired Equivalent Privacy (WEP) mechanisms by switching to the stronger Advanced Encryption Standard (AES) encryption, which can use 128-, 192-, or 256-bit key lengths, as compared to WEP's 40-bit keys. AES is not only stronger than WEP because of key length, but it also uses a more powerful encryption algorithm.
- It addresses issues related to the use of static keys in WEP with a dynamic rekeying mechanism called the Temporal Key Integrity Protocol (TKIP). Although manual updates will be required for all devices—this probably also means firmware upgrades for all devices—it will make communications much more secure by updating keys dynamically and automatically.
- It supports plug-in authentication subsystems that perform user authentication (rather than device authentication) and can include RADIUS, Kerberos, or PKI (these topics are covered in Chapter 6, "PKI, Key Management, and Attacks").

In the meantime, security experts recommend that administrators who do use 802.11b network enable WEP, assign a well-designed encryption key, and disable automatic DHCP logins for unknown devices (or entirely) on wireless segments. These simple steps do not eliminate all vulnerabilities, but they do make keeping wireless Ethernet segments as safe and secure as possible much easier.

EXAM TIP

Know the Basics of EAP For the Security+ exam, only general familiarity with EAP—that is, what it means and what it works with—is required. You don't need to learn all the details of its encryption or how to install and configure EAP.

Other security improvements to 802.11 are also underway, sometimes collectively called 802.1X, that might eventually offer enhanced security capabilities as well—if and when such efforts are adopted and widely deployed. 802.1x relies on the Extensible Authentication Protocol (EAP, RFC 2284) for its authentication needs. EAP is utilized both in wireless and wired LANs, which allows for a common authentication technology to be used over several media types. EAP is a flexible authentication technology and can work with smart cards, Kerberos, one-time passwords, X.509 certificates, public key encryption, and others. EAP messages are encapsulated into 802.1x packets and are marked as EAP Over LAN (EAPOL). Because IEEE 802.1x is an open standard, individual manufacturers can introduce enhancements as they see fit.

The authentication process works as follows. Before any communication can occur, a client (initiating party) sends a connection request to one of the wireless access points in the area. *Access points* are analogous to hubs or switches in wired networks, but they are also employed for access request verification purposes *(authenticator)*. The authenticator marks all initial communication with the initiating party as unauthorized, and only EAPOL messages are accepted while in this mode. All other types of communication—HTTP, Post Office Protocol (POP3), Dynamic Host Configuration Protocol (DHCP), and more—are blocked until supplied credentials are verified with an authentication server.

Upon receiving an EAPOL request from the initiating party, the wireless access point device requests logon credentials and sends them to the designated authentication server. Remote Authentication Dial-In User Service (RADIUS)—more on this in a few sections—is commonly employed for authentication purposes; however, 802.1x does not make RADIUS mandatory. If supplied, credentials are successfully validated by the server, an EAP-success request is issued to the initiating party, and regular communication can begin. Otherwise, if the server fails to validate supplied credentials, the communication session request is rejected. This authentication process is depicted in Figure 2.1.

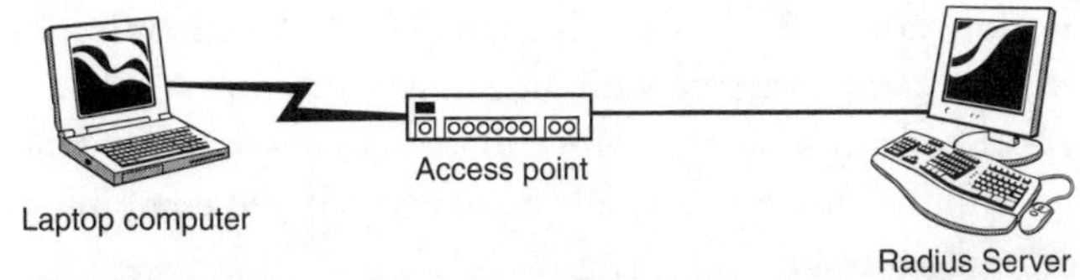

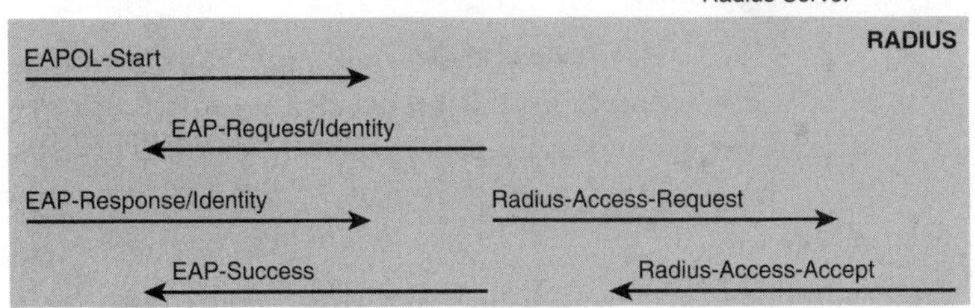

FIGURE 2.1
Wireless access authentication.

The 802.1x standard allows for a more secure and reliable wireless communication environment than previous implementations. It has the following advantages:

- **The 802.1x standard employs an 128-bit RC4 algorithm for data encryption**—This is an improvement over the 40-bit encryption used in 802.11b. Longer encryption key bit lengths make decrypting data intercepted in the "open air" somewhat more difficult and make other known attacks to weaker encryption more time-consuming to mount. The standard also implements dynamic key management, which allows switching WEP encryption keys in the course of each communication session. Normally, dynamically changeable keys are more difficult to forge, and authentication sessions are impossible to replay. However, WEP's 128-bit scheme is subject to cracking if data is captured over time because this enables the guessing of keys and breaking of encryption. For this reason, most experts recommend that wireless implementations use additional encryption, such as IPSec or some VPN technology, to prevent easy interception of wireless communications.

> NOTE
>
> **The Wireless Encryption Protocol**
> Also called WEP, this is part of the basic 802.11 technology. It permits use of 56- or 128-bit keys with various methods for assigning and managing encryption keys. WEP is quite easy to crack, often because implementers leave well-known default keys in place or because documented key attacks work easily to permit WEP traffic to be decrypted.

- **802.1x uses widely accepted industry standards that are proven to be reliable**—These include EAP, RADIUS, and Transport Layer Security (TLS). Wireless EAP clients conform to the single sign-on (SSO) concept, so in effect, after RADIUS authentication is completed successfully, wireless clients can access network services company-wide.

This functionality is possible because RADIUS authentication networks easily integrate with other authentication systems. TLS provides mutual authentication, data integrity, encryption algorithm negotiation, and key exchange between communication end points.

- **802.1x blocks all network activity up until the point where the client successfully establishes its identity with authentication servers**—One of the 802.11 standard shortfalls is that the communication system is vulnerable during a short period of time allocated for client authentication purposes.
- **No fundamental changes have occurred between the 802.11 and 802.1x standards**—This enables companies that already have 802.11 deployed to seamlessly transform their technology to a more secure 802.1x environment.

Securing Virtual Private Networks

The Internet is still growing rapidly: Communication speeds and quality, as well as the amount of transferred data, are increasing constantly. At the same time, Internet access costs are declining. These factors stimulate great demand from both consumers and businesses.

For businesses, Internet access is an absolute necessity. In addition to customer interaction, remote administration and "work from home" concepts have also taken hold, primarily because of their cost efficiencies and convenience. As in the real world, where it is sometimes important to hold private conversations only between specific parties, the same holds true for Internet communications. Technology is needed to secure remote communications and ensure that communications theft or eavesdropping is difficult, if not altogether im possible.

The most secure method to safeguard point-to-point communications is a dedicated communications channel for each such link. Unfortunately, this approach imposes high costs and complexity and is subject to limited availability. For example, imagine a salesperson who travels around the country among temporary offices. It's simply impractical to install a high-speed dedicated communications pipe to every possible location where a connection is (or might be needed).

This helps explain why dial-up access services, Remote Access Servers (RAS), can seems like a good solution. But this technology demands that remote users dial in to a specific server and incurs long-distance charges when users outside the local area code need access. Likewise, as a company grows, so does its need for remote access, which means more telephone lines must be ordered and installed on the remote access server. In turn, monthly phone service charges go up, as do long-distance fees.

By using the Internet to handle the nonlocal portions of the "access equation," however, users can call their nearest Internet service provider (ISP)—almost always a local call. Likewise, the remote access server can establish a big-bandwidth connection to the Internet locally to ensure its capability to handle a given number of connections at any one time. By layering extra software to secure these communications, you can keep these connections (and the conversations they carry) safe and secure. This notion explains the origin of the term *virtual private network*: It uses the public Internet to create a private link between pairs of parties. In fact, a VPN can be used for remote access, where remote users pay only the price of a local telephone call, or it can be used to connect two or more private LANs via the Internet. When used for single-party remote access, a VPN is said to be operating in point-to-point or call mode; when used to interconnect two LANs, a VPN is said to be operating in gateway or site-to-site mode.

Obviously, open transmission of confidential information via public networks is unacceptable because it is highly unsecure. When using the Internet as a transport, you have absolutely no control over routing paths involved, nor can you prevent eavesdropping on such traffic. Thus, when dealing with data transfer over a public network, security must be the number-one concern.

A VPN provides an integrated suite of security controls. It ensures that information travels the wire in encrypted form, that both sender and receiver are established and verified, and that data is not altered in transit either by error or intent. The concept of VPN communications is based on establishing a secure tunnel between LANs or remote clients—a tunnel that is free from outside inspection or interference. To establish such a tunnel, specific VPN software and protocols must be used, as described in the following section. In some cases in which a VPN handles significant amounts of traffic, specialized hardware can be used to provide proper levels of throughput and performance.

By definition, a *VPN tunnel* is a logical connection established between two end points. All information that traverses the VPN is encapsulated within the protocols the VPN uses. In fact, VPNs use encryption and authentication to protect all information traveling inside the tunnel.

VPN Protocols

Plenty of protocols have been used for tunneling at various times, but only two were ever widely used: the Point-to-Point Tunneling Protocol (PPTP), developed by Microsoft, Copper Mountain Networks and others, and the Layer Two Tunneling Protocol (L2TP), developed by Cisco Systems. The IP Security (IPSec) protocol provides an additional level of security, because it supports specific security associations (to manage and control communications access) and because it uses strong encryption.

The basis for both PPTP and L2TP is the Point-to-Point Protocol (PPP), which operates at Layer 2 in the OSI Network Reference Model. All Transmission Control Protocol/Internet Protocol (TCP/IP), Sequenced Packet Exchange (SPX), and NetBIOS Enhanced User Interface (NetBEUI) communications are encapsulated into PPP, which in turn is encapsulated within either PPTP or L2TP. That way, a multiprotocol VPN tunnel is supported no matter which protocol is used on the LAN side of the point-to-point connection the VPN uses.

> NOTE
>
> **Downside of IPSec** One of the downsides of IPSec is its indifference to controlling access on the Application layer of the Open System Interconnection (OSI) model. IPSec is only concerned with the Network and Transport layers of OSI.

Both PPTP and L2TP have various advantages and disadvantages. Today, the most widely accepted mechanism to strengthen security for encapsulated traffic is IPSec. Two thirds of all modern VPN solutions use IPSec. When combined, the tunneling protocols and an extra IP security layer ensure the same level of security over a public WAN as if that information were traveling over LAN media.

Most VPN solutions establish bidirectional trust between communication parties. Some non-IPSec solutions provide one-way (unidirectional) trusts using alternatives to VPN tunneling. In a unidirectional connection, if some kind of security breach occurs, only the destination network is affected. Such solutions are flexible in choosing virtually any authentication and encryption algorithms and can be more useful where bidirectional trust is not required.

Information Protection

Information is protected in a VPN tunnel using encryption, authentication, and access control. Data transmitted on the wire can be read only by recipients who possess valid encryption keys. The most commonly used VPN encryption algorithms are Data Encryption Standard (DES 56-bit), Triple DES (168-bit), and various implementations of the Advanced Encryption Standard (AES). The industry is moving away from relying on DES because it is no longer considered sufficiently secure.

All parties involved in a VPN tunnel must successfully establish their identities before the tunnel can be established. Data verification is a process in which a hash value is computed by applying a hashing algorithm to a portion of data of any size. The result of the computation is a relatively small value that changes completely if there is any change in the data from which it was calculated. The hash is submitted along with the data that produced it, and at the receiving end, the hash value is recomputed and then compared to the original hash value. If the two values match, the recipient is assured that the data has not been intentionally modified or accidentally damaged in transit. Most popular hashing algorithms include Message Digest version 5 (MD5) and the Secure Hashing Algorithm, version 1 (SHA1). For a more thorough discussion on hashing and message signing, see the section "Recognizing and Administering Security Controls—Email Communications," later in this chapter.

> EXAM TIP
>
> **Virtual Private Networking** VPN gives users the ability to securely connect to a private network over a public network (usually the Internet).

Identity verification is integral to the security process because all parties involved must be sure that their peers are who they say they are. Identity verification is gradually moving away from traditional username and password authentication and toward digital certificates (X.509). Within the so-called public key infrastructure (PKI), certificate authority (CA) servers issue, manage, and verify such certificates and help to support a widely available public key system. Popular CAs, such as VeriSign, Entrust, and Thawte, can service certificate verification requests using the Lightweight Directory Access Protocol (LDAP) or HTTP. Besides PKI, systems also rely on biometric scanners (retina or fingerprint scanners) or other widely used authentication systems such as RADIUS or TACACS (these systems are discussed in Chapter 6).

> NOTE
>
> **QoS** Quality of service (QoS) can be used in conjunction with VPN links to prioritize traffic and optimize VPN channel bandwidth utilization. This approach grants higher priority to time-sensitive traffic such as streaming video or Voice Over IP (VoIP) services.

Understanding the Public Key Infrastructure

VPN relies heavily on PKI, which is discussed in greater detail in the section "Recognizing and Administering Security Controls—Email Communications," later in this chapter. PKI allows parties to engage in communications in secure VPN tunnels without prior arrangements, such as key exchange or establishing trust relationships. In the absence of PKI, virtual private network solutions are limited to vendor-specific frameworks (hardware/software/algorithms), which translate into higher deployment and maintenance costs. Depending on the vendor and the solution provided, it might not always be easy or even possible to implement a VPN system with a few thousand clients even within one company. Fortunately, industry participants realize the importance of PKI and are backing digital certificates. Examples of this can be found in products such as those from CheckPoint (which now integrates a CA into its offerings) and TimeStep.

VPN Solution Providers

A number of high-profile players in the industry offer hardware and software VPN solutions. Among the leaders, not surprisingly, are Microsoft, Cisco, and Intel. AT&T, 3Com, Nortel, Symantec, CheckPoint, and several other companies also feature VPN solutions in their product line-ups.

RADIUS

Corporate IT infrastructures often involve complex, heterogeneous environments of disparate systems. Such infrastructures sometimes have difficulties reacting to business challenges, not to mention keeping pace with technological advancements. As a company grows, its IT infrastructure invariably gets bigger. Unfortunately, so do the risks of downtime (and the duration for such downtime when it occurs).

Environments that fall victim to ineffective planning or whose planning fails to take future needs into proper account, are most vulnerable to downtime and outages. Under some circumstances—such as when essential business transactions are lost or stymied—outages can paralyze an entire company and cause serious financial losses. In some cases, IT departments in large corporations estimate that one hour of downtime can cost millions of dollars in lost revenue.

When business operations depend on a working network infrastructure, administrators need access to fix such problems to bring the business back to work as soon as possible.

By deploying PPP, VPN, and terminal server software (such as pcAnywhere, Microsoft Terminal Services, and so forth), organizations can permit network clients to work and administer networks remotely. Although its other productivity advantages are well-known, such capabilities can also significantly reduce downtime. Let's say company XYZ is a 24/7 ASP shop, and one of its critical servers goes down at 2:34 a.m., while all its systems engineers are asleep. Network monitoring teams that are onsite 24/7 are supposed to identify the issue immediately and contact a designated engineer. Instead of having to travel from home to the office, a proper remote access solution means that the engineer has all the technology he needs to fix problems within minutes directly from home.

Although broadband access is becoming increasingly available in North America and Europe, dial-up often remains the best way to connect to an enterprise network. But regardless of the type of connection used, remote access also puts the security of corporate infrastructures at risk. Unfortunately, this means that network managers often have to choose among expensive hardware solutions or proprietary systems that might not be compatible with applications in use. This situation proves that some kind of standard authentication and access control mechanism could be useful, not only to provide necessary services and controls, but also to make multivendor remote access systems possible.

In fact, the RADIUS protocol was developed by Livingston Enterprises to support server access, authentication, and accounting services. A fifth draft of RADIUS was tabled before the IETF in June 1996. Presently, however, the RADIUS specification (RFC 2058) and the RADIUS accounting standard (RFC 2059) are nominated for approval as common standards. RADIUS and TACACS+ (you can learn more about TACACS+ later in the chapter in the section titled "TACACS+") have introduced unified systems that provide key services to support user access to systems and resources, including the following:

- **Authentication**—To establish user identities
- **Authorization**—To verify user access permissions
- **Accounting**—To track resource consumption or use

Collectively, these three capabilities are important enough to occur together often in discussions of information security. As a key component in providing information security, they are collectively called *AAA* (pronounced "Triple-A," like the automotive club). By design, both RADIUS and TACACS+ provide these services for remote users.

RADIUS is based on a client/server technology. Any network access server (NAS) is considered a RADIUS client, so long as it is configured to work with RADIUS server software that can be deployed either on Unix or Windows Server (NT/Windows 2000) computers. In design and capability, NAS devices are similar to AS-series Cisco dial-in devices. All client/server communications in RADIUS are UDP based: A client passes requests to the server and acts in accordance with the corresponding response received from the server. RADIUS servers that receive client requests to validate a user and establish whether that user can access requested resources gather all the information necessary to service that user and send it back to the RADIUS client.

For other RADIUS servers, or for user validation servers belonging to other systems common to modern networks, a RADIUS server can act as an authentication proxy server (a middleman, in other words). This authentication process works as follows:

1. By seeking to gain access to a corporate network, a user initiates a call to the NAS server (in this scenario, a local directory or network server takes the role of the RADIUS client).

2. NAS requests the user to supply his username and password (if the Password Authentication Protocol [PAP] is used as an authentication protocol) or a challenge phrase (if the Challenge-Handshake Authentication Protocol [CHAP] is used as an authentication protocol). Other authentication protocols (such as Microsoft's MS-CHAP) can also be used in some implementations.

3. The user supplies the requested information to the local directory or NAS.

4. NAS submits those user credentials to the RADIUS server and awaits a reply. Some implementations (for example, Windows 2000) use a technique called *user impersonation* whereby the system uses cached or stored user credentials, acting on behalf of the user who's requesting access.

5. The RADIUS server issues a reply of accept (access is allowed and access controls apply), reject (access is denied), or challenge (a further challenge-response is required before an accept or reject message is issued).
6. NAS takes action based on the reply it gets from the RADIUS server, along with any optional parameters (such as access control lists, information about user rights, and so forth).

In RADIUS, both authentication and authorization functions are combined. As long as a match is found in the user database, and as long as the password provided by the user matches the password on record, the RADIUS server issues an accept reply along with session parameters. Typical parameters include the service type (shell or framed), the protocol type, the IP address for the remote user, a list of objects the user is authorized to access, and a static routing entry to be added to the NAS server if needed.

RADIUS accounting functions are used independently from the first two *A*s (authentication and authorization). Accounting in RADIUS relies on providing resource usage information upon initiation and completion of each user session. Thus, companies can implement billing or security applications to monitor how much time certain resources were in use, how many packets were exchanged, how many bytes were sent or received, and so forth. This is especially useful for ISPs and other service vendors who meter or charge by usage levels.

All transactions between a RADIUS client and a RADIUS server use a shared *secret* for mutual identification needs. This secret is never transmitted on the wire. All exchanges of user information, account names, and passwords are encrypted, thereby eliminating threats based on eavesdropping or interception. One of RADIUS's major drawbacks is its combination of authentication and authorization into a single process (it's assumed that if the user and password match, the remote user's identity claim is valid).

Among RADIUS software vendors, Microsoft's Windows 2000 includes Internet Authentication Service (IAS) Server software, whereas Cisco Systems implements RADIUS client support in its Internetwork Operating System (IOS) software that controls most of its routers, switches, and network access equipment.

TACACS+

TACACS is an acronym for Terminal Access Controller Access Control System. It is also an access management protocol originally developed by Bolt, Beranek, and Newman (BBN) for the defense network known as MILNET (military network). TACACS is fundamentally similar to RADIUS. An extended version of TACACS, called XTACACS, was released in 1990 and is documented in RFC 1942. TACACS was further developed and modified by Cisco Systems a few times, resulting in a new proposal known as TACACS+. TACACS+ offers a wider variety of services but is fully compatible with previous versions of the TACACS protocol.

Like RADIUS, TACACS+ is a client/server-based technology in which a client is a NAS and a TACACS+ server is a software service (daemon) running on a Unix or Windows NT/Windows 2000 platform. The service listens to incoming requests on TCP/IP port 49, which is reserved specifically for this use. All original versions of TACACS and their mutations utilize TCP or UDP port 49.

One of the key components of the TACACS+ protocol is its isolation of authentication, authorization, and accounting functions within AAA, whereas RADIUS combines the first two of these functions. Furthermore, identification is optional and depends on the situation, so it might not be required at all or might be used only in special circumstances for specific reasons. With that in mind, separation of authentication and authorization allows the use of various protocols for various purposes; for example, the TACACS+ protocol can still be used for authorization on the network, while Kerberos v5 is used for authentication on the same network. After NAS receives a positive acknowledgment from a Kerberos server that the user successfully established her identity, it issues a secondary request to the TACACS+ server without additional authentication procedures. NAS communicates that the Kerberos server validated the user's identity, and a TACACS+ server issues the information necessary to authorize user access to network resources. This permits easy integration of TACACS into environments where reasonably secure authentication services are already available.

> **EXAM TIP**
>
> **RADIUS Versus TACACS** RADIUS combines certain services, such as authentication and authorization, whereas TACACS keeps each of these components separate.

A more detailed review of TACACS+ architecture yields the following picture. As with every reliable security system, TACACS+ has three key areas that do not depend on each other—the three elements of AAA. These are covered in the following sections.

Authentication

Because plenty of authentication protocols are available these days, it is important not to rely on any single one in case the industry moves away from it in the future. At the same time, support for many such protocols ensures great flexibility and interoperability within mixed environments. TACACS+ supports PAP, CHAP, the Serial Line Internet Protocol (SLIP), the AppleTalk Remote Access Protocol (ARAP), hardware authentication devices, Kerberos, and Telnet. This ensures that users can use the same username/password combination regardless of their authentication preferences or requirements. TACACS+ might be extended to include support for other protocols not mentioned in the preceding list—for example, KCHAP (a Kerberos-based implementation of CHAP). It is noteworthy that all traffic traveling between a NAS and a TACACS+ server is encrypted using a preshared secret key and an MD5-based hashing algorithm. This helps ensure reasonable confidentiality for all such communications.

Authorization

TACACS+ provides a mechanism necessary to communicate authorization information to a NAS, and it includes security settings and context information that applies to specific user sessions. TACACS+ allows only positive or negative authorization. In cases where authorization fails, a reject reply is communicated to the NAS; otherwise, an accept reply is sent along with other applicable session information, such as the number for an access control list that the NAS is to apply to the session just authorized.

Accounting

Accounting is a process of recording user actions, resource usage based on time and volume of information, resource access, and the like. In a TACACS+ system, accounting can serve two purposes: billing and security. Accounting in TACACS+ features three types of activity records: start, stop, and update. Start records indicate when a resource is first requested and when its usage began. The converse is true about stop records. Update records are posted between start and stop records to indicate that a resource remains in use.

Accounting records contain the full set of information received during the authorization stage, as well as other data such as timestamps for initial and final resource access and resource usage information. Thus, they can be used to indicate which resources were accessed, at what time, and to some extent for what purpose while a user session is underway. This can provide useful security data, as well as usage monitoring information, and can therefore be tracked in intrusion detection systems (IDSs).

L2TP/PPTP

In the mid-1990s, two companies started developing separate VPN protocols: Microsoft drove PPTP, and Cisco drove the Layer Two Forwarding (L2F) protocol. As a result of security issues discovered with PPTP, Cisco and Microsoft united their efforts on the VPN front and created the Layer 2 Tunneling Protocol, (which is a hybrid of PPTP used with L2F). Later, L2TP became an Internet industry standard as described in RFC 2661 and other related RFCs. Knowledge of both PPTP and L2TP invariably helps when choosing the most appropriate technology to secure remote access services in a VPN.

Both PPTP and L2TP are based on PPP and essentially work as extensions. PPP functions at the Data Link layer of the OSI model and was first developed to provide data encapsulation and transmission services over peer-to-peer connections. PPP is an important component of both L2TP and PPTP. It features the Link Control Protocol (LCP), which is responsible for setup, configuration, management, and termination of peer-to-peer connections, and the Network Control Protocol (NCP), which encapsulates various Network layer protocols for subsequent transportation over a peer-to-peer connection. Because of NCP, remote links established with PPP are compatible with most popular LAN protocols, including TCP/IP, Novell's IPX/SPX (or NWLink in Microsoft environments), and NetBEUI, (which is still used in some small home and office networks).

PPTP

PPTP allows tunneling in PPP connections on IP networks by means of VPN connections. Thus, a remote connection (tunnel) can be established between a client from network A and a gateway in network B, imitating a local connection from network B's perspective. This tunnel, maintained on the gateway in network B, has an IP address local to network B. All traffic sent to that local IP address is redirected by the gateway back to the remote client in network A. The two main connection types where PPTP can be used are over the Internet or via a dial-up connection (PSTN).

NOTE

When PPP Is Not Mandatory PPP is not mandatory when establishing a VPN connection. Today, more and more VPN connections originate from broadband cable "last mile" users. In the case of xDSL, and for some cable modem installations, Point-to-Point Protocol Over Ethernet (PPPoE) is used instead. Because PPP is a point-to-point communication protocol, it is made redundant if the client already has a dedicated Internet connection. For example, with cable, the client is connecting from one LAN (cable ISP) to another (corporate network). It is basically the same as VPNing between two computers sitting on the same physical LAN in that there is no need to preestablish a network connection between the client and the ISP before the VPN connection can be made between the client and the PPTP server.

PPTP encapsulates virtual network packets into PPP, which are, in turn, encapsulated into generic routing encapsulation (GRE) packets and transmitted in the form of IP datagrams between the parties. In other words, after the PPTP tunnel is created, user data is transmitted between the client and PPTP server in IP datagrams containing PPP packets. These IP datagrams are created using a modified version of the GRE protocol. In parallel to the encapsulated data channel, another TCP session is established for control purposes. This control session is initialized by the client and uses TCP port 1723 on the server. It is a bidirectional channel used for signaling and session status information exchange between the client and the server.

PPTP does not mandate the use of specific authentication algorithms. Instead, it provides a framework for the negotiation of these algorithms by the parties involved.

For the purposes of user authentication, PPTP can use any of the PPP authentication protocols, including CHAP, EAP, Microsoft Challenge Handshake Authentication Protocol (MS-CHAP) version 1 or version 2, Shiva Password Authentication Protocol (SPAP), or PAP.

L2TP

Layer Two Tunneling Protocol is another extension of the PPP protocol, which is created by combining PPTP and L2F. L2TP is critical to building VPNs for dial-up access because it combines the best qualities of PPTP and L2F.

The L2TP specification does not describe authentication and encryption methods. Because L2TP is a data link extension of PPP, it can handle any of the supported protocols implemented higher in the OSI networking model. Unlike PPTP, however, L2TP requires protocol support on the ISP's routers, which can be a setback. However, L2TP allows the creation of IP, as well as x.25, Frame Relay, and ATM tunnels.

L2TP encapsulates and transfers PPP frames and data over IP networks in the form of UDP packets. Two components are not featured anywhere else in this discussion: the L2TP Access Concentrator (LAC) and the L2TP Network Server (LNS). The L2TP tunnel directs user requests via LAC to a central network server LNS, which is either a router or a server and also the endpoint for all PPP sessions. L2TP can be used in conjunction with IPSec to encrypt information in the tunnel creating the equivalent LAN security over public unsecured networks. Thus, L2TP/IPSec is considered the best approach when implementing VPN connections.

During the first authentication phase in L2TP/IPSec, clients and servers use digital certificates issued by a CA. The client exchanges public keys (certificates) with the server, creating a security association (SA).

After L2TP finishes authenticating the participants from the hardware perspective, another authentication pass occurs at the user level. In this phase, any of the authentication protocols described in the previous sections can be used (PAP, CHAP, MS-CHAPv1, MS-CHAPv2, SPAP, or EAP). L2TP over IPSec encrypts the entire session, so even clear-text password authentication using PAP is considered secure inside such a tunnel.

SSH

Imagine the following scenario: A publishing company has two departments at different sites: editorial and printing. A file ready to be published is transferred from one office to the other. After the file is printed, a few major discrepancies are found in the submitting department, and it's definitely not what they wanted to print. And, of course, one side says that it sent exactly what needed to be printed, and the other side says it printed exactly what the first side submitted.

The problem is that the publishing department folks could not compare the information they received with something stored in its location. So, in essence, to really be sure that the submitted file is what it needs to be, you would have to actually carry or snail-mail the file on a disk from office to office and then send it by email or FTP. This defeats the whole point of electronic transfer. Furthermore, you can't be sure that the version on disk isn't damaged or altered as well.

In fact, the idea of a standard against which to compare the data has been around for some time. It's called a *digital signature*, and information being transmitted is passed through a mathematical formula (encryption algorithm) to calculate a unique checksum value *(hash)*. The hash is encrypted with a private key and attached to the message. The recipient uses the sender's public key to read the hash and then attempts to recalculate that hash using the same process the sender used. If the two values match, the information has not been damaged or altered in transit.

This concept is fundamental to many data protection and security systems, and Secure Shell (SSH) is no exception. SSH is an open standard widely used in many systems for remote administration and file transfer. SSH is effectively a secure Telnet client, designed to replace clear-text telnet sessions because they are highly unsecure. The same issue also applies to FTP, which is designed to transfer files but does so in the clear. Because remote administrators often need to transfer a few files back and forth, SSH comes in handy and naturally replaces both FTP and Telnet. SSH uses port 22 (whereas FTP uses port 21 and Telnet listens on port 23). Likewise, SSH can be used to tunnel other, less secure protocols, including POP3 and IMAP (common email messaging protocols).

SSH in Action

All SSH communications are encrypted using the International Data Encryptions Algorithm (IDEA) or any of the following symmetric encryption algorithms: three-key Triple DES, DES, or Blowfish. Rivest, Shamir, & Adleman (RSA) methods are used for key exchange, and all the keys are destroyed and regenerated every hour. (Keys are not stored anywhere after they are destroyed.) The RSA host authentication method is used with RSA keys to verify communicating parties' identities, where every communicating party has its own unique and private RSA key. Encryption is used to prevent IP spoofing, and public key verification is used to stop DNS and Routing spoofing. SSH protects from the following attacks and acts of mischief:

- **IP spoofing, or IP source routing**—Occurs when an attacker replaces the source IP address in his packets to make it seem as if the request is coming from a trusted IP address. This is a well-known attack. SSH provides protection against such attacks even in LAN boundaries.
- **DNS spoofing**—Occurs when an attacker forges name server records in the DNS.
- **Username/password interception, or eavesdropping on data transmission by intermediary hosts**—This is a passive attack.
- **Real-time data modification**—Occurs when an intermediary host hijacks active communication and impersonates both parties to both parties (that is, participates as the sender from the recipient's view and vice versa). The attacker receives information sent by the real sender, modifies it as he sees fit, and forwards it to the recipient on behalf of the sender. The recipient does not suspect anything.
- **Authentication replay attacks**—Occurs when the attacker records the stream of data while a legitimate user is authenticating, dissects all user replies from the stream, and attempts to play back replies during his own attempt to establish a connection.

SSH has no mechanisms designed to protect a workstation using other well-known or newly discovered attacks. If a hacker gets into a workstation where SSH is used and gains root access privileges, he can then modify the SSH application to his liking. Security is also undermined if someone gets access to your home directory.

IPSec

As this chapter mentioned in the context of VPNs and L2TP/PPTP tunneling, today's networks are increasingly connected and accessible to the outside world to permit remote access via the Internet. Two types of attacks are possible in every scenario in which two or more remote parties authenticate with each other to establish a trusted private connection over unsecure public networks.

The first such attack is based on traffic interception because that traffic uses public network links. The second such attack is enabled when a network is configured to accept remote connections. Although it might never happen, there is always the risk that unauthorized or unwanted users can exploit this capability to steal or compromise private information or crash one or more systems remotely.

Companies rely on IPSec to protect them from attacks involving information theft. IPSec allows all TCP/IP transmissions, inside and outside the corporate LAN, to be secured with encryption. In the early days of IPSec, a major setback was the processing overhead from constant data encryption and decryption. When performed at the operating system (software) level, encryption and decryption take processing power away from average desktop machines. Given average processing power in modern computers, this is no longer a major issue; furthermore, many mid-to-high–end network interface cards now offer hardware support for IPSec encryption/decryption functions. This offloads the processing overhead associated with encryption and decryption from the operating system onto an onboard NIC processor.

IPSec is based on the following concepts:

- **Network resource protection**—Users can access only those services they are expressly allowed to use.
- **Identity verification**—Uses public key certificates to ascertain user identity and permits stronger authentication/identification schemes (biometrics, token cards, smart cards, and so forth).
- **Communication security**—Occurs only with full encryption of the information traveling the wire. It's ideal for solutions that rely in part or fully on public communication networks such as the Internet (VPN, Terminal Services, and similar remote access applications).

IPSec has a certain structure that is described in publicly available RFC standards developed in the IP Security Working Group at the IETF. IPSec conducts authorization of users, ensuring that the information is traveling from and to those who are allowed to use this information, and it ascertains that users are really who they claim to be. IPSec employs data integrity mechanisms described in this chapter to ensure that information is not damaged or altered in transit and that unauthorized people cannot read such communications.

IPSec uses three main security control elements: an authentication header (AH); an encapsulated security payload (ESP); and a protocol for exchanging encryption keys, called the Internet Key Exchange (IKE) Protocol. Finally, IP compression (IPcomp) is used to compress raw IP data. In addition, AH and ESP can be used independently of each other.

AH is an identification record that includes the user's digital signature; it is inserted in the headers of all packets. Digital signatures establish user identity and allow the recipient to ensure that the information is neither damaged nor altered in transit. However, AH does not actually encrypt anything in the packet payload; it only serves the purposes mentioned in this paragraph. The most popular bit lengths used in authentication headers are 128-bit MD5 and 160-bit SHA1 digital signatures.

> NOTE
>
> **Digital Certificates** Digital signatures and private/public key encryption are sufficiently strong that they are also computationally intense. In plain English, this means that digital certificates provide keys that can be used to encrypt and decrypt less strong (but still powerful) secret keys that two or more parties can share. Those secret keys are used to encrypt and decrypt ordinary message traffic, to keep the computational overhead involved more manageable. In other words, asymmetric encryption (which is extremely strong and uses public/private key pairs that are 512 bits in length or longer) makes it possible to exchange a shared key for symmetric encryption (which is weaker and uses a single key of anywhere from 40 to 256 bits in length, depending on the exact algorithm in use).

ESP provides confidentiality through encryption. The receiving end uses ESP to decrypt the contents of the encrypted packet, and a pre-shared secret key is used by both parties. Under most circumstances, no one else possesses that secret key, so protection from eavesdropping is virtually guaranteed. ESP can also be used as an alternative to AH to verify user identity. If both parties have not already shared a set of keys, IKE facilitates secure key exchange.

Another technique used in the IPSec suite is IPcomp. In traditional dial-up connections, PPP compresses data before it is encrypted. In the absence of PPP, IPcomp provides the same service—namely, compressing raw IP data prior to its encryption.

IKE is also associated with a framework known as the Internet Security Association and Key Management Protocol (ISAKMP). ISAKMP defines how an SA can be formed and keys exchanged securely. Using UDP port 500, IKE defines a protocol that is used to generate keys and establish SAs between the two end points of an IPSec encryption channel (IKE SA). Where no shared keys are available, IPSec participants must agree on a session encryption key to use for symmetric encryption of the information traveling the wire (usually DES, 3DES, or Blowfish). The Diffie-Hellman (DH) algorithm is used to generate a session key, and the key is safely transferred to the other party using public key encryption mechanisms. This is safe against man-in-the-middle attacks because of the very nature of public encryption, as explained in a previous note.

IP Security Solutions

The main advantage of using IPSec within infrastructures that might have been deployed before it was developed is backward-compatibility. IPSec easily traverses routers and switches installed long before the birth of that standard (and remains firmly rooted to the Internet Protocol). IPSec therefore can also be used effectively on public networks, where everything (hardware, software, cabling, and so on) can be described only as totally heterogeneous. In fact, IPSec solutions can be categorized as either transport solutions—when TCP headers remain unprotected and the actual data within every packet is encrypted (using ESP)—or tunneling solutions—where each transmitted packet is encrypted in full, including all the headers, and then is transmitted over the network encapsulated into a new set of IP headers (AH plus ESP).

Vulnerabilities

Where vulnerabilities are concerned, every technology is subject to some drawbacks. However, it must be noted that recent developments, such as public cryptography, have had a positive impact on the quality of security. PKI is now used in nearly everything from IPSec, to email, to the Web, to integrated network logons, to remote access, to administration. Public cryptography is a strong security technology that has proven to be nearly flawless. Where weaker encryption algorithms have been broken (such as DES), weaker, shorter key lengths (DES uses only 56-bit keys) are judged responsible.

Given today's trends, a 2,048-bit key should keep data safe until 2015 (give or take a year or two), unless some mathematical breakthrough occurs to significantly speed up the prime factoring techniques used to calculate private keys or some other revolution of comparable significance arises in computing techniques. (Some experts have predicted that quantum computing techniques could crack even 2,048-bit keys nearly instantly, but quantum computing is currently a theoretical possibility rather than even an experimental technology.)

PKI is a reliable standard for protecting against many of the most serious vulnerabilities, such as man-in-the-middle attacks, wiretapping or eavesdropping, impersonation that results in theft of legitimate credentials, authentication replays, active and passive interceptions, and hijacking. However, PKI does not secure corporate environments from things such as software bugs. Here is example that is not directly related to PKI but still applies in principle: Bruce Schneier discovered a serious PPTP bug in Microsoft's RAS service. Although it does not allow attackers to gain unauthorized access, it allows them to crash unpatched Windows NT systems and cause downtime and, hence, successfully conduct denial-of-service attacks. Very unpleasant, yes, but does it constitute information theft or communication security breach? Not quite.

Another significant source of communication security problems stems from social engineering and other matters seemingly unrelated to technology (a buddy's laptop with saved VPN passwords, sticky notes with passwords stuck on the monitors, disgruntled employees who retain network access after termination, and so forth). Properly planned communication security strategy is nearly unbreakable, but you must keep in mind that a chain is only as strong as its weakest link. This helps explain why other parts of this book emphasize physical security and implementation of appropriate employee or user training and security policies.

Recognizing and Administering Security Controls—Email Communications

Understand communication security in wireless, wired, and application-specific environments.

Email communication, according to some sources, dates back to 1971 when the first computer message was sent back in the ARPAnet days. Email has come a long way in the last 30 years or so, and it is really hard to think of any modern organization that does not depend on email on a daily basis. Furthermore, email proved to be the killer app in the 1990s, given human strivings to communicate. Not surprisingly, a vast majority of viruses arrive via email these days, and email has also been the subject of several privacy-related concerns.

Email threats can be categorized into the following areas:

- Spam
- Hoaxes and chain letters
- Impersonation and social engineering
- Viruses and other malware attachments
- Rich content (HTML), client scripting, and links outside corporate firewalls
- Embedded content (MIME)
- Software bugs
- Communications privacy

There are ways to deal with most, but unfortunately not all, of these potential threats. Educated and conscientious users should be able to avoid a vast majority, or perhaps even all, of these problems; however, given the sizes and politics of organizations and human nature, it is not always possible to rely solely on education and mindfulness to prevent their occurrence. The following sections describe some potentially useful technological solutions that should be pursued above and beyond education and consciousness-raising.

S/MIME

S/MIME stands for Secure Multipurpose Internet Mail Extensions. The MIME standard specifies how email clients handle messages that contain not only plain-text ASCII characters, but also graphics, attachments, and rich content. The S/MIME standard implements encryption for message content using RSA's public key encryption technology. All major email application vendors (including Microsoft, IBM, Novell, and Netscape) support S/MIME, currently at version 3 (RFCs 2630-2634).

The process of making your email communications comply with S/MIME begins when a user requests a personal digital ID from a trusted authority. (For intracompany communications, this can be a private CA server, but for external communications, it must be issued by a public CA). The user generates a private key and submits a request to the CA; the request also contains her personal information including name, organization, address, and email address.

After going through a formal identity verification process, the CA issues an X.509 certificate that contains the following data:

- A public key generated for the user
- Date of certificate issue
- Date of certificate expiration
- Root CA and issuer information with CA's public key, key length, and encryption algorithm in use
- Digital signature information

This certificate is much like a driver's license, whereas the CA is a licensing body similar to the Bureau of Motor Vehicles.

In public-key cryptosystems, a public key needs to be available to all recipients of encrypted messages. Private keys stay on each sender's machine, are sensitive, and should be backed up and stored safely. If you lose a private key, you are out of luck and the information it is used to encipher will likely be lost. When a sender encrypts a message, data contained in that communication is encrypted with the receiver's public key. The receiver of this encrypted message can use only her private key to decrypt the message content. A public key is normally used only to encrypt communication and, therefore, is useless to attackers who intercept an encrypted message or public key. Only the private key can be used to decrypt messages encrypted with the public key; this is the security foundation upon which asymmetric cryptography firmly rests.

WARNING

Pay Attention to How the Message Encryption Process Really Works
It is a fairly popular misconception to assume that messages get encrypted to the sender's private key and decrypted by the sender's public key. If this were the case, the attacker would be able to decrypt intercepted communication using a public key attached with the sender's X.509 certificate.

For the entire encryption/decryption process to work, public keys need to be distributed to potential senders of messages so they can be encrypted using that public key. A public key could be distributed manually using a disk with a copy of the sender's digital certificate, but at a certain point, its efficiency fails. (How do you distribute a certificate to all the strangers in the world with whom you initiate communication using a disk?)

In private-key cryptosystems, such distribution is the only acceptable distribution approach because anyone with that key is able to encrypt AND decrypt messages. However, in public-key cryptosystems, we do not care if someone eavesdrops and intercepts a copy of our public key because it is not used to decrypt message payloads or other sensitive data, so we can safely exchange such keys via email in the form of X.509 digital certificates. Figure 2.2 depicts the message encryption process.

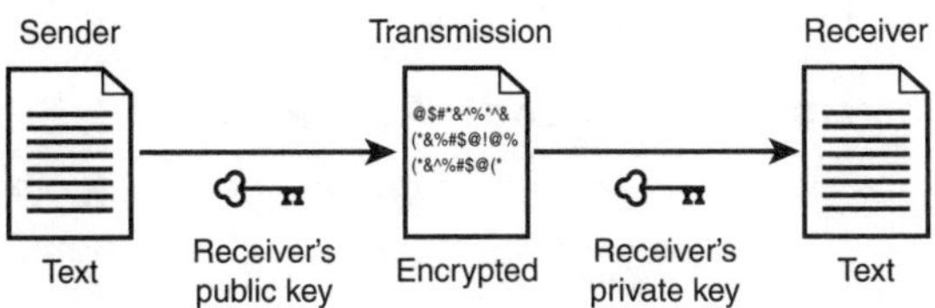

FIGURE 2.2
Message encryption.

Some of the most prominent and reliable asymmetric cryptography key management algorithms include DH, RSA, Digital Signature Algorithm (DSA), and Digital Signature Standard (DSS). Among symmetric cryptography algorithms, IDEA, CAST by Carlisle Adams and Stafford Taveres, DES, 3DES or Triple DES, AES, and TwoFish are used.

Encryption strength is characterized not only based on the algorithm, but also on key length in bits. The longer the key length, the more difficult it becomes to crack encrypted messages (and hence the more processing power and time it takes to encrypt/decrypt messages). Speaking of cracking, it's generally understood that the brute-force approach works best when cracking a symmetrical key (trying all possible combinations), whereas factoring is faster for asymmetric key pairs (trying to figure out a private key through access to its public key counterpart).

Still, even the fastest processing facilities today are not even close to breaking average-strength public key encryption. It is also understood that symmetric encryption works about a thousand times faster than asymmetric encryption. Table 2.1 shows the most common cryptology algorithms.

TABLE 2.1

MOST COMMON CRYPTOLOGY ALGORITHMS

Algorithm Name	*Algorithm Type*	*Algorithm Use*	*Key Bit Length*
Diffie-Hellman	Asymmetric	Crypt	Up to 8,192
RSA	Asymmetric	Crypt/Sign	Up to 16,384
DSA	Asymmetric	Sign	Up to 1,024
DSS	Asymmetric	Sign	Up to 1,024
IDEA	Symmetric	Crypt	128

continues

NOTE

For More Information on Algorithms
Please note that Table 2.1 is massively simplified and presents only information directly relevant to the Security+ exam. For more details, visit `http://kremlinencrypt.com/crypto/algorithms.html`. This page contains information on some 40 algorithms.

TABLE 2.1 *continued*

MOST COMMON CRYPTOLOGY ALGORITHMS

Algorithm Name	*Algorithm Type*	*Algorithm Use*	*Key Bit Length*
CAST	Symmetric	Crypt	128, 256
DES	Symmetric	Crypt	56
3DES	Symmetric	Crypt	DESx3 = 168
AES	Symmetric	Crypt	128, 192, 256
TwoFish	Symmetric	Crypt	128, 192, 256
MD5	Hashing	Sign	128 digest
SHA	Hashing	Sign	160 digest

NOTE

CRL Replaced by OCSP The CRL process is being replaced by the Online Certificate Status Protocol (OCSP). OCSP overcomes the need to download lists frequently to stay current with the status of certificates. Instead, it queries the server that owns the certificate in question and requests status of the certificate only when necessary. This approach is more efficient.

PKI exists to facilitate distribution and management of public keys, and it consists of CAs and certificate servers. The root CA sits at the top of a trust hierarchy and defines a container for a few other trusted CAs that issue certificates and perform identity checks. Certificate servers store user information and maintain CRLs.

Digital certificates issued by a CA have two timestamps: when the cert was issued and when it expires. CRLs can be used to expire certificates that are otherwise valid based on those two timestamps. When a certificate is revoked for any reason, it is placed on the CRL. CRLs are checked regularly by other users of public certificates, and when the expiration date is reached, that entity is removed from the CRL to reduce maintenance and lookup overhead.

How does the recipient of a digital certificate determine that it is valid? A public key for the CA who issued this same X.509 certificate lets the client software easily verify the sender's identity claim securely (the query is encrypted using the CA's public key and is sent to the issuing CA).

S/MIME allows digital signing of email messages, which has a twofold security benefit. First, you demonstrate your identity to the recipient of your communication (this is an identification benefit). At the same time, by providing information only you should possess, you cannot later claim that you never sent that message (this is called *nonrepudiation* in security terms). Therefore, digital signing provides assurances to both parties and eliminates most chances of impersonation. In fact, the process employed makes forging a digital signature nearly impossible.

S/MIME digital signing works backward from message encryption: Instead of encrypting a message using a public key that belongs to the intended recipient, the sender uses his private key and a message digest to create a signature. A *message digest* is the value that results from hashing message content, and it is a short but unique summary of whatever data is contained in the message. In most cases, a digest is no more than several hundred bits in length, as specified by the protocol in use (128-bit for MD5 digests, for example). If any bits in the original message change, this results in a different message digest value. On the receiving end, the signature is recalculated using the same hashing algorithm on message content, and if the resulting value matches the one extracted from the signature, the receiver verifies that the message is unchanged. To extract the message digest value from the signature, the sender's public certificate is used. Thus, the sender's identity is verified as well. If the two values do not match, something is wrong with either the sender or the contents. Figure 2.3 shows the message signing process.

WARNING

Pay Attention to How the Message Signing Process Really Works
Contrary to message encryption, message signing uses the sender's private key (and a hash) to sign and the sender's public key is used on the receiving end to verify user identity and message integrity. In both cases, no private keys travel anywhere! Private keys are confidential and must be stored safely.

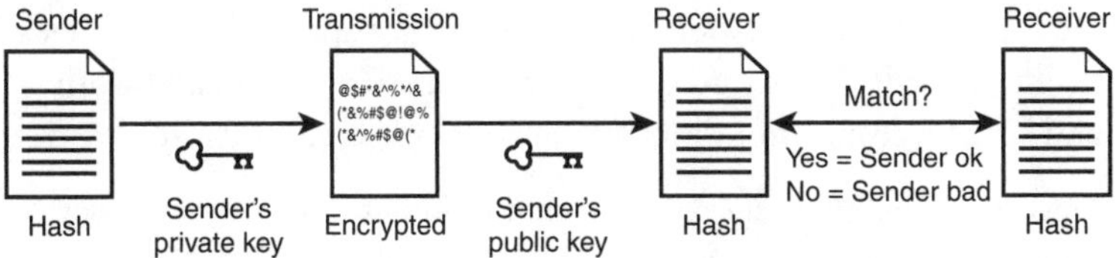

FIGURE 2.3
Message signing.

Up to a certain point, one of the main roadblocks to S/MIME technology was the price tag on even personal certificates available from public CAs. In cases where there is a central (or satellite) CA, identity verification expenses will occur—for example, VeriSign. However, personal X.509 certificates are now available at no charge from Web-of-trust CAs, such as Thawte. The good thing about Thawte is that it is a widely recognized and accepted CA and its certificates are supported by major email client vendors out of the box. To get a certificate through a Web of trust, you usually are required to meet with an affiliate of the Web face-to-face and produce a few pieces of identification.

NOTE

Key Escrow and Recovery Policy Mandate In recent developments, the U.S. government has been trying to mandate key escrow and recovery policies. In other words, Uncle Sam wants its law enforcement agencies to keep a copy of our private keys just in case we use email for malicious purposes. However, if someone has your private key, that person can read messages addressed to you and sign communications on your behalf. Even half-decent CAs are strongly against this privacy violation and usually let it be known in respective service agreements when people sign up. The crucial point in the whole process is that you, and only you, have the only copy of your private key. Only then can privacy be guaranteed.

PGP

PGP was designed by Phil Zimmerman in the early '90s and is available to the public both at no charge and as commercial software. PGP stands for pretty good privacy, and it is essentially the same thing as S/MIME, with a few important exceptions. It is a hybrid cryptosystem that utilizes symmetric cryptography for actual message encryption and asymmetric cryptography for digital signatures and key distribution and management. It also employs so-called session keys and plain-text compression to further complicate things for would-be message interceptors.

While a user is typing a message, PGP records all keystrokes and mouse movements, thereby creating a unique session key. It is virtually impossible for such a session key to be duplicated. After the user is done typing and clicks the Send button, PGP compresses all the plain-text components in the message, as well as the compressible attachments. Some known attacks try to brute-force an encrypted message by matching known strings to encrypted portions of the message. Plain compression eliminates any possibility that this attack could succeed. Furthermore, compressed messages save bandwidth and speed transmission times for messages of significant size.

Next, the message is encrypted with a unique session key used with symmetric encryption, most commonly IDEA, CAST, or Triple DES. The main benefit of using symmetric encryption for actual message encryption is the speed: They work at least 1,000 times faster than asymmetric algorithms. Now the message is encrypted and ready to be sent, but you also have to transmit the secret key to the recipient so that the message can be read—this is where asymmetric encryption comes into play. Instead of encrypting the entire message with the recipient's public key, only the session key is encrypted and is transferred with the encrypted message. PGP relies on RSA (up to 2,048 bits) and DH/DSS (1,024-bit signature, 4,096-bit encryption keys) algorithms for public key encryption.

> NOTE
>
> **PGP** At the time of this writing, PGP is at version 7.0.3. A freeware copy can be obtained at `http://www.pgpi.org/products/pgp/versions/freeware`. More information about PGP can be found at `http://www.pgpi.org` (international, free version of the site/product) or `http://www.pgp.com` (United States, commercialized version).

On the receiving end, the recipient uses his private key to retrieve the secret session key, which is then used to decrypt the entire message. As far as digital signatures and hashing go, the PGP process employed is essentially the same as that for S/MIME. So essentially, PGP has processing speed advantages over S/MIME using conventional cryptography for message encryption while relying on public cryptography to facilitate the key distribution process.

Because of recent changes in company ownership, the future of PGP is uncertain at this time, nor it is clear what development directions the product will take in the future. This uncertainty provides a good example of the risks associated with using a vendor product for security purposes. Even though PGP is widely used, it can still become a potentially severe problem if vendor support should ever cease entirely.

Vulnerabilities

Now that this chapter has discussed two mainstream methods of content protection and identity verification (S/MIME and PGP), we cover a series of other email-related security threats and discuss protection mechanisms available for each such case.

Viruses and Attachments

Email is the number one source of viruses and other malware introduced to organizations these days, with some IT security organizations estimating this at 80% or more. This is hardly surprising, given the fact that so many users are unaware or not informed about such threats. Attackers focus their efforts on email users, disseminating Trojans, worms, and other destructive mechanisms in the form of attachments.

In every IT organization today, security controls that block certain types of attachments must be in place, regardless of their true purpose or content. These files must include all forms of executables (`*.exe`, `*.bat`, `*.cmd`, `*.pif`, `*.vbs`, `*.com`, and `*.js` to name a few). It shouldn't matter who is sending what in which direction, be it an important customer or a high-flying executive. The trouble with viruses is that they spread, often without the knowledge or consent of those who spread them. So, if you catch one infected executable at the cost of blocking 10,000 legitimate files, at the end of the day, the company may be saved. Table 2.2 lists file attachments considered potentially unsafe in a Microsoft environment (see KB Q290497 for more information on unsafe attachments).

TABLE 2.2

POTENTIALLY UNSAFE EMAIL ATTACHMENTS

File Extension	*File Type*
`.ade`	Microsoft Access project extension
`.adp`	Microsoft Access project
`.asx`	Windows Media Audio/Video
`.bas`	Microsoft Visual Basic class module
`.bat`	Batch file
`.chm`	Compiled HTML Help file
`.cmd`	Microsoft Windows NT Command script
`.com`	Microsoft MS-DOS program
`.cpl`	Control Panel extension
`.crt`	Security certificate
`.exe`	Program
`.hlp`	Help file
`.hta`	HTML program
`.inf`	Setup Information
`.ins`	Internet Naming Service
`.isp`	Internet Communication settings
`.js`	JScript file
`.jse`	JScript Encoded Script file
`.lnk`	Shortcut
`.mdb`	Microsoft Access program
`.mde`	Microsoft Access MDE database
`.msc`	Microsoft Common Console document
`.msi`	Microsoft Windows Installer package
`.msp`	Microsoft Windows Installer patch
`.mst`	Microsoft Windows Installer transform; Microsoft Visual Test source file
`.pcd`	Photo CD image; Microsoft Visual compiled script
`.pif`	Shortcut to MS-DOS program
`.prf`	Microsoft Outlook profile settings
`.reg`	Registration entries
`.scf`	Windows Explorer command

File Extension	*File Type*
`.scr`	Screensaver
`.sct`	Windows Script Component
`.shb`	Shell Scrap object
`.shs`	Shell Scrap object
`.url`	Internet shortcut
`.vb`	VBScript file
`.vbe`	VBScript Encoded script file
`.vbs`	VBScript file
`.wsc`	Windows Script Component
`.wsf`	Windows Script file
`.wsh`	Windows Script Host Settings file

The most common mechanism to implement such protection is an antivirus program for your corporate mail server that checks incoming and outgoing messages on-the-fly. It is important not to run antivirus scanners on systems on which they weren't designed to run; this can do more harm than the viruses from which they offer protection. A good example is Microsoft Exchange Server, which is essentially built on a database engine that manages one or more message stores. Naturally, this database includes transaction logging capabilities. The trouble with antivirus software not specifically written to work with Microsoft Exchange is that it can recognize known virus patterns within the stream of data written to a transaction log. If this happens, depending on what action the antivirus software takes, you can lose some or all of the data stored on your Exchange Server.

Good mail antivirus software should be able to check incoming messages for viruses, block certain types of attachments, offer profanity and address filters, and scan text to keep spam off your corporate network. (We cover spam in a few paragraphs.) A pretty good scanner goes the extra mile and offers scans for known risks within certain types of attachments (for instance, archive files, such as `*.zip`, or Word documents, `*.doc`). Keep in mind that virus definition files are sometimes updated daily, so make sure your program of choice is able to run scheduled updates at whatever frequency you choose. You might also want to deploy desktop antivirus solutions that are email client-aware.

> NOTE
>
> **Antivirus and Security Tools Resource** A superb antivirus and security tools resource for all emailing needs can be found at `http://www.slipstick.com/addins/antivirus.htm`.

Unfortunately, the presence of antivirus software is not always enough to ensure that no viruses can penetrate the boundaries of your systems or networks. This is true for several reasons. One of those reasons is that it is absolutely impossible for antivirus vendors to know about every existing virus. (A *virus* is defined as any piece of malicious code written to do harmful things. A virus is not necessarily deployed worldwide to bring down thousands of systems and cause an immediate response. It can be written just to launch an attack on your particular company in retaliation or for any other reason, and not known to anyone other than the sender.)

Microsoft Office is a popular office productivity tool that is installed on nearly every computer running a Microsoft operating system. With Office, Microsoft has created a superb product that includes a built-in programming environment to support easy integration with other systems and programs. This gives programmers unparalleled flexibility in customizing Office and developing applications for environments familiar to most users. Alas, such openness and flexibility also create a prime target for attacks. To help prevent such attacks, even older versions of this productivity suite include built-in code execution controls, as shown in Figure 2.4.

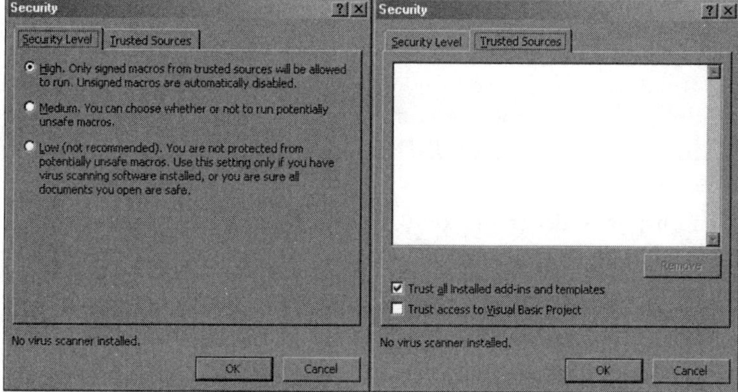

FIGURE 2.4
Built-in macro virus protection in Microsoft Word.

As a matter of sound security policy, you should enable macro virus protection in your Office installations. However, do not be fooled by the security this control delivers. Most macro viruses, when launched, attempt to disable this setting to open the system to future attacks. This control offers three settings: low, medium, and high protection.

Unless your organization uses applications written for the Office environment, set this control to High to disallow all macro code from executing by default. If your organization relies on macros and VBA code to add functionality to Office, use code signing to distinguish safe code from potentially unsafe code and permit only signed code to execute.

Microsoft is also a dominant vendor of email client software. Outlook Express handles POP3, SMTP, Internet Message Access Protocol (IMAP4), HTTPMail, and Network News Transport Protocol (NNTP) client needs; Outlook express primarily targets the home consumer market. The full-blown version of Outlook (97/98/2000/XP) included with higher-cost versions of Microsoft Office targets corporate customers and includes Exchange, POP3, SMTP, IMAP4, and LDAP support with advanced calendaring and organizer features. Not surprisingly, these two applications have come under steady and constant attack, so Microsoft now offers built-in protection against common mail client exploits as part of these packages.

Fundamentally, email attacks on Outlook (and similar packages) take one (or both) of two major approaches. One approach uses programmatic mail generation and address book access through either collaborative data objects (CDO) or Messaging Application Programming Interface (MAPI) object models and application programming interfaces (APIs) to send copies of itself to additional victims. The other approach takes the form of attachments that destroy or steal data and cause disruptions or that install back doors for remote access and control. Often, both approaches are combined. Self-propagation is particularly dangerous and has caused major meltdowns when a single user gets infected and propagates the virus to all entries in his email address book. Unsuspecting recipients open infected attachments because they trust the sender. Such a wave of infections can grow exponentially, sweeping the Internet, bringing thousands of systems down, and bogging down networks with unwanted traffic.

Starting with Outlook version 2002 (found in Windows XP), it is impossible by default to open any attachment considered potentially harmful. Outlook purposely blocks access to such attachments and informs the user about its action. Changing this setting requires a Registry edit, which should be performed only by advanced users cautious enough to avoid infection. A security patch is also available that introduces the same functionality for Outlook 2000.

This feature can be frustrating at first because you might have to ask people to resend archived attachments, but an ounce of prevention in this case is worth a pound of cure. For average corporate users, this approach provides the best built-in protection.

> NOTE
>
> **Removing Unsafe Attachments in Outlook** To allow potentially unsafe attachments to be accessed in Outlook 2002, you have to modify the `Level1Remove` value in `HKEY_CURRENT_USER\Software\Microsoft\Office\10.0\Outlook\Security` key. For more information, please refer to Microsoft Knowledge Base article Q290497, available online at `http://support.microsoft.com`.

This feature works for outgoing mail as well. You can't send any attachment deemed harmful (for example, any file with an executable file extension is blocked). Another security control that is helpful in stopping the spread of viruses is CDO and MAPI access protection. Every time a process attempts to access an address book or create and send an email programmatically, a dialog box pops up to ask the user to allow or disallow such activity explicitly. As shown in Table 2.2, the list of attachments blocked by Outlook is extensive. This provides a safety net in case the corporate antivirus solution is not good enough to recognize a potential threat.

One of the latest trends on the virus front is to combine vulnerabilities in other areas with email weaknesses. Instant messaging software developed by AOL/Netscape, Microsoft, and ICQ has become quite popular but not, alas, without security incidents. Attackers can employ client-side scripting (more on this in the next section) to gain access to a contact list and steal list member contact information, as well as your email address.

What can happen next is a phone call from an upset friend asking why you sent an attachment that destroyed his computer system and caused problems at work. You are ignorant (and innocent) in this attack; the real sender impersonates your address, hijacks your credibility, and sends an email with a forged From: address with the virus attached. This illustrates that the main weakness in email remains the human factor and the trust people build over years of relationships. As far as email goes, you should not to trust anyone or open any attachments you do not specifically request or expect to receive.

Another item to consider when dealing with email threats is online (often free) email services. Although most well-developed services have built-in scanning systems in place, remember that antivirus systems protect from most, but not all, harmful executables, and not all online services offer virus scanning. You should install a content filtering server, firewall, or proxy server that can block access to such sites in the workplace. Aside from whatever protection against malware it might afford, this technique can also save company dollars on employee productivity that might otherwise be wasted.

In the Windows environment, group policy objects (GPOs) can offer additional controls over unwanted executables. GPOs are available in Windows 2000 and later versions (alternative system policies can also be defined in Windows NT) and enable system administrators to define which users can execute which programs. Programs not on the list of allowed programs are not allowed to run. If the set of programs used in an enterprise is not extensive or changes are seldom, you can implement another virus execution control in the form of a GPO that allows only a predefined list of programs to run. This approach might not be feasible in all environments, but when combined with other virus controls, it offers additional protection for those who use it.

Finally, it's absolutely imperative to educate users about email attachments. People should never open unsolicited executable attachments. The chances of a cautious and aware user becoming infected with a virus are significantly lower. Thus, training is essential and is likely to produce the best results in avoiding infection.

The following is a list of security controls that can be employed to make email applications as safe as possible:

- Increase user awareness.
- Deploy an antivirus solution on the email server.
- Implement content filtering (email server and Internet gateway).
- Deploy secure email client software (patched Outlook 2000, Outlook XP).
- Deploy a desktop antivirus solution that supports whatever email client is in use.
- Tighten productivity software security settings (Macro virus protection in Microsoft Office).
- Consider implementing HTTP traffic controls such as a proxy server; block access to free online email services.
- Consider enforcing a list of allowed programs through GPOs.
- Consider deploying host intrusion prevention systems such as Entercept and Okena's Stormwatch.

NOTE

Don't Rely Solely on Antivirus Programs Note that you should not rely solely on antivirus programs for email security. Often, destructive virus-like programs are written to attack a select few targets, and such programs might never be reported to antivirus coders. If such a program eventually gets on an update list or signature file, minor modification and recompilation can make it a different program, which can again become destructive. Also, it always takes time for coders to release updates when a new virus hits, and it also takes time for updates to be deployed.

Rich Content (HTML), Client Scripting, and Outside Links

Email messages formatted as HTML pages are as common these days as interactive or data-driven Web sites—they are everywhere. HTML support is a feature in most email clients, and it is a convenient form of communication. But with convenience comes security threats: HTML technology and browsers that render such content are subject to major security holes. As if that is not enough to worry about, HTML emails allow marketers (and spammers) to collect information about readers, up to the point where they can track purchasing habits and target banner advertising to your interests on sites you frequent. As scary as this might sound, this is not new and can constitute privacy violations as well as pose security risks.

The main threats that come in HTML form can be described as follows:

- ActiveX objects and Java applets
- Client-side scripting (VBScript, JavaScript)
- The `<iframe>` tag
- Outside links
- Personally identifiable information in cookies
- Bugged images
- The `<meta refresh>` tag

ActiveX objects are system components that can be initialized and scripted from a variety of environments, including HTML-formatted email messages. These components are installed as part of an operating system (`FileSystemObject` in Windows 2000, for example), can be written as part of application development processes, or can be written and employed by attackers. Granted, ActiveX objects are versatile and can do nearly anything, depending on how they are written. This includes installing back doors, launching destructive attacks inside a corporate LAN, transmitting information back to attackers, capturing keystrokes, deleting or submitting files, and more.

In the Windows world, Outlook Express and Outlook both rely on Internet Explorer to handle HTML content; therefore, HTML email security settings are controlled through Internet Explorer settings. Later in this chapter, we review Internet Explorer security settings and zones in great detail in the "Recognizing and Administering Security Controls—Web Presence" section. For the time being, we mention only a few important related vulnerabilities.

An HTML script can use both ActiveX controls that come preinstalled with the system and those supplied externally. External controls are downloaded by a Web browser, such as Internet Explorer. Internet Explorer enables users to differentiate between controls that are marked as safe and ones that aren't. If a malicious piece of code appears on your system unsigned (without some trusted publisher's digital signature), a warning pops up to alert you that some controls could not be initialized because they are not marked safe. (This behavior is controlled through Internet Explorer settings.) If a similar piece of code gets on your system, you are prompted by default to review the publisher's certificate and choose whether you want to install this control on your system. This also strongly suggests that users should be trained to refuse such permission if there's any doubt about the origin, importance, or potential trouble-making capabilities of unknown ActiveX objects or controls.

A good example appears whenever you visit `windowsupdate.microsoft.com` for the first time. It also raises an interesting question: Does the presence of a digital signature automatically mean that an ActiveX control is safe? Of course not! In fact, there have been cases in which certificates were issued to sign malicious code and later had to be revoked. As a rule, you should trust only large, well-known, established companies. Macromedia, Symantec, and comparable companies can be classified as trustworthy. Another good suggestion is to accept ActiveX controls only when absolutely necessary and when their purpose is well-known and well-understood.

The fact that an ActiveX control is marked as safe is not a convincing reason to install it. By the same token, allowing client-side scripts to run without user knowledge is dangerous. The Windows operating systems come with many ActiveX components preinstalled, and all of them are marked as safe for scripting. This enables client-side scripts to engage those components and cause massive destruction, from deleting files to running arbitrary code on a system.

It is highly recommended that Internet Explorer settings be controlled strictly. You should disallow all unsafe controls and scripts without prompting and allow only scripts and safe controls to be run with user acknowledgement. Disabling client scripts altogether can affect how Web sites appear to users, and a good Web site design should include client-side scripting only when absolutely necessary. Outlook XP now automatically blocks client-side scripts.

A few control mechanisms can be employed to standardize and lock down Internet Explorer and rid the network of controls and scripts not marked as safe. Internet Explorer settings are controlled through the Internet Explorer Administration Kit (IEAK) and GPO in Windows 2000 running in the Active Directory environment, and network filtering can be done using hardware and software solutions similar to proxy services with content filtering enabled.

The `<iframe>` tag is used in HTML to allow flexible use of frames; it can display content from Web sites other than host HTML files. It is also used as a vehicle for automatic code execution attacks (such as Klez). Within the `<iframe>` tag, an attacker can embed a MIME attachment that contains VBA macro code. When an infected email is previewed or opened or a Web page viewed, `<iframe>` executes the embedded attachment on the user machine, triggering the code automatically. To add insult to injury, `<iframe>` bypasses Internet Explorer security zones, essentially giving attackers carte blanche. Microsoft released a patch that addresses `<iframe>` vulnerability, but the problem is that not all users patch their systems regularly, which is why a few more epidemics that exploit `<iframe>` remain likely. Generally, all HTML messages containing `<iframe>` should be blocked using content filters.

Outside links inserted into emails can contain references to Web sites that lure unsuspecting users with attractive financial offers, pleas for help to find a missing child, and so forth. Such sites can then deploy HTML attacks using any of the methods described elsewhere in this section. The `<meta refresh>` tag redirects users automatically after a certain period of time to a site of the attacker's choice, as configured within this tag. Although the first method of attack requires user action (for example, clicking a link), attacks that use automatic refresh are more dangerous because no user action is necessary and the process is essentially automatic.

Personal or identity information stored in cookies is another risk that stems from HTML content. *Cookies* are small text files stored on your computer that can contain general information, such as browsing preferences, but they can also include personal identity data, such as name, address, or credit card numbers. Malicious sites can scan for such cookies and gather valuable information, thereby breaching your privacy. Internet Explorer 6 solves this issue by implementing much stricter privacy policies that block third-party cookies by default and that reject any cookies that attempt to write personal identity information.

Bugged images allow senders to receive notifications automatically when a user opens submitted email. This happens without intervention or clicks from the user when the email is generated in a preview pane or is opened. Harmless as this might seem, this technique allows senders to learn about a user's environment and obtain IP addresses, browser and operating system version information, and other potentially useful information for later attacks. This is implemented in the following HTML code:

```
<p><img border="0" src="http://www.some-spam-company.com
➥/open_email.asp?reference=######" width="275"
➥ height="63"></p>
```

Basically, this code sends an HTTP `GET` request to `http://www.some-spam-company.com` for `open_email.asp` and communicates a tracking reference number, `reference=######`, using ASP's `QueryString`. The `Open_email.asp` program invoked in the URL contains code that might be similar to the following:

```
<%
on error resume next

'Query reference number from image request
strParentID = request.querystring("reference")

'Query user parameters, including address,
➥browser version, and browser capabilities
strAccept = request.servervariables("HTTP_ACCEPT")
strAcceptLang = request.servervariables
➥("HTTP_ACCEPT_LANGUAGE")
strReferer = request.servervariables("HTTP_REFERER")
strUserAgent = request.servervariables
➥("HTTP_USER_AGENT")
strRemoteAddr = request.servervariables("REMOTE_ADDR")
strRemoteHost = request.servervariables("REMOTE_HOST")

'Open database connection and insert event information
➥along with other parameters
➥ (simplified for demo purposes)
```

```
set Conn = session("cnn")
Set rsAct = Server.CreateObject("ADODB.Recordset")
strSQLAct = "INSERT INTO Activity ([ID]) VALUES
➥('" & strQueryString & "')"
Set rsAct = Conn.Execute(strSQLAct)

'And finally - return requested image!
response.redirect "some_logo.jpg"
%>
```

This block of code inserts tracking information into a database and redirects the `GET` request to a requested JPEG file. All the user sees in his browser is a logo or some other picture (which can also match background color and might not be visible at all).

This is a simplified example that shows how easy capturing information is when users open HTML email. But information gathering is only one side of this coin. This technique is also useful for spammers (more in the following paragraphs) who can record reference numbers with email addresses during mass mailings and then use such callback information to match emails with active users. Thus, whenever a user opens a tracked message this act confirms that his address is live. Next, the user gets a continuing stream of unsolicited email that never stops.

> NOTE
>
> **For More Information on Various Email Issues** For more information on Outlook HTML security, please visit `http://www.slipstick.com/outlook/htmlmail.htm`. If you want to learn more about implementing HTML conversion rules, visit `http://agricola.myweb.nl/outlook2002.html`.
>
> A content filtering solution, Mail Essentials, can be found at `http://www.gfi.com/mes`.
>
> To protect your LAN from disseminating browser and internal address information and prevent attacks, use firewalls, NAT, private addressing, and proxy servers.

On top of the security and privacy problems HTML brings to networks, HTML tags introduce plenty of overhead and can reference large images that are downloaded automatically. Obviously, plain-text messages are smaller in size and do not pose any of the HTML risks. By now, it should be obvious that HTML email is not always safe. The bad news is that in many email clients you might not be able to turn off an HTML display, but a few workarounds are available. Administrators should consider implementing content filtering on email servers; by using content filters, you might be able to convert messages from HTML to plain text on-the-fly or even to reject HTML messages deemed harmful and generate a non-delivery report (NDR). If you use Microsoft Outlook 2000 or 2002, you can implement rules that run scripts to convert HTML messages to plain text every time HTML email arrives. A simplified listing might look like this:

```
Sub HTMLToPlainText(oMsg As MailItem)
    If oMsg.GetInspector.EditorType =
      ➥olEditorHTML Then
        oMsg.BodyFormat = olFormatPlain
        oMsg.Save
    End If
End Sub
```

Embedded Content (MIME)

MIME continues to be a source of serious security problems. It allows emails to include embedded images, files, and other content, and attackers can use vulnerabilities found in software to execute such attachments without user intervention or acknowledgment. These attacks are often deployed in an email that contains an executable attachment and exploits buffer overflow or MIME handling flaws found in the most popular email programs.

Incorrect MIME handling results in execution of MIME attachments when a user clicks an email message, so there is no need to launch harmful attachments to fall victim to such attacks. Even if a user attempts to right-click a message to delete it, that action can be sufficient to infect vulnerable systems. This is why systems administrators must keep up with Microsoft and other software vendors' patches and update their systems regularly. Most recently, although the Nimda and Klez worms capitalized on MIME handling exploits, properly patched systems were not infected.

Spam

Spam is defined as unsolicited email—in other words, junk mail. The content of the email does not matter; if senders submit it for their own purpose or gain, or it is something that recipients do not want in their mailboxes, such a message is considered spam. Gone are the days when simple mass-mailing applications were employed to send a few messages to a large number of recipients. Modern spammers employ various technologies to harvest email addresses and deploy spam. Spam bogs down network bandwidth; puts additional stress on email systems; wastes employee productivity; and above all is extremely frustrating to everyone, consuming time and sometimes money. Unfortunately, this problem has no real solutions that can guarantee 100% efficiency when filtering spam.

Anti-spam rationale builds on the notion that Internet users must not purposefully annoy each other and should not transmit any traffic to each other unless it is of interest to both parties. The two fundamental approaches to mass-mailing are *opt-in schemes* and *opt-out schemes*. The only scheme that makes sense is the first one, wherein users subscribe to mailing lists of interest (that is, they explicitly express an interest in mail on specific topics). Opt-out schemes are the ones that created spam in the first place:

> NOTE
> **General Spam Rationale** For more information on a general spam rationale, please visit `http://mail-abuse.org/rbl/rationale.html`.

They build on the notion that advertisers send unsolicited mail first, with instructions on removal from the list to those who are not interested. Unfortunately, even reading such instructions means that recipients have already been spammed. Worse yet, replying to such email often means that you have only confirmed that your email is active. Therefore, instead of stopping spam, requesting removal from opt-out lists only produces more!

Among other technologies, spammers often employ bugged messages to track mail-read events and detect live email addresses. To gather new email addresses, Internet-crawling software follows links from one page to another in a tangled Web of cross-referenced Web sites and collects strings that match email address patterns. Have you ever noticed that even a newly opened email account on free sites, such as Yahoo! and Hotmail, gets spam even if you haven't advertised or used it yet? Such address harvesting tools explain why.

The latest trend in address gathering is to employ software that connects to a mail server and acts as if it is about to send an email, running through an SMTP session to the point where message data should be transferred. During this process, the sender tells the destination email server who the recipient of this email message is and the server is supposed to reply if the recipient exists on the server. This is the information spammers want most. They go through a massive amount of auto-generated recipient addresses for that domain. Some email systems silently accept messages and then attempt to deliver them internally, but this does not invalidate the technique. Bounced emails are processed automatically, and if no bounce occurs within five days, the address is valid. This explains why users sometimes get one- or two-line email *probes* (which are useless messages) that leave them scratching their heads trying to understand who the sender is and why they need to know that John left Sarah a voice message.

Relaying is another method responsible for massive amounts of spam. Often, spammers do not have the resources or are not willing to expose their own addresses because they risk disconnection when they send spam. Relaying allows spammers to use unsecured intermediary public SMTP servers to offload bandwidth and processing requirements. All SMTP servers must reject mail not destined to their networks, as well as mail relayed through other unsecured servers (conducting a reverse DNS lookup when a new connection attempt is made).

All things considered, a vast amount of spam is sent on a single-recipient basis from legitimate sources (such as online e-tailers and established names in e-commerce) that do respect user privacy and do unsubscribe upon request. Why is it spam? Because recipients have probably never explicitly expressed a desire to receive offers; nonetheless, corporations assume that because someone buys their product once, that person is interested in learning about other offers from the company. These kinds of opt-out schemes do work, but sometimes processing requests can take a few days. (They are probably in a queue along with millions of other unsubscribe requests.)

A number of factors must be analyzed to decide whether a piece of email should be classified as spam and therefore be blocked or whether it's legitimate email. The following lists some common rules email analysis tools apply to decide whether email is legitimate (matches the conditions as stated) or spam (violates the conditions as stated):

- The IP address of the sender SMTP server resolves to the mail-from domain (using a reverse DNS lookup).
- The receiving SMTP server is either the destination domain server or a designated relay server (in other words, the mail is not relayed through multiple, unrelated, public SMTP servers).
- A limited number of recipients appears in the To and CC fields (this is somewhat vague but still sometimes useful).
- The subject does not contain known strings (for example, "FREE VACATION").
- The message body does not contain certain known patterns (same as a preceding bullet) or profanity.
- HTML messages do not contain bugged images (iframes and client scripts should be added to the list, but they are not directly related to spam).
- The sending SMTP server is not blackholed (described later in this section).

Two solutions to the spam filtering problem can maximize investments of time and money, but they still are not as effective as one might want. A legitimate piece of email is always in jeopardy of not getting to its recipient, or vice versa, while a piece of spam does get through. One of these solutions is content filtering, which is usually somewhat expensive. An example of content filtering is PerlMx from `http://www.activestate.com/`, which can be deployed as a standalone email filtering gateway and works with any existing corporate email server.

The other solution is a subscription to real-time blocking lists similar to the one found at `http://mail-abuse.org/rbl`. Real-time *blackholing* is a third-party system that works by blocking any IP traffic from or to offending ISPs that are known for tolerating spam. Putting an offender on the list isn't easy, so if your company's ISP appears on that list and it affects your business, consider switching providers. Mail-abuse requires victims of spam to do all they can to contact offending ISPs and resolve the situation with them. If this fails, only then are victims allowed to nominate offenders with the blocking organizations; further, they must provide proof of offense and document their efforts to contact individuals responsible for dealing with abuse issues. After an offender is listed, thousands of subscriber networks automatically stop accepting any traffic from the offending ISP, and it quickly becomes their priority to cooperate. This strategy works to some extent but is subject to all kinds of problems as well—primarily those related to ever-changing domain names and addresses as spammers seek to avoid blocks and whole blocking of names and addresses that can include blameless and legitimate email senders.

Hoaxes and Chain Letters

Depending on user awareness, hoaxes can become a source of inconvenience for administrators. A typical hoax comes in the form of an email advising users that the computers they are working on are infected with a time-bomb virus that supposedly will activate itself and destroy their systems in X amount of time. The email goes on to advise that they should delete a certain file or several files from their `C:\Winnt\System32` directory to avoid this horrible situation.

Depending on which file is targeted for deletion and whether the operation succeeds, the user can create a situation in which her computer can no longer boot. On the other hand, the user might experience other severe problems that would require administrative time and incur losses of employee productivity. There is no real protection from hoaxes, other than raising user awareness. Just like viruses, hoaxes can result in catastrophic losses of data in worst-case situations; however, because user action is required to cause damage, education can foil such attacks.

A *chain letter* is a piece of communication that, for one reason or another, encourages users to forward it to as many people as possible. Reasons can vary from a less-than-funny joke to a plea for help for a dying kid, to signing a petition to save the Amazon rainforest, to money giveaways. Although no significant harm occurs in propagating chain letters, they often disclose users' email addresses and waste company time and bandwidth. As with hoaxes, the best protection against chain letters is user education and awareness.

Impersonation and Social Engineering

Misrepresentation of identity and intent to gain access to information or for other unlawful purposes has been around since day one. In the past, amateur high-school kids hacking away on 9,600-baud modems relied heavily on impersonation. Nowadays, this threat is not as widespread as it was, but it is by no means nonexistent. Impersonation can come in the form of a phony phone call or a forged email that asks for passwords or something of similar value. The email also might accuse certain people of wrongdoing or impersonate a co-worker.

No systems can automatically safeguard a company from social engineering; therefore, the best way to protect employees from acts of mischief is through education, as with hoaxes and chain letters. In addition to awareness, a company might want to institute standard policies for dealing with passwords or other sensitive information. Users should be encouraged to report suspicious or out-of-the-ordinary requests and to preserve emails for further investigation should it be deemed necessary. The use of digital signatures can help ensure that email content has not been tampered with and that the sender is who she claims to be. Other than digital signatures, company policies, and user awareness, not much can foil such activities.

For more information on social engineering, please refer to the "Recognizing Vulnerabilities and Taking Action—Instant Messaging" section in this chapter.

Software Bugs

Software bugs and patching should be the single most important area of administrative efforts in pursuit of email security. As discussed in this section, many email exploits and virus infections take advantage of known vulnerabilities in popular software that covers the biggest user bases—namely, Microsoft Outlook Express and Microsoft Outlook. Some of these flaws derive from Internet Explorer libraries email clients use to render HTML content. Other vulnerabilities exploit operating system flaws. The importance of maintaining current patches cannot be overemphasized, so the best protection against software bugs is subscription to security advisories from Microsoft, Bugtraq, and other security-focused Web communities. Administrators should visit `http://windowsupdate.microsoft.com` at least once a month to evaluate which new security releases can benefit their companies. As a general rule, all security releases should be installed on all systems, unless they break existing mission-critical functionality. If that's the case, the mission-critical application should undergo an immediate review and risks should be assessed.

Privacy of Communication

As an email travels across nations and continents, it can traverse many email servers that have logging enabled. Such logging can leave a copy of a clear-text message open to administrators, and possibly to hackers as well. As it travels the wire, such email is also susceptible to sniffers because plain-text encoding is easy to decode. To protect company data against potential theft or unwanted disclosure of email, rely on S/MIME or PGP and employ strong public encryption to render data intercepted en route indecipherable.

Some companies opt to include a legal warning at the bottom of each message that leaves their systems. This alerts potential interceptors about legal repercussions that might follow if they use this information in any way, but it is more of a scare tactic than a real strategy to deter information theft or disclosure.

Recognizing and Administering Security Controls—Web Presence

Understand communication security in wireless, wired, and application-specific environments.

Areas of security on the Web can be split into protocol-level security and application-level security. *Protocol-level security* deals with issues such as securing communications between clients and servers and making them unreadable if intercepted. *Application-level security* deals with issues such as Web server software vulnerabilities, plus all the issues stemming from faulty design and coding of Web applications, which can expose otherwise secure systems and make them susceptible to destructive attacks.

Protocol-level security is normally easier to implement because of well-understood and well-explained industry standards. Application-level security depends on systems administrators to patch and configure Web servers and developers who code Web applications. This is a gray area that is open to as many faults as humanly possible.

SSL/TLS

SSL technology is described in more detail in the following section of this chapter dealing with directory security. *SSL* is a widely supported security control employed for Web traffic security, among other things. SSL and TLS reside just above the Network layer of the OSI network reference model; they are available to higher layers in the protocol stack, such as HTTP and LDAP. In essence, any application can be coded to support secure connections using SSL. SSL-enabled Web server technology is convenient for Web application developers because their code does not change. All the work required to establish a secure communication channel between the Web server and a client is done by the browser and the Web server.

As shown in the following section of this chapter, SSL works by establishing a secure channel using PKI, which eliminates a vast majority of man-in-the-middle attacks, session hijackings, impersonation attempts, information theft, and authentication replays. This technology made e-commerce feasible and is still used worldwide for secure online shopping today.

According to the approved IETF standard, all URLs secured with SSL use the `https://` protocol prefix instead of the unsecure `http://` protocol prefix.

HTTP/S

Secure Hypertext Transfer Protocol (HTTP/S) is considered a runner-up to SSL—not really a competing but rather a complementary technology. The main difference between HTTP/S and SSL is that SSL establishes a secure session and can be used to transfer any number of information items, whereas HTTP/S is used with HTTP to encrypt individual messages. HTTP/S has not gained a lot of popularity in the community, although it, too, is an IETF standard.

Vulnerabilities

Only a few SSL vulnerabilities have been documented. First are two cipher strengths employed by the SSL standard—40-bit encryption (long open to the entire world) and 128-bit encryption (until recently, this was allowed to be distributed only within the USA and Canada). Breaking 40-bit encryption is relatively easy, so a determined hacker (or the government) who intercepts messages encrypted with 40-bit strong algorithms can get the information out in a reasonable amount of time. This makes communications based on older, weaker versions of SSL relatively unsecure. The problem is easy to remedy, however—any companies and organizations that still use the older, weaker 40-bit technologies must upgrade to the newer 128-bit technologies as soon as is feasible.

Second, certain vulnerabilities can be associated with X.509 certificate spoofing, or DNS spoofing, performed by a man-in-the-middle attacker. A crucial step in client/server authentication is the client's verification that the server has a fully qualified domain name (FQDN) as listed on the certificate. In some cases, an attacker can fool a client's browser into thinking that communication is underway with the server listed on the certificate when that communication is actually occurring between the client and an attacker and between the attacker and the (real) server. When this happens, an attacker can take complete control over all information exchanged between the parties involved.

The four steps a client goes through to authenticate a server are as follows:

1. The server certificate's validity span is checked against the date and time on the client's machine. If the server's certificate has expired, a warning is displayed to the user that this server can no longer be trusted. The client also checks the CRL to ensure this certificate has not been revoked.

2. The issuing CA for the server certificate is checked against a list of trusted CAs on the client side. This list is built in to the browser software and updated periodically.

3. The client checks the authenticity of the server by comparing information found in the CA's public keys presented to the client by the server and located during step 2.

4. Finally, the client checks whether the server listed on the certificate is the server the client communicates with. This protects against man-in-the-middle attacks.

If all these checks yield a positive result, the client is satisfied that the identity of the server is genuine and valid. The server, for its part, can be configured to allow anonymous client connections or can require client certificates as well, thereby establishing bidirectional authentication and trust. This does not affect the security of the channel in any way; it's just an option that can apply in certain situations (as when accessing the company intranet from the Internet, for example).

> NOTE
>
> **SSL Security** For more information on SSL security, refer to Netscape's documentation at `http://developer.netscape.com/docs/manuals/security/sslin/contents.htm` and/or `http://developer.netscape.com/tech/security/ssl/howitworks.html`.

Beyond the previous vulnerabilities, numerous holes and bugs exist in browsing software, which make the Web a very popular avenue for attack. Most of these threats were covered in the email security section earlier in this chapter. (HTML content delivered via email is just as good a target for attack as an ordinary Web page; sometimes both can be coordinated.) Here, we summarize this information:

- **JavaScript and VBScript**—Java was meant to be safe and was designed to work in a *sandbox*, which is a secured environment on the client side. Unfortunately, many sandbox implementations have proven faulty, which allows attackers to access the user file system and manipulate information to which they are not supposed to have access. Furthermore, both JavaScript and VBScript are client-side scripting technologies that can do harm by scripting accessible objects registered on the system (for instance, getting a list of the buddies from your instant messaging software and sending it back to the attacker). As if that was not enough, attackers and script-kiddies can cause a great amount of annoyance by taking control of your browsing environment, redirecting browser sessions wherever they want, and opening as many new windows as they please. Java implementation flaws are being discovered quite often, and security flaws vary from being able to access user files to redirecting all traffic to a third-party Web site.
- **ActiveX**—ActiveX is dangerous to allow on Web pages users visit because of two reasons. First, an ActiveX object can be written to do pretty much anything on a system, just as if it were a standalone application. Unsigned ActiveX objects (not signed with the vendor's digital signature) must be banned from the network altogether. Those that are signed should be used only when absolutely necessary and when the vendor is a trusted, established, well-known company. There are known cases where malicious code was signed with a legitimate certificate. Another reason even safe ActiveX controls are dangerous is that the operating system includes built-in ActiveX controls, marked as safe. Any savvy attacker can employ a script to initialize and take advantage of built-in ActiveX objects.
- **Buffer overflows**—Buffer overflows are one of the most common ways to cause denial-of-service (DoS) attacks, lost data, and downtime. A buffer overflow works by supplying a piece of data to the client (or server) application that is too large for it to handle and that uses more memory than provisioned by developers who neglected to screen out oversized or bad requests. A buffer overflow attack overwrites portions of memory used by other applications and can cause failures or crashes or enable system-level access to commands and code that should be unable to operate at such a level of privilege.

- **Cookies**—Questionable Web sites can use cookies to store personal identity data, such as date of birth, name, address, and credit card numbers. Attackers can employ scripts to locate such information and use it to their benefit. They can also allow other questionable Web sites to track your visits, which violates your privacy.
- **CGI and ASP**—CGI and ASP Web applications running on a server are also vulnerable to buffer overflow attacks that can enable hackers to upload and execute code or commands at will, crash servers, or make services inaccessible by sending invalid data for processing that causes code loops and high CPU utilization.

How do you protect your company from Web attacks on both client and server sides? Here's a good set of rules to follow:

- Use the latest software versions (yes, this works to the benefit of software vendors but makes a lot of sense from a security perspective, as well).
- Patch your software often; subscribe to reputable, well-known mailing lists that track newly discovered information that can affect the products in use.
- Disable client-side scripting (this renders some sites slightly less usable). Use the Security Zones feature in Internet Explorer to list exceptions, but make sure Internet Explorer is patched because some vulnerabilities are associated with security zones as well.
- Disable unsigned ActiveX objects; enable prompting for user permission when signed objects are used.
- Disable scripting of objects marked as safe.
- Disable cookies with personal identity information (enabled by default in MSIE 6.x).
- Implement proxy server and a content filtering solution to rid the network of unsafe coding embedded in Web pages (such as controls, scripts, and `<iframe>` tags) and to protect your privacy (most proxies can hide browser headers).

The first two elements in the preceding list apply to both servers and clients; the remaining elements in that list apply as makes most sense.

RECOGNIZING AND ADMINISTERING SECURITY CONTROLS—DIRECTORY

Understand communication security in wireless, wired, and application-specific environments.

Directory services in various forms have become widespread to make disparate, vast, or both disparate and vast systems work in concert. Directory services provide centralized user information lookup, resource location, authentication, and other applications for geographically dispersed and heterogeneous systems. Because directory services can also be crucial to system security, it is vital to protect them adequately. The next few sections provide an overview on how this can be implemented and what kinds of risks you should watch for.

SSL/TLS

SSL and TLS standards implement communications security control just above the Transport layer of the OSI model, where TCP and UDP protocols reside. TLS stands for Transport Layer Security and is based on SSL, but it uses a completely different protocol. SSL and TLS are used to secure communications traveling across the Internet at a higher level in the OSI network reference model as compared to L2TP and IPSec. SSL and TLS have an advantage over IPSec in certain circumstances, such as when security must be configured differently for individual applications. SSL/TLS security controls can also be built in to applications—for example Web servers and Web browsers.

The SSL protocol was invented by Netscape Communications, and in version 3 the protocol was proposed for use as a standard protection mechanism for Internet communications. SSL supports data encryption, digital signing using the Message Authentication Code (MAC) algorithm, and mutual authentication at the socket level by both client and server. SSL has been most successfully employed by higher-level application protocols, such as HTTP. It provides security controls for fundamentally unsecure communication mechanisms and has proven absolutely crucial for secure delivery of consumer services, such as e-commerce, online banking, financial services, and others. TLS was proposed and developed by the IETF to extend SSL version 3 authentication functionality.

SSLv3 functions as described in the following steps:

1. The SSL client initiates communication with the SSL server.
2. The SSL client submits an initial set of parameters containing the SSL version it uses, all encryption methods the client understands, and a random stream of bytes.
3. The SSL server replies to the SSL client with its initial parameters containing the SSL version, the encryption mechanism it picked from the list submitted by the client, the session ID, and a random stream of bytes.
4. The SSL server submits its X.509 digital certificate to the client that contains the server's public key and other data.
5. The SSL server requests the client's digital certificate as part of the client authentication and public key exchange.
6. The SSL client authenticates the SSL server using the server's digital certificate. (This includes standard verification of expiration date, if the certificate is listed on the CRL, and if the CA that issued this certificate is trusted by the client. It also verifies the server's digital signature by comparing the server's hashed domain name with a locally calculated hash of the same FQDN.)
7. The SSL client creates a temporary session key and encrypts it to the server's public key.
8. The SSL client submits the temporary session key to the SSL server.

9. The SSL client submits its own public key in the form of a X.509 digital certificate for authentication and key exchange purposes.
10. The SSL server authenticates the SSL client using the certificate submitted in step 9. The SSL server conducts all the checking that the client did in step 6.
11. The SSL client and SSL server calculate a new session key based on the temporary session key the client created and submitted to the server in step 7.
12. The SSL client and SSL server create a secret session key independently of each other, without sending it between the parties.
13. The SSL client and SSL server exchange and agree on encryption settings and let each other know that all future messages should be encrypted according to these specs.
14. The SSL client and SSL server exchange messages encrypted to the secret session key. These messages acknowledge successful session establishment and begin an SSL-secured session.

Both the SSL client and SSL server can exchange messages and inform the other party if an error is detected. The SSL standard also allows both parties to renegotiate the encryption algorithm in use during any session.

LDAP

A vast majority of companies operating in the twenty-first century employ various operating systems, databases, billing systems, and so on to boost productivity. Although all these systems increase worker efficiency, security remains a key element in this process. Every resource in the overall system needs to be assigned access parameters and security descriptors. Likewise, every application can have its own security management system. But without special setups or additional development, multiple security systems can have nothing in common. This leads to excessive repetition of administrative labor and information duplication. Over time, administration can become unmanageable and too expensive.

From the user perspective, everything can seem even messier: Users need to enter login names and passwords to log on to their networks; then they must enter their credentials for database access. Also, if an administrator fails to issue a digital certificate, users might not be able to access an enterprise resource planning (ERP) system, for example. Thus, some centralized security system is obviously needed to facilitate access control and authentication for all network services and resources.

LDAP is a potential bridge between directory services and various applications, whether they be file servers, network services, or database servers. LDAP is an industry standard that enables users to have single user accounts that can access all available network services and applications. By permitting developers to write custom applications that can query a centralized object and security repository, such as directory services, LDAP helps make the so-called "single log-on" real.

The Comité Consultatif International Téléphonique et Télégraphique (CCITT) X.500 standard specifies a basic structure and functionality model for directory services. X.500 is fairly complex and has several disadvantages; besides, its implementation relies on certain OSI protocols. As a result, the X.500 standard was neither widely accepted nor implemented in the TCP/IP networks that represent most operational network architectures in use today.

The X.500 standard describes both a structural model for directory services as well as the protocols used to access those services. Directory Access Protocol (DAP) is a set of rules that describes how a client should interact with directory services. DAP had numerous shortcomings and consumed an inordinate amount of system resources and bandwidth, so the industry had to refine this specification further before it could become a workable standard.

IETF came out with a lightweight version of the DAP protocol, named LDAP1 in RFC 1487. LDAP1 is easier to implement on TCP/IP networks and specifies LDAP clients and LDAP gateways. LDAP1 allows Internet users to query, delete, add, and edit information stored in X.500 directories. Thus, it defines a TCP/IP interface for X.500 directories.

Before it was widely implemented, however, this standard was developed further. LDAP2 (RFC 1777) introduces the concept of an LDAP server and allows the creation of autonomous LDAP directories. LDAP3 (RFC 2251, currently in use) enhances LDAP2, eliminates some limitations, and makes LDAP fundamental to building distributed information systems in large and complex environments. Classic examples of directory services include Microsoft Active Directory in Windows 2000 and Novell Directory Services in Novell NetWare. Both of these environments claim compatibility with LDAP3.

The standard described in RFC 2256 specifies a common schema for all LDAP directories, one that is compatible with X.500 directory schemas. This common schema is implemented in all LDAP directories and is designed to supply company information, organizational structure, and employee information. LDAP administrators can extend this common schema beyond standard specifications to support custom applications. A good example is the Microsoft Exchange 2000 installation process, during which the Microsoft Active Directory Schema (itself compatible with X.500) is extended to include Exchange-specific objects and properties.

X.500 Versus LDAP

An LDAP server can be implemented as a standalone application that uses an LDAP gateway to interact with an X.500 server, or it can be provided as part of an X.500 server. Standalone LDAP servers use the same namespace and directory schema as X.500 but support fewer commands while providing comparable functionality.

Unlike X.500 clients, LDAP clients do not need to worry about object references. The LDAP server takes care of them and redirects requests to appropriate directory servers, returning either the set of data requested or an error. If one directory server gets a request for data that does not reside on that server, that request is redirected to whichever server has the required data using either chaining or referral methods.

Functionality

LDAP directory services are based on a client/server architecture that enables clients to open connections, authenticate with LDAP servers, query and edit objects stored in a directory, and close connections upon completing their work. LDAP services vendors provide APIs for most popular programming languages, including C++, Perl, Java, Visual Basic, and so forth. This enables developers to integrate their products with ease. Besides APIs, several LDAP tools are available for both Windows and Unix environments, and the latest Internet browsing software also supports searching LDAP directories.

The following list briefly describes LDAP functions. Each of these functions can operate either in synchronous or asynchronous mode:

- **Search (ldapsearch)**—Searches a directory for specific information and returns a set of objects that matches the query.
- **Add (ldapadd)**—Enables the adding of new objects to a directory, the specifying of object parameters, and the defining of a distinguished name (DN).
- **Delete (ldapdelete)**—Removes objects from a directory. Containers that are not empty can't be removed, so if a container must be deleted, the program that works with an LDAP directory has to enumerate all the leaf objects of the container and iterate through them, deleting child objects individually. Only then can the parent object be removed.
- **Modify (ldapmodify)**—Allows changing, removing, and adding object properties as well as the values of those properties.
- **Bind**—Opens a connection between the client and the server. In the process, client authentication credentials are provided for access control purposes.
- **Unbind**—Closes the connection between the client and the server.
- **Abandon**—Interrupts the server-side execution of any commands issued in asynchronous mode.

Security

Because LDAP is a client/server application, it relies on traditional methods that are not specific to LDAP. In fact, SSL is the security mechanism of choice for LDAP authentication and data encryption. It ensures that each party establishes the other party's identity and that communication does not get intercepted or altered in transit.

Access control in an LDAP directory services environment is implemented using the following elements and approaches:

- Individual and group user accounts
- User login requirement
- Definition of actions permitted by each user or groups of users on each of the objects (individually or collectively)

Users and groups are defined as LDAP directory objects, just as any other object stored in LDAP. A special LDAP class, `person`, represents users in the directory, but other derivatives of this class exist, namely `inetOrgPerson` and `OrganizationalPerson`. Objects of the class `person` have a varied set of properties, including `userPassword` and `userCertificate`. If one of these properties is set, LDAP treats the object as a registered user of the system. The unique name (DN) of this object is the login name used by the user to log on to the network authenticating with LDAP.

Not only is the `userPassword` field used to store encrypted passwords, but it also contains information about the algorithm used to encrypt it. This information is in a format similar to `{encryption algorithm} encrypted password`—for example, `{sha}DFDj#jD97JFf`. The `UserCertificate` field stores the X.509 certificate in a binary format. Combined or separately, these fields serve to authenticate bind requests to LDAP directories. The simpler of the two is username/password authentication, which basically compares user-supplied information to the user's object as stored in the LDAP directory. The second method involves digital certificates and is more complex. It uses SSL to verify the client certificate with the one stored in the directory.

X.500

It is safe to assume that anyone can get in touch with any other person on the planet as long as that person has a telephone number (and of course a telephone) and the person dialing has the number to dial. To find which number to dial, you must obtain the number from that person or access a telephone directory. The problem here occurs when a user in Tokyo wants to dial a user in Toronto because Tokyo isn't likely to have access to Toronto telephone directories. It would be helpful to have a single, global telephone directory that serviced arbitrary lookup requests, such as the one coming from Tokyo for a number in Toronto.

The X.500 directory standard was developed in 1988 by ITU-T, which also created the X.25 and X.400 standards. An X.500-based directory can contain network information; email addresses; telephone numbers; and any other information needed for specific purposes, such as user authentication. Users and applications alike can rely on an X.500 directory to find telephone numbers (in the case of a user) or, for instance, network addresses (in the case of an application).

X.500 Functionality

The most important features found in X.500 functionality include

- X.500 is accessible to any application written to X.500 standards.
- X.500 is a distributed, global directory that gives users a single resource for all queries.
- One user can access the directory from any location; many users can access the directory from a single location.
- X.500 supports various transport protocols to make it as accessible as possible.
- The X.500 architecture allows the use of gateways to increase directory accessibility.

X.500 Components

X.500 directories consist of three main components: a directory information base (DIB), various directory system agents (DSAs), and various directory user agents (DUAs). A DIB is a collection of information that X.500 makes accessible. This collection is distributed, where no single organization has control over any portion of significant size. Such organizations are DSAs, and X.500 software applications for end users are DUAs. A special type of DUA, called an administrative DUA (ADUA), works for administrative purposes.

X.500 Protocols

DSA uses four protocols:

- The Directory Access Protocol is used between DUAs and the directory.
- The Directory System Protocol (DSP) is used between DSAs while a client request is processed. DSAs are aware of each other and routinely exchange information when trying to find any requested resource (they're called *cooperating* DSAs).
- The Directory Information Shadowing Protocol (DISP) supports directory information distribution.
- The Directory Operational Binding Management Protocol (DOP) works between DSAs for administrative purposes.

By implementing X.500-compliant directory services, companies can build distributed platform-independent databases that can interact with the global X.500 directory.

Information Security in X.500

Often, a company has proprietary information it wants (or does not object) to share with the public. In earlier examples, this could have included personnel information; however, with the latest headhunting trends, this might not be the best idea. Still, technical support contact information and sales offices contacts are something all companies should advertise publicly. Although this is true, some information needs to be shared but have access to it limited and controlled. For this purpose, X.500 uses access control lists (ACLs).

The X.509 standard was developed as a way to secure X.500; ironically, because it covers other significant areas of the OSI reference model, it is also widely accepted by the industry in other areas. In fact, X.509 is more popular than the X.500 standard it originally was developed to secure.

As this chapter describes, encryption can be symmetric or asymmetric. *Symmetric* encryption uses a secret key that both parties must share to enable communication. *Asymmetric* encryption uses PKI infrastructure and is more convenient for public use. X.509 uses asymmetric encryption. Digital certificates enable the exchange of public keys and serve to establish identity on untrusted networks.

Replication

Replication enables multiple identical copies of a database to be maintained. Replication ensures that such copies (called *replicas*) are updated and remain true to the data stored in the central database (the *master* database). At the same time, you often need to maintain multiple, bidirectionally synchronized master databases.

Replication offers reduced query times because a query is sent to a local replica, normally located on a local network. Also, when replicas are available, no single database server has to service all user requests. Furthermore, replication offers reliability and fault-tolerance characteristics. If any single copy of the database becomes inaccessible or gets corrupted and lost, other valid replicas can still handle user requests and prevent downtime.

Replication assumes real-time data updates, which means all updates must be both timely and accurate. Should an error occur, there is a high risk that snowballing replication errors can render a replica useless. This also can make systems vulnerable to attacks and exploits. Thus, it is no surprise that the replication process has a definite set of rules that must be followed closely to avoid service interruptions or security risks.

LDUP handles replication in LDAP space and assumes that all resources to be synchronized share the same underlying structure, or *schema.* In the real world, this is unlikely to be true. Synchronization between incompatible platforms and between nonstandard systems is challenging at best. Microsoft's Active Directory uses a proprietary alternative to the LDUP replication methodology.

Replication Models

The IETF offers two models for directory replication methods:

- **Multimaster replication**—Records can be written and updated on several replicas without notifying other masters in the replication space.
- **Master-slave or single-master replication**—Only one server is granted the authority to write and edit replicated data, whereas all other replicas in the replication space are read-only copies transferred from that master (this is considered to be a multimaster replication subset).

X.500 Replication

In effect, LDUP's replication characteristics are similar to those originally introduced with X.500, where three update models exist, as follows:

- Simultaneous update of all replicas
- A master election structure, where only a subset of replicas in the distributed database are updated immediately
- Selection of a single master replica where all updates must be submitted to the server on which that replica resides

The first model is not feasible to implement because of the nature of globally distributed databases: You can't ensure that all systems worldwide will be accessible at the time of replication. The master election model is acceptable for LANs but, again, in a global, untrusted environment, this system is susceptible to failures. Thus, the selection of a single-master replica has emerged as the best solution for distributed directories, and it facilitates the most straightforward information concurrency controls.

RECOGNIZING AND ADMINISTERING SECURITY CONTROLS—FILE TRANSFER

Understand communication security in wireless, wired, and application-specific environments.

FTP is used to transfer information between computers. FTP is based on a client/server architecture, in which an FTP *client* is a software application that sends and receives files to and from an FTP *server*. An FTP server is a network server that stores and makes files accessible through FTP server software. Many Web servers on the Internet offer FTP service as one of the ways for administrators to upload modified Web site content. Many of these FTP servers permit anonymous access, so users can upload or download files without using any special login parameters. FTP also supports account- and password-based authentication.

FTP is completely vulnerable to sniffer attacks because all authentication information is transferred in clear text. Furthermore, all data is transferred in a readable format, so anyone can intercept this information. In a sense, anonymous FTP servers configured with read-only access are safest because usernames and passwords do not have to travel across the network for a session to be established. This avoids the common case in which such intercepted passwords can be used in other hacking attempts against the system.

One could argue that read-only anonymous FTP servers remain popular, especially with software vendors for public driver and patch file downloads and for open source distributions—and one would be right!

S/FTP

The Secure File Transfer Protocol (SFTP) uses the SSH technology described in the "SSH" section in this chapter to create a secure tunnel for file transfer. Even if an attacker manages to intercept SFTP communication, the chances of unauthorized decryption are nearly nil. Where read/write file transfer is required, or where user authentication is needed, most experts recommend that administrators deploy SFTP servers rather than plain-vanilla FTP servers because this prevents open disclosure of login credentials.

Earlier implementations often used a utility call SCP (secure copy) to provide a secure alternative to plain FTP; today, SSH V2 includes SFTP as part of its built-in capabilities.

To initiate a new SFTP session, an SFTP user typically uses a command that looks like this:

```
sftp <username>@<hostaddress>
```

SFTP does not rely on FTP daemons, such as `ftpd` or `wu-ftpd`, which further increases security. Statistically, `wu-ftpd` is the daemon that is most commonly attacked, so elimination of this service foils many well-known attacks.

To run SFTP, the `sshd` daemon (or the equivalent runtime process) must be installed and running on the server. When a connection attempt occurs, `sshd` verifies the validity of that request with the SSH server. SFTP uses SSH2, which secures that connection as tightly as possible. SFTP has two advantages over FTP:

- Passwords are never transmitted over the wire in clear-text format, which means sniffers are useless in attacks on SFTP sessions.
- Data transferred within SFTP sessions is encrypted, which makes it nearly impossible to launch man-in-the-middle attacks or to use passive data capture with subsequent brute-force decryption.

SFTP is simple to use, and after a session is established, numerous commands like those found in FTP support directory navigation, session parameter configuration, and various file operations (read/download, write/upload, move, delete, rename, and so forth) can be used. Here's a list of common commands associated with SFTP (note the similarities to the Unix shell and thus also to FTP):

- `quit`—Quits the SFTP client application.
- `cd [directory]`—Changes the current remote directory.
- `lcd [directory]`—Changes the current local directory.
- `ls [-r][-l][file...]`—Lists files in a remote directory. The `-r` option performs recursive lookups of directories (by default, directories are not listed). The `-l` option lists the rights assigned to files on the system.

- `lls [-r][-l] [file...]`—This is the same as `ls` only for local files.
- `get [file...]`—Requests a file transfer from the SFTP server to the local machine. Directories are copied recursively, including all directory contents.
- `put [file...]`—Uploads files from the local computer to the remote server. The same recursive copy works for `put` as for `get`.
- `mkdir [dir] or rmdir [dir]`—Creates a directory on or removes a directory from the SFTP server.

SFTP takes a heavy toll on client and server systems because of its use of encryption. Connection transfer speeds are reduced as compared to clear-text FTP, and CPU and memory requirements are higher. However, most experts agree this is a reasonable overhead in exchange for improved network security. Please note also that numerous GUI-based tools exist to replace command-line operation of SFTP—such as WinSCP (`http://winscp.vse.cz/eng/`).

Blind FTP/Anonymous

As described in the opening of this section, many systems still allow anonymous FTP access. A massive amount of data is stored on such anonymous servers, ready to deliver driver downloads, product documentation, patches or software updates, music, and so forth. Anonymous FTP allows users access without requiring any credentials.

All the services a computer system offers must be configured properly, yet this vital step is often ignored or omitted. On anonymous systems, failure to properly secure the access or scope is an obvious oversight that can render such systems vulnerable to attack. Thus, when some servers are configured to allow posting files to readable directories, this action can open that system to potential attacks. Generally speaking, write directories and read directories should reside in the same container or on the same server (if possible).

Hackers share lists of servers known to be vulnerable to attack or wide open for their use; loosely configured FTP servers are no exception to this practice. Such lists often include writeable directory locations and paths to pirated software. This explains how pirated software is often shared, where an unwitting server owner must bear the expense of the bandwidth used. Credit card numbers, software serial numbers, and passwords are also shared this way. Because the owner of the server on which such information resides can be held liable for making that information publicly accessible, this situation can lead to legal action—aside from the risks involved in letting hackers loose on a system.

Likewise, if writeable FTP directories fill up faster than anticipated and no system checks are in effect, serious storage problems can take time to diagnose. Disk quotas can address this situation by imposing storage limits. But if such quota limits are reached, legitimate users might not be able to use the system, creating a denial-of-service (DoS) condition. Yet another risk is hitting the maximum number of allowed connections (or if none are set, the maximum imposed by system or hardware capabilities). After that maximum number is reached, legitimate users can no longer access the server, resulting in a classic DoS condition.

FTP Vulnerabilities

Many FTP servers run on Unix-based systems and include FTP installations as part and parcel of system capabilities brought up years ago. In some cases, system administrators might not even be aware that their servers offer FTP access. So many FTP vulnerabilities are well documented that unpatched or unmonitored servers can be open to numerous attacks or exploits. Modern implementations might not yet offer known vulnerabilities, but they are sure to fall prey to new attacks over time. Thus, system administrators must keep abreast of new security advisories for all the platforms they manage.

`wu-ftpd` is a well-known and improved version of the original `ftp` daemon from Washington University. One of the most popular attacks against this service was developed in 1996–1997, and it targets buffer overflows in FTP commands. Unchecked it can cause systems to crash or provoke memory dumps. It can even be launched by anonymous FTP users; therefore, the memory dump created is completely readable because, when an anonymous user owns a file (as is the case here), anyone can access it. Because memory dumps can contain cached passwords and other sensitive information, this is a huge potential security problem.

Thus, such attacks against `wu-ftpd` servers could (and did) result in anonymous attackers gaining root privileges on the system, thereby enabling them to run any programs they might choose to execute. Total system compromise is the normal next step in this process.

Most FTP servers are vulnerable to DoS attacks if configured without an appropriate Network layer security infrastructure. Numerous DoS vulnerabilities are well documented, and there will likely be more to come. The most popular attacks use buffer overflow techniques, of which new examples continue to occur. One of the latest such exploits was documented in 2001, in which the following command crashed vulnerable servers by locking them into an infinite code loop, leaking memory, and causing excessive CPU processing throughout the duration of the attack:

```
ls */../*/../*/../*/../*/../*/../*/../*/../*/../*/../
*/../*/../*/../*
```

Packet sniffing is another classical attack that FTP is incapable of combating in its own right. Packet sniffing can normally occur only on a local cable segment or at an upstream Internet service provider, so you need to take steps to avoid potential compromise through sniffing (when it comes to network segments outside your immediate control, this requires the use of secure FTP or some type of encrypted VPN tunnel to prevent clear-text transmission of files and credentials).

EXAM TIP

The best way to secure any server is to disable all unneeded services; use encryption with all services that are mission critical; patch your systems often; implement continuous monitoring; and remain aware and alert about new attacks, exploits, and vulnerabilities as they are publicized.

Enough well-known vulnerabilities exist in FTP services that an exhaustive catalog would require a book of its own. You don't need to learn the details involved in launching specific attacks. What really matters is that FTP is open to attack and is thus a predictable target.

This means that preemptive steps to avoid FTP (by using SFTP) or to obscure FTP traffic (by encapsulating it in some type of secure tunnel) represents the best way to foil potential attacks. Likewise, you need to monitor current security advisories and patch and update systems as new security fixes become available.

Other common things often overlooked include proper system configuration. Don't assume that any system is set up properly. Review all its settings, preferably with a well-known and well-built security checklist (most vendors and many security companies or publications offer such checklists to the public). Network layer security and intrusion detection systems are also appropriate, but they go beyond the topic of this chapter (they're covered in Chapter 4, "Intrusion Detection, Baselines, and Hardening"). All these observations hold true not just for FTP, but for all other network services your servers might provide.

Recognizing and Administering Security Controls—Wireless

Understand communication security in wireless, wired, and application-specific environments.

Wireless communications, reviewed in part earlier in the chapter in the "Recognizing and Administering Remote and Wireless Access" section, enable certain technologies that make it easier to deploy and use networks than ever before. Unfortunately, several significant threats are associated with transferring data across the open air, including eavesdropping and data interception, man-in-the-middle attacks, impersonation and authentication replays, and so forth. Wireless security controls address most of these risks, but some create new risks. The following sections review security controls employed for wireless communications.

WTLS

The Wireless Transport Layer Security (WTLS) is the security layer in the Wireless Application Protocol (WAP). WTLS is designed to provide privacy, data integrity, and authentication facility for WAP services.

WTLS is designed specifically for the wireless environment and is indispensable because of the very nature of wireless communications. WTLS is crucial because it enables communicating parties to be sure about who they are communicating with and ensures that information is not broadcast through the atmosphere as clear text. WTLS must be deployed wherever wireless communications occur because mobile networks do not provide complete end-to-end security by default. Even with WTLS, numerous potential methods of attack are already well known and documented. Thus, you should not wait and see how reliable WTLS really is (this also explains the impetus for the 802.11i and 802.1X initiatives mentioned earlier in this chapter).

Fundamental to WTLS is the widely used TLS v1 security layer originally developed as an extension to SSL technology. Because of the broadcast aspect inherent to wireless technologies, modifications to make TLS wireless friendly were necessary. These modifications address lowered bandwidth consumption, as well as datagram-based connections, the limited CPU and memory capabilities common in many mobile devices, and cryptography issues.

For wireless applications, WTLS is considered more effective than TLS or SSL. It functions much like TLS and relies on public cryptography and X.509 certificates to handle traffic between WAP gateways and mobile devices. So-called "mini X.509 certificates" (deliberately abbreviated versions of ordinary X.509 certificates that don't require as much data transfer when exchanging credentials) can be used in the wireless world as well.

The most commonly found communications pattern between WAP clients and service origin servers is depicted in Figure 2.5.

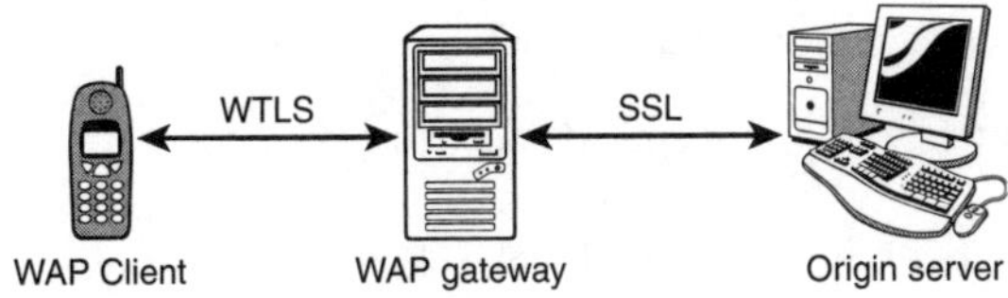

FIGURE 2.5
Wireless communication pattern.

The service provider WAP gateway encodes and converts necessary protocols and ensures that communication is secure. One of the major drawbacks to this system lies in the implementation of its security capabilities. WTLS operates between mobile devices and WAP gateways; however, WAP gateways use SSL/TLS to communicate with service providers, so a WAP gateway must decipher an encrypted stream from the sending network and then re-encrypt it for the destination network. This is where information is most prone to attack and interception.

This problem is known to service providers and standards development teams alike, and the industry is brainstorming on new standards to eliminate this vulnerability. WAP 2.0 addresses the problem, but it is still in the development and proposal stages and is not yet a valid standard.

802.11x

The IEEE 802.11 standard (sometimes called the 802.11x family of standards to refer to the numerous elements it contains) defines a group of protocols used in various wireless communication systems. The Media Access Control (MAC) and Physical Layer Device (PHY) protocols specify how devices should access broadcast media and how information should be physically transferred over wireless networks. These two protocols are crucial to all other elements in the 802.11x family and define how several types of wireless networks operate at those levels.

802.11 employs three physical data transfer technologies:

- Infrared spectrum (IR)
- Direct sequence spread spectrum (DSSS)
- Frequency hopping spread spectrum (FHSS)

Because IR is a lightwave-based technology, it is sensitive to weather conditions and must be situated so communicating parties are within each other's line of sight. These two limitations normally confine infrared technology to use only within a single set of premises. DSSS and FHSS operate in the 2,400MHz–2,483.5MHz spectrum, usually described more simply as 2.4GHz. DSSS/FHSS antennas can be either directional (such as satellites) or omni-directional.

Directional antennas increase reception distance at the cost of reducing coverage angles; thus, they are best for wireless bridging of several offices or other stationary sites. *Omni-directional* antennas are used mostly for end user access (wireless access points). This technology allows transfer speeds of up to 2 megabits per second (Mbps).

FHSS divides its operating spectrum into 79 channels, with 1MHz per channel. Both parties agree how they will "hop" between such channels before regular transmission begins. Each transmission in an 802.11 network uses unique hopping sequences to minimize chances that more than one device will attempt to transmit on the same channel at any given moment, thereby causing a collision. In addition to media access contention management, hopping also makes FHSS significantly more secure because the transmission frequency changes every tenth of a second. Without the correct hopping code, data interception is impossible. This technology was borrowed from law enforcement and military radio communication technologies.

DSSS divides the spectrum into 14 partially overlapping channels and uses up to 3 channels simultaneously to inhibit signal interception. Thus, these channels must be 25MHz apart to prevent crosstalk. To minimize the number of retransmissions because of noise, every bit in DSSS is translated into a redundant bit pattern (called a *chipping code*) that is transmitted over several channels. This approach increases the signal's resistance to interference and serves to amplify the signal without additional power, resulting in longer transmission ranges. DSSS transfer speeds add up to 6Mbps, or 2Mbps per channel times three. DSSS equipment is more complex and costs more than FHSS equipment.

802.11 defines two types of equipment involved in transmissions. First is the client, which is usually a computer equipped with a wireless network interface card (NIC) and an access point (AP). The client serves as a gateway between wireless and wired networks. Second is the AP, which consists of a wireless transmitter and receiver, a wired NIC, and some software that manages channels and security (and also handles translation and decryption/encryption for traffic moving between wired and wireless network segments).

The 802.11 standard has two extensions. 802.11a uses a different transmission spectrum in the 5GHz area and enables speeds of up to 54Mbps due to a different radio signal modulation technology: orthogonal frequency division multiplexing (OFMD). Drawbacks of this standard are shortened reception range and higher power consumption requirements—definitely a disadvantage for mobile devices.

802.11b, the second extension, is also known as Wi-Fi (wireless fidelity). It relies on DSSS technology but increases transfer speeds to 11Mbps. If the quality of the signal suffers from external interference or other environmental conditions, Wi-Fi automatically slows down by design.

Standards 802.11d, 802.11e, 802.11f, 802.11g, 802.11h, and 802.11i are still in the development and proposal stages, and they primarily focus on increasing transmission security and algorithm efficiency.

NOTE

For More Information on 802.11 For more information on the 802.11 set of standards, please navigate to `http://grouper.ieee.org/groups/802/11/`.

WEP/WAP

WAP allows users of mobile phones and other wireless devices to access and interact with various information services on the Internet. It was designed to address bandwidth concerns as well as to deal with display limitations. This is because the majority of mobile device displays lack color and offer only very small screens on which to display data (mostly to keep device costs low). WAP integrates telephone services with microbrowsing, allowing mobile phone users to access simple Web sites designed for such use. WAP works for various applications, including e-commerce, online banking, information services, and more. It is also forcing cellular providers to enhance their services to stay competitive in the marketplace.

When HTTP and TCP were designed, wireless communication limitations weren't on the agenda of their governing bodies. HTTP is too complex, packet structures are too lengthy, and security standards are too bandwidth-hungry to make sense for wireless use.

Data packets are significantly smaller in WAP because it uses a simple binary format. Likewise, the WAP protocol is optimized for longer wait times and low bandwidths typical of wireless channels.

A specifically designed Wireless Markup Language (WML) is a derivative of XML; Web developers can use it to make their Web sites and services accessible to wireless devices, including even the two-line displays built into older cell phones. A special WML Web browser is usually part of mobile phone software that's embedded into the electrically erasable programmable read-only memory (EEPROM) that's hard-wired into such devices, but it can also be written into a plug-in SIM card. Some useful applications of this technology apply to systems management, where administrators can monitor their servers even while stuck in morning traffic. Likewise, salespeople can use their cell phones to access lists of incoming orders or obtain contact information for potential sales leads.

WAP supports several transport protocols by design; this is considered an advantage. WAP is also forward compatible with a new standard-in-development called *Bluetooth*. WAP appears to have a bright future, with the WAP Forum developing security, data storage standards, billing and authorization systems, additional transport-level protocols, and more. In addition, mobile phone manufacturers such as Nokia and Motorola are developing their own WAP application servers.

WAP does not compress data; however, WML commands are compressed. The minimal loadable unit of data in WML is one *deck*, or 1,400 bytes. All WAP applications must be extremely efficient, and many of them normally use templates and variables, which enable both client-side and server-side caching.

As mentioned earlier, WAP is based on a client/server architecture and WAP gateways facilitate access between servers and clients. Gateways are necessary for Internet access, short message service (SMS) text messaging between providers, and data transmission services such as Circuit Switched Data (CSD) and General Packet Radio Service (GPRS). Each WAP gateway decodes information coming from either the phone client or the Internet server and translates it to whichever destination network format is required. WAP gateways also provide DNS services, translate Wireless Transport Protocol (WTP) packets into TCP and vice versa, and handle WTLS operations as covered in the "WTLS" section earlier in this chapter. A microbrowser embedded in mobile phones is part of the WAP programming model; it interacts with the WAP gateway.

WAP applications must be limited because of mobile hardware restrictions and bandwidth concerns. Nonetheless, WAP is a convenient tool to access all types of information and services, including weather forecasts, public transport schedules, news, ticket and hotel reservations, translation services, and email. WAP technologies have yet to win user support, though, and have not yet made a significant market impact. HTML does not convert to WML easily, Web and WML browsers are not cross-compatible, and security standards are still emerging. In short, WAP is more of a gee-whiz technology than a useful service today.

Recognizing Vulnerabilities and Taking Action—Instant Messaging

Understand communication security in wireless, wired, and application-specific environments.

Instant Messaging (IM) is an Internet service that enables users to communicate in real-time using text messages and to exchange files (pictures, music, and so on) with one another. Although the concept of real-time chat is not new (Internet Relay Chat [IRC] has been around for a decade or longer), average consumers started chatting only when the latest user-friendly programs, such as ICQ, MSN Instant Messenger, Yahoo! Instant Messenger, and AOL Instant Messenger, became available.

IM might prove to be the next killer Internet application, and it might even partially replace email. IM combines the best features of voice conversations (real-time, somewhat emotional) and email (impersonal, convenient). The trouble, however, is that IM vendors are battling fiercely to develop a common standard for instant messaging while still respecting competition and freedom of choice. As key vendors iron out their differences, upstarts are also developing their own software that supports all known proprietary chat protocols, thereby allowing users to intercommunicate no matter which service provider they favor.

On new systems, IM software often comes preinstalled; if it's not, IM software is probably one of the first things a new user will install. Microsoft and Netscape promote their IM technologies aggressively, and users don't seem to mind. In March 2002, Osterman Research stated that 30% of companies already rely on IM software for company communications and 42% have approved its use in the near future. Another company, Gartner, claims that 70% of businesses will end up using IM for mission-critical or production purposes. As with other convenient technologies, however, IM poses potential security concerns and is already prey to numerous well-documented exploits and vulnerabilities.

The most important IM questions from a security perspective are

- Are these technologies safe?
- Is the communication confidential?
- Is it reliable enough to conduct the company's business?

It is important to realize that popular software, be it open source or commercial, usually has an array of vulnerabilities that attackers are eager to discover and exploit. As with other programs, when IM software flaws are discovered or exploits occur, that news is communicated to its custodians and patches are released. Again, this underscores the importance of monitoring security advisories and responding quickly to potential threats or vulnerabilities. Although some small fraction of the bugs might not be discovered or documented until after a large-scale exploit occurs, such routine attention heads off most potential problems.

EXAM TIP

Instant Messaging Also called IM, this is an Internet service that provides real-time communication capabilities using text-based messaging.

Vulnerabilities

Besides the attacks described in the following sections, some serious vulnerabilities are inherent to instant messaging software. They include, but are not limited to, the following:

- **Impersonation attacks**—Attackers can send messages on behalf of another person using client-side scripts and the IM object model. Among other vulnerabilities, this allows hackers to send links to attacking Web sites through IM.

- **Information theft**—Attackers can steal contact information from your contact lists. By combining this vulnerability with the preceding one, they can send viruses to those people while impersonating you.
- **Privacy and activity indicators**—IM software permits users (and attackers) to determine whether a person is online, sometimes without that person's consent. This identifies possible targets for attack and victims for impersonation.
- **Malware propagation**—Worms can get into a system, steal address book data, and propagate themselves using IM file transfer tools.

As in other situations, the human factor remains one of the biggest problems for IM security. Because a hacker can impersonate you and send malicious material to people on your contact list, they can open files or provide information you otherwise wouldn't. As with other applications in which humans can easily subvert built-in security, the key here is to educate users not to handle files they don't expect nor to provide sensitive information to others simply for the asking.

Packet Sniffing

A network sniffer, or *packet sniffer*, is an application that captures all traffic traveling past a network interface attached to some network. Packet sniffing is useful for network troubleshooting and software developers; however, it can also be used to eavesdrop on unencrypted traffic (unencrypted email, Web packets, IM, and more).

When people communicate via IM, they do not realize their communication is probably hopping around numerous times through various networks and routers. On any network segment along this path, someone can use a packet-sniffing tool to intercept such communications. However, scanning through a large number of packets to extract something useful is very difficult. Thus, attackers also employ *communication filters*, software to detect and identify specific types of communication currently underway.

When attackers get access to some wire, they attach a network device to that network segment. Next, they install a communication filter to capture packets that contain specific strings or patterns, such as the "password" keyword. If a pattern in the filter matches traffic from the wire, that packet is recorded for subsequent analysis.

Flat, unswitched local area networks are particularly vulnerable to sniffing attacks because every packet traveling between two hosts is broadcast to all nodes on the network segments to which each host belongs. Thus, a sniffing device or program could be connected to any port or installed on any machine on the same segment. A few years ago, switching technology became sufficiently inexpensive to be widely accepted as a standard LAN building block. In many installations, switches replaced broadcast hubs and were used to micro-segment LANs into numerous virtual segments. Switches also establish point-to-point channels between pairs of hosts as they initiate conversations. This alleviates the problem of sniffing but does not eliminate it completely (especially if attackers can access the switch itself).

In the real world it is at least difficult, if not impossible, to gain access to ISP facilities and install sniffers there. Therefore, the biggest source of sniffing threats stems from LANs and public facilities. Cable modem technology is particularly prone to sniffing-based attacks, because all users on a cable segment can see (and therefore sniff) all traffic on that segment. Companies or organizations that support remote access for cable modem-based users should definitely use more secure implementation, preferably those based on IPSec.

Because so much information used in popular messaging software now takes the XML format using the HTTP protocol, traffic vulnerability to sniffing is actually on the rise. The latest trend is to convert everything to XML formats. Unfortunately, this also means that using HTTP without SSL or TLS is tantamount to sending information in clear text from the hacker's perspective. This explains why sniffer attacks are both insidious and potentially very dangerous because they can decode and reveal lots of sensitive information.

To prevent information leaks, you can't rely on communication programs that use no encryption mechanisms; you must use IPSec or VPN solutions to secure communications both on the local network and for all remote access. If IM services are deployed for business purposes, use applications similar to Microsoft Exchange Server 2000, which enables you to operate your own IM server that might or might not interact with the rest of the world. As a matter of security policy and user education, users should also be coached on which types of communication and file transfer are appropriate using IM outside organizational boundaries—if indeed such use is permitted at all.

Social Engineering

The main objective behind instant messaging is communication. Such communication is real-time, fast, and convenient, but it's also easily impersonated. How can users be sure that their communication partners are who they claim to be? In instant messaging, social engineering takes a new form.

Social engineering can be loosely defined as any attempt to gain unauthorized access to systems or resources by means other than software or hardware hacking. The rules of this game are to outsmart co-workers or strangers to gain knowledge or information that can compromise system security.

Social engineering attacks are particularly dangerous for IM users because they work for anyone who can speak or type; no significant technical expertise is needed. A little bit of psychology and some insight into the victim's character or habits is usually enough to mount a successful attack, under the right circumstances.

Assume two legitimate corporate users are known to each other: user John, an outside contractor, and Michael, a company representative. Michael and John work together regularly, so each is listed in the other's IM contact list. Assume further that Michael's computer security gets compromised and a hacker takes over and copies his contact list by exploiting some known vulnerability that isn't yet patched or fixed.

Here's how that hacker can impersonate Michael and catch an unsuspecting John off-guard:

Hacker says: `Yo, John buddy. Sup?`

John says: `All is well. What's going on?`

Hacker says: `Hey listen, I am really busy. I'm in and out. Have a bit of a problem here, need your help bud. Our big boys need some useless reports - your admins created my user account just yesterday but warned if the password gets lost I'll have a chat with the management... :-\`

John says: `Bud, you weren't born yesterday - you know how it is...`

Hacker says: `Yeah, for sure... sorry to bug ya - next one is on me!`

John says: `Umm... Err... Okay. I'll go bug my admin.`

John says: `Username is Michael, password is Qwsd34G. You will have to change it once you are in.`

Hacker says: `Buddy - you saved my day! I owe you one - thanks a bunch!`

Safeguarding against such an attack is very difficult. The only way to institute some sort of protection is to refrain from using IM for business purposes or institute a firm policy whereby no sensitive information is permitted to travel using IM (this might also necessitate creating a separate automated process to serve password lookup requests, for example). As always, user training is imperative and will cost the company time (and money). An alternative method is to use subtle authentication that could not be intercepted by packet sniffers due to obvious uselessness, as in the following example:

Michael says: `John, how's your doggy doin'?`

John says: `I don't have a dog, Michael. I've got a cat.`

Authentication is successful; Michael types in the challenge phrase and John responds with the secret answer. The key is to avoid using unsecure channels to transmit or exchange sensitive data. If Michael asks for a password, John could also say, "I'll call you with that information." That's because corporate policy forbids sending passwords via email or IM but allows it to be communicated if the other party is accessible through a phone number known to both parties. In highly secure environments (where national security might be involved), such information can usually be transmitted only in a face-to-face meeting between the parties involved where impersonation becomes virtually impossible.

Attacks

Attacks described in this section are not specific to IM software; instead, they are well-known attacks that have been successfully deployed against many platforms and types of software. This is something that developers did not anticipate, nor do such vulnerabilities often surface until after a release. Some attacks exploit the very way in which communication works and can be foiled only by utilizing so-called intrusion detection systems (IDSs) or firewalls.

Denial-of-Service Attack

One IM application proved to be vulnerable to transferring (accepting) any file with `%s` characters in its name. Simply creating a file named `%s%s%s%s%s%s%s%s%s%s.jpg` and sending it to the victim was enough to cause the victim's computer to crash.

The following is another exploit that uses the same approach to crash `explorer.exe` in Windows Me:

```
%s%s%s%s%s%s%s%s%s%s%s%s%s%s%s%s%s%s%s%s%s%s%s%s%s%s%s%s%s%s%
➥s%s%s%s%s%s%s%s%s%s%s%s%s%s%s%s%s%s%s%s%s%s%s%s%s%s%s%s%s%s%
➥s%s%s%s%s%s%s%s%s%s%s%s%s%s%s%s%s%s%s%s%s%s%s%s%s%s%s%s%s%s%
➥s%s%s%s%s%s%s%s%s%s%s%s%s%s%s%s%s%s%s%s%s%s%s%s%s%s%s%s%s%s%
➥s%s.jpg
```

It also causes crashes in Windows 98 when attempting to view that file's properties window.

Buffer Overflow

A buffer overflow attack capitalizes on bad coding in applications running on a victim's computer. Numerous applications are vulnerable to this kind of attack. It's a pervasive (and therefore effective) attack technique for many Internet services and their client applications.

Assume that a user is requested to enter her name and the programmer who wrote the application has allocated 100 bytes to store that input. If the user enters 200 symbols, that requires 200 bytes of storage. What sometimes happens is that the allocated 100 bytes are filled up but an additional 100 bytes are also written immediately following the 100 bytes allocated in memory. This extra data overwrites whatever information should be contained in the second 100 bytes. In many cases, when this happens a hacker can choose the correct array of symbols to overflow the buffer and then be able to execute arbitrary code on the system. The consequences of such an attack can be grave indeed.

VBScript/JavaScript

Many IM applications allow images to be substituted directly in the typing area. Although this functionality makes IM user friendly, it also poses a security risk. If an attacker inserts an intentionally damaged picture, the victim receives a JPG file icon instead of a picture. The exploit occurs when the user attempts to save that conversation. The picture is saved as follows:

```
<BINARY><STYLE><DATA ID="1" SIZE="66">JPG picture data
➥</DATA></BINARY>
```

You can send an HTML file that masquerades as an image (naming it with a JPG image extension) to insert some VBScript or JavaScript into that file if that file begins with the string `</DATA></STYLE></BINARY>`. That script is executed if the conversation is saved and viewed later.

Privacy

Privacy is an issue with free IM software vendors who depend on advertising revenues. Ad banners arrive from Web servers, and some user information is included in standard HTTP `GET` requests by design. This information can include the user's IP address, among other parameters. Here again, such data can be abused by either the software vendor or a sniffer.

In addition to collecting such information, which still seems to be within acceptable norms (it is part of the HTTP functionality), advertisers can attempt to put cookies on a computer to track user visits to their Web sites or affiliate sites. This information also can be analyzed without the user's knowledge or consent for use in surveys or to compile statistics, target ads, observe spending habits, and so on. This is a gray area; some people question whether this is ethical.

Clearly, IM software is both convenient and widely used. Alas, IM services are also highly unsecure at present. Things might come to a point where vendors agree on a single IM standard that implements security mechanisms similar to those found in Web communications. Today, businesses should not rely on free or popular instant messaging software to convey sensitive information. Until the major players create secure IM implementations, organizations should look at alternative implementations that address security—such as Project SCIM software (`http://www.projectscim.com`), which offers a secure chat window that can send encrypted messages and files to designated contacts on command.

CASE STUDY: BEAR, TRAP, AND ASSOCIATES

ESSENCE OF THE CASE

Here are the essential elements in this case:

- Install a VPN server in the Santa Barbara office.
- Install VPN clients in all other offices and migrate WAN links to VPN links over the Internet.
- Implement a certificate authority infrastructure and issue clients their own certificates. Configure the server with its own certificate and enable SSL/TLS. Configure the server to require clients to furnish valid certificates for authentication.
- Implement SSH to secure data feeds.

SCENARIO

Bear, Trap, and Associates (BTA) is a company that deals with financial markets worldwide. Currently, the company has branches across the United States and offices in Canada, the UK, Germany, Hong Kong, Japan, and Australia. All the offices have dedicated high-speed WAN links in their remote facilities that connect them to the central HQ office in Santa Barbara, CA. BTA's primary products include financial trading software, data feed services, and a stock and options trading portal on the Internet.

BTA wants to achieve several objectives. First, it wants to replace expensive dedicated WAN links with less expensive but highly secure alternative links. Next, the company wants to secure its data feed transfers between itself and its clients. Third, the company wants to implement tight controls over who accesses its trading portal on the Web and to guarantee that all communications are both private and secure. The company prefers to issue its own digital certificates for client authentication because the client base is limited and fairly stable.

ANALYSIS

The first step is to implement a VPN solution between the offices and cut costs involved in supporting WAN links. Security is of utmost importance to BTA, so encryption should use strong cryptography algorithms and lengthy keys (2Kb or longer). As for the solution itself, designers are free to choose between hardware solutions such as the Intel Shiva VPN and Cisco products, or software solutions such as those provided with Microsoft Windows 2000 Server and Microsoft ISA Server 2000. Hardware solutions take the ciphering load off VPN servers, but they don't come cheap, so actual implementation decisions will depend on company priorities and budgets.

Case Study: Bear, Trap, and Associates

The next step to achieving the desired result is to implement a certificate authority and enroll all customers. The CA will generate client certificates and assign them to user accounts. Clients must be trained or assisted in making the necessary configuration changes to support certificate-based authentication.

Going forward, the Web server farm must be configured to disallow any communications except those in which valid digital certificates are proffered. Web servers must also be enabled to support SSL/TLS as a key project requirement.

BTA has developed prospecting software for traders. The software includes a module that connects to the dedicated server farms and downloads stock data in hourly increments. Although such data files store information in application-encrypted form, the username/password authentication is vulnerable to intercepts and other attacks. By implementing SSH instead of using an FTP server, the company will significantly improve the security of its network and be better able to protect its customers.

Chapter Summary

Communications security is crucial in a world that is increasingly dependent on public networks such as the Internet, where so many useful and essential services are deployed online (online banking, Web-based email services, and online shopping, to name just a few). Although usually considered fundamentally unsecure, the Internet makes our lives more efficient and convenient.

Various communication security mechanisms are available for pretty much anything that is connected to some type of network. In the past, such security controls were weak and attackers were eager to exploit vulnerabilities and hack into loosely secured systems to show off their talents or simply wreak havoc. Security is clearly a critical aspect of communication technologies—up to the point where it can make the difference between a discarded standard with great functionality and an accepted standard that might lack functionality but is sufficiently strong in security to meet user needs.

Many communications standards and best network design practices now implement public key encryption mechanisms to enable application-independent security controls. This technology makes for reliable communication security and is currently available for almost any communication technology or application. Indeed, given modern processing capabilities, public key encryption is strong enough to even hide private information from governments.

KEY TERMS

- Digital signature
- Encryption algorithms
- Hashing
- IP Security (IPSec)
- Layer Two Tunneling Protocol (L2TP)
- Lightweight Directory Access Protocol (LDAP)
- Point-to-Point Tunneling Protocol (PPTP)
- Pretty good privacy (PGP)
- Public key infrastructure (PKI)
- Remote Access Dial-in User Services (RADIUS)

Chapter Summary

- Secure Multipurpose Internet Mail Extensions (S/MIME)
- Secure Hypertext Transfer Protocol (HTTPS)
- Secure Shell (SSH)
- Secure Sockets Layer/Transport Layer (SSL/TLS)
- Terminal Access Controller Access Control System Plus (TACACS+)
- Virtual private network (VPN)
- Wireless Transport Layer Security (WTLS)
- X.500 directory
- X.509 digital certificate

Nevertheless, the biggest threat to security remains in the software used to implement online services and create Internet infrastructures. Too many developers create applications by trying to get the best functionality or provide a huge selection of features and options, without thinking enough about potential exploits and security holes they might be unintentionally building into their software. Hackers look for such errors and exploit them, deploying devastating attacks that cause billions of dollars in damage every year and that lead to service disruptions and information theft.

To really protect the communications infrastructure from potential break-ins, data interception, and other unauthorized activity, you must think outside the box. Strong communications security means nothing without strong LAN security, strong database security, strong Network layer security, proper software configuration, and ongoing patching and service pack maintenance. In other words, a company or organization must have tight security controls all around, not just in those areas that are apparently more vulnerable than others. The chain of security is only as strong as its single weakest link.

APPLY YOUR KNOWLEDGE

Exercises

2.1 Creating a VPN Server in Windows 2000

This exercise demonstrates how to create a VPN server on a Windows 2000 Server platform. This VPN should enable clients to establish new VPN connections with that server.

The following assumptions are made in this exercise: The server is dual-homed, has one interface connected directly to the Internet, and uses PPTP for tunneling.

Estimated Time: 5 minutes

1. Click Start and select Programs, Administrative Tools, Routing and Remote Access.
2. In the Routing and Remote Access Service Administrator program, click the server and select Action menu Configure and Enable Routing and Remote Access.
3. The Routing and Remote Access Server Setup Wizard will appear. Click Next.
4. Select Remote Access Server. Click Next.
5. In the Remote Clients Protocols window, enable all the protocols the remote clients will use while connected to the server. These protocols must be listed in the Protocols box. When you are done, click Next.
6. In the Network Selection window, select the network adapter that is connected to your LAN. Click Next.
7. In the IP Address Assignment window, select Automatically if your network has DHCP servers configured. If that is not the case, select from a specified range of addresses and configure a range of available IP addresses for clients. Click Next when you are finished.
8. In the Managing Multiple Remote Access Servers window, decline setting up a RADIUS server right now and proceed by clicking Next.
9. In the Completing the Routing and Remote Access Server Setup Wizard window, click Finish. You now have configured the VPN server.
10. Before your VPN server can begin functioning, you must allow users to log on to the VPN server. Do this individually on a per-user basis or by using Remote Access Policies in the Routing and Remote Access MMC snap-in (the Allow Access If dial-in permission is enabled).

    After logon access has been configured, Windows 2000 and Windows XP users can access the VPN server by going through a network connection wizard and creating a new VPN connection. Users must still provide their Windows 2000 logon credentials to log on.

2.2 Connecting to a VPN Server from Windows 2000

This exercise is a continuation of the previous one and shows how to create a VPN client connection using Windows 2000.

Estimated Time: 5 minutes

1. Right-click My Network Places and click Properties.
2. Double-click Make New Connection. The Network Connection Wizard will appear.
3. On the Network Connection Wizard welcome screen, click Next.
4. Select the Connect to a Private Network Through the Internet option. Click Next.

Apply Your Knowledge

5. On the Public Network page, select which connection should be dialed first when connecting to this network. If you are connecting to a server on your local network or already have dedicated, always-on Internet access such as cable or DSL, select Do Not Dial Initial Connection. Otherwise, select the connection to dial. Click Next.
6. On the Destination Address page, provide the IP address or FQDN name of the VPN server to which you want to connect. Click Next.
7. On the Connection Availability page, choose whether this connection should be available only to the user currently logged on (you) or all users using this computer. Click Next.
8. On the Completing Network Configuration page, type the name for this connection and click Finish.
9. The Connect Virtual Private Connection dialog box appears. Click Properties.
10. On the Security tab, select the appropriate password security settings.
11. On the Networking tab, make sure that all the services you need are installed and are bound in the correct order.
12. Provide the username and password and click Connect.

Review Questions

1. What are the choices when it comes to selecting a tunneling technology for VPN?
2. What is the process used to sign messages using digital signatures in the PKI security model?
3. Describe the process used to encrypt communications using a public/private key pair in the PKI security model.
4. What are the main differences between the S/MIME and PGP email security mechanisms?
5. What are the main differences between the symmetric and asymmetric encryption technologies?
6. Describe the process used to authenticate a client requesting a connection in the 802.11x standard.
7. What is the main security risk in the WAP paradigm?
8. What are the benefits of using SSH-based file transfer technology instead of FTP?

Exam Questions

1. You are an independent consultant working on a security project for ITproConsult.com Corporation. Your project manager asks you to design a secure Exchange-based emailing environment. Which of the following steps would you consider taking to provide the highest possible security, while minimizing administrative effort along the way? (Choose all that apply.)

   A. Install an Exchange-aware antivirus solution.

   B. Install a file system antivirus solution on the Exchange server.

   C. Install a MAPI-compatible antivirus solution on each user's workstation.

   D. Install a content filtering solution on the Exchange server.

   E. Implement S/MIME or PGP.

Apply Your Knowledge

2. The company wants to secure its Web services and provide a guarantee to the online customers that their credit card information is securely transferred. Which technology would you use?

   A. VPN

   B. SSH

   C. S/MIME

   D. SSL/TLS

3. You need to secure communications between remote offices located in Melbourne and London and the head office in New York.

   Required Result:

   Any type of communication between any of the offices must remain completely secure and be impossible to decrypt. In addition, receivers must be sure that the sender's identity is verifiable and trusted.

   Optional Desired Results:

   Legacy plain-text authentication programs should be secured without the need to migrate to a superior technology.

   Processing power requirements for the encryption and decryption of packets should be kept at a minimum.

   Proposed Solution:

   Implement a VPN solution between the satellite offices and headquarters. Use hardware, such as Cisco's VPN concentrator, to facilitate endpoint encryption.

   Evaluation of Proposed Solution:

   Which result(s) does the proposed solution produce?

   A. The proposed solution produces the required result but neither of the optional results.

   B. The proposed solution produces the required result and one of the optional results.

   C. The proposed solution produces the required result and both of the optional results.

   D. The proposed solution does not produce the required result.

4. You are authenticating a server using X.509 certificates, but your DNS is compromised. An attacker intercepts this communication and authenticates to the server on your behalf, at the same time impersonating the server to you. What type of attack is this?

   A. DoS

   B. Man-in-the-middle

   C. Authentication replay

   D. Ping of death

5. Why is it unsafe to allow signed code to run on your systems?

   A. The fact that the code is signed guarantees only that the code belongs to a certain entity, not that it is absolutely harmless.

   B. Malicious users are known to have attempted obtaining legitimate certificates to sign harmful code, with some success.

   C. Scripts can be used to employ signed code that comes preinstalled and signed with the operating system.

   D. All of the above.

APPLY YOUR KNOWLEDGE

Answers to Review Questions

1. When it comes to selecting a tunneling technology for VPN, the choices are the Point-to-Point Tunneling Protocol (PPTP) or Layer Two Tunneling Protocol (L2TP). The first one is a protocol often used in older Microsoft implementations (Windows NT), but the second is widely implemented with IPSec to provide the most reliable industry standard solution for VPN connections.

2. Digital signing works as the reverse of message encryption. The sender uses his private key and a message digest to create a signature. The message digest is the resulting value from hashing message content; it is only a short summary of any amount of data contained in the message and is limited to several hundred bits as specified in the protocol in use (128 in the case of MD5). If any number of bits in the original message change, a totally different message digest value results. On the receiving end, the sender's public key is used to decipher the message digest, which is calculated again using the hashing algorithm over the message content. If the resulting value matches the one extracted from the signature, the receiver sees that the message has not been tampered with in any way. The sender's identity is verified because a message digest is retrieved using the sender's public certificate.

3. When a sender encrypts a message, data contained in that communication is scrambled to the receiver's public key. The receiver of this encrypted message uses his private key to decrypt the message contents. The public key is used only to encrypt communication and is therefore completely useless to attackers who intercept the encrypted message or public key. Only the private key can be used to decrypt messages.

4. PGP is considered a hybrid cryptosystem that uses symmetric cryptography for actual message encryption and asymmetric cryptography for digital signatures and key distribution and management. It also employs so-called session keys and plain-text compression to further complicate things for message interceptors. PGP works faster than S/MIME without any concessions in the security.

5. Symmetric encryption technologies use a secret session key for both encryption and decryption of the secure communication. A way to securely exchange this secret key between the communicating parties via an open network is needed. Thus, this key must be preshared offline. This problem is addressed by asymmetric or public encryption, where the public key of the recipient is used to encrypt information that can be read only with the recipient's private key.

APPLY YOUR KNOWLEDGE

6. The wireless authentication process works as follows: Before any communication can occur, the client (initiating party) sends a connection request to one of the wireless access points in the area. Access points are analogous to hubs or switches on wired networks, but they are also employed to verify access requests (authenticator). Authenticator marks all initial communication with the initiating party as unauthorized, and only EAPOL messages are accepted while in this mode. All other types of communication are blocked at this point (HTTP, POP3, DHCP, and so on) until the moment when supplied credentials are verified with an authentication server. Upon receiving EAPOL requests from the initiating party, the wireless access point device requests logon credentials and sends them to the designated authentication server. If the supplied credentials are successfully validated by the server, an EAP-success request packet is issued to the initiating party and regular communication can begin. Otherwise, if the server fails to validate the supplied credentials, the communication session request is rejected.

7. The WAP gateway of the service provider encodes and converts necessary protocols and ensures that communication is secure. One of the major drawbacks of this system is its security subsystem. WTLS is used between mobile devices and WAP gateways; however, WAP gateways use SSL/TLS to communicate with service providers, so the WAP gateway's function is to decipher one encrypted stream and encrypt it for the destination network. This is where information is prone to attacks and interceptions.

8. All SSH communications are encrypted with IDEA or any of the following symmetric encryption algorithms: three-key Triple DES, DES, and Blowfish. The RSA host authentication method is used with RSA keys to verify communicating parties' identities, with every communicating party having its own RSA key. Encryption is used to prevent IP spoofing, and public key verification is used against DNS and routing spoofing. In short, file transfer technologies based on SSH are not vulnerable to data interception, impersonation, or session hijacking. FTP is vulnerable to almost every attack available.

Answers to Exam Questions

1. **A, D, E.** To secure the Exchange server against potential known virus attacks, you need to install an Exchange-aware antivirus software solution, not a file-system antivirus software. Workstations do not need email antivirus software because email is checked at the server. Content filtering is a good idea to protect the network against spam. S/MIME is preferred over PGP in this particular scenario because it delivers better operating system/Outlook integration, but it is not mandatory, so PGP is also acceptable as a correct answer.

2. **D.** SSL/TLS is used to secure Web communications and ensure that customer information is securely transferred. VPN is not used to secure public anonymous connections to Web servers, but instead is used to provide secure remote access services to the company's agents. SSH is used to secure file transfers and terminal sessions, and S/MIME is used to secure email communications.

Apply Your Knowledge

3. **D.** The solution does not meet the required result. Technically, the solution would meet both of the optional results and the required result if it were implemented somewhere in North America. Certain export restrictions might prohibit the use of strong encryption outside North America; hence communications between international offices might not be impossible to decrypt because of a shorter encryption key length.

4. **B.** The attack described is a man-in-the-middle attack, also known as active interception.

5. **D.** All of the statements are true about signed code.

Suggested Readings and Resources

Online Material

1. Cryptographic Algorithms (`http://kremlinencrypt.com/crypto/algorithms.html`).
2. "How SSL Works" (`http://developer.netscape.com/tech/security/ssl/howitworks.html`).
3. IEEE 802.11 WG "Hot Topics" (`http://grouper.ieee.org/groups/802/11/`).
4. The Mail Abuse Prevention System (MAPSSM) Realtime Blackhole List (RBLSM) (`http://mail-abuse.org/rbl/rationale.html`).
5. Modern Hacker's Desk Reference (`http://cyborg.virtualave.net/mhdr.htm`).
6. SecurityFocus (`http://www.securityfocus.net`).

Publications

1. McClure, Stuart, ,Joel Scambray, and George Kurtz. *Hacking Exposed Network Security Secrets and Solutions, Third Edition.* Berkeley, CA: McGraw-Hill Osborne Media, 2001.
2. Microsoft Corporation. *Windows 2000 Server TCP/IP Core Networking Guide.* Redmond, WA: Microsoft Press, 2002.

OBJECTIVES

This chapter covers the following CompTIA-specified objectives for the Communications Security section of the Security+ exam.

Understand the basic security concepts of network devices.

- It is important for you to understand the basic security concepts of network devices, such as firewalls, routers, switches, and so on, so you can protect the environment and outgoing and incoming communications on these devices.

Understand the basic security concepts of storage media devices.

- It is important for you to understand the basic security concepts of storage media devices (such as the various types of cable and removable media) so you can protect the environment and outgoing and incoming communications on these devices.

Understand the basic security concepts of security topologies.

- It is important for you to understand the basic concepts of security topologies (such as security zones, VLANs, NAT, and tunneling) so you can protect the environment and outgoing and incoming communications.

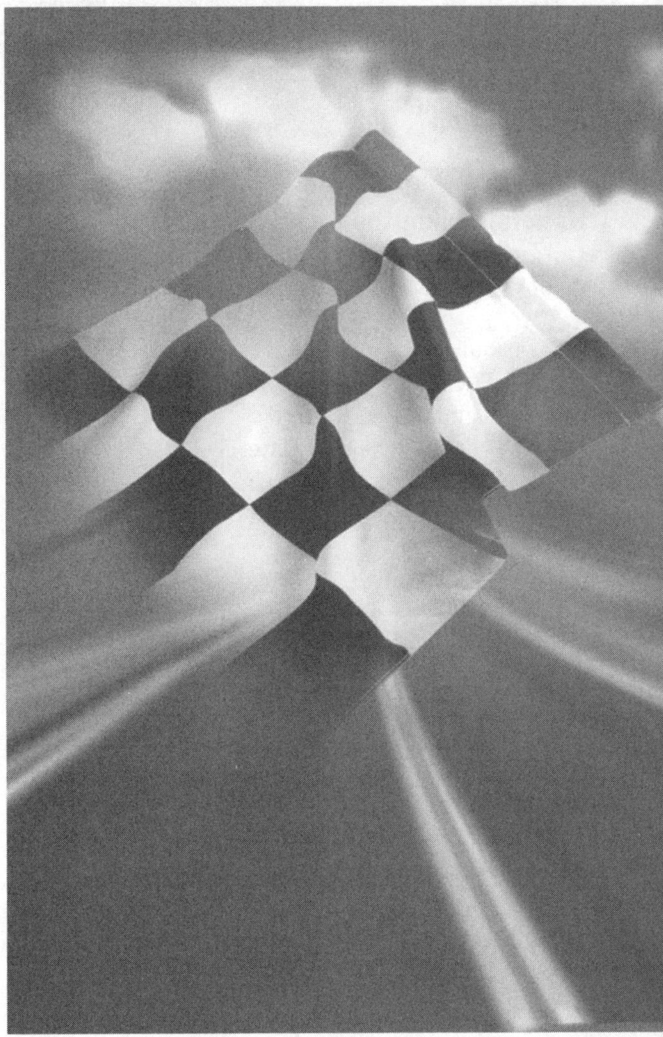

CHAPTER 3

Devices, Media, and Topology Security

OUTLINE

Study Strategies

- One of the most important topics of this chapter is security topology and firewalls, which are security controls designed specifically to protect the infrastructure. Be sure you understand the types of firewalls and security topology configurations.
- If you have access to a Cisco router, Unix machine, or Windows 2000 machine (better yet, all three), make sure you are familiar with features such as access lists and IP filtering.
- Set up one or more of the security topologies in your lab.

INTRODUCTION

This chapter takes you through the basics of media, devices, and security topology. Protecting communications includes more than securing the software technologies and protocols covered in Chapter 2, "Communication Security." The infrastructure, including all network devices, servers, and data, also requires security controls on all levels to ensure company-wide network security.

UNDERSTANDING THE BASIC SECURITY CONCEPTS OF NETWORK AND SYSTEM DEVICES

Understand the basic security concepts of network devices.

Network devices—such as routers, firewalls, gateways, switches, hubs, and so forth—create the infrastructure of local area networks (on the corporate scale) and the Internet (on the global scale). Securing such devices is fundamental to protecting the environment and outgoing/incoming communications. You also have to be aware of security risks and controls available in the public switched telephone networks (PSTN) infrastructure because PSTNs are often used for computer communications. This section of the chapter introduces the security concepts applicable to physical devices, network topologies, and storage media.

Firewalls

EXAM TIP

Know that a firewall is a hardware or software system designed to protect one network from another network, and be familiar with the various types of firewalls.

A *firewall* is a hardware device or software application installed on the borderline of secured networks to examine and control incoming and outgoing network communications. As the first line of network defense, firewalls provide protection from outside attacks, but they have no control over attacks from within the corporate network. Some firewalls also block traffic and services that are actually legitimate.

A firewall is designed to protect one network from another network.

Because network security is concentrated on configuring the firewall, or at least is built around it, a compromised firewall can mean a disaster for a network. For smaller companies, though, a firewall represents the best investment of time and money. All things considered, a firewall is as indispensable as the Internet itself; however, you should not rely on it exclusively for top-to-bottom network protection.

Increasingly, companies are also deploying firewalls outside the edges of networks, as well as between network segments and even on individual machines, where justified.

Three basic types of firewalls are available, in addition to one—the stateful inspection firewall—that combines the features of the three basic types. Firewall architectures include the following:

- Packet-filtering firewall
- Circuit-level gateway
- Application-level gateway
- Stateful inspection firewall

Packet-Filtering Firewall

Packet-filtering architecture involves checking network traffic for source and destination addresses, source and destination port numbers, and protocol types. Packet filtering allows an administrator to exclude traffic based on its source and destination addresses, and, depending on the device, it can also exclude traffic aimed at specific protocols and ports or traffic that is sent to or from particular addresses. This architecture functions on the Network layer (layer 3) of the Open System Interconnection (OSI) model. Most quality routers (not just firewalls) have packet-filtering functionality built in. Devices made by Cisco Systems, the undisputed leader in the area of network devices in general, employ access lists provided as a feature of the Internetwork Operating System (IOS). For Transmission Control Protocol/Internet Protocol (TCP/IP) traffic control, the two types of access lists are *standard* and *extended*.

Only extended lists allow you to check for all the previously listed characteristics and include some other conditions, such as secondary connections. These access lists can be applied to different interfaces to screen network traffic in both directions or in either direction on each interface. You can apply an access list filter to the external interface so the router will discard prohibited packets before it has to spend CPU time on making a routing decision. All packets that are not explicitly permitted are effectively rejected. Similar solutions that come built into the operating system can be found in Windows NT and its TCP/IP implementation, Windows 2000 with the same protocol features plus IP Filtering in the local policies, many Unix-like operating systems, and specialized firewall platforms.

Packet-filtering solutions are considered generally less secure than circuit-level architectures because they still allow packets inside the network regardless of the communication pattern within the session. Thisopens the system to denial-of-services (DoS) attacks (buffer overflow exploits in “allowed” applications on target machines, connections exhaustion, and so on).

Circuit-Level Gateway

Circuit-level architecture involves monitoring TCP/IP session requests between trusted hosts on the LAN and non-trusted hosts on the Internet. This monitoring, performed on the Session layer (layer 5) of the OSI model, is done to determine whether a requested session is legitimate. When hosts establish a session in TCP/IP communications, they conduct a procedure called *handshaking*, in which peers agree on communication parameters in TCP SYN requests and TCP ACK responses. The firewall ensures that these session establishment packets occur only when prescribed. It also verifies the validity of the sequence numbers used in TCP to reassemble packets in the correct order, as shown in Figure 3.1.

TCP Three-Way Handshake

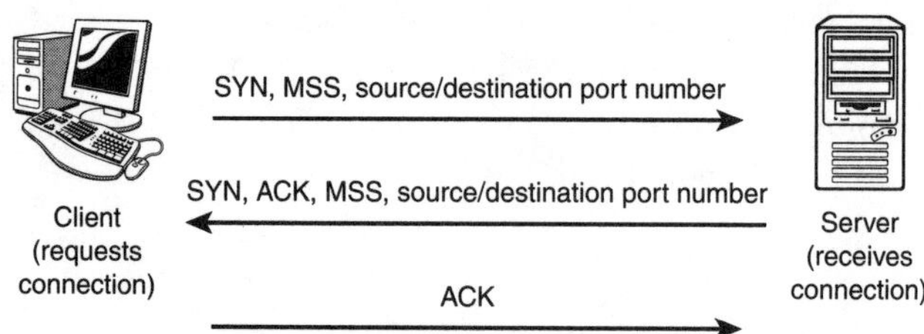

FIGURE 3.1
A normal handshake.

Popular attacks, such as DoS, are often launched when an attacker begins the TCP three-step handshake sequence with a SYN packet (and thereby begins to establish a connection) that is never completed. Instead, the attacker emits another SYN packet and initiates another connection that is also never completed (when repeated thousands of times, it causes problems). This attack, called a *SYN flood*, forces a victim system to use up one of its finite number of connections for each connection the initiator opens. Because these requests arrive so quickly, the victim system has no time to free dangling, incomplete connections before all its resources are consumed. TCP/IP standards suggest acceptable timeout periods that assume a timeout will handle some type of congestion or outage adequately. However, a massive number of connection attempts can occur during the normal default timeout period, thereby exhausting system resources and making the system unavailable for legitimate users. These attacks are detected and prevented in circuit-level architectures where a security device discards suspicious requests. If you receive 2,000 SYN (connection) requests per minute from a single host, you should become suspicious. Security devices can also be configured to do some or all of the following:

- **Block any future communications from a suspicious host**—This can be problematic if an attacker is using a spoofed source address. Legitimate traffic from that address will be blocked as well.
- **Throttle back the rate of responses to requests**—You can honor a certain number of requests per minute and discard the rest.
- **Expire unanswered initialization requests much more quickly than the default TCP/IP recommendations.**
- **Notify an administrator of a potential attack in progress.**

In fact, some of these techniques are not unique to firewalls and borderline devices, but instead should be considered for company-wide deployment. This is referred to as *hardening* a TCP/IP stack.

NOTE

How to Harden a TCP/IP Stack A good source of information on how to harden a TCP/IP stack in Windows 2000 is published in the Knowledge Base at `http://support.microsoft.com/default.aspx?scid=kb;en-us;q315669`. Microsoft is focusing more efforts on security; however, many of the new security features are not well known and are disabled in default configurations. This article points to a few modifications in the Registry, such as those that make a Windows 2000 TCP/IP stack more sensitive to recognizing SYN attacks, reduce the maximum number of allowed connections, and reduce the keep alive setting to expire silent connections more quickly.

The following are the most commonly used reconnaissance and attack methods:

- **Ping sweep**—An automated procedure of sending Internet Control Message Protocol (ICMP) echo requests (also known as PINGs) to a range of IP addresses and recording replies. This can enable an attacker to map your network.
- **Port scan**—An automated procedure of initiating sessions on every specified TCP port to see whether the host replies. If it does, a service is running on the target port of the machine. Different services run on default ports. For example, FTP usually runs on port 21, and HTTP usually runs on port 80. Port scanning programs check ports and use responses from these ports to guess which services are running on a machine. Publicly available programs such as nmap (available from `http://www.insecure.org`) and nessus (available at `http://nessuso.org`) use target system responses to valid and invalid data to guess the manufacturer or operating system versions of a system and to list vulnerable ports and services on scanned machines. This is known as *fingerprinting*. These programs can be used to find and close security holes on your network by simulating attacker reconnaissance and exploit behavior. Do not use them without prior consent and knowledge of your network administrator.
- **Email reconnaissance**—A probe in the form of a legitimate email sent to a nonexistent recipient in an attempt to obtain a nondelivery-report (NDR) reply. These reports sometimes reveal important email infrastructure elements, such as IP addresses and hostnames. Spammers use a form of email probing for different purposes, as noted in Chapter 2.
- **SYN flooding or DoS**—One of the first attacks to be tried against a target, it's perpetrated as described in the previous paragraph. The well-known Ping of Death and User Datagram Protocol (UDP) Bomb belong to the DoS category because they make a target machine unavailable as the result of a buffer overrun and a crash. These DoS attacks are not application specific and can be prevented by a firewall.

- **Application-specific DoS attacks**—Many applications do not take sufficient safeguards against malicious user input. Buffer overruns occur when attackers intentionally send more data than an application is designed to handle, causing the application to crash. A firewall cannot prevent this type of attack without preventing all communication with a particular application. This type of attack can be prevented by ensuring that applications run on your network have been tested against this type of attack.

- **IP spoofing**—An attack in which the source is disguised by using a different address as its source address. Potentially, the attacker not only escapes liability, but also appears to be a trusted source who has permission to access the system. Authentication methods, rath. firewalls, should be used in this case.

- **Packet sniffing**—As described in Chapter 2, packet sniffing is an effective reconnaissance method employed by attackers in a shared medium such as flat Ethernet. A firewall really can't do much against this technique, but applications aimed at detecting network nodes running in promiscuous mode can be used.

- **Trojan horses, back doors, spyware**—A common way to gain control over a remote system is by installing a small application on a target machine. A *Trojan horse* is an application that is hidden in some other type of content, such as a legitimate program. It can be used to create a new, secret account called a *back door*, or it can be used to run *spyware*, which collects user keystrokes for analysis. Trojan horses can also be used to infect and control affected systems, destroy and expose valuable company information, or use your systems as launching pads for further attacks from the inside. After an internal system is infected, a firewall is not very effective protection, although it can prevent certain types of traffic from flowing between the attacker and the infected host or between the infected host and other potential victims. Some Application-layer (layer 7) firewalls offer content filtering, which can help keep malicious Java applets and ActiveX controls out of your network. You must remember that a firewall is just a first line of defense—it should never be viewed as a cover-all insurance policy.

EXAM TIP

It is important that you understand DNS transfers.

- **DNS transfer**—An attempt to issue an `ls -d <domain name>` command against a DNS server in a bid to list all DNS server records (tantamount to getting a map of a fortified city about to be invaded). All DNS servers must be configured to refuse such a listing if the request does not originate from a preconfigured DNS replication partner. DNS was designed to be a system open for querying, but a DNS lookup is not the same as asking for a list of all a server's DNS records. If a DNS software vendor does not allow disabling of the `ls` command, consider implementing a separate DNS server for publicly accessible services, such as those located in the demilitarized zone (DMZ), or switch software vendors.

NOTE

Attackers Look for Vulnerable Systems Many attackers look for vulnerable systems, not caring who owns them. These attackers are seldom interested in uncooperative systems, but they shouldn't be the basis of your security policy.

A Pretty Good Reconnaissance Tool LANGuard Network Scanner can be downloaded from `http://www.gfi.com`. A free, limited version is available that is still very useful for security configuration and verification purposes.

A Comprehensive List of Vulnerabilities Go to `http://www.astalavista.com`. In addition to vulnerability walkthroughs, you can look through security tutorials on a host of topics, get privacy protection information, and download several tools. (Be cautious installing the tools, though; be sure you are not installing a Trojan horse or other malware.) Also check out the BugTraq section of `http://www.securityfocus.com` and the CERT advisories at `http://www.cert.org`.

Some reconnaissance probes can reveal more than enough information for an attacker to proceed with his plan. If a potential attacker doesn't know about your infrastructure and cannot probe it, chances are you are safe, at least until the next attacker tries.

You cannot guarantee that your ISP will monitor its network for such activity and prosecute port scanners and ping sweepers. Therefore, you want your firewall to catch these reconnaissance attempts, log the source information, and alert administrators on-the-fly. Ping sweeps are simple to protect against, but you should be aware that ICMP requests might be rejected or discarded and that this difference is important to attackers. Actively rejected ICMP echo requests mean that the target host is alive, which gives the attacker information. To protect against this probe, a firewall needs to discard the packet silently so the attacker's ICMP requests appear to be sent to an unused IP address. The same goes for port scanning: a decent firewall detects a port scan in progress and rejects further requests from the source IP address, sending a real-time alert to the administrator.

Many times, attacks are daisy-chained in a bid to get as much information or cause as much damage as possible. For example, an attack can begin with a ping sweep and when a host replies, a port scan is launched. The port scan can find the SMTP (email) port. Next, an email probe is sent to reveal information about the type of email software the server is running, resulting in a non-delivery receipt (NDR reply). Then, the attacker can test that specific email server for known vulnerabilities to see whether it is patched or can be exploited.

IN THE FIELD

ATTACK EXAMPLE

An attacker receives an email from someone's free Web email account—a very safe and anonymous communication medium. He uses the email's headers and notes the message's path from the very first communication point until it reached him. This first point is the IP address of the email sender as it was assigned by her ISP. Next, the attacker uses `PING`, `nslookup`, and `whois` to find the ISP's domain name, address, and administrative contacts, as well as which name servers are responsible for that domain. Then he issues an `ls -d` command against one of the name servers and, with luck, receives a full list of IP addresses and hostnames used on that ISP's network. Using a ping sweep to locate active hosts and then port scanning to detect services on those active boxes, he launches attacks against vulnerable applications.

If the ISP uses descriptive names in its DNS, an attacker can learn about physical connection types and the estimated bandwidth of the target. In a worst case scenario, if crashing or breaking into that machine is not possible, social engineering can still work for the attacker.

A good firewall also prevents non-application-specific denial-of-service attacks and, in some cases, even provides content filtering if it is an Application-level gateway.

Application-Level Gateway

An *Application-level gateway* is known as a *proxy*, and it functions on the highest layer of the OSI model: the Application layer. A proxy server basically inserts itself between an internal client (inside the network perimeter) and an external server (outside the network perimeter) for the express purpose of monitoring and sanitizing external communications. (For example, a proxy can remove references to internal or private IP addresses from client communications before emitting them onto a public network segment, thereby hiding information about network internals and details from outsiders.)

When a packet travels all the way up the TCP/IP stack on a proxy server, software developers can implement application-based security controls. Therefore, user access can be controlled on an individual basis, group policies can be applied, content types can be restricted, and so on. The higher up the OSI model that a proxy can operate, the more controls that can be implemented; however, there might be some costs in either performance or flexibility. Some applications will not run properly (because the protocols they use can't be proxied), or such applications might need to be specially configured to operate in the presence of a proxy server (such implementations are called *proxyable* or *proxy aware* when they can be made to work with a proxy server).

Stateful Inspection Firewall

The fourth type of firewall architecture, *stateful inspection*, combines the aspects of the three basic architectures explained in the previous sections. Stateful inspection firewalls not only examine packets at the Network layer, but also gather information about the packet's communications session from all layers to determine whether a packet is valid in the context in which it is received. For example, when a communications session is opened, the session is recorded in a state table. Subsequent session packets are checked against this state table to verify that they are valid in the context of the session. A packet that is already part of a valid session does not have to be compared to all the rules, which speeds up processing. Packets that do not make sense in the context of an open session can be discarded. Likewise, packets that attempt to exercise questionable or unwanted commands or activities can be blocked, and questionable patterns of activity (attempts at dangling synchronization, invalid segment sizes, and so forth) can be discarded. This prevents potential attacks from getting underway or denials of service from succeeding, but requires complex custom configurations to work.

Granted, firewalls residing higher up the OSI model can perform the same inspections that lower-level implementations can, but they are more complex to write (leaving the potential for overlooked back doors and lots of bugs), more complicated to maintain, and less complicated to attack as a result of the first two. However, providing that the software was written correctly and is deployed and maintained correctly, this provides the best security level.

Other Firewall Considerations

In addition to the four core firewall architectures, a few other elements that administrators have to consider are involved in the designing of a firewall solution:

- Network policy
- Service access policy
- Firewall design policy
- Authentication policy

Network Policy

Network policy deals with general network use issues, subdivided into *high-level policy* and *low-level policy*. High-level policy deals with "why"; low-level policy deals with how to place administrative controls on the network. On the high level, companies normally stipulate which applications can be used on the network, which applications can communicate with the outside world, which applications can talk to local clients from the outside, and which conditions must be met for exceptions to be allowed.

Low-level policy details specifically which commands will be used on the firewalls to actually lock them down. Many companies are missing this important element, which in turn leads to on-the-fly, poorly designed solutions that are not effective as security controls. If the company grows dependent on an on-the-fly solution and the engineer who implemented it leaves the company, successors will have to figure out why and how it works. After network policy is defined, the high-level portion should be communicated to the new and existing employees who need to be aware of what is allowed on the network and how it is allowed.

Service Access Policy

Service access policy, an extension to the network policy and overall organizational guidelines, should deal with issues of communications between the local network and remote services available on the Internet (and vice versa). Firewalls can be used to exclude the internal use of unauthorized external services and the unauthorized external use of internal services.

Firewall Design Policy

Firewall design policy refers to one of the two fundamental ways firewalls deal with the traffic rules defined by the administrators. They allow what is expressly permitted and deny the rest, or they deny what is expressly prohibited and allow the rest. For obvious reasons, "deny-all unless expressly permitted" is much more secure than the opposite. Every packet goes through the list from top to bottom, and if a match is not found, the packet is rejected. Thus, entries representing the most frequent kinds of traffic should be placed higher up the list to make a quick match and minimize overhead.

Authentication Policies

Authentication policies deal with issues of establishing secure, effective user authentication. Older methods of authentication, such as clear-text passwords, are no longer considered secure. The authentication methods used in today's networks must be secure enough to be useless in the hands of an interceptor. (Many technologies that can be used for this purpose are discussed in Chapter 2.)

In most cases, Application-level authentication is involved on a per-application or per-user basis without the involvement of firewalls. This is also true about lower-level network services, such as virtual private networking (VPN), where specialized devices establish a tunnel.

Generally, firewalls should not be called on to perform authentication services for general users or access. All that a firewall should be called on to handle is the traffic it should block (when rules or filters are violated) or allow to pass through for a connection to be established (when no untoward or unwanted patterns, addresses, or activities are detected). Firewall authentication policy comes into play only for firewall configuration. Whenever possible, use only secure methods for remote access to security devices. Telnet sessions, although quick and easy to establish, are inherently unsecure and can jeopardize network control. Instead, use secure shell (SSH) wherever possible. If a firewall does not support SSH, create a third-party SSH server for management purposes in the demilitarized zone (see the "Security Zones" section later in the chapter for more about DMZ and security zones). Then, configure the firewall to allow SSH in and to allow Telnet connections only from within the DMZ on the internal interface. This protects the public portion of the management session and (generally) 95% of the risk is eliminated. You can use a VPN link as an alternative to an SSH session; either way, communications will be encrypted and indecipherable to snoopers.

Even hardware firewalls are running highly specialized software that allows them to be configured and monitored remotely. All password and Telnet session protection rules apply in a standard fashion. That is, don't use Telnet to manage security devices remotely; this is tantamount to putting an expensive bleeding-edge digital security lock on your front door and advertising the passkey in the local daily. Use SSH where possible. If your firewall does not support SSH, create a third-party SSH server for management purposes in the demilitarized zone, and configure the firewall to allow SSH in and to allow Telnet connections only from within the DMZ on the internal interface. This protects the public portion of the management session and (generally) 95% of the risk is eliminated. You can use VPN as an alternative to SSH.

As always, use complex passwords of eight or more characters with mixed case and at least one digit and one punctuation mark. Programs are available that force users to choose secure passwords by refusing passwords that appear in the dictionary, are too short, or do not contain at least a few nonalphabetic characters.

Passwords should never be birthdays, family member or pet names, nicknames, or other easily guessed words. Passwords should also never be shared with anyone, especially not by email, via instant message, or over the phone. Passwords should not be stored on or around your workstation, and you should not use the password "remembering" features of popular browsers.

Passwords should be changed on a regular basis. Most companies use a rotation period between one and three months. More frequent password changes tempt employees to write passwords down, and less frequent password changes increase the chances of a password being discovered through either guessing or simple mistakes.

Periodic audits of accounts and automatic account expiration can ensure that users do not retain access to restricted areas after they no longer need it.

Be sure that the highest privilege levels are assigned to no less than two and no more than four senior engineers for fail-over purposes. (That is, if one engineer is on vacation, the other one is not likely to be absent, too.)

NOTE

Secure Password System A more secure form of password system is available for both Unix and Windows hosts. Called S/KEY (sometimes denoted as SKEY, or winkey for Windows clients), this technology uses one-time hashed 64-bit values as defined in RFCs 1760 and 2289 to prevent passphrases from ever traversing the network in the clear. The facility generates one-time passwords (which can be used only once, based on a user password associated with the `skey` command). Users get a string of six English words in return, which can be used to log in once to a system. Many routers, firewalls, and other network devices now work with this type of facility.

NOTE

Finding More Information on Firewalls Point your browser to `http://csrc.nist.gov/publications/nistpubs/800-10/node1.html`. Another good introductory firewall document from Cisco is available at `http://www.cisco.com/warp/public/cc/pd/rt/800/prodlit/fire_wp.htm`.

EXAM TIP

Know that a router is an OSI Network layer (layer 3) device that connects two or more networks and routes traffic between them; they also act as packet filtering and circuit-level firewalls.

Configure alerting and lockout for failed login attempts. In addition, allow configuration changes only from certain hosts inside the internal network or from a particular local subnet to increase the chances that your security infrastructure will not be compromised catastrophically.

Routers

A *router* is a physical network device (usually running proprietary software) that is used to connect several network segments into one network or an existing large network into smaller subnets. Routers operate on the Network layer of the OSI model and unite multiple physical network segments into a single seamless, logical network by understanding how to forward traffic from a sender to ultimately reach an intended receiver. This means that routing behavior is influenced strongly by the protocols in use. To some extent, therefore, understanding routing also requires understanding how Network layer protocols behave.

Various LAN protocols that were developed many years ago are still around. They do, however, employ certain techniques that are famous for not scaling well as an enterprise grows. You must take network protocols into account when considering routing designs. Some protocols require you to design specialized solutions to compensate for nonscalable or less secure protocol features. Broadcasts and service advertisements are just two types of protocol features that can require special routing solutions (or workarounds). The next few paragraphs discuss the following protocols: NetBIOS Enhanced User Interface (NetBEUI), Internetwork Packet Exchange/Sequenced Packet Exchange (IPX/SPX), and TCP/IP protocols, for example.

NetBEUI supports only local, bridged (flat) networks; has no addressing capabilities; is not routable; and relies on broadcasts entirely. This protocol is fairly old, but it can still occur in some remote locations—most likely because of legacy application issues. NetBEUI is the easiest protocol to deploy because no configuration is required. Owing to broadcast traffic overhead and lack of logical or physical organization, NetBEUI is not recommended for networks with 30 or more nodes. It is therefore the worst protocol for scalability and should not be the focus for security efforts because it supports no security features.

IPX/SPX is a routable Novell protocol that is still widely used. Although Novell switched to TCP/IP recently, IPX/SPX has a significant deployed base and remains supported and widely used. IPX has one significant scalability shortcoming: The more servers and network resources added, the more broadcast traffic is generated in the form of periodic service advertising protocol (SAP) announcements. SAP packets inform the network about resource availability. When scaling, it might not be desirable to propagate such advertisements owing to traffic overhead or for security reasons (an advertisement is also an invitation, after all).

Routers can help mitigate issues by dividing a larger broadcast domain into smaller subdomains. By acting as a SAP relay agent, routers can aggregate and forward all broadcast advertisements from any NetWare system only as required. Remote segments need to receive directed summarized updates, sent to other routers on other subnets. You can also implement access lists to control access to specific protocols from specific subnets and to limit distribution of SAP information, thereby controlling who can locate (and access) network resources.

TCP/IP is the de-facto standard protocol for all new networks, whereas other protocols are maintained only for legacy applications or backward-compatibility. TCP/IP has been around for several decades and provides numerous built-in techniques for effective control of transmissions over LANs and WANs alike. It has an elaborate addressing scheme well suited for subnetting and routing, although some proprietary environments can still affect overall network design. Consider older Windows Networking built on TCP/IP with Windows Internet Naming Service (WINS), Dynamic Host Configuration Protocol (DHCP), Remote Access Service (RAS), and computer browser issues. Most importantly, TCP/IP scales extremely well.

Generally speaking, you should not mix protocols, unless business requirements dictate otherwise. Multiprotocol environments are more difficult to maintain, more difficult to troubleshoot, and less efficient because each protocol imposes overhead and maintenance traffic that subtracts from available bandwidth. Furthermore, recall from the firewall section of this chapter that the smaller an attack surface is, the lower the likelihood of it being hacked. Each protocol has its own vulnerabilities, and some protocols rely on broadcasting service advertisements, which are inherently unsecure.

However, if using such protocols is a business requirement, routing provides solutions that can contain broadcast traffic within specific subnets and make the overall network more efficient and secure. In addition, routers can employ access lists to reject unwanted traffic.

As the basis of the network infrastructure, routers must be secured both physically and logically using the guidelines discussed in the "Other Firewall Considerations" section earlier in this chapter. Routers can be configured from a physically attached console or via a network connection such as an SSH session.

A router directs a packet to its network or Internet destination using routing protocols to exchange information and determine routing decisions. These concepts and protocols could fill a book, but for this discussion, just be aware that routing exists in an intranet between routing devices and on the ISP network between a border gateway router and a router.

Routers maintain routing tables that are consulted every time a packet needs to be redirected from one interface or segment to another. Routes can be added manually to the routing table—a very secure but less-manageable method, depending on the size of the network—or be updated automatically using routing protocols such as the following:

- Routing Information Protocol (RIP)/RIPv2
- Interior Gateway Routing Protocol (IGRP)
- Enhanced Interior Gateway Routing Protocol (EIGRP)
- Open Shortest Path First (OSPF), Border Gateway Protocol (BGP)
- Exterior Gateway Protocol (EGP)
- Intermediate System-Intermediate System (IS-IS)

Protocols such as RIP, IGRP, and OSPF are used internally to propagate route information as it changes, such as when a link goes down or the network needs to converge or become aware of the downed segment. BGP and EGP are used externally to exchange route updates between your gateway router and the ISP. Some routing protocols send updates at preconfigured intervals; some replicate the updates immediately as they are triggered.

Routing protocols employ different techniques to prevent routing loops (when a packet is rerouted indefinitely without finding the destination). Some of these techniques are

- Counting to infinity
- Route poisoning
- Split horizon

Later revisions of each of these routing protocols authenticate a replicating partner in a different way, and knowing how each works is extremely important in avoiding trouble situations, such as these:

- A hacker sending a route update to your network and poisoning (marking as downed) an important route to cause a DoS condition
- The creation of a routing loop that overloads the router and causes the network to become very slow and appear overutilized
- The update of a route to send all outbound traffic to a different host, which would then forward it to the ISP, launching an active interception or man-in-the-middle attack

Of course, no matter how secure the routing protocol, the first rule is to change the default password on the router itself. Failing to create a unique password practically invites attackers to wreak havoc on your network.

Switches

Sometimes referred to as microsegmentation, *switching* increases the performance of traditional media by reducing collision domains and facilitating media access. Classic switches operate on the Data Link layer (layer 2) of the OSI model and can be considered a multiport bridge with high-port density.

Switches have superceded more traditional hubs (multiport repeaters), which are no longer capable of accommodating adequate media access. In addition to facilitating congestion and media-contention problems, a hub is considered highly unsecure because it enables a flat network (a network segment with many network nodes sharing the same communication channel and seeing communications of every other network node in the segment), which is vulnerable to packet sniffers. (A switch can provide protection against a casual user attempting to pry into the network but needs additional security, such as port access control and MAC filtering, against ARP poisoning, sniffers, and other more advanced threats.)

Over time, networks designed on traditional Ethernet technologies grew in size, and network node density was constantly increasing. At the same time, software was developing and introducing new network-intensive client/server applications that exercised lengthier and more bandwidth-intensive transmissions. Software advancements introduced multitasking in the Windows world, adding to the existing functions in the Unix environment, and added to the stresses on the aging Ethernet network technologies.

Here is a simple explanation of the slowdown:

1. Before a workstation can transmit, it listens to the wire and attempts to sense existing activity in the network segment.
2. If a transmission is sensed, the workstation must wait a random amount of time and sense again until the wire is clear of transmissions.
3. When the wire is transmission-free, the workstation can commence its own transmission. However, when more than one workstation attempts to transmit a signal on the wire at the same time, a collision occurs and the segment is jammed.
4. Transmitting workstations then wait a random amount of time and attempt to retransmit.

This regime is characteristic of shared media such as Ethernet and is called collision sense multiple access/collision detect (CSMA/CD) to describe the type of circuitry involved. Apple Computer implements a similar approach called collision sense multiple access/collision avoidance (CSMA/CA). This differs from CSMA/CD in that it uses explicit signals ready to send (RTS) and clear to send (CTS) before accessing the network media—this approach avoids collisions rather than detecting them (hence, the difference in their names).

As the number of workstations attempting transmissions on a network segment increases, the chance of a collision increases. With more transmissions and collisions, the network becomes oversaturated and slows down.

A *collision domain* is a collection of network nodes that belong to the same shared network segment. LAN switching effectively splits broad collision domains into smaller domains or even dedicated network segments and significantly reduces or completely eliminates collisions and transmission delays. It also effectively doubles transmission capabilities by using full-duplex technology, meaning it uses all four pairs of CAT5 cable: two pairs to transmit and the other two to receive signals.

With recent improvements in switching technology, cost per switch port has steadily decreased, turning switching into a sound technology investment. In addition to fixing media-contention issues, a switch can help prevent packet sniffing and increase overall network security. You should implement switching if media contention problems exist or if the chances of attracting a sniffer are high (for example, in your business's guest offices or conference rooms where the public can access corporate LAN services). Although switches can enhance network security, they are not security devices per se and should not be considered a replacement for purpose-built security devices.

Switch security, as with firewalls and routers, requires both physical and virtual security controls. A switch has proprietary software that enables remote configuration of the switching operating system. Restrict physical access to devices where you can—at the network access point if possible or deeper into the distribution and core layers of the network. Employ strong authentication and password policies to secure virtual and local console access to the device's operating system and configuration.

EXAM TIP

Know that a switch operates at the Data Link layer (layer 2) of the OSI model and that it can be used to create virtual LANs.

Wireless and Mobile Communications

Wireless communications security was discussed in detail in Chapter 2. You need to remember that Wireless Application Protocol (WAP) applications are vulnerable to attacks at the WAP gateway. At this point, data streams are decrypted from Secure Sockets Layer (SSL) and are encrypted into Wireless Transport Layer Security (WTLS) for transfer to WAP devices. There is a brief time when the data stream is unencrypted. So, if the gateway infrastructure is not adequately protected, the entire WAP system is at risk. This vulnerability is especially common in developing countries where infrastructure investments can take budgetary precedence over security investments.

Some companies that don't specialize in mobile communications might provide WAP applications and services. These companies usually pass their WAP traffic to a third-party WAP gateway. The WAP traffic leaves the provider's protected (we assume) network encrypted in SSL. When it is decrypted at the gateway before being reencrypted in WTLS, it can be compromised; the provider has no control over the security of the WAP server.

Providers could avoid this vulnerability by operating their own WAP servers, but this is not a practical solution for two reasons: WAP broadcasting requires very costly equipment investments, and the technology is difficult to maintain and upgrade. It would be prohibitively complex to coordinate switching WAP clients between WAP service providers.

WAP communication cannot be considered safe in its present implementation. Therefore, WAP devices are inherently unsecure as well. In addition to the WAP specification flaw, mobile devices are easily lost or stolen. A company must be aware of these risks and consider which, if any, WAP implementations are suitable for its purposes.

Corporate wireless 802.11x-based infrastructures, on the other hand, have matured, and most types of known attacks are extremely difficult to conduct in the presence of strong authentication and encryption technologies. Risks primarily are attributed to the nature of mobile devices: They are small, valuable, and preferred over other personal items among thieves. All security discussions about physical and virtual device security in the context of switches, routers, and firewalls also apply to wireless access point devices used at the access level of the wireless network infrastructure.

Modems

Modems are gradually becoming a relic of "last mile" communications. They are being supplanted by high-speed cable and DSL connections that are significantly faster and not much more expensive than dial-up access. Although modems still can be found in some corporations and small/home office environments, most companies now use a more centralized administration and security model. A corporate network environment provides a single point of access to the Internet for all workstations and is guarded by a firewall or other security controls.

Some companies might still rely on modems, and some migrated environments might still have unused (and possibly forgotten) modems installed and connected to telephone lines.

Another reason companies might have modems and modem pools attached and connected to their networks is RAS, which is covered in Chapter 2 and in the following section.

No matter how good its firewall, a network's security can be compromised through a single PC connected to both the network and a modem.

War-dialing attacks take advantage of network-accessible modems administrators have forgotten or did not know how to secure. A *war dialer* is an automated software application that dials a given range of phone numbers to determine whether any are actually serviced by modems—indicated by returning dual tone multifrequency (DTMF) tones—and accepting dial-in requests. Telecommunications providers employ anti-war dialing software that attempts to detect war-dialing activity and disable any subsequent attempts; unfortunately, this protection works only if the numbers are dialed in sequence.

After a dial-in request has been accepted by a victim modem, the attacker can initiate password-cracking routines and compromise the system in a matter of time. Real-time attack-alerting systems are unlikely to detect a war-dialing attempt because the attack takes place in a seldom- or never-used part of the system. Fortunately, because modem communications are being replaced by more secure technologies, war dialing has become an unlikely threat for a LAN.

NOTE

Finding More Information on War Dialing Point your browser to `http://www.att.com/isc/docs/war_dial_detection.pdf`. This is a white paper on war-dialing detection written by AT&T.

Conventional dial-tone modems, with their low throughput, are relatively easy to flood with useless traffic. This is just one way to cause a denial of service through modems.

Dial-tone modems have two basic operation modes: transmission and command. When switched on, a modem enters command mode and awaits instructions from the terminal to begin transmissions. After communication has been established, the modem looks for certain patterns in the data flow that signal it to drop the connection and return to command mode.

The Hayes Corporation developed and patented one such sequence consisting of three escape sequences bounded by two pauses in the communication stream. The two pauses mark the escape symbols as an actual termination request, not a coincidental matching pattern in the data stream. To avoid paying royalties to Hayes, some equipment manufacturers have devised their own (sometimes incompatible or faulty) techniques. Attackers could create wide-scale disconnects by sending a normal data pattern containing certain character sequences (that these “alternative solutions” would interpret as termination requests) via email messages, mailing lists, and IRC chat sessions.

Cable and DSL modems are not vulnerable to dial-tone modem attacks, but an always-on connection to the Internet presents its own dangers. Encryption and firewall solutions must be used for protection against potential attacks over high-speed residential media.

Always-on access significantly increases the chances that an attacker will find and compromise a system. Often home users are not technically sophisticated enough to take the appropriate safeguards against attacks. Any system connected to the Internet should employ a properly configured firewall.

Cable modems also present an additional vulnerability because they provide Internet access using a shared coaxial cable. Potentially, all traffic to and from a machine connected to a cable modem is visible to other cable users in the area. Any cable modem traffic that accesses a network must be encrypted to prevent network compromises.

RAS

Remote Access Server (RAS) technologies are described in detail in Chapter 2. Modern technologies such as VPN use standard corporate network infrastructures such as firewalls and existing authentication systems. A dial-up modem pool, however, is an RAS device that is fairly distinct from the rest of the network. The following security controls can be used to protect the RAS point of entry to the corporate network:

- Using strong authentication
- Forcing callback to a preset number
- Using two-factor authentication
- Allowing dial-in only
- Restricting users who are allowed to dial in
- Restricting dial-in hours
- Using account lockout and strict password policies
- Restricting allowed protocols
- Restricting access to specific servers
- Configuring real-time alerting system
- Enforcing and review RAS logging

The items on this list can be complimented by other techniques.

Strong authentication helps protect against war dialers and unauthorized attempts to gain access to an otherwise secure environment. The Challenge-Handshake Authentication Protocol (CHAP), described in RFC 1994, or Microsoft's extended CHAP, described in RFC 2433, is a more secure approach than sending passwords in clear text where they can be intercepted on a PBX switch. (You learn more about telecom and PBX in the next section.) Challenge handshake authentication is much less vulnerable to replay attacks because the challenge is not the same every time.

The callback feature disconnects the incoming dial-in request and immediately initiates a call-back connection, to either a predefined number or a number specified by the user. Using a predefined call-back number is more secure because it eliminates the war dialing threat and controls the telephone numbers that can establish connections. Callback virtually assures the identity of the person at the other end, but it does not eliminate PBX eavesdropping or software bugs in RAS software that can cause significant trouble.

Two-factor authentication can be used when a callback policy is impossible—for example, when a user travels frequently. Devices such as the Cisco AS Series use a password and a second identifying piece of data provided by a physical device that contains a small clock chip and a special algorithm to generate codes. Neither the password nor the device alone can be used to gain access.

Restricting dial-in hours can limit potential exposure to attackers seeking access and trying to brute-force a password by repeatedly dialing in and trying new combinations. Often, automated attacks try to establish connections outside standard business hours to avoid immediate intervention by network security administrators.

A strict lockout policy can also help prevent brute-force attacks. After a designated number of failed login attempts, the system should automatically disable a user account.

RAS logs should be reviewed frequently and systematically, looking for connection attempts from unfamiliar phone numbers, repeated connection attempts, connection attempts at odd hours, and any other activity that seems suspicious.

Restricting dial-in access to one or a few servers limits network exposure in the event of a successful break-in.

Restricting dial-in access to just one or a few network protocols can also limit the effects of a successful break-in.

A real-time alerting system that notifies an administrator of suspicious activity as it occurs can help prevent or curtail unauthorized access. Real-time alert systems must be monitored, however, so it is most effective to use them in combination with either 24-hour monitoring or limited dial-up hours.

Like all network devices, RAS modem pools should be located in a highly secure place (such as a server room) that guarantees physical security and is accessible only to authorized administrative personnel. The platform used for dial pools, such as a Cisco AS-series access server, also should be secured as described earlier in the "Firewalls," "Routers," and "Switches" sections.

When all the previous security controls are implemented, the RAS environment becomes fairly secure and poses a challenge to potential attackers. However, these controls will not protect (even cumulatively) from the following three items:

- PBX vulnerabilities
- RAS software bugs, buffer overflows, and DoS attacks
- Social engineering

Historically, RAS software bugs were abundant in Windows applications and on the Windows NT platform in particular, but this has improved a great deal since the release of Windows 2000. Regardless of the operating system brand and version, vendor security patches should be applied as soon as they are available.

Social engineering is a favorite method of gaining access to otherwise impregnable systems, and combined with a public PBX infrastructure, this poses a threat that is not feasible to contain.

Telecommunications/PBX

Attackers have targeted telecommunications infrastructure for years. Originally, attackers sought to gain free long-distance service. As the Internet became more popular and dial-up access became a de-facto communication technology for residential and corporate RAS connections, telephone switch access also meant that an attacker could eavesdrop on communication sessions and decode all the transmitted information. Clear-text authentication, Telnet, email, and File Transfer Protocols were all in danger of being intercepted—even in a seemingly secure scenario where a user dialed in to a corporate network and accessed corporate resources from within the corporate infrastructure.

Some PBX hacking efforts were concentrated on accessing local loops that are out of commission. Local loops are numbers that belong to a telephone company and are no longer in public service but are still active. These decommissioned numbers allowed hackers to rack up thousands of dollars in long-distance charges that the telephone company could not bill to anyone because the numbers were no longer registered.

Another attack on telephone company infrastructure that is of more interest to our discussion allows a hacker to gain access to one or more telephone company switches. Switches have secret dial-in numbers that allow the telephone company and switch manufacturers to dial in and administer the switch remotely. Instead of regular username/password combinations, some manufacturers, such as Nortel Networks, employ a pool of challenge phrases that are presented to the dialer on a random basis. The dialer is expected to respond with a matching answer to get into the system. After the dialer is in the switch, she can wiretap any line, hijack a dial tone, and establish complete control of the lines serviced by that switch. Getting the challenge/response codes from the telephone company or the manufacturer isn't easy, but some switches use default usernames and passwords without implementing any sophisticated security controls.

> **EXAM TIP**
>
> Be familiar with why telecom and PBX equipment is susceptible to attacks and how to reduce the likelihood of attacks.

An attacker can use social engineering to trick a telephone company or manufacturer employee to give away the secret telephone number to a switch in a telephone conversation. One of the most famous convicted hackers in the U.S. claimed that he had control of telephone company switches that serviced all of Nevada. The level of detail he presented makes his claim plausible and also makes it seem probable that something similar could happen again.

IDS

Intrusion detection systems (IDSs) are designed to provide the network with more sophisticated protection than that offered by firewalls. IDS can come in different packages: as a standalone hardware device that eavesdrops on traffic, as a software application for a dedicated server, or as hardware add-in modules for existing firewalls. IDSs can be categorized based on three main parameters:

- **Active or passive analysis**—A passive IDS system monitors attacks in progress and just tells the administrator that her network is under attack. An active IDS system takes a preconfigured action against the intruder to protect the network against an attack in progress.
- **Host or network analysis**—Host-based IDS resides on network hosts and monitors system logs, communications, file systems, and processes for suspicious activities. Network IDS monitors network traffic and looks for suspicious traffic. A key tool used by IDS is signature matching. A *signature* is a string of data used to identify a potential attack; it includes a definition of the protocol and header information and packet data that is characteristic of an attack.
- **Misuse or anomaly analysis**—Misuse IDSs are designed to look for network traffic patterns, such as host port scanning, that match attack patterns stored in the attack pattern database. If network traffic matches one of the known patterns, an action or alert is triggered. Anomaly IDSs use norms that are established by the network administrator to define what is acceptable traffic and what is suspicious traffic. An example might be the number of ICMP echo requests that are allowable in a given time frame. Any traffic pattern outside the norm triggers an action or alert.

Both IDS and firewalls protect networks, but where and how they do so differs. Firewalls are designed to prevent attacks before they happen by keeping offending traffic offsite. If attackers are smart enough to get through a tightly locked firewall, the IDS comes into play. It detects attacks that penetrated the first line of defense. Therefore, the IDS acts as a safety net for firewalls. Also, IDS can prevent application-specific attacks that the majority of firewalls are indifferent to and are designed to catch attacks in progress within the network as well, not just on the boundary between private and public networks.

NOTE

Getting More Information on IDS
For more information and pros and cons of each method employed in IDSs, visit `http://www.cisco.com/warp/public/cc/pd/sqsw/sqidsz/prodlit/idssa_wp.htm`, a Cisco white paper on the art of IDS.

EXAM TIP

Be familiar with the various types of IDS.

Be familiar with the FCAPS.

The biggest advantage of the more sophisticated IDS is the capability to conduct stateful packet matching. That is, not only are certain packets filtered on a per-packet basis, but the whole communication session is also examined with a knowledge of which types and quantities of packets are normally expected. IDSs can provide an excellent level of protection against attacks of all kinds, but they require tuning to become an effective tool in your network. With so many variations and approaches to monitoring, you need to select the approach from which your company would benefit the most. IDS is discussed more thoroughly in Chapter 4, "Intrusion Detection, Baselines, and Hardening."

Network Monitoring/Diagnostic

Certain accepted practices in the industry are not yet standards but are pioneered by the companies or organizations that make standards. One of these practices deals with network monitoring and diagnostics. The industry recommends a structured approach to network management that includes fault management, configuration management, accounting management, performance management, and security management. This approach is referred to as *FCAPS*. This section discusses the framework of FCAPS and provides an overview of network monitoring protocols and security-related issues.

FCAPS is not a proprietary framework. It was developed by the International Organization for Standardization (ISO) to address network management issues. FCAPS, as originally defined, specifically focuses on the technical aspects of running the network infrastructure. It does not include the management of expenses, people, or software and server hardware (except for the network interface cards).

However, today's networks and business requirements are more integrated, to the extent that a major network fault or security breach can bring a large corporation to a standstill. Therefore, most companies have integrated network and systems monitoring and management practices anyway. This is usually because of cost savings, advanced management software that is available, personnel issues, or business limitations. The following sections cover integrated network and systems monitoring and management practices.

Fault Management

Fault management embodies all the tasks and duties related to network monitoring and troubleshooting. It is paramount to establish that a problem exists in the network in the shortest amount of time, determine what the cause is, eliminate the cause, verify that the service has been restored, and document (or *log*) the problem in a fault documentation or system monitoring log.

Configuration Management

Configuration management encompasses network configuration, device configuration, and all network and otherwise relevant settings. Support personnel must know the network configuration to troubleshoot a problem in a timely fashion. Personnel turnover, network size, and configuration complexity necessitate configuration documentation. Network items such as IP addresses, DNS settings, DHCP settings, subnet masks and default gateways, router configurations, network maps, and other network configuration information should be kept up-to-date and accessible to support personnel. Having this documentation on hand can help determine whether a router configuration has been tampered with and is also invaluable when recovering from a catastrophic network event.

Accounting Management

Accounting management consists of knowing exactly what a network system is built with and includes recording the exact model numbers and specifications of all network components and equipment and gathering and keeping all hardware and software inventory data up-to-date and available. Combined with other data provided by FCAPS, this is a valuable source of information for determining where the system needs tuning or upgrading to increase productivity or eliminate network bottlenecks or security risks. This segment of FCAPS is also concerned with billing users, if appropriate, and measuring and logging network resource usage.

Performance Management

Performance management involves baselining the network and analyzing trends to detect network problems and plan upgrades to, a replacement of, and development of the network infrastructure. The idea behind performance management is to identify problems before they occur by analyzing all network statistics and relevant indicators. It involves periodically benchmarking or measuring network statistics and comparing them with acceptable standards as identified in the network design documents. Criteria can include such values as data transfer rates, network and segment utilization, CPU usage, collision rates, broadcast rates, CRC error rates, queuing issues, and so on. Knowing network baselines can make certain types of attacks or consequences obvious. Performance management is closely tied with fault, configuration, accounting, and security management.

Security Management

EXAM TIP

Be familiar with the various types of management.

Security management is one of the most important areas of FCAPS and one that directly concerns this discussion (although you might have noticed that all areas of FCAPS enhance network security in one way or another). Security encompasses data encryption and integrity, authentication, securing data transmissions and network nodes, and managing overall security requirements by weighting them against usability of the network and ease-of-use from a user's perspective. Security management involves a thorough understanding and analysis of available technologies—both hardware and software. Designing and implementing a secure network isn't enough. Security must be proactively managed to avoid new exploits, repair newly discovered design flaws, upgrade and enhance existing operating systems and embedded software, and take advantage of new security and data protection technologies.

Simple Network Management Protocol

The Simple Network Management Protocol (SNMP, RFC 1157) was developed in the 1980s as a temporary solution to the network management problems that arose from growing network infrastructures. Although it had a simple and effective design, it was meant to be a stop-gap measure until better solutions were developed.

However, over time, it has become apparent that these other solutions have enormous financial and infrastructure demands and that only large companies can afford them. Therefore, SNMP has become a widely deployed de-facto standard for network management.

The benefits of SNMP-based solutions include but are not limited to the following:

- Industry standard
- Hardware independent
- Relatively simple to code
- Extensible and customizable

The purpose of SNMP is to enable the flow or exchange of management information between network nodes and enable management of the network environment. The SNMP protocol is an Application-level protocol and is implemented by an SNMP agent. SNMP management infrastructure consists of three main components:

- **SNMP managed node**—Any network-enabled device running an SNMP agent—for example, a hub, router, switch, Unix station, or Windows station.
- **SNMP agent**—A software agent that stores and retrieves device-specific information from its Management Information Base (MIB) and that is aware of local aspects of hardware or software. SNMP agents interact asynchronously with the SNMP network management station to supply information about exceeded thresholds and warnings and to apply changes (set thresholds) received from the management station.
- **SNMP network management station**—The focal point of the SNMP infrastructure that makes all management information available to NOC operators. It displays a list of warnings and errors reported by the agents, allows a certain amount of configuration control, and provides exhaustive statistical information on network operation. Management stations query agents, configure thresholds, and acknowledge warnings. This is used as yet another defense front in the overall corporate security domain.

Figure 3.2 shows the SNMP architecture.

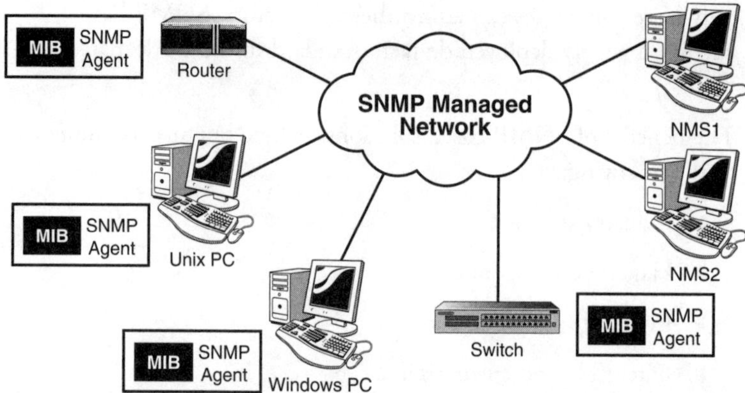

FIGURE 3.2
SNMP architecture.

In Microsoft environments, an SNMP managed node is a Windows workstation; an SNMP agent is a software component called SNMP Service; and the SNMP network management station is third-party enterprise software. A few predominant network management station products exist, with HP OpenView being the most well-known product. Similar solutions are available from Sun, IBM, and DEC, and an open source network management product called OpenNMS is also available.

The SNMP protocol exists in three versions: SNMPv1, SNMPv2, and SNMPv3. SNMPv3 was approved as an Internet standard by the Internet Engineering Standards Group in March 2002. Its primary difference from prior versions is that it provides security mechanisms to authenticate the origin of data, verify the integrity of data, ensure the privacy of data, and make messages time sensitive to prevent replay attacks.

It is important to recognize that SNMP agents are implemented by a variety of vendors and that each implementation can be affected differently by inherent protocol vulnerabilities. Some SNMP implementations might contain decoding problems that make a device vulnerable to denials of service, buffer overflows, or hostile takeover attacks. Countermeasures include disabling SNMP, filtering outside access to SNMP services and ports, and allowing only SNMP traffic on management networks. See the CERT Advisory CA-2002-03 for vulnerability and workaround information about specific SNMP implementations.

SNMP Management Information Base

SNMP defines standards for device information organization and communication between agents and management stations. The following are two standards that are included in SNMP:

- **Structure of Management Information (SMI)**—Covered in RFC 1902, this is an OSI standard that governs how a data structure should be organized. The purpose of maintaining a database of management information is to make the information easily accessible and organize it in a logical manner. Management information within devices is organized into a hierarchical structure of objects that have properties and values. SNMP follows the logical structure, objects, properties, and values as defined by SMI. SNMP is employed to read these values and adjust them as appropriate.
- **Abstract Syntax Notation One (ASN.1)**—The syntax standard for all SNMP messages between agents and network management stations. Because ASN.1 is a standard, it provides reliable interoperability between different vendors.

Management Information Base (MIB), now in its second revision (MIB II, RFC 1213), is the data storage facility that houses SMI-compatible data structures in the SNMP agent. MIB exposes vendor-specific and device-specific information to the SNMP agent running on the device, thereby making it available to the management infrastructure. Examples of data available through MIB are an IP address, routing table, open TCP sessions, subnet mask, free disk space, current CPU utilization, and so on. For each object stored in the MIB, several properties are defined, such as the name of the object, unique identifier, description, data type, and access permissions. When requesting the object data, properties are returned with corresponding values.

Certain object properties, such as CPU utilization or number of FTP sessions, are read-only; others can be configured from the central location.

Messages, Communities, and Trap Destinations

Management stations and agents exchange information over UDP using the default port 161 for general messages and default port 162 for traps. Normally, the network management station sends a request for data and an SNMP agent retrieves that data from the MIB and delivers it back to the network management station. However, the SNMP agent is also allowed to initiate communication with the station when a trap event occurs. A *trap event* is a trigger for an alarm to be generated and delivered to the management station. An alarm can be generated by unauthorized system usage, by exceeding configured thresholds, or by some types of hardware failure. The four major types of messages are explained in the following list:

- `GET`—Used and initiated by the management station to request information from the managed node. This request is accepted and processed by the agent.
- `GET-NEXT`—Used in the same way as `GET` to request the next object after the first object in a group was requested. This sort of enumeration is convenient for requesting arrays of data. For example, when retrieving a list of open TCP connections, a few different connections can exist, but they all belong to the same type of object in the MIB.
- `GET-BULK`—Used to indicate that maximum datagram transfer size should be used when pulling large amounts of management data, initiating the transfer from the management station. Again, the agent is the processing and transmitting component in this case.
- `SET`—This type of message is used when a MIB object property value must be changed, providing that it has read/write access permissions. This communication is sent from the management station and accepted and processed by the agent committing the changes to its MIB.
- `TRAP`—Also known as `NOTIFY` message. Trap events trigger trap messages to be sent from the agent to the management station. These trap events are defined by the management station and usually represent critical device conditions. The agent submits these traps, and the management station processes them, generating an alarm. Alarms can be acknowledged after they have been looked at by the network management personnel. SNMP traps are submitted on an asynchronous basis.

- `INFORM`—Allows the exchange of trap information between several management stations without having to query agents again.

Trap Destinations

Every agent has to be configured with at least one trap destination to be capable of sending traps. A *trap destination* is essentially an IP address, an IPX address, or the hostname of a target management station running SNMP management software that can accept and process traps and generate alarms. Trap destination is a very important security configuration that, if modified, can reveal a lot of information about the host and network infrastructure to unauthorized individuals.

Communities

All agents and management stations must belong to an SNMP community. *Communities* can be thought of as shared strings, and their purpose is to provide a basic form of authenticating SNMP messages. They can almost be thought of as workgroups or domains in the SNMP world, although they share absolutely no relationship. SNMP and management stations that belong to the same community can accept messages from each other and communicate as defined in the community properties. Depending on your SNMP agent implementation, you could set whether this should be a read-only communication and from which hosts the SNMP agent should accept messages.

You need to define hard-to-guess community strings to prevent security holes from appearing in the network. The trouble with community strings in SNMPv1 and SNMPv2 is that they are passed in plain text, which makes them vulnerable to packet sniffing. After a community string becomes known or is guessed, an attacker can gain a lot of information about the host being queried, pivotal configuration settings, and potential system vulnerabilities. In SNMPv3, additional privacy measures make the detection of the community string more difficult.

Specifics of SNMPv2

SNMPv2 is based on the first version of the protocol and is designed to extend the functionality of its predecessor somewhat. Similar to SNMPv1, SNMPv2 is based on SMI. However, it introduces new data types and enhances some existing ones. It also implements SMI modules, the capability to group different information into modules, and capability and compliance statements.

SNMPv2 implements two new protocol operations, or message types: GET-BULK and INFORM, which aren't supported in the previous version. Also, packet data units (PDUs) formats are not compatible between the two protocols. Because of message format and type enhancements, the two versions are effectively rendered incompatible.

To manage all SNMP devices regardless of their version, an SNMPv2-based management environment has to either use SNMP proxies to translate messages between versions or use management products that are capable of identifying and adapting to the version of SNMP running on each managed device. SNMP *proxies* act as intermediaries between management hosts and managed devices that do not share the same communication standard. Their purpose is to receive messages from the management host, analyze the request, and issue the appropriate version command or commands to the target device. Proxies collect the response or responses and forward these to the network management station. In some instances, one SNMPv2 request is translated to several SNMPv1 requests due to message type enhancements in v2.

Recent versions of Cisco IOS software support all three versions of SNMP standards and eliminate the need for proxies when managing Cisco hardware.

RMON

The Remote Monitoring (RMON) specification can be considered an extension to the SNMP standard and is based on RFC 1271. It was defined in the early 1990s and is based on the similar standards as SNMP. It also relies on the MIB structure of information and SMI. As seen in RFC 1271, availability of RMON statistics and information can prove pivotal in designing and assessing network security. Its purpose is to deliver network information grouped into the following major monitoring elements:

- **Statistics group**—Contains statistical information collected by an RMON probe from each of the configured interfaces on the device. It provides detailed counter information, characterizing network traffic on each monitored interface. Reported numbers include
    - Packets dropped, sent
    - Bytes sent
    - Broadcast packets and multicast packets
    - CRC errors, runts, giants, collisions
    - Fragments, jabbers
    - Counters for packets in the byte size ranges of 64–128, 128–256, 256–512, 512–1024, and 1024–1518
- **History group**—As the name suggests, this group includes information that is sampled over a period of time at regular intervals and is stored for later analysis. It includes items sampled, sampling intervals, and number of samples.
- **Alarm group**—If alarm thresholds are configured on an RMON-monitored device, statistics data is sampled periodically to be compared to threshold values. If threshold levels are exceeded, an alarm is generated and posted to the alarm table.
- **Host group**—Contains basic statistical information on the hosts discovered in the network. This information includes host addresses, number of packets sent and received, number of multicast and broadcast transmissions, and other pertinent information.
- **HostTopN group**—Designed to prepare top lists of hosts based on certain configurable criteria. It can be used to compile top error lists, for example, and identify major sources of errors and faulty or improperly configured equipment in the network. It also can reveal break-in attempts and brute-force incursions. Information included here is statistics, hosts being rated, and duration and sampling rate of the compilation.

- **Matrix group**—Stores statistics on conversations between participating hosts. Each time a new conversation is initialized, it is verified with the group and is added if missing. Information in the matrix group includes source and destination addresses, packet counts, bytes transferred, and number of errors. This information can prove indispensable when analyzing and planning network usage, as well as when designing IDSs.
- **Filter group**—Contains streams of packets that are logged if they match a specified formula. This allows for detailed application-based or protocol-based communication statistics analysis on a given device. It can also be used for event generation. Criteria that can be specified include various packet parameters.
- **Packet capture group**—As the name implies, it allows the logging and analysis of actual packets. Parameters that can be specified include capture buffer size, status, and number of captured packets.
- **Event group**—Controls event generation and notification on a monitored device. It works together with the alarm group, controlling the amount and periodicity of alerts. It provides information about the event type, event description, and time of the latest occurrence.

Implementing all these groups isn't mandatory, and most vendors opt to implement the groups that provide the most basic and fundamental information first. However, some of the groups are dependent on others and cannot be implemented without implementing other groups as well. For example, the alarm group depends on the implementation of the event group.

RMON can provide crucial information for the following security purposes:

- Network security and real-time host metrics and configuration.
- Network monitoring and operations information critical to supporting networks and ensuring proactive monitoring, including alarms.

- Matrix information that describes data flows, characters, and quality and supplies network and security designers with one of the most critical parts of information needed to ensure effective designs.
- Packet capture, traffic analysis, and decoding capabilities necessary for troubleshooting and design.
- Historical information for trend analysis, baselining, and performance monitoring, needed to effectively design and support networks. It is used by both groups: network operations and network architecture/engineering personnel.
- Network accounting and billing applications can use data provided by RMON for business and financial purposes.

Cisco Systems includes RMON functionality in its IOS software. However sophisticated, this information is only as useful as it is accessible. Centralized RMON configuration management, analysis, and tuning is necessary, and several software packages are available to be deployed as add-ons to HP Openview, IBM, Sun, and DEC solutions. Some can even be operated independently without the need for implementing expensive management infrastructure.

NETWORK MANAGEMENT STATIONS

Network management stations collect a large amount of critical network information and are considered to be the most likely targets of intruder attacks. These network management stations are very visible in the network because most systems "chat" with the station on a consistent basis. Make sure network management stations are secure physically and network-wise. It would be reasonable to implement a separate management subnet and ensure that it is protected by at least a router with an access list.

You should be aware that the traffic between monitoring agents and management stations can slow down your network if you have a large number of hosts. Polling can take from as little as 800 bytes to up to more than 2 kilobytes per host. Multiply this by the number of hosts on your network, and the traffic load can become prohibitive.

Workstations

Workstation security is often overlooked, but this is one of the most attractive areas to intruders because it is the path of least resistance to deploying an attack. It is not unusual for users to be naive and to occasionally click links when they read "click this link" or to open emails with potentially suspect or downright ominous subject lines, especially if the company is not in an IT-related industry. Average non-IT users are not as aware of Internet risks as their IT counterparts are. (Note the usage of the word *average* here. It means that in every environment, you are likely to encounter exceptionally aware and, unfortunately, exceptionally unaware individuals. A single case of exceptional unawareness is enough to bring a network down.) Unfortunately, Internet risks are not the only risks that can exist in an organization. Basic user protection controls from Internet risks are covered in Chapter 2, but the following is a list of other risks you must protect against:

- Workstation and laptop theft
- Natural disasters, fire (arson)
- Physical access by unauthorized personnel (visitors)
- Physical failures of workstation components

See Chapter 7, "Physical Security, Disaster Recovery, and Business Continuity," for more information on these subjects.

You can't prevent things such as natural disasters and physical failures of components; however, you can prevent catastrophic information loss when a disaster occurs by implementing a corporate-wide backup policy. A comprehensive policy should mandate the storage of all company files on a dedicated network server that is located in a secure environment and that runs nightly backups. Backup tapes should be properly labeled with date and volume information, rotated, and stored offsite for further protection. One item many administrators overlook is the testing of backup media. It is not enough to run a nightly backup; the backup must be tested to ensure that it can actually be used to restore data. In addition, you might want to test the tape on various devices to ensure it works on other devices and not just yours.

In the area of theft, two solutions are available. The most obvious is a security lock. Every laptop comes with a hook for a security lock that can be used to deter all theft attempts. Similar locks exist for desktop workstations, as well. (These devices are particularly useful in schools, universities, walk-in printing shops, Internet cafes, and other public places that can be difficult to control.) To protect the information that must reside on a laptop or workstation, encrypt individual files or encrypt the file system. The Windows Encrypting File System (EFS) makes it impossible to read file information without appropriate login credentials.

If your company has regular visitors who might pose a risk, consider buying disk drive locks to ensure that critical information cannot be extracted using a disk drive. Some manufacturers now produce workstations without floppy drives. Securing floppy access also prevents employees from bringing in infected files. In addition to physical prevention, train employees to always log off or lock their unattended workstations. Combined, these methods will also prevent a visitor from booting a system from a floppy drive.

Servers

Everything discussed in the workstation section applies just as well to the servers. Naturally, servers are more sensitive to attacks. Therefore, all servers (and as much network equipment as possible) must be isolated in a server room or an ISP co-location facility and must be locked to prevent any type of unauthorized physical access. Visitors to these premises must be justified and supervised. No matter how rigorously your software is configured to guard your network from hackers, if a nighttime cleaning person can accidentally switch off the box while dusting it or knock a $15,000 piece of equipment over, your protective measures have failed. One major corporation spent thousands of dollars investigating how someone was sabotaging server backup tapes, only to find that the magnetic interference from a motorized floor buffer was erasing the tapes in their storage rack. Make sure that access to the room is limited to authorized personnel only; use server racks that have locking capabilities; and when selecting server hardware, assess its physical security controls in addition to its other features. We talk more about locking down servers in Chapter 4.

UNDERSTANDING THE BASIC SECURITY CONCEPTS OF MEDIA

Understand the basic security concepts of storage media devices.

Chapter 2 provided details of securing communications on most layers of the OSI model except the Physical layer (layer 1). If an attack is launched against the signal on the wire, hackers might be able to copy information as it flows in the form of bits. This might not be as dangerous if an appropriate software encryption mechanism is employed in the transmission. Depending on the communication medium, hackers might be able to steal either information or bandwidth.

Coaxial Cable

Coaxial cables are made of a core wire with an outer metallic shield used to reduce interference. Often, the shield is made of a metallic Web, with or without an additional metal-foil wrapping surrounding the core conductor. The cable is then surrounded by a plastic covering, called a *sheath*. Coaxial cables are no longer deployed en masse, but they are still abundant in legacy environments. Two types of coax cables are used: 10BASE-2 and 10BASE-5. On a 10BASE-2 cable, a signal can travel a distance of 185 meters at a speed of 10Mbps before it appreciably attenuates. On a thicker 10BASE-5 cable, signals can travel a distance of up to 500 meters at the same speed.

Because the electrical signal is conducted by a single core wire, someone can easily tap the wire by piercing the sheath. He would then be able to eavesdrop on the conversations of all the hosts attached to the segment because 10BASE-2 coaxial cabling implements broadband transmission technology and assumes many hosts connected to the same wire. Coaxial cable is still popular in campus areas, especially 10BASE-5 (or Thicknet), because of its greater transmission length. Coaxial cables have no physical transmission security and can be easily tapped without interrupting regular transmissions and without detection.

UTP/STP

Unshielded twisted pair (UTP) is the main cabling type in LANs today. Seven types of UTP cable are available, but the most popular and widely deployed is category five (CAT5). CAT5E allows transmissions of up to 1Gbps at a distance of 100 meters, and it is made up of eight individual wires twisted in pairs (hence the name). Twisted pairs prevent crosstalk between the wires. UTP has no shielding and is prone to radio frequency interference (RFI) and electromagnetic interference (EMI); however, its installation is relatively simple and its cost low. In *half-duplex* deployments, only four of the eight wires are used and a device might not simultaneously transmit and receive. In a *full-duplex* (switched) environment, all eight wires are used: Two pairs are used to send, and the other two pairs are used to receive data. UTP uses RJ45 cable connectors for cable termination and connectivity. UTP is used in Ethernet topologies and is a shared communication medium unless a switch is used, in which case Unicast communications are conducted between the devices involved.

STP is analogous to UTP with a slight modification: It is *shielded*, which means it can withstand EMI and RFI much better than UTP does. STP is used in token-ring topologies.

Both UTP and STP can be tapped, although it is physically a little trickier than tapping coaxial cable because of the physical structure of STP and UTP cable. The major difference from coaxial cable is the connection method. Whereas coaxial cable runs from computer to computer, twisted pair cabling runs from computer to concentrator—hub, repeater, bridge, switch, Multi-Station Access Unit (MSAU), and so on. Therefore, the service is more vulnerable to abuse and theft in those concentration spots. You need to keep concentrators in the server room (if cabling distances permit) or in wiring closets. At a minimum, keep distribution and core devices secured from unauthorized access. At the same time, authorized personnel must have ready access to patch panels, and cables must be clearly marked and available for visual inspection.

Fiber

Fiber-optic cabling has many advantages over more traditional twisted pair cabling. Fiber is designed for short- and long-range transmissions at speeds higher than 1Gbps. It uses light pulses for signal transmission, making it immune to RFI and EMI. However, some disadvantages are that it is still quite expensive compared to more traditional cabling, it is less forgiving of physical stress, and it is more difficult to install.

As far as security is concerned, fiber cabling eliminates the tapping of electrical signals that is possible in the case of twisted pair and coax. Tapping fiber cable without service interruption and specially constructed equipment is impossible, which makes stealing service or eavesdropping on traffic significantly more difficult.

Infrared, RF, and Microwave

One obvious disadvantage of open-air signal transmission technologies is the lack of clearly defined boundaries. Wired networks have a physical signal path that can be secured. In broadcast, however, it is theoretically possible for anyone to tune a receiver to the frequency of your transmission and eavesdrop on it without anyone knowing about it. In the early days of wireless LAN technologies, it was even possible to use network services without authenticating. All an intruder had to do was to choose a site and do a site survey by scanning the frequency bands to find services. Signal spread spectrum technology made wireless transmission somewhat more secure, but only to a certain point. Frequency-hopping sequences are not secret; instead they are openly published standards.

EXAM TIP

Know which types of media are susceptible to which types of interference.

The fact that modern wireless facilities have security controls that prevent unauthorized use of the medium and services does not make the open-air medium safe from eavesdropping. IR transmissions are considered safer than radio transmissions because the communicating devices use an invisible light spectrum range and require a direct line of sight with each other. This makes eavesdropping on the communications without being noticed more complicated. But the technology itself is not technically immune to eavesdropping; infrared signals can be recorded using cameras with infrared filters. The only way to be sure of wireless communication security is to use strong authentication algorithms such as PKI and to encrypt all your communications.

Removable Media

Removable media poses a security risk because of two main problems. First, classified or confidential information can be stolen, destroyed, or misused. The loss or exposure of business, financial, or consumer information can cause serious damage to a company's competitiveness or reputation. Second, system, policy, or infrastructure information can give intruders enough information to mount future attacks.

Why do companies use removable media? With the storage density and capacity available today, using removable media might not seem relevant. However, even if a company has a few storage area network (SAN) devices that provide terabytes of storage space, it still needs to back up its files and databases. Remember, offsite storage of backups is a crucial part of a disaster recovery plan. The second reason that some companies might still have large amounts of sensitive information on removable media is because they have relied on removable media at some point in the past to control access or provide additional storage and the media has not been disposed of yet.

Various types of removable media include tape, CD-R, hard drives, flash cards, and smart cards, and they are covered in detail in the following sections.

Tape

Tape devices use magnetic storage and are extremely popular in backup technologies because of the amount of data that can fit on a storage unit (tape). It is the medium of choice for backing up mission-critical systems that often contain sensitive customer information, databases, and files. Tape backups are also widely used to back up system configuration and account information, which means they often contain system Registry and network user account databases.

Several backup types can be employed in disaster recovery strategies, and they are not specific to tape devices. (See Chapter 7 for full coverage on backups.) For the purposes of this discussion, the security person needs to be aware of the most popular backup strategies, which are as follows:

- **Full backup**—Contains the entire set of data being backed up and is most sensitive to theft because the information it contains is readily available in full.

- **Incremental backup**—Works with the full backup and does not contain a full copy of the information. Instead, it contains all the information that was modified between the time of the incremental backup and previous incremental or full backup. In case of theft, incremental information taken out of context might or might not represent value to the offender, but it certainly represents risk to the company.
- **Differential backup**—Similar to incremental, with the only difference being that the archive flag is not reset after the differential backup is run. This causes every differential backup to copy information changed since the last full backup, regardless of when the last differential backup was made. This backup strategy is more risky in respect to theft because larger chunks of sequential data can be stored on tape the further away from the last full backup it gets.
- **Copy backup**—Very similar to a full backup in that it takes a complete snapshot of the system at the time of backup. The only difference between copy backup and full backup comes into play in database environments where transactional logging is employed. A copy backup takes a copy of the system as it is running at that moment, whereas a full backup commits the logs to the database first and then backs up the database. From a security perspective, the loss of a tape with a copy backup is tantamount to losing a tape with a full backup.

In addition to these backup strategies, companies employ tape rotation and retention policies to have a safety net if something goes wrong.

Backup is just one small part of an overall disaster recovery and contingency plan. Despite obvious security threats, backups must be done on a regular basis for every computer whose physical failure or loss would cause any amount of inconvenience. Every company should determine its own rotation and retention strategies, depending on the needs and nature of the information. Tapes that are going out of rotation and into archive must be stored offsite in safe deposit boxes or similar secure environments. Offsite storage ensures business continuity in the case of natural or manmade disasters. See Chapter 7 for more information.

CDR

Recordable or rewritable compact discs (CD-Rs or CD-RWs, respectively) can be used for the same purpose as tape backups in smaller companies where information might not change as frequently or where the volume of information is smaller. However, CDs are typically used for backup or distribution of individual projects to clients, offline content distribution, proprietary software or algorithm transfer, or similar purposes. This does not diminish the sensitivity of the information, and hence protection measures discussed in the previous section apply to CDs as well.

If a CD is no longer useful or is not working correctly, it must be made safe to discard. Formal as well as physical processes can be used to do this.

Disposal of Media

The following three concepts apply to all removable media units:

- **Declassification**—A formal process of assessing the risk involved in discarding particular information. You should consider all possible situations if this information ends up in the wrong hands, becomes known to the public, and so forth. Is it possible to use it against the company? Is it proprietary? Would it damage the company's market posture or competitive plans? Would it cause litigation or civil or criminal liabilities? If the information being discarded is innocuous or obsolete and therefore does not present any risk to the company, it can safely be declassified if no other threats are uncovered through the risk assessment.
- **Sanitization**—The process of removing the information from the media as fully as possible, making it almost impossible to restore it even for data recovery specialists. Sanitization has no effect on the classification of the information. Depending on the media type, sanitization might or might not apply. To sanitize media, you can use a process such as magnetic degaussing or magnetic overwriting.
- **Destruction**—Physically destroying the media and, therefore, the information stored on it. Other than destruction, there are no safe methods of completely removing all traces of information stored on a removable media device.

Because of the nature of CDs and CD-Rs, sanitization is not applicable to these media, and either declassification or destruction should be used (or both). Concerning destruction, only authorized, cleared personnel should ever have access to the media decommissioned for destruction.

Every company should have media disposal policies in place. It is important to follow company disposal standards and to know what obligations contracts with other companies or agencies impose on media disposal requirements. A listing of Department of Defense media disposal standards can be found at `http://www.cerberussystems.com/INFOSEC/stds/sanitize.htm`.

Hard Drives and Disks

Hard drives and disks are magnetic media, and in addition to destruction and declassification, sanitization can be used. The processes employed by sanitization are

- **Degaussing**—Also called *demagnetizing*, it is applicable to magnetic storage devices. Degaussing works by applying a reverse magnetic field to the magnetic media and reducing magnetic density to null. This makes all the previously stored data unreadable. Degaussing is considered very safe.
- **Overwriting**—Applicable to magnetic storage devices, it involves an operation of completely rewriting every addressable bit pattern on the media with a single bit pattern (all 0s), verifying that the operation was successful, rewriting the bit pattern again using the opposite bit pattern (all 1s), and verifying again. This process must be repeated as many times as is required by the classification level of the information being sanitized.
- **Disconnection**—For volatile memory devices such as RAM, all sources of power must be disconnected including backup and BIOS batteries and the computing device must be grounded before sanitization is considered complete.
- **Removal of information**—For laser printers and copiers on which a large amount of declassified information is printed and copied, you need to remove traces of the classified information from the drums for the device to be considered sanitized.

NOTE

Physical Security on Computer Systems Just because systems don't include ports for removable media (such as a caddy for removable hard drives) doesn't mean somebody can't attach such a device. Today, compact USB-based hard disks small enough to fit on a keychain offer up to 2GB of storage space and can conceivably be mounted on any system with a USB port. Not only does this underscore the overwhelming need for physical security on computer systems (thereby denying intruders the opportunity to use such devices), but it also argues that publicly accessible machines should be locked down so that unwanted devices cannot be mounted or used on that equipment.

Flashcards and Nonvolatile Memory

Flashcards and EEPROM devices are contained in many devices of varying sizes and purposes and can contain traces of classified or confidential information, such as customer data in the case of flashcards or proprietary software in the case of EEPROM. Companies should consider sanitizing or destroying these components when upgrading or discarding equipment.

Smart Cards

Smart cards are widely used in cell phones and mobile devices to store customer ID information for providers to identify their subscribers in the network. They also store a personal phone book, Short Message Service (SMS) messages, and a log of incoming and outgoing calls. In corporate computing requirements, smart cards are replacing conventional username/password authentication mechanisms because they allow personal X.509 digital certificates to be used for user authentication and network logon purposes. Remember from the encryption discussion in Chapter 2 that digital signatures are impossible to forge and X.509 certificates are used in digital signing. Therefore, the company must be extremely vigilant regarding how these smart cards are used, distributed, and serviced. A single lost or stolen card can pose a company-wide risk of an intruder gaining unauthorized access to the site.

Smart cards often carry employee and company credentials printed on them, which makes identifying the target easy. Clearly, the right smart card in the wrong hands is a recipe for disaster. Therefore, companies must institute and enforce extremely strict smart card policies that make employees treat these identification devices with extreme caution and report lost or stolen cards immediately. Administrators, in turn, can revoke issued certificates or disable user accounts, making the smart card a piece of useless plastic.

Another area of concern for the company in this case is disgruntled employees and headcount reduction. A process must be in place to ensure that all employees leaving the company relinquish their cards in a timely fashion. Administrators can then put the certificates stored on the cards on the revocation list and reprogram the cards to issue to new employees.

EXAM TIP

Know the types of removable media and the security risks involved with each.

UNDERSTANDING THE CONCEPTS OF SECURITY TOPOLOGIES

Understand the basic security concepts of security topologies.

The concepts of security topologies are based on firewalls and their application to specific network design scenarios. Topologies consist of hardware devices and security zones that are created with these devices. The remainder of this chapter provides an overview of how firewalls are used to segment the network into security zones and create various security topologies. The following security topics are covered in more detail in the following sections:

- Security zone topologies
- VLANs
- NAT
- Tunneling

Security Zones

The three major types of security topologies are as follows:

- Bastion host
- Screened host gateway
- Screened subnet gateway

Various combinations of these three basic security topologies can yield additional categories that combine the benefits and disadvantages of the fundamental topologies, but for the purposes of our discussion we will concentrate on these three.

Bastion Host

A *bastion host* is a dual-homed device—that is, a device with two network interfaces. It can be a specialized hardware device (Cisco PIX, Checkpoint Firewall, and so on); a router running access lists (most Cisco and other routers are capable of this); or a PC running Windows 2000 or later, Unix, or another operating system that supports routing rules definitions or traffic-filtering mechanisms. Any routing between the interfaces on the dual-homed device is disabled and specialized software (IP Security in Windows 2000, Cisco IOS, and so on) is configured to allow only certain types of traffic through while excluding the rest of the traffic.

This type of firewall secures the network by filtering communications based on different configurable criteria, such as port numbers (traffic type), source or destination IP addresses or IP subnets, whether the connection is a secondary connection to an already established communication session (file transfer requests of an FTP session), and so on. Regardless of hardware configuration, IP forwarding (routing) must be disabled between the two network interfaces and the process of forwarding packets between interfaces must be controlled by specialized software. A bastion host is used to connect the outside network (unsecure extranet) with the inside network (secured intranet), and in most cases, it is one of the first devices public traffic hits on its way into your network.

The more specialized this device or software is, the more unlikely it is that someone will be able to exploit a flaw in its overall design. Therefore, it is highly recommended that only specialized devices or machines dedicated to securing the network border be used as bastion hosts. The number and diversity of features and applications running on any given device are sometimes referred to as the *attack surface.* Keeping the attack surface small makes a more secure bastion host.

In addition to the purposes outlined previously, a specialized solution is more likely to maintain desirable performance levels without introducing bottlenecks and lags.

Bastion host solutions are most common to small corporate networks, small branches or remote locations, and home office or telecommuter environments. Figure 3.3 depicts the basic elements of a device built as the bastion host.

> NOTE
>
> **Dedicated Hardware and Software for Specific Purposes Is Secure** For smaller companies that are short on cash, this might seem too expensive, but using cobbled-together solutions opens the infrastructure to potentially devastating attacks that could ruin a small business. If you have a Web server exposed to the public, it should be just that: a Web server (that is, it should not host mailing and database applications). This is especially true about firewalls of any type or topology. A firewall device is the first line of defense against network intrusions, and the less software features that are installed on it, the smaller the attack surface is.

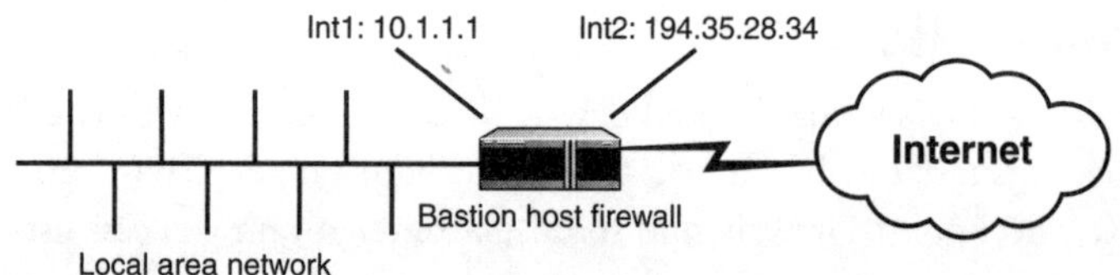

FIGURE 3.3
Bastion host firewall.

Screened Host Gateway

A *screened host gateway* is a packet-filtering device, usually also a router, which communicates only with a designated application gateway inside the secured network. No other traffic is allowed in or out of a screened host gateway. The basic functionality is the same as a bastion host; however, a few important differences exist. Unlike with a bastion host, the network design incorporates an application gateway. Traffic coming in from the Internet is filtered based on what is considered to be safe. If a data stream is deemed safe (based on the configuration), it is forwarded to the application gateway. The application gateway then determines how to handle this stream and redirects it to an appropriate information server or workstation in the network. The process works in reverse for outgoing communications. The screened host gateway ignores all outgoing traffic that is not coming from the application gateway.

An application gateway is a one-interface device, whereas a screened host gateway is a dual-homed device (just as a bastion host firewall is). Therefore, an application gateway does not need a special subnet—it can be just another network node in the corporate or production subnet as far as network design is concerned. An application gateway also runs a few application services (hence, the name), redirecting traffic it receives from the borderline filter to the systems inside the network. The borderline filter (screened host gateway) can also be configured to allow redirection of certain types of traffic considered to be safe directly to the systems inside the network. DNS requests or Telnet sessions are examples of such traffic.

Compared to a bastion host, the screened host gateway scenario is more likely to let certain types of offending traffic slip through unnoticed. In the case of a bastion host, all rules are configured on one device (if it's a pool of devices serving several redundant connections, the same configuration can be applied to other devices in the pool). With application gateways, two devices need to be configured very carefully: the borderline packet filter and the application gateway itself. This leaves room for unnoticed configuration errors and loopholes that might not be discovered until an attack has been executed, which is too late. Another reason this solution is less secure is because the packet filter is configured in a rather generic fashion, usually allowing "all or none" requests of configured types, which forwards all those requests to the application gateway indiscriminately. Because the application gateway's attack surface is significantly greater than that of the bastion host, greater potential exists that the application gateway can be compromised.

Application gateways do provide greater flexibility, albeit at the expense of security. It might be more convenient to take advantage of the modularity implemented with the two types of devices in this scenario, each responsible for its own functions. Packet filtering rules can be difficult to configure and even more difficult to maintain on one device where you have to manage permit/reject rules for more than one internal system in the absence of an application gateway. The difficulty of creating rules for a single device that must allow only specific types of traffic to reach only specific hosts can create security holes. With a bastion host, administrators often create rules that are too permissive, especially after receiving numerous complaints from special case users who cannot receive legitimate traffic. In these instances, a screened host gateway can be more secure.

Figure 3.4 depicts a typical screened host gateway deployment set of elements.

Screened Subnet Gateway

The third type of topology is called a *screened subnet gateway.* Screened subnet gateway architecture includes two screened host gateway devices that isolate the LAN from the Internet, creating what is known as a *screened subnet,* or *DMZ,* between them. The architecture also includes a proxy server (bastion host).

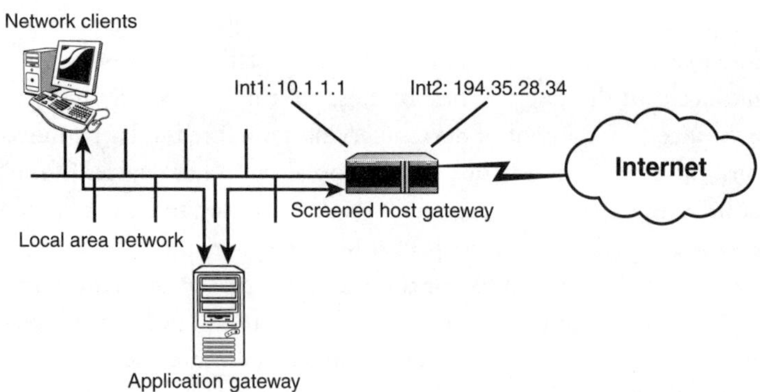

FIGURE 3.4
A screened host gateway.

This architecture is essentially a combination of the bastion host and screened host gateway architectures discussed in the previous section. Traditionally, this approach offers the best solution because traffic is controlled more granularly and the design has built-in redundancy; it isolates the internal network with more than one layer of security. Public inbound traffic is restricted to and is allowed only in the DMZ subnet. Outbound traffic flows through the DMZ, which creates anonymity for the requesting clients on the LAN. The only obvious disadvantage of this mixed architecture is that it is more complex than the other two; however, the complexity is partially offset by the fact that different components of this mixed architecture have their own functions and areas of responsibility. In effect, the planning requires the most effort, not the actual configuration.

Consider the deployment scenario depicted in Figure 3.4. In the DMZ are application servers the public needs to be able to access to communicate with internal clients. You would therefore place certain critical application systems inside that subnet, as shown in Figure 3.5. For example, your email servers, Web servers, DNS servers, FTP servers, and other public-facing information servers would need to be located in the screened subnet. This does not compromise the security of these application systems because at least one bastion host still exists on the borderline between the DMZ subnet and the unsecure extranet. This bastion host would be configured to allow communications initiated from the public, nontrusted clients specific to the applications the DMZ servers provide (in this case, SMTP [TCP port 25], DNS [TCP 53], FTP [TCP 21], and HTTP [TCP 80]).

All other communications from the public to internal clients on the LAN or any other communications not explicitly allowed into the DMZ would be rejected. Optionally, you could place a rule to forward certain requests to certain internal machines, but this has to be justified by corporate or production requirements.

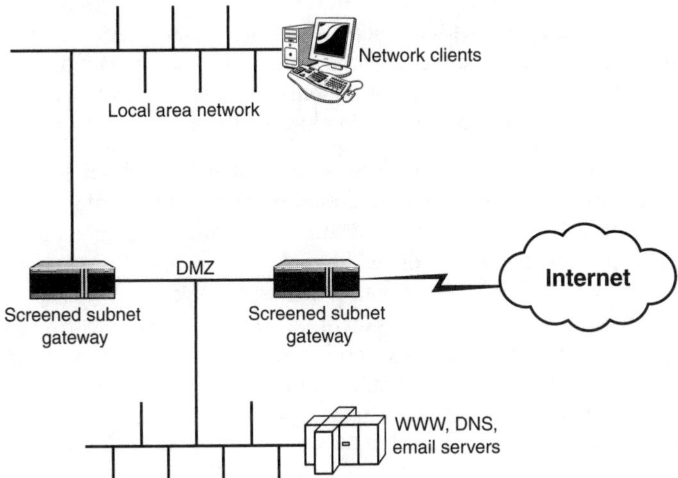

FIGURE 3.5
A screened subnet gateway.

Now, you can install any other application gateways in the DMZ to make external resources available to your internal clients, and vice versa. This application gateway can provide an extra layer of security in cases where Application-layer security is necessary. Thus, administrators can have control over traffic leaving internal networks and initiating bidirectional communications with the outside world on a user level. Good examples of an application gateway are a CERN-compliant proxy server, Microsoft Internet Security and Acceleration (ISA) Server 2000, or some similar software product. From an internal client's perspective, they can either be configured to talk to the outside world directly, only receiving email, DNS, and corporate intranet Web services from the DMZ, or be restricted to talking only to application gateways and information servers in the DMZ. An external borderline bastion host would then be responsible for blocking outbound communications that originate internally.

With a screened subnet topology, two local subnet IP addresses are needed to implement this architecture. One subnet address is used within the DMZ, and another subnet (which can be subnetted further) is used for internal network segments.

IP ADDRESSING

A few words need to be mentioned here about IP addressing. Using publicly routed IP addressing for your LAN design is very unsecure. Not only does it allow direct communications between outside hosts and internal clients (at least in theory), but it also wastes scarce public IP address space. After Internet Protocol Version 6 (IPv6) is widely accepted and deployed, more IP addresses will be available for public communications. Nonetheless, even without the problem of scarcity, using private addressing internally is much more secure and much more maintainable.

The "Network Address Translation" section that appears later in this chapter provides more information on public and private addressing. For the moment, suffice it to say that the combination of NAT plus private IP addresses helps avoid the need to renumber internal networks if an organization ever contemplates changing from one service provider to another. Because ISPs are the primary source of public IP addresses, you can sidestep the need to renumber entire networks (only the public interfaces in your network need to change) only by avoiding the use of public addresses.

EXAM TIP

Know the three major types of security zones.

Disadvantages of this architecture are the complexity of implementation and the possibility of firewall policy violations when conduits are administratively allowed from the borderline firewall through the DMZ and into the internal network. However, this second disadvantage is not unique to the screened subnet scenario. This scenario is by far the most flexible and secure topology because of its capability to completely eliminate inside/outside communications and conduct everything through a strictly controlled middleman called the DMZ.

DMZs

A DMZ can be viewed as a layer of privacy between the corporate infrastructure and the Internet, exposing only those systems that must be known to the public. Strict authentication and encryption can add to the security the two firewall devices provide to make the internal network impenetrable. Demilitarized zones can also be created with just one firewall device with three network interface cards on board, as depicted in Figure 3.6.

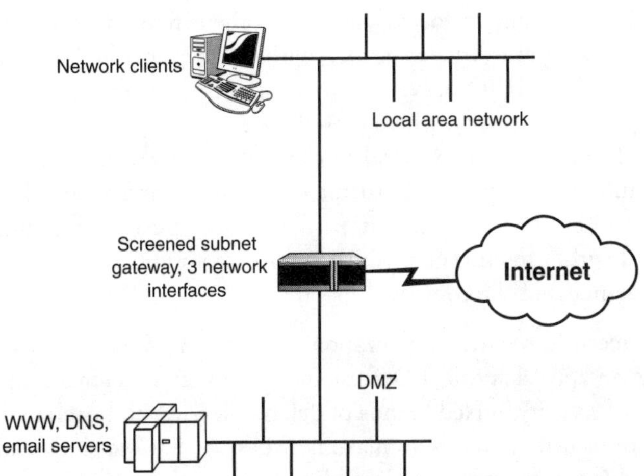

FIGURE 3.6
An alternative DMZ configuration.

In Figure 3.6, an intranet and the Internet are separated by a single device and both of these segments are attached to separate interfaces. The third interface is attached to a separate network segment that effectively is an alternative DMZ and an extranet. This alternative solution compromises a little bit of security (an intruder has to break only one firewall as opposed to two), but with proper planning, good hardware, and solid configuration, this is highly unlikely. Companies can opt to use this method in situations where security is a must but the budget does not allow for two well-designed firewalls.

Intranets

As can be inferred from the discussion in the preceding section, an *intranet* is the portion of a network that belongs to and is controlled by a company. It is not necessarily just the inside LAN segment; it can also include the DMZ segment, WAN links to remote locations, and the remote locations. The definition of an intranet is somewhat blurry, and opinion varies as to whether a DMZ can properly be considered part of the intranet. However, one rule is that if a portion of the infrastructure belongs to the company and the communications links are managed and secured by the company, these elements are encompassed in the definition of an intranet.

Security requirements for intranets (with the exception of the DMZ) are usually significantly lower than with extranets or the Internet, although this might not be true in certain organizations. (A good example is a university, where firewalls are used to protect staff networks from student networks.) In classical examples, some access separation exists between departments, branches, and geographical locations, but by and large, company resources are accessible and trusted within the intranet, which is open to authorized personnel and members of the company.

More recently, security organizations such as SANS have been advocating an approach called Defense in Depth that calls for multiple layers of security, mixed brands of defense devices, and overlapping areas of security coverage to make network penetration significantly more difficult for attackers. In addition, the deployment of security devices within the intranet can help contain breaches of network security and limit the scope of an attack.

Extranets

The notion of an *extranet* is even blurrier than that of an intranet. It refers to the practice of allowing partners, whose network space is outside the company's control, to use some of the resources available on the intranet, usually in the DMZ.

The extranet is a public portion of the company's IT infrastructure that allows certain resources to be accessed by outside users, such as partners and resellers, with proper authorization and authentication. The DMZ serves as a security cushion between the extranet and the intranet. Although it is technically located within the intranet, the DMZ can serve as the extranet as well. Resources on the extranet trust and honor only requests that have been authenticated using a reliable authentication technology such as PKI or digital certificates.

Virtual Local Area Networks

A *virtual local area network (VLAN)* unites network nodes logically into the same broadcast domain regardless of whether they are physically united. A VLAN can create a logically stable environment when computers are not physically stationary or are not physically close. For example, network administrators and technical personnel can roam a complex corporate environment but, regardless of their physical connection locations, still need access to their administrative resources.

At the same time, a VLAN can allow one broadcast domain to be split into two or more domains that restrict access to certain network resources. This can be a handy addition to user management and security strategy for the company.

VLANs are implemented using a technology known as *tagging*. The 802.1Q standard defines a Q-tag mechanism that allows marking frame headers with tags that identify VLANs. VLAN-aware network devices look for Q-tags in frames and make appropriate forwarding decisions. A VLAN is therefore a software solution that enables the creation of unique Q-tag identifiers to be assigned to ports on network switching devices. One switch port can be a member of many VLANs.

Network Address Translation

Network address translation (NAT) enables the use of public IP address space by devices that use private IP address space. A NAT device creates and maintains mappings between private IP address space, invisible to the outside world, and public IP address space that can communicate with external resources.

Private address ranges, defined in RFC 1918, are special address ranges in class A, B, and C networks that can freely be used by organizations internally. Their key feature is that addresses within these ranges are considered nonroutable on the Internet. If your organization is connected to the Internet, it is recommended that private address ranges be used on the LAN.

Private addressing through NAT provides three major benefits. First, routable network address space is preserved because the Internet community is running out of available addresses rather quickly. The second benefit is that because private addressing is nonroutable, it is harder (but not impossible) for intruders to penetrate the perimeter of your network. Third, if you change Internet service providers, your public IP address changes, but your private network addresses can remain the same.

As a security measure, NAT deprives intruders of the direct access to LAN workstations that they would have with public IP addresses. Instead, intruders must break through the NAT and, in most cases, a firewall that secures the Internet connection.

Workstations communicate with outside networks through the NAT device. Each outgoing request dynamically creates a mapping on the NAT device, and NAT proceeds with the outgoing request, acting as a proxy. When it gets the reply, it looks up the mapping and forwards the information to the original requester. In the same fashion, static mappings can be created to instruct NAT to forward certain requests to certain hosts on the inside network.

In a variation of NAT called port address translation (PAT), the idea is the same, but instead of creating address-based mappings, port-based mappings are employed on a higher level up the OSI model. This becomes useful in situations where IP addresses on the public interface of a NAT device are scarce, allowing many internal IP addresses to be mapped to a single external IP address and differentiating between the channels using port assignments.

NAT can also be used for address translation between multiple protocols, which measurably improves security and provides for more interoperability in heterogeneous networks. For more information about NAT, see RFC 2663 at `http://www.ietf.org/rfc/rfc2663.txt`.

The private address ranges are as follows:

- **Class A**—10.0.0.0 network is reserved for private addressing. Valid host IDs are from 10.0.0.1 to 10.255.255.254.
- **Class B**—172.16.0.0–172.31.0.0 networks are reserved for private addressing. Valid host IDs are from 172.16.0.1 to 172.31.255.254.
- **Class C**—192.168.0.0 network is reserved for private addressing. Valid host IDs are from 192.168.0.1 to 192.168.255.254.

For companies that do not have and do not plan to have any Internet connectivity, any network address range will work as long as it accommodates the company's host number needs.

> NOTE
>
> **NAT Does Not Work Well with IPSec**
> A NAT device must strip the headers off incoming packets and attach its own headers before sending the packets on. This might not be possible in the IPSec channel where information is encrypted.

Another address range to keep in mind when designing IP address space is Microsoft's Automatic Private IP Addressing (APIPA). Microsoft implemented APIPA in Windows 98 and Windows 2000 clients. If these workstations are configured as DHCP clients and no DHCP server is available at the time of a DHCP lease request, a client automatically is configured with an address from 169.254.0.1 to 169.254.255.254.

Tunneling

Tunneling, also known as *virtual private networking (VPN)*, poses some particular security challenges. When using VPN with firewalls, you need to define a set of firewall rules that permits the tunneling. Unfortunately, after a VPN tunnel is created, it is considered a communication channel that has already passed necessary security checks. In most popular solutions, VPN traffic is not filtered by a firewall. After establishing a communications channel, a remote user could funnel any traffic through, bypassing the rules instituted by the firewall. Furthermore, when encryption is used in a tunnel, filtering is impossible because the firewall does not see the contents due to end-to-end encryption between the peers.

Some topological solutions are possible for these problems. One such solution is to deploy the VPN host in parallel with an internal firewall and then force decrypted traffic to pass through the firewall. Another possible solution is to use the VPN features of some firewall products such as PIX and Checkpoint firewalls. In addition, the threat of malicious traffic traveling through VPN is greatly reduced if the remote host employs adequate security measures. This can require more IT support for remote users, especially less technically sophisticated users, but it can greatly enhance security.

NOTE

Creating VPN Solutions for Home Offices When creating VPN solutions for the purpose of telecommuting and working from home, keep in mind that requiring the use of an application gateway for public Web and DNS traffic for remote users can cause performance problems at higher volumes. Such a requirement means the client must send and receive large volumes of encrypted traffic that could safely travel directly between public Web sites and the remote client without having to go through the corporate VPN channel. Encryption/decryption, unless it is performed by dedicated hardware, is resource intensive for both the client and server. Be sure to factor in the costs of dedicated hardware or existing hardware upgrades when evaluating solutions.

CASE STUDY: BRIGHT PICTURE SOLUTIONS, INC.

ESSENCE OF THE CASE

Here are the essential elements in this case:

- Secure the corporate environment using a set of firewalls.
- Set up a DMZ segment and place publicly accessible servers and services in that segment.
- Secure customer communications using any of the means discussed in Chapter 2. (This can include using public encryption algorithms and digital certificates for authentication purposes.)
- Plan, test, and implement a disaster recovery procedure, including tape backups.
- Ensure that the information stored on the backup tapes in-house and offsite is accessible only to authorized and cleared personnel, and ensure that security guidelines are honored.
- Secure the server room and communication patch panels, and implement user policies that would mandate server-side information storage.

continues

CASE STUDY: BRIGHT PICTURE SOLUTIONS, INC.

continued

SCENARIO

Bright Picture Solutions, Inc. (BPS) is in the printing and publishing business. The company has several branches across the United States and offices in Canada, the UK, Germany, Hong Kong, Japan, and Australia. It serves retail customers through many specialty shop locations in major cities in these countries, and it deals with a large number of wholesale customers through the Internet and wholesale printing and pickup outlets. Publishers can submit their work requirements and content through the Internet and pick it up or have it delivered. The company has experienced a fair amount of growth and expects continued growth as well.

BPS wants to achieve several objectives. First, it wants to ensure that its IT infrastructure is secured from Internet-based incursions. Second, the company wants to secure data feed transfers between its clients, partners, and the company. Third, the company wants to ensure business continuity in the event of a disaster by designing a comprehensive disaster recovery plan. This plan must also ensure that customer information and publishing materials will not be lost in the event of a system outage.

ANALYSIS

The process should begin with the company creating a secure network infrastructure. On the local LAN and in the DMZ, private address ranges should be used to reduce the risk of direct communication between potential intruders and the DMZ systems, bypassing firewall and NAT devices.

All servers accessible to the public will go into the DMZ, and communications between these hosts and outside systems will be tightly screened by the firewalls. Communication encryption should be configured between the clients and partners of the company according to the policy.

Partners need access to certain systems located in the DMZ, and they need more privileges and services made accessible than retail customers who might use the Web servers. This access effectively translates into an extranet concept, so in effect, the company will be implementing extranet functionality in the DMZ segment.

A disaster recovery solution must be implemented to ensure that no single point of failure exists and that the customer submissions and information databases are recoverable in case of a catastrophic failure. Tape backups should be planned to rotate on a weekly or bi-weekly basis, and archive tapes should be sent offsite for safe storage twice per month.

All server equipment must be locked down in a secure, ventilated, and humidified server room. The same requirements apply to cabling racks, patch panels, and network infrastructure equipment such as distribution and core switches and routers.

CHAPTER SUMMARY

This chapter provided an overview of basic security concepts and controls that can be used by administrators to secure physical devices and media. One of the most important topics, controlling who can access the network and how, was further expanded.

Firewalls are the focal points of overall network access policy. Several types of firewalls provide network security on various levels of the OSI model. However, they are all designed for one purpose: to keep the intruders out. Depending on their architectures, firewalls can recognize less complex attack patterns and alert administrators or take action to restrict all communications from the source of an attack. Firewalls can be used to implement three basic security topologies, ranging from a standalone security device; to a standalone security device limited to talking to one or more application gateways; to multiple security devices transforming a portion of the intranet into a secure, publicly accessible zone called a DMZ. Email, DNS, and Web servers are typically placed in the DMZ zone where strict access rules apply to all incoming connections.

In addition to securing the network with physical devices, administrators must ensure that communication and storage media as well as critical network devices are secure. This means cabling concentrators and infrastructure equipment must be locked in server rooms or wiring closets, and physical server access must be monitored, restricted, and tightly controlled.

Removable media security concerns most organizations because of backup technologies and the vast acceptance of magnetic tape devices as de-facto standard backup media. Backup is one of the major components of a disaster recovery plan. Backup media must be properly labeled, guarded, and archived offsite. An archiving plan should also include the decommissioning of archived backups.

KEY TERMS

- Degaussing
- Demilitarized zone (DMZ)
- Extranet
- FCAPS
- Firewall
- Intranet
- Intrusion detection system (IDS)
- Magnetic overwrite
- Network address translation (NAT)
- Public branch exchange (PBX)
- Public switched telephone network (PSTN)
- Reconnaissance
- Remote monitoring (RMON)
- Router
- Shielded twisted pair (STP)
- Simple Network Management Protocol (SNMP)
- Switch
- Unshielded twisted pair (UTP)
- Virtual local area network (VLAN)

APPLY YOUR KNOWLEDGE

Exercises

3.1 Configuring Windows 2000 Server IP Filtering

This exercise demonstrates how to configure IP filtering on a Windows 2000 Server using the Local Security Settings MMC console. Windows 2000 has built-in security controls that can help restrict certain traffic from entering the server or the network segment it is servicing. This should not be used as an alternative to hardware firewalls, but the idea is similar.

The following assumptions are made in this exercise: The server is a member or a standalone box, there is a DMZ segment, the server was built to host the company Web site, and HTTP is not being used.

Estimated Time: 7 minutes

1. Select Start, Programs, Administrative Tools, Local Security Settings.
2. In the navigation tree, right-click IP Security Policies on Local Machine, and then select Manage IP Filter Lists and Filter Actions. The configuration applet appears.
3. Before you can define IP filter lists, you need to create a new filter action. Click the Manage Filter Action tab.
4. On the Manage Filter Action page, click Add. A wizard dialog box pops up. Click Next.
5. In the Name text box, type `Block` and click Next.
6. From the Filter Action list, select Block and click Next. Click Finish. The filter action for rejecting unwanted traffic is created. Now you can use it to define access lists.
7. Switch back to the Manage IP Filter Lists tab, and click Add. On the IP Filter List page, click Add again to define a new IP filter.
8. A wizard dialog box appears; click Next. In the source address drop-down box, select Any IP Address. Click Next.
9. In the Destination IP Address drop-down box select My IP Address. Click Next.
10. In Protocol Type, select TCP and click Next.
11. On the IP Protocol Port page, leave the From This Port option unchanged. Click To This Port, and type `80` for the Web server port; then click Next.
12. Click Finish. The IP filter for Web traffic has been created.
13. Repeat steps 7–12 one more time to add definitions for port 3389 to allow terminal server connections for remote server management.
14. When you're finished, type the name for your list and click Close. Click Close again to go back to the Local Security Settings MMC console.
15. Now that you have IP filter lists and filter actions defined, you can create an IP security policy. Right-click IP Security Policies on Local Machine and select Create IP Security Policy.
16. A wizard appears. Click Next. Type the name for your policy and click Next.
17. Uncheck the Activate the Default Response Rule check box and click Next. Click Finish to create the new policy, and the policy properties window will appear.
18. Uncheck the Use Wizard check box at the bottom of the page and click Add.
19. On the following page, select the All ICMP Traffic rule and click the Filter Action tab. Select Block Action and click OK. Notice that the policy has been updated with the new rule.

APPLY YOUR KNOWLEDGE

20. Repeat steps 18 and 19 for all IP traffic (assign a block action) and your custom IP filter list (assign a Permit action). Click Close to finish and go back to the MMC. Note that a new policy has been created in the right pane.
21. To activate the policy, right-click the policy and select Assign. The policy takes effect immediately. Now test that the only traffic allowed to the box is Web and Terminal Services traffic.

This exercise shows how to protect a Web server from receiving unwanted traffic. If planned carefully, all servers of significance, at least in the DMZ, should have a similar security control implemented as a second line of defense in addition to the firewall. This ensures that the servers are still hard to crack on an individual basis even if the firewall is compromised.

You can use the import/export feature of the IP Filtering snap-in to define policies once per each server type and then distribute them to other boxes that have the same functions to save time. Please note that this type of security does restrict unwanted traffic to the box, but that is all it does. Web server security should be carefully considered and implemented, including the Web server software and the Web applications the server is running. For IP filtering to work, you must have the IPSEC Agent service running.

3.2 Configuring an IP Access List on a Cisco Router

This exercise is an extension of the previous exercise, and it demonstrates how to create a similar IP access list on a Cisco router.

This exercise assumes that a router running IOS software has a minimum of two network interfaces, one of which is connected to the Web server segment of the DMZ. The DMZ interface has an IP of 10.1.1.3/24, and the Web segment interface has an IP of 10.1.20.1/24.

Estimated Time: 5 minutes

1. Start a Telnet session and connect to the router's IP address (10.1.1.3/24). Log in and switch to the privileged mode by typing **`enable`**.
2. Enter configuration mode by typing **`config t`**.
3. Define an access list by issuing the following command:

   ```
   access-list 110 permit tcp any
   10.1.20.0 0.0.0.255 eq www
   ```

   This command creates access list 110 (if no access lists were previously defined as number 110) and adds a permit rule to allow Web traffic from any host to pass into the Web segment.
4. For detailed access-list usage syntax, type `access-list ?`.
5. You might want to add more traffic rules to allow Terminal Services management traffic in. For example, type the following:

   ```
   access-list 110 permit tcp any
   10.1.20.0 0.0.0.255 eq 3389
   ```
6. Don't forget that an implicit `access-list 110 deny ip any any` exists at the end of any IP list. To make troubleshooting easier later in the process, you might want to add this command, too.
7. Enter DMZ interface configuration mode (assuming it is the first Ethernet interface on the box, type **`int e0`**).
8. To assign access list 110 to interface `e0` to screen all incoming traffic out (and prevent it from being forwarded to the Web segment interface), type **`ip access-group 110 in`**.
9. To save the configuration changes, exit the interface and terminal configuration modes and type **`write mem`** to copy running configuration into startup configuration. Test your setup.

APPLY YOUR KNOWLEDGE

Review Questions

1. What is the purpose of a firewall and what are the three main architectures of firewalls?
2. What are the three basic security topologies created using firewalls?
3. What is the purpose of an IDS? How is it different from a firewall?
4. What are the main architectures of IDSs?
5. What is the purpose of access lists employed on routing devices?
6. Explain NAT functionality and the reasons for using NAT.
7. Describe the protocols used in network monitoring and management.
8. What are the basic physical access security controls? Explain each.

Exam Questions

1. Your company is in the process of setting up a DMZ segment. You have to allow file sharing and Windows management console traffic from internal systems to enter the DMZ segment. Which TCP ports do you have to open? (Choose two.)

   A. 110

   B. 139

   C. 135

   D. 161

   E. 131

   F. 23

2. Your company is in the process of setting up a DMZ segment. You have to allow FTP and Web browser requests from internal systems to enter the DMZ segment. Which TCP ports do you have to open? (Choose three.)

   A. 20

   B. 21

   C. 25

   D. 80

   E. 110

   F. 135

3. During regular security audits and log checking, you suspect that the organization is under attack and someone is using or is attempting to use resources on the internal network. You are confused because the IP addresses in the log files belong to trusted partner companies. Which of the following is likely to be happening?

   A. Hijacking

   B. Replaying

   C. Spoofing

   D. Social engineering

4. During regular security audits and log checking, you notice that one of your users is accessing files after midnight, when she is normally never active on the network outside normal business hours. When you ask her whether she has been working late at night, she denies having done so. Which of the following is most likely to explain what's occurring?

   A. Hijacking

   B. Replaying

APPLY YOUR KNOWLEDGE

C. Spoofing

D. Social engineering

5. You are securing the network with firewall technologies. You want to prevent certain types of traffic from certain IP addresses and subnets from entering your secured segment of the network. Which technology should be used to achieve this?

   A. NAT

   B. VLAN

   C. Static packet filter

   D. IDS

6. What type of firewall technique monitors the connection throughout the communication session, checking the validity of IP packet streams?

   A. Static inspection

   B. Stateful inspection

   C. Dynamic inspection

   D. Non-stateful inspection

7. Your company has a firewall that talks exclusively to an intermediary host that verifies the validity of requests at the Application level, authenticates and hides user identity, and serves as a communications portal. In addition to the firewall, what else is used in this setup?

   A. Switch

   B. Router

   C. Subnet screener

   D. Application gateway

Answers to Review Questions

1. A firewall is a hardware device or a software application installed on the border of secured networks with the purpose of examining and controlling incoming and outgoing network communications. Firewalls are the first line of network defense. The three basic architectures of the firewalls are packet filtering, circuit level, and application level. One more architecture type includes all three of the basic types: stateful inspection.

2. A bastion host is a dual-homed device (a device with two network interfaces). Any routing between the interfaces on that device is disabled, and specialized software (IP Security policies in Win2K, Cisco IOS, and so on) is configured to allow certain types of traffic in while keeping the rest out of the network.

   A screened host gateway is a packet-filtering device, usually also a router, which communicates only with a designated application gateway inside the secured network. No other traffic is allowed in or out of the screened host gateway. Basic functionality is the same as a bastion host. If a data stream is deemed safe (based on the configuration), it is forwarded to the application gateway. The application gateway then determines how to handle the stream.

   A screened subnet gateway includes two screened host gateway devices that isolate the LAN from the Internet, creating what is known as a screened subnet or demilitarized zone (DMZ) between them. The architecture also includes a proxy server (bastion host). This architecture is essentially a combination of the bastion host architecture and screened host gateway architecture.

APPLY YOUR KNOWLEDGE

3. An IDS is an intrusion detection system. Its purpose is to detect known attack patterns in communication streams. An IDS is designed to detect more sophisticated attacks than those that firewalls can handle on-the-fly. Firewalls are designed to prevent attacks before they happen by keeping offending traffic offsite. If attackers are smart enough to get through a tightly locked down firewall, this is where the IDS comes into play: It detects attacks in progress that were able to penetrate the first line of defense. Usually, IDS does not prevent attacks but generates alarms about attacks in progress, acting as a safety net for firewalls.

4. Active or passive analysis, host or network analysis, and anomaly or misuse analysis are three main IDS architectures.

5. Access lists can be configured on routing devices to effectively act like packet-filtering firewalls. This should not be used as the first line of defense, but it certainly can be used to create security fallback mechanisms in the network in case of a firewall compromise.

6. NAT is used to enable address translation between private, nonroutable addresses and external public address for communication in the public network. This is achieved using mappings that the NAT device creates and maintains. Each outgoing request dynamically creates a mapping on the NAT device, and NAT proceeds with the outgoing request, acting as a proxy. When it gets the reply, the NAT device looks up the mapping and forwards the information back to the original requester. In the same fashion, static mappings can be created to instruct NAT to forward certain requests to certain hosts on the inside network.

   By using NAT, you can preserve scarce public routable IP addresses and provide an additional layer of security because internal systems are not directly accessible using public addresses. Also, in the event of a service provider change, you do not have to reassign new IP addresses to your internal networks.

7. The Simple Network Management Protocol (SNMP) was developed as a temporary solution to network management requirements arising from growing network infrastructures. The purpose of SNMP is to enable the flow or exchange of management information between network nodes and to enable a network management environment. Three versions of SNMP are available. The most recent version, SNMPv3, provides authentication and data integrity safeguards that the first two versions do not have. The Remote Monitoring (RMON) specification can be considered an extension to the SNMP standard. It is based on similar standards to SNMP and relies on Management Information Base (MIB) structures and SMI. The purpose of RMON is to deliver network information grouped into nine major monitoring elements. Availability of RMON statistics and information can prove pivotal in designing and assessing network security.

8. To secure infrastructure equipment from potential theft and unauthorized physical access, all vital equipment (servers, routers and switches, cable patch panels, modems, backup devices and removable media, and so on) must be stored in an isolated location with controlled and restricted access. This location must be humidified and ventilated and should be monitored by video surveillance systems.

APPLY YOUR KNOWLEDGE

Answers to Exam Questions

1. **B, C.** To enable file transfer using Windows sharing, traffic for port 139 needs to be allowed to pass through the firewall. You might want to consider opening ports 137 and 138 to allow NetBIOS traffic for name resolution to work, but port 139 is sufficient for sharing if you are planning to reference DMZ servers by IP addresses or use manual WINS entries or lmhosts files in the internal segment. Port 135 must be open to allow RPC traffic (remote procedure calls are used extensively by Windows management tools).

2. **A, B, D.** Ports 20 and 21 are associated with FTP, where 20 is used for file transfer data and 21 for command and control data. Port 80 is associated with HTTP, the protocol Web browsers use to request service and receive responses. Port 25 (answer C) is associated with the Simple Mail Transfer Protocol and is not mentioned in the requirements. Port 110 (answer E) is associated with POP3, the protocol many email clients use to download email from a server to a local machine.

3. **C.** Spoofing is the most likely reason for this confusion. Spoofing allows attackers to misrepresent the source of the requests and masquerade as valid sources. Hijacking (answer A) involves taking over an existing session by seeking to anticipate next-packet sequence values and "jumping into" a traffic stream before the legitimate user can respond. Replaying (answer B) involves capturing and reusing historical (previously legitimate) traffic to try to compromise security and gain unauthorized access. Social engineering (answer D) involves an attempt to talk human users into divulging access information (accounts, passwords, and so forth) to enable unauthorized users to compromise security and use legitimate credentials to gain access.

4. **D.** Social engineering involves an attempt to talk human users into divulging access information (accounts, passwords, and so forth) to enable unauthorized users to compromise security and use legitimate credentials to gain access. Somebody has obtained this user's account and password information and is using it to access resources to which she's entitled. At the bare minimum, disabling this account and providing her with a new account/password combination is warranted (and it might make sense to monitor the old account to try to locate or identify the malefactor). Hijacking (answer A) involves breaking into active sessions, which does not match the pattern you've observed. Replaying (answer B) involves capturing and replaying previous legitimate network activity to compromise system security; this doesn't match the pattern, either. Spoofing (answer C) involves reporting a network address that doesn't actually match the intruder's real address; it doesn't match the pattern, either.

5. **C.** Static packet filtering is the simplest solution available to implement basic filtering of network traffic based on source, destination addresses, and protocol types.

6. **B.** Stateful inspection monitors the connection throughout the communication session, checking the validity of the IP packet stream.

7. **D.** An application gateway is used in some security topologies to act as the intermediary between users and services. Application gateways communicate and service all requests through the firewall.

APPLY YOUR KNOWLEDGE

Suggested Readings and Resources

Online Material

1. HOW TO: Harden the TCP/IP Stack Against Denial of Service Attacks in Windows 2000 (`http://support.microsoft.com/default.aspx?scid=kb;en-us;q315669`).
2. Keeping Your Site Comfortably Secure: An Introduction to Internet Firewalls (`http://csrc.nist.gov/publications/nistpubs/800-10/node1.html`).
3. Local Area Detection of Incoming War Dial Activity (`http://www.att.com/isc/docs/war_dial_detection.pdf`).
4. White Paper: Internet Security for Small Businesses (`http://www.cisco.com/warp/public/cc/pd/rt/800/prodlit/fire_wp.htm`).
5. White Paper: The Science of Intrusion Detection System Attack Identification (`http://www.cisco.com/warp/public/cc/pd/sqsw/sqidsz/prodlit/idssa_wp.htm`).

Publications

1. Chappell, Laura. *Advanced Cisco Router Configuration.* Indianapolis, IN: Cisco Press, 1998.
2. Microsoft Corporation. *Windows 2000 Server TCP/IP Core Networking Guide.* Redmond, WA: Microsoft Press, 2002.

OBJECTIVES

This chapter covers the following CompTIA-specified objectives for the Communications Security section of the Security+ exam:

Understand the basic security concepts of intrusion detection methodologies.

- **Network based**
- **Host based**
- **Honeypots**
- **Incident response**

▶ The primary purpose of this objective is to help you understand the various approaches to detecting intrusion in a corporate local area network (LAN).

Understand security baselines.

- **OS/NOS hardening**
- **Network hardening**
- **Application hardening**

▶ To secure an environment completely, you must look beyond securing the borderline between the LAN and the Internet. The goal of this objective is to help you understand the methods used to secure applications and network hosts using security controls applicable and specific to that level and the corporate security policy.

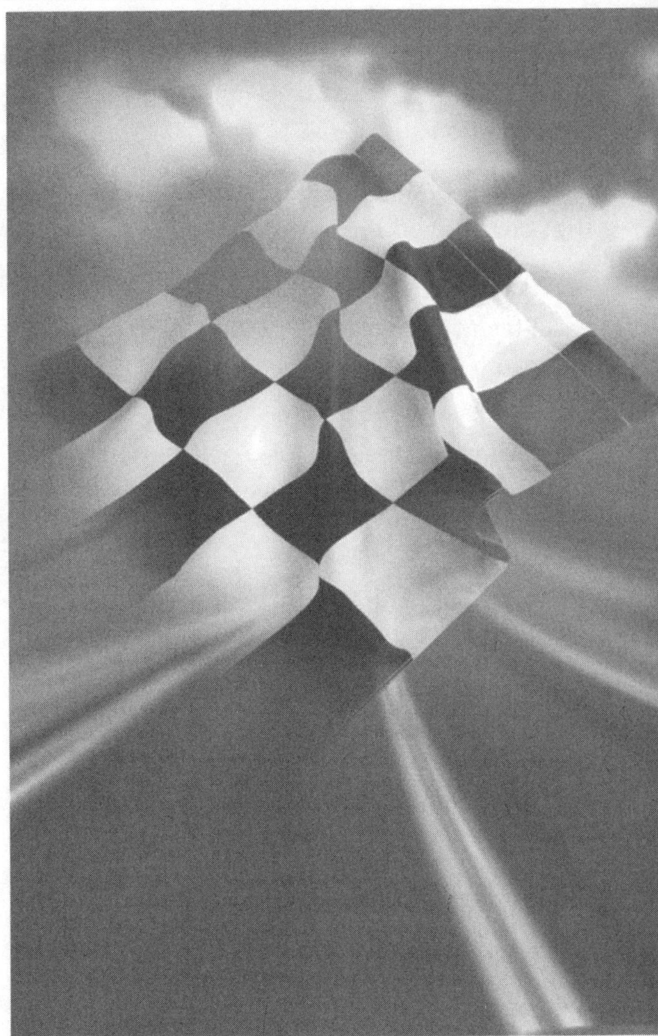

CHAPTER 4

Intrusion Detection, Baselines, and Hardening

Outline

Study Strategies

- Install a Windows 2000 server running IIS and configure it to conform to high security standards using suggestions in the chapter along with Microsoft's security baseline templates.

INTRODUCTION

This chapter will help you understand the two main divisions of intrusion detection technologies: *network-based intrusion detection systems* and *host-based intrusion detection systems.*

You also investigate honeypots. A *honeypot* is a decoy box designed to attract hackers. It usually has all the logging and tracing enabled, and its security level is lowered on purpose. Honeypots are not security mechanisms in their own right; they are valuable additions to otherwise strong systems security-wise.

The next part of this chapter introduces *incident response handling procedures.* The basic premise of incident handling and response is that the company needs to have a clear action plan on what each response team member needs to do and when it has to be done. Next, we move on to help you understand security baselines and more specific steps of locking down various parts and types of servers and networks. A security baseline is defined in the company's security policy and is a model set of security-related modifications, patches, and settings that underpin the technical implementation of security.

NETWORK-BASED INTRUSION DETECTION

Understand the basic security concepts of intrusion detection methodologies.

IDS stands for *intrusion detection system.* As clear as this definition is, the industry is segmented as far as the application of IDS methodologies is concerned. Various organizations claim to have the best intrusion detection system. Yet if examined, they all use different approaches or combinations thereof—and oftentimes the very definition of what constitutes an intrusion is not the same. In the following sections, we will review the various approaches to detecting intrusion in a corporate local area network (LAN).

The two main categories of IDSs are *network-based intrusion detection systems* and *host-based intrusion detection systems.*

The essence of a network-based intrusion detection system is in its purpose to analyze network traffic in real-time. It uses raw packets traveling the network as the source of information and most often is implemented as a standalone, dedicated device that has one or more network interfaces running in a promiscuous mode. These systems usually feature an intrusion recognition module, either hardware or software, that uses one or more of the many analysis approaches, such as pattern matching, stateful inspection, protocol decode, heuristic analysis (frequency or threshold excess), or anomaly analysis, to catch would-be attackers.

Regardless of the architecture of the system, whether it is host-based or network-based, IDSs look for so-called *intrusion signatures.* A signature is a set of very specific conditions that constitutes an intrusion or suspicious activity if matched.

Network-based IDSs have a complete picture of the network segment they are configured to protect. They "see" entire network packets, including the header information. Therefore, they are in a better position to distinguish between network-born attacks and host-based IDSs. Depending on the implementation of a personal firewall (wrapper) in host-based IDSs, header information and therefore network pattern recognition might simply be out of reach for host-based detection systems.

Network-based systems are centralized and, therefore, have very low maintenance requirements. They are positioned to detect outside intrusions, but in addition, they can detect network-based intrusion patterns originating from within the segment they are protecting.

The main advantages of using a network-based intrusion detection system are summarized in the following list:

- **Covering up the trails and altering the logs of a network-based intrusion detection system are difficult.**
- **There's a lower total cost of ownership (TCO)**—It is cheaper to maintain one IDS centrally, and easier to manage its configuration and updates.
- **Detects attack patterns within the network and malicious intent, as well as the attacks themselves**—With a network IDS, you can learn about communication patterns of the attacker, what she was trying to break into, and whether the attempt succeeded or failed.

- **Network-based IDSs can see attacks host-based IDSs might not be aware of, depending on implementation**—In some host-based systems, the IDS application itself is implemented higher than the Network level of the Open System Interconnection (OSI) model, most commonly at the Application level. This prevents it from seeing packet header information that is visible to network-based IDSs.
- **Network-based IDSs do not depend on the operating system(s) in use**—This is well-suited for heterogeneous environments in which rare or custom operating systems are used. This, again, translates into lower TCO because personnel does not need to be trained to support an application on different operating systems.
- **If your IDS is configured to take some action in response to an attack or suspicious activity, it can immediately drop a connection before further harm is done**—This prohibits further attempts of the same type or from the same source. This happens on-the-fly and prevents the attacker from any further attempts network-wide.

WARNING

Warning for Configuring IDS to Take Action Caution must be exercised when configuring your IDS to take a particular action in response to an attack or suspicious activity. Consider the following example: Because the source IP can be easily spoofed, an intruder could simulate an attack, forging her IP address and replacing it with the address of your own mail server sitting in the DMZ; therefore, active IDS can start dropping legitimate mail server connections.

When a suspicious or offending event is detected by the network-based IDS, one or more of the following can occur:

- It submits an alarm to administrative console.
- It submits an alarm to a network management station via a Simple Network Management Protocol (SNMP) trap.
- It submits an email to the appropriate personnel directly or via a distribution group (which in turn can be forwarded to a pager or cell phone).
- It allows you to view the suspect session.
- It stores a record in the log describing the event(s).
- It stores the entire session in the form of raw packet data.
- It reacts by resetting the suspect network connection.
- It reacts by reconfiguring a firewall.
- It reacts in a different way as programmed or configured by the administrative personnel.

EXAM TIP

Be sure you are familiar with the basic differences between NIDS and HIDS. You don't have to memorize all the material in this chapter, but knowing the advantages of each system would certainly help.

In the following sections, pattern matching, stateful inspection, protocol decode analysis, heuristic analysis, and anomaly analysis approaches to network IDS are discussed in more detail.

Pattern Matching

Pattern matching network-based IDSs (NIDSs) are the simplest systems, and they work much like antivirus software: A central box on the network takes each packet and compares it against a database of signatures (formats of packets known to be offending). This approach is the least flexible of all, but at the same time, it is a building block for more advanced NIDS and works very quickly.

NIDS administrators can additionally specify what the system should be looking for in the traffic. This can be based on Transmission Control Protocol (TCP) flags, source or destination addresses, port numbers, protocol types, or even strings in the data portion of the packet. And here lies one of the biggest problems of pattern matching: How do you catch a Trojan installed in your network that does not use a fixed port? You cannot define a rule to detect this Trojan because it is not associated with one protocol.

To better assess whether pattern matching applies to a particular situation, consider the following:

- It is the simplest method of NIDS.
- Configuring pattern-matching NIDS is fairly easy.
- It works very fast compared to other NIDS methodologies and therefore can handle more traffic. (It can be placed closer to the backbone where traffic gets aggregated, which means fewer locations, less specialized hardware, and less costly hardware.)
- Pattern matching uses highly specific signatures, which yields extremely reliable results when looking for signatured patterns.
- Nonetheless, if the signature is not specific enough, pattern matching can potentially generate a massive amount of false positive alerts and flood the system with useless data.
- If an attacker happens to modify any one parameter the signature specifies, the signature becomes outdated and practically useless, making the network vulnerable to the modified attack. NIDS will generate false negatives, allowing the offending traffic to go unnoticed.

- Another significant disadvantage of pattern matching is that it might require more than one signature to deal with the same vulnerability because of the specific nature of this methodology. By the same token, pattern matching applies to one packet and therefore is incapable of dissecting attacks based on data streams or communication patterns.

> NOTE **Sample Signatures** To view a sample collection of current signatures, point your browser to `http://www.iss.net/security_center/advice/Intrusions/default.htm`.

Similar to antivirus software, keeping signature databases updated is very important because hacker techniques evolve every day. In addition, new attacks and vulnerabilities are developed and found often.

Perhaps the main shortcoming of pattern matching is its inability to span checks across several packets. This is where stateful inspection comes in handy.

Stateful Inspection

Stateful matching, or *stateful inspection*, is a step beyond pattern matching. It recognizes the need to match patterns outside a single packet, looking for signatures in data streams instead. A stateful inspection NIDS reassembles the fragments of the same communication in the right order and compares them against the signature database. If the attacker splits a command that was defined in the signatures into more than one packet, stateful inspection will catch it, whereas simple pattern matching will not. NIDS maintains TCP stream information for each session.

Because stateful inspection is effectively an extension to pattern matching, most of the advantages and disadvantages remain the same, with slight modifications. To better assess whether stateful inspection applies to a particular situation, consider the following:

- It is almost as simple as pattern matching.
- Configuring stateful inspection NIDS is fairly easy.
- It works more slowly than pattern matching because of the need to maintain session information.
- It uses highly specific signatures, which yield extremely reliable results when looking for signatured patterns.
- With stateful matching, evading detection is a little harder for hackers.

- If the signature is not specific enough, stateful inspection can potentially generate large numbers of false positive alerts.
- If an attacker happens to modify any one parameter the signature specifies, the signature becomes outdated and useless, making the network vulnerable to the modified attack. NIDS will generate false negatives, allowing the offending traffic to go unnoticed.
- Stateful inspection might require more than one signature to deal with the same vulnerability because of the specific nature of this methodology.

Protocol Decode Analysis

Protocol decode analysis is another step ahead for signature-based NIDSs and can be thought of as an enhancement to stateful inspection and pattern matching. Protocol decode methodology works by applying protocol rules as they are prescribed in requests for comments (RFCs) while searching for suspicious traffic. This allows the analysis of packets in the context of protocols they are using, looking for irregularities in header field values and lengths, and searching for patterns therein.

Protocol decode is effectively an extension to both pattern matching and stateful inspection—most of the advantages and disadvantages remain the same, with slight modifications. To better assess whether protocol decode suits a particular situation, consider the following:

- It is a more complicated variation of pattern matching NIDS.
- It takes more effort to configure protocol decode NIDS.
- It works more slowly than pattern matching because of the need to maintain session information, and it is a little slower than stateful inspection because of the expanded search options.
- It uses less-specific signatures, which allows capturing more of the offending traffic with fewer rules (it still uses signatures).
- It is trickier for hackers to evade detection with protocol decode; they have fewer options available to transmit data unnoticed.

- It can be very accurate if the signature is defined properly, reporting fewer false positive alerts.
- One of the shortcomings of protocol decode NIDS is that some RFC references do not set very specific protocol requirements. This leaves some room for optional protocol features or field values, which makes defining a signature that would alert reliably more difficult.
- Another issue associated with protocol decode NIDS is the actual coding of the product; it must be accurate and sophisticated enough to parse protocol data reliably.

Despite a shortcoming in the area of protocol standards (or lack thereof in some specific areas), protocol decode is a step forward in making a signature-based pattern-matching NIDS a little less susceptible to variations on behalf of hackers.

Heuristic Analysis

Heuristic analysis still uses signatures in much the same way, looking for patterns. Its major improvement over the pattern-matching family of NIDS methodologies is its capability to think—that is, statistically analyze the traffic. This method can sometimes be referred to as frequency, threshold, or excess algorithm, and it is based on the idea that a certain pattern might be detected a few times before it is considered suspicious or harmful.

Consider a port scan reconnaissance. It usually probes a large number of defined ports, its requests usually come from one source but are most often destined to the same machine, and it uses TCP SYN flags to tell the destination port it wants to establish a connection. Obviously, a few attempts to connect from one machine to another cannot be considered an intrusion. However, if the number of attempts to establish connections on many different ports in a short period of time exceeds some predefined threshold, this activity is halted and an alarm is fired. Organizations can set their own thresholds based on what they do and do not consider acceptable. By manipulating these values, an adjustment is made to the ratio of false alarms to true alarms; the lower the threshold, the more alarms you get, and the more of those alarms are usually false.

To better assess whether heuristic analysis applies to a particular situation, consider the following:

- It is one of the most complicated variations of pattern matching NIDS that also introduces statistical elements to the analysis.
- It might take significant effort to configure heuristic analysis NIDS and set all the thresholds to their optimal values in each given network.
- It uses signatures together with threshold and frequency analysis to detect some hacker activity other methodologies do not recognize.
- It makes most of the reconnaissance approaches visible to network personnel, hampering hackers' ability to learn the system without drawing some attention.
- It can be very accurate if the signature is defined properly and the threshold is set appropriately, reporting fewer false positive alerts.
- One of the shortcomings of heuristic analysis NIDS is that sometimes you must adjust detection algorithms to better conform to what the organization is trying to protect itself from.

All in all, heuristic analysis provides significantly more complex logic that watches the network activity and detects suspicious or illegal activity that other methodologies just cannot catch.

Anomaly Analysis

Anomaly-based analysis looks for traffic that is considered abnormal. To single out abnormal traffic patterns, the system has to be taught (or learn) what is considered normal in the first place. A theoretical approach to this problem is that either systems can be preconfigured with a vast variety of traffic profiles that can be considered safe and assume the rest is an anomaly or systems can be programmed to learn from what they see on the wire, compile new traffic profiles, and assume they are safe. After the learning phase is complete, NIDS is activated.

Anomaly detection is considered to be the universal cure for all IDS/NIDS problems known today. Of course, such a cure is still not known to the industry, and currently, anomaly methodologies are seen largely in the area of academic research. Very few commercially available NIDSs provide anomaly detection solutions. In theory, anomaly detection is a sound approach to IDS because of its fundamental difference from the rest of the methodologies reviewed in these paragraphs: Instead of looking for known attack patterns, which are frequently modified and expanded, anomaly NIDS looks for safe traffic and denies the rest. It is similar to packet filtering technology where you would normally define what to allow and the rest would be denied, although it is much more complex to configure. To better assess whether anomaly-based analysis applies to a particular situation, consider the following:

- Among the obvious advantages of a hypothetical anomaly-based NIDS, administrative overhead is almost nonexistent because after the device is configured, you do not have to update attack signatures, as opposed to pattern-matching systems.
- The greatest strength of such a system is its capability to detect unknown attacks.
- One disadvantage is that to be successful, anomaly-based NIDS implementation depends heavily on the learning process—that is, how the system has been configured. If the safe traffic profile database is incomplete or inaccurate, the system can potentially generate a great amount of false positives. At the same time, if it does detect an attack, it will be incapable of distinguishing between them because no attack profiles would ever be defined, so essentially the system will be alerting you about "something that has happened."

NOTE

The Ideal IDS Solution Speaking of the ideal IDS solution, there is none. The choice of the algorithm depends heavily on which attacks system administrators are trying to protect the environment from. Ideally, the NIDS of choice includes all the methodologies discussed, except maybe anomaly detection because this technology can be too unrefined to implement just yet. For reconnaissance attacks, heuristics works best. For the rest of the attacks, mixes of protocol decode and stateful or simple pattern matching are the best approaches at this time.

Active Detection

Active detection mechanisms involve some action taken by the intrusion detection system in response to a suspicious activity or an intrusion (in essence, it is reactive detection). This potential action is configurable and varies from product to product, but it can involve connection termination or automatic firewall reprogramming to deny all further communications from the source of suspicious activity.

In addition to some action active detection systems can take, they can feature a mix of responses usually associated with a passive detection system.

Passive Detection

The passive detection concept has an IDS present in the network in a silent fashion; it does not interfere with communications in progress, but it can react in a certain way. For example, an IDS can send an administrative alert if a suspicious activity has been found in log files or network traffic, or it can record a communication session for further analysis or forensic evidence.

HOST-BASED INTRUSION DETECTION

Understand the basic security concepts of intrusion detection methodologies.

Opposite of network-based intrusion detection systems, *host-based intrusion detection* is built around the analysis of logs on each host (also in real-time or very close to real-time mode). This often is expanded further into the analysis of events and conditions as they are triggered. Every time a log changes, the IDS compares the change to the database of suspicious patterns to see whether this latest log event changes the set of matched conditions.

Host-based IDSs in many instances are more complex than network-based systems because host-based systems monitor many other things in addition to network traffic specific to the host on which the system is running. They can also be configured to monitor any of the following:

- Ports used by the system or incoming connections
- Processes running on the system and how the list compares to the baseline
- Checksums of important system files to see whether any of them have been compromised

In addition to active network traffic analysis on the host itself, it can feature content filters and antivirus modules to protect from viruses, unsigned controls and applets, client scripts, and spam.

Host-based can be architecturally subclassified into two categories:

- **Host wrapper, or personal firewall**—Best used for monitoring network-related activity and communication attempts in to or out of the monitored host.
- **Host agent**—In addition to the preceding item, it is capable of monitoring operating system events and conditions, such as monitoring system files and running processes.

Host-based and network-based approaches are complimentary rather than competing, and they both have their own strengths and weaknesses. Many successful intrusion detection systems have been built using mixes of both methodologies, and ultimately, this is what all system administrators or security engineers should consider for their environments.

Security systems that employ host-based approaches in their detection mechanisms typically provide better protection from both outside and inside attacks. Although network-based IDSs can break a connection and reprogram a firewall, they are less flexible in taking action to prevent an attack originating from within (inside the network that does not usually contain any firewalls). In addition, internal attacks might not match against any network-related attack signature but instead use allowed network connection patterns to cause harm.

Host-based systems are more complex to maintain because every host connected to the network must have the software installed, maintained, and upgraded/updated as required. In addition, host-based systems need careful supervision by attentive security personnel who are familiar with every monitored workstation and typical patterns of user activity, logon times, file transfers, connectivity, and so on. Although many systems are designed to prevent intrusions, no one system can fully ensure that the host it is protecting is impenetrable, so careful supervision and alert follow-up by personnel can potentially eliminate some of the limitations host-based systems might be vulnerable to. It helps that more and more solutions allow centralized distribution of configuration and updates to individual host IDSs.

We must also note here that IDS (of any type) is only as good as its configuration; chances are slim that the system will get fully configured from the very first try, generating as few false positive or false negative signals as possible. So, in essence, the purpose of IDS is to learn about attacks and adapt to learned patterns to prevent them in the future.

Databases of known signatures are available that you can use to begin with, but these databases are quickly outdated as new patterns are discovered.

Advantages provided by the host-based intrusion detection system are summarized in the following list:

- **Its capability to catch intrusions that network-based IDSs are likely to miss**—This is the first and most obvious advantage of a host-based IDS. Dial-in intrusions and physical access to the actual server are unlikely to cross any network wires, so in effect, they are invisible to network-based IDSs.

- **Network-based IDSs cannot see inside encrypted tunnels, and visibility is usually limited in switched environments**—End-to-end encryption exposes only tunnel addressing and encapsulation information for the network to route the packets successfully; however, the information inside the tunnel is out of reach. In switched networks, hosts communicate via a dedicated switched channel on which information travels from one port of the switch to another one and is not broadcast to anyone else, which makes it difficult for IDS. In some switch implementations, though, you can set up a port to receive a copy of all traffic for management or billing purposes, and it addresses IDS concerns. This is called *spanning a switch.*

- **Host-based IDSs work with event logs**—Because they work with event logs, they are in a better position to understand whether an attack actually happened and what the result was. The system might ignore suspicious activities that actually do not do any damage.

- **Host-based IDSs are more than just network traffic scanners**—In addition to scanning incoming and outgoing traffic, they can monitor file system activity, user logon/logoff events, program installations, and other activities on the actual workstation (at locations much higher than the Network layer). This strength comes at the expense of performance and might not necessarily be the best option to monitor such user activity. In Windows 2000 environments, more efficient ways to control user behavior are available.

- **Lower cost of entry**—A network-based IDS provides a total solution for network-based detection and therefore costs significantly more to implement (but less to maintain). Host-based systems require an installation of an agent on each individual workstation, with every individual agent costing a fraction of the network-based IDS price. It costs less to begin the implementation but more to maintain it.
- **No dedicated hardware is required**—This is because every protected host on the network actually has an agent installed on it, so there really is no need for additional dedicated and specialized hardware in most cases.
- **Real-time detection and response operating systems nowadays allow applications to subscribe to system events**—These are events such as log write events that allow "consumer" applications to be immediately notified of the event and receive a copy of event information if requested. Quite a contrast to the old approach of polling the log periodically, this concept enables host-based IDS developers to be immediately notified, analyze, and react to an event that might constitute a security breach. Of course, a bit of a delay is necessary to process and analyze the event, but it is quite negligible.

As far as IDS response options are concerned, host-based IDSs are usually capable of carrying out the following:

- Submitting an alarm to an administrative console
- Submitting an alarm to a network management station via an SNMP trap
- Submitting an email to the appropriate personnel directly or via a distribution group (which in turn can be forwarded to a pager or cell phone)
- Storing a record in the log describing the event(s)
- Reacting by logging the offending user off the system
- Reacting by disabling a user account
- Reacting in a different way as programmed or configured by the administrative personnel

NOTE

Choosing Which IDS Suits Best
When choosing between NIDS or host-based IDS, consider the mix of both. In an ideal world, every host that exists on a secure network segment should have some type of specific solution that can interact with the system intimately, looking for events of attack from any side—be it a user, virus, or network exploit. To gain a better view of the big picture, NIDS would be deployed as well.

The big issue with host-based IDS is the overhead it places on the system. Network operating systems have their own protection mechanisms, and when configured properly, they are in the best position to quench the need for host-based IDS.

EXAM TIP

Be sure you understand the definition of a virus and know the categories of viruses and how they work. This could prove useful on the exam both inside and outside the scope of IDS technologies.

HONEYPOTS

Understand the basic security concepts of intrusion detection methodologies.

Up to this point, we have been looking mostly at protecting the system, network, or communication from a break-in or any other security vulnerability. A *honeypot* is the ultimate defense feature that works exactly in the opposite way; it is a decoy box designed to attract hackers. A honeypot usually has all the logging and tracing enabled, and its security level is lowered on purpose.

The general school of thought on honeypots is that after a hacker spots a vulnerable system, she would return more than once. The hacker can also give out the location and vulnerabilities of the system to peers of the hacker community for various reasons, not the least of which is to gain more visibility and respect. Honeypots are *not* security mechanisms; they are valuable additions to systems with strong security configurations.

Honeypots are implemented largely for three reasons:

- A honeypot can potentially distract an attacker from the systems that present real value, a successful attack on which would be disastrous to the company.
- By monitoring successful "attacks" on honeypots, system administrators can learn about hackers and their techniques and strengthen the real production environment against these attacks.
- Information collected about hackers gaining unauthorized access to these decoy boxes can be used by the legal department to practice or execute complaints, investigation, and prosecution of attackers, potentially deterring further attempts to gain unauthorized access to the resources of the company.

While setting up a honeypot, administrators should keep in mind that the decoy box has to be interesting to hackers. This usually means that it has to appear as though it is a real production system, runs similar applications, and contains similar information.

If the company has a serious reputation as a security-conscious organization, a decoy system that is too easy to access will probably raise suspicions and intruders with experience will most likely leave the system before enough information is recorded. Likewise, a honeypot that is very noticeably modified from the original operating system settings or functionality will, in many cases, raise similar suspicions. It is very important to find the right balance of features to gain enough insight into hacker activity while still attracting it.

At the same time, be careful not to make this decoy box a launching pad for attacks into the production network or other production servers that don't need the hacker's attention. This is why it is important to still have control over what is going on with the dummy box. Consider the following locations for the honeypot:

- **Outside all firewalls**—This is dangerous because administrators have very little to no control over a decoy that can easily be used to launch attacks into the network and is likely to attract some attention.
- **Inside the DMZ**—This location has moderate chances of attracting attention due to firewall protection and relative invisibility, but for the same reason, this method allows administrators to control how the decoy is used and what kind of traffic enters or leaves the box.
- **Inside the production network**—At this location, it is very unlikely that an external attacker will ever get to it, and therefore it offers limited use as far as external attacks are concerned. However, that might not necessarily be the case with attacks originating from within.

To record the session or otherwise gather forensic information about honeypot visitors, you can use any form of logging that might apply to the situation, including operating system logging, firewall logging, sniffers, and protocol analyzers.

Administrators can choose to build their own honeypots or use one of several commercially available honeypot implementations. There are pros and cons to each of the two choices; for example, a honeypot built in-house can more accurately represent the type of information the company is likely to have. It also is less likely to scare attackers who might be familiar with the commercial honeypot products, and it will likely cost less. In addition to these considerations, commercial honeypot technologies have not matured yet and can contain their own flaws and vulnerabilities.

All things considered, honeypots are valuable additions to network security feature sets and controls that should be at least considered for deployment in any network environment. As long as they do not attract angry swarms of hackers waging attacks in response to being caught or convicted once or twice, they should serve the purpose of practicing security in environments exposed to real attacks. In addition to providing insightful information into hacker practices, honeypots also serve the purpose of training personnel in incident response.

INCIDENT RESPONSE

Understand the basic security concepts of intrusion detection methodologies.

Regardless of how strict security policies and procedures are, incidents do happen from time to time in most organizations. It is important to realize that proper incident response is just as vital as security itself, and its presence (or absence) can make the difference between improving security and customer relations and running the business into the ground. A company that does not learn from its mistakes, no matter how costly, is tantamount to species that do not adapt to changing environments—both will eventually become extinct. By the same token, customers who might have been affected by intrusion have the right to know what exactly happened, why it happened, who is responsible, and what is being done to prevent an outage or information loss in the future. Customers need to see that the company has enough expertise to deal with the problem.

Organizations of larger sizes normally should have *incident response teams* consisting of several members from more traditional departments. Granted, this team is not a full-time commission; rather, it is a collection of people who have obligations to act in a coherent, predefined manner in case of an incident. A model response team typically consists of the following team members:

- Special security response or general information systems security member
- IT department member (if not same as above)
- Legal team representative

- Management contact
- Public relations member

The basic premise of incident handling and response is that the company needs to have a clear action plan on what each response team member needs to do and when it has to be done. An incident response team usually deals with the following (it is advisable to document any actions response team members are taking for further documentation, analysis, and reports):

- **Initial assessment**—Determine whether it is a false positive (one of the two types of a false alarm), determine whether the attack is still in progress, and get some preliminary information as to what type of attack the organization is dealing with and what the potential damage areas and severity are.
- **Initial communication**—Personnel assigned to the alarm, if suspecting a real incident, should notify the appropriate people as soon as possible. Usually, network operations center (NOC) monitoring personnel receive network alarms and alerts first-hand; if this is the case and the alert has been determined to be real, NOC people are responsible for contacting security engineers as soon as possible.
- **Initial containment of the incident**—Set priorities and follow them closely. They vary depending on the organization, but the list usually begins with protection of classified data, then business and proprietary data, and then actual systems (be it hardware or software). The key question is, "Do I pull the plug?" The security response team has to be clear about what to do. Business decisions that weigh the operation's continuity dollars against further risk from an attack that might still be in progress need to be made long before the real attack. When customer privacy is at risk, bad publicity can cause much more damage to the business than actual sales revenue lost from the server being taken offline for a few hours. The secondary objective is not to scare the intruder away, in pursuit of gaining more information about her.

- **Intrusion evaluation**—Determine the origin of the attack, its purpose, the type of attack, the tools and mechanisms used, and the systems and files that were accessed successfully or unsuccessfully. The key is to understand what actually happened (on more of a scientific level rather than an impulsive one) and how severe the attack was. Every imaginable security check is an appropriate addition to the list of actions in this category. Everything from major hardware components and settings to the most insignificant security-related setting on the operating system/application level, firewall and operating system logs, and other security checks is appropriate.
- **Forensic evidence collection**—Actions from the plan category are likely to yield some meaningful results. The next action plan item is gathering all the information learned about the incident up to this moment. Be sure you store it in a secure location on secure media, in case it is needed for potential legal action. Depending on the size of the data, you should take a snapshot of the affected system(s) or even a full backup that includes all the inflicted damage, plus add firewall and/or router logs, sniffer session data, IDS logs, and security alerts—anything that can later prove the incident and its perpetrators. You also should use recordable CD-ROM media that cannot be erased without completely destroying the disk and that cannot get demagnetized by accident. Store it in a secure place, such as a safe deposit box, and access it only for the purposes of prosecution and forensic evidence.
- **Communication of the incident in public**—In contrast to the initial communication (the purpose of which is to bring the problem to the attention of the right people within the company), public communications can be subdivided into several categories. First of all, the incident of a bigger proportion or repetitive pattern should be communicated to municipal, provincial, or federal law enforcement agencies, especially if customer privacy or financial loss can be involved. Second, the incident should be reported to IT security companies and other expert groups (such as product vendors) that can provide some expert help in mitigating the risk and develop and distribute attack signatures or patches so that other companies can get immunity to this particular attack if it is new.

Third, where applicable, customers should be notified as soon as there is something to be communicated that includes a non-technical description of what happened, what is being done to fix it, the impact, and the estimated time of availability. This communication is time-sensitive when service downtime or customer privacy is involved (for instance, credit card database theft is a highly time-sensitive issue). Fourth, if the company is large enough, and the event is worthy of a news story, expect to be contacted by the media. It is important to keep in mind that denial will cause more damage than has already been inflicted, but equally important, there needs to be one person authorized to speak to the media. This person should usually be from the management or public relations team. Incident handling personnel must be alerted not to leak any information accidentally and instead redirect all media queries to the appropriate team member who will handle the responses in a consistent, official fashion.

- **Service restoration**—Next, the incident response team needs to evaluate whether the systems should be repaired, restored, or completely rebuilt. This will depend on the actual system complexity and the extent of the damage, as well as on the security breach. If it was a known one-time exploit, it might be sufficient to simply lock down your Web servers or firewalls. To the contrary, if it was an unknown attack or an attack that is known to leave undesired effects on the system (Code Red is one of the recent examples), it might be in the best interests of the company to completely reinstall the affected parts of the system. This is where backup policy comes in handy—knowing the duration of the attack and having the backup rotation and archiving in place is very important.
- **Incident report preparation**—Contrary to public communication, this report is an internal document that puts everything in perspective, from the minute the incident was noticed at the NOC monitoring station until the minute the service was restored. It outlines all the actions taken and the results achieved step by step, drawing up the timeline of the incident response. This report serves many purposes, from filing management reports, to analyzing response effectiveness, to keeping records as additional courtroom evidence, to documenting the event for further training and record keeping, to supporting outages that exceed service level agreement (SLA) thresholds.

- **Damage calculation**—This ultimate dollar figure should look beyond actual and obvious losses associated with service outages and business interruptions. It should also include costs incurred by any secondary processes, such as legal fees, loss of proprietary information (industrial espionage), system downtime costs (actual outage, angry customers leaving the company as a result, possible financial liabilities for violating the SLA obligation, and so on), labor costs, hardware/software costs, consulting fees, bad reputation and publicity (unhappy customers and media discouraging potential customers), and any other costs stemming from the incident.
- **Summary and updates**—After all the dust settles, gather the entire security response team for a meeting and review the process and timelines in detail (this is where the incident report comes in handy). Analyze each step's effectiveness, timeliness, and results. It also helps to review the usefulness and suitability of security policies as they apply to the current situation. Draw conclusions, decide the best way to protect against this incident in the future, and implement and document the necessary security changes. Analyze risks in other parts of the system and decide whether obvious variations of this attack (if any) can cause more damage and how to protect against that. The security response team lead needs to ensure that every person on board did the best she could and performed the most appropriate action given the circumstances. This person also needs to look at the situation from a distance to see whether the overall strategy of the department is useful or where it needs changing or fixing.

UNDERSTANDING SECURITY BASELINES

Understand security baselines.

A *security baseline* is defined in the company's security policy and is a model set of security-related modifications, patches, and settings that underpin the technical implementation of security.

Companies should have post-installation configuration and audit guides (automated, where possible) that implement security policies. These settings include but are not limited to the following:

- Registry enhancements and lock-downs
- Auditing and logging configurations
- File system security tightening
- Services and applications configurations
- Custom security tools, where applicable

Security policies must be reviewed and updated on a regular basis, so security baselines can constantly improve. To cope with the ever-changing nature of the baseline, tools are available from operating system vendors that check system settings and report inconsistencies. In addition, companies are encouraged to develop their own, more application-specific baselines on top of the basic security configurations touted by software vendors.

There needs to be a process of change management, and ideally, all changes to the production environment should be reviewed by security personnel. A new patch can be a great fix for a bug in the application or service, but it is important to always keep the right balance between features/fixes and security. In other words, if the new patch addresses application problems while sacrificing security, the change management process should be able to catch it. The change management process is a topic of a separate discussion and is mentioned here in the context of protecting security baseline settings from ad-hoc changes.

Baselines can exist in several versions and should really be tailored to server functions and locations in the network. As far as security settings are concerned, a one-size-fits-all approach is unrealistic; it can lead to restricting functionality of internal systems beyond acceptable thresholds. In addition, this same security baseline can be considered an under-par policy for public systems such as DMZ Web or email servers. This is not to say it is admissible to have lax security baselines for internal systems; this is a common situation that hackers try to use to their advantage. Internal servers are likely to be running a different set of services that need a different kind of lock-down.

From time to time (as determined by the company's security policy), the security engineer should audit production systems and verify that all the security-related settings are still in effect and unchanged, comparing the systems to a post-installation audit guide (which also changes in accordance with the security baseline updates). Automated tools are welcome in audit practice, and recent initiatives by industry consortiums have laid foundations of a universal management paradigm that vendors are implementing in the operating systems.

The Distributed Management Task Force (DMTF) has developed and is perfecting a new standard designed to unify computer management environments, making network management, server management, and desktop management essentially the same integrated environment. This paradigm, commonly referred to as *WBEM* (stands for *Web-Based Enterprise Management*), is based on the Common Information Model (CIM) standard and relies on the Hypertext Transfer Protocol (HTTP) for CIM data transmission. Messages are formatted and encoded based on the xmlCIM Encoding Specification. Because security settings are integral to the overall management information base of an operating system, WBEM provides an Application Programming Interface (API) for pulling security-related information from the audited systems, such as Registry settings, driver versions, file system permissions, installed patches information, and so forth.

DMTF board members include 3Com, BMC, Cisco, Compaq, Dell, HP, IBM, Intel, Microsoft, NEC, Novell, Sun, and Symantec. As you can see, this initiative is a serious attempt to build a new management standard based on the benefits and flaws of SNMP and Remote Monitoring (RMON) and extend the model to span the entire information technology infrastructure and promote interoperability.

The most common operating system provider today is Microsoft, which shipped its implementation of the WBEM standard with Windows 2000 and Windows XP and made a separate add-on package available for Windows NT 4 systems. From Windows 2000 on, the Windows Management Instrumentation (WMI) is an integral component of the operating system, even more so than SNMP. IBM implemented its Desktop Management Interface (DMI) version in IBM Director hardware management package and integrated it with Microsoft's WMI, making DMI information available to WMI.

Other hardware vendors are taking similar steps as well. This results in a tight integration in the domain of hardware, software, and network management. Operating system and hardware alerts and management information can now easily be ported into existing network management infrastructure.

Furthermore, security audits can be automated and done much more often with much more precision, almost entirely eliminating the human factor. Thus, a one-hour server audit can be scripted and processed in under 60 seconds. In addition, results can be presented in a variety of forms, including graphical or statistical. Compared to baseline and other servers, reports can be submitted by email or stored in a database. A management summary report can also be automatically compiled, and the information can later be analyzed in the database. The possibilities are really endless.

The following lists a few tools and management products available for this platform. Although some of these tools collect security baseline-related information from sources other than WMI/WBEM, some are based entirely on WMI or use it in some way. In either case, the information presented is largely available through WMI:

- MS Systems Management Server
- MS Operations Management 2000 Server
- MS Security Baseline Analyzer tool (MSBA)
- HFNetChk tool
- Custom WMI scripting

The latest developments introduced in Windows 2000 now allow you to create server baseline settings in the form of templates. The Microsoft Management Console (MMC) Security Settings management tool enables easy importing of these templates, making automated security baseline implementation a breeze. Furthermore, the Security Configuration and Analysis MMC snap-in enables collective management of all security settings (including the Registry) in one central location that can be applied to as many servers as necessary. This can further be expanded into the use of Group Policy Object (GPO) policies in an Active Directory environment, which is effectively an elaborate extension to the System Policy concept in the Windows NT family of operating systems.

OS/NOS Hardening

Operating system/network operating system hardening is an ongoing process of creating, implementing, and maintaining a secure configuration on your platform, be it Windows, Unix, Cisco, or any other environment. The next few paragraphs discuss the actual tools, settings, and concepts associated with implementing security baselines specifically as they apply to the situation.

The assumption is made that you are working with a Windows 2000 Server system. Although the Security+ exam does not focus on any one operating system in particular, Windows 2000 and Microsoft in general represent much of the IT environment in a large share of businesses, and the concepts learned on the Windows platform mostly apply to other platforms, such as Unix.

Getting back to the post-installation configuration guides and audits, they should include all types of information relevant to the post-installation configuration and audit routine; they have to include a security section with the appropriate security baseline settings fused into the guide. Examples of basic operating system security settings that would normally be included in the baseline are as follows:

- **Verify the operating system build number as well as major and minor service pack revision numbers**—For example, in Windows 2000, the operating system build number is always 2195 and needs no checking; however, the major service pack number makes all the difference in the world. At the time of this writing, Service Pack 3 is the latest one; be sure it is installed (more about service packs in the following sections).
- **Check the network driver versions**—Although more important for the purposes of network subsystem performance and functionality than security, it is not uncommon for the latest versions of drivers to feature fewer bugs and some security enhancements or fixes.
- **Verify configuration of remote management services**—For example, Terminal Services and Telnet. Decide which remote management services are allowed, and if any are, how application-specific security needs to be configured (such as authentication and encryption options).

- **Disable all unnecessary services running on the system**—Windows 2000 has many services enabled by default that aren't necessary in most deployments. Consider leaving only the services that are absolutely necessary for the system itself plus all the services that must be enabled to support core business requirements or applications. Figuring out which services specifically need to be disabled can be difficult, but once they are determined, the process should be documented and automated (through security templates, DOS batch, or WMI Windows script). By removing the services you do not require, the attack surface is decreased and there are fewer chances that the next discovery of buffer overflow vulnerability in a certain service will affect your servers.
- **Configure SNMP settings**—If the company is using some sort of SNMP solution, be sure that you are using very hard-to-guess community string names and that the SNMP agents on the Windows machines are set to accept only read-only requests from the management station. Configure the community string and other settings, or make sure the service is disabled.
- **Sync time zone and Windows time service settings**—These are seemingly unimportant settings, but the system places timestamps on all log records. Therefore, it is crucial that your time settings are correct and synched with the domain controller. In the absence of Windows 2000 domain controllers (if you are running standalone servers or Windows NT 4 PDC/BDCs), Windows time service normally posts errors in the event log. You can set the network time protocol (NTP) server to synchronize time by using this formula: `net time /setsntp:<server>`, in which *<server>* refers to a private or public Unix server running an NTP daemon (such as a local university or research or military facility).
- **Set event viewer settings**—By default, Windows sets log sizes to 512KB, but in most deployments, activity on the server warrants much larger logging file sizes. Set all log files to what is considered normal for your enterprise—usually this is between 4,096KB and 8,192KB (note that a logging file that's too large will degrade system performance). Set all log files to overwrite events as needed.

- **Rename local guest and administrator accounts**—The guest account is disabled by default in Windows 2000. It is a highly recommended practice to rename both guest and administrator built-in accounts, which makes launching brute-force attacks harder.
- **Ensure that all accounts with administrative privileges are configured to use long, alphanumeric, and mixed case passwords.**
- **Ensure that administrative group membership is restricted to only those individuals who must have administrative access.**
- **Configure the logon screen to hide the last logged on user.**
- **Institute password age requirements**—Also, be sure that passwords cannot be immediately reused (that is, a new password needs to be different from the old one).
- **Review account lockout policies**—Also, make sure that after a small number of unsuccessful attempts, the account gets locked out for an extensive period of time (or indefinitely, requiring administrative interference).
- **Configure the systems with the legal warning message that anyone accessing the system would normally see**—This makes it easier for the legal department to prosecute attackers when enough forensic evidence is gathered.
- **If file sharing must be enabled on the system, use IP Security Policies**—Also, configure IP filters to allow access only to NetBIOS/SMB ports from the hosts required to have access, and deny the rest. It goes without saying that the "hidden" shares should be removed and share-level permissions should be assigned carefully. Otherwise, be sure file sharing is unbound from all network adapters and removed from the list of installed network services.
- **Make sure that the Microsoft Data Access Components (MDAC)/Open Database Connectivity (ODBC) subsystem is upgraded to the latest version**—Do this if the server is involved in any kind of database hosting or interaction, such as ActiveX Data Object (ADO), Remote Data Service (RDS), Data Access Objects (DAO), and other database libraries.

The most current version is 2.7.9001 as of this writing; the version shipped with Windows XP.

- **Use HFNetChk, MBSA, or Windows Update tools to scan the system for the missing security patch information**—Also, update the server as prescribed (more in the following sections).
- **In the Microsoft world, it is recommended that the latest version of Internet Explorer be installed and updated to the latest set of security patches**—Some of the server components require a certain version of Internet Explorer, and the more recent it is, the greater the likelihood of having a stable and secure version available. The latest Internet Explorer package installs the best libraries written to date, some of which can be used by other products on the server.
- **Evaluate whether you need to install a full version of Resource Kit, or whether you need to copy specific tools onto the system**—Some tools might be imperative for remote administration or necessary when a suspicious process is running on the system and you need to either find out more information about the process (such as image path) or instantly kill it. Some Resource Kit utilities might prove to be useful security tools; others might help hackers.
- **Review security-related Registry settings**—Several extremely important settings in the Registry cannot be overlooked. Some of the settings are actually implemented in the server security templates provided by Microsoft, but nonetheless, administrators and security engineers need to know that these Registry settings exist and should be included in the security audit. Examples of such settings are TCP/IP stack tightening settings (`EnablePMTUDiscovery`, `SynAttackProtect`, `EnableDeadGWDetect`, `KeepAliveTime`, `NoNameReleaseOnDemand`—`HKLM\SYSTEM\CurrentControlSet\Services\Tcpip\Parameters`) and the infamous `RestrictAnonymous` setting (`HKLM\SYSTEM\CurrentControlSet\Control\Lsa`). Restrict anonymous setting controls NULL (anonymous) session requests for enumeration of system resources.

- **Consider implementing the `NoLMHash` Registry value in the `HKLM\System\CurrentControlSet\Control\Lsa` key**—Do this if all Windows systems on your network are Windows 2000 SP2 and later because it prevents Windows from generating comparatively weak password hashes for backward-compatible authentication. This can make a difference between a successful and failed brute-force password cracking attack.
- **Scan your system with an IP sweeper (port scanner) and determine which ports are open for no good reason**—Either disable those services and applications or implement IP filtering on the server to manage access to these ports.
- **Turn off some of the ICMP functionality on the public boxes**—Make the boxes "deaf" to ICMP echo requests to hinder reconnaissance attacks.
- **Determine whether NetBIOS is used by any of the applications running on the server**—If not, you should turn off the Computer Browser service and disable NetBIOS in the TCP/IP properties.
- **Check the `boot.ini` file to ensure that the boot time delay has been set to 0 seconds**—Do this to avoid potential situations in which someone can reboot the server and choose a different operating system or boot options.
- **It might be advisable in many installations to have cmdcon (recovery console) deployed with every installation of Windows**—Although it has no effect on securing the installation, it can definitely help you recover from a successful attack. In many cases, of course, the best recovery is reinstallation, but cmdcon might be needed to restore the system to some usable condition to retrieve data or forensic information.
- **The system Registry has to be secured from anything but administrative influence**—Use Registry Access Control Lists (ACLs) to assign permissions to Registry values. Special consideration should be given to the `Run`, `RunOnce`, and `RunEx` values because they can be used to initialize malicious software upon reboot (the same goes for the Startup folder in the Programs menu, which can be restricted using NTFS permissions). Revoke access privileges of nonadministrative personnel from the `HKLM\System\CurrentControlSet\Control\SecurePipeServers\winreg` key to limit remote access to the Registry.

- **Remove the OS/2 and Posix subsystems from the Windows system by deleting the respective Registry values from `HKLM\System\CurrentControlSet\Control\Session Manager\Subsystems`**—Be sure you leave the `debug`, `kmode`, `required`, and `windows` values, and remove the `optional`, `os2`, and `posix` values. In addition, remove the `Os2LibPath` value from the `Environment` subkey and remove `os2.exe`, `os2srv.exe`, and `os2ss.exe` from the `system32\dllcache` and `system32` directories. Finally, remove `system32\os2 directory`. This reduces the attack surface and potential vulnerabilities from the system.
- **Pay attention to the Recycle Bin settings**—It is not secure to leave purposefully deleted files in the Recycle Bin because they are not deleted if they're simply moved to the bin. Configure the bin to remove files permanently (in the Recycle Bin properties).
- **Review auditing options**—Also, be sure all the auditing options on the operating system level that need to be enabled according to your security policy are enabled. This is accessed by selecting Local Security Settings MMC, Local Policies\Audit Policies category. Many security options must be considered under the Local Policies\Security Options category, so be sure the audit includes them in detail.
- **In addition to all the tools listed thus far, all the settings can collectively be stored and managed in one central security settings database**—The MMC tool Security Configuration and Analysis allows you to create, manage, apply, and analyze all the security settings collectively in one file or tool. This applet is not accessible from Administrative tools by default, so be sure to add it from the MMC snap-ins list.

Security configuration in no way is limited to these inspections; rather, this is just a beginning that is likely to eliminate the most gaping holes.

EXAM TIP

One of the most important things to remember when locking down a mailserver is to ensure that mail relaying is switched off—it is enabled by default on most operating systems. When the mail server allows relaying, it effectively means that external users on the Internet can use the mail server in question to send mail outside the organization that owns it, effectively using that server as an intermediary.

File System

File system security can be controlled on two levels: the *share level* and the *file system level*. The problem with share-level access control is that it applies only to network-based requests for file access.

To secure access from users and applications using the system locally, you must have some kind of file system-level control. In Windows 2000, several file systems are available, but only one provides security controls: NT File System version 5 (NTFSv5). NTFS associates every file system object with an ACL and defines which system objects (user accounts) have access to the files and what type of access is allowed.

In addition to NTFS, Windows 2000 provides the Encrypting File System (EFS) service, which takes file system security to the next level. EFS enables users to encrypt their files with digital X.509 certificates, which guarantee information privacy as long as the control of the certificate is uncompromised. Where NTFS permissions can be revoked by the administrator, files encrypted with a user's certificate are no longer accessible even to the administrator. Furthermore, if the user loses control over his certificate, files encrypted with that certificate must be discarded because they are no longer accessible to anyone.

It is hardly sufficient to just ensure that your systems are running NTFS. As far as file system security is concerned, in prior versions of Windows running on NTFS, it has been wide open and even unauthenticated users could potentially gain access to and execute system utilities and even upload their own executables. Clearly, giving Full Control to the Everyone group is not the best idea. To take advantage of the NTFS features, proper permissions have to be assigned. Security templates in Windows 2000 address this problem and set restricted NTFS permissions on the following system directories:

- `%system_drive%`—Administrators are granted full control privileges, System is granted full control, and Authenticated users are granted read/execute/list folder contents/read.
- `%system_root%\repair`—Administrators are granted full control privileges, Creator and Owner are granted full control privileges, and System is granted full control privileges.
- `%system_root%\security`—Assigned the same ACL as the previous directory.
- `%system_root%\temp`—Assigned the same ACL as the previous directory.
- `%system_root%\system32\config`—Assigned the same ACL as the previous directory.

- `%system_root%\system32\logfiles`—Assigned the same ACL as the previous directory.

In addition to these settings, about a hundred system executables get assigned ACLs that limit access only to members of the Administrators group.

For those systems not installed on NTFS volumes, you can convert them from File Allocation Table (FAT) or FAT32 systems to NTFS. This process does not destroy any data, but it needs a reboot and you can't reverse this change. You use the `convert` command to convert the volume.

While operational, the system uses the `pagefile.sys` file for virtual memory needs. This file contains memory pages flushed to disk and represents another security risk associated with the file system. Be sure that the page file contents are flushed upon reboot; this can be controlled in Security Options in the Local Security Settings MMC.

Considerations other than file system permissions have to be kept in mind while securing the file system. For Win16 applications to work on much improved operating systems, they have to be capable of accessing files using the 8.3 naming format. For Windows 2000, two filenames must be maintained for each file: the native long filename (LFN) and an 8.3 name generated for backward-compatibility. Potential attackers can capitalize on shorter filenames because they are more easily revealed or guessed if they are the only method available. In addition to this, an overhead is added by 8.3 naming, so you should disable 8.3 names. The Registry key with the value that controls this feature is `HKLM\System\CurrentControlSet\Control\FileSystem`, and the value is `NtfsDisable8dot3NameCreation`.

When NTFS permissions are used and file sharing is enabled, keep in mind that the most restrictive permissions are effective permissions when combining share-level and file-system permissions. That means whichever setting is more restrictive takes effect. Furthermore, the No Access setting overrides all other assigned access levels. When working with the same type of permissions (for instance, just share-level or just file-system), if one user belongs to several groups and these groups are assigned different privileges on the same resource's ACL, permissions are combined and are cumulative (the No Access rule still applies). As a final note, under no circumstances should administrators use the Everyone system group when defining ACLs on any resource because the Everyone system group assumes all access attempts. It should really be called Anyone.

This also includes the users who are not authenticated (anonymous users). Instead of Everyone, use the Authenticated Users group, which includes only users who have already been authenticated by the system.

Updates (Patches, Service Packs, and Hotfixes)

Before we proceed, we need to define what exactly we mean by *patch*, *service pack*, and *hotfix*:

- **Service pack**—This is a major update for an operating system or product it is designed to patch. Effectively, a service pack is a collection of patches released to date since the operating system or product was shipped (every service pack is cumulative). It is usually pretty large in size, so the best way to deploy it is to download it once and then use automation techniques to distribute the service pack locally. Generally, service packs are crucially important updates and should be deployed on every operating system installation as soon as possible, provided that existing applications are not impaired by this update.
- **Hotfix**—Also called *quick fix engineering (QFE)*, hotfixes are software fixes written to address specific problems certain customers are experiencing. These are not fully tested patches available to the general public, and the prevailing school of thought is that most users do not need this fix, unless they are experiencing that specific problem. As new service packs are released, some hotfixes do get some serious testing and subsequently are included in service packs.
- **Security patch**—When new vulnerabilities are discovered, hotfixes are written to eliminate the vulnerabilities. The difference between a hotfix and a patch is that a security patch is tested and is mandatory for all users to avoid potential break-ins. It is a race between the company releasing the patch, the hacker community, and security administrators. Generally, as new vulnerabilities are discovered, they immediately receive a lot of attention and hackers try to exploit these vulnerabilities, hoping that system administrators will be slow patching the servers. (In some cases, a lot of bureaucracy is involved in the change management process, which introduces significant delays.)

> Patches can be of three categories: the ones that fix low-risk problems, ones that fix moderate risk problems, or ones that fix critical problems. They also can apply to client applications and subsystems integral to the workstations, which might not be as difficult to test and deploy. Server-side patches conceivably need testing and evaluation whether they are actually necessary in a particular deployment (whether the risks described in the security advisory actually apply to the server in question).

Granted, you might not be able to chase all the patches that get released almost on a weekly basis, but you must have a process that evaluates potential risks of the newly discovered vulnerability as it relates to your particular business. In some cases (exploit outbreaks on the Internet, such as the Code Red and Nimda attacks in most recent history), it might be a matter of hours when servers in your organization are exposed, and it can be crucial to put all other assignments on hold and concentrate on immediately mitigating the risk (that is, apply the patch on one server, let it soak for a few hours, and then deploy on the rest). In situations such as this one, a regular change management process should be circumvented and an emergency patching process should be followed, if one exists. Security policies must establish the emergency process alternative to regular change management motions. In either case, a rollback path must be available that administrators can follow in case of an unsuccessful update (sometimes urgent patches are released lacking a full testing cycle and problems are found after the rollout).

Generally, patch management processes should follow steps similar to the following:

1. **Risk analysis**—Risks of deploying the patch should be weighted against risks of not deploying it. In certain circumstances, new waves of attacks are still using old or recently discovered vulnerabilities, and the existing environment might already be immune to them. Security advisories are helpful during this step.

2. **Planning**—You should determine which systems in particular need patches, which patches they need, who will be responsible for implementation, when it should occur, and other administrative items.

3. **QA testing**—In a classic change management approach, all changes, no matter how insignificant, must be rigorously tested. This is especially true in environments running custom applications. QA testing length is determined by the urgency of the issue, and at times it mandates very short QA cycles.
4. **Deployment**—The person assigned during planning executes the plan and communicates the change. Several tools can be used to help deploy the patches, including but not limited to Windows Update, Software Update Services (SUS), and custom scripted mechanisms.
5. **Monitoring**—The NOC monitoring station is notified and requested to pay special attention and monitor affected servers. If an issue is evident, appropriate engineers should be contacted immediately.
6. **Review/Rollback**—After the dust settles, a meeting is called to analyze the steps taken and the degree of their effectiveness and success. The emergency/change management process can be reviewed and updated at this time. If the rollout proved to be unsuccessful, a rollback to the previous configuration is made.

In deploying patches in Microsoft environments, several tools are available to help with patch inventory scans and distribution. The first and most obvious is the Windows Update mechanism designed to work with the `http://windowsupdate.microsoft.com` site. When the site is visited for the first time, it prompts the user to accept a Microsoft ActiveX component that essentially implements the process. Next, an up-to-date patch definition Extensible Markup Language (XML) file maintained by Microsoft is downloaded to the client computer, and then the ActiveX control's logic checks system settings, system files' checksums and versions, and Registry settings. Then, results are displayed in the browser, and the user can download selected patches and apply them as part of the same process. This utility is great for ad-hoc patching, but in a big environment, individual patching and inventory checks might not be an option. Also, online services might not always be accessible due to occasional outages on Microsoft's side or the company's network architecture.

An optional workaround is to manually download all the patches in a centralized location and create an installation script that applies the patches. Although perfectly acceptable, depending on the size of the network, it can also be a burden.

Alternatively, the Automatic Update service (an optional component that can be installed) can be set to check for updates on a periodic basis, alerting the user of new updates available for his platform. Additionally, it can download the patches and even features the option to automatically install the downloaded patches. It is a dangerous way of configuring the service, but it can be combined with other tools to make it the best desktop update mechanism available. A connection to the Internet is needed for the Automatic Update service to work on its own.

The next option is Software Update Services (SUS). The SUS concept is essentially the same as the Windows Update and Automatic Update service combined, although it introduces some important improvements to the patch management process that might suit many production environments. First, it replaces the Windows Update online servers with an internal company server running SUS Service. This eliminates the need to download patches more than once, preserving bandwidth. In addition, individual servers no longer need the Internet connection to communicate directly with the Microsoft update services. The new process essentially allows system administrators to review, download, and test patches locally. After approved, the patches are published on the internal server, specifying which computers must download these patches and update their components without further intervention. On the client side (with clients in this case being desktop and server systems), the Automatic Update service is employed with minor modifications, effectively being set up to work with the local patch distribution server. SUS needs either Active Directory or, in the absence of it, a slight modification in the Registry that tells the update services on client systems where to look for updates. In addition, administrators can specify time for these deployments and specifically block servers and desktops from downloading some of the patches that do not apply to them.

SUS seems to be based on two separate patch management techniques that are quite impractical in the real world where change management, combined with large corporate environments, can create administrative nightmares. SUS takes the concepts employed in these two techniques and makes them suitable specifically to those environments in which a strict change management process is in place—at the same time eliminating much of the manual labor.

In addition to these methods, implementing a process in which patch inventory would be compiled on a regular basis, preferably automatically, is useful. In this area, the HFNetChk command-line tool comes in handy. It can be employed with a variety of command-line switches where you can specify hostnames to be scanned, the level of detail to be included in the report, and the output form (or location) of the report. HFNetChk uses much the same patch definition XML file as the Windows Update process; the only difference is that it can optionally use a local (previously downloaded but still up-to-date) version of the XML file. There are no deployment considerations—it is a command-line utility administrators are free to use wherever they like. To take this process one step further, a Web-based interface can easily be programmed to work with a SQL database to specify which computers should be queried, pass the parameters to the command-line utility, parse the text files generated as the result, and import the data back into the database. The process can be further automated and implemented in a form of a system service running on the administrative machine. Of course, having this information in the database enables all kinds of reports and analysis to be done and is indeed a very powerful option; however, custom programming is somewhat of a requirement.

As an option to the HFNetChk tool and all the solutions built using it as the engine, a custom WMI script can be utilized to query patch inventory from the server and, likewise, be incorporated into a similar database solution, as described in the preceding paragraph. A sample listing of such a script is shown in Listing 4.1. It uses Microsoft Excel to generate a report and can collect patch information either from the local machine or from a set of remote servers.

LISTING 4.1

A SAMPLE LISTING OF A CUSTOM WMI SCRIPT

```
' This script collects patch inventory information
➥from either
' a local computer or one or more remote computers.
' This is a demonstration of WMI usage

On error resume next
set oXL = CreateObject("Excel.Application")
oXL.visible = true
set oWB = oXL.workbooks
oWB.add
```

```
if msgbox("Are you collecting patch inventory locally (as
➥ opposed to remotely)?", vbyesno, "Local/Remote?")
➥=vbyes then
   servername="."
else
   username = inputbox("Please enter your domain\
➥username:")
   password = inputbox("Please enter your password:")
   servername = inputbox("Please enter one or more IP
➥ addresses you wish to collect inventory from." &
➥ vbcrlf & "Use comma to separate server addresses:")
   If trim(servername)="" or trim(username)="" or trim
➥ (password)="" then
      msgbox "Either username, password, or servername(s)
➥  were empty. Please run the script again and
➥ enter these values."
      oxl.quit
      'set owb = Nothing
      set oxl = Nothing
      wscript.quit
   end if
end if

servernames = Split(servername, ",", -1, 1)
runs = UBound(servernames)
x = 0

for i = lbound(servernames) to ubound(servernames)
   OutQuery = RunQuery (trim(servernames(x)), username,
➥ password)
   'now add to excel
   for v = lbound(outquery)+1 to ubound(outquery)+1
      if x = 0 then
         oxl.sheets.item(1).cells(v,1+x).Value =
➥ outquery(v-1,0)
         oxl.sheets.item(1).cells(1,1).interior.color
➥  = RGB(255,130,50)
         oxl.sheets.item(1).cells(v,1+x).font.bold =true
➥   'Interior.colorindex=5
      end if
      oxl.sheets.item(1).cells(v, 2+x).value =
➥  outquery(v-1,1)
   next
oxl.sheets.item(1).cells(1, 2+i).interior.color =
➥ RGB(255,130,50)
x=x+1
next

bugstop

oxl.sheets.item(1).range("A1:IV65535").font.size = 8
oxl.sheets.item(1).range("A1:IV65535").font.name = "Arial"
oxl.sheets.item(1).range("A1:IV65535").columns.autofit
oxl.sheets.item(1).range("A1:IV65535").rows.autofit
oxl.sheets.item(1).range("B1:IV65535").
➥ Style.HorizontalAlignment = 4
```

continues

LISTING 4.1 *continued*

A SAMPLE LISTING OF A CUSTOM WMI SCRIPT

```
oxl.sheets.item(1).range("A1:IV65535").
➥ style.verticalalignment = 1

if msgbox("Do you wish to save this report now?",vbyesno,
➥ "Save Report")=vbyes then
   oxl.save '"C:\inventory.xls"
end if
set oxl = Nothing

if err.number <> 0 then
  msgbox "Error: " & err.number & ", " &  err.description
else
   msgbox "Patch inventory report has been generated",
➥ vbInformation, "Success"
end if


'==========================================
' this function does all the work.
' The upper part of the code collects user input
' and feeds the parameters to this function, then
' presents the results.
' Usage: RunQuery(servername, username, password)

On error resume next
Function RunQuery(byval ServerName, byval username,
➥byval password)

'This array will be used to house all the data collected
'during each run.
' It will be returned to the caller, which can then present
' the data in any format deemed appropriate, put it in a
' SQL, or do whatever.

Dim myArr(8,1)

'first, we define MyLocator object to use Web Based
' Enterprise Management library.

set MyLocator = CreateObject
➥("WBEMScripting.SWBEMLocator")

' we call Bugstop every now and then to trap errors

BugStop

' Now, we initialize WMIcon object and establish a
' connection to the server name that was provided in the
' function call, we also use credentials passed with the
' servername. Local computers need no password, so these
' can be null. For remote connections, passwords and
' usernames are mandatory.
```

```
Set WMIcon = myLocator.ConnectServer(ServerName,
➥"root\CIMV2", username, password)
BugStop

'this is the main loop that collects info from WMI
' WMIobjectset collection represents the resulting set of
' objects returned from the query passed as a parameter to
' the ExecQuery method

Set WMIObjectSet = WMICon.ExecQuery("SELECT *
➥FROM Win32_ComputerSystem")
BugStop

' now we enumerate all the objects within the result set
' and collect properties

for each WMIobj in WMIObjectSet
   MyArr(0,0)="Netbios Name"
   Myarr(0,1)=WMIobj.name
   Myarr(1,0)=""
   myarr(1,1)=""
err.clear
Next

bugstop

' Basic idea is the same going forward. First we query,
' and then collect data from the result set.
' We can reuse existing connection, which speeds the
' process up.
' Next piece of code collects QFE information.

Set WMIObjectSet = WMICon.ExecQuery("SELECT *
➥FROM Win32_QuickFixEngineering")
   totalpatches =0
for each WMIobj in WMIObjectSet
   totalpatches = totalpatches+1
   myarr(2,0)="Total number of patches"
   myarr(2,1)=totalpatches
   myarr(3,0)="Installed patches KBIDs"
   myarr(3,1)=wmiobj.hotfixID & ", " &
➥wmiobj.servicepackineffect & vblf & myarr(3,1)
   err.clear
Next

' And, repeat one more time to collect a few operating
'system parameters - version and service pack.

set wmiobjectset = WMIcon.execquery("SELECT
➥* FROM Win32_OperatingSystem")
for each WMIobj in WMIobjectset
   myarr(5,0)="Operating System"
   myarr(5,1)=wmiobj.caption & ", Version " &
➥wmiobj.version
   myarr(6,0)="Service Pack Level"
```

continues

LISTING 4.1 *continued*

A SAMPLE LISTING OF A CUSTOM WMI SCRIPT

```
   myarr(6,1)=wmiobj.servicepackmajorversion & "." &
➥wmiobj.servicepackminorversion
next

err.clear
RunQuery = myarr
End Function


'=========================================
Function BugStop()
if err.number <> 0 then
   msgbox "Error: " & err.number & ", " & err.description
   err.clear
   'owb.close
   oxl.quit
   'set owb = Nothing
   set oxl = Nothing
   wscript.quit
end if
End Function
```

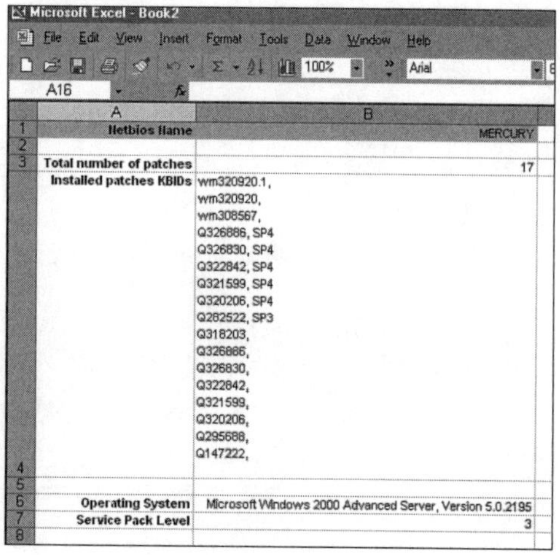

	A	B
1	Netbios Name	MERCURY
2		
3	Total number of patches	17
4	Installed patches KBIDs	wm320920.1, wm320920, wm308567, Q326886, SP4 Q326830, SP4 Q322842, SP4 Q321599, SP4 Q320206, SP4 Q282522, SP3 Q318203, Q326886, Q326830, Q322842, Q321599, Q320206, Q295688, Q147222,
5		
6	Operating System	Microsoft Windows 2000 Advanced Server, Version 5.0.2195
7	Service Pack Level	3
8		

FIGURE 4.1
Sample output of the script.

Figure 4.1 show an example of what this script outputs.

This script demonstrates how WMI can be tapped for administration and security purposes; granted, the script can be modified to take input from any source and produce output in any format. It can also be expanded to include any other administrative and security information available through WMI.

> **NOTE**
>
> **A Good Source of Information** To find out how to take full advantage of WMI, check out the WMI SDK kit on Microsoft's Web site. It features a thorough help file with plenty of samples and a WMI Object Browser—sort of an explorer of all the objects and properties of the WMI object model. This helps you write the scripts and find the correct properties to include in the report.

Perhaps the biggest advantage of this custom approach to patch management is its flexibility. Administrators can fuse this information into existing database-driven IT solutions that their company might already have in place. By the same token, administrators can code their own alerting mechanisms to ensure that the patch set is the same across the servers of similar types. The script can grab the set of patches from the server, compare it to the patch inventory baseline maintained in the management database or against a freshly downloaded XML definition file, and send an email or page a security engineer if a difference is found. After it is optimized, this process can make a huge difference in eliminating known vulnerabilities and keeping the environment updated.

Network Hardening

In addition to all the previous discussions of firewall and IDS techniques, routers themselves need to be secured and maintained to eliminate as much potential vulnerability as possible—this is referred to as *network hardening*. As far as hosts on the network are concerned, in an ideal world, they should have their own IP filters configured according to the corresponding baseline. Filters can be created once and then distributed to the servers where this particular baseline applies. Some might see it as a bit of overkill, but in reality, this provides an additional layer of security and serves as a safety net to the firewall protection. In addition, managing every bit of traffic on the firewall can sometimes be difficult. What administrators can do instead is allow specific types of traffic collectively into the DMZ and then set up IP filtering on the server level to process only traffic types that are relevant to that server.

In addition to serving as a safety net to the firewall, this technique also protects the servers from attacks originated from within, such as when a virus arrives in an email, a user opens it, and it goes looking for vulnerable Web servers on which to spread itself. It never hurts to have additional layers of security; it is rather a matter of choosing the right balance between security and manageability.

But, besides firewalls and servers, we also have routers and switches—the very brains of networking. A compromised routing device can prove a costly experience for any company. Let's look at the options available when securing a routing device. (For the purposes of this discussion, the assumption is made that this hypothetical device is a Cisco router running IOS software. IOS is a stripped-down and very specialized version of Unix, and many router implementations follow Cisco's example: a hardware box that runs proprietary software. In some cases, even the configuration commands are similar.)

When securing a router, the following areas have to be considered:

- Physical security (discussed in previous chapters)
- Firmware security
- Router configuration security (static and dynamic configuration security)
- Remote access and administration security
- Interface and protocol security (network traffic security)

When it comes to routers, security-wise they are no different from the rest of the environment. The same change management process applies. The security policy and incident response process must cover network devices as well.

Firmware Updates

Cisco devices run the Internet Operating System (IOS) software, stored in flash memory. Just like any other operating system, it contains vulnerabilities that are discovered every now and again. Cisco also constantly improves performance of IOS and adds features, some of which are security-related. All in all, router software changes quite frequently, and it can be a real challenge to maintain IOS updates across a network of significant size. You also must keep in mind that testing of the latest IOS often does not catch all the bugs every time it is released. Therefore, administrators have to choose the right balance for their environments between new features/bug fixes and the potential introduction of new bugs and stability issues. As a general rule, you should keep the environment updated using a recent, but not the latest, version of the IOS. It is wise to wait for a month or two after the release to ensure it is stable. Then, you can roll it out in your QA environment, let it soak for a week or two, and finally upgrade your production routers—providing that no problems are discovered during the testing.

Depending on the flash memory size, a Cisco router can have more than one operating system image and offer administrators an option of which version of operating system to boot from. More traditionally, a router has just enough flash memory to store one image. In any case, make sure the new operating system being loaded has operating memory requirements that are satisfied by the hardware on which the IOS is being upgraded. This step is crucial in determining whether the upgrade is technically possible or whether a hardware upgrade is required as well. The rest of the steps are as follows:

1. Download the IOS image and place it on the network. Cisco IOS supports three update mechanisms: File Transfer Protocol (FTP), Trivial FTP (TFTP), and NAS Change Proposal (NCP). FTP seems to be the best option because it has some rudimentary authentication mechanism associated with it. In either case, be sure the service used for upgrade purposes does not remain enabled on the production network. Enable it only to perform an upgrade.

2. Verify flash/RAM memory sizes and existing IOS version by running the `show version` and `show flash` commands.
3. Back up the existing IOS image and running configuration. Use the `copy flash tftp` command if you are using TFTP as a transfer mechanism. For the running configuration, use the `copy running-config tftp` command.
4. If you are upgrading borderline routers, you should shut down the external interface for the time being. Use the `shutdown` command in the interface configuration mode.
5. Now you perform the actual upgrade. Use the `copy tftp flash` command to download the new IOS image from the TFTP server. When the process completes, reboot the router.
6. Verify the current router configuration, IOS version, and available memory sizes after the upgrade is complete. Cancel the shutdown on the external interface by using the `no shutdown` command in the interface configuration mode.

Configuration

When configuring a routing device, the following checklist can provide some guidance as to what to look for:

- **Router users are limited to administrative personnel**—The password and the enable password (the password you are prompted for when you type the enable command and go into privileged mode) have to be complex and kept strictly confidential.
- **Console, AUX, and VTY access should be limited and controlled**—In the case of AUX and Console, this is very much related to physical router security. In the case of VTY, there should be only one or two ports available at any given time.
- **Use SSH instead of Telnet for more secure router administration.**
- **Disable any unnecessary network services, leaving only the bare minimum.**
- **Shut down any other interfaces not used, such as Ethernet or serial interfaces.**

- **Clearly define which ports and protocols are allowed into the network**—This is not hard to do if one or two firewalls have already been configured. Armed with this information, the administrator is in a much better position to define access lists.
- **Implement access lists, strictly following documentation compiled as a result of the previous step**—For detailed information on configuring access lists on a Cisco router, refer to the exercises section in Chapter 3.
- **Consider security benefits of static routing as opposed to convenience of using a dynamic routing protocol**—You can use dynamic routing inside the network, and if at all possible, resort to static route configuration on the borderline routers.
- **If you are using routing protocols, ensure that deployed versions utilize integrity mechanisms**—In addition to successfully detecting routing loops, they have to ensure that route updates are coming from a trusted, authenticated source.
- **Logging must be enabled**—The router has a buffer that keeps the most recent log records until it fills up; then the buffer is overwritten. To keep up with the security policy standards, you should set up a syslog server and direct log records from a router to that server. Not only does this enable you to keep a history of events and collect forensic information, but it also helps protect it from being altered in case of a router compromise. In addition, various syslog servers can introduce rudimentary IDS logic to the processing of syslog messages (one of the examples is Private I).
- **The time and date on all routers must be adjusted to the current time**—This is for reasons similar to those outlined in the operating system hardening discussion. It should also be synchronized with an NTP server.
- **Logging should be reviewed on a daily or otherwise regular basis.**
- **SNMP should be configured to use difficult-to-guess community strings or disabled altogether**—If an intruder guesses a community string, he will be able to read vital configuration information and operational data off the device.

Application Hardening

The final phase of securing an environment is application lockdown. Applications are as secure as the more fundamental components they rely on, such as the operating system and network (meaning that no matter how carefully the house is built, if it has no solid foundation, it will probably fall apart very soon). A massive amount of exploits and vulnerabilities is nonetheless found in applications, simply because they are designed to communicate. The purpose of a Web server, a DNS server, or an email server is to be open to the public, albeit in a limited, highly specialized sense. Still, it is enough for one port to be open to consider security implications when deploying server applications. In many cases, it is up to the vendor to keep releasing security and performance patches and keep up with the hacker community, but some of the more popular server types have their own security-related configurations.

Web Servers

Without doubt, public service Web servers are the most abundant type of servers on the Internet, and they are the most likely target for exploits and break-ins. Apache on the Unix platforms and Internet Information Services (IIS) on the Microsoft platform are the two most popular Web server types and, not surprisingly, they are the most frequently targeted ones. Microsoft's IIS has had the largest number of exploits discovered to date.

Setting any performance-related discussions aside, it is a half-myth/half-truth that IIS is the least secure Web server platform in existence. It is hard to argue that IIS is secure when massive worldwide attacks are successfully launched against it as often as every few months. It has to be noted, however, that the success of those attacks is oppositely proportional to the attention administrators pay to Web server security. Armed with the appropriate knowledge, administrators can secure IIS as tightly as Microsoft's source code allows, which is pretty tight.

IIS is and will remain a popular platform because of its development ease and versatility, and this is why your Web server should be one of the key parameters when defining security baselines.

IIS6 is announced to bring major changes to performance as well as security, which will only make the security situation more important as the number of deployments grow. Whereas Web server security configurations used to be largely "tweaks" that not many people were aware of, now the process is rather straightforward with the help of the IISLockDown utility that also uses the URLscan ISAPI filter.

IISLockDown (currently version 2.1) automates the process of securing an IIS server. This tool allows an administrator to select which features and services she wants to leave enabled and remove/disable the rest. It offers a choice of server template and implements respective security baselines, providing the administrator with optional control of the process. Furthermore, it removes unused ISAPI DLL script mappings, removes unneeded directories from the file system and virtual directories from the IIS server, and changes ACLs on the file system content exposed by the Web server. It also locks down access to system tools and directories and installs URLscan—perhaps the best utility ever released for IIS servers.

The purpose of URLscan is to monitor and filter Web server requests. The idea to create something of URLscan type probably was triggered by the massive outbreak that Code Red caused in mid-2001. URLscan is essentially an ISAPI filter that, hypothetically speaking, isolates the IIS core from the outside world, checking every request to the Web server before the Web server sees it. URLscan configuration is fairly flexible and allows administrators to

- Deny various URL sequences known to be harmful and used in many exploits (directory traversals, trailing dots on directory names, backslashes in URLs, alternative stream access, escaping after normalization, and multiple CGI processes to be accessed in single URL)
- Deny various static files from being requested via a URL (`.ini`, `.log`, and so on)
- Deny unused script mappings (`.ida`, `.idq`, `.printer`, and so on)
- Deny executables that can be run on the Web server (`.com`, `.exe`, and so on)

- Deny all but allowed OR allow all but denied file extensions (any extension such as `.gif`, `.css`, `.jpeg`, `.html`, `.exe`, `.bat`, `.com`, and so on)
- Deny certain HTTP methods (`DELETE`, `PUT`, `COPY`, `MOVE`, and so on) while allowing others (`GET`, `POST`, and so on)
- Deny certain headers (`Translate:`, `If:`, `Lock-token:`)
- Perform normalization of URLs (one-pass or two-pass)
- Control whether dots are allowed in paths other than to demarcate file extension
- Log all rejected activity, including IP addresses and URLs
- Redirect rejected requestors to a URL that can contain legal warnings, among other explanations

After URLscan is configured (the `.ini` file contains all the settings) and the Web service is restarted for the change to kick in, URLscan instantly becomes a crucial security control that filters a lot of invalid, harmful requests. A sample logging recorded on a typical day can look similar to the following:

```
[09-03-2002 - 01:30:45] Client at 24.141.93.35: URL
➥contains extension '.exe', which is disallowed.
➥Request will be rejected.  Site Instance='2',
➥Raw URL='/scripts/root.exe'
[09-03-2002 - 01:30:46] Client at 24.141.93.35: URL
➥contains extension '.exe', which is disallowed.
➥Request will be rejected.  Site Instance='2',
➥Raw URL='/MSADC/root.exe'
[09-03-2002 - 01:30:49] Client at 24.141.93.35: URL
➥contains extension '.exe', which is disallowed.
➥ Request will be rejected.  Site Instance='2',
➥Raw URL='/c/winnt/system32/cmd.exe'
[09-03-2002 - 01:30:49] Client at 24.141.93.35: URL
➥contains extension '.exe', which is disallowed.
➥Request will be rejected.  Site Instance='2',
➥Raw URL='/d/winnt/system32/cmd.exe'
[09-03-2002 - 01:30:49] Client at 24.141.93.35: URL
➥normalization was not complete after one pass.
➥ Request will be rejected.  Site Instance='2',
➥Raw URL='/scripts/..%255c../winnt/system32/cmd.exe'
[09-03-2002 - 01:30:49] Client at 24.141.93.35: URL
➥normalization was not complete after one pass.
➥Request will be rejected.  Site Instance='2',
➥Raw URL='/_vti_bin/..%255c../..%255c../..%255c../
➥winnt/system32/cmd.exe'
```

```
[09-03-2002 - 01:30:49] Client at 24.141.93.35: URL
➥normalization was not complete after one pass.
➥Request will be rejected.  Site Instance='2', Raw
➥URL='/_mem_bin/..%255c../..%255c../..%255c../winnt/
➥system32/cmd.exe'
[09-03-2002 - 01:30:50] Client at 24.141.93.35: URL
➥normalization was not complete after one pass.
➥Request will be rejected.  Site Instance='2', Raw
➥ URL='/msadc/..%255c../..%255c../..%255c/..%c1%1c..
➥/..%c1%1c../..%c1%1c../winnt/system32/cmd.exe'
[09-03-2002 - 01:30:50] Client at 24.141.93.35: URL
➥contains high bit character. Request will be
➥rejected.  Site Instance='2', Raw URL='/scripts
➥/..%c1%1c../winnt/system32/cmd.exe'
```

In this record, you can clearly see that a year and a half after Code Red stormed the Internet, the author's Web server is still receiving entire batches of Code Red-like URL requests trying to find an exploit on the IIS server. This is probably the reason the IIS server generally has a reputation as the least secure Web platform: Microsoft used to include it in default installations of operating system too often. People are running Web servers on their home workstations without even knowing about it, never mind the Web server security configuration details! These workstations have been compromised for more than a year now, and most of their owners don't know their machines are infected, which spreads the virus. The Web server from which this log sample was taken was receiving a heavy stream of similar requests for a year. This is just one of the reasons it is extremely important that Web server security is configured before the plug goes into the network adapter.

Securing a default Web server is easy. What is more challenging is developing custom applications while keeping the whole security issue in mind. This is one of the reasons for the overwhelming popularity of exploit searching in the Web server area. Unlike, say, email servers, Web servers run custom applications that are often designed very poorly from the security perspective. These applications often concentrate development efforts in the functionality and user experience areas.

IN THE FIELD

ABC CORP'S WEB SERVER SECURITY

The following is an example to illustrate this school of thought and to switch away from Microsoft vulnerabilities for the time being.

While consulting for a real corporation with the imaginary name ABC Corp., we were asked to find security vulnerabilities in the company's Web server, which was running Allaire's (Macromedia) ColdFusion software. The Web server configuration was quite tight, but upon some scrutiny of the user interaction processes implemented by developers through the Web interface (having no inside information of any kind), we walked away and in less than two hours launched a custom-written application that crawled the site. This application attempted to guess the member IDs in the URL requesting their profile and parsed the names and contact information into a database. The next morning we had a database of several tens of thousands of member profiles with addresses, telephone/fax numbers, and emails.

This was almost the entire database of member profiles ABC Corp. had behind several firewalls and with strict access control. In the real world, what would happen next is that not only would ABC Corp. experience a massive privacy blow, but this database would most likely also be put up for sale. Competitors would buy it, and their sales personnel would go after ABC Corp.'s members. The news would leak to the media, and ABC Corp.'s reputation (and business) would be ruined. The hacker would get some cash for the effort and gain respect in her community. By logging IP addresses, a hacker can easily get someone in the great unknown to run the software overnight in exchange for a moderate monetary reward, covering up her tracks. Case closed. And so is ABC Corp.

It goes without saying that IIS servers, as well as Apache (or any other Web server, for that matter), must be thoroughly patched very soon after a new vulnerability is discovered and the patch is released. It is extremely important to be half a step ahead in learning about the Web server vulnerabilities; you should subscribe to a security alert list that keeps you in the loop. In the case of Microsoft's IIS, the same patch management technologies described previously apply, thanks to tight cross-product integration.

Although patching Web servers is simply a matter of due diligence, the real challenge remains to write "smart" applications. Even with the tightest of Web servers, ABC Corp. is exposed beyond belief without realizing it. A smart application should be able to detect and prevent such massive break-ins and espionage. There is as much vulnerability out there as there are custom Web-applications, and thus the quest continues. Web server vulnerabilities are one of the main administrative headaches because Web server holes are sought so much.

NOTE

Web Server Security This is a topic worthy of a book in its own right. A few paragraphs in this chapter are a solid starting point; they are not written to cover the topic in detail, however.

A good set of security whitepapers on IIS and other popular products is available from the National Security Agency at `http://www.nsa.gov`.

In addition to the NSA, Microsoft's site contains many security whitepapers, at `http://www.microsoft.com/security`. This site contains security information from the source on just about anything with a Microsoft logo.

Apache-specific information is accessible through `http://www.apache.org`.

For Web server security information of a more general nature, navigate to `http://www.w3.org/Security`.

WARNING

Control DNS Server Updates A few words need to be said about DNS and SQL servers. DNS server updates in the form of zone transfers need to be controlled and restricted to prescribed replication partners only if the request is coming from an authenticated source. That is rule number one in DNS security.

Remember the `ls -d` command from discussions in previous chapters? Using the nslookup tool, you can connect to any DNS server and retrieve the entire database of hostnames and IP addresses if the `ls -d` command is unrestricted. Likewise, it is dangerous not to control who your zone transfer partner is. Keep in mind that IP addresses should no longer be acceptable as authentication parameters because IP address information can be spoofed.

NOTE

Additional Study It is highly recommended that you get a copy of the *Security Operations Guide for Windows 2000* for additional study in environments where Windows 2000 plays a role.

Other Servers

Compared to the Web servers and custom applications, configuring security in the rest of the standard server types is significantly easier. It is also usually limited to the settings available in the management interface of the server in question, as well as all service packs and security patches released by the software vendor.

The latest version of the DNS standard allows dynamic updates, Dynamic Domain Name System or Service (DDNS). This is a useful feature in the internal DNS system, but it can prove quite harmful if enabled on external DNS servers. Companies are advised to architect their DNS systems so that they are split in two: internal and external. The external system is placed into the DMZ and becomes available to the public; however, it should not reveal any hostname information other than what is absolutely necessary for public access—for example, email and Web servers. The internal system is subsequently used to service the internal part of the namespace, where dynamic updates are acceptable. The internal system can be configured to forward DNS requests it cannot answer to the external server. It can also contain the records from the external DNS system, ensuring that local clients are able to find the DNS server and, at the same time, necessitating maintenance of only one set of external host records on the external DNS server.

Speaking of database servers—and this usually means some implementation of the SQL standard—the same patch and service pack rules apply. In addition, the local equivalent of the `sa` account must have a complex password assigned to it (watch out for SQL implementations that might not allow you to change the `sa` password, forcing it to remain blank). If possible, you should use integrated authentication with the operating system, allowing centralized management of user accounts as opposed to worrying about several user account databases. Be sure that users are assigned only to those database objects they really need access to.

CASE STUDY: PENTATONIC SOUND SYSTEMS, LLC

ESSENCE OF THE CASE

Here are the essential elements in this case:

- Secure the corporate environment using a set of firewalls.
- Set up a DMZ segment and place publicly accessible servers and services in that segment.
- Lock down and patch the Web server farm, and place database servers inside the internal network; block access to the services with IP filters, allowing only specific IP addresses to connect to specific services.
- Plan, test, and implement a network intrusion detection system that combines all pattern-matching technologies.
- Ensure desktops are patched against known vulnerabilities and implement an automated patch rollout process.

SCENARIO

Pentatonic Sound Systems is a major supplier of audio equipment to hundreds of entertainment complexes across the USA and Canada. The company has branches in 10 major North American cities. It also serves retail customers through many specialty shop locations and the Internet. Companies and clients can submit orders via the Internet and pick up the merchandise or have it delivered. The company is enjoying a great deal of strength in sales figures and is planning to continue in the same direction.

Pentatonic Sound Systems wants to achieve several main objectives. First of all, it wants to ensure that its IT infrastructure is secure from potential incursions from the Internet on a desktop level. Next, the company wants to secure its Web application infrastructure and also be able to securely communicate with partners and between branches of the company. Most importantly, the company wants to ensure that its internal network is free from outside interference.

ANALYSIS

The process should begin with the company creating a secure network infrastructure. On the local LAN and in the DMZ, a private address range should be used to reduce the risk of direct communication between potential intruders and the DMZ systems bypassing firewall and NAT devices.

continues

Case Study: Pentatonic Sound Systems, LLC

continued

All servers accessible to the public will go into the DMZ, and communications between these hosts and outside systems will be tightly screened by the firewalls. In addition to firewalls, the company should commit resources to implementing network-based IDSs to monitor the company's internal networks for potential hacker activity.

Partners and retail customers are welcome to use the Web servers for researching and procuring the equipment, but these Web servers must be secured through patching and configuration.

In addition, Web applications should be architected so that a firewall separates the Web server farm from the database servers and the Web server farm from the rest of the world.

User desktops should be locked down through automated patching using AD software publishing, SUS services, or any other custom or commercial patch deployment system. In addition to patching, administrators must implement security policies to ensure that user activity is within well-defined boundaries.

Chapter Summary

KEY TERMS

- Active detection
- Anomaly-based IDS
- Demilitarized zone (DMZ)
- False negative
- False positive
- Heuristics analysis
- Honeypot
- Host intrusion detection system
- Incident response
- Intrusion detection system (IDS)
- Network intrusion detection system (NIDS)

This chapter has provided an overview of intrusion detection technologies. It was concluded that IDSs can be subcategorized into two main divisions: network-based intrusion detection systems and host-based intrusion detection systems. The essence of network-based intrusion detection systems is in their purpose to analyze network traffic in real-time. They use raw packets traveling the network as the source of information and are most often implemented as standalone, dedicated devices that have one or more network interfaces running in a promiscuous mode. These systems usually feature an intrusion recognition module—either hardware or software—that uses one or more of the many analysis approaches, such as pattern matching, stateful inspection, protocol decode, heuristic analysis (frequency or threshold excess), or anomaly analysis.

This chapter also reviewed the concept of honeypots. A honeypot is the ultimate defense feature that works in exactly the opposite way from traditional security items. It is a decoy box designed to attract hackers. It usually has all the logging and tracing enabled, and its security level is lowered on purpose. Honeypots are not security mechanisms in their own right; they are valuable additions to otherwise strong systems security-wise.

Chapter Summary

Next, the chapter looked at the incident response handling procedures. The basic premise of incident handling and response is that the company needs to have a clear action plan on what each response team member needs to do and when it has to be done. An incident response team usually consists of members from various departments (from the CEO and legal to press people to IT experts to external contacts for forensic analysis help). The incident response team deals with items such as initial assessment, initial communication, initial containment, intrusion evaluation, evidence collection, communicating to the public, restoring the services, and then analyzing whether the action plan addressed the situation properly. Team members need to document any actions they are taking for further documentation, analysis, and reports.

From that point on, we discussed security baselines and more specific steps of locking down various parts and types of servers and networks. A security baseline is defined in the company's security policy and is a model set of security-related modifications, patches, and settings that underpin the technical implementation of security. Companies should have post-installation configuration and audit guidelines (automated, where possible) that implement security policies. These settings include, but are not limited to, Registry enhancements and lock-downs, auditing and logging configurations, file system security tightening, service and application configurations, and custom security tools.

- Passive detection
- Pattern matching
- Protocol decode analysis
- Security baseline
- Signature-based IDS
- Stateful matching
- Threshold and excess analysis

APPLY YOUR KNOWLEDGE

Exercises

4.1 Configuring Windows 2000 IIS Server

This exercise demonstrates how to configure IIS on a Windows 2000 Server using the MMC console and supplemental configuration tools. Windows 2000 has built-in controls that help secure the IIS server.

The following assumptions are made in this exercise: The server is a member or a standalone box in a DMZ segment, and the server was built to host the company Web site but does not currently have IIS installed.

You will have to download the IIS Lockdown Utility from Microsoft's Web site (the current version of this tool is 2.1).

Estimated Time: 10 minutes

1. First you need to install IIS on the machine; if this has already been done, skip to step 6.
2. Select Start, Settings, Control Panel, Add/Remove Programs, Add/Remove Windows Components.
3. A list of Windows components appears. Scroll down and click Internet Information Services (IIS); then click Details.
4. Select the following components: Common Files, Internet Information Services snap-in, and World Wide Web Server. Click OK, and then click Next.
5. If your server has Terminal Services installed, a prompt appears for you to choose in which mode Terminal Services is running. Select the appropriate option (Remote Administration mode in most cases). Click Next. You are prompted to provide a location of Windows 2000 installation files. Click Finish when the process is completed.
6. Navigate to where the `iislockd.exe` utility has been downloaded and execute it. A wizard appears; click Next.
7. You are prompted to consent to a license agreement. Select I Agree, and click Next.
8. Next, you have to select which security baseline template you want to apply. This depends on what the server was built for, but for the purposes of this exercise, select Dynamic Web Server (ASP enabled) and check the View Template Settings check box. Click Next.
9. On the following screen, you are prompted to select which services you want to keep and which ones the utility will disable. The default configurations for these settings are influenced by the baseline you chose in step 8. Leave the settings unchanged and click Next.
10. On the Script Maps page, the file associations that are prohibited from being processed by the IIS server are displayed. All but the Active Server Pages should be disabled. Click Next.
11. An additional Security page provides a few more options for disabling standard IIS components, scripts, virtual directories, and samples. You can also restrict access to system utilities (this includes about a hundred command-line utilities located in the `system32` directory). Finally, an option to disable WebDAV extensions is provided. Review the settings and click Next.
12. On the next page, you are asked whether the URLscan filter should be installed. Install it, review the settings, and click Next.
13. A review screen will appear with a brief summary of all the settings as configured in the previous steps. Click Next to proceed with the lockdown.

APPLY YOUR KNOWLEDGE

14. After the process finishes running all the steps, a report screen will appear. Review the results and click Next. Click Finish.

15. As a final step, review the configuration of the URLscan filter located in the `%system_root%\System32\inetsrv\urlscan` directory. Review the URLscan logs in the same directory to see whether your server is receiving any malicious requests. This log is also useful when troubleshooting a URLscan configuration if it is rejecting access to legitimate applications running on the Web server.

This exercise shows how to protect an IIS server from processing unwanted traffic. It is not enough to just run through these steps. After this basic configuration, you need to ensure that the operating system is patched to the fullest—and that includes all the latest service packs and every security patch available for IIS. In addition to these, consider applying one of the Microsoft-provided security baseline settings databases or applying Registry modifications manually to reduce the attack surface, eliminate vulnerabilities and security holes, and provide further hardening against denial-of-service attacks.

Review Questions

1. What is the purpose and five main traffic analysis techniques of the IDS?

2. What is the difference between active and passive IDS?

3. What is the difference between host-based and network-based IDS?

4. What are honeypots and what is their purpose in the network?

5. What is the purpose of having a proper incident response strategy in place?

6. What is the purpose of a security baseline?

Exam Questions

1. Your company is in the process of setting up an IDS. You want to scan for irregular header lengths and information in the TCP/IP packet. Which IDS methodology is suitable for this purpose?

   A. Pattern matching

   B. Stateful inspection

   C. Protocol decode

   D. Heuristic analysis

   E. Anomaly analysis

2. Your company is in the process of setting up an IDS. You want to scan for data strings contained in packets, and you want to ensure that packets are searched in a continuous fashion, not on a packet-by-packet basis. Which IDS methodology is suitable for this purpose?

   A. Pattern matching

   B. Stateful inspection

   C. Protocol decode

   D. Heuristic analysis

   E. Anomaly analysis

3. You are securing the network with IDS technologies. You want to be able to see malicious intent activity as well as provide some security and monitoring for users who are VPNing outside the network.

APPLY YOUR KNOWLEDGE

Which IDS types are better suited for this job? (Choose all that apply.)

A. Network-based IDS

B. Host-based IDS

C. Server-based IDS

D. Router-based IDS

4. You are setting up a network IDS to look for attacks on a Microsoft IIS server farm. Which signature sets would you need to deploy?

A. All signatures from the IDS library

B. All signatures for the MS IIS server

C. All signatures for the MS TCP/IP stack

D. All signatures for the HTTP protocol

E. B and C

5. Which of the following are components of network-based IDSs? (Choose all that apply.)

A. Sensor

B. Rules

C. Controlled access router

D. Controlled access workstation

Answers to Review Questions

1. IDS stands for intrusion detection system. These systems usually feature an intrusion recognition module, either hardware or software, that uses one or more of the many analysis approaches—pattern matching, stateful inspection, protocol decode, heuristic analysis (frequency or threshold excess), or anomaly analysis.

2. Active detection mechanisms involve some action taken by the intrusion detection system in response to a suspicious activity or an intrusion. For example, it might be able to adjust the firewall configuration to prevent the source from accessing the network again and send a reset signal to terminate the current session. The passive detection concept has an IDS present in the network in a silent fashion. It does not interfere with communications in progress, but it can react in a certain way. For instance, an IDS can send an administrative alert if a suspicious activity has been found in log files or network traffic.

3. A network-based intrusion detection system analyzes network traffic in real-time. It uses raw packets traveling the network as the source of information. These systems usually feature an intrusion recognition module, either hardware or software. Host-based intrusion detection is built around the analysis of logs on each host. This often is expanded further into an analysis of events and conditions as they are triggered.

4. A honeypot is a decoy box designed to attract hackers, usually has all the logging and tracing enabled, and has its security level lowered on purpose. Honeypots are set up for various reasons, which can be anything from hacker distraction to intruder apprehension to research and analysis.

5. Regardless of how strict security policies and procedures are, incidents do happen from time to time in most organizations. It is important to realize that proper incident response is just as vital as security itself. Proper incident response keeps customers aware and hopefully satisfied that the problem is dealt with in a professional and responsible manner. It also increases the chances of successful apprehension and minimizes service interruption through a coordinated and rehearsed team effort.

APPLY YOUR KNOWLEDGE

6. A security baseline is a subcomponent of security policy and is a model set of security-related modifications, patches, and settings that underpin technical implementation of security. Companies should have post-installation configuration and audit guides (automated, where possible) that implement security policies.

Answers to Exam Questions

1. **C.** Protocol decode dissects the headers in a TCP/IP packet and compares them against the standards defined in the RFCs, where applicable.

2. **B.** Stateful inspection looks for strings in the data portion of the TCP/IP packet stream on a continuous basis.

3. **A, B.** A combination of both systems is likely to provide the best protection. Network-based IDS is the best option for monitoring malicious intent, but it will not see tunneled data traveling the VPN connections users establish outside.

4. **E.** B and C are the best sets of signatures to use in this case. It is important to keep in mind that only the necessary portion of the IDS signature sets should be applied on the monitoring devices to keep the number of checks to a minimum to not overburden the devices on a saturated network segment. In this particular case, Apache vulnerability signatures are most likely to be irrelevant and therefore should not be included. The HTTP library, likewise, is general in nature and does not cover all the protocols made accessible by the IIS server.

5. **A, B, C.** All three are components of a typical network-based IDS.

APPLY YOUR KNOWLEDGE

Suggested Readings and Resources

Online Material

1. The Apache Software Foundation (`http://www.apache.org`).
2. CERT Coordination Center. "Identifying tools that aid in detecting signs of intrusion" (`http://www.cert.org/security-improvement/implementations/i042.07.html`).
3. List of intrusions detected by Network ICE (`http://www.iss.net/security_center/advice/Intrusions/default.htm`).
4. Microsoft Security and Privacy Web site (`http://www.microsoft.com/security`).
5. Network Security Library. "Network- vs. Host-based Intrusion Detection" (`http://secinf.net/info/ids/nvh_ids/`).
6. SANs Institute. "What Is a Honeypot?" (`http://www.sans.org/newlook/resources/IDFAQ/honeypot3.htm`).
7. "The Science of Intrusion Detection SystemAttack Identification" (`http://www.cisco.com/warp/public/cc/pd/sqsw/sqidsz/prodlit/idssa_wp.htm`).
8. "Security Operations Guide for Windows 2000 Server" (`http://www.microsoft.com/technet/treeview/default.asp?url=/technet/security/prodtech/windows/windows2000/staysecure/default.asp`).

Publications

1. *Windows 2000 Server TCP/IP Core Networking Guide.* Redmond, WA: Microsoft Press, 2002.

OBJECTIVES

This chapter covers the following CompTIA-specified objectives for the Communications Security section of the Security+ exam.

Understand the various encryption algorithms used in cryptography.

- Encryption is a necessary evil in today's secure environments with the increased sophistication of hacking tools and the growing number of hackers with lots of time on their hands. Modern encryption can provide an excellent way to protect your network and computer data. By studying and learning the various types of encryption algorithms and how they work, you can better understand how encryption interacts with various security applications, design concepts, and operating system security features.

Understand the concepts of using encryption in a secure environment.

- Encryption is an often misunderstood aspect of security, and it is amongst the most important to understand for an effective security implementation. The objective covered in this section will help you better understand how the popular encryption methods can be used to improve the security of your network and data.

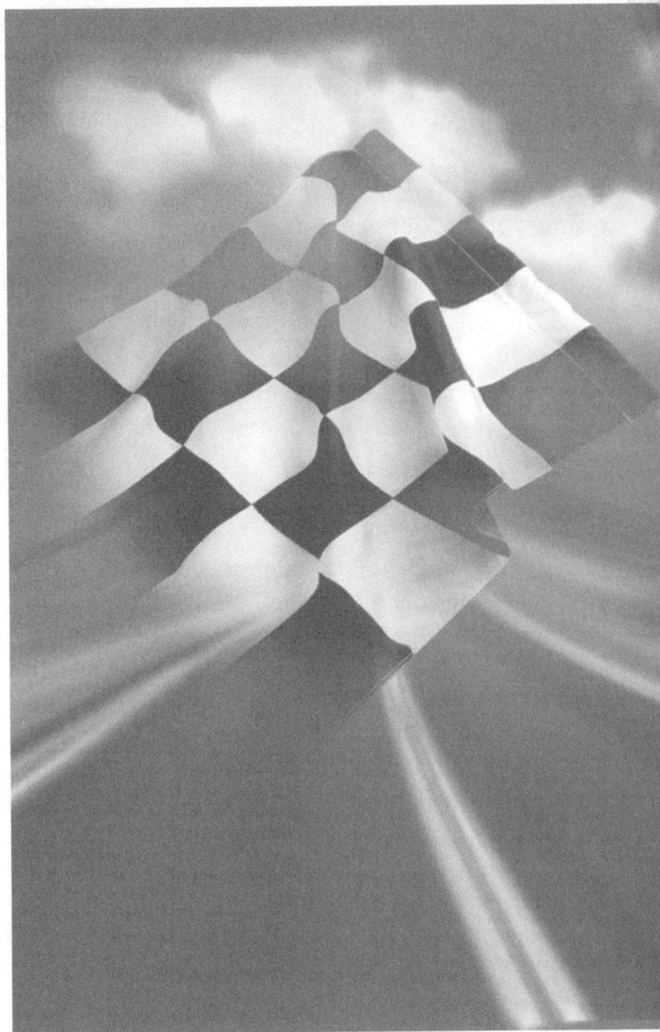

CHAPTER 5

Cryptography Algorithms

Outline

Study Strategies

- Encryption is one of the cornerstones of security; understand the ins and outs of encryption and how it fits in with network and system security in general.
- Learn how each major, popular encryption method performs its function as well as which features it has. Doing this will help you better understand which encryption method will work best in which situation.
- Test and understand how common desktop applications that feature encryption, such as pretty good privacy (PGP), can be used to augment an already secure network environment.
- Take some time to implement popular operating system features that utilize encryption to see how encryption affects typical operating system functionality.

Introduction

There have been growing concerns over the security of sensitive personal and business data. With the growing abilities of hackers and the proliferation of business networks connected to the Internet, much of your important data can be left exposed to anyone with the skills and motivation to get your data. One practical method of securing this data is the use of cryptography (the concept and study of encryption and decryption) in the form of encryption algorithms applied to data that is passed around networks or even stored on hard drives. Ideally, encryption is used to change regular readable data into unintelligible garble that no one can read without the matching key on the other end to unscramble the data. Although the concept itself is basic, implementation on a larger scale in the IT world has taken a while to gain the momentum seen today. Cryptography and encryption are certainly not new (the military has been using them for decades), but they are relatively new players in many popular operating systems, such as Windows 2000.

The use of cryptography and encryption is on the rise, but there are often misconceptions or just a plain lack of knowledge when it comes to this often-complex subject. Understanding the fundamentals of cryptography and encryption's role in system security and how it affects your network and (most importantly) the end user experience is important for any security professional or administrator to know.

This chapter reviews and details many popular cryptography and encryption methods as well as how they can be used in your network environments. Complete volumes could be written just on the individual encryption algorithms, but this chapter provides only the necessary background into encryption to help you properly understand encryption and how it can bolster the security of your networks, workstations, and servers.

Encryption Algorithms

Understand the various encryption algorithms used in cryptography.

At its most basic level, an *algorithm* is simply a set of steps that can be sequenced and repeated each time. In encryption, the algorithm is used to define how the encryption is applied, how the data held inside is encrypted, and how the data is decrypted on the other end.

Think of the algorithm as the guidebook to how any particular encryption method is applied. The method of applying encryption to data or information can also be called a cryptography *cipher*.

Most people wouldn't understand or really need to know the internal details of how an encryption algorithm works. However, knowing the fundamental design of any given encryption algorithm can provide insights into how it will perform, as well as how secure it is. With that information in hand, you can select which algorithm is going to do the job for your given situation because some algorithms are better suited for different tasks.

Each algorithm in the following sections would typically be considered better than no encryption at all; however, it is very important to not get a false sense of security when it comes to any encryption algorithm. The main reason is that even the most secure encryption algorithms could become tomorrow's has-been method. With the advancing sophistication and knowledge of today's hackers and crackers as well as with the advent of *distributed computing* (using many computers to process a single task), the days of a completely unbreakable encryption are likely behind us.

NOTE

The Art of Using Cryptography
Using cryptography to mask the actual meaning of written text has been commonplace since before the Roman Empire. However, the Romans were one of the first people known to have used the substitution method of taking one letter of the alphabet and substituting it with another. For instance, A would correspond with F, B would correspond with G, and so on. This type of cryptography is often called the Caesar system because Julius Caesar was one of the first to use it for military applications. The previous method, for reference purposes, would be annotated to read C6—C for Caesar and 6 meaning the letter that A matches (in this case, F).

Keys to Encryption

Before any discussion of encryption methods can occur, the fundamentals of current encryption must be understood. The basis for encryption will always be the establishment of trust between two hosts or systems. After a trust is established, encrypted data can flow and communication, data, or the authentication process that is being encrypted will be protected and you can be fairly sure that it is as secure as it can be. What helps establish this trust and provides the basis for almost every major encryption algorithm designed is the *key exchange* method.

In a key exchange, both a *public key* and a *private key* are generated and for a secure communication to commence, the keys must be exchanged between hosts. To allow for this, the public key is distributed to whomever needs it. This can be accomplished in a variety of ways, including as part of an email or a file or as part of authentication that is accomplished as a series of data passed back and forth in the form of handshakes.

After the keys have been matched up and verified, the data is decrypted and authentication can commence or the network connection can securely start. As long as the private key information is kept safe, there is little chance of any type of security breach—unless the hacker is able to simulate or fake an authoritative connection using the public key. This also assumes that the hacker has managed to secure the appropriate key data and is able to do something with it—this is no small task, but it has been done before. Hence the warning that encryption, for all its benefits and strengths, should not be considered a completely bulletproof security technology.

Hashing

To set the stage for many of the following encryption methods, you first must learn how hashing and signing work. An *encryption hash* takes the data found in documents and other data and computes this information into a section of data measured in bits, which is then called a *hash value.*

Hashing, in encryption terms, is typically used for information you don't want to be decrypted. This is because, after the hash is applied, decryption is almost impossible if you don't know how the hash was generated or what the actual information used to create the hash was, which defeats the purpose.

Although permanently locking the information in a hash might seem counterproductive, the methodology has definite uses when information simply needs to be verified. Items such as passwords, confirmation codes, and account numbers can be hashed. This is how it works: The data is encrypted, and then during the transfer and authentication of data, the user or software enters the appropriate information, presumably on a safe terminal or server. This user- or system-entered data is hashed, and the original hash value is compared to the one input by the user or system. If the hashes match, the data is verified as factual and the transaction can commence, keeping the actual information safe and transferring only the hash across any public network, which as you learned earlier, is of little use to most people.

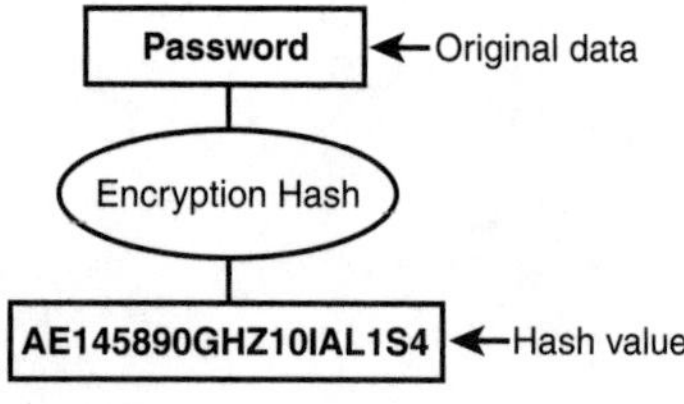

FIGURE 5.1
Basic example of a simple encryption hash.

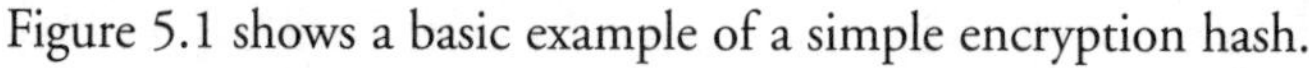

Figure 5.1 shows a basic example of a simple encryption hash.

DICTIONARY ATTACKS

It is very important to note that one potential attack against a hash algorithm is a *dictionary attack*. An example of a dictionary attack is as follows.

Say the source against which the hash algorithm is applied to make the resultant hash is made up of your dog's name Fluffy. If a hacker captures the appropriate data from a network communication and then runs what is called a *brute-force dictionary attack* against that hash, the hacker can possibly break the hash by going through the dictionary word by word, generating hashes to compare against the captured hash. Breaking the hash requires knowledge of what type of hash algorithm is used and, in some cases, a lot of time and system resources. This depends on how strong the bit strength of the hash being used is. This is why, in particular to the use of passwords on your workstation or network, you need to use complex passwords that are not made up of anything in a dictionary. Today's brute-force dictionary attack software engines can work at an incredible rate and will only get better as time goes on.

NOTE

Bit Strength You will hear the term *bit strength* mentioned quite often in regard to encryption methods. This term is used as a general signifier for how strong the particular encryption method or hash being used is. The longer the hash used is (measured in bits), the more secure it technically should be, the more processing time the hash takes to generate, and the larger it will be when passing the information over a network. Keep in mind that encryption strength can also fluctuate based on the algorithm used. A strong encryption is typically 128-bit. Anything this level or higher typically has limited use outside of North America with exceptions for some trusted countries around the world. This is mainly due to export laws limiting the export of software using strong encryption to foreign countries that might have a more nefarious use for keeping data or communications locked away.

Signing a Hash

Signing is a method that enhances hashing. After the data is hashed, another encryption layer is put on the hash that signifies that the data is in fact from one person or source. This layer of encryption provides another level of data integrity so that the destination verifying the information in the hash knows that the data came from where it says it came from.

Verifying the source via signing can be accomplished using the source's private key, which as such, verifies that the data is from the source. When this type of signing is used, it might seem that you are leaving the private key in jeopardy of being captured because you are identifying the person or source. Although this is true to a degree, think back to the previous hashing example when the bank card transfers the PIN. The private key on the PIN is still hashed (so the data is kept private) and then compared on the other end.

NOTE

Hashing Example An excellent example of hashing is when you use your bank card at a grocery store and you use a terminal at the register to make your payments. You swipe your card and then enter your PIN. When the PIN is entered, it is hashed and that information, as well as the hash information stored on the card and at the bank, is compared and verified; then your transaction can go through, assuming funds are in place. In this case, no sensitive PIN or password information is passed along over the wire and your information is kept safe.

Secure Hash Algorithm

One method of hash encryption, pioneered by the National Security Agency and widely used in U.S. government encryption, is the *Secure Hash Algorithm (SHA-1)*. SHA-1 can generate a 160-bit hash from any variable length string of data, making it very secure but, as you can imagine, very resource intensive.

SHA encryption is designed very much like the Message Digest (MD) series of encryption algorithms (MD2, MD4, and MD5) that you will learn about in the next section. However, because of the higher bit strength of the SHA-1 algorithm, it is 20%–30% slower to process than the MD family of algorithms.

It is important to know that SHA-1 isn't limited to government use and can be applied in any number of applications as a method of encrypting data. It can be used to digitally sign data to help ensure that information is from the correct source and is unaltered. Even given its strength, it is still fast compared to other types of encryption and suitable for signing data. One aspect SHA-1 and other related message digest-type encryption methods benefit from is that any given data will not be encrypted the same way twice, even from the same system. This makes the encryption harder to break because of the variety and, as such, much harder to input fake data if the source data is intercepted and potentially altered.

Message Digest Series Algorithms

The *Message Digest (MD)* series of encryption algorithms (MD2, MD4, and MD5) was developed by Ron Rivest many years ago. The main design philosophy was to have a fast, simple, and secure encryption algorithm optimized to run well on Intel-based systems. As mentioned, MD-style encryption is the basis for the SHA-1 encryption algorithm and, as such, is designed similarly. MD generates a unique one-way hash of up to 128-bit strength out of any length of data. Similar to SHA-1, no two chunks of data have the same resultant hash, which helps increase the security of the encryption.

As you can ascertain from the different versions of Message Digest listed, there has been some refinement to the algorithm over the years. The most commonly used are MD4 and MD5, which are both faster than MD2. In addition, both MD4 and MD5 produce a 128-bit hash; however, the hash used in MD4 was successfully broken a while back.

This spurred the development of MD5, which features a redeveloped cipher that makes it stronger than the MD4 algorithm while still featuring a 128-bit hash.

Ron Rivest's name will also come up later this chapter; he is one of the creators of the RSA (Rivest, Shamir, and Adleman) asymmetric encryption algorithm as well as the Rivest Cipher (RC) series of symmetric encryption algorithms widely used today.

RSA is amongst the most respected and widely active encryption-focused organizations in the world. It accounts for many of the more popular encryption algorithms used today. You can read more about RSA and find out more about its current encryption algorithms at `www.rsa.com`. Both RC and RSA algorithms are covered in more detail a little later in the "Rivest, Shamir, and Adleman Encryption Algorithm" and "Rivest Cipher" sections of this chapter.

EXAM TIP

Be sure you know that MD is a symmetric hashing algorithm.

Symmetric Encryption

Symmetric encryption is an encryption methodology that simply passes a key one way, with that key being verified with a matching key on the other end. One drawback of this particular situation is that every party participating in communications with the source must have the exact same key on the other end to compare the information. If the key is compromised at any point, it is impossible to guarantee that a secure connection has commenced. Signing, as you learned earlier, can help protect against this type of situation but isn't always used or perfect for that matter.

One benefit of symmetric encryption is that it is typically very fast. This is true because, when you encrypt the data for transport, the system performing the encryption has to encrypt only a miniscule amount of data, which keeps the process very quick. Other types of encryption, such as asymmetric encryption (which is covered later), can generate large amounts of data and use a lot of system resources. This can become a factor when you take into account network bandwidth and server performance.

Even given the possible risks involved with symmetric key encryption, the method is used quite often in today's society mainly for its simplicity and ease of deployment. On top of that, it is generally considered very strong as long as the source and destination that house the key information are kept secure. Figure 5.2 shows how symmetric encryption works.

NOTE

Effective Symmetric Encryption One simple way to increase the effectiveness of symmetric encryption is to change the key or PIN, as in the bank card example earlier, on a regular basis. Another way is to support the symmetric encryption with another level of encryption using, for example, a different symmetric key such as signing the data. Another common practice is to apply some type of asymmetric encryption to the data or authentication process to take the guarantee of secure data one step further. You will learn more about asymmetric encryption later in this chapter in the "Asymmetric Encryption Algorithms" section.

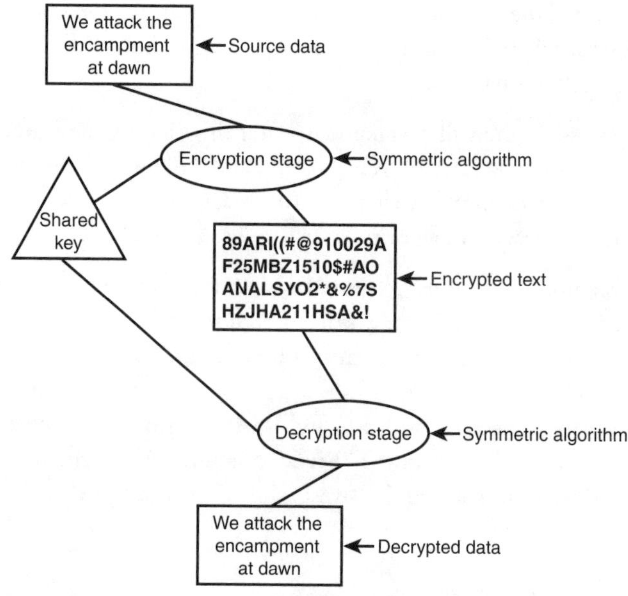

FIGURE 5.2
Diagram of how symmetric encryption works.

Data Encryption Standard Encryption

The Data Encryption Standard (DES) encryption (also referred to as Data Encryption Algorithm) was adopted for use by the National Institute of Standards and Technology in 1977. DES, as such, has been around for a long time in the industry and is still used today in a wide variety of areas.

The older DES and the newer, stronger Triple DES (3DES) are used by companies and software applications to provide data security. You will learn more about 3DES later in this chapter in the "Triple Data Encryption Standard" section.

DES is designed as what is called a *block cipher*. When a block cipher encrypts the data, it does so in 64-bit chunks (or *blocks*) of data. When encrypted, the same key is used to both encrypt and decrypt the data, helping keep performance maximal and easing implementation.

A unique feature of DES is referred to as the *diffusion and confusion technique*. This technique takes each 64-bit block of encrypted data and splits it into two; then each piece is run through the algorithm, applying the encryption key to each one separately. This process is repeated to the same data 16 times with DES and is called a *round*.

With each successive passing through a round, the key used to encrypt the data is changed slightly, which helps increase the strength of the algorithm. After the rounds are complete, the bit strength of DES is equal to 56 bits, making it one of the weaker encryption methods used for security today.

As you learned in the previous section, DES has been around since the 1970s, making it a widespread and well-adopted encryption algorithm. Similar to other symmetric algorithms, it is quick and easy to implement. However, it does suffer from the typical issues of having difficulties securely distributing keys to the systems or users needing them to communicate securely with the host. However, you will likely encounter DES encryption in your travels. If you would like to learn more about DES and how it works, visit `http://www.nist.gov/` for more information on the ins and outs of DES encryption.

Triple Data Encryption Standard

As you learned in the previous section, DES encryption uses a (by today's standards) relatively weak 56-bit encryption algorithm. Even with this weakness, it provides enough security for basic protection. When the data sensitivity and security needs of DES are stretched too thin, most users turn to the Triple Data Encryption Standard (3DES).

When encrypted, the data is passed through a 56-bit DES key providing the basis for encryption; then the data is decrypted using a different 56-bit DES key and passed once again through with the original key to finalize the bit strength at a robust 168 bits. Because of the design feature of 3DES, it also lends itself to protecting against something most other symmetric encryption algorithms cannot—*man-in-the-middle* attacks. In a man-in-the-middle attack, a hacker tries to intercept data and interject his own encrypted data into the mix to perform one task or another.

Although it is not as fast as DES (because 3DES must effectively run DES three times), it is still one of the faster encryption algorithms available because it is a symmetric algorithm. One benefit of 3DES is that, if an organization already has DES in place, updating to 3DES is a relatively effortless migration because DES and 3DES both use the same software and hardware. This keeps the organization from having to invest in new solutions.

> NOTE
>
> **3DES Decryption** It might seem confusing to encrypt the data with one key and decrypt it with a different one, but in effect, decryption and encryption are the same process. In the case of 3DES, however, it is designed that way so that when the decryption is performed during the second stage, it isn't with the original key, which changes the data that the third run of the algorithm with the original key sees. This is what 3DES uses for increased strength and protection against hacking because there are effectively two different keys applied, which makes reconstructing data very difficult.

Advanced Encryption Standard

In the past few years, there has been speculation that DES and 3DES are past their prime and do not offer the necessary levels of security that today's connected environments require. Listening to the input from the industry and also noticing that DES was in fact over 25 years old, the National Institute of Standards and Technology (NIST) commenced development and research to select a successor to DES. The standard it chose is called the Advanced Encryption Standard (AES).

Several competing encryption algorithms were submitted for approval to the AES standard with a few defining requirements. First, the new algorithm had to support 128-bit, 192-bit, and 256-bit strength encryption keys. In addition, it also had to support a wide array of hardware, including 8-, 32-, and 64-bit processors as well as *smart cards* (which are cards that can be used as an enhanced type of debit or ID card capable of performing a variety of functions, including security).

Of the competitors submitted, some of the main candidates included the RC6, Twofish, and Rijndael encryption algorithms—each with its own take and design on what the NIST was looking for. In October 2000, the Rijndael submission was selected as the new AES encryption algorithm. The Rijndael home page can be found at `http://www.esat.kuleuven.ac.be/~rijmen/rijndael/` with information on the algorithm, including information on books written specifically about this new block cipher.

AES is similar to DES in that it can create (as mentioned previously) keys from 128-bit to 256-bit in length and can perform the encryption and decryption of data on up to 128-bit chunks of data (in comparison to the 64-bit chunks of the original DES). And similar to 3DES, the data is passed through three layers, each with a specific task such as generating random keys based on the data and the bit strength being used. After going through three layers, the data is encrypted with the keys through multiple encryption rounds, like DES, and then the data has the final key applied. Similar to DES and 3DES, AES is still a symmetric encryption algorithm and as such, uses only a single key for the encryption and decryption of the data.

NOTE

Old Encryption Strength Over New
As an interesting comparison in strength, on a given system that could potentially crack the original DES encryption algorithm, it would take somewhere around 150 trillion years to break the Rijndael encryption algorithm. That is quite an improvement in security for an algorithm that is still very efficient and fast!

AES is still relatively new; therefore, it might not be widely used for some time, but it is currently used in government applications for sensitive but unclassified information that doesn't require the most secure encryption possible. If you are interested in downloads and very technical information on AES, the NIST site has everything on AES; it can be found at `http://csrc.nist.gov/encryption/aes/`.

Carlisle Adams/Stafford Tavares Encryption

Carlisle Adams/Stafford Tavares (CAST) is a relative unknown public encryption algorithm; yet it is used for many versions of the popular and well-respected PGP line of software. Similar to DES, CAST is a block cipher capable of 128-bit or 256-bit strength encryption keys. It is also a fairly strong cipher that has proven very resilient to most forms of attack, short of brute-force dictionary attacks. More often than not (with the current iterations of CAST), this type of attack has turned out to be particularly fruitless. It is worth noting that lesser-strength offshoots of the CAST design have been defeated or exhibited some weaknesses in one way or another; however, the most widely used version of CAST (for example, in PGP) has thus far been fine.

Like DES, CAST-128 breaks the data into 64-bit chunks when applying the encryption algorithm. CAST-256, on the other hand, applies the encryption to larger 128-bit chunks of data. CAST is fast and, even for its relative obscurity and the fact that little information is available on it, it is well respected in the encryption community. Two Request for Comment (RFC) documents have been released on the two latest iterations of CAST (CAST-128 and CAST-256). You can find them at `http://www.faqs.org/rfcs/rfc2144.html` and `http://www.faqs.org/rfcs/rfc2612.html`.

Rivest Cipher

As far as widely available commercial applications go, the Rivest Cipher (RC) series of encryption algorithms is the most commonly implemented cipher for encryption security. The RC series was developed by RSA security along with its popular RSA encryption algorithm, which you will learn about later in this chapter.

The RC series algorithms (RC2, RC4, RC5, and RC6) are all similarly designed and are considered symmetric encryption algorithms.

Each is a varying design on the now familiar block cipher method used with DES. Each version of RC has its own take on the block cipher design, as well as its own capabilities. Take a look at the following list that outlines the major features of the RC series of algorithms:

- **RC2**—Encrypts the data in 64-bit blocks. One of its unique features is that it can use a variable length encryption key ranging from 1 to infinity, making the bit strength entirely dependent on what you want to implement.
- **RC4**—A variation on the block cipher called a *stream cipher.* With a stream cipher, the encryption is applied against the whole chunk of data in real-time as it is generated. RC4 supports various lengths of encryption keys, with 128-bit strength being the most common in North America and 40-bit strength being the exportable version used in most other countries because of the aforementioned export restrictions.
- **RC5**—In most cases, this is similar to RC2 because it is a block cipher and can have variable-length encryption keys. In addition to this, RC5 supports a variable amount of data for the block size instead of being limited to 64-bit blocks, as RC2 is. In most cases, a 128-bit strength key applied over 16 or so rounds provides the best compromise between security and performance with the RC5 algorithm.
- **RC6**—Released in 1998. After people noticed a possible chink in the armor of the RC5 algorithm, Rivest designed the RC6 algorithm, which fixes the issue with RC5 (the way the encryption applies itself during particular key rounds). Keep in mind that this was a potential problem, but it was determined that fixing it sooner rather than later was a priority for this popular line of encryption algorithms. In addition to this fix, some improvements were made to the performance of how RC5 handles 128-bit blocks of data, leading to overall performance benefits when configured for this. Otherwise, RC6 is quite similar to RC5.

EXAM TIP

Be sure you know that the various forms of RSA are symmetric encryption algorithms.

As you can see, the RC series of algorithms has seen a lot of development over the years. The robust nature of the cipher has made it one of the most popular types of symmetric encryption algorithms in use today.

Blowfish Encryption Algorithm

Designed by Bruce Schneier, Blowfish is a block cipher that, like RC6, can encrypt using any size chunk of data. In addition to this, Blowfish can perform its encryption with any length encryption key—up to 448 bits—making it a flexible and secure symmetric encryption algorithm.

In the encryption world, Bruce Schneier is an affluent member who makes significant contributions in many areas. Recently, Schneier developed a new encryption algorithm called *Twofish* that is similar to Blowfish in design and uses 128-bit blocks. It also supports a variety of encryption key bit strengths (128-bit, 192-bit, and 256-bit). With the lessons learned with Blowfish and a more finely tuned cipher, Twofish can outperform Blowfish quite nicely. In fact, Twofish was one of the candidates for the Advanced Encryption Standard proposed by the NIST; it was not selected for the standard but was considered one of the top entries.

International Data Encryption Algorithm

Originally created around 1990, the International Data Encryption Algorithm (IDEA) went through several variations before arriving at its final acronym. Originally called the Proposed Encryption Standard (PES), it was later renamed and refined to the Improved Proposed Encryption Standard (IPES). After even more refinement, it was ultimately named IDEA in 1992. In its final form, IDEA is capable of encrypting 64-bit blocks of data at a time and uses a 128-bit strength encryption key.

Many consider IDEA a solid and reliable encryption algorithm when the 128-bit key is employed. Even given its capabilities over the standard DES design, IDEA has yet to gain any major popularity or use, especially in the face of other strong candidates such as 3DES and RC6.

Asymmetric Encryption Algorithms

As you learned earlier in this chapter, two major types of algorithms are in use today: *symmetric*, in which one key is kept private all the time, and *asymmetric*, which uses two keys—a public key and a private key.

In the asymmetric encryption model, a public key is always available to whoever is going to encrypt the data sent to the private key's holder. That key is maintained on the host system or application. Quite often the public encryption key is made available in a number of fashions. Examples of this are email or centralized servers that host a pseudo address book of published public encryption keys.

For instance, when someone wants to send secure email to a user, she obtains the target user's public encryption key and encrypts the message with that key. Because the message can be unencrypted only with the private key, only the target user can read the information held within. Ideally, for this system to work well, everyone should have access to everyone else's public keys. In a corporate environment, this isn't as much of a problem as it is over a network such as the Internet. Slowly but surely, however, the asymmetric method of encrypting data is catching on and its use is on the rise. Figure 5.3 shows how asymmetric encryption works.

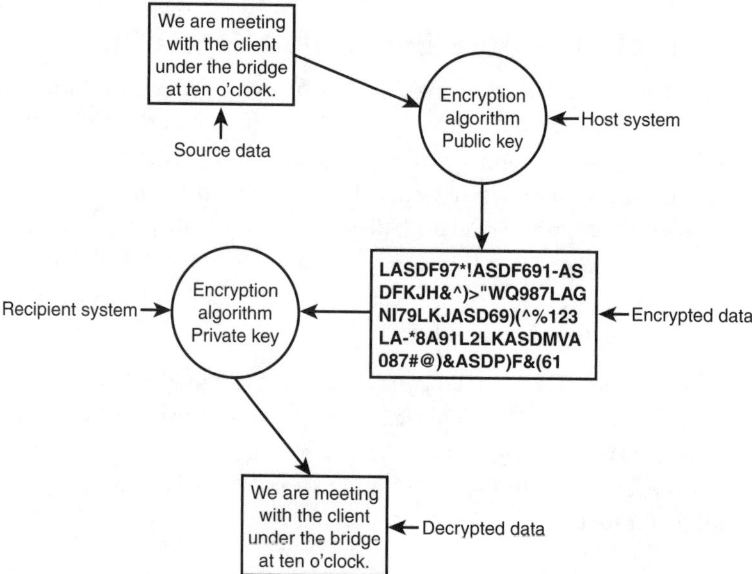

FIGURE 5.3
Diagram of a how asymmetric encryption works.

A wide array of asymmetric algorithms have been designed; however, very few have gained the widespread acceptance seen with symmetric algorithms. Some things to keep in mind while reading about the following asymmetric algorithms are that some are capable of different features, including built-in digital signatures (which you will learn more about later this chapter) as well as generally stronger encryption algorithms.

Also, because of the additional overhead generated by using two keys for encryption/decryption, more resources are required to use asymmetric algorithms. This is partially why asymmetric algorithms haven't necessarily caught on as well as symmetric algorithms have. However, because of their added strength and ease of use, their popularity is on the rise.

Finally, you might also hear asymmetric algorithms called *public key encryption* because of the use of the public key as the focal point of the algorithm. The one environment in which public key encryption really shines is on networks such as the Internet. This is mainly because the safe public key is all that needs to be distributed. Because nothing harmful can be done with the public key, it is useful over the Internet where data can pass through many hands and is vulnerable to interception and abuse. Symmetric encryption works fine over the Internet as well, but the limitations on providing the key securely to everyone that needs it can be difficult. The following sections cover some of the more popular asymmetric encryption algorithms available today.

NOTE

Asymmetric Algorithms Rules Some general rules for asymmetric algorithms are as follows:

- The public key can never decrypt a message that it was used to encrypt the message with.
- Private keys should never be capable of being determined through the public key (if it is designed properly).
- And finally, each key should be capable of decrypting a message encrypted by the other key. For instance, if a message is encrypted with the private key, the public key should be capable of decrypting it.

History of Asymmetric Algorithms It's important to note that asymmetric algorithms aren't necessarily the new kid on the block anymore. In fact, MIT developed the first asymmetric encryption algorithm in the 1970s. Although not the oldest algorithm, it has been around long enough to become a proven method of securing data, even with its somewhat slow performance.

Rivest, Shamir, and Adleman Encryption Algorithm

In 1997, Ron Rivest, Adi Shamir, and Leonard Adleman (RSA) invented the RSA encryption algorithm, which is the foundation for other RSA-developed encryption algorithms. RSA Laboratories (the company founded by the same inventors) is responsible for many of the major encryption advancements in the past couple of decades and can be credited for helping push encryption into the mainstream by developing encryption products that can be used as complete cryptographic solutions.

As mentioned, the RSA algorithm is used as the foundation for many encryption algorithms of differing design and focus.

Two of the major encryption algorithms developed out of the RSA algorithm are the *RSASSA-PSS* and *RSAES-OAEP* encryption algorithms. RSASSA-PSS stands for the RSA Signature Scheme with Appendix-Probabilistic Signature Scheme, and RSAES-OAEP stands for RSA Encryption Scheme-Optimal Asymmetric Encryption Padding. You learn more about the design of these two encryption algorithms shortly.

RSA was involved in the AES bid initiated by NIST to replace DES encryption as the default standard. RSA, being a progressive encryption organization, did not limit its activity to the AES bid. RSA also worked on the European counterpart to the NIST bid called New European Schemes for Signature, Integrity, and Encryption (NESSIE) at the same time. NESSIE is slightly different from AES in that it is a long-term (three-year) plan that will examine a variety of aspects of encryption and designs to come up with an appropriate solution. Some of these aspects include stream ciphers, asymmetric and symmetric encryption, and how to handle digital signatures.

As part of the bid for NESSIE, RSA contributed three of its major encryption algorithms: RC6 Block Cipher, RSA-OAEP Encryption Scheme, and RSA-PSS Signature Scheme with Appendix. As an aside, RSA has also been keeping busy in an almost identical bid put out by the Information-Technology Promotion Agency (IPA) in Japan, called CRYPTREC. Similar to efforts in Europe and the U.S., IPA is also trying to develop encryption standards to keep up with the ever-growing data integrity and security concerns.

You learned about the RC6 encryption algorithm earlier in this chapter; now take a look at the other two new offerings presented as part of the NESSIE and CRYPTREC bids.

RSA Signature Scheme with Appendix-Probabilistic Signature Scheme

This hybrid encryption standard uses the asymmetric RSA encryption algorithm and combines it with the Probabilistic Signature Scheme (RSASSA-PSS) encoding algorithm that is used to apply a form of digital signature to increase the veracity of the data encrypted by the algorithm. PSS was developed by Mihir Bellare and Phillip Rogaway and combined with the RSA algorithm (with some tweaking and adjustments) to create a stronger, more secure method to digitally sign the RSA algorithm.

This is necessary because, although the RSA algorithm itself can generate its own digital signatures, those signatures aren't entirely secure. Therefore, a more sophisticated method of digitally signing the RSA algorithm was required—hence, the PSS extension to the RSA algorithm.

PSS encrypts its data in equal length chunks, making the length of the encryption vary from situation to situation. As well, with this algorithm no rhyme or reason is apparent to the hacker on how the encryption hash method is applied. As such, with seemingly variable hash algorithms and variable length chunks of data, PSS becomes an extra layer of strong encryption for RSA to reside under while providing secure digital signatures.

RSA Encryption Scheme-Optimal Asymmetric Encryption Padding

Also developed by Mihir Bellare and Phillip Rogaway, this encryption algorithm is similar to the RSASSA-PSS encryption standard in that it uses asymmetric RSA encryption with public keys. The difference is that it does not provide a built-in facility for digital signatures. The encryption hash in RSAES-OAEP is truly randomized, making it very difficult to predict and break. Even if OAEP were broken, the attacker would have to work his way through RSA, which in itself is no easy task.

The OAEP component of RSAES-OAEP is typically used for encrypting smaller chunks of data, such as encrypting encryption keys themselves to provide an extra layer of authenticity and security. You might see OAEP used in other software and in conjunction with other encryption algorithms; however, because it is an RSA product, it will likely be used only with RSA algorithms.

Diffie-Hellman

Sometimes called the Diffie-Hellman key exchange, Diffie-Hellman is an early key exchange design in which keys that are assumed to be secret are passed over an unsecured network path (such as the Internet). The keys are passed in a way that they are not compromised using encryption algorithms to verify that the data is arriving at its intended recipient.

> NOTE
>
> **For More Diffie-Hellman Information**
> Although the standard isn't that widely used today outside of PGP, the key exchange designs and fundamentals developed in Diffie-Hellman live on in other products. For more information and details on the internals of how Diffie-Hellman works, as well as additional history on the design, visit `http://www.rsasecurity.com/rsalabs/faq/3-6-1.html`.

M. Hellman and W. Diffie developed this standard back in the mid-1970s in a document titled "New Directions in Cryptography." The initial documentation on this method is often referred to as one of the more influential discussions and developments in the growth of asymmetric, or public key, cryptography. It set the stage for today's popular asymmetric encryption algorithms.

El Gamal Encryption Algorithm

As an extension to the Diffie-Hellman design, in 1985, Dr. El Gamal took to task the design requirements of utilizing encryption to develop digital signatures. Rather than focusing just on the key design, El Gamal designed a complete public key encryption algorithm using some of the key exchange elements from Diffie-Hellman and incorporating encryption on those keys. The resultant encrypted keys reinforced the security and authenticity of public key encryption design and helped lead to future advances in asymmetric encryption technology.

A fantastic presentation on encryption in general, but using El Gamal for its examples, can be found on the RSA Web site at `http://www.rsasecurity.com/rsalabs/staff/bios/mjakobsson/teaching/encryption_files/frame.htm`. This document goes into more detail on how the mathematics of encryption is done, but it also provides general insight into how the encryption process is followed. It is definitely a worthwhile read if you are interested in how the intricacies of an encryption algorithm work.

Merkle-Hellman Knapsack Encryption Algorithm

The Merkle-Hellman Knapsack encryption algorithm was originally published in 1978 and dubbed *knapsack cryptography*. As an interesting note, Shamir (from RSA fame) originally broke the first iteration of this encryption algorithm, and Merkle subsequently decided to hold a simple contest to see how the algorithm would stand up. The prize for breaking the original algorithm was $100, and breaking the improved multiple iteration cipher was worth $1,000. This was pretty good money in the late 1970s, and it came out of Merkle's pocket. Both were eventually cracked, and Merkle paid out the crackers.

Because of this, you likely won't see the Merkle-Hellman algorithm in use anywhere—particularly because some trapdoors are built into it just in case a user needs to get at the data. Because it was broken and these trapdoors exist, there is little need to use the algorithm as anything more than reference and the basis for future encryption development.

Elliptic Curve Cryptography

Another public key encryption is called *Elliptic Curve Cryptography (ECC)*. As you have ascertained by now, mathematics is the cornerstone of any encryption algorithm, and ECC is no exception. Back in the mid-1980s, Neal Bolitz and V.S. Miller developed, through a series of published documents on cryptography, a method in which elliptic curves could be used to calculate simple but very difficult-to-break encryption keys to use in general-purpose encryption.

One of the key benefits of ECC encryption algorithms is that they have a compact design because of the advanced mathematics involved in ECC (something that is beyond the scope of this title). For instance, an ECC encryption key of 160-bit strength would, in actuality, be equal in strength to a 1,024-bit RSA encryption key. This difference alone suggests the compact nature and obvious performance benefits involved with a smaller key (160 bits versus 1,024 bits) and the robust strength of a strong encryption method would have a variety of uses. In fact, some of the key markets ECC encryption algorithms are being targeted and recommended for are applications such as digital signatures, general software, data encryption, smart cards, wireless equipment such as phones, and most hardware solutions.

Throughout this section on the various encryption algorithms, you have learned how each type of symmetric and asymmetric algorithm performs. One thing you haven't seen yet is how bit strengths compare to each other when looking at asymmetric and symmetric algorithms in general. The following list sheds some light on why symmetric algorithms are favored for most applications and why asymmetric algorithms are widely considered very secure but often too complex and resource intensive for every environment.

This list shows a typical comparison between symmetric key strength on the left and an asymmetric key strength on the right:

- 64-bit key strength = 512-bit key strength
- 112-bit key strength = 1,792-bit key strength
- 128-bit key strength = 2,304-bit key strength

EXAM TIP

Be sure you know how hashing, symmetric, and asymmetric encryption work, and the definitions of each.

As you can see, a dramatic difference exists in the strength and consequently the overall size of asymmetric encryption keys. For most environments today, 128-bit strength is considered good enough; therefore, symmetric encryption might do the trick for you. Of course, your mileage might vary, and if you want to simplify how you distribute keys, asymmetric encryption might be the best option for you.

There are many aspects that you will have to consider to determine which method or combination of methods you should use. The following sections of this chapter examine how encryption can help best augment security and how encryption will work in your environments.

CONCEPTS OF USING ENCRYPTION

Understand the concepts of using encryption in a secure environment.

In many situations, using encryption can make a huge difference in how secure your environment is—from a workstation level, to a server level, to even how data is transferred to and from your business partners. As mentioned before, encryption is becoming more and more important because of the number of people connected to the Internet and on networks daily. This situation is amplified when you take into account the increasing sophistication of users and the propensity for mischief that some of these users have.

As it stands today, encryption isn't a technology that requires little thought. More often than not, it needs careful consideration to answer many questions, which include

- How will encryption affect the performance on my network, as well as the servers and workstations attached to that network?
- In what way will my end users interact with encryption? What type of encryption will they experience on an end-user level? Will server or simply network encryption be all that is implemented?

- What additional costs will encryption bring to my organization and, in particular, the department that manages it? Will we need additional hardware, software, and training? Even if all these things stay the same, how many hours will be required to implement encryption?
- What real, tangible benefits will encryption bring to my organization? Can this be tempered against the costs to make encryption worthwhile?
- Do my business partners or other organizations I communicate with use encryption? If so, what do they use and how do we integrate with them? How will this affect my decision on what types of encryption to implement?
- How will the encryption algorithm, software, and other methods I implement today scale with what I want to do tomorrow and my organization's long-term IT and business goals?

As you can see from the preceding questions, a great deal of consideration and research is required before you even start to think about implementing encryption into your organization. The following sections discuss how encryption can work in environments to promote confidentiality of sensitive data, integrity of data and authentication, as well as digital signatures and access control.

EXAM TIP

Understanding how these concepts work with today's encryption technologies is imperative to how you secure the environments in which you are working—both locally on workstations and on the network through servers and network traffic. While reading about the effects of encryption on network security in the coming sections, think about the solutions described in the previous sections on encryption algorithms and how those solutions could be used in any number of situations.

Confidentiality with Encryption Technologies

One of the key benefits that implementing encryption can bring to your organization is the promise of confidentiality. In fact, if you think about it, the capability of encryption to provide confidentiality is important to today's companies as well as to individuals in countries that restrict free speech and monitor the messages and emails posted and sent on the Internet.

Like any open environment in which sensitive information is shared, the most important thing to most people is keeping the information secret and not letting anyone know they are sending the data. It is not unheard of to have large corporations hire people to spy on and try to capture sensitive data being transmitted on competitors' networks as a means to gain a competitive edge.

NOTE

Fight for Free Speech Part and parcel with this idea of government control of encryption is the U.S. government who, back when PGP was gaining popularity and exposure in the media, tried to force the software to be taken down and made unavailable to public consumption. (PGP is the email program that uses encryption and is available for free to anyone who wants to download it in North America.)

Part of the government's argument against PGP was that it could not control the information people were sending. In cases where criminals were involved, they could use encryption and seemingly hide their online activities and data from the prying eyes of the government. Eventually, the public's right to use encryption (and PGP in particular) won out, but you can be sure the government has been busy working on ways to get around the problem of encryption.

This type of activity took a sharp rise recently with the increased awareness of the lax security and typically unencrypted data being passed around many companies with wireless networks. (You can find more on wireless encryption later in this chapter in the "Wireless Encryption" section.)

Fast forward to the individual sitting in an Internet cafe in a foreign country (often the only way these people can access the Internet). You have governments so afraid of what their citizens might see from the outside world that they restrict what people can see in addition to recording and monitoring what information they post. Encryption enables people to take this control away from the government; therefore, publicly available, strong encryption isn't very popular with these types of governments—unless it's for their own use.

On one hand, being able to use encryption can easily be seen as a good idea. Protecting your information and effectively using your right to free speech is very important. On the other hand, you can sometimes see the government's viewpoint as well. For example, it has been discussed widely that the terrorist activities in the U.S. and abroad are hidden and secured using some form of encryption that helps these individuals hide from the very people trying to investigate them. So, on the one hand, you have your freedom to say whatever you like, and on the other hand, you have the people trying to protect you from those who would do harm. Therefore, the people trying to protect you are unable to do their job as effectively as they could otherwise because of encryption.

The battle over what the government can and cannot look at will be debated for many years to come. Yet, the simple fact is that publicly consumable encryption is available, and it can provide that extra level of protection now and will most likely continue in some form for the foreseeable future. The protection that you take for granted now—encompassing anything from encrypting your new product patent on your local network to the text in the email that you sent to your friend across the country—could be compromised if the government has its way. However, thanks to lobbyists, this might never come to pass. Whatever your take on the ramifications of it, confidentiality is one of the premium features of encryption and will continue to be that way forever.

Ensuring Data Integrity with Encryption

Ensuring that the data you send arrives unmodified is something people often take for granted. However, given the Internet's popularity, this is not something we can necessarily take for granted any longer. This is not to say that every bit of data is prone to attack or will come under the scrutiny of hackers—not in the least. However, if you have data that is sensitive or you need to ensure that the recipient is assured that the data being delivered is actually from you, you should consider one of the other major benefits of encryption: *integrity*.

Integrity can take on many forms. On the one hand, data integrity can be provided using encryption (assuming you have a secure algorithm). As you learned in the preceding section, if the key has been changed or the data modified, the recipient might not be able to open or decrypt the data, depending on the encryption algorithm used.

In the case of digital signatures (which you will learn about in the following section), you can also provide verification that the data is in fact from you. Once again, if the digital signature can't be unencrypted, it might have been modified and you will know it is not from who it says it should be from. This allows the recipient to either discard the data or possibly request another copy or confirmation directly with the sender.

Similar to confidentiality, integrity is a huge aspect of what corporate America and other organizations around the world require when dealing with the transfer of data over unsecured networks. In many cases, contractors that deal with the government (in particular, the armed forces) have to run a minimum specified level of encryption before they are even allowed to do any kind of work. This is due to the sensitive nature of the information transmitted. For some contractors, there must be a minimum level of overall security compliance that encompasses not only encryption, but also certain security practices. This is something to keep in mind if you or your organization ever plans to work with a branch of the government that requires this type of security.

By selecting the correct encryption algorithm or the correct combination of algorithms and digital signature schemes, you can increase both the confidentiality and integrity of your data.

Digital Signatures

As you have learned, *digital signatures* attempt to guarantee the identity of the person sending the data from one point to another. The point of this verification is to prevent or alert the recipient to any tampering with the data. Ideally, if a packet of data is digitally signed, it can bear only the original mark of the sender. If this mark is different, the receiver knows that the packet is different from what it is supposed to be and the packet either is not unencrypted or is dropped altogether. This works based on the encryption algorithm principles learned previously. If you can't determine what the original data was in the encrypted data (in this case, the signature), faking the data and actually getting it past the receiver as legitimate data is much harder.

The basic design of a digital signature is as follows: A small amount of data (it can be randomly inserted data or part of the actual data to be transferred) is encrypted using the prescribed algorithm (either the source encryption or a specifically selected algorithm for the task). That small amount of data (typically smaller than the chunk of data being sent) is bound to the core data being sent as well as to the identity of the sender (in most cases, the public key). Ideally, this situation provides the authentic signature with the key so the recipient can verify the digital signature on any data sent with that signature, thus ensuring that the data is unmodified and sent by the authentic sender.

When creating a digital signature, the software being used to generate the signature sends the data being transferred through a hash algorithm. After the data is sent through this hash, an output is generated in the form of a fixed-size chunk of data called a *message digest.* The message digest is unique for every chunk of data passed through the hash algorithm, which makes it difficult to replicate.

If the algorithm used to create the message digest is of quality design (taking appropriate secure design fundamentals into account), it should be able to guarantee the following:

- The original data cannot be re-created out of the message digest, and vice versa.
- There should never be replication of a message digest between two separate files because the algorithm used should create entirely different end results when the data passes through the hash.
- Message digests should always be generated by using the entire piece of data being sent.

To add to the security of the message digest, the resultant data is then encrypted using the sender's private key. The unique message digest and consequential signing with the private key should be enough to guarantee authenticity. Finally, this resultant digital signature is attached to the data and transferred. The digital signature should be encrypted as well to increase the security. Figure 5.4 shows how the creation of a digital signature works.

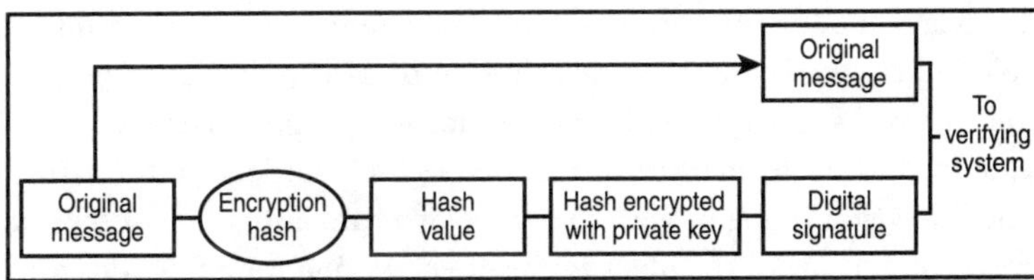

FIGURE 5.4
Diagram of a how the creation of a digital signature works.

After the recipient gets this digitally signed data, the sender's public key is used to decrypt the data and subsequently the message digest, which if the decryption is successful—meaning the sender's public key decrypts the data—the signature is authenticated and the data can be trusted. This is true only because the message digest was encrypted using the sender's private key and, as you learned, only the public key can decrypt the private key, and vice versa. After it is determined that the data is from the true source, the data is run through the same hash the source system used to generate the message digest again. If the message digest sent with the data and the digest generated on the recipient's end are the same, the data is deemed as authentic and untouched. Figure 5.5 shows how the data is verified on the recipient side.

FIGURE 5.5
Diagram of how the data is verified on the recipient side.

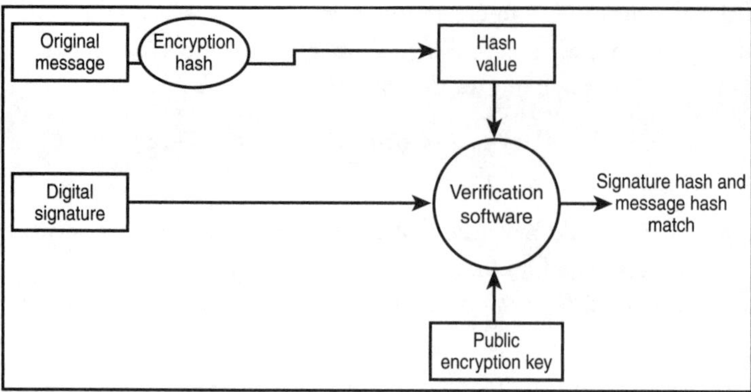

As you can see, the act of digitally signing data is resource intensive and in the grand scheme of things time intensive, as well. The methodology does, however, allow for a fair assumption that the data being sent is authentic and from whoever was the actual sender.

Establishing User Authentication with Encryption

In today's modern operating systems, encryption has an increasing role in helping secure the authentication of users to workstations and networks. Encryption for authentication purposes has even extended to small smart cards that can secure your login information and allow you to log in with the swipe of a card and a PIN. Let's not forget about one of the older forms of encryption for authentication: ATMs and your encrypted PIN. Secure authentication is likely one of the most common applications for encryption mainly because the small amount of data used to pass user and password information along. This helps keep network resource and traffic use in check. In addition to this, you of course have the very sensitive nature of a user's login information, which using encryption can help protect. If that information falls into the wrong hands, encryption in other areas might not actually do you any good if the hacker can freely manipulate data by posing as an authentic user.

Encryption is finding its way into almost every operating system available, including Windows 2000 workstations and servers. Of particular interest in Windows 2000 is the inclusion of basic data encryption on a user's or server's hard drive called the *Encrypting File System (EFS)*.

EFS requires that the hard drive with the data being encrypted use the NTFS file system and allows for fairly seamless encryption of data in a given folder or group of folders. One concern with EFS is that to have some control over which data is encrypted and who can see it, any administrator on that system can go in and review the information decrypted. On one hand, this enables administrators to retrieve data for a user who has been fired, for example. At the same time, however, it compromises the security in that more than one person has access to that encrypted data. In addition, if the user's password was compromised and someone logged in as that user, that person would have full access to the encrypted data as if it were never encrypted in the first place.

Another useful security feature of Windows 2000 is the inclusion of *Public Key Infrastructure (PKI)*. PKI, as the name suggests, uses asymmetric encryption to provide both a public and private key for users who want to access the system. This type of setup is often used to connect workstations to servers and is of particular interest to server administrators with remote users connecting to the server from the Internet. PKI provides confidentiality; secure authentication; and *nonrepudiation*, which is a service with the capability to provide proof of the origin and integrity of data.

An excellent introduction to Windows 2000 PKI and the possibilities of encryption and authentication can be found at `http://www.microsoft.com/technet/treeview/default.asp?url=/technet/prodtechnol/windows2000serv/evaluate/featfunc/pkiintro.asp`. PKI is also covered in more detail in Chapter 6, "PKI, Key Management, and Attacks."

In addition to PKI, you can take advantage of *Kerberos* authentication in Windows 2000. Kerberos is like the proverbial guard dog at the front door to your network. This type of authentication is based on symmetric encryption and was first developed by MIT as part of its Athena project. Windows 2000 includes support for Kerberos, albeit in a slightly modified form than historically used to this point.

In Windows 2000, Microsoft added extensions to Kerberos that can help the initial authentication with Kerberos take place using secure digital certificates, rather than the typical public key-type authentication Kerberos normally uses. Although you can still use the original method, secure digital certificates are another new security feature in Windows 2000, so including support for them was essential. Another excellent document on the Microsoft Web site discusses Kerberos in Windows 2000 (`http://www.microsoft.com/technet/treeview/default.asp?url=/TechNet/prodtechnol/windows2000serv/deploy/kerberos.asp`). It is also worth a read if you are simply interested in this authentication method.

With authentication on your mind, the next section expands and explains nonrepudiation and how it can improve or help establish the veracity of your authentication methods.

Nonrepudiation

Nonrepudiation is intended to provide, through encryption, a method in which there is no refuting where data came from. This definition never takes into account the possible compromise of the workstation or system used to create the private key and the encrypted digital signature. The following list outlines four of the key elements nonrepudiation services provide on a typical client/server connection:

- **Proof of origin**—The host gets proof that the client is the originator of particular data or an authentication request from a particular time and location.
- **Proof of submission**—The client gets proof that the data (or authentication, in this case) has been sent.
- **Proof of delivery**—The client gets proof that the data (or authentication, in this case) has been received.
- **Proof of receipt**—The client gets proof that the data (or authentication, in this case) has been received correctly.

It is acceptable to say that, if the digital signature came from this computer and some form of nonrepudiation is in place then it came from that person; however, it isn't a 100% guarantee because of variables that might be out of the control of the nonrepudiation service. For instance, a user might walk away from her computer for a lunch break and forget to lock the system or log out. Over that lunch hour, another employee could use that user's computer to log into servers to which he normally wouldn't have access. Because the server is convinced through authentication and nonrepudiation that the person connecting is the one who is the owner of the private key, this rogue user can easily get access to whatever he wants—assuming either he knows the password or the user's account allows him in automatically.

Nonrepudiation is intended to provide a more reliable method of ensuring that whoever is authenticating to a system is indeed the intended user. For nonrepudiation to be more reliable and accurate, though, a trusted third party must be involved in the process. This third party can provide the following benefits:

- Both parties involved in the communication or data transfer have their proof of identity stored at the third party. This would ideally provide better security than the proof just sitting on a workstation hard drive, for instance.
- The third party provides the stored proof of identity as necessary for verification purposes. This can be both from the processing side of things when systems are trying to verify identities and providing evidence should the authenticity of the proof of identity ever come into question.
- In some cases, a trusted third party takes data from one source, packages the data, and stamps it as authentic—already taking the steps to guarantee whomever sent the data is who they say they are and that the data is then passed down to the recipient after they are confirmed. This intermediary service adds some complexity and time into the equation, but if you want strong assurance that whoever is sending the data is who they say they are, this is a good way to go about it.

As the previous description might suggest, nonrepudiation is provided as a service, likely built into the operating system or as part of whatever software is handling the encryption and decryption of your data or authentication methods. In many implementations of nonrepudiation, when data is encrypted, extra data is attached to the digital signature. This data is called the *nonrepudiation bit* and is similar to a personalized rubber stamp used to emblazon everything you encrypt. This bit helps provide another level of verification that you are who you say you are. Of course, many would argue that a small bit of data is hardly much better than a regular digital signature. For the most part, that is very true, but like anything else, the more information you can provide with your original ID, the better.

Nonrepudiation can be a very complex and an ever-changing topic. How you go about ensuring true nonrepudiation will always be in question because guaranteeing who the actual sender is can be difficult. Some of these problems are addressed in the following section on access control and how encryption and access control work together.

Access Control with Encryption Technologies

Access control in an organization can take on many forms. In most environments, access control can encompass something as simple as limiting which directories users can open to something as involved as defining what content users can and cannot view on the Internet. Access control can be an important aspect to implement in an organization when you want to have the best possible control over what your users can see and, potentially, what they can send from and bring into the network. The less potentially dangerous data and connections coming in and out of your network, the less chance of there being a security issue (in particular, viruses). It makes sense that the less you let in or out, the less you have to worry about.

Access control is typically the most effective when you combine it with encryption—for example, in Windows 2000, using Kerberos to encrypt the authentication process or using PKI to secure remote connections to a server. Any way of controlling access (using a password, setting rights, setting user policies, and so on) helps augment security. However, when you combine it with encryption, you get the benefits of confidentiality and integrity as well.

Access Control via XACL

A newer method of implementing access control is through a secure version of the Extensible Markup Language (XML). This version of XML is specifically designed for access control and is called XML Access Control Language (XACL). XML documents can be written to provide a variety of services, and they are particularly useful in company intranets where having centralized services accessible through the Web is quite handy. XACL is a newer development that allows granular access control to resources by using XML on such pages. The capability to control what the end user can see and use makes XACL a powerful tool for companies. This version of XML could also prove to be something that companies extend to the Internet—particularly, companies providing customers services over the Web might find this method of access control optimal.

XACL encompasses encryption because XML was designed to allow developers to take advantage of today's strong encryption algorithms.

So, any XML document can use encryption to provide more robust access control as well as data integrity and confidentiality. IBM has a lot of information and documentation on XACL on its Web site at `http://www.trl.ibm.com/projects/xml/xacl/`. XML and XACL are not in mainstream use yet, but they are gaining popularity. Becoming familiar with XML technology is a good idea not only for understanding how security can be augmented with it, but also so you can see how XML can affect security for your organization.

Wireless Encryption

A growing concern over the past year and a half has been the overall security frailty of wireless networks. With wireless networking technology exploding worldwide, it was only a matter of time before serious security issues cropped up.

One of the main security-related problems with wireless networking is that a wireless solution is easy to set up and is relatively inexpensive. As a result, many wireless stations and cards have been sold. Yet, many using and administering these wireless networks are inexperienced users and administrators who set up wireless networks without any or very little security.

To help ease installation concerns, most wireless networking equipment is configured without any security features, such as encryption or any type of access password. This was done so these new users could get up to speed as quickly as possible and with a minimum of support calls to the company's help desk. One major problem with the removal of basic security features is that inexperienced users and administrators probably never configure these devices to have security features after the initial setup. This obviously leaves major holes and exposures to user and company data.

Security of wireless networks was not a big concern in people's homes and businesses until the summer of 2001, when hackers started demonstrating how to jump on to, access, and monitor wireless networks without being in the same building. This was demonstrated with simple antenna equipment purchased at a Radio Shack or, in some instances, rudimentary antennas built with Pringles cans and connected to laptops. These antenna amplifiers enabled the hackers to extend the range of their laptop wireless cards far enough to connect to wireless networks from a parking lot or even a few blocks away!

Not only were these hackers able to join a network and surf the Internet for free, but in many cases, they also captured sensitive information because no encryption was enabled and the data was passing freely around the wireless network.

IN THE FIELD

WIRELESS NETWORK SECURITY

The number of unsecured wireless networks shown in the San Francisco downtown area were staggering to say the least. To find out how many unsecured networks existed, the people performing the demonstration simply drove around in a van with their antenna pointing out the window and watched the networks pass by on their notebook's wireless connection manager, which comes with the wireless network cards. There won't be any names mentioned in this title, but needless to say this was alarming considering some of the large organizations that were completely vulnerable, including some large IT organizations.

Many valuable documents outline how to properly secure a wireless network. At a minimum, a password should be required to join a wireless network. (This is not the same as your network password used to log in to your server, but the wireless network itself.) This stops people from just hopping on your network and taking a free ride. Ideally, encryption should be used, but—as you now know—encryption is a big resource hog and wireless networks perform at just over 11% of what a typical wired network does. Add the extra bandwidth and overhead of encryption on your wireless network, and your performance can quickly be reduced. However, some encryption is typically better than no encryption at all. Yet, it is important to not let encryption become a security blanket because it might not be the total solution you hope.

One such pitfall exists with the Wired Equivalent Privacy (WEP) implementation included in most modern wireless networking devices. WEP was a response to the initial security concerns about wireless networking. Most people were urged to take advantage of it and enable it to boost the security of their wireless networks to supposedly the same security levels they would experience on their regular wired networks. The problem is that many organizations' regular wired networks that the WEP purports to match in security, aren't as easily accessible.

When you look at the fact that your wired network is housed within your building with no external access and then compare that to a wireless network where a hacker using a Pringles can simply sit and collect enough data to crack your WEP encryption and reconstruct network data, WEP doesn't appear to help that much at all.

Although all hope seems lost when securing wireless networks, there are signs of improvement from wireless manufacturers. Plus, when all else fails, you can take advantage of the encryption included in your operating system or from a third-party application designed to encrypt your sensitive data or communications. If some hacker is riding your wireless network and capturing data, she will have a harder time breaking into your email if you have a solid encryption algorithm protecting it.

Case Study: Tiny Monsters Creations

ESSENCE OF THE CASE

Here are the essential elements in this case:

- Which methods of access control can be used in this situation? What would be the best way to integrate access control into its Web page plans?
- TMC wants to have stores log in with as much security as possible, but the company also needs to keep bandwidth costs down. Which encryption method would you recommend for a good balance of resource utilization and performance?
- If TMC absolutely wants to know for sure (within reason) which user is logging in, which service could it use to best accomplish this?
- If TMC does not decide to use an XML-designed Web site for data entry but wants to dump data directly into the accounting server, what would be the most secure method of achieving this?

SCENARIO

Tiny Monsters Creations (TMC) is a large chain store of children's clothing and accessories with locations all over North America. TMC has been growing at a phenomenal rate and recently opened more than 20 new stores, bringing its grand total to 50. TMC wants to centralize its business, including record accounting, to its Boise, Idaho, office. To this point, the record accounting has strictly been couriered in paper format monthly from each location to the Boise office. Besides being costly, the data must be reentered by hand into the company's accounting server to be processed as a whole—which is also very time-consuming.

To rectify the situation, TMC would like to have the stores connect to a Web site where the data would be dumped from its Internet service provider into its accounting servers.

continues

CASE STUDY: TINY MONSTERS CREATIONS

continued

ANALYSIS

In this situation, if XML is being implemented, the easiest method of providing access control is to use XACL to control access to certain areas of the site. For instance, if TMC wants only managers to have access to the payroll section of the Web site, this could be accomplished using XACL.

To keep bandwidth usage and costs down and to keep performance up when using encryption, a symmetric encryption algorithm with at least 128-bit encryption should be used. In this case, 3DES or AES would be a good choice. However, SHA-1 or MD5 might be a better selection because of their proven track records, ease of implementation (a larger variety of software developers experienced with using the algorithm are available), and wider support in many software applications out of the box (especially over the newer AES).

One of the most effective ways to ensure that TMC could verify who is sending the data is through nonrepudiation services. However, implementing encrypted digital signatures can provide the best balance between veracity and performance.

Ultimately, one of the best ways to verify is to have the user call and verify that she did send the data. If decryption is successful, the data is very likely from the source and integrity can be ensured.

The most secure way would, of course, be to continue to do what the company is doing now. However, because that isn't the goal of the redesign, the best way is to enable an asymmetric encryption algorithm—likely the RSA algorithm, but ECC might be a consideration as well for its performance and strength properties. Of course, you would earn extra points if you recommended using asymmetric encryption and ensuring that the entire network is secured. In addition, you could also implement PKI and have the users log directly in to the domain using encrypted authentication.

Ultimately, many solutions exist to these situations, but as you can see, the solution varies depending on many circumstances, such as performance, integration, and reliability. With more than 50 stores to roll into the new program and at least as many users to train, user impact is certainly an issue that should be addressed in a proposed environment such as this.

CHAPTER SUMMARY

Throughout this chapter, you learned about the fundamentals of encryption, including encryption algorithms and the ways in which many of them function. It is important to remember these fundamentals of encryption and how they can be applied to your environments to provide more effective security.

As you learned, a variety of symmetric encryption algorithms are available for use today. In essence, symmetric encryption methods are the weakest of the current encryption methods. However, they typically provide very strong security that can be used for authentication, file encryption, and securing data sent over network connections. Among the most common and popular types of symmetric encryption used today are the 3DES, MD, and RC algorithms. Each brings its own capabilities to the table, but all function in essentially similar ways. An important aspect to remember in regard to symmetric encryption is that comparatively speaking, it requires fewer system resources and performs better (meaning encryption and decryption happen more quickly). This is mainly because of the smaller nature of the encryption keys and the fact that only one key is used to process both ends of the connection.

Asymmetric encryption will undoubtedly provide the utmost in security, but at a price. With very large encryption keys compared to symmetric encryption keys, asymmetric encrypted data takes longer to transfer across networks because more data must be sent along with the original data and it takes longer to both encrypt and decrypt. Even given these handicaps, the use of asymmetric algorithms, such as the popular RSA algorithm, is on the rise because they do provide the strongest overall encryption solution available today.

Simply knowing which encryption algorithms are available and the basics of how they work isn't enough if you plan to use any type of encryption in your organization. You must understand the fundamental uses and caveats that come with using encryption. Confidentiality and integrity are of the utmost concern to most companies and organizations. With the threat of hackers and corporate espionage present, encryption is quickly becoming a necessity to provide security. Being able to send data without worrying about who might be viewing it or ensuring that the data you send or receive will arrive intact and without modification is very important when money and possibly people's lives depend on it.

KEY TERMS

- Algorithm
- Asymmetric algorithm
- Block cipher
- Cipher
- Dictionary attack
- Digital signature
- Distributed computing
- Elliptic Curve Cryptography (ECC)
- Encrypting File System (EFS)
- Encryption hash
- Extensible Markup Language (XML)
- Hash value
- Key exchange
- Man-in-the-middle attack
- Message digest
- Nonrepudiation
- Nonrepudiation bit
- Private key
- Public key
- Public Key Infrastructure (PKI)
- Round
- Smart card
- Symmetric encryption
- Wired Equivalent Privacy (WEP)
- XML Access Control Language (XACL)

CHAPTER SUMMARY

Encryption can help accomplish these goals, but you must remember that encryption might not be the ultimate fix for your security needs. A good security implementation takes encryption into account as a major focus, but ensuring that the rest of your network and computers are secure is just as important.

Digital signatures can help provide an extra element of verification when dealing with encryption. When you need to know for sure that the data you have received is in fact whom you expect it to be from, digital signatures can help provide the necessary confirmation. Nonrepudiation services can help augment current digital signature standards by providing an extra level of verification if you are concerned about the veracity or reliability of your digital signature solution.

APPLY YOUR KNOWLEDGE

Exercises

5.1 Enabling Encrypting File System in Windows XP

This exercise demonstrates how to create a folder on your system and enable it for use as an encrypted folder using the integrated Encrypting File System in Windows XP. Keep in mind that although this lab focuses on Windows XP, the procedure is the same when using Windows 2000, which also supports EFS.

Remember that to enable EFS on Windows 2000 or Windows XP, you must have at least one partition formatted as an NTFS partition for EFS to work. FAT32 partitions lack the security features EFS requires.

Estimated Time: 10 minutes

1. Locate and double-click My Computer on your desktop. Alternatively, click the Start button and then click My Computer.
2. In My Computer, locate and double-click the NTFS-enabled partition on which you want to create the EFS folder—for example, `C:\`.
3. Select File, New, Folder from the menu bar. Rename the new folder you created **EFS**.
4. Right-click the EFS folder you created in step 3, and select Properties from the pop-up menu. The EFS Properties dialog box opens (see Figure 5.6). Click the Advanced button to open the Advanced Attributes dialog box.

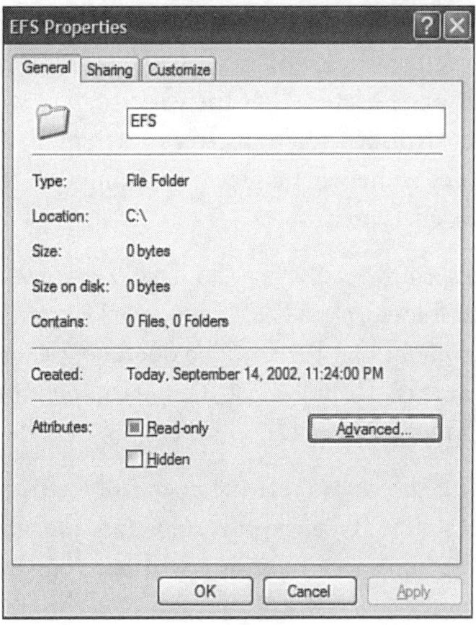

FIGURE 5.6
The EFS folder's Properties dialog box.

5. Locate the check box next to the Encrypt Contents to Secure Data option in the Advanced Attributes dialog box and select it (see Figure 5.7). Now EFS is enabled for that folder. Click the OK button to apply the setting change, and click OK on the EFS Properties dialog box.

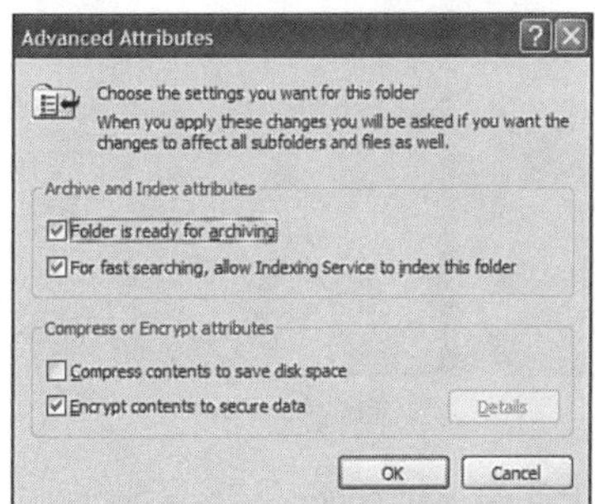

FIGURE 5.7
Setting the folder's Advanced Attributes to enable EFS for the EFS folder.

APPLY YOUR KNOWLEDGE

6. Double-click the EFS folder to open it. If you are running Windows XP, in the Details information box on the left side of the window, you will see the Attributes folder listed as Encrypted. Also the folder name will be green, meaning that the folder is encrypted.

7. To see how easily you can have encrypted files in this folder, select File, New, Text Document from the menu bar. Rename the document **`Encrypted Text.txt`**. Double-click the file to open it in Windows Notepad.

8. With the empty text file open in Notepad, type **`This file is encrypted`** and close the window. A dialog box appears asking whether you want to save the file. Click Yes to return to the EFS directory. Now your directory should look similar to Figure 5.8. Congratulations, you have created an encrypted file folder and file using EFS!

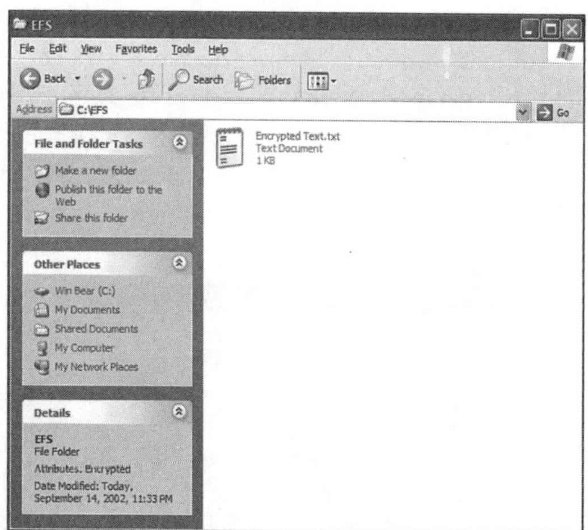

FIGURE 5.8
An encrypted folder with encrypted text file using EFS.

9. Finally, click the Back button on the menu bar to return to your partition's folder listing. Select File, New, Text Document from the menu bar. Leave the document named as is, and then click and drag the file into your EFS folder. Double-click the EFS folder; both files are there and encrypted. Any new files created in that folder will be encrypted, and any files copied or moved into that folder will also be encrypted.

As an optional step, try logging out and logging in as a user on the system that does not have administrator access. You can see and open the EFS directory you created, but if you try to open any files you have in the EFS-enabled directory, you receive an `Access Denied` message. Although not the most descriptive explanation, this is what Windows 2000 or Windows XP does to let users know they don't have access to the encrypted files.

5.2 Installing PGP Under Windows XP

In this exercise, you install PGP email on Windows XP. This exercise focuses on Windows XP, but the steps should apply to any major Windows operating system. You must have Outlook Express installed for this exercise; it is installed by default in Windows 2000 and Windows XP. You can also download it for free from `http://www.windowsupdate.com`.

PGP is available as freeware and is available for download from `http://web.mit.edu/network/pgp-form.html`. Before you can download PGP, you have to answer some questions on where you live and other legal issues to ensure the software is going to be used in appropriate locations because of the strong encryption it uses. Answer Yes to all the questions on the Web form if they apply, and proceed to the download page. After you download the latest freeware version for your OS (PGP Freeware v6.5.8 as of this writing), save the file to your desktop.

Apply Your Knowledge

Once there, extract the files (the program is packed in a Zip format) to a folder on your desktop called `PGPSOURCE`; then proceed to step 1 of the exercise.

Estimated Time: 15 minutes

1. Close any email applications you have open on your system. Locate and double-click the `PGPSOURCE` folder on your desktop. Read the `whatsnew.txt` file, and then double-click Setup.exe. PGP setup unpacks the files and prepares for installation.
2. At the Welcome screen, click the Next button to continue to the Software License Agreement window. Read through the contents of the agreement and if you agree, click the Yes button to continue to the Important Product Information window. You should have already read this information prior to running setup; if not, do so now.
3. In the User Information window shown in Figure 5.9, enter your name and company information. Then click the Next button to continue to the Choose Destination Location dialog box.

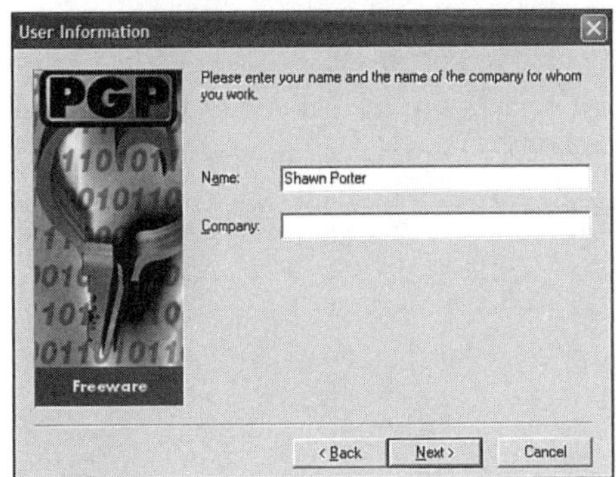

FIGURE 5.9
The PGP User Information set up window.

4. In the Choose Destination Location dialog box, the default installation path is already entered into the Destination Folder text box. Leave this as the default and click Next.
5. The Select Components dialog box appears. Three main plug-ins are used to allow PGP to interact with your email software. Select the email program you have installed or want to use for testing, and deselect any that you do not have installed. For this exercise, ensure that PGP Qualcomm Eudora Plugin and PGP Microsoft Exchange/Outlook Plugin are deselected and that PGP Microsoft Outlook Express Plugin is selected. Your Select Components dialog box should look similar to Figure 5.10. Click the Next button to proceed.

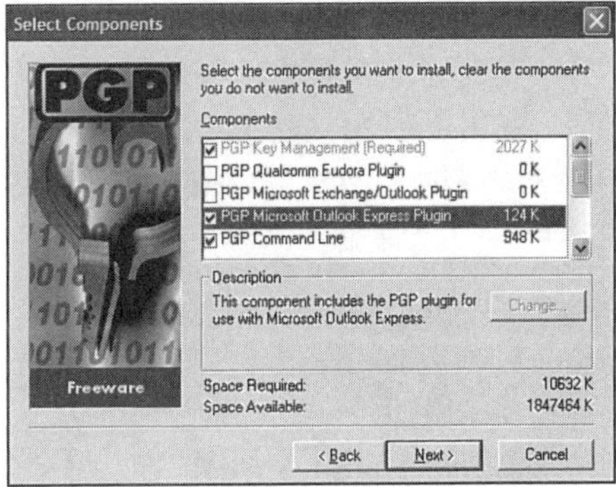

FIGURE 5.10
The PGP Select Components window with PGP Microsoft Outlook Plugin selected.

6. In the Ready to Start Copying Files window, view the information for this installation and click the Next button to start installing PGP. After the files have been copied, a question box appears and asks whether you have existing keyrings you want to use. Click No.

APPLY YOUR KNOWLEDGE

7. After the installation is complete, the Setup Complete dialog box appears. Select the check box next to the Launch PGPkeys option to remove the check mark. (PGPkeys are covered in the next exercise.) Click the Finish button to finish installing PGP.

5.3 Creating a Set of Public and Private Keys in PGP

In this exercise, you use your fresh PGP installation from Exercise 5.2 to generate a public and private key pair using the PGPkeys utility. With a set of public and private keys, you can encrypt emails and file attachments and send them to other people who use PGP.

Estimated Time: 15 minutes

1. Open the PGPkeys utility by selecting Start, Programs, PGP, PGPkeys. PGPkeys opens and you are presented with the Key Generation Wizard welcome screen. Click Next.
2. The next dialog box asks you to enter the email address and name you want associated with the key pair you are generating in this exercise. After you enter your information into the two text boxes, your dialog box should look similar to Figure 5.11. Click Next.

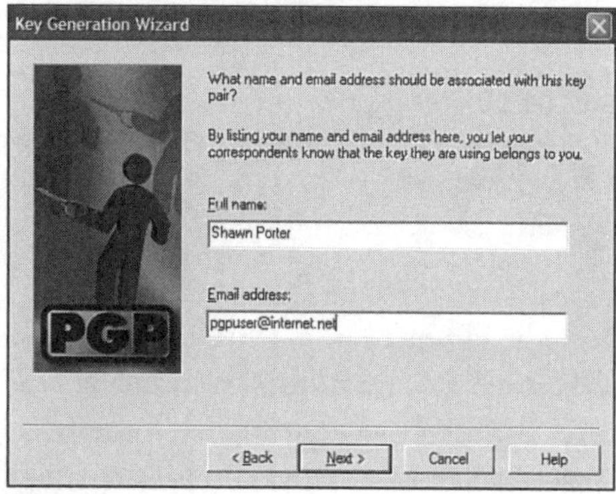

FIGURE 5.11
Using PGPkeys to associate a name and an email address with a new key pair.

3. The next dialog box displays a choice of two types of encryption with which to generate your key pair: Diffie-Hellman/DSS and RSA. For this exercise, select the radio button next to Diffie-Hellman/DSS, as shown in Figure 5.12. Click Next.

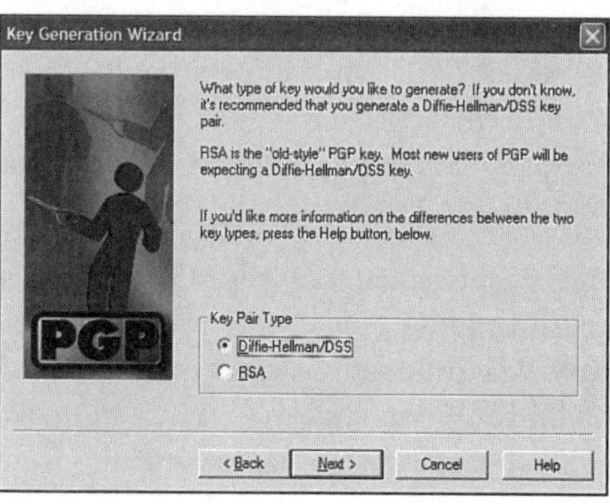

FIGURE 5.12
Selecting the type of encryption used to generate a key pair in PGPkeys.

4. In the next window, you select which key pair size (bit strength) you want to make this key pair. Remember that the larger they are, the slower the process is. For this exercise, select the radio button next to the 1536 Bits (1536 Diffie-Hellman/1024 DSS) option, as shown in Figure 5.13. Click Next.

APPLY YOUR KNOWLEDGE

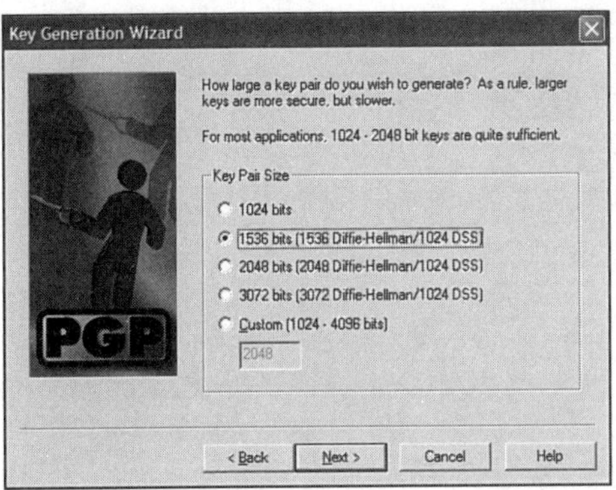

FIGURE 5.13
Selecting the bit strength of the key pair you are generating in PGPkeys.

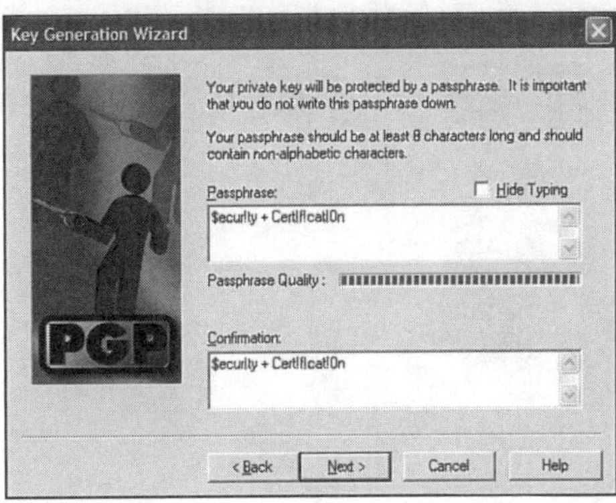

FIGURE 5.14
Entering and confirming a passphrase in the PGPkeys utility.

5. In the next window, you set the expiration for your key pair. For security purposes, you might want your keys to stop working after a certain amount of time so you can create new keys. This can obviously become a key management nightmare with anyone receiving your messages and files. For this exercise, select the radio button next to Key Pair Never Expires. Click Next.

6. Now you must enter a passphrase, which is used to secure your private key. The passphrase must be at least eight characters long and should contain nonalphanumeric characters such as !, @, %, and *. For this exercise, enter **`$ecur!ty + Cert!f!cat!0n`** in the Passphrase text box. Notice in Figure 5.14 how we have unhidden the passphrase by disabling the Hide Typing check box.

   You will also notice that the Passphrase Quality meter increases the more characters you enter. In the Confirmation text box, you must enter the exact same passphrase again. So, if you are creating a large, complex passphrase, you should unhide your entry so you do not make a mistake; however, if you are in an unsecured environment, it might be better to leave it hidden. Enter the passphrase again into the Confirmation text box and click Next.

7. PGP uses your passphrase to generate your key pair based on your previous settings; as shown in Figure 5.15. After you see the complete message at the bottom of the window, click Next.

APPLY YOUR KNOWLEDGE

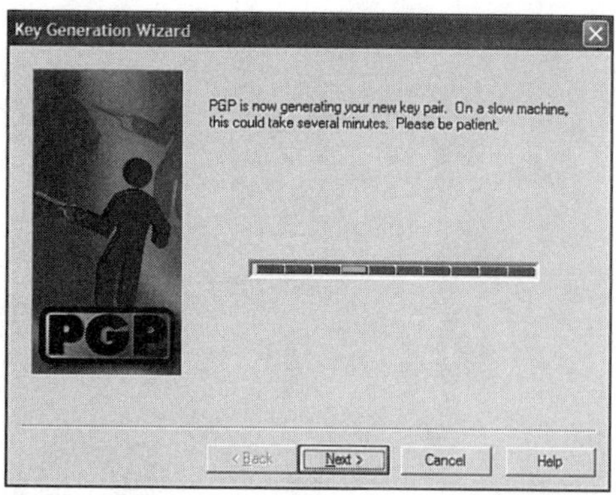

FIGURE 5.15
PGP is generating a key pair using the PGPkeys utility and a confirmed passphrase.

8. The next window asks whether you want to send your public key to the PGP root server where other people wanting to obtain the key can do so easily. For this exercise, you will not send your key to the root server; however, you can do it later from the PGPkeys utility. Leave the check box next to the Send My Key to the Root Server Now button unchecked. Click Next to proceed to the final window of the Key Generation Wizard.

9. Click Finish to complete the wizard. The PGPkeys utility opens and displays the default keys from members of the PGP team and Network Associates as well as your new key, as shown in Figure 5.16.

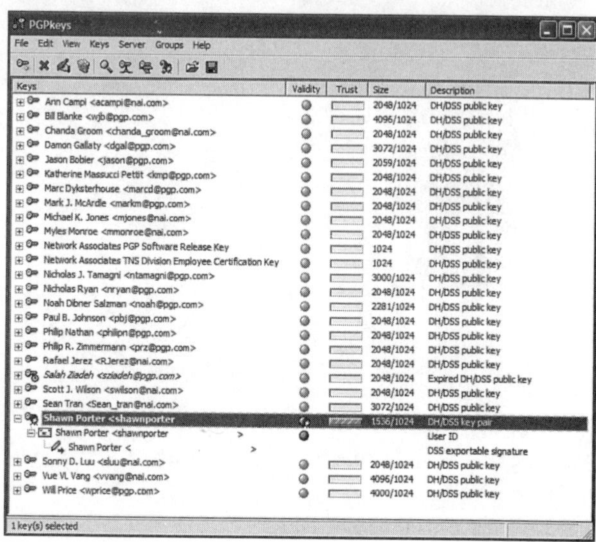

FIGURE 5.16
The PGPkeys utility showing your key and other keys installed in the software by default from the PGP team.

You have created your own PGP key pair. Leave this window open for Exercise 5.4.

5.4 Setting Options in the PGPkeys Utility

In this exercise, you configure the options for the key pair you generated in Exercise 5.3. PGPkeys enables a fair amount of customization, such as types of cipher, how encrypted email is handled, and of course how to manage the keys of people you communicate with. In this exercise, you configure some of the email options as well as choose which encryption algorithm to use by default.

Estimated Time: 10 minutes

1. If you closed the PGPkeys utility in Exercise 5.3, reopen it by selecting Start, Programs, PGP, PGPkeys. PGPkeys opens and you are presented with the list of keys installed on your system.

APPLY YOUR KNOWLEDGE

2. From the menu bar, select Edit, Options. The PGP Options dialog box opens, as shown in Figure 5.17.

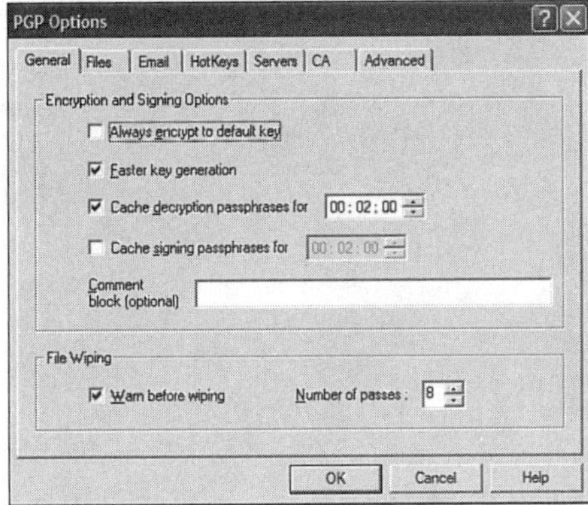

FIGURE 5.17
The PGPkeys PGP Options dialog box's General tab.

3. On the General tab, select the check box next to Always Encrypt to Default Key and leave all the other options at their defaults.

4. Click the Email tab. Select the Encrypt New Messages by Default check box to have PGP encrypt anything you send out. Also, check the Sign New Messages by Default check box to include your PGP signature, which people can use to verify that the message did in fact come from you. Finally, check the Automatically Decrypt/Verify when Opening Messages check box to have PGP decrypt messages without you having to do so manually each time. After you have set these options, your tab should look similar to Figure 5.18.

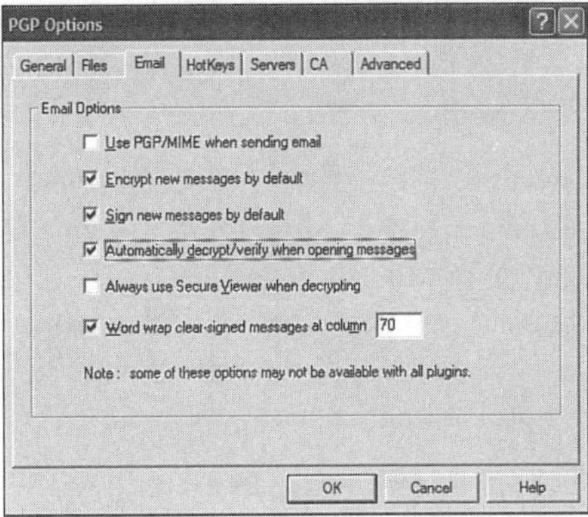

FIGURE 5.18
Setting email options in the PGPkeys utility.

5. Click the Advanced tab to set which encryption algorithm you want to use. Your selections are CAST, IDEA, and TripleDES. Click the arrow next to the Preferred Algorithm drop-down box and select TripleDES. Your Advanced tab should look similar to Figure 5.19.

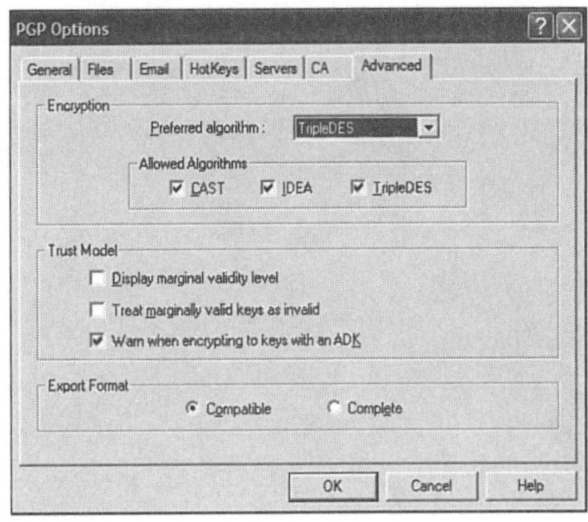

FIGURE 5.19
Setting encryption algorithm options in the PGPkeys utility.

APPLY YOUR KNOWLEDGE

6. Click OK to accept these changes and return to PGPkeys. Click the X in the upper-right corner of the window to close PGPkeys.
7. A window opens explaining that the keys you created are very important and a backup should be made in case you experience a fatal hard drive crash and lose your data. Click the Save Backup Now button to open the Select Public Keyring Backup Destination window.
8. Navigate using the Save In drop-down menu to the EFS folder you created in Exercise 5.1, and once there, click the Save button. This saves your keyring to the folder; then you are asked to save your secret keyring file. Click the Save button to save it in the same folder. PGPkeys closes and your keys are backed up.
9. Double-click the My Computer icon on your desktop to open it, and double-click the partition in which you created your EFS folder. Locate and double-click the folder. As you can see in Figure 5.20, both of your backed up files are encrypted, providing an extra level of security for those files.

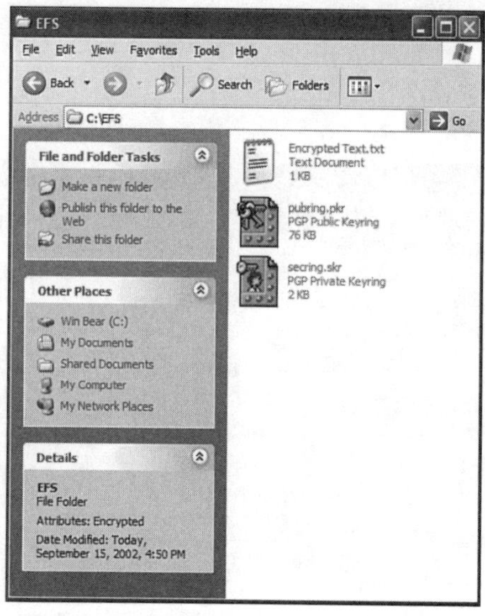

FIGURE 5.20
Backed up PGP Keyring files encrypted in a folder enabled with EFS.

   After you view the encrypted files, click the X in the upper-right corner to close the EFS folder window.

You should actually save those backup files on a floppy disk or CD-ROM and store them in a secure place such as a safe. Network servers that are secured work well, and as shown in this exercise, EFS folders can be employed to increase the security of the backed up files.

APPLY YOUR KNOWLEDGE

Review Questions

1. You are going to create a large archive of files and want to encrypt these files to secure them while you send them to your business partners and colleagues. Which encryption method would be the most efficient method to do this?

2. After sending several encrypted emails, recipients are complaining that they have no way of knowing for sure that the emails are from you. What can you do to allay their concerns?

3. The president of your company has decided that you need to implement some type of secure method of authentication on the network after concerns that a competing company might have hired a hacker to try to retrieve sensitive information. Which common component built into Windows 2000 and other operating systems would allow for that?

4. You are developing a new piece of software that will be used by a large Internet Web site dedicated to selling large-ticket items. The company wants to ensure that encryption is used not only on the Web site, but also within the company to ensure that the data from these customers and transactions is as secure as possible but still fast. Which symmetric encryption algorithm and key strength would you implement in this case if you want the fastest possible encryption?

5. Your department manager has decided that digital signatures aren't enough to verify the sender, and she wants to implement a nonrepudiation service to help provide an extra level of veracity to encrypted data sent from your department. She is adamant that this will be all the company needs to guarantee to recipients the integrity of the data. What are some concerns that you might want to bring up about implementing a nonrepudiation service?

Exam Questions

1. What is a potential concern to weaker encryption algorithms as time goes on?

   A. Hackers using distributed computing might be able to finally crack an algorithm.

   B. Performance of the algorithm will worsen over time.

   C. Keys generated by users will start to repeat on other users' systems.

   D. Newer versions will make the original obsolete.

2. Which type of algorithm do the MD series of encryption algorithms (MD2, MD4, and MD5) use?

   A. Asymmetric encryption algorithm

   B. Hashing algorithm

   C. Digital signature

   D. Private Key

3. To secure wireless networks, a protocol was developed to perform basic encryption on data passing over the network in hopes that it would provide security on par with that of a regular wired network. What is the name of that protocol?

   A. Wireless Application Environment (WAE)

   B. Wireless Session Protocol (WSP)

   C. Wireless Encryption Protocol (WEP)

   D. Wired Equivalent Privacy (WEP)

APPLY YOUR KNOWLEDGE

4. In encryption, which type of algorithm involves data being broken into chunks of varying sizes (dependent on the algorithm) and the encryption being applied to those chunks of data?

   A. Symmetric encryption algorithm

   B. Elliptic curve

   C. Block cipher

   D. Asymmetric encryption algorithm

5. When the NIST put out the call to have a new algorithm replace the aging DES as the standard encryption algorithm used for general consumption in government organizations, there were several entrants. Which algorithm eventually won?

   A. Rijndael

   B. 3DES

   C. RC6

   D. Twofish

   E. CAST

6. Which type of algorithm generates a key pair of a public key and a private key that are then used to encrypt and decrypt data and messages sent and received?

   A. Elliptic curve

   B. Asymmetric encryption algorithm

   C. Symmetric encryption algorithm

   D. Block Cipher

7. Which of the following algorithms are examples of a symmetric encryption algorithm? (Choose all that apply.)

   A. Rijndael

   B. AES

   C. Diffie-Hellman

   D. RC6

8. Which of the following algorithms are examples of an asymmetric encryption algorithm? (Choose all that apply.)

   A. 3DES

   B. Elliptic curve

   C. CAST

   D. RSA

9. When encrypting and decrypting data using an asymmetric encryption algorithm, you do what? (Choose all that apply.)

   A. Use only the private key to encrypt and only the public key to decrypt.

   B. Use only the public key to encrypt and only the private key to decrypt.

   C. Can use the public key to either encrypt or decrypt.

   D. Use only the private key to decrypt data encrypted with the public key.

10. In a block cipher, the data is broken into blocks of data and the encryption algorithm is then applied against those blocks of data multiple times. When a block cipher does this, what is it called?

    A. A round

    B. A chunk

    C. A nonrepudiation service

    D. Brute-force encryption

APPLY YOUR KNOWLEDGE

Answers to Review Questions

1. Although an asymmetric encryption algorithm such as RSA or Diffie-Hellman provides the most secure method of encrypting these files, a symmetric encryption algorithm such as 3DES is a more efficient method. This is especially the case if you have a large quantity of files that would be encrypted and sent on a frequent basis.
2. The easiest method of allowing the email recipients to verify that you are in fact the sender of the message is to use digital signatures. Programs such as PGP allow you to attach digital signatures to every email you send. You can then send this along, and the recipients can verify the signature is from you.
3. Public Key Infrastructure (PKI) is available in Windows 2000 and other operating systems. It allows for secure authentication methods, which can help provide control over who accesses your system. Using PKI with the addition of some type of stronger overall security plan should help defend against any such intrusions.
4. In this situation, two encryption algorithms come to mind. CAST is a popular, fast, and very secure method that is worth looking into because of its established status on the encryption scene. This is mainly because more widespread support and information is likely available for the algorithm. This is always a concern when trying to integrate encryption into custom-written software. Ultimately, if a learning curve is not a concern, AES might be the better selection. AES is designed for strong encryption and performance and can be customized to varying degrees to enable the customer to ramp up the strength of the algorithm as required.
5. Although nonrepudiation services are a good idea overall, one particular concern is that guaranteeing that the data (nonrepudiation bit or not) is actually from that user is almost impossible. Also, one user could use another's terminal, which can invalidate the guarantee that nonrepudiation could provide. Suggest that, part and parcel with nonrepudiation services, a complete workstation security plan is put into place that requires additional security measures, including good physical security (locking terminals when users leave them and so on). It still can't guarantee 100% security, but the combination would be very hard to refute if followed through with.

Answers to Exam Questions

1. **A.** As computers get faster, the ability of hackers to use distributed computing as a method of breaking encryption algorithms increases. With computer performance in some cases increasing by 30%–50% a year on average, this could become a concern for some older algorithms.
2. **B.** Although the Message Digest series of algorithms is classified globally as a symmetric key encryption algorithm, the correct answer is hashing algorithm, which is the method the algorithm uses to encrypt data.
3. **D.** Wired Equivalent Privacy (WEP) was developed after engineers started to notice how completely vulnerable wireless networks were without any kind of security implemented. The problem occurred in many cases in which anyone could connect to the network and see what was on it without having to be in the building.

APPLY YOUR KNOWLEDGE

4. **C.** When data that is going to be encrypted is broken into chunks of data and then encrypted, the type of encryption is called a block cipher. Depending on the block cipher, some chunks can be any size from 1KB to the whole file, whereas others have a set size, such as 64KB or 128KB.

5. **A.** Rijndael was the eventual winner of the new AES standard, although the other algorithms do provide very solid performance and security. Rijndael was selected because of its capability to scale upward for future use as well as the flexibility in configuring how the algorithm operates.

6. **B.** Although many types of algorithms use public and private keys to apply their encryption algorithms in varying methods, the type of algorithms that perform in this way are called asymmetric encryption algorithms (or public key encryption).

7. **A, B, D.** Because Rijndael and AES are now one in the same, they both can be called symmetric encryption algorithms. Cipher 6 (RC6) is symmetric, as well. Diffie-Hellman uses public and private keys so it is considered an asymmetric encryption algorithm.

8. **B, D.** In this case, both elliptic curve and RSA are types of asymmetric encryption algorithms. Although the elliptic curve algorithm is typically a type of algorithm that is incorporated into other algorithms, it falls into the asymmetric family of algorithms because of its use of public and private keys, just like the RSA algorithm.

9. **D.** Answers A and B are both incorrect because in public key encryption, if one key is used to encrypt, you can use the other to decrypt the data. Answer C is incorrect because the public key cannot decrypt the same data it encrypted.

10. **A.** In a block cipher, the process of breaking the files into smaller blocks of data and then applying the encryption to these blocks is called a round. Each time encryption is applied to a block of data, it is called a round. Dependent on design, block ciphers use different numbers of rounds to achieve their goals.

APPLY YOUR KNOWLEDGE

Suggested Readings and Resources

Online Material

1. AES page at the NIST Web site (http://csrc.nist.gov/encryption/aes/).
2. El Gamal encryption discussion document on the RSA Web site (http://www.rsasecurity.com/rsalabs/staff/bios/mjakobsson/teaching/encryption_files/frame.htm).
3. How Encryption Works reference Web site (http://www.howstuffworks.com/encryption.htm).
4. Microsoft Kerberos deployment Web page (http://www.microsoft.com/technet/treeview/default.asp?url=/TechNet/prodtechnol/windows2000serv/deploy/kerberos.asp).
5. Microsoft Public Key Infrastructure introduction Web page (http://www.microsoft.com/technet/treeview/default.asp?url=/technet/prodtechnol/windows2000serv/evaluate/featfunc/pkiintro.asp).
6. National Institute of Standards and Technology Web site (www.nist.gov).
7. Request for Comment document for CAST-128 (www.faqs.org/rfcs/rfc2144.html).
8. Request for Comment document for CAST-256 (www.faqs.org/rfcs/rfc2612.html).
9. Rijndael Web site (www.esat.kuleuven.ac.be/~rijmen/rijndael/).
10. RSA-based Cryptographic Schemes Web site (http://www.rsasecurity.com/rsalabs/rsa_algorithm/).
11. Security books, journals, bibliographies, and publications listing Web site (http://www.cs.auckland.ac.nz/~pgut001/links/books.html).
12. W3C XML Encryption Working Group Web site (http://www.w3.org/Encryption/2001/).
13. XML Access Control Language (XACL) Web page at IBM (http://www.trl.ibm.com/projects/xml/xacl/).

Publications

1. Krutz, Ronald, and Russel Dean Vines. *The CISSP Prep Guide: Mastering the Ten Domains of Computer Security.* Indianapolis, IN: John Wiley & Sons, 2001.
2. Russel, Crawford. *Microsoft Windows 2000 Server Administrator's Companion.* Redmond, WA: Microsoft Press, 2000.

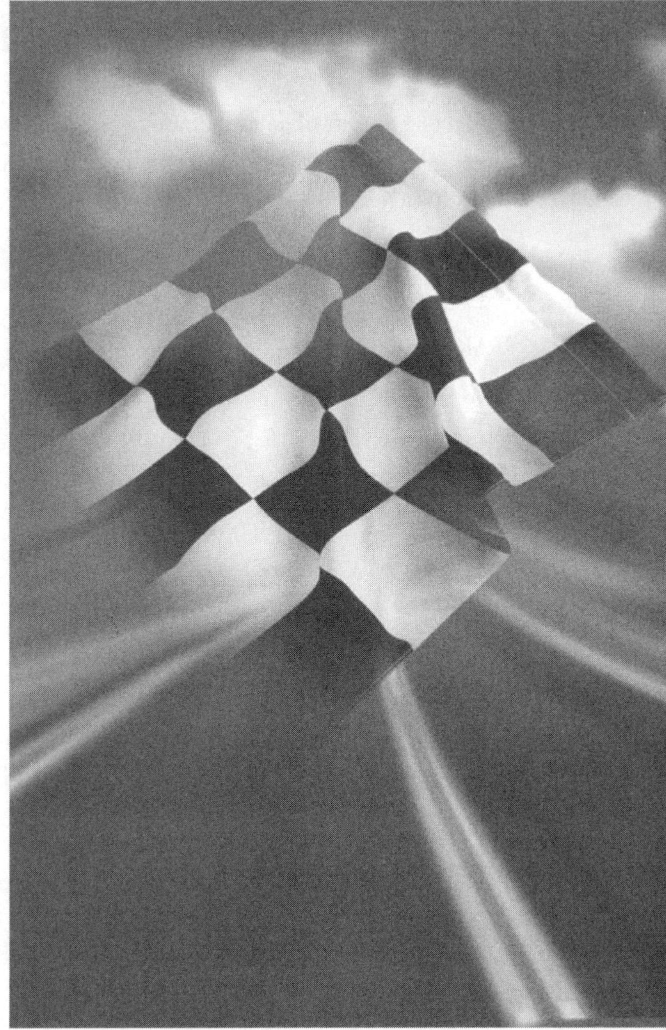

CHAPTER 6

PKI and Key Management

Objectives

This chapter covers the following CompTIA objectives for the Security+ exam.

Understand the basic security features and operational concepts involved with digital certificates.

- This objective will help you understand the basic security features and operational concepts involved with digital certificates. These include the following:
  - Digital certificates
  - Certificate revocation
  - Trust models

Understand the concepts involved in a digital certificate.

- This objective is designed to educate you on the basic concepts involved in a digital certificate. Because a digital certificate can provide a means for a user to identify himself, management policies and procedures must be in place ensure its integrity for the user community to trust it.

Recognize and understand the essential standards and protocols associated with a Public Key Infrastructure (PKI).

- For a PKI to be effective, it must adhere to the standards and protocols that have been created and accepted for its use. Without standards, the solution would be relevant only to the organization that deploys it. This would prevent it from being able to interact with other organizations or solutions, which would severely limit its capabilities.

OBJECTIVES

The following is a list of areas that are covered in this chapter:

- PKIX/PKCS
- X.509
- SSL/TLS
- ISAKMP
- CMP
- XKMS
- SMIME
- PGP
- HTTPS
- IPSec
- CEP
- FIPS
- Common Criteria
- WTLS
- WEP
- ISO17799

Understand the concepts involved in key management and the digital certificate lifecycle.

▶ This objective will help you understand some of the more interesting concepts involved in key management and the digital certificate lifecycle. These concepts include methods for key generation, storage, and destruction.

The following list represents the activities most often associated with a digital certificate:

- Centralized versus decentralized
- Storage
- Escrow
- Expiration
- Revocation
- Suspension
- Recovery
- Renewal
- Destruction
- Use

OUTLINE

Study Strategies

- Design a public key infrastructure (PKI) solution that can be used in your organization. This will help you understand the structure of a PKI solution.
- Write a security policy that specifies structure, standards, protocols, and key management elements for a PKI. This will help you understand the guidelines that need to be put in place to have a successful deployment.
- Set up an IPSec virtual private network (VPN) connection with another corporate office and a partner organization. This will enable you to test your knowledge of IPSec and the differences between connections for your own company and your partners.
- Sign up for an SSL, email, and public key digital certificate from a public certificate authority (CA) (such as Verisign). After you have the digital certificates, install them in your personal computer software and test their usage. After you have successfully tested their usage, go back to the CA and revoke your certificates. This will take you through the user experience of creating, utilizing, and revoking a digital certificate from a solution.

INTRODUCTION

The concept of public key infrastructure (PKI) enables you to bring strong authentication and privacy to the online world. By using public key cryptographic techniques and encryption algorithms, you can provide a means to identify users and ensure that no one but the intended recipients of data can have access to the data or any other network resources. Up until this point, we have discussed the specific technologies and individual modules that can make up a technical solution. With the introduction of PKI, we can introduce you to the elements of a security solution that provide integrity and privacy to information but are not specific to any vendor or application.

PKI is a solution that includes technological, procedural, and personnel elements. The key technological components of a PKI solution are the *private key*, *public key*, and *certificate authority* (which creates and oversees the digital certificate). The procedural elements are the security policies that govern the use of the technological components, and the personnel elements are the cultural requirements of the user community that uses the solution. The user community's belief in the technological and procedural elements of the solution makes it effective. Without this, the solution is useless.

The purpose of a PKI solution is to give a user a means of identifying himself in the electronic world. This is done through the use of *asymmetric cryptographic techniques* and the creation of *digital c ertificates*. A user utilizes a complex math algorithm to create a public key and private key pair. The public key is distributed to anyone with whom he wants to establish secure communications. The private key, on the other hand, is kept in the sole possession of the user and is never disclosed to anyone else.

After a user has created a key pair, he needs to have his identity validated by a trusted third party. He submits his public key to this third party and authorizes it to investigate him to prove his identity. This third party is known as the *certificate authority*. After the certificate authority has affirmed that a user is who he claims to be, it then adds its digital signature to the private key and adds information about the user to create an X.509 digital certificate.

Any user who chooses to trust the digital certificate of another user has to trust only the third party that investigated the user to ensure his identity. In this way, the certificate authority essentially becomes an insurance agency. If a user with a digital certificate signed by a certificate authority is somehow found to be invalid, the affected users can seek retribution through the certificate authority.

This chapter further discusses the concepts and technologies involved in a PKI solution. The various uses of PKI are reviewed, as are the standards and protocols that build the foundation of PKI. Operational concepts and the pros and cons of different options that can be used in PKI solutions are also examined.

DIGITAL CERTIFICATES

Understand the concepts involved in a digital certificate.

Understand the basic security features and operational concepts involved with digital certificates.

Providing identity in the electronic world requires a solution that not only can be easily used by an individual, but can also be verified by a trusted third party. This is accomplished using a *digital certificate*, which becomes the equivalent to a passport on the Internet. It binds you to your electronic transactions and allows you to prove that you are who you claim to be. This validation is vital to any business that trusts the third party willing to validate your identity and credentials. The key components of the digital certificate are

- The user's public key
- Information about the user
- Certificate information, including the expiration date, certificate authority (CA) that issued the certificate, and other information
- The digital signature of the CA that issued the digital certificate

Digital certificates by themselves are only a technical tool and meaningful data bits organized in some structure. They require policies and procedures to define how they should be used and managed.

Without these policies and procedures, they are useless. These policies and procedures are defined in certificate policies and certificate practice statements.

Certificate Policies

Digital certificate policies are statements used to govern the use of digital certificates. They are defined in the Internet Engineering Task Force (IETF) X.509 standard as a set of rules that indicate the applicability of a certificate to a particular community and class of application with common security requirements. These policies should have the following characteristics:

- They should be clear and concise so everyone who uses digital certificates can understand them and understand what the digital certificates mean to their organization.
- They should be endorsed by senior management within the organization to ensure effectiveness.
- They should be no more than a couple of pages in length.
- They should contain bulleted statements that give the reader a high-level understanding of the usage guidelines of the digital certificates issued by a particular authority.

Certificate Practice Statements

A *certificate practice statement* is a document that defines the practices and procedures a CA uses to manage the certificates it issues. It gives an in-depth view of the management and use of digital certificates. These documents are extremely detailed in nature and should contain scenarios and examples that help users understand how to properly use the certificates in the organization utilizing the certificate.

REVOCATION

A digital certificate can be used to electronically provide an identity to an individual. This creates significant risks if this certificate is compromised in some way. A key element of the utilization of digital certificates is the capability to *revoke* the privileges of the user if the organization or entity that issued the credentials deems it necessary. This is done through a process called *revocation*, which deems the certificate invalid.

Certificate Revocation Lists/CRL Distribution Points

A CA needs to be able to publicize the fact that it has deemed certain certificates to be invalid so businesses and individuals relying on the CA's authority know certain certificates should not be used or trusted going forward. This is usually accomplished by creating *certificate revocation lists (CRLs)*. These lists are generated on a regular basis by the CA as defined by its certificate policy. After these lists are generated, they should be made available to all the entities using trusting certificates issued by the CA.

Two models are employed: the *push model* and the *pull model*. In the push model, the CA distributes the CRL to all participating entities. In the pull model, the CA publishes the CRL in the public domain where anyone who would like to verify the validity of a digital certificate it has issued can access it.

Online Certificate Status Protocol

The *Online Certificate Status Protocol (OCSP)* is defined by the IETF in Request for Comment (RFC) document number 2560. It is a protocol approach to validating certificates issued by the CA. Instead of having to retrieve a CRL from a CA, a user can use OCSP to query the CA in real-time to check the validity of the certificate in question. This protocol helps overcome the problem of CRLs becoming too large to manage and maintain by the CAs that issue them. By using OCSP, a CA can manage one central database of revoked certificates, which can be queried by any interested party. This removes the need for CRL creation and distribution.

TRUST MODELS

PKI works only if organizations are willing to trust the CA issuing certificates. Within a PKI, multiple certificate authorities can be used for a particular solution. For example, a large corporation might have a corporate CA and CAs for each division within the company. Each of these divisional CAs establishes policies for its own portion of the organization, but that CA still needs to have a trust association with the corporate CA, usually known as the *root* CA. This is known as a *trust model.*

Trust models for PKI solutions involve two major concepts—cross certification and hierarchies. *Cross certification* is a process that enables distinct CAs from different organizations to act on each other's behalf in a functional solution. *Hierarchies* enable a single CA solution to have subordinate CAs in place to provide localized support in operational solutions. Each of these has its own particular challenges as well as benefits.

Cross Certification

Cross certification is when two or more distinct CAs choose to establish a trust relationship with each other. In this relationship, they each agree to trust the digital certificates that the other has issued as though they had issued them themselves. This enables users to interact with other organizations securely with the digital certificates issued by their organization's CA. An example of this is when two distinct organizations are working together in a partnership that requires users to interact with each other's corporate resources to complete their business initiative. Each user would utilize his own digital certificate issued by his own organization to access the resources of the other organization.

Bridges

CA bridges act as central points where multiple CAs can cross certify to allow communication across these organizations. This enables a CA to cross certify with a single CA instead of having to cross certify with multiple CAs to communicate with each other.

This is useful when you are working with a consortium of organizations that need to communicate securely. Cross certification can be a time-consuming and intricate process. If all the organizations agree to certify with a CA bridge, they have to certify only with this CA to enable secure communications with their users within the consortium.

Hierarchies

In PKI deployments, where multiple CAs are deployed within a single organization, a hiearchial structure is usually employed for trust management. In this structure, a *root CA* is placed at the top of the hierarchy and then multiple CAs are placed underneath the top layer. The CAs underneath the root CA have the public keys in their certificates signed by the root CA.

Hierarchial models enable the policies and standards of the organziation to be enforced throughout the infrastructure. This is because the root of the certificate chain during any verification process is always the root CA of the organization. This root and the policies and standards it represents supercede any of the subordinate CAs in the hierarchial structure.

Hierarchial structures work well with homogeneous organizations but tend to not work well in peer-to-peer relationships, such as business partnerships. In the hierarchial model, a root CA must exist. In a peer-to-peer relationship, however, no clear root is defined because both parties tend to want to be treated as equals and have their policies and procedures enforced. This actually becomes a business problem that has to be examined by the leaders of all the organizations involved to establish the appropriate security policies. Figure 6.1 shows the CA structure from the root level down.

You now understand the basic structure for utilizing and managing digital certificates. The next section looks at the globally accepted standards and protocols that are used to effectively deploy a PKI solution.

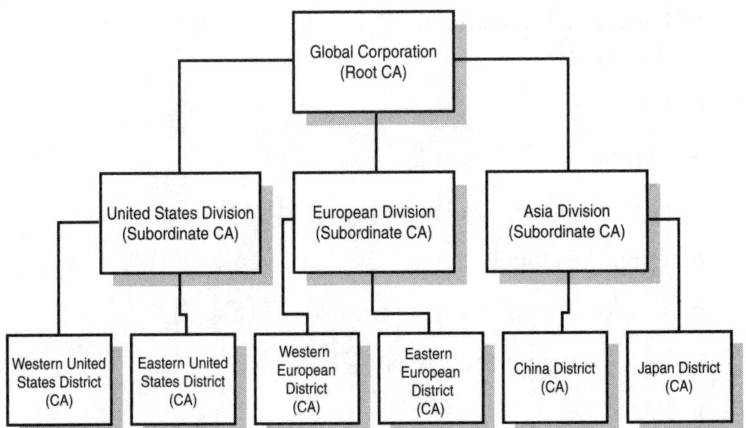

FIGURE 6.1
The CA structure from the root level down.

IDENTIFYING AND DIFFERENTIATING STANDARDS AND PROTOCOLS

Recognize and understand the essential standards and protocols associated with a public key infrastructure (PKI).

Multiple standards and protocols are associated with a PKI, and each one has a specific purpose and might or might not be needed in a PKI solution. In this section, we briefly cover the following standards and protocols associated with PKI:

- PKIX/PKCS
- X.509
- Secure Sockets Layer (SSL) Protocol
- Transport Layer Security (TLS) Protocol
- Internet Security Association and Key Management (ISAKMP) Protocol
- Certificate Management Protocol (CMP)
- XML Key Management Specification
- Secure Multipurpose Internet Mail Extensions (S/MIME)
- Pretty good privacy (PGP)

- Hypertext Transfer Protocol over Secure Sockets Layer (HTTPS)
- IPSec
- Certificate Enrollment Protocol (CEP)
- Federal Information Processing Standard (FIPS)
- Common Criteria
- Wireless Transport Layer Security (WTLS)
- Wireless Equivalent Privacy (WEP)
- ISO17799

PKIX/PKCS

Public Key Infrastructure for X.509 Certificates (PKIX) is an IETF working group established in 1995 to create standards for X.509-based PKIs. It is currently focused on the following five areas:

- **Profiles of X.509 version 3 Public Key Certificates, and X.509 version 2 Certificate Revocation Lists (CRLs)**—This provides a description of the digital certificate fields and the extensions that must be supported for the certificate and CRL. It also defines certificate validation paths and the cryptographic algorithms that must be supported.
- **Management Protocols**—This document provides the specifications for data structures for PKI management messages and the corresponding functions their system must be capable of supporting in connection with these messages. It also describes a basic protocol for transporting PKI messages.
- **Operational Protocols**—These protocols describe how the Lightweight Directory Access Protocol (LDAP), File Transfer Protocol (FTP), and Hypertext Transfer Protocol (HTTP) can be used in the operations of a PKI solution.
- **Certificate Policies and Certificate Practice Statements**—This document describes the relationship between digital certificate policies and digital certificate practice statements. It also provides a structure for authors of certificate policies and practice statements to follow to create a complete document.

It identifies key areas that should be considered in the development of these documents.

- **Timestamping and Data–Certification/Validation Services**—This document defines the criteria for a trusted third party to create timestamp information to certify that data existed at a particular point in time. The data certification and validation services define a method to verify the possession of data and validity of the digitally signed documents and certificates associated with the data in question.

The Public-Key Cryptography Standards (PKCS) were produced by RSA Laboratories, a division of the RSA Corporation, in an effort to create globally accepted specifications for the development of PKI solutions. This effort initially resulted in the production of 15 documents that make up the PKCS specification library. Recently, some consolidation of the documents has occurred, so the resulting documents are as follows:

- **PKCS #1: RSA Cryptography Standard**—This document describes multiple elements of the RSA PKI cryptographic solution. First, it describes a method known as *rsaEncryption*, which is used to encrypt data using the public key cryptographic system created by the RSA Corporation. PKCS #1 also describes the syntax for public/private keys that are identical to the X.509 standard; therefore, these keys can be used on nonproprietary systems outside the RSA Corporation's product suites.

  The third element of PKCS #1 is its definition of three digital signature algorithms: md2WithRSAEncryption, md4WithRSAEncryption, and md5WithRSAEncryption. These are used to create digital signatures for X.509, Privacy Enhanced Mail (PEM), and CRLs.

- **PKCS #2**—This document no longer exists, and its functionality has been integrated into the PKCS #1 document.

- **PKCS #3: Diffie-Hellman Key Agreement Standard**—This document describes a method for using the Diffie-Hellman key agreement solution. This solution enables two parties who have not previously exchanged secret key information to be able to agree on a secret key that is known only to each other.

This key can then be used to encrypt other data transmitted between two parties.

- **PKCS #4**—This document no longer exists, and its functionality has been integrated into the PKCS #1 document.
- **PKCS #5: Password-Based Cryptography Standard**—This document describes a method for encrypting a data string, such as a private key, with a secret key that has been derived from a password. The result of this method is another data stream. This is useful when a user needs to transfer her private key from one computer to another. It accomplishes this by defining two key-encryption algorithms: pbeWithMD2AndDES-CBC and pbeWithMD5AndDES-CBC. These algorithms use the Default Encryption Standard (DES) in a cipher-block chaining mode and derive the secret key from a password using either the MD-2 or MD-5 hashing algorithm.
- **PKCS #6: Extended-Certificate Syntax Standard**—This document describes a syntax that can be used in extended digital certificates. An extended digital certificate consists of an X.509 public key certificate with a set of attributes that has been digitally signed by the issuer. The purpose of extended attributes is to supply a mechanism to provide certification of information contained in a certificate beyond the public key. This information can include identification information about the user of the certificate, such as email and organizational information.
- **PKCS #7: Cryptographic Message Syntax Standard**—This document describes a syntax for data streams, such as digital signatures and envelopes, that can have cryptographic algorithms applied to them. The syntax also enables nesting of data, which means that one person can sign a digital envelope that has already been signed by another person. The specification also allows for attributes to be authenticated within a message as well as the message itself. An example of this is the authentication of the message and the time the message was signed.
- **PKCS #8: Private-Key Information Syntax Standard**—This document describes a syntax for private-key information. This includes the private key portion of a public-key cryptographic algorithm as well as a set of attributes associated with this key.

The attributes are used to provide a user with a way to validate information such as the distinguished name in a certificate that she receives.

- **PKCS #9: Selected Attribute Types**—This document defines the attribute types for use in PKCS #6 extended certificates, PKCS #7 digitally signed messages, and PKCS #8 private key information.
- **PKCS #10: Certification Request Syntax Standard**—This document describes a syntax for certification requests. These requests should include a distinguished name, public key, and set of attributes (which are optional) that have all been digitally signed by the requester. The request should be sent to a CA, which then converts the information provided in the request into a properly formatted X.509 public-key certificate.
- **PKCS #11: Cryptographic Token Interface Standard**—This document defines an application programming interface (API) called Cryptoki for cryptographic devices, including (but not limited to) smart cards and PC cards that store cryptographic information and perform cryptographic functions. It is designed to be vendor and technology independent so it can be used by any organization on any hardware platform. The computer system that interfaces with the API recognizes it as a cryptographic token.
- **PKCS #12: Personal Information Exchange Syntax Standard**—This document specifies a format for storing and transporting a user's private keys, digital certificates, and attribute information. This specification has several modes for ensuring privacy and integrity of the information. The most secure of these requires the source and destination systems to have trusted public and private key pairs usable for digital signatures and encryption available. The lower security option uses a password system when key pairs are not available.
- **PKCS #13: Elliptic Curve Cryptography Standard**—This document is currently under development. It is intended to cover the PKI capabilities that will take advantage of elliptical curve cryptography.
- **PKCS #15: Cryptographic Token Information Format Standard**—This document establishes a specification that defines how public/private keys, digital certificates, and application-specific information can be stored on media.

This is known as the Cryptographic Token Information Format.

X.509

The X.509 standard (currently in version 3) provides authentication services for a system. This means that the X.509 standard provides a mechanism for verifying the identity of a person whose system is claiming to be someone or something. The X.509 standard has three key elements: the *public key certificate*, the *attribute certificate*, and the *certificate revocation list*:

- **Public key certificate**—This certificate binds a user or system's identity to a specific public key.
- **Attribute certificate**—This certificate binds data items to a user or system by using a name or public key certificate. This certificate is typically used to convey user or system permissions.
- **Certificate revocation list**—This list (as discussed earlier) lists certificates that are no longer valid prior to their expiration dates.

The X.509 standard also defines a specific format of required data for digital certificates. Currently, this format requires the digital signature of the CA as well as the following fields to be compliant to the standard:

- **Version**—This identifies to which version of the X.509 standard the certificate complies. Currently, there are three versions defined by the IETF.
- **Serial Number**—The CA that creates the certificate assigns a unique serial number for each certificate it issues. This information can then be used to identify specific certificates for activities such as revocation.
- **Signature Algorithm**—This identifies the cryptographic algorithm.
- **Issuer**—This is the name of the CA that signed the certificate.

- **Validity Period**—This defines the period during which a certificate is valid. This period is noted with both a start and end time. It can be any duration—from a few seconds to any stated date. Typically, this period is set to one year for normal operations, but it can be different based on the security policy with which the certificate is associated.
- **Subject Name**—This is the name of the entity identified in the public key associated with the certificate. This is more often known as the distinguished name (DN). It uses the X.500 directory standard, which allows it to be queried accordingly. It is also meant to be unique across the entire Internet infrastructure.
- **Subject Public Key Information**—This is the public key of the entity being named in the certificate, cryptographic algorithm descriptor, and optional key parameters associated with the key.

Figure 6.2 shows a sample certificate.

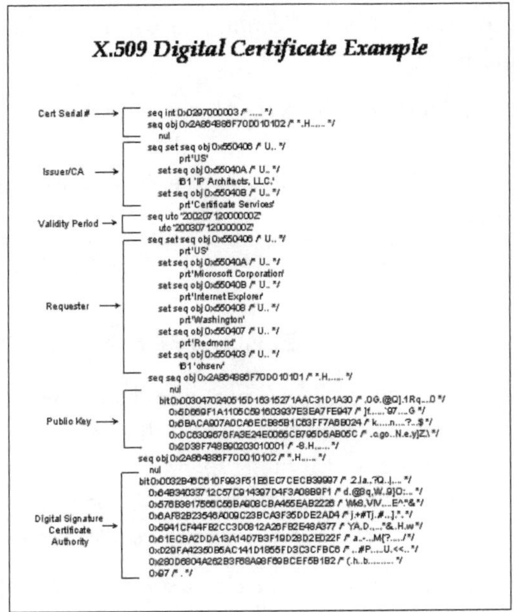

FIGURE 6.2
A sample certificate.

The extensions field, which was introduced in version 3 of the X.509 standard, is an optional field. It was created to satisfy the need for more informational fields for PKI solutions. The two types of extensions are *private* and *standard.*

Private extensions are user definable and can include information specific to a type of system being used. An example of a private extension can be found in the Secure Electronic Transaction (SET) specification where private extensions include the hashed root key as well as tunneling parameters.

The standard extensions include the following:

- **Keys**—This field defines things such as the valid usage period for the private key associated with the public key in the certificate and the intentions and restrictions associated with the digital certificate.
- **Subject/Issuer**—This field allows for alternative names and attributes to be defined for a certificate.
- **Policies**—This field was put in place to support cross-certification activities. This enables attributes from the certification and application policies to be included in the certificate.
- **Certification Path**—This field defines in what way the key can be used, the length of the key, the subject names, and the required security policies that need to be in place to use the certificate.

The Secure Sockets Layer Protocol

The *Secure Sockets Layer (SSL)* protocol is probably the most widely known of the digital certificates used, even though the user community using it doesn't know it is doing so. SSL was created by Netscape Corporation and is primarily used to enable secure communication between a Web browser and a Web server.

SSL works at the Session layer in the Open System Infrastructure (OSI) stack and is designed as a client/server solution. It uses public key cryptography to authenticate a server to a client and optionally establishes an encrypted channel for secure communication for a specific session.

SSL uses a 40-, 56-, or 128-bit key and the RC4 stream encryption algorithm to ensure privacy within the communication. It is different from a traditional PKI infrastructure because it does not require either the client or the server to have a personalized X.509 certificate. It only requires the server to have a personalized certificate, and it can use a browser-generated session certificate for the client side of the solution.

SSL provides the following three primary security functions for a system:

- **SSL server authentication**—This function takes place on the client side (that is, the Web browser) and enables a user to validate the identity of the server with which he is communicating. This is done by examining the SSL certificate that has been presented by the server and verifying that it has been issued by a trusted CA.
- **Client side authentication**—This function enables the server to verify the client's identity. It uses the same techniques as the server-side authentication function; however, in this case, it examines the client's SSL certificate.
- **Encrypted SSL connection**—This function creates an encrypted session for sensitive data to be transmitted over public networks. The client and the server share their public keys with each other during a handshake process and create a temporary secure channel for communication. After this handshake is complete, a negotiation takes place in which both sides agree on an encryption algorithm to be used, and then a shared secret is generated for the session that enables the use of this algorithm.

The SSL Record and SSL Handshake Protocols

SSL also includes two subordinate protocols: the *SSL record protocol* and the *SSL handshake protocol*. The SSL record protocol defines the format attributes used to transmit data, whereas the SSL handshake protocol uses the SSL record protocol to exchange the public keys between the two systems and authenticate the server to the client. It also sets the parameters to establish a secure communications channel between the user and server and optionally authenticates the client to the server.

The Transport Layer Security Protocol

Transport Layer Security (TLS) is the open standard that is considered the successor to SSL. It supports all the same functionality and properties of SSL and also adds some minor improvements in functionality. Because SSL is licensed by vendors, it cannot be considered an open standard available to the general public for use. This is the primary reason TLS was created.

It is important to understand that TLS and SSL have some of the characteristics of a PKI, but they lack the capability work with attribute certificates or CRLs. This limits their capability to provide functionality beyond offering basic user authentication and establishment of a secure channel for communications. This does, however, provide these protocols with the advantage of requiring less infrastructure for their use, which makes them easier to set up and maintain.

Internet Security Association and Key Management Protocol

The Internet Security Association and Key Management Protocol (ISAKAMP) defines a common framework for the creation, negotiation, modification, and deletion of security associations in VPNs. It also defines the packet payload characteristics for exchanging key generation and authentication information. These characteristics are completely independent of the following: the technique used to generate the key, the chosen encryption algorithm, and the authentication mechanism being utilized. It simply provides a standardized format that is globally accepted for packaging and receiving these requests. It also can be used on any transport protocol, which makes it very flexible.

Certificate Management Protocol

The Certificate Management Protocol (CMP) defines a mechanism for advanced management functions associated with the use of digital certificates within a PKI solution. These advanced management functions include certificate issuance, exchange, invalidation, revocation, and key commission. CMP can also operate on any transport protocol.

These are all important functions for managing the operational capabilities of a PKI solution.

XML Key Management Specification

The XML Key Management Specification (XKMS) defines protocols for distributing and registering public key information for use in XML signatures. It is made up of two elements:

- **XML Key Information Service Specification**—This protocol enables an application to transfer the processing of public key information associated with an XML digital signature, encryption, or other pubic keys to a service. It also includes capabilities that allow the identification of public key information required for a transaction and enumerates the relationship of these keys to the identification information with which they are associated.
- **XML Key Registration Service Specification**—This protocol enables key owners to register their key information for use in the XML Key Information Service Specification. This is the mechanism users or applications would use to make the system aware of key information they want to use in XML procedures.

Secure Multipurpose Internet Mail Extensions

The Secure Multipurpose Internet Mail Extensions (SMIME) specification is intended to provide security services to email systems and is designed to integrate with the popular Multi Purpose Internet Mail Extensions (MIME) platform. SMIME provides email privacy using encryption and authentication via digital signatures. Each of these can be used independently of each other or used together to provide a high degree of email security. The encryption algorithms it supports for privacy purposes are DES, Triple-DES, and RC2.

SMIME has been integrated into many popular email applications, such as Microsoft Outlook, Eudora, and Netscape Mail. Because of this integration, users will find that using SMIME is very simple and transparent after they make the applications aware of their SMIME digital certificates. SMIME is also very scalable because it uses a hierarchical structure usually within the PKI to establish user credentials.

This allows it to be extremely scalable within an enterprise deployment.

Pretty Good Privacy

Pretty good privacy (PGP) is an application created by Phillip Zimmerman. It is similar to SMIME in that it uses private/public keys and encryption algorithms to provide authentication and privacy to email messages. PGP is both a specification and an application. There are some limitations of scalability and deployment for PGP. It uses a key ring server approach for key management that requires users to query specific servers for key information unless they choose to transmit the keys between themselves. Because it is an application, it has not been readily incorporated by messaging software vendors into its products. It is, however, available from the PGP Corporation, which has integrated it into popular email packages. The problem in this case is the extra cost associated with the purchase of licenses and the extra overhead of managing and supporting a separate application on the user's system.

Hypertext Transfer Protocol over Secure Sockets Layer

The Hypertext Transfer Protocol over Secure Socket Layer (HTTPS) was also designed by the Netscape Corporation. It is essentially the transmission of data using the Hypertext Transfer Protocol (HTTP) over SSL (as its name implies). The use of this protocol is denoted by preceding a Web page request with the `https://` request header. It differs from SSL in that it is used specifically for HTTP data communication. SSL can theoretically be used to transfer other data types, but it is mostly used for this purpose.

IPSec

The IPSec Internet protocol suite has modernized Internet Protocol (IP) security. The IPSec protocol suite utilizes cryptographic techniques to ensure data confidentiality, and digital signatures and digital signature verification algorithms to authenticate the source of data transmissions. IPSec also brings a new level of interoperability to Internet communications that never existed before its introduction.

Because it is an IETF standard, it does not rely on proprietary protocols or applications to establish encrypted and authenticated links between network nodes. By utilizing the IPSec protocol suite in virtual private networking (VPN) solutions, organizations can exchange sensitive data over public networks, such as the Internet, with the knowledge that the parties they are exchanging the data with are the intended receivers, that the data was kept confidential during the communication, and that the data did not change during the communication.

IPSec is primarily used for VPN applications at this time. This is primarily because it provides an organization with the capability to leverage its existing Internet connectivity for secure communications with remote locations and business partners. Because of the interoperable nature of the IPSec protocol suite, business partners can communicate with each other without having to purchase identical vendor-specific equipment. IPSec also provides strong authentication capabilities, data integrity, and data confidentiality services that allow for a higher level of assurance to be achieved than most organizations currently have when performing secure communications.

The way the IPSec protocol suite achieves its higher level of assurance for data transport is through the use of multiple protocols. These protocols include the Authenticated Header (AH) protocol, Encapsulated Secure Payload (ESP) protocol, and Internet Key Exchange (IKE) protocol, which is discussed in the following sections. Each of these protocols can be used independently of each other to provide specific heightened security capabilities, but when used together, they create an extremely powerful suite of capabilities. These capabilities can be used to ensure high levels of data security during data transport over public networks such as the Internet.

Authenticated Header

One of the protocols included in the IPSec protocol suite is the Authenticated Header. The AH protocol provides data integrity, authentication, and optional anti-replay capabilities for IP data packets. It does not provide data confidentiality capabilities. It does, however, provide integrity protection for the packet payload and most of the IP header. AH also ensures that the fields that identify the source and destination of IP packets are valid and have not been modified during transmission.

This is accomplished by using digital signature techniques or one-way hash functions. The following are the six elements that make up the authenticated header as defined by the IETF RFC 2401:

- **Next header**—Indicates what the higher-level protocol following the AH is (that is, ESP, TCP).
- **Payload length**—This is an 8-bit field that specifies the size of the AH.
- **Reserved**—This is a placeholder for a future function.
- **Security parameter index (SPI)**—SPI is a pseudorandom 32-bit number that specifies the security settings being used by the transmitter to communicate with the receiver. This includes the encryption algorithms being used, which encryption keys are being used, and the information about the validity period for these encryption keys.
- **Sequence number**—The sequence number is a counting mechanism that increases incrementally each time a packet is transmitted using the parameters setup in the SPI. It identifies the packets and enumerates the number of times packets have been transmitted using the same SPI. The sequence number protects receiving nodes from replay attacks in which an attacker copies a packet and then resends it in an attempt to confuse the receiver.
- **Authentication data**—This is the integrity check value (ICV) for the packet. The originator creates a keyed one-way hash of the packet payload and attaches this hash value to the packet as the authentication field.

Encapsulated Security Payload

The Encapsulated Security Payload (ESP) is the portion of the IPSec protocol suite that addresses the confidentiality of the data being transmitted within an IP data packet, and it also has authentication capabilities. ESP uses symmetric encryption techniques to encrypt the IP data packet payload; the symmetric encryption algorithms that must be supported to be compliant to IETF standard are DES, 3DES, RSA, CAST, and Blowfish.

The ESP does not encrypt the IP header or information, which includes the information required for routing—it encrypts only the packet payload, which ensures the confidentiality of the data. The following elements make up the ESP as defined by the IETF RFC 2401:

- **Security parameter index (SPI)**—SPI is a pseudorandom 32-bit number that specifies the security settings used by the transmitter to communicate with the receiver. This includes the encryption algorithms being used, which encryption keys are being used, and the information about the validity period for these encryption keys.
- **Sequence number**—The sequence number is a counting mechanism that increases incrementally each time a packet is transmitted using the parameters setup in the SPI. It identifies the packets and enumerates the number of times packets have been transmitted using the same SPI. The sequence number protects receiving nodes from replay attacks in which an attacker copies a packet and then resends it in an attempt to confuse the receiver.
- **Payload data**—The data contained in the IP packet.
- **Padding**—Padding is used to prevent attackers from using packet sniffers to estimate that amount of data transmitted in some encryption algorithms. Padding techniques use random data that can range from 0 to 255 bytes in length and generally insert this random data after the valid payload.
- **Pad length**—This field specifies the amount of padding that is in place in a specific packet payload so it can be properly identified and stripped from the packet during the decryption process.
- **Next header**—The next header field in the IP packet identifies the types of data being carried in the packet as well as the protocols being used.

The SPI and sequence number are not encrypted, but they are authenticated. On the other hand, the payload data, padding, pad length, and next header are encrypted to ensure confidentiality. An optional field is also included in the ESP—the authentication field.

The authentication field contains the integrity check value and is calculated after the encryption function has been completed on the ESP.

The ICV is a digital signature that is computed using the ESP (not including the authentication field itself). The originator creates a keyed one-way hash of the packet payload and attaches this hash value to the packet as its authentication field. The IPSec standard specifies that the HMAC symmetric signature work with hash algorithms SHA-1 or MD-5. The recipient can then validate that integrity of the payload data by using hash algorithms to hash the payload data after it has been decrypted with the same one-way hash algorithm, which the originator used. If the two hash output values are identical, the recipient can be confident that the data was not modified during the transmission.

ESP can operate in two modes: *transport* and *tunnel* mode. In the transport mode the packet payload is the only part of the packet that is encrypted, which means the original packet header is undisturbed in this case. This has the advantages of reducing the overhead added to the packet size and allowing the routing elements in the network to view the final destination address of the packet. This information can also be used for quality of service (QoS) capabilities and routing services by the routing elements encountered during packet transmission across the network. The downside to using transport mode is the exposure of the originator and receiver IP header data. An attacker could potentially perform traffic analysis techniques on these packets during their transmission and gain insight about the activities being performed.

ESP tunnel mode encrypts both the packet and the payload in a new IP packet. In this case, all traffic is passed to the IPSec device, and it then acts as a proxy element for this traffic. The IPSec device performs all encryption and encapsulation activities without having to modify any of the other systems in the network. Tunnel mode also protects against traffic analysis because the attacker can decipher only the tunnel end points, which are the IPSec devices. They can't decipher the actual source address or destination address.

Internet Key Exchange

The Internet Key Exchange (IKE) protocol is the method used for public key exchange, secure association (SA) parameter negotiation, identification, and authentication. IKE is actually a hybrid of three existing key management schemes: the Internet Security Association and Key Management Protocol (ISAKAMP), Oakley, and the Secure Key Exchange Mechanism (SKEME). IKE creates an authenticated and secure tunnel between the originator and the receiver and then negotiates the security associations for IPSec. This process starts by the originator and the receiver authenticating themselves to each other to communicate their respective keys to each other. To accomplish this, both parties must agree on a common authentication protocol through a negotiation process. The two common methods for this negotiation process are as follows:

- **Preshared keys (shared secret)**—The same key is preinstalled on both the originator's and receiver's host. Both parties then initiate an asymmetric key exchange with each other using the Diffie-Hellman key agreement algorithm. This enables both parties to establish an SA where they can transfer data securely and set up an initial set of parameters for data transfer via the SPI. Authentication then is performed by both entities computing a one-way keyed hash of the preshared key and transmitting the resulting hash value to each other via the previously established SA. Next, both parties perform a one-hash operation using the previously agreed upon (and previously used) one-way hash algorithm and compare the output values from this function. If the values are identical, both parties have the same secret key, which means they have authenticated to each other. After the authentication process has been completed and agreed on by both parties, the key exchange for the symmetric encryption algorithm can take place using the previously established SA.

- **Public key cryptography**—A key exchange using public key cryptography involves multiple steps. The first step in the process is for both parties to initiate an asymmetric key exchange using the Diffie-Hellman key agreement algorithm. This enables both parties to establish an SA where they can transfer data securely and set up an initial set of parameters for data transfer via the SPI. After this SA has been established, both parties can transmit their public key data through this SA to each other. This then enables strong authentication to take place if a properly formatted X.509 certificate is used. After the public keys have been exchanged and a new SA has been established, the key exchange for the symmetric encryption algorithm can take place via the new SA.

The IKE protocol functions in two phases. During the first phase the two entities, which are attempting to communicate securely with each other, set up a secure channel to negotiate security associations with each other. This phase does not take into account actual authentication of the two entities to each other. In phase two of IKE, the actual SAs are negotiated between the entities via the secure channel that was created in phase one of the process.

In addition, two modes are specified in the IKE protocol: *main mode* and *aggressive mode*. Main mode performs the key exchange separately from the SA proposal activity to conceal the identity of the IKE agent, enabling peer authentication of IKE agents.

Aggressive mode reduces the number of messages involved with an IKE exchange. The drawback to this mode is that it does not conceal the IKE agent identities. The primary difference between the two modes is the amount of operations that take place during the IKE negotiation process. If you were establishing a secure tunnel with a recipient for the first time or in a highly volatile environment, you would most likely want to use the main mode of operation. If you have already established SA relationships with a recipient before and you feel comfortable with his environment, it might be more appropriate to use aggressive mode to reduce the number of processes involved with the IKE activity.

Security Association

The best way to ensure effective communication using authentication and encryption capabilities is to have a system that accounts for the individual elements of each connection. In the IPSec protocol suite, this mechanism is known as the *security association (SA)*. An SA contains all the information involved in communicating with another node securely. These elements include

- The mode and keys of the authentication algorithm used in the AH
- Which protocols, encryption algorithm, and keys will be used to authenticate the communication
- The encryption algorithm mode and keys used with the associated encryption algorithm for the ESP

- Cryptographic synchronization information, including presence and size, to be used with the chosen cryptographic algorithm
- Specification of the timing for key change
- Validity period of the keys used
- Validity period of the individual SA being established
- The mode and keys of the authentication algorithm used in the ESP
- Source address for the SA being established
- Sensitivity level descriptor

The individual security associations used for communication paths you establish to different nodes can be different for each node. This allows you the flexibility to have different levels of security based on the security policy criteria you have set up with the entity with which you are going to communicate.

An example where this can be used is when you are setting up an encrypted IPSec-based VPN with various corporate offices located in multiple countries. Each country will have its own legal statutes that specify which encryption algorithms can be used and the size of the encryption keys that can be used within its borders. Using an encrypted IPSec-based VPN solution, you can compensate for the boundaries set by the statutes by using individual SAs to establish different levels of encryption for each connection to your location. This alleviates the problem of having to set all the connection settings to the same encryption algorithm and least common denominator for key size, which was the traditional solution to this problem.

Certificate Enrollment Protocol

The Certificate Enrollment Protocol (CEP) is a proprietary protocol created by the Cisco corporation. It allows Cisco Internet Operating System-based devices to acquire and use digital certificates from CAs. The primary use for this protocol is in the deployment of IPSec VPNs when using Cisco devices and digital certificate authentication.

Federal Information Processing Standard

> **NOTE**
>
> **Cryptographic Modules** A *cryptographic module* can be any combination of hardware, firmware, or software that implements cryptographic functions, such as encryption, decryption, digital signatures, authentication techniques, and random number generation.

The Federal Information Processing Standard (FIPS) is issued by the U.S. government for the evaluation of cryptographic modules that can be used in U.S. solutions provided to the U.S. government. The portion of the standard usually associated with PKI is FIPS 140-2, which specifies the security requirements that need to be met by a cryptographic module used in a security solution that protects unclassified information within computing and telecommunications systems.

The FIPS 140-2 standard was created by the National Institute of Standards and Technology (NIST) and specifies the criteria for implementing cryptographic modules. These cryptographic modules can be hardware or software systems that encrypt or decrypt data or perform other cryptographic operations, such as the creation or verification of digital signatures. The standard specifies the following four increasing levels of security with specific requirements for each level:

- **FIPS 140-2 Level 1**—This is the lowest level of security specified by the standard. It requires the use of a single, approved cryptographic algorithm or security function and does not specify any physical security requirements for the cryptographic module. It also does not require any special considerations for the operating system with which the cryptographic module will interact.
- **FIPS 140-2 Level 2**—This level of the standard adds physical security and user authentication requirements to the cryptographic module. The module must have the capability to show evidence of being tampered with. The key here is that the portion of the module that enables access to the cryptographic key material must show evidence of being tampered with. This can be done with seals, locks, or tamper-evident tape.

  The user authentication aspect of the level 2 standard requires role-based security to be employed, meaning a user must be authenticated to the system under a defined role. Examples of roles can be administrator or operator. These roles will both have distinctively different functions and capabilities as they relate to operating the cryptographic module.

Level 2 also has requirements for a higher level of security to be present in the operating system with which the cryptographic module interacts. It must comply with the common criteria protection profiles and be evaluated at the common criteria assurance level of EAL2. The common criteria profiles and assurance levels can be found at `http://csrc.nist.gov`.

- **FIPS 140-2 Level 3**—This level of the certification standard adds a higher level of assurance for the physical attributes of the module. It specifies requirements for the device to be able to not only show evidence of tampering, but also to react to the tampering. A reaction usually is the destruction of the critical security parameters and keying material (including the private key) that the cryptographic module uses.

  The user authentication aspect of level 3 requires the same role-based authentication as level 2 but also requires individual user authentication. Therefore, a user would have to authenticate to the module and then assume one of the roles defined by the system.

  Level 3 also requires the capability to enter or back up the critical security parameters in physically separate interfaces. This is typically done using secure devices that resemble keys and have the capability to store their portions of the cryptographic material safely.

  The level 3 specification also has requirements for a higher level of security to be present in the operating system with which the cryptographic module interacts. It must comply with the common criteria protection profiles and be evaluated at the common criteria assurance level of EAL3 and also add a trusted path function. The common criteria profiles and assurance levels can be found at `http://csrc.nist.gov`.

- **FIPS 140-2 Level 4**—This level of the certification standard adds the highest levels of assurance for both the hardware and software elements of the cryptographic module. It requires the module to meet all the requirements of level 3, plus be evaluated at the common criteria level 4.

  It also specifies requirements for the device to be able to not only show evidence of tampering, but also be highly tamper resistant.

In addition, the module must recognize and react to all attempts of tampering. A reaction is usually the destruction of the critical security parameters and keying material (including the private key) that the cryptographic module uses. This level also adds an environmental protection element to the cryptographic module and requires the module to be capable of responding to changes in temperature and voltage.

Common Criteria

The *common criteria* specification is a document designed to set a baseline for security evaluations of security devices and solutions beyond U.S. standards. It does this by using information from U.S., Canadian, and European standards and specifications. It describes security functionality in the following distinct classes of requirements:

- Security audit
- Communication, cryptographic support
- User data protection
- Identification and authentication
- Security management
- Privacy and protection of security functions
- Resource utilization
- Access
- Trusted path/channel

Common criteria also defines two distinct types of evaluation outputs: a *protection profile* and a *security target.* The protection profile establishes a set of requirements for a specific environment or solution, whereas the security target specifies the security requirements for a specific hardware or software product.

Wireless Transport Layer Security

Wireless Transport Layer Security (WTLS) is the security layer for the Wireless Application Protocol (WAP). It is used to establish secure communication channels between microbrowsers (most often seen in mobile phones and PDAs) and WAP-enabled servers. It closely resembles SSL/TLS in the way it functions and establishes secure connections. It uses digital certificates to authenticate a server to a client and uses public key cryptography to establish the secure channel.

WTLS differs from SSL/TLS in certain ways so it can be optimized for use with mobile devices. It supports datagrams in high-latency environments, such as times when very little bandwidth is available. It also uses a wireless, optimized key handshake that supports dynamic key refreshing. This allows it to migrate to different WAP servers during a session that is characteristic of a mobile computing situation.

Wireless Equivalent Privacy

The Wireless Equivalent Privacy (WEP) standard is used mainly in 802.11 wireless networking solutions. WEP is designed to protect wireless local area network (LAN) connections from eavesdropping. It also can be used to prevent unauthorized users from using network resources via an 802.11 gateway. It operates at the Physical and Data Link layers of the OSI model, which prevents it from providing end-to-end security—it would require a secondary protocol to provide this level of security.

WEP uses the RC4 encryption algorithm and a shared-secret authentication mechanism for authenticating a host to a wireless gateway and for establishing the secure channel between them. The standard does not specify how the key is generated or which parameters should be used to create strong keying material. Typically, the same key is transmitted to both parties via a communication method such as email, postal mail, or a verbal communication technique.

ISO17799

ISO17799 is a detailed security standard that is composed of 10 major sections. It is quickly gaining in popularity because it is considered a global standard instead of a standard created by the U.S. and then adopted globally. Each of the sections covers a different topic of interest. The sections and their purposes as defined by the standard are as follows:

- **Business Continuity Planning**—To counteract interruptions to business activities and critical business processes from the effects of major failures or disasters
- **System Access Control**—To control access to information, to prevent unauthorized access to information systems, to ensure the protection of networked services, to prevent unauthorized computer access, to detect unauthorized activities, and to ensure information security when using mobile computing and tele-networking facilities
- **System Development and Maintenance**—To ensure security is built into operational systems; to prevent loss, modification, or misuse of user data in application systems; to protect the confidentiality, authenticity, and integrity of information; to ensure IT projects and support activities are conducted in a secure manner; and to maintain the security of application system software and data
- **Physical and Environmental Security**—To prevent unauthorized access, damage, and interference to business premises and information; to prevent loss, damage, or compromise of assets and interruption to business activities; and to prevent compromise or theft of information and information processing facilities
- **Compliance**—To avoid breaches of any criminal or civil law, statutory, regulatory, or contractual obligations and of any security requirements; to ensure compliance of systems with organizational security policies and standards; and to maximize the effectiveness of and to minimize interference to/from the system audit process

- **Personnel Security**—To reduce risks of human error, theft, fraud, or misuse of facilities; to ensure that users are aware of information security threats and concerns and are equipped to support the corporate security policy in the course of their normal work; and to minimize the damage from security incidents and malfunctions and learn from such incidents
- **Security Organization**—To manage information security within the company, to maintain the security of organizational information processing facilities and information assets accessed by third parties, and to maintain the security of information when the responsibility for information processing has been outsourced to another organization
- **Computer and Operations Management**—To ensure the correct and secure operation of information processing facilities; to minimize the risk of systems failures; to protect the integrity of software and information; to maintain the integrity and availability of information processing and communication; to ensure the safeguarding of information in networks and the protection of the supporting infrastructure; to prevent damage to assets and interruptions to business activities; and to prevent loss, modification, or misuse of information exchanged between organizations
- **Asset Classification and Control**—To maintain appropriate protection of corporate assets and to ensure that information assets receive an appropriate level of protection
- **Security Policy**—To provide management direction and support for information security

Up until this point, we have discussed the management structure for digital certificates as well as the standards and protocols that are available to use them. In the next section, we discuss the management structure for the keys themselves. This includes the critical elements that must be taken into account to properly protect and account for the private key material that is the most important element of a PKI solution.

Understanding and Explaining Key Management/Certificate Lifecycle

Understand the concepts involved in key management and the digital certificate lifecycle.

The critical element to any PKI solution is the ability to manage the digital certificates and the key pairs that are used. Different uses have different requirements. For instance, a corporate implementation usually requires a key escrow capability to comply with corporate security policies, but an individual often does not want her private key to be accessible to anyone but herself.

Centralized Versus Decentralized Key Management

PKI solutions have different methods of creating and managing digital certificates based on their security policy. In a *centralized key management* solution, the CA generates both the private and public key for the user. It then takes this key and adds the appropriate user information (usually to comply with the X.509 format). After the key pair has been generated and the CA has added its digital signature, it distributes the certificate and key pair to the user and optionally distributes the digital certificate to a directory service where other users can access the certificate.

Centralized key management allows the organization that is operating the PKI solution to have complete control over the creation, distribution, modification, and revocation of electronic credentials it issues. This is useful in situations where a high level of control is desired. It does, however, introduce certain problems as well. The primary issue is the acceptance of the user base for this type of control. With privacy becoming a growing concern for many individuals, the idea of a centralized system generating and having copies of credentials that could be used for legally binding transactions is not favorable.

Centralized key management systems also require significant infrastructure elements (that is, multiprocessor servers, large disk arrays, and secure facilities) and processes to operate. One of the often overlooked, but extremely important, areas is the transmission of the private key material back to the user's local computing solution. Because the private key material is considered one of the most sensitive elements of the solution, a secure channel must be established and the user must be positively authenticated prior to transmitting the private key material to the user.

Decentralized key management, on the other hand, allows a user to generate the private and public key material and submit the public key portion to the CA for validation and signature. The CA can still take on the role of distributing the finalized certificate to a directory service, but it no longer has the capability to store the private keys for future uses. This enables the user to maintain complete control of the private key, which is considered one of the most sensitive portions of the PKI solution. In this case, though, the CA must validate that the key material was generated properly and all the policies involved with the creation of the key pairs were adhered to.

Key Storage

After the key pairs have been generated and the digital certificate has been issued by the CA, the key pair now has real meaning. This also means that both the private and public key must be stored appropriately in such a way that their integrity is maintained but they are still easy enough to use so the user finds them to be beneficial in activities where their use is required. This can come in the form of either hardware or software storage mechanisms.

Hardware Versus Software Key Storage

The two possible options for storing keying material in a PKI solution are *hardware* and *software*. Hardware devices are usually associated with higher levels of security and assurance than software because they can have specialized components and physical encasements to protect the integrity of the data stored in them. Hardware devices also tend to be more efficient in operation than software because they are a dedicated solution—they can dedicate resources to PKI functions, unlike their software counterparts.

Hardware typically has a higher cost associated with it than software, however, which is one of the reasons it is not used in some PKI solutions.

Software solutions for key storage do not have the same high level of security associated with them compared to their hardware counterparts. The benefit of software storage is the capability to easily distribute the storage solution to all the users with a very low cost. Software also makes the keys extremely easy to transport from computer to computer and enables the same set of keys to be used simultaneously on multiple systems (although this is not often recommended).

Software storage solutions attempt to protect keying material by enforcing strong authentication for access to the keys (such as the use of tokens) as well as storing key material in volatile memory space when in use. This helps reduce the risk of a copy of the key being left in latent memory on the system when it is not in use.

Private Key Protection

The private key is the more sensitive of the keys and requires a higher level of protection than the public key does. Because of this, special care needs to be taken when protecting private keys, especially the root key for a CA. If the private key is compromised, the public key and certificate associated with this key are no longer valid. An advisory could use this key to assume the identity of an individual or a system until the compromise has been detected. This is especially dangerous if the root CA private key is compromised. If an advisory is able to take control of the private key of the CA, she can issue false credentials using the key. This would cause the CA operator to have to revoke all the active keys generated using the CA and reissue new keys to all the users. Because of the high risk associated with the CA keys, hardware storage solutions are often used for private keys.

The general user's private key also requires a high security posture. In most cases, the private key is, at a minimum, protected by a password. In some cases, a user might also choose to store his private key on a smart card or PC card he carries with him as well. When using the smart card or PC card solution, the user must have the actual card with the keying material stored on it, as well as the password required to access the private key material.

Key Escrow

Private key escrow is probably one of the most sensitive topics in the PKI community. Private key escrow occurs when a CA or an entity maintains a copy of the private key associated with the public key that has been signed by the CA. This allows the CA or entity to have access to all information encrypted using the public key from a user's certificate, as well as create digital signatures that can bind a user to a transaction. This can be very dangerous if the key is misused and is often not favorable to a public PKI solution.

A corporate PKI solution usually includes a key escrow element. In most cases, an employee is bound by information security policies that allow a corporation to have access to all intellectual property generated by a user for the company as part of that person's terms of employment. A corporation must have the ability to access data an employee generates to maintain the operations of the business.

Key escrow also helps an organization overcome the problem of lost or forgotten passwords. Instead of having to revoke and reissue new certificates, the organization can generate a new certificate using the private key that is in escrow.

Digital Certificate Expiration Periods

A digital certificate will, in most cases, have a validity period associated with it. This validity period can be as short as a few seconds or as long as any calendar dates you specify. This validity period is usually indicated in a specific field within the certificate. A typical validity period for a certificate is one year for most applications. Shorter validity periods are usually not favorable because of the lengthy process of issuing a new certificate to the user and notifying all the current users of the individual's new certificate and how to obtain it.

Certificate Revocation

Certificate revocation takes place when a certificate is no longer valid. This can occur for any number of reasons (the private key is compromised, the user lost the private key, credentials are no longer valid, and so on). The important part of revocation is that you need to be sure to notify the user community that trusts the certificate that it is no longer valid.

Most often this is done through using CRLs, which were discussed earlier in this chapter in the "Certificate Revocation Lists/CRL Distribution Points" section. In sensitive solutions, the security policy might require users to verify the validity of the certificate each time they use it to verify another user's identity or credentials.

Certificate Suspension

Certificate suspension takes place when a certificate is being investigated to see whether it should be revoked. Suspension allows a certificate to stay in place but not be valid for use, authentication, or permissions purposes. Suspension still has the same issue of notification that revocation has. The only difference is that the user community does not have to retrieve new credentials; they only have to be informed that the current credentials have changed in status and are temporarily invalid for use.

Status Checking

Status checking relates to the concept of verifying the status of a particular certificate. The three basic status levels in most solutions are as follows:

- Valid
- Suspended
- Revoked

Protocols such as OCSP (discussed earlier in this chapter) or CRLs can be used to verify the status of a certificate. The validity can be checked by going to the CA that issued the certificate or to an agreed upon directory server that maintains a status database for a particular organization's certificates. In most cases, the application using the certificate has a function available that initiates a validate check for a particular certificate.

Recovery

Recovery involves a process for restoring a private key and public key pair from a backup and regenerating a digital certificate by using these keys. This activity should be initiated only when the private and public keys have been corrupted but are still considered valid and trusted. In most cases, it is beneficial to have the user's private and public keys backed up. The private and public keys of the CA should always be backed up and stored in a safe location for business continuance and recovery purposes.

After the private and public keys have been recovered for a user, a new digital certificate can be generated by the original issuing CA with the original attributes included. This means the user can continue to use this certificate as she did before she needed to use the recovery function.

M of N Control

M of N Control is the concept of backing up the public and private key material across multiple systems or devices. This method is designed to ensure that no one individual can re-create her private and public key material from the backup. The key materials are backed up and then mathematically distributed across several systems or devices. In most operational cases, three people are defined with separate job responsibilities and from separate portions of the organization. This is intended to prevent collusion between the individuals for the purpose of recovering the keys without proper permission. The mathematical equation supports any number of users up to 255 for the splitting activity. In most cases, though, no more than 5 are used for the purposes of operational efficiency.

Certificate Renewal

Digital certificates have a validity period associated with them, and at the end of the validity period, a new digital certificate needs to be issued. If the user has not changed her permission requirements or private and public key information, this process can be a simple one. The CA has to validate only that the person is who she claims to be and then generate a new certificate based on the current public key.

The CA also adds the current certificate to the revocation mechanism (that is, CRL) if the user renews the certificate prior to its validity period expiring.

Certificate and Key Pair Destruction

When a key pair and certificate are no longer valid and must be destroyed, multiple activities must take place—depending on the purpose of the key pair and certificate. If the key pair is used for digital signature purposes, the private key portion should be destroyed first to prevent future signing activities with the key. If the key pair is not used for signature purposes and is used only for privacy purposes, you might need to archive a copy of the private key. This is because the private key might need to be used to decrypt archived data that was encrypted using it.

The digital certificate should be added to the CRL as soon as the certificate is no longer valid. This activity takes place regardless of the archive or nonarchive status of the private key for future use. Depending on the sensitivity of the key in question, it might also be necessary to contact the individuals who use this certificate and trust the credentials it represents to inform them to no longer trust this certificate because it is no longer valid.

Key Usage

Digital certificates and public/private key pairs can be used for multiple purposes, including privacy and authentication. The security policy of the organization using the key and the CA defines the purposes and capabilities of the certificates it issues.

Privacy is achieved by using only the public key encryption purposes. In this case, a user receives the public key of the individual or entity with which he wants to communicate securely. He then uses this key to encrypt the data that he transmits securely.

Authentication is achieved by adding a digital signature element to the communication being transmitted. The creation of a digital signature requires the user to access his private key. If the user has properly protected his private key, the receiver of the communication is able to feel comfortable that the communication was transmitted by the issuer.

The receiver can also verify that the key is still valid by accessing the CA that issued the key if it is in the form of a digital certificate.

In some cases, both authentication and privacy are desired for a communication. This combination of purposes offers the highest levels of privacy and authenticity for the data. In this case, the public key of the individual or entity who is receiving the data is used to encrypt the data and the private key of the sender of the data is used to create the digital signature that binds the transmitter to the data being sent.

Multiple Key Pairs (Single, Dual)

In some cases, an individual might want to have multiple key pairs. This is especially true in corporate situations where a user might need to digitally sign information and encrypt information but wants the ability to have her personal credentials kept out of the key escrow policy. In this case, the individual is issued a key pair and certificate that is used only for encryption purposes and another key pair and certificate for digital signature purposes only.

Chapter Summary

In this chapter, we examined the concept of the public key infrastructure and the functions it enables. We began the chapter with a discussion of the digital certificate and the policies and procedures required to support it. We then looked at the concept of trust and how it relates to PKI in the form of trust models. We also talked about one of the most challenging portions of a PKI operation: cross certification.

To understand the capabilities of PKI, we examined the standards and protocols that currently exist to support and operate it in great detail. Each of these standards and protocols provides a specific function that needs to be taken into consideration when using a PKI solution. Currently, the most widely used of these are PKIX, SSL/TLS, HTTPS, and IPsec. These can be considered the foundational technologies for PKI deployments because they all solve current issues well enough for a corporation to invest in them at this point. With this investment in place, the gradual adoption of the other standards and protocols will happen as the adoption of the technology is solidified in operational solutions.

KEY TERMS

- Attribute certificate
- Authenticated header (AH)
- CA bridges
- Centralized key management
- Certificate Enrollment Protocol (CEP)
- Certificate Management Protocol (CMP)
- Certificate practice statement
- Certificate policy
- Certificate revocation
- Certificate revocation list

CHAPTER SUMMARY

- Certificate suspension
- Cross certification
- Cryptographic module
- Decentralized key management
- Diffie-Hellman Key Agreement
- Digital certificate
- Federal Information Processing Standards (FIPS)
- Keyed-Hash message authentication code (HMAC)
- Internet key exchange
- IPSec
- ISO17799
- Key escrow
- M of N Control
- Message authentication code (MAC)
- Online Certificate Status Protocol (OCSP)
- Padding
- Pretty good privacy (PGP)
- Secure Multipurpose Internet Mail Extensions (SMIME)
- Security association (SA)
- Security parameter index (SPI)
- Sequence number
- Wireless Equivalent Privacy (WEP)
- X.509

The chapter's final area of focus was key management and the certificate lifecycle. This area focused on the functions and management issues of a digital certificate from its inception until its destruction. It also discussed key areas that are often controversial, such as key storage and key escrow activities.

APPLY YOUR KNOWLEDGE

Exercises

6.1 Multinational Corporate PKI

The Global Corporation has decided to deploy a PKI solution across its enterprise. This is a multinational organization with 30,000 employees worldwide. The corporation is comprised of three divisions that report to a central operating body based in the U.S.

Each division has profit and loss responsibility for its own operating body but is dependent on corporate headquarters for policy and standards support. Each division also has an independent information technology department. The directors of each of department report in to the corporate information officer of the Global Corporation.

The information technology standards for Global specify a Microsoft Windows 2000 operating system for all user systems. Global also uses the Microsoft Office 2000 suite as its application suite. It has proprietary programs and Customer Relationship Management (CRM) software that have Web interfaces which support SSL communication paths.

The Global Corporation wants to use the PKI to enable secure communications across its divisions and to its partners. It also wants to use secure messaging capabilities for sensitive email communications and digital signatures to authenticate these messages. There is also a strong desire to enhance the security of its critical internal information systems. The users of these systems currently use username and password combinations and do not use any strong authentication techniques.

The questions you need to ask yourself for this exercise are

1. Who should define the security policy for the PKI?
2. What type of trust model would be most appropriate for this type of PKI?
3. Which protocols should be used to enable the secure electronic messaging capabilities?
4. Which protocols should be used to establish secure communications with the corporation's partners?
5. What are the international implications of this type of solution?
6. How many CAs should be deployed in this solution?

6.2 User Access Control in a Corporate Environment

You are the chief information officer in a mid-sized corporation that provides services to the U.S. government and private organizations. You have been asked to deploy an access control solution that is stronger than the current username and password system. The corporation also wants this solution to be used for both the Web environments and application suites that are used in the corporation.

The corporation has offices throughout the U.S. as well as multiple departments with different user requirements. The sales department employees require access to the Web-enabled systems while they are traveling to access pricing information and generate quotes for their customers. The finance department requires access to payroll systems that are using CRM applications that do not yet have Web interfaces available to them.

Because of the size of the corporation and current company conditions, there is currently a high degree of turnover. The corporation is working on remedying this situation but would like to have a way to ensure that it is able to access the intellectual property of all employees even after they have left the organization.

APPLY YOUR KNOWLEDGE

Corporate security policies are in place that require users to relinquish intellectual property at the time of resignation. Unfortunately, some users have used commercial software to encrypt their hard drives and have not relinquished the password required to decrypt them prior to their departure.

The questions you need to ask yourself for this exercise are

1. What type of CA structure should be deployed in this situation?
2. What type of certificates will be needed to satisfy the requirements of the sales department?
3. Which standards will need to be adhered to for the solution to be used for the entire customer base of the corporation?
4. How can you prevent users from using encryption techniques to encrypt their hard drives so the corporation cannot access them?
5. How will you use the PKI solution to set permission levels for different types of users?

Answers to Exercises

6.1 Answers

1. The security policy of the PKI should be defined by corporate headquarters. The top level of the organization should define all the policies and procedures associated with the PKI, and the executive staff should endorse these policies.
2. A hierarchical trust model is the most appropriate for this type of PKI. The corporate entity will act as the root CA, and each division will then have subordinate CAs to this root.
3. The SMIME protocol would be the most appropriate secure messaging protocol for this environment. This protocol allows the users to encrypt and digitally sign the messages they are sending. Because the Global Corporation standardizes on the Microsoft Office Suite for the applications, it can use the embedded SMIME functions included in Microsoft Outlook.
4. The IPSec protocol suite is the most appropriate protocol set to use to communicate with the partners. IPSec will enable Global to use strong authentication using digital certificates to authenticate with the partners and establish encrypted tunnels over the Internet for private communications. Because the IPSec protocol is a standard, the partners will not be forced to buy vendor-specific equipment but will need to use equipment that supports the IPSec protocol suite.
5. Because the Global Corporation has international divisions, it must comply with local encryption laws for each country. Depending on the country it's in, Global might have to use weaker levels of encryption or possibly supply the government with a means to access the data being transmitted over the encrypted connection. Auditing standards also vary from country to country and must be complied with according to local laws.
6. There should be a total of four certificate authorities deployed in this solution: one root CA for the corporation as a whole and an individual CA for each division.

APPLY YOUR KNOWLEDGE

6.2 Answers

1. In this case, there should be a single CA for the entire organization. Even though multiple departments exist, separate CAs don't need to be put in place for each one. This would only confuse the situation and cause higher costs for managing the solution.

2. The sales department will require client-side SSL certificates to enable authentication with the Web interfaces.

3. The corporation provides solutions with the U.S. government, which means it needs to adhere to the Federal Information Processing Standards (FIPS) for these solutions. If the users will use their certificates to authenticate with U.S. government resources or use them to establish secure communication channels, they must store their CA's private key in a FIPS 140-1-rated device. The government entity with which they are communicating will define which rating level must be met through their security policy.

4. In this case, you would use key escrow techniques to maintain a copy of the user's private key. In most cases, you would deploy the CA infrastructure in a centralized fashion in which the CA generates the private and public key for the user. The CA can then retain a copy of this key prior to transmitting it to the user.

5. This can be accomplished either by using the extension settings in the X.509 certificate or through the use of attribute certificates. The attribute certificates offer you more flexibility than the X.509 certificate but require you to create yet another certificate for each user.

Review Questions

1. Why would a CA use the Online Certificate Status Protocol instead a CRL?

2. What functionality does a CA bridge offer?

3. Which portion of the IPSec protocol suite can provide privacy to an IP packet?

4. What is the difference between a centralized and decentralized key management system?

5. Why would a CA issue multiple key pairs to a user?

Exam Questions

1. Which of the following is not included within a digital certificate?

   A. Information about the user

   B. The user's public key

   C. The user's private Key

   D. The digital signature of the issuing CA

2. Which of the following best describes a certificate policy?

   A. A set of rules that indicates the applicability of a certificate to a particular community and class of application with common security requirements.

   B. A set of rules that defines the usage of certificates by the user community of an organization.

   C. A document that states the procedures for deploying and operating a certificate solution.

   D. A document that certifies the validity of the CA.

APPLY YOUR KNOWLEDGE

3. Which of the following would you use if you wanted to check the validity of a digital certificate?

   A. Certificate policy

   B. Certificate revocation list

   C. Corporate security policy

   D. Trust model

4. Which PKI trust model would be used by a CA with multiple subordinate CAs?

   A. Cross certified

   B. Hierarchical

   C. Bridge

   D. Linked

5. Which trust model is most appropriate for a business partner relationship?

   A. Cross certified

   B. Hierarchical

   C. Bridge

   D. Linked

6. Which of the following PKI functions do SSL/TLS protocols not support at this time? (Choose two.)

   A. Authentication

   B. Certificate revocation lists

   C. Encryption

   D. Attribute certificates

7. Which of the following integrates with current messaging platforms as a service to provide secure messaging?

   A. SMIME

   B. Secret Agent

   C. PGP

   D. HTTPS

8. Which portion for the IPSec protocol suite provides authentication and integrity but not privacy for a packet?

   A. Encapsulated security payload

   B. Internet key exchange

   C. Authenticated header

   D. Security parameter index

9. Which of the following encryption algorithms must be supported for a product to be compliant to the IPSec security standard?

   A. DES

   B. Blowfish

   C. RSA

   D. All of the above

10. Which mode of IKE reduces the number of messages involved in a key exchange operation?

    A. Fast

    B. Main

    C. Low secure

    D. Aggressive

APPLY YOUR KNOWLEDGE

11. In decentralized key management architecture, the user is responsible for which function?

    A. Creation of the private and public key

    B. Creation of the digital certificate

    C. Revocation of the digital certificate

    D. Creation of the CRL

12. Which of the following is not a function of the HTTPS protocol?

    A. Transportation of data over an SSL connection

    B. Creation of a connection for secure communications

    C. Authentication of a user or server

    D. All of the above

Answers to Review Questions

1. The Online Certificate Status Protocol would allow the CA to maintain a database of revoked certificates instead of having to generate CRLs and publish them to all its users. This database could be publicly available and could reduce the burden of maintaining contact information and addresses of all the users of the certificates it issues.

2. A certificate authority bridge allows two separate CAs to communicate with each other without having to cross certify with each other. This means that the CAs can work with each other, but they do not have to allow each other to generate credentials on their behalf.

3. The ESP can provide privacy to an IP packet. It can also use encryption to scramble the data and hide the source address of the packet if tunnel mode is selected.

4. A centralized key management solution allows the CA to have complete control over the generation, escrow, and distribution of private and public key pairs as well as the digital certificate itself. In a decentralized model, the user generates the public/private key pair and then submits her public key verification and signature to the CA.

5. Multiple key pairs for a user are attractive because they allow a user to have a pair of keys for encryption and one pair for digital signature purposes. This enables users to submit their private keys that they have used for encryption to an escrow system for recovery purposes without jeopardizing their personal credentials.

Answers to Exam Questions

1. **C.** A user's private key should never be distributed outside of the user's control.

2. **A.** A certificate policy is intended to set the rules of use for digital certificates in an organization.

3. **B.** The CRL provides a detailed list of all the certificates that are no longer valid for a CA.

4. **B.** A PKI structure with a single CA and multiple subordinate CAs would benefit the most from a hierarchical structure because it allows the top CA to be the root CA and control trust throughout the PKI.

APPLY YOUR KNOWLEDGE

5. **A.** Cross certification enables multiple CAs to produce credentials on the behalf of the other. In a business partner relationship, both parties will most likely want to be able to allow users to access the entire solution the partners are providing. Cross certification enables either CA to grant users access to others' systems.

6. **B, D.** SSL/TLS does not support either certificate revocation lists or attribute certificates.

7. **A.** SMIME is a protocol, not an application, and is widely accepted by the application community. It is currently integrated with the most popular corporate email systems, including Microsoft Outlook, Exchange, Lotus Notes, and Eudora.

8. **C.** The AH portion of the IPSec protocol suite is intended to provide authentication so the receiver can be confident of the source of the packet. It does not use encryption to scramble the packet payload, though, so it cannot provide privacy for the packet.

9. **D.** The IPSec protocol suite requires multiple public domain encryption algorithms to be supported to be compliant. All these are included in the list of required algorithms. It does not endorse the use of proprietary algorithms because they are not freely available to the community at large.

10. **D.** The aggressive mode of IKE is used after a certain degree of confidence of identity has been established between the two communicating parties. This function can be used to reduce the overhead of the IKE process on computing systems.

11. **A.** In a decentralized key management scheme, the user creates both the private and public key and then submits the public key to the CA to allow it to apply its digital signature after it has authenticated the user.

12. **B, C.** Hypertext Transfer Protocol over SSL is intended only to provide HTTP functionality over SSL. SSL itself provides the secure connection and authentication capabilities.

Suggested Readings and Resources

Online Material

1. Internet Engineering Task Force. Request for Comment Document number 2401, "Security Architecture for the Internet Protocol" (`http://www.ietf.org/rfc/rfc2401.txt?number=2401`).

2. Internet Engineering Task Force. Request for Comment Document number 2459, "Internet X.509 Public Key Infrastructure Certificate and CRL Profile" (`http://www.ietf.org/rfc/rfc2459.txt`).

3. National Institute of Standards and Technology. "Security Requirements for Cryptographic Modules" (`http://csrc.nist.gov/cryptval/140-1.htm`).

4. RSA Corporation. "Public Key Cryptography Standards" (`http://www.rsasecurity.com/rsalabs/pkcs/`).

Publications

1. Housely, Russ, and Tim Polk. *Planning for PKI.* New York: John Wiley and Sons, Inc., 2001.

OBJECTIVES

This chapter covers the following CompTIA objectives for the Security+ exam.

Understand the basic security concepts and usage of physical security.

- **Access control**
- **Social engineering**
- **Environment**

▶ This objective is designed to focus the reader on physical protection mechanisms. The best encryption and firewalls in the world won't help you if someone walks away with the server.

Understand the basic security implications of disaster recovery.

- **Facilities**
- **Equipment**
- **High availability**
- **Backups**
- **Secure recovery**
- **Utilities**
- **Vendor support**

▶ Even with the best of plans, disasters will still strike. Planning, preparation, maintenance, and execution of a disaster recovery plan all help minimize the effects. This objective covers these topics in detail.

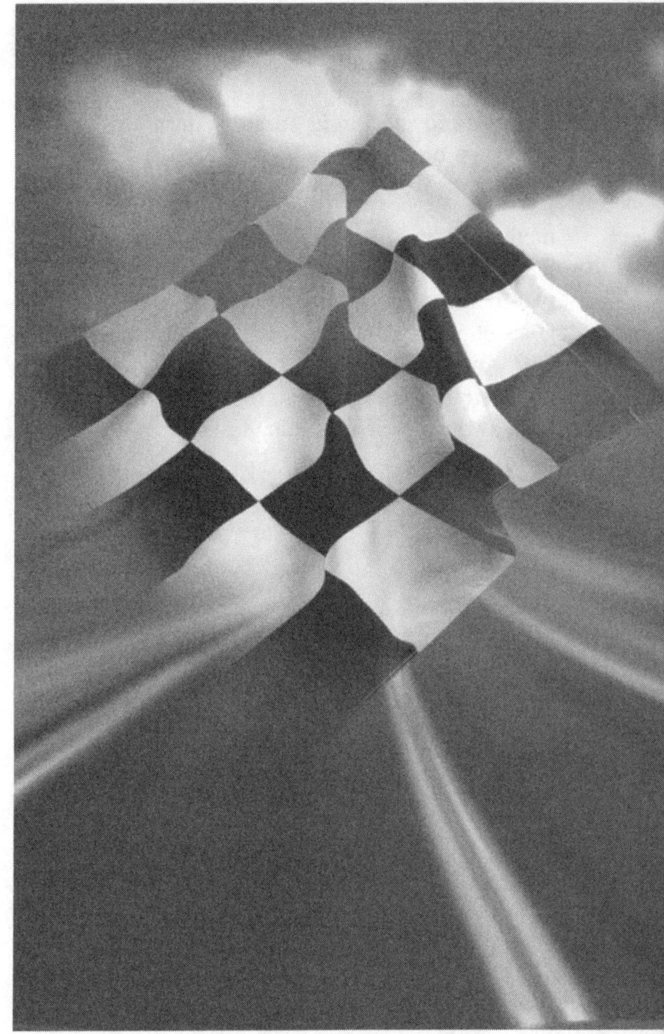

CHAPTER 7

Physical Security, Disaster Recovery, and Business Continuity

Objectives

Understand the basic security implications of business continuity.

- In conjunction with disaster recovery is the implementation of a *business continuity plan.* If services fail or facilities are destroyed, a disaster recovery plan helps focus on immediate tasks and short-term goals of getting the business's doors open again. The objective of business continuity, however, is a longer-term look at how to recover from a disaster such as the loss of a building or facility.

Outline

Outline

Study Strategies

- This chapter focuses on two key areas: physical security and disaster recovery. Be sure you understand these two concepts and the steps for properly deploying each.
- When new concepts are introduced, write them down along with a definition for later study and research.
- Use the case studies at the end of the chapter as well as your own experience to apply the information discussed. Try to find real-world examples in your own environment.

INTRODUCTION

A large majority of our focus in this book so far has been protecting data from attacks, alteration, or manipulation. We now shift the focus from protecting the data to protecting the systems, people, and buildings that store and use the data in day-to-day operations.

Understanding and implementing software encryption, firewalls, cryptography, and Public Key Infrastructure (PKI) is all for nothing if an intruder can simply walk into your building or offices and walk away with your physical computer systems. Encrypting your stored data will only prolong the process of getting at the data. If theft occurs and someone has physical ownership of a server, even the toughest encryptions can be broken.

Chapter 1, "General Security Concepts," discussed a brief history of computers. Theft in the days of the mainframe computer was not a big concern. The mainframes were simply too large and often too complex to be considered a target for theft. Plus, they were housed in specific rooms and required cooling and maintenance that few companies (never mind individuals) could manage. An enormous shift has occurred over the last 20 years, however. Every worker seems to have a desktop computer for doing her job in today's environment. The ease of maintenance and small size of the modern server have allowed large companies, by using newer network design topologies, to distribute these systems throughout the corporation in smaller, more efficient server rooms. This has had the positive effect of pushing data closer to users but a negative impact on physical network security.

Instead of one large server room with a single point of entry that's easily protected and watched, companies have many server rooms and multiple points of entry for a would-be thief. It is up to you as a network administrator and security engineer to design a system that is secure yet usable. A system is considered very secure if it's buried in a block of concrete but would represent little benefit to users if they couldn't get to the data stored on it. The real task becomes managing the compromise between the ultimate secure network with no usability and the easily used network with no security. Let's not forget cost, either. Network security costs corporations tens of thousands of dollars every year in support and maintenance after security measures have been put in place. With your tasks now before you, let's look at physical security in more detail.

IN THE FIELD

THE IMPORTANCE OF PHYSICAL SECURITY

The following events actually occurred. We were consulting with a medium-sized company of about 750 employees. The IT department maintained the network and was also the security team and disaster recovery planners. They had done a good job preparing their systems for what-if scenarios such as long- and short-term power failures, air conditioning unit mishaps, water damage, and other natural and man-made disasters. However, they had overlooked a key function of disaster recovery and physical data security by storing all their backups onsite.

After some recommendations, discussions, and additional budget reconfiguration, the company invested in a faster and more efficient backup system. By doing so, they gave themselves enough time to duplicate the backups and store the second set of tapes offsite. The process of convincing the managers and executives to absorb the cost of the new system and have their budgets reduced paid off like few projects do.

About two months after deploying the new system, an executive left the company. The separation was seen as amicable by all involved. The night following the departure of the executive, the main data center was broken into. The damage done allowed the disaster recovery plan to be tested to its fullest.

Four gallons of cleaning fluid had been poured into the three server cabinets. The wiring in all the patch panels had been pulled out and all the hot-swappable server hard drives had been removed and destroyed. The onsite tapes had been removed from the tape storage area and rendered useless with a set of large speaker magnets.

The intruder was careful not to set off any alarms that would notify authorities and did most, if not all, of the damage, in about 10 minutes (educated guess). The only thing that allowed the company to recover the next day was the offsite storage of backups and a competent disaster recovery plan. Where the system had failed was the aspect of physical security that let the individual accomplish his goals in the first place.

PHYSICAL SECURITY

Understand the basic security concepts and usage of physical security.

EXAM TIP

When working through this particular section, concentrate on the fire suppression systems and environment section because they are common elements for almost all networks.

As illustrated by the previous "In the Field" section, physical security is as important, if not more so, than information security. Given enough time, energy, and intellect, physical access can overcome all other security measures.

Understanding and implementing physical security involves understanding a different set of vulnerabilities and threats. Computer security highlights issues with attackers gaining access to systems through software or hardware mechanisms and attacking data in transit or in storage through electronic means. Physical security, and the associated planning, identifies physical dangers to the hardware and buildings that store the equipment on which the data resides. The following list describes some of the threats encountered when planning physical security:

- An intruder or outside agent breaking into a building and stealing or damaging networking hardware and resources
- An employee or inside agent gaining unauthorized physical access to a protected area or server system
- Natural disasters, such as tornadoes, hurricanes, earthquakes, and floods that threaten the building and its contents
- Man-made disasters, such as fires and chemical spills, that can have the same effect as a natural disaster

In each case, a company must identify an event's occurrence probability, estimate its impact, and implement measures that help reduce the effects should the disaster actually occur. One of the first steps to physical security is physical access control.

Physical Access Control

Physical access control is similar to the data access control discussed in Chapter 1. There are mandatory, discretionary, and role-based access control mechanisms to physical facilities just as there are with data.

Mandatory physical access controls are commonly found in government facilities and military installations where users are closely monitored and very restricted. Users are often allowed in very few areas and are not free to roam about. Users also are not given the capability to let others in or modify entry methods because security personnel is monitoring them. It is much easier to implement mandatory control over physical equipment and facilities than over data. Scalability issues don't have as big an impact when dealing with facilities because facilities remain static when compared to data growth. In addition, after they're set up, physical access controls require far less maintenance than their data counterparts.

When using discretionary control to a building or room, it is generally delegated or distributed to down-level parties responsible for the contents of the building or room. This is different from mandatory control, where the authority to get into different areas is centrally controlled and monitored.

Finally, role-based access methods for physical control identify groups of people who have common access needs and allow them to get into different locations with the same key or swipe card without additional help or interaction from the security department. This is again a hybrid of both mandatory access control (MAC) and discretionary access control (DAC), as previously illustrated in the data model in Chapter 1. The security department coordinates the secure setup of the facility and surrounding areas, identifies the groups allowed to enter various areas, and allows them access based on their group membership. Users in this model generally have some security training and often are allowed to grant access to others by using an escort or guest badge procedure.

Setting up any of these methods requires a secure facility to start with. The first stop for us, then, is physical barriers. After that, we cover these other physical security items: location, building materials, shielding, and fire suppression.

Physical Barriers

Physical barriers, such as fences and water, play a key role as both a visual and physical deterrent to intruders. The use of physical barriers involves

- Planning
- Deploying

- Monitoring
- Maintaining

Planning

Implementing physical barriers, like most aspects of security, requires planning. The land, building, areas inside the building, and even individual offices need to be evaluated for possible security risks. Any large job is best approached by looking at smaller pieces of the whole. Tackling physical security planning is best done by looking at the perimeter of the building first and then working inward toward the smallest spaces to be secured. To give you a better idea of what to implement, let's take a look at some of the available resources and barrier types that can be used.

The grounds and perimeter of a building are mostly a matter of taste or choice. Some companies don't have this issue to worry about because their facilities are located in downtown buildings or office complexes. If you do have grounds or a campus environment, security is again a balance between aesthetics and functionality.

No-man's Land

Often, buildings that house secure or important information and systems have an area of cleared land surrounding them. This area is often referred to as *no-man's land*. The area might encompass only the front section of the building, where the normal entry points are, but the open space more likely surrounds the entire building as a protective measure. This area should offer no hiding places, such as shrubs, trees, or even other small buildings on the grounds. It is odd to think that an area of clear land would represent a physical barrier, but if it's well lit and monitored, this type of barrier can be an excellent first line of defense, turning away most casual intruders. This type of barrier is also an excellent passive deterrent that lets everyone know you are serious about protecting your property and its contents.

Fences

The next most common deterrent is a fence, moat, or similar device that usually surrounds the entire building. The fence can be made of a visually pleasing material, but it serves the purpose of turning away unwanted people and vehicles. Fences can be made of concrete blocks, chain-link, wood, and even boulders and can be mixed to form a more pleasing configuration.

Some companies have been known to use a concrete block in the back of a building with chain-link fencing attached on the sides and finally wood and boulders in the front to add a bit of style. In any case, the fencing should be inspected and maintained on a regular basis, and the areas within the fencing should generally be well lit.

The height of the fence is important, as well. A standard 4' garden fence will only keep out a curious individual. A 6' fence usually represents a more serious obstacle, and a 10' fence is an obvious sign to most that you do not want people in that area unless they proceed through an approved access point. If barbed wire is used at the top, it simply adds to the effect. To help reduce the "prison" appearance associated with large chain-link fences (especially ones with barbed wire at the top), companies often plant bushes or trees in front of the fence to help break up the look.

Water/Moats

Water has been used as a physical barrier for hundreds of years. Moats, or water surrounding part or all of a facility, are excellent physical barriers. They also offer the added benefits of being very low profile and pleasing to the eye. If moats are used as physical deterrents, the depth of the water should be considered, as well as the added maintenance of keeping the water free of trash, algae, and so on when you implement them. Generally, the moat should be deep enough to prevent vehicles from crossing and should force an individual to swim at its deepest part. Care should also be taken so that people (especially children) can't fall in and drown.

External Lighting and Cameras

Additional security measures for the perimeter of a building or campus should also include lighting and, if possible, cameras. Intruders rarely welcome a brightly lit area, so the better the lights, the bigger the deterrent. Employees will also appreciate the increased safety associated with a well-lit outside area. Cameras offer the benefit of centralized monitoring of the perimeter. Fewer security personnel are required when using cameras, and the monitoring central station can be placed in an optimum position for quick response to incidents or accidents.

External Motion Detectors

Motion detectors can be used both inside and outside buildings. When used outside, motion detectors can alert security personnel of intruders or unwanted activity on the company's grounds. The sensors can be based on

- Light
- Sound
- Infrared/Heat
- Ultrasonic

Light-based motion detectors are typically used inside and are discussed in the "Internal Motion Detectors" section later in the chapter.

Sound-based sensors, if used outside, must be adjusted properly to avoid setting off false alarms. If the facility is in a remote location, wildlife and even the wind can set off sound-based motion sensors. These alarms are comprised of microphones and monitoring chips that react when sound is produced in the monitored area, above a preset threshold (this is the area where adjustments can be made). These devices should be used in conjunction with other mechanisms, such as cameras, to help prevent reactions to normal events such as deer, dogs, cats, and the occasional stiff breeze.

> **WARNING**
>
> **Don't Rely on One Security Measure** A common mistake is to rely on one security measure too much. Monitoring cameras is a tedious job, and people doing so are likely to be bored and might even fall asleep. You should mix activities of security personnel and mix security measures, too. Having personnel walk the perimeter occasionally in addition to monitoring camera output will help them overcome boredom. Using motion sensors and alarms in conjunction with cameras can prevent someone from sleeping through an event.

Infrared and heat-based motion sensors are only good at night when used outside. The system should be calibrated much like sound sensors to avoid false positive readings. The system is built to react to a change in temperature or infrared signature (such as the introduction of a human body) in the area being monitored. Because of the radiant heat given off by objects, sensors are typically set to look at very small areas, such as doorways and windows.

The final type of sensor to consider is ultrasonic. An ultrasonic motion sensor is probably the one most accurately described by the term *motion sensor*. These detectors work on the premise of emitting a small ultra-high frequency wave. The transmitter and receiver are usually located in the same device. After it's turned on, the transmitter sends out timed pulses of sound, and the receiver receives a return wave from surrounding objects. The system also identifies holes in the monitored area (no bounce-back areas such as doorways) and creates a baseline for the return of the signals sent by the transmitter (see Figure 7.1).

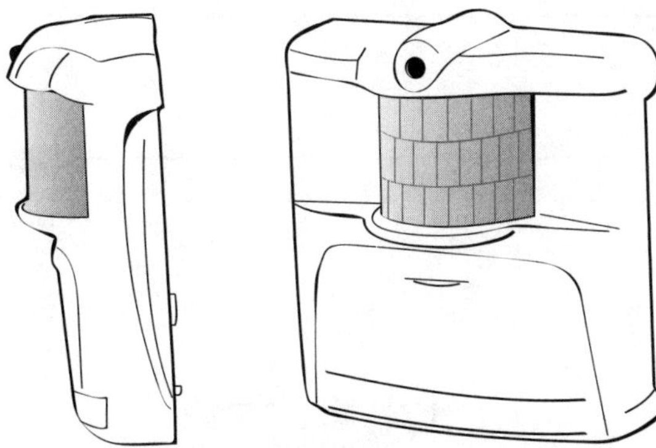

FIGURE 7.1
Ultrasonic sensor and protection pattern.

If an object enters the area and disturbs the baseline expected by the receiver, an alarm goes off.

External Doors and Windows

Doors and doorways should represent the first line of defense of the building itself. If protection is your goal, you can't save money by implementing weak doors. Steel doors represent the best deterrent, although steel reinforced wooden doors work as well. Doors, similar to the other barriers we have discussed, represent a visual deterrent. Make sure they are maintained and functional at all times. Corporate desires can play a role in this. A building using nothing but solid steel doors can look like a prison or bunker, so companies often have a set of glass doors at the main reception area with steel doors blocking the entrance to the rest of the building from the reception area. Figure 7.2 shows a double entry lobby area.

The locks and locking mechanisms should be capable of withstanding the force of an attempted entry. Doorways should be well lit, and if cameras are used, outside doors should be in the field view of at least one camera. External doors should be alarmed and monitored for open/closed status. Additional alarms can be put in place to notify security if the door has been opened too long or is blocked open, allowing unauthorized or unregulated entry.

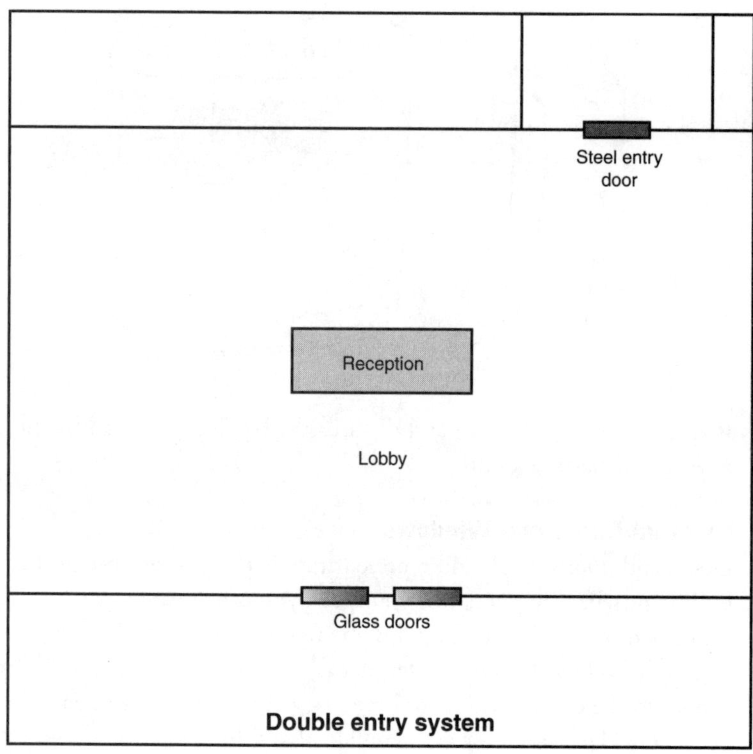

FIGURE 7.2
Double entry lobby configuration.

Windows should have locking mechanisms, and building security alarms should monitor the open/closed condition of all the windows that are an entry risk. The ground floor windows on secure buildings often do not open for ventilation. This precaution makes breaking into the building from the ground floor more difficult; however, caution should be taken that you do not trap people inside while trying to secure the building from outside intruders. Ground floor windows that do not open should have a release mechanism so they can be pushed out in the case of an emergency evacuation of the building.

Although we are still only in the planning phase of physical barriers, you now have a good idea of perimeter and external building security. It is time to move our focus to the building's interior.

Mantraps

A mantrap gives security personnel time to view a building entrant before allowing full access or entry into the interior of the building space. The mantrap is illustrated in Figure 7.3.

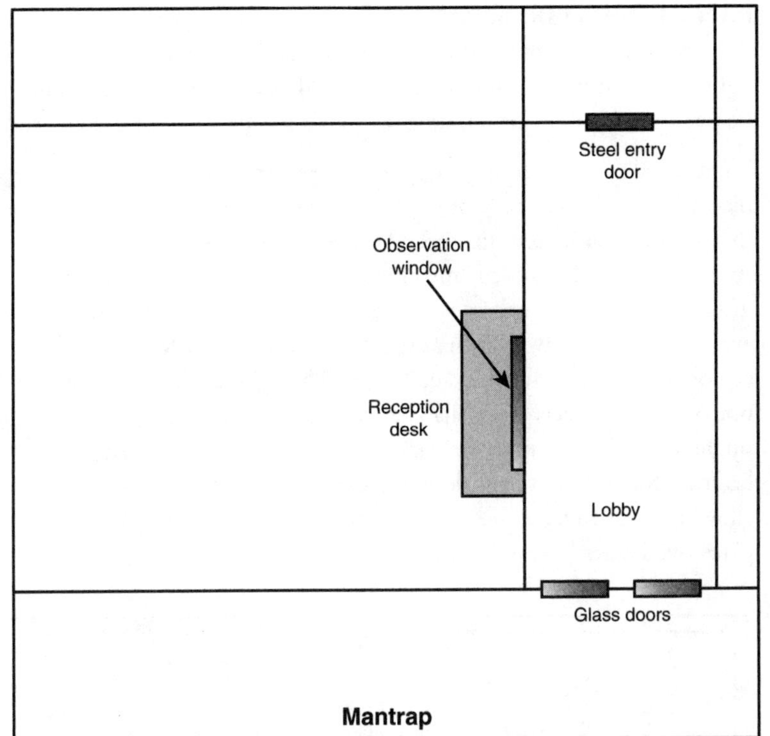

FIGURE 7.3
A mantrap layout.

The benefit of this is that, if an intruder happens to succeed at getting by the security on the outer door, both doors will be locked and the intruder will be caught in the holding area. In some cases, the outer door must be closed and locked before the inner door can open. These locks are often electronic and can be passive or active locks.

A *passive* electronic lock opens if the electricity is turned off; an *active* lock remains locked. The risk is that if an intruder has cut electricity to the building, doors secured by passive locks could be unlocked and other security mechanisms could be shut down. Active locks have the same stipulation as windows that don't open: The active lock mechanism needs a bypass so in an emergency, such as a fire or other problem that requires evacuation of the building, people are not trapped inside the building.

Internal Motion Detectors

As previously mentioned, the four common motion detectors are light, sound, infrared, and ultrasonic. All these motion detectors can be deployed inside your building, as well.

Light-based motion sensing equipment is generally comprised of two pieces. The first piece generates a beam of light and projects it across the area to be protected; the second piece is a photosensitive receiver. After the system is enabled, any object blocking the beam of light (for instance, passing through it) will cause an alarm to go off. Other events can occur as well, such as the door automatically locking and a call being placed to the local authorities. The light can be visible or not. Visible light acts as a visual—as well as physical—deterrent but might allow the system to be bypassed if a way around the visible light beams is found. You might decide to deploy both types of systems, allowing an intruder to see only a fraction of the actual protection in place (see Figures 7.4 and 7.5).

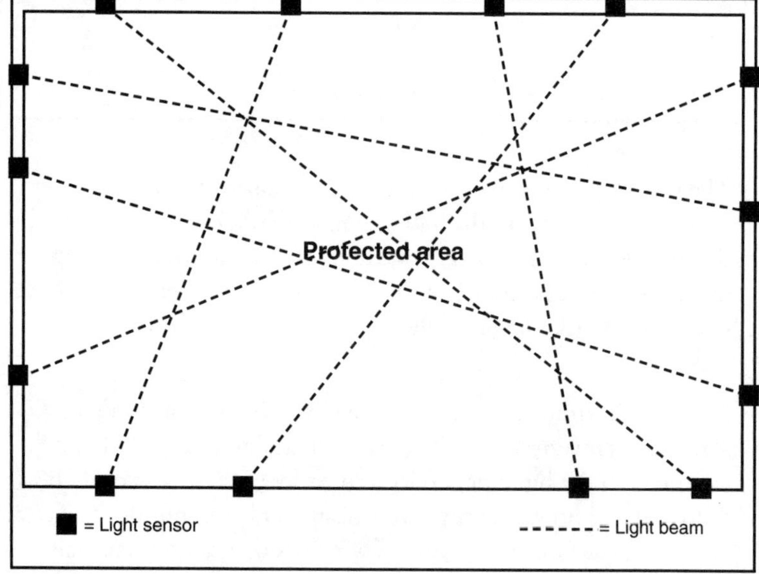

FIGURE 7.4
Light-based protection in a spider web configuration.

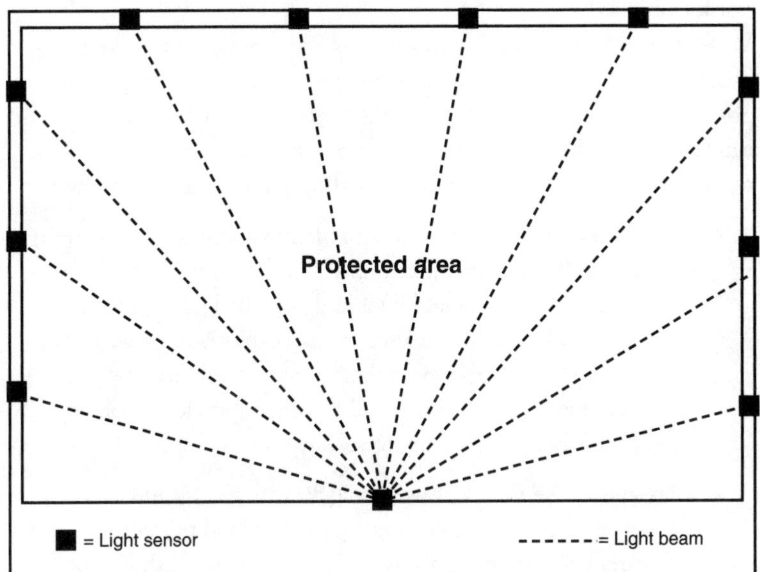

FIGURE 7.5
Light-based protection in a fan configuration.

Sound-based motion detectors are more easily deployed inside a building than outside. Internal sensors work just as their external counterparts but can be configured to be more sensitive than outdoor detectors. Even though they are more sensitive, they cause false alarms less frequently because the internal building is less susceptible to unknown noises. When deploying these sensors inside, be careful of common noise-making equipment such as air conditioners and automated/robotic equipment that can move at night, causing a false alarm.

Infrared, heat, and ultrasonic systems deployed indoors are the same as their outdoor counterparts. These systems can be tuned just as the sound-based systems to be more sensitive because of the controlled nature of an inside structure. For each system used indoors, common changes in heat (because of heating systems or equipment) and movement of air and equipment should be taken into account when placing and tuning the devices to help prevent false alarms.

Locks

When considering locks, you must consider functionality. The locks should be easy to work for those who are allowed access and should pose a significant deterrent to intruders. Realize that given enough time and the right tools, any lock can be defeated. The main characteristics that come into play when deciding on locks are as follows:

- **Strength**—Locks are often rated to help you decide between various models and manufacturers. You should identify the average length of time it would take to defeat the lock and which methods would need to be used (torch, explosives, crowbar, bolt cutters, and so on). Use locks that provide maximum defense at an affordable cost. A lock used to protect a bicycle is probably not appropriate when trying to secure entry into a building.
- **Material**—The materials used in locks vary greatly and influence the cost of the locks. Steel, aluminum, iron, and titanium are just a few examples of materials used. The lock material should be capable of withstanding repeated efforts of forced entry.
- **Cost**—This can play the biggest role in your decision, but again be careful about trying to save your budget by being cheap. Good locks of any kind are expensive. A solid steel door would be useless with a cheap, domestic doorknob.
- **Aesthetic**—We have discussed the fact that many companies like to avoid making the workplace look like a prison. Many styles of locks are available and still offer the necessary visual and physical deterrent.

Normal key locks are readily available and offer an excellent solution in many cases. In large companies with many doors and secured areas, however, physical keys and physical key management (described so as not to be confused with crypto keys and crypto key management) can become a considerable issue. The classic movie portrayal of a night security guard with a key ring of hundreds keys is a good example of the problem that can be caused. To help overcome this problem, other lock types can be deployed instead of or in conjunction with key lock systems. The following list contains a brief description of some of these lock types:

- **Cipher locks**—These locks typically have a punch code entry system. The price range for these types of locks varies widely between manufacturer and model so be sure to do your homework. See Figure 7.6 for an example.

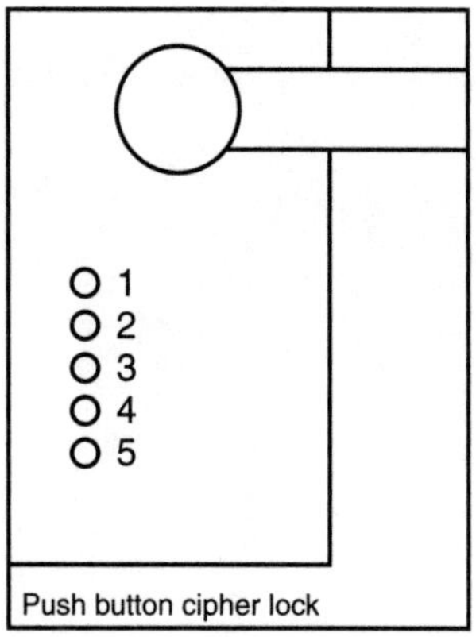

FIGURE 7.6
The push button method of the cipher lock.

- **Wireless**—These systems work on a card or token held by an authorized entrant close to the receiver. The receiver mechanism reads the card and, based on the information it contains, automatically opens the door or electronically disengages the locking mechanism for a short time (the classic 5-second buzz). Remember that, if your lock system uses electricity, you have to decide on a passive or an active lock behavior.
- **Swipe card**—This lock is similar in function and design to the wireless system. It requires that the user insert or swipe a card to open the door (similar to a bank ATM). This can be a problem in areas of a company where people often carry loads of paperwork or other items, so remember to take into account the common behaviors of your people when considering any lock type.
- **Biometrics**—Biometric systems and devices were covered in Chapter 1 with a focus on computer security. Physical security can also use the biometric methods and integrate them into a door lock mechanism. Table 7.1 is provided as a quick review.

TABLE 7.1

BIOMETRIC REVIEW

Biometric	*Description*	*Issues*
Fingerprint	This involves the scanning and matching of a thumbprint or fingerprint.	This type of system is typically controlled by an external computer system. It's noninvasive and easy to use. It is not a common door lock mechanism, so support and maintenance might be a problem.
Hand/Palm geometry	Identity is based on a person's palm or hand profile.	This is one of the most common forms of biometric door entry systems. Similar to the fingerprint system, this is noninvasive, easy to use, and readily available for doors. Some systems come with a built-in computer and can function as a standalone mechanism.
Voiceprint	A user identifies herself by speaking into a microphone.	This type of system is typically controlled by an external computer system and is noninvasiveand easy to use. It isnot as common as hand/palm geometry.
Facial geometry	A user is identified on the profile and characteristics of her face.	This is a relatively new form of authentication. Finding a system integrated into a door lock mechanism can be difficult. It is, however, noninvasive and easy to use.
Iris profile	The colored part of the eye is used to properly identify an individual.	This is becoming a very popular option to replace the more invasive retinal scanner system. It is easy to use and noninvasive.
Retina scan	The blood vessel pattern at the back of the eye is read to properly identify an individual.	This system is the classic system portrayed in movies. It requires that glasses be removed and is more invasive than any other system. This technology has been around for a long time and is well supported.
Signature	An individual signs electronically, and the signature is matched to a database.	It would be unusual to see this as a door entry method, but it's possible.

The preceding sections give you a better idea of what is available for physical barriers. Armed with this information, the planning phase continues with a timeline for upgrades and new installations. Influences on your decision to deploy physical barriers include

- Building ownership
- Building location
- Cost
- Technological expertise

If you own the building you want to secure, the planning and deployment of physical barriers is typically a quicker process. Building codes and zoning restrictions should be researched to identify proper procedures and potential problems with certain types of physical barriers (a moat or no-man's land are good examples). Necessary permits for the upgrades should be applied for in advance of the actual deployment. If you do not own the building, obtaining permission from the building owner and other tenants will likely be required. This can add time to the planning phase, require a more detailed reporting process, and increase the overall cost of the deployment.

Building location can have a significant influence on which barriers are deployed. If your company is located in a downtown office building, constructing a moat around the building is not practical. If you don't occupy the entire building, additional restrictions on access barriers might apply. In this case, a mantrap on the first floor might not be desired or approved by the other tenants.

Cost is always a large influence on any project. The cost of advanced security systems can be very high, and getting budgets and funding approved can be difficult, particularly because no profitability is associated with the cost of security. Management must buy in to the security project, or it will rarely leave the planning stage.

Physical barriers associated with security have steadily grown in their technical complexity. Training or hiring staff to support new security mechanisms should be examined in the planning phase to avoid delays and disappointments. Monitoring, repair, and maintenance add significant costs to the overall operations of the company, as well. Whether you choose to accomplish these tasks in-house or contract these services to an outside company should be identified early in the process and placed in the budget.

The planning phase is complete when you create a timeline for the project and order the actual equipment. This can be complex enough that companies often contract the security system deployment to experts. The timeline should identify how long deployment and training should take and include milestones and a target completion date. The plan should be reviewed and adjusted as necessary throughout the lifecycle of the project. Now that we have a well-developed plan in hand, it is time to deploy the system.

Deployment

Deploying physical barriers usually involves the physical installation of the devices, training personnel on their use, and debugging unforeseen issues. If proper planning was accomplished, the deployment phase should go smoothly.

Authorized installers and certified building contractors should be used for the installation of all physical barriers to ensure that they meet local, state, and government building codes. Many of the systems discussed require additional electrical wiring and proper installation of transceivers; using authorized installers will give you a warranty of support and functionality should something go wrong during the installation and testing of the new equipment. If new physical barriers such as moats, fences, and a no-man's land are developed, using qualified contractors ensures that the job is done properly and to code. As mentioned in the planning phase, this process can be complex and time-consuming. Many companies therefore choose to outsource the deployment of the equipment to people who specialize in security system installation exclusively. If the building is a new construction project instead of a reconfiguration of an existing building, many of the processes discussed so far can be built in to the normal phases of construction.

As you deploy the new security systems, training on system use should begin. The timing of training should be coordinated so that training completion and physical deployment finish at about the same time. The final phases of training should take place on the company's new security system whenever possible. This ensures the new systems are working properly and that the personnel have been trained to an appropriate level to use and monitor the devices.

As a final note for the deployment phase, problems occur in most projects, and security is no different. You need to put a debugging phase in your plan after the deployment. Cameras might be in the wrong place or not focused properly, no-man's land might turn into a swamp after a good rain, cipher locks might get set to the wrong combination, and motion detectors might be too sensitive initially. By allowing time up front to work through these problems, you are more likely to set expectations properly and finish the project on schedule.

Monitoring

The type of physical barriers deployed will help you identify monitoring procedures. You will have a choice of hiring and training personnel within the company or outsourcing monitoring to an outside security firm. Either case requires the development of proper procedures, including incident handling.

Procedures should include daily activities and outline responsibilities for security personnel. When deploying key card entry systems, for example, you need to outline procedures for issuing key cards to new employees and handling lost or stolen key cards. You also need to outline the proper entry methods to be used if the system is offline, and how to report problems and breeches of security to the proper internal and external authorities. A comprehensive list of procedures would take up too much of this book. It is important that you understand how to develop the procedures for your situation, define proper monitoring methods for each of the security measures deployed in your company, and ensure that security personnel understands and follows them.

The procedures should be flexible and a constant work in progress. Security personnel should have a method to update procedures when needed, and employees should have a method for making suggestions to improve the security and usability of the system. Periodic checks of the systems should be planned, and reviews of procedures should include live tests of all systems to ensure that they are in proper working condition.

Maintenance

After your security system is in place, you need to ensure that it remains in good working order. The entire security system should be put on a regular maintenance and inspection schedule because without proper maintenance, the security systems we have discussed are worthless. Some examples of regular inspection procedures include the following:

- **No-man's land**—Inspect the area for debris, and keep the area mowed. The idea is that this area represents an unobstructed view of people approaching the facility. Nothing should be stored in this area that presents a visual obstacle.
- **Fences**—Inspect fencing regularly for normal wear and tear as well as deliberate attempts to gain access. If the fence is painted, it should be repainted on a regular basis to maintain its appearance.
- **Water/Moats**—Keep water free of debris, and make sure it doesn't become a breeding ground for insects. Installation of a water pump and filter can solve both of these problems. Make sure that the water level is maintained and that any safety fencing for small children is in good working order.
- **Motion sensors**—Because motion sensors are often placed near the ceiling and in corners of areas, they are prone to collecting dust and spider webs. Regular maintenance should include cleaning these areas and inspecting the physical transceivers for damage. The system should also undergo regular live testing to ensure it works.
- **Outside lighting/cameras**—Replace broken bulbs and cameras immediately! Too often these items are left malfunctioning for extended periods of time. Replacement parts for these devices should be onsite at all times. Lighting and cameras represent one of the best visual and physical deterrents, so these devices should be always be in good working order.
- **Doors/Windows**—Inspect doors and windows for broken parts (hinges, glass, locks, and so on), and replace as necessary. As with fences, if doors and windows are painted, a regular schedule for repainting should be implemented.

- **Mantraps/Locks**—Inspect and test all locks and locking mechanisms routinely, and replace any broken or malfunctioning locks immediately. If locks are electronic, test their behavior with the power off to ensure that active and passive lock behaviors are correct.

If maintenance is overlooked, the system will begin to degrade. The visual deterrent of these security measures will be compromised if left to deteriorate. Old paint on rusty doors, fencing that is falling down, loose doorknobs, and cracked windows let a potential intruder know that you are not maintaining your security systems. Additionally, if security mechanisms are left in a poor or nonfunctional state, employees will bypass the security to get their jobs done. This will compromise the entire system and render the investment of time and money worthless.

REVIEW BREAK

- Physical barriers are an integral aspect of physical security.
- When using physical barriers you must plan, deploy, monitor, and maintain them to get the most out of them.
- Barriers include no-man's land areas, fences, water, lights, cameras, motion detectors, doors, windows, mantraps, and locks.
- Locking systems can rely on advanced technologies, including wireless key entry systems and biometrics systems.

Social Engineering

Social engineering is an attack form based on deceiving a user. In Chapter 1, we examined it from the perspective of someone trying to gain access to information systems. The threat of social engineering can also be seen when dealing with physical security. Remember that social engineering seeks to exploit human nature and human behavior: Most of us are good-natured and trusting and will seek to help out someone in trouble. Without proper training, this type of behavior can be played upon to gain access through physical barriers.

The following are some common ways social engineering can be used to gain entry into a building or restricted area:

- **Grabbing/holding a door**—When attempting to gain access through an outside door, an intruder typically sits in a car or stands slightly away from the secured door area and waits. When an authorized employee gains access through the door, the intruder approaches and holds it open on behalf of the employee or attempts to catch the door just before it closes. This is sometimes referred to as *piggybacking*.
- **Talking**—This method relies on the intruder's ability to interact with employees. When attempting to gain access to a restricted area or building, the intruder makes an excuse such as losing an entry badge, leaving keys at home, or being unable to get the entry system to function properly. The intruder then asks the employee let her in.
- **Impersonation**—This is the classic movie-style approach. An intruder poses as a repair technician or building maintenance worker. Dressed in a proper uniform and carrying a toolbox, this approach is often very effective. The intruder might even successfully gain a temporary access badge in such a disguise. An intruder can also pose as a guest or new employee in an attempt to gain entry.
- **Observation**—Using this technique, an intruder simply watches over the shoulder of an employee as he types his pass code to get through a secured door system.
- **The struggle**—In this technique, the intruder approaches a door timed with the arrival of an employee. The intruder is usually carrying an armload of books and papers and fumbles about trying to get to a badge or key while struggling with the armload of cargo. The approaching employee typically helps without any additional encouragement.

To avoid the situations previously listed, employees should be instructed on how to handle these events. Intruders do not typically attempt entry through the main (or front) doors. Side doors, back doors, and freight or delivery entries offer a greater chance for success for the intruder and therefore are often targeted.

The company can set policies and locking mechanisms disallowing normal employee access through these areas and then train employees to report any suspicious behavior. In addition to training, you can implement specific types of physical barriers, such as a turnstile, that prevent actions such as piggybacking. The turnstile entry system shouldn't allow more than one person through at a time and should prevent an employee from passing her pass card or key back through the turnstile system.

The employee should be trained to direct or escort an outsider to the security desk for proper processing. If a confrontation is possible, the employee should immediately avoid entry at the current location and proceed to the main entry or security desk. Employees should also be taught not to allow any unknown persons into the facility. As a final step, door code systems should be configured with a 911 or hostage code. If the employee is forced to punch in a door code, the code will open the door, but will also alert the security desk of a problem.

Environment

Environment is a broad term used to describe the physical conditions that affect and influence growth, development, and survival. Although it is a term generally used to describe animals and their surroundings, it can also be used to describe the condition that affects a business and its physical security. The environment of a building or security area (both inside and out) will have a major influence on your physical security plans and considerations. We will confine our discussion of the environment by examining the following:

- Building location
- Building materials
- Shielding
- Wireless technology
- Fire suppression systems

Location

The three rules of real estate are location, location, and location. Security is no different. Whether constructing a new building, buying an existing building, or renting space, location will influence decisions about physical security. As we look at security (from the point of view of the environment) and specifically the location of the facility, realize that some decisions will involve which type of barriers to deploy and how many barriers to use, whereas other security decisions might involve how and where you place key data centers and equipment within a building. Additional location considerations can influence where you choose to allow entry and exit. When choosing a location, many factors are blended to achieve the desired result for both business and security needs. Think of the following questions, and you'll begin to see how the location of a building or office plays a role in the security environment:

- What type of neighborhood is the facility in? Is it an office park, a warehouse, or a downtown building?
- What is the general population of the area? Are there many other businesses or residential structures? Is it in an isolated part of town?
- What is the crime rate in the surrounding area?
- What is the average time it takes for police and fire to respond in an emergency in the area?
- Is the building or office owned or rented? Can you adjust the physical surroundings?
- Which natural disasters could strike because of the placement of the building? Is the area susceptible to fires, flooding, hurricanes, and so on?

Based on the answers to these and other similar questions, you should begin to develop a good idea of which types of physical security are possible, what security is necessary, and how your facility's location can influence your choices. For example, if the facility is located in a warehouse district and has few or no residences surrounding it, it can be a good target for intruders. Physical barriers in such a situation should include lighting, cameras, fences, and onsite security personnel.

Remember that you are not just protecting the building from human intruders. Be cautious in your evaluations; don't overlook the possibility of natural disasters that could intrude into your facility. Identify barriers that could help prevent the intrusion of fire, water, and wind. Although natural elements are not out to steal your data, these elements can steal your ability to get to your data by causing the destruction of the systems used for storage.

You must analyze the potential dangers from such natural disasters and plan to reduce their impact when possible. Let's look at our fictitious building in a warehouse district again. After analysis, we discover that the area our building is in is prone to flooding in the spring. Protecting our servers from physical damage should now include plans to keep computers, electronic equipment, wiring closets, and other similar devices out of the basement and lower floors. If planned and deployed correctly, proper placement of the equipment should cost the company little money upfront and yet provide significant protection from possible loss of data due to flooding.

Location, as shown in the previous paragraphs, can influence security decisions and the deployment of security measures. Another variable that comes into play in the environment of security is the material of the building itself.

Building Materials

When evaluating the environment for security purposes, its important to look at the actual construction materials used throughout the building. The three most common materials that will influence you are

- Concrete
- Wood
- Steel

Concrete requires some special attention, particularly if you work in a facility you do not own. Most leases can accommodate the needs of the business if the property is rented, but be sure to get permission prior to altering the structure for the sake of security. Concrete poses several unique problems as well as providing some significant benefits when planning and deploying a security layout.

Concrete represents a formidable physical barrier. It is difficult to penetrate without special tools, thus assuring the company of controlled access. If properly constructed, concrete walls can also inhibit electrical signals, making it difficult for a would-be information thief to use special equipment designed to eavesdrop on passive electrical signals (see the next section, "Shielding"). Using concrete as the primary construction material also has an added benefit of being resistant to fire, flooding, and wind damage.

A significant drawback to using or dealing with concrete as the primary construction material is that altering the layout is difficult after it is in place. Special tools are required to drill through concrete for running wires, setting doors, placing windows, and wall mounting special equipment. Moving walls after they're poured is impossible without destroying the existing wall and building a new one. Wireless technologies (covered in more detail later in this chapter) are difficult to use in concrete buildings because of the thickness of the walls and the use of iron or steel reinforcement bars (rebar).

Wood, as a construction material, is easier to work with and is, by far, the most popular construction material for inside walls and partitions in modern office buildings and corporate facilities. It offers the freedom to reconstruct and remove walls fairly easily and inexpensively. However, wood offers far less protection from the elements when used for outside walls. It will suffer greater damage from fire and water should the building catch fire or be flooded. Interior wood walls are often covered with sheet rock or drywall and offer only modest protection from eavesdropping equipment and brute-force entry.

Steel is rarely used as a standalone material. Typically, it is combined with both wood and concrete to provide greater strength and load bearing capabilities in larger buildings. The most likely use of steel is as I-beam floor and ceiling supports. Steel poses a more significant problem than even concrete does when used as a construction material. Steel beams can often interfere with cabling runs as well as wireless technologies. As with concrete, special equipment must be brought in when trying to drill through steel beams, and moving a steel beam to accommodate a security change is impossible.

To overcome some of the presented problems, companies commonly use a combination of all three building materials. The exterior walls of a building are often made of concrete with a reinforced grid of steel I-beams. In addition, steel and concrete beams are used in strategic load-bearing areas in the interior to ensure the building is safe and can withstand the necessary loads. Wood walls are used to further split the interior space into smaller more manageable areas. Figure 7.7 shows the basic layout of a single floor.

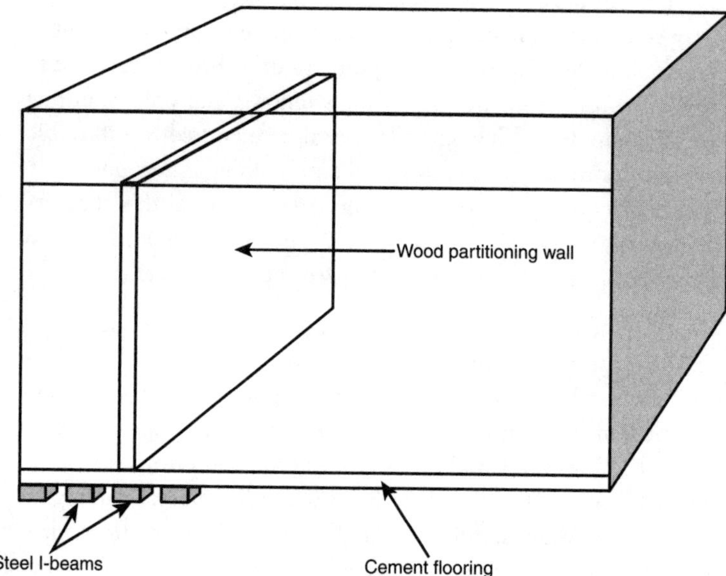

FIGURE 7.7
Single floor layout.

Besides interior walls, drop ceilings are used for a greater amount of flexibility when running needed resources such as water pipes, electrical wiring, and data cables. A word of caution is warranted here. Several security risks are posed by using the space between the drop ceiling and the floor above (called the *plenum space*). An intruder or thief can use the area to gain access to your network data cables, to sabotage electrical current to a vital area, or as an access method (see Figure 7.8).

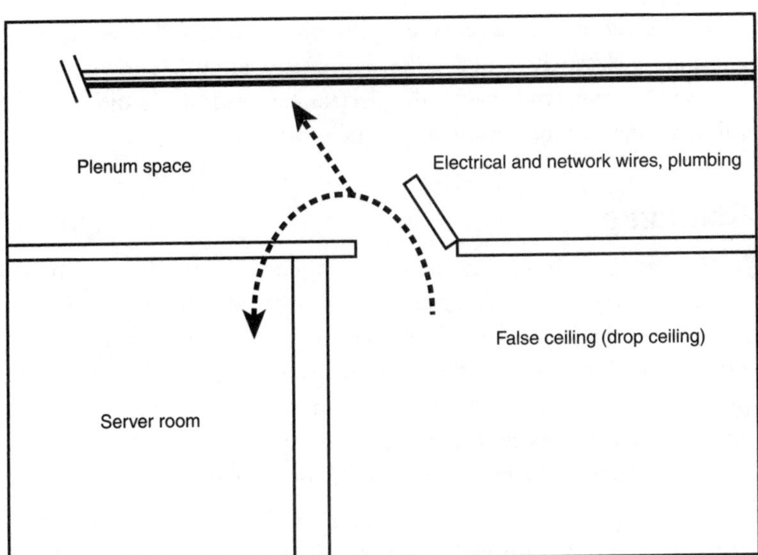

FIGURE 7.8
Access through plenum space.

Protection can be provided in these areas by using metal conduit (metal tubing), motion sensors, and wire cages (see Figure 7.9).

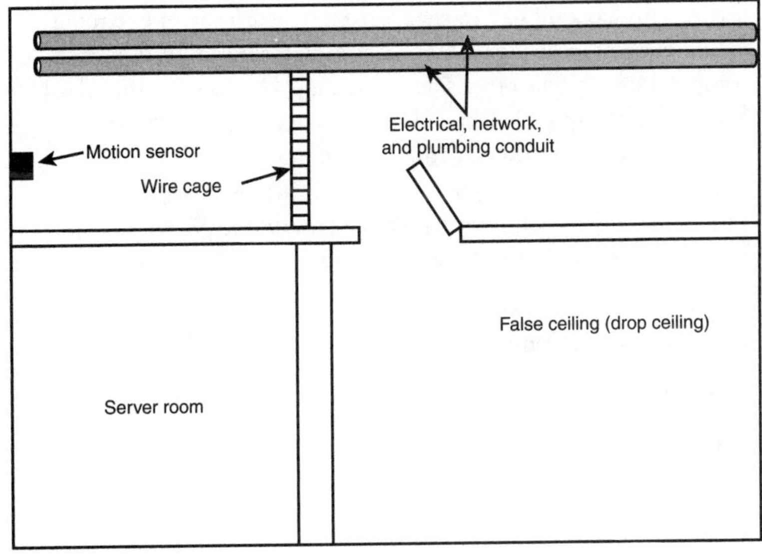

FIGURE 7.9
Protecting data centers with wire cages.

Going deeper into the discussion of environment includes a look at controlling electricity—not in the classic sense of outlets and circuit breakers but from the view of the electronic eavesdropper and shielding that can be used to block such forms of intrusion.

Shielding

When dealing with security and discussing the business or work environment, every possible risk must be evaluated. One risk that can often be overlooked is that of electronic emissions or emanations. Electrical equipment generally gives off electrical signals. Monitors, printers, fax machines, and even keyboards use electricity. What if you could create a receiver that could pick up leftover electronic signals? These signals are said to leak, bleed, or emanate from common computer and electronic equipment. If you have ever set a computer monitor close to a TV screen and been able to see computer output on the TV, you have a basic idea of what we are talking about.

Shielding seeks to reduce this unwanted output from computers and related equipment. The shielding can be local to the device or encompass an entire room or building depending on the perceived threat. This has a bit of a movie feel to it, where a spy in one room with a piece of receiving equipment is monitoring an unsuspecting computer user on the other side of the wall. The user is losing classified or secret corporate data without even realizing that the loss is occurring. Although this is admittedly an unusual form of theft (called *electronic eavesdropping*), it has been proven a viable method, and a billion-dollar industry has grown around the practice of shielding equipment so that such loss has a minimal chance of occurring.

To give you a better idea of what's available in the area of shielding, we're going to concentrate on two specific types:

- TEMPEST
- Faraday Cage

TEMPEST

TEMPEST is thought to be a code word developed by the U.S. government in the 1950s. It can also be an acronym built from **T**ransient **E**lectro**M**agnetic **P**ulse **E**manation **ST**andard.

Most documentation on the Web and public documents published by the government point to TEMPEST as a simple code word used to describe standards and methods implemented to limit or block electromagnetic emanation (radiation) from electronic equipment.

TEMPEST has, over the years, grown in its definition to include the study of the process of electromagnetic emanation (EME) as well as the standards used to control it. TEMPEST can also be used to describe equipment that has been protected based on the standards, which can lend a bit of confusion to any discussion. Much of the TEMPEST standard remains classified, but sufficient information exists in the public domain to allow for a good understanding of the standards as well as the practice of protecting electronic equipment.

TEMPEST equipment includes the following:

- Computers (in this case, the actual CPU/motherboard)
- Hard drives
- Monitors
- Fax systems
- Scanners
- Keyboards
- Mice

These individual pieces of equipment are protected through extra shielding that helps prevent electrical signals emanating from the cords used to carry electronic signals or the devices themselves (as in the case of a computer monitor). This extra shielding is thought to be a metallic sheath surrounding connection wires for mouse, keyboard, and video monitor connectors or can be a completely shielded case for the motherboard, CPU, hard drive, and video display system. This protection should prevent the transfer of signals through the air or nearby conductors such as copper pipes, electrical wires, phone wires, and other similar materials.

You are likely to find TEMPEST equipment in government, military, and corporate environments that process government/military classified information. Some large private corporations that work with the government or develop new and highly valuable products also might use TEMPEST-protected equipment. Several government directives require agencies and corporations to protect the government information processed at their respective facilities from EME eavesdropping.

Because of these government directives, a few companies have specialized in the manufacture, conversion, installation, and maintenance of equipment designed to meet the TEMPEST standards. Even with these companies, the cost associated with deploying TEMPEST-based network equipment is still very high and cost prohibitive for most companies. The real threat of electronic eavesdropping is not well known because of the shroud of government classification. Numerous Web-based articles imply that information was stolen this way during the cold war and government self-inspections have been successful at stealing information in this manner, so the possibility must be assumed real.

It will probably make better sense to protect an area within a building rather than protecting individual pieces of equipment. An alternative to (or maybe in conjunction with) TEMPEST is the idea of isolating a small section of a building or, in extreme cases, the entire building itself with a protective shield that will counter attempts to steal data by electronic eavesdropping methods.

Faraday Cages

A more efficient way to protect a large quantity of equipment from electronic eavesdropping is to place the equipment into a well-grounded metal box. This configuration is referred to as a Faraday cage. The box can be small enough for a cell phone or can encompass an entire building. The Faraday cage is named after its inventor, Dr. Michael Faraday. The original idea behind the cage was to protect its contents from electromagnetic fields. The basic configuration of a Faraday cage is shown in Figure 7.10.

The cage involves surrounding an object or objects with interconnected and well-grounded metal. Initial cages were solid metal, but additional research found that a wire mesh would do as well. Each of the six sides of the box must be properly connected to allow current to flow freely and easily from any point to ground. The metal used today is typically a copper mesh that is attached to the walls and covered with plaster, drywall, or another cosmetically pleasing finish. The wire mesh acts as a net for stray electric signals either inside or outside the box. When looking at a flow from outside to inside, the metal conducts these stray signals to ground and prevents them from interfering with equipment inside. When looking at the flow of electricity from inside to outside, the Faraday cage prevents EME from being captured and processed.

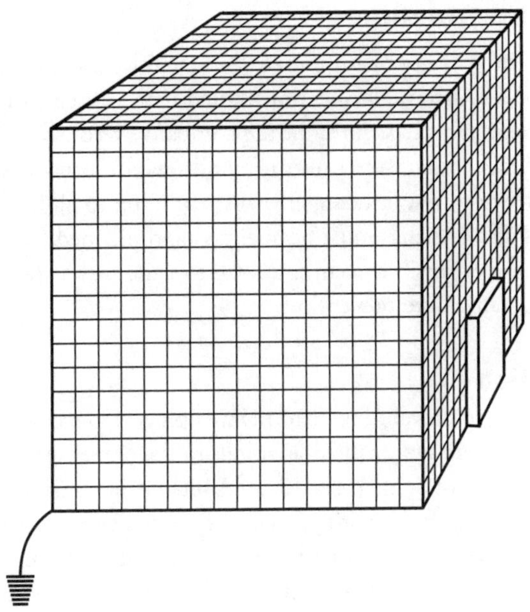

FIGURE 7.10
Configuration of a Faraday Cage.

Protecting a room is probably the most feasible for non-government and non-military businesses. It is possible, however, to protect an entire building by using the outside walls as the basis for the Faraday cage. Unconfirmed documents and articles speculate that some overseas U.S. embassies are protected in this way. The process is the same as protecting a room, simply deployed on a larger scale. In some cases, the iron rebar used in the outside walls can provide some level of protection. It is important to remember that the metal mesh must be completely interconnected and well grounded to achieve the best protection.

If you use the rebar, it must be welded together or tied tightly with wire at all the overlaps to achieve the desired result. One notable problem with using rebar as the mesh is the size of the holes or spacing. If the spacing is large enough, the cage will allow EMEs to leak out of the protected area, negating the desired result.

Getting the rebar close enough together can increase the cost of the building so much that covering the walls with copper mesh is more feasible and more protective. A modification of the Faraday concept includes the basic wire mesh concept but with the added feature of a low voltage current applied to the system to generate electronic white noise. This electric charge produces an output similar in frequency to the equipment being protected and makes distinguishing true data signals from the generated noise nearly impossible.

WARNING

Well-Grounded Doesn't Mean Grounded Multiple Times A lack of understanding at a client's site led a building contractor to ground each of the four corners of a building. This behavior was completely counter to the term *well grounded*. During a summer storm, the ground was soaked with rain. When lightning struck nearby, the four grounding rods created an effective circuit and conducted the lightning into the building. The result was severe damage to the building's electrical equipment, including the computer systems that were supposed to be protected from such an event. Well grounded implies a clear and defined *single* path from the mesh of the Faraday cage to the ground outside.

Fire Suppression

The physical security of equipment and facilities must include a discussion on fire safety. This section started with a discussion of the environment and the security of the company's resources. Not all environments contain the threat of floods, wind, tornadoes, or hurricanes. Fire, however, is a danger that is common to all business environments and one that must be analyzed and planned for well in advance of any possible occurrence. One of the first steps in a fire safety program is fire prevention.

Prevention

The best way to prevent fires is to train employees to recognize dangerous situations and report these situations to the proper internal department immediately. Some basic examples include recognizing odd odors, identifying faulty wiring, incorrect use or placement of heating systems, and so on. Correct response training is also critical when a fire is actually discovered. Knowing where a fire extinguisher is and how to use it can stop a small fire from becoming a major catastrophe.

Additional prevention techniques take us back to the beginning of the chapter and our discussions of electronic detection mechanisms. Many of the newer motion and ultrasonic detection systems used for physical security also include heat and smoke detection systems used for fire prevention. After they're installed, these systems alert the monitoring station of smoke or a rapid increase in temperature. Because people are not in all parts of the facility all of the time and because human response time can be delayed, not all prevention techniques will work. If a fire does break out somewhere within the facility, a proper fire suppression system can avert major damage.

> WARNING
>
> **Adhere to the Laws** Keep in mind that, as we discuss these systems, numerous federal, state, county, and city laws and ordinances can apply to the deployment and monitoring of a fire suppression system. It is your responsibility to ensure that these codes are properly met or exceeded whenever possible.

Wet-Pipe Sprinkler System

Fire requires three main components to exist: heat, oxygen, and fuel. Take away any one of these three components and the fire goes out. A common way to fight fire is with water. Using water attempts to take away two of the required components: oxygen and heat.

A wet-pipe fire suppression system is probably the one that most people think of when discussing an indoor sprinkler system. The term *wet* is used to describe the state of the pipe during static operations (no fire). The pipe in the wet-pipe system has water under pressure in it at all times. The system is built out of a grid of pipe material, which can be made of copper, plastic, or another approved composite.

The pipes are interconnected and have sprinkler heads attached at regularly spaced intervals. These systems function primarily on heat, not smoke.

If a fire breaks out in a protected section, the temperature rises rapidly in an area located directly below the fire. The sprinkler system can be activated in several ways, but the four most common are as follows:

- Mechanical fusible links
- Electric thermal detectors
- Flame detectors (UV or IR)
- Heat strips

In a system with fusible links, the sprinkler heads have a stopper held in place with tin solder or some other bonding agent that is designed to melt at an appropriate temperature. The activation temperature range can vary from a low of 130° to a high of 175° Fahrenheit. After the stopper melts, it opens the head valve and allows water to flow from the sprinkler head and hopefully extinguish the fire below.

Electric thermal detectors, flame detectors, and heat strips are also based on a response to the rapid rise in temperature. However, they control the activation of the system electronically (instead of mechanically).

As we discuss sprinkler systems, keep in mind that electronic equipment and water don't get along very well. Remember, though, that you are trying to protect the building and its contents. Fires that start outside electrical areas (such as your server room) are well served by water-based sprinkler systems. Also keep in mind that all these systems should have both manual activation and manual shutoff capabilities. If a mistake has been made or a situation is under control, you want the capability to turn off a sprinkler system to prevent potential water damage. (Some of the systems are rated to pump out 80 gallons per minute through each active sprinkler head.)

A common misconception about sprinkler systems is that after a single valve is opened, all the valves in the system begin discharging water (or chemicals). This is not true. Most systems are designed to activate only one head at a time. This works effectively to put out fires in the early stages. Several manufacturers' Web sites claim a common statistic stating that, in a fire situation, an average of only four valves (sprinkler heads) is activated before the fire is out.

Dry-Pipe Sprinkler System

Dry-pipe systems work in exactly the same fashion as wet-pipe systems with one exception: The pipes are filled with pressurized air instead of water. The stoppers work on the same principle listed previously with a temperature threshold. When the stopper melts, the air pressure is released and a special valve in the system opens to allow water to flow into the pipes and extinguish the fire.

You might want to leave the pipes empty of water for a few reasons. The first and most common reason is that the pipes are in an area of the building that is unheated and susceptible to freezing (such as a storage warehouse). The pipes also might be along an outside wall as part of a refit on an older building. If the outside temperature drops below freezing in such a situation, it is important to have a dry-pipe system. The last reason for justifying a dry-pipe system is the delay associated between the system activation and the actual water deployment. Enough of a delay occurs that it is feasible for someone to manually deactivate the system before water starts to flow. Although this sounds counter to the desired result of putting out the fire, this might be necessary for one good reason: Some laws require a sprinkler system even in areas of the building that house electrical equipment. In such a case, companies can deploy a dry-pipe system and a chemical system together (see the following section). The delay in the dry-pipe can be used to deploy the chemical system first and avoid serious damage to the running equipment from a water-based sprinkler system.

Chemical Systems

Chemical systems can be wet or dry and are generally credited with the capability to put out fires more quickly than straight water-based systems. Unlike water, a chemical-based suppression system tries to separate the fuel from the oxygen. This is achieved by coating the fuel or rapidly depleting the available oxygen supply in the area around the fuel. Chemical systems have the added benefit of being capable of putting out fires involving many types of fuel, including wood, oil, metals, fabric, chemical, and electrical. Dry chemical systems are commonly used in areas in which electrical equipment is in use because they are less likely to ruin the equipment they've been deployed to protect. The activation of chemical systems is the same as water-based systems.

REVIEW BREAK

- Social engineering is an easy, low-cost, and very effective method for an intruder to attempt to gain access to your facility.
- Employee training and awareness of social engineering techniques should help prevent such attacks or at least reduce their chance of success.
- Environment influences security and involves variables such as location, building materials, electronic shielding, and fire suppression systems.
- Shielding can encompass a small area of the building or include the entire building. Faraday cages, tempest equipment, and other precautions can be deployed to help protect equipment from electronic eavesdropping.
- Fire suppression systems are built around wet or dry pipe installations and wet or dry suppression materials (such as water or chemicals).

DISASTER RECOVERY AND DISASTER RECOVERY PLANS

Understand the basic security implications of disaster recovery.

What do you do when the worst happens? The answer to that question should be found in your disaster recovery plan (DRP). Your ultimate goal is to protect your facility and its equipment. If the worst happens and, despite your best efforts, the facility is damaged or destroyed, a well-designed plan can be the difference between staying in business and going down for the count. Modern business now relies on the computer for data storage and processing. In the 1980s computers were a nicety; today they're a necessity. The first step to creating a competent DRP is identifying the company's critical business flow and the resources associated with that flow.

Companies are generally in business to make money. Some, such as the military and government, are in business to serve.

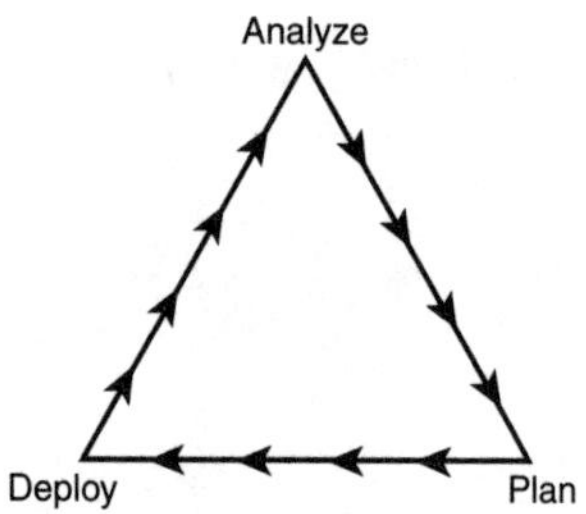

FIGURE 7.11
Disaster recovery planning process.

Regardless of which type of business you are in, the DRP process starts by examining the core product(s) supplied and the resources required to produce the product(s). This is the analysis stage. The other steps of the DRP process form the DRP triangle, as shown in Figure 7.11.

Analysis

Many approaches to analysis are available when trying to build a DRP. Numerous books and articles state that all possible disasters should be considered, including fire, flood, tornadoes, hurricanes, typhoons, and so on. However, this analysis should actually be accomplished during the analysis stage of physical security, as covered earlier in the chapter.

A better approach for true disaster recovery planning is one of a top-down view of the network. By looking at the network first as a whole and then as a collection of pieces, you can better evaluate what to do if certain pieces are rendered nonfunctional. The key understanding here is that, despite your preparations and best effort for physical security, a disaster has struck and rendered part or all of the network useless. Many times in DRP meetings, people lose sight of the big picture and immediately get lost in the details of how to recover phones, lights, specific computer systems, and so on. It is important to start with a general overview and then get input from each and every area of the company.

As many people as possible should be brought into this initial analysis stage. This is one process where more heads are better than one. Many of the department heads, as well as workers, will be able to point out potential problems because of their unique understanding of the flow of the business and the functions that surround and support it.

An example illustrates the analysis process. Let's assume you are a system and security administrator for a law firm. Here are some questions that would help you build a DRP:

- Which resources are required for immediate recovery in the event of a complete network loss?
- Do we need Internet connectivity to continue business operations?

- What data is required?
- Which equipment will need to be put in place for operations to be brought back online (switches, routers, servers, desktops, and so on)?
- Where will we get power in the event of a complete loss of city power?
- If the building and its contents are destroyed, where will we get replacement software?
- If the building is destroyed, what possible alternative locations can be used for business operations?
- How will clients be contacted and notified of the situation? Who is responsible for making contact?
- If only part of the building is rendered unusable (due to flood or fire), are there other parts of the building that can be used for temporary recovery?
- How and who will start the employee notification process in the event of a disaster?
- Which departments are dependent on each other to function properly?
- In what order should the recovery process take place? Should certain pieces be put together before others?
- What physical security will be available at a new location, or if still in the current building, will physical security be in place?
- If phones are out, how will clients and employees be able to contact the business?
- What is the estimated time to complete the steps in the DRP and get the business back online?

The list of questions could go on for many pages. The important thing to gain is an understanding of the process and the types of questions that should be part of the initial analysis process. A member from each department should make up the analysis team to create the most complete DRP. Note that the questions do not center around equipment exclusively. Your equipment needs people and power to run, and a business needs clients to stay in business.

The final step in analysis is to assign a monetary value to each section of the recovery process. This is required for proper budgeting and financial evaluation. If you spend $2 million to recover a business that's worth only $1.8 million, there is something wrong with the plan. The only way to discover such inconsistencies is to properly evaluate the expense associated with the DRP. After the analysis phase is complete, you can set budgets and goals and subsequently plan to meet those goals.

Planning

The analysis phase helps you discover specific resources required to get the business back on its feet and the doors open after a disaster has struck. The replacement or reconditioning of these resources should translate to specific goals for your company and its DRP. Some of this section is generic by design because each industry, company, and department has specific issues and needs that have to be met for recovery. However, some areas can be discussed that are common to most, if not all, businesses.

Facilities

It is important to clarify the distinction between protecting your systems from viruses, regular hardware failures, and the occasional network failure and a DRP. As part of a broad security plan, your computers, data, and networking equipment should be protected and updated as necessary with the latest software and hardware devices designed to do so. A DRP looks at much more catastrophic events and should address business issues in a completely different way than a standard security plan.

True disasters are uncommon compared to the more routine system, service, or electrical outages. When a real disaster does strike, it can be devastating. An example is hurricane Hugo. When it struck south Florida, it didn't just cause flood and wind damage; it leveled the town of Homestead and the surrounding area. Buildings were literally taken down to the cement foundation. Had the hurricane struck just a few miles further north, the metropolitan area of Miami would have suffered the same fate. Realistic disaster planning should include an action plan to relocate in the event that the entire facility is destroyed.

Several options exist to help the company relocate and get back to business:

- Hot site
- Warm site
- Cold site

Hot Site

A *hot site* is a site that is up and available 24/7. These sites allow the company to walk in, sit down, and continue normal business operations, usually within hours of the loss of a facility. These sites typically mirror the configuration of the main corporate facility, including software and available data and even using the same servers (down to the names of the systems).

The hot site should be located far enough from the facility being protected to avoid the disaster striking both facilities. There is a fine line when trying to determine how far is far enough. A hot site that is too far away might not be practical for employees to get to every day, and a facility that is too close can suffer the same damage as the protected facility.

Hot sites can either be set up and run by the company or be a prearranged contract between the company and a provider who specializes in the maintenance and delivery of emergency services. Regardless of the solution chosen, hot sites offer the advantage of a very quick return to business and the ability to test a DRP without affecting current operations. The major drawback to a hot site is the enormous cost associated with duplicating all or part of the company's current functionality.

Warm Site

A *warm site* is a scaled-down version of a hot site. The site, in this case, is generally configured with power, phone, network ports, and other base services. A warm site typically doesn't have computers and other specific resources because it is assumed that the company will bring its own or contract for these services through a third party on an as needed basis. This type of site is one of the more common for companies that need a fast turnaround after a disaster but can't afford the expense associated with a full hot site.

The advantage of the warm site is the considerable reduction of cost when compared to a hot site. Because the warm site is really just office space and or warehouse space, the site can serve multiple clients simultaneously. If exclusive use of the facility is required, a hot site is probably the best solution. Additional consideration must be given to the process of getting computers, data, and company specific resources to the site in the case of a disaster. This involves other service contracts with hardware vendors and telecommunications companies. Another drawback to a warm site can be a limitation on testing your company's DRP. Testing can be done, but a separate clause or agreement in the contract should specify when and how often a DRP test can take place.

Cold Site

A *cold site* is the weakest of the DRP options but also the cheapest. These sites are generally just a prearranged request to use facilities if necessary. The site can be a simple empty office or warehouse space with little else available or be configured in terms of business resources. Electricity, bathrooms, and space are about the only things guaranteed in a cold site contract. This is an optimum solution for companies that can't afford the other solutions. This might also be an optimum solution for a company with considerable expertise and access to redundant resources from other areas of the company, such as branch or regional offices.

> **EXAM TIP**
>
> Concentrate on the differences and similarities between hot, warm, and cold sites.

The configuration of the cold site is the sole responsibility of the company or contracted third party. A common approach is to take a few resources from each of a number of branch or regional offices to outfit the cold site and get it up and running in as short a time as possible. Cold sites are not an optimum choice when a fast turnaround to a functional site is required or desired because it can take several days (or even weeks) to get equipment in place and data restored to a necessary level for functionality. The cold site is a common option for a longer-term business continuity plan when facilities will be unavailable for an extended time (covered in detail later in the "Business Continuity" section of the chapter).

Equipment

As mentioned in the previous section on sites, a considerable worry just after a disaster from a business point of view is having equipment available for your users to use. Several solutions exist for procuring systems, including pulling from other sections of the company, purchasing new equipment off the shelf, or having a preexisting service agreement with a hardware vendor.

The possibility of replacing equipment must be considered even if a loss of facility has not occurred. Flood, fire, wind, and other partial disasters can rob you of functionality of parts of the network. Based on your analysis and plan, you should have an idea of which systems need to be replaced so you can return to business. Using the analysis, contracts can be put in place to ensure that these systems are available for deployment within an acceptable time frame.

The type and number of systems needed should be reviewed carefully. Some software and operating systems are particular about what hardware is required to run correctly. Systems backed up to tape on one type of machine might not properly restore to a different machine. This process should be completely debugged before it is ever needed to ensure a smooth transfer of capabilities.

Don't just look at computers in the case of equipment and your DRP. You will also likely need switches, routers, firewalls, phones, phone switches, and their configurations, too. A detailed configuration document should also be kept for each piece of equipment to aid in the recovery process.

High Availability

Some of your business functions and resources might not tolerate even small delays in availability. Assuming your company does $2.4 million a day on the Web, it would make sense to have your Web systems built with some considerable redundancy. The basic calculation to identify the cost of being offline would be as simple as dividing $2.4 million by 24 hours, which equals a flat cost of $100,000 per hour lost. This calculation doesn't take into account the loss of goodwill or the perceived loss of trust by the customers. Protecting that business and your client base would be well worth it. Other resources such as power and certain types of data (other than Web) can also require highly available configurations.

To achieve high availability, companies duplicate small sections of their networks at alternative locations. The resources duplicated can be entire servers, subsets of data on the servers, data warehouse files, and so on. This is similar to the behavior of a hot site but on a much smaller scale. Although this configuration can be deployed and managed completely under the control of the company, it can also be contracted out for an additional level of confidence and security.

Servers and their data can be duplicated offsite and then retrieved if a disaster hits, or users can simply be redirected to the backup location, making their data quickly available. Another means to make data available quickly is through backups.

Backups

Backups are the most common way that companies protect their data from loss. Backups can be accomplished in numerous ways:

- **Magnetic tapes (DLT/DAT)**—Using tapes is cheap and easy and can be automated.
- **Disk duplication or disk imaging**—Disk duplication can be done from one disk to another (mirroring) or accomplished through software that images the contents of the drive and builds a file that can be stored offsite. This is a slightly more involved process and can be partially automated.
- **CD-ROM burning**—This is the simple process of moving data from a hard drive to a write-once or write-many CD-ROM system. The basic process can be automated but is limited to a small volume of data (approximately 700MB of data).
- **DVD-ROM burning**—Similar to CD-ROMs, DVDs can hold anywhere from 4GB to 17GB of data. The process is the same as for CD-ROM burning.
- **Direct offsite/over the Web**—This is a newer option being explored by companies to give them the opportunity to have single-step offsite backups. Companies subscribe to a backup service and allow a third party to back up key servers and data. This can also be done within the company if the expertise exists.

No matter which way you choose to back up your data, back it up! You should ensure that you also have offsite copies of your backups to help you recover in case the entire facility (along with your onsite copies) is destroyed. Normal backups should include all data that is produced by your users and cannot be easily reproduced. You don't need to back up application files and operating system files with daily backups because they can easily be reinstalled if necessary from the original CD-ROMs or floppies. A complete discussion that would work for everyone and every situation is outside the scope of this book, but don't take that as a lack of emphasis. Backing up your data is one of the cornerstones to recovery—whether it is a single file or an entire data center in your company.

Backing up and restoring data is a serious security issue as well. If someone has the right to back up your data, that person could potentially take the tapes offsite and recover the data, removing file permissions as he did so. This would leave all data available for viewing. Some operating systems can help prevent this behavior by assigning permissions to the tapes, but a backup operator can easily overcome most of these protections. In some higher-security environments, backup and restore operations are completely separate functions assigned to different teams of people to help prevent this type of behavior. In very secure environments, two- or three-person teams are used during backup and restoration operations and the entire process is captured on camera so the temptation to remove data from the site is minimized.

Backups are required to help fulfill physical security and the protection of your data in case of a catastrophic event. However, backups also expose you to a security risk of losing the data if someone steals the tapes or copies the data on them. Minimize this risk by analyzing the situation and putting the appropriate measures in place. The second half of the backup process is your ability to restore the data. Normally, this is done onsite with the tapes or other media. There is, however, a newer option to recover data over the Web or through a recovery service.

Secure Recovery

Secure recovery services provide a large number of advantages to small- and medium-sized companies that need offsite storage and security and don't have the money or expertise to deploy these services in-house. Numerous companies provide offsite data backup and recovery, so it is up to you to do your homework and find one that suits your particular needs. Most companies tailor a package to match your requested schedule and needs. Look for some of the following options when dealing with offsite storage:

- 24/7 access to data
- Secure facility
- Bonded employees
- Monitored facility
- Automatic backup capability

- Reports for successful and failed backups
- Reports for successful and failed restores
- Secure backup and restore procedures

Anytime you consider outsourcing a part of your organization, make sure that the company has references and is willing to work with you on any issues. You should test the capabilities of the chosen provider and seek a trial period before signing a long-term contract for its services.

Utilities

Computers need power, and disasters can take it away from you. When creating a DRP, one of the most common resources lost is power. Your business might not even be hit by the tornado, flood, hurricane, or fire, but you can still suffer if knocked off the power grid. The most common way to overcome the power problem is to supply your own. We are not talking about intermittent power problems commonly solved by UPS devices. Here again, we are talking about a sustained loss of power lasting several days or weeks due to a natural or manmade disaster that could put your business in jeopardy if not resolved.

One way to supply your own power is through the use of a gas-powered generator. Generators come in many sizes and ratings, so time needs to be spent properly sizing the generator to your needs. The utility company can help you determine your current usage and inform you of the reason and length of the more recent outages. This information will help you determine the size of the generator and the amount of fuel that needs to be kept on hand in case an outage does occur. If the data and systems are deemed critical, an additional generator might be required to provide for full redundancy.

Scheduled testing should be done to ensure that the system is working properly and can supply the necessary power for the business to run efficiently and for the estimated duration of the outage. Most generators can be tied in to the existing electrical grid so that, if power is lost, the generator starts supplying power immediately. A good example of a business that requires this type of configuration is a hospital. Hospitals cannot afford to be without utilities for very long and typically have dual-generator systems to ensure that their business and clients are protected.

Vendor Support

Throughout this section of the chapter, we have discussed the replacement of equipment and services should a disaster strike your business. One way to help ensure that replacements are available is to sign agreements before the disaster occurs. These agreements are referred to as *service-level agreements.*

Service-Level Agreements

Service-level agreements (SLAs) are signed contracts between you and the vendors you commonly deal with. These contracts can be for services such as access to the Internet, backup, restore, or even hardware maintenance. The SLA can also help you guarantee the availability of computer parts or even entire computer systems if a disaster destroys your existing systems.

SLAs can be thought of as insurance against a particular event. It might seem expensive until the first time you need it. These agreements can vary widely between vendors and vary just as widely in their expense. Therefore, a comprehensive cost analysis should be conducted to ensure that the SLA is cost efficient and properly focused on the needs of the company. As an example, an SLA might require a vendor to supply your company with replacement servers within 36 hours if your current servers are destroyed (no matter what reason). This service costs you a predetermined amount of money. Also, an SLA usually lasts for a year but can be longer or shorter depending on your needs and the capabilities of the vendor.

Code Escrow

Companies today rely on software of all types to do business. Much of today's software is off-the-shelf and can be upgraded or replaced by simply purchasing a new copy of it from a vendor or retailer. But what if your company has invested $25,000 or $35,000 in a special software package or custom-built software program? For some large companies, it is not uncommon to spend hundreds of thousands of dollars having code developed. How can you protect your company if the software programming company goes out of business? What will you do if the programmers refuse to fix bad code?

Software companies rely on their programs to make money. These are seen as intellectual property, and they do not typically give the programs to others in raw language (called *source code*).

If they did, anyone could simply copy a program and redistribute it under a different title, in effect, stealing the intellectual property of the software company. This is where a problem arises: You need to protect your ability to get to the program code if the software company goes out of business or refuses to live up to stated contracts, and the software company needs to protect its intellectual property.

The solution to this is *code escrow*, which is similar to a SLA but pertains specifically to software. It is an agreement between the developers and the company to deposit code to a third party company, and this agreement should specify when the code can be released to the purchasing company. The agreement might state that if the software company goes out of business, refuses to update problematic code, or refuses further development of code, the purchasing company can have access to all the information in the code escrow library.

The information on deposit should include the program's source code and instructions that are specific enough that a competent programmer who's well versed in the programming language used (C, C++, Visual C, and so on) would be able to understand the code and its intended purpose. Setting up a code escrow protects both the software purchaser and the developer from unforeseen problems.

Deployment

We started this section by talking about disaster recovery and DRPs. The idea is to protect your company and its resources from the unforeseen. The final step in the process is deployment. After analysis is complete and planning has been accomplished, you should have a complete roadmap to deployment. This is typically the easiest phase if the first two steps have been done correctly.

Deployment will include signing contracts for

- Hot, warm, and cold site facilities
- SLAs for equipment
- SLAs for services such as backup and Internet access
- Code escrow

In your deployment plan, you should include periodic testing of the system and drills for employees to ensure they know their roles when the time comes. Make sure that your DRP is a work in progress. It should be constantly updated to reflect changes in the work environment and changes in the business and its needs.

Business Continuity

Understand the basic security implications of business continuity.

Whereas disaster recovery seeks to fix systems, utilities, facilities, and business functions in the short-term, business continuity plans extend the idea of the DRP to cover an undetermined amount of time. A common approach to developing a business continuity plan is to return to the DRP and ask, "What if we were offline for a year instead of a week or two?"

Each of the main areas of the DRP should be revisited and reevaluated for long-term issues and problems, and a time frame should be set for the transition from disaster recovery to business continuity. Even though the plans are similar, a separate business continuity statement or plan should be created and reanalyzed with the same frequency as the DRP.

EXAM TIP

Make sure you understand the differences between disaster recovery and business continuity, the key elements of both, and how each is used in an overall security plan.

CHAPTER SUMMARY

KEY TERMS

- Business continuity plan
- Cipher lock
- Code escrow
- Cold site
- Disaster recovery plan (DRP)
- Dry-pipe fire suppression
- Electromagnetic emanations (EME)
- Environment
- Faraday cage
- Hot site
- Mantrap
- Moat
- No-man's land
- Plenum
- Service level agreement (SLA)
- TEMPEST
- Warm site
- Wet-pipe fire suppression

We started this chapter by focusing on the physical protection of the facility and its resources. The methods discussed are summarized in Table 7.2.

TABLE 7.2

PHYSICAL BARRIERS

Barrier	*Description*
No-man's land	A wide expanse of clear, flat land that allows for easy view of anyone approaching the facility.
Fences	Fences can be made of a wide variety of materials, but they're all meant to do one thing: stop unwanted entry through nondesignated areas.
Water/Moat	This is useful as both a physical barrier and an eye-pleasing addition to the landscape. It's very effective at stopping entry by vehicle.
External lighting/cameras	Lighting and cameras let would-be thieves know you're serious about security.
External motion sensors	These devices can see and hear where humans can't. They provide a wide variety of capabilities, including sound, heat, light, infrared, and ultrasonic.
External doors/windows	These external access points into your building should be strong and imposing without making the facility look like a prison.
Mantraps	Used as an internal physical barrier, a mantrap consists of two doors that can be locked to capture an unwanted individual.
Internal motion sensors	These function like their outdoor counterparts but can be more sensitive and more reliable when properly deployed.
Locks	A wide range of locks exists to help you protect your facility both indoors and outdoors. Deploying the correct locks in the right situation can make all the difference.
Biometrics	Discussed first in Chapter 1, biometrics offer some of the most secure forms of entry on the market.

Chapter Summary

In addition to physical barriers, we also discussed the environment of the facility and its effects on physical security. Factors such as building materials, location, and fire protection mechanisms all play a significant role in how you handle the variables of physically protecting your data and the systems that store it.

The next section discussed what to do if your physical security is overcome by a disaster. Analysis, planning, and deployment are the essential steps to any good DRP. By properly analyzing your risks and the costs, you can better plan what to do when things go wrong. We identified common issues that affect each business, such as the following:

- Facilities
- Equipment
- High availability
- Backups
- Secure recovery
- Utilities
- Vendor support

We also discussed the fact that each business will have its own unique issues that need to be addressed in the company's DRP.

If the facilities of the company are wiped out on a long-term basis, a business continuity plan is the main document used for action and ongoing support of business objectives.

APPLY YOUR KNOWLEDGE

Exercises

Use the following exercises to practice the principles of physical security and disaster recovery.

7.1 The Marketing Firm

Estimated Time: 20 minutes

You are the network and security administrator for a marketing firm and have been asked to come up with a new security plan for a new downtown office—the company has just leased the first two floors of a new downtown location. Several executive offices will be on the ground floor and will occupy corner offices. Because of this, the company wants to ensure that data cannot be eavesdropped off of these computer systems.

Additionally, there have been several attempts in the past to steal the client database and other project information off company computer systems. Some of these attempts have come from employees, and one attempt to steal data came from an outsider who gained access to the facility. Access to these systems and certain areas of the building must be strictly controlled.

Use the following case study questions to apply the principles of security you have learned throughout the chapter:

1. Which type of security would you recommend for the executive offices on the first floor?
2. Which physical security configuration would be best deployed to prevent access to company servers and data systems?
3. What security can be implemented to prevent outsider access to the internal company offices?
4. Which external barriers could be put in place to prevent outside access to the windows at the ground-floor level?
5. Which consideration would most influence the type of security that is deployed for the marketing firm?

7.2 The Manufacturing Plant

Estimated Time: 20 minutes

Your team has just been hired to survey a site for the construction of a new manufacturing plant. The company will be working with the government and must have a secure facility to win the desired government contracts. Your job is to evaluate the site and make recommendations about physical security.

Access to the grounds must be strictly controlled, and entry into the facility should be based on an access methodology that is extremely difficult to compromise. The building must be protected from electronic monitoring and the grounds need to be monitored at all times.

Use the following case study questions to apply the principles of security you have learned throughout the chapter:

1. What type of security would you recommend for the grounds outside the facility?
2. What physical security configuration would the grounds need to be monitored at all times?
3. Which physical security access methodology would you deploy for gaining entry into the building?
4. Which security mechanism could be put in place to prevent electronic monitoring of the design building?
5. Which consideration would most influence the type of security that is deployed for the manufacturing firm?

APPLY YOUR KNOWLEDGE

Review Questions

1. List four types of physical barriers and describe each.
2. Which three access control methods can be used for physical access?
3. What are some features to look for when evaluating or purchasing locks?
4. What are some common social engineering attacks?
5. What is a Faraday cage and how does it work?
6. What is TEMPEST?
7. How does a dry-pipe fire sprinkler system work?
8. What are the three common types of sprinkler systems used in fire suppression?
9. What are the three types of sites used in disaster recovery, and how do they differ?
10. Which methods do companies use to guarantee certain levels of response and service during and after a disaster?

Exam Questions

1. Which of the following motion detector systems is best deployed inside a building?

    A. Ultrasonic

    B. Infrared

    C. Light

    D. Sound

2. Which of the following best describes a Faraday cage?

    A. A metal box or wire mesh that completely surrounds a device, room, or building. Well insulated from the ground, it blocks incoming and outgoing electronic signals.

    B. A metal box or wire mesh that completely surrounds a device, room, or building. It is well grounded and blocks transient incoming and outgoing electronic signals.

    C. A metal box or wire mesh that completely surrounds a device, room, or building. After each side is independently grounded, it blocks incoming and outgoing electronic signals.

    D. A metal box or wire mesh that partially surrounds a device, room, or building. It is well grounded and blocks transient incoming and outgoing electronic signals.

3. Which of the following best describes a hot site? (Choose two.)

    A. It needs setup time.

    B. Facilities might be shared with other companies.

    C. It's available 24/7.

    D. The company needs to bring its own equipment.

    E. The facility is completely preconfigured and ready to occupy.

4. Which of the following physical barriers would best stop a vehicle from approaching a facility? (Choose two.)

    A. A moat

    B. A clear area of land surrounding a building

APPLY YOUR KNOWLEDGE

C. A metal fence

D. Steel doors

E. Lights

F. Cameras

5. Which of the following is NOT true when discussing physical security?

   A. Physical security attempts to control unwanted access to specified areas of a building.

   B. Physical security attempts to control access to data from Internet users.

   C. Physical security attempts to control the impact of natural disasters on facilities and equipment.

   D. Physical security attempts to control internal employee access into secure areas.

6. Which of the following best describes a disaster recovery plan?

   A. A DRP reduces the impact of a flood on a facility.

   B. A DRP attempts to manage risks associated with theft of equipment.

   C. A DRP is a plan that sets up actions for long-term recovery after a disaster has hit.

   D. A DRP is an immediate action plan used to bring a business back online immediately after a disaster has struck.

7. Which phase of the disaster recovery plan process involves identifying critical systems and functions in the company?

   A. Analysis

   B. Planning

   C. Deployment

   D. Testing

8. What is TEMPEST?

   A. TEMPEST is a process of securing information on a local computer system.

   B. TEMPEST is a standard for identifying systems that are susceptible to electromagnetic interference.

   C. TEMPEST is a standard for identifying systems that have special protection from emanating electronic signals.

   D. TEMPEST is a method of protecting systems from electromagnetic emanations by enclosing them in a solid metal or metal mesh box.

9. What is the difference between a wet-pipe and a dry-pipe fire suppression system?

   A. A dry-pipe system uses dry chemicals.

   B. A wet-pipe system uses wet chemicals that deploy after the pipe loses air pressure.

   C. A dry-pipe system uses air to suppress fires.

   D. A wet-pipe system has water in the pipe at all times.

10. Which method is most commonly used by companies to protect data?

    A. Offsite, secure recovery

    B. Onsite backup

    C. High-availability systems

    D. Site redundancy

APPLY YOUR KNOWLEDGE

11. What is a service level agreement?

    A. A method by which a company can guarantee a level of service from another company.

    B. A method of procuring services after a disaster has struck.

    C. A method of protecting servers and computers from disasters.

    D. A method of protecting a facility from disasters.

12. Which of the following best describes a business continuity plan?

    A. A business continuity plan seeks to reduce the impact of a flood on a facility.

    B. A business continuity plan attempts to manage risks associated with theft of equipment.

    C. A business continuity plan is a plan that sets up actions for long-term recovery after a disaster has hit.

    D. A business continuity plan is an immediate action plan used to bring a business back online immediately after a disaster has struck.

13. Which of the following motion detector systems works by sending out high-frequency sound and responding to changes in the return pattern?

    A. Ultrasonic

    B. Infrared

    C. Light

    D. Sound

14. What is the best way to provide fault tolerance for utility power in the case of a disaster?

    A. Solar power

    B. Gas/diesel generator

    C. Windmill power

    D. UPS

15. Which of the following best describes a cold site? (Choose two.)

    A. It needs setup time.

    B. Facilities are not shared with other companies.

    C. It's available 24/7.

    D. The company needs to bring its own equipment.

    E. The facility is completely preconfigured and ready to occupy.

Answers to Exercises

7.1 Answers

1. Because this is a leased facility and it's already built, it's unlikely that a Faraday cage could be deployed properly. The best method for protecting the executive offices is to use TEMPEST type equipment. Although the sale of TEMPEST equipment is strictly controlled, there are similar alternatives for nongovernment entities.

2. The best configuration is to centralize the servers in a centrally located room in the company's occupied floors and set access methods so that only designated personnel can gain entry.

APPLY YOUR KNOWLEDGE

This could be done with swipe cards, cipher locks, or even biometrics if necessary.

3. An analysis of the prior attempts should be conducted. If social engineering was used, a training program should be implemented and deployed for employees to teach them how to avoid such attacks. If the attempt was made through standard entry methods, entry into the facility should be limited to the reception area and should include swipe card, cipher lock, or electronic lock access methods.

4. Because the building is not owned, the marketing firm would have to request physical barriers be put into place. Some options include a fountain or landscape architecture that prevents direct access to the executive office area outside the building. Fencing could be used, but it would be an obvious attempt to limit access and wouldn't be very aesthetically pleasing.

5. The fact that the marketing firm doesn't own the building or the any of the facility would be the one of the largest concerns with deployment of physical security measures.

7.2 Answers

1. Because the manufacturing firm desires strict control of entry into the grounds, owns the land, and is building a new facility, use of a no-man's land should be considered along with fencing. The system should restrict access to a single point of entry if possible.

2. Use of cameras would be best for the proper monitoring of the grounds.

3. Because the firm wants an access methodology that is extremely difficult to compromise, biometrics with a mantrap would be an excellent recommendation.

4. Because of the new construction, a Faraday cage should be deployed for the area of concern or for the whole building if it makes financial sense.

5. The manufacturing company not only owns the property, but also is building new. It will offer the greatest amount of influence for the security configuration.

Answers to Review Questions

1. Answers will vary; see the beginning of the chapter for a discussion on physical barriers and descriptions.

2. MAC, DAC, and RBAC.

3. Strength, cost, material, and aesthetic.

4. Talking, impersonation, observation, struggle, and holding/grabbing a door.

5. A Faraday cage is a solid or mesh metal box used to trap and ground stray electrical signals. The box completely surrounds the protected equipment and is well grounded to dissipate stray signals traveling to or from the cage.

6. TEMPEST is a government standard that describes methods implemented to limit or block electromagnetic emanation (radiation) from electronic equipment.

APPLY YOUR KNOWLEDGE

7. A dry-pipe sprinkler system works by filling the pipes with pressurized air. When triggered, the air pressure is released, opening a valve and filling the pipes with water. The system allows the pipes to be placed in areas that normally freeze.
8. Wet-pipe, dry-pipe, and chemical.
9. A hot site is available 24/7, expensive, already set up, and ready for immediate startup in case of a disaster. A warm site is available on short notice, can be shared with other companies, has most of the basic networking equipment, and typically has no computers. It's less expensive than a hot site. A cold site is the least expensive site; can take days to set up; and has only basic electricity, heating, and plumbing. All computers and other equipment must be supplied by the company.
10. Service level agreements or SLAs.

Answers to Exam Questions

1. **C.** Light-based sensors are best deployed inside a building. If deployed outside, they are ineffective during daylight hours.
2. **B.** A Faraday cage completely surrounds the protected area and is well grounded.
3. **C, E.** A hot site is best characterized by being immediately available 24/7 with no configuration necessary.
4. **A, C.** The only barriers listed that could actually hinder the approach of a vehicle are a moat and a fence. The others let you see the approach but not slow or stop it.
5. **B.** Preventing Internet users from getting to data is data security, not physical security.
6. **D.** A DRP is an immediate action plan to be implemented following a disaster.
7. **A.** The analysis phase is the correct phase for identifying critical resources and processes when developing a DRP.
8. **C.** TEMPEST describes methods and standards to protect and reduce electronic emanations from computers.
9. **D.** A wet-pipe system constantly has water in it. It is the only correct statement of the four listed.
10. **B.** Onsite backup is the most common way for companies to protect their data.
11. **A.** A service level agreement is a contract between two companies that guarantees service.
12. **C.** A business continuity plan looks at the long-term actions taken by a company after the disaster has taken place.
13. **A.** Ultrasonic systems work on ultra-high sound waves.
14. **B.** The most reliable backup for utility power is a gas/diesel generator. Although wind and sun could supply backup power, they rely on natural conditions. UPS systems are for short interruptions in power.
15. **A, D.** The best description of a cold site is one that has only basic electricity, plumbing, and heating resources. The rest must be brought in and set up, requiring time and equipment.

Apply Your Knowledge

Suggested Readings and Resources

Online Material

1. Davis, Warren, Ph.D. "How Does a Faraday Cage Work" (`http://www.physlink.com`).
2. Department of Defense Trusted Computer System Evaluation Criteria (`http://www.radium.ncsc.mil`).
3. McNamera, Joel. "The Complete, Unofficial TEMPEST Homepage" (`http://www.eskimo.com/~joelm/tempest.html`).
4. "Modern Protection: Elemental Faraday Cage" (`http://www.boltlightningprotection.com`).
5. Nelson, Michael. "Fire Suppression in Historic Places of Worship" (`http://www.sacredplaces.org`).
6. Pawliw, Borys. "TEMPEST" (`http://whatis.techtarget.com`).

Publications

1. Fennelly, Lawrence J. *Effective Physical Security.* Burlington, MA: Butterworth-Heinemann, 1996.
2. Garcia, Mary Lynn. *Design and Evaluation of Physical Protection Systems.* Burlington, MA: Butterworth-Heinemann, 2001.
3. Harris, Shon. *All in One CISSP Certification Exam Guide.* New York: McGraw-Hill Publishing, 2002.

OBJECTIVES

Understand the basic security concepts and use of security policy and procedures.

- Much of what information system security deals with is avoiding security incidents and recovering fully when incidents do occur. These activities are only possible as a result of the required planning for developing and implementing a comprehensive security policy. This objective covers the areas a security policy addresses and the procedures necessary for implementation.

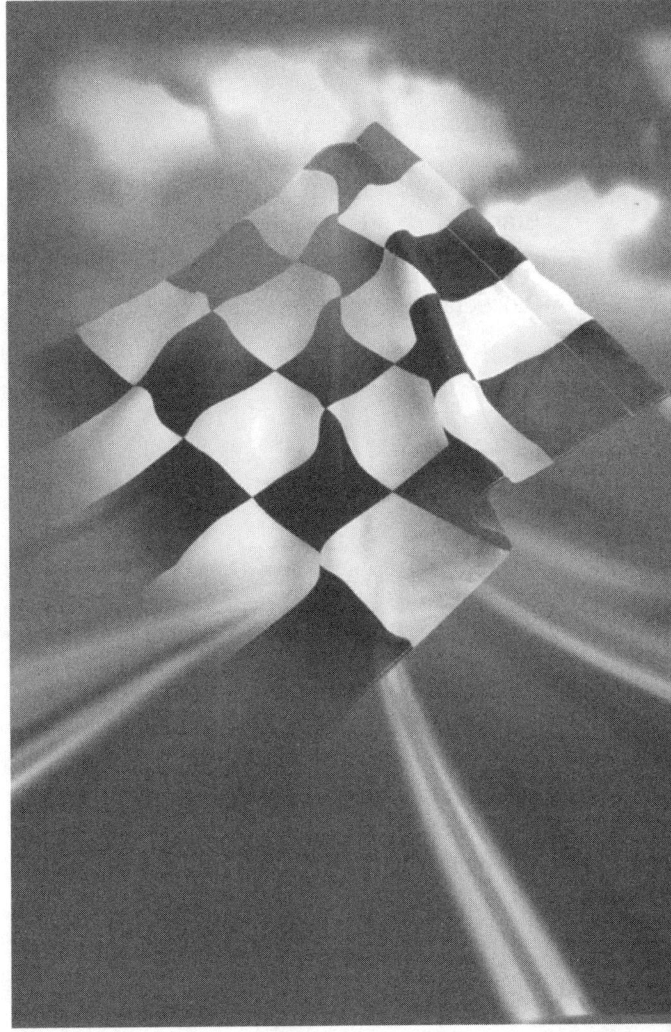

CHAPTER 8

Security Policy and Procedures

OUTLINE

STUDY STRATEGIES

- A solid security policy is the most important topic to consider when studying information system security. It directs all other discussions. Be sure you know the purpose and general content of a security policy.
- Understand the differences between policies, standards, guidelines, and procedures. Understand the need for each.
- Although a strong security policy should protect an organization from intrusions, no organization is immune. Understand the process of identifying and reacting to an intrusion.

INTRODUCTION

This chapter discusses the structure of a complete security policy. Although all security policies are different, they all share several central themes. In this chapter, we discuss which common areas a security policy should cover. We also cover industry- and organization-specific areas. As you study the material in this chapter, remember that a security policy is a set of proposals designed to ensure a secure operational environment. These proposals vary from friendly suggestions to mandatory rules you must follow, most of which are the latter. It is more important for you to understand the security policy concepts and their applicability to an organization than it is for you to memorize a list of policy components.

Consider any type of organization. Think about the many ways the security of your chosen organization could be compromised. Then consider how you would write a set of recommendations to ensure protection from each of the possible vulnerabilities you envision. Can you envision all possible vulnerabilities? From whom else should you solicit input? To whom is each section of the security policy targeted? This is the nature of security policy development.

The difficulties in creating a successful security policy are plentiful but not impossible to overcome. A good security policy has many contributors and at least as many target audiences. So, what constitutes good? The answer is simple: A good security policy is one that satisfies your security needs. Although it appears that this answer does not help at all, it really helps organize the security policy development effort. You must start with a vision of your mission instead of starting the process by listing restrictions you think will protect the system. Carefully identify the security goals, and then identify the procedures and controls necessary to reach the stated goals.

In short, a *security policy* is a set of instructions on how to conduct business and interact with an information system while maintaining an acceptable level of security. The acceptable level of security is expressed in terms of confidentiality, integrity, and availability. After you identify what a secure system is to your organization, you can establish rules to get you there.

Before we move into the material and discuss the security policy details in earnest, be aware there is another, equally important, reason for a security policy. Although a security policy sets forth rules to ensure a secure information system, it provides another type of security through its existence. Investors, board members, officers, employees, regulatory personnel, legal personnel, and scores of other people associated with an organization place a great deal of weight on the security policy. The quality of the policy indicates how sophisticated an organization is as well as how well it can deal with security threats. A well thought-out security policy can provide intangible value to an organization and help remove some fears of future security liabilities by providing accountability.

Creating a solid security policy is a difficult task but one that can provide a substantial reward. You do not have to suffer a catastrophic intrusion to prove the value of your security policy. The process to create the policy will have certainly decreased the organization's overall vulnerability and increased its ability to react to events when they do occur. In addition, the security policy can provide the assurance that the organization has done its homework and is acting as a proper custodian of its assets.

> **EXAM TIP**
>
> **Policies** As you study for the Security+ exam, focus on the general content of a sound policy, not the specific details.

An acceptable guideline for security policy development is the Generally Accepted System Security Principles (GASSP) created by the International Information Security Foundation $(ISC)^2$. GASSP represents the consensus of committee members in the areas of security principles, practices, and opinions. This project provides an excellent overview of what a sound security principle should contain.

You need to understand the following terms to discuss security policy development. There is a lot of confusion between the following terms, so be sure you understand the definition of each one and how it differs from the other terms:

- **Policy**—A broad statement of views and position. A policy states high-level intent with respect to a specific area. It generally includes both statements of expected performance and consequences of noncompliance. Policies are made compulsory and reinforced by standards, guidelines, and procedures.
- **Standards**—These are usually best practices for specific platforms, implementations, operating system versions, and so on. Standards are usually mandatory and provide for uniform application of a technology across an organization.

- **Guidelines**—These are different from standards in that they are generally not mandatory and provide specific details on how standards should be implemented. Guidelines are more flexible than standards that allow for variations in specific applications, when necessary.
- **Procedures**—These specify how the policies shall be put into practice in an environment. Procedures provide the steps required to carry out policy elements. Whereas policies state the intent, procedures provide the how-to instructions.

EXAM TIP

Differences Know the differences between policies, standards, guidelines, and procedures and what each is.

The terms previously defined are frequently used to refer to documents that are included in a security policy. For the purpose of discussion in this chapter, let us take a closer look at each term.

Policies

So, what is in a security policy? A *policy* details certain rules and requirements that must be followed in an organization. Regarding information and network security, policies usually cover a single area. An *acceptable use* policy, for example, explains how to appropriately use computing facilities. Other policies cover various business units, providing a high-level outline of conditions you must meet to consider your area secure.

Standard

A *standard* describes requirements that must be met by everyone. These standards are generally specific to a system or procedure. Standards provide the first level of details on how you will achieve the goals set forth in a policy. For example, your security policy might contain a standard that documents how to handle files that contain sensitive information. The standard would outline the specific goals you must meet when storing and transferring such files, instead of listing each step in the process.

Two fairly new InfoSec standards are gaining widespread acceptance. ISO 17799 and its predecessor, BS 7799, are both standards that define best practices in InfoSec. The earlier standard, BS 7799, was first published by the British Standards Institution in 1995.

An updated and expanded version of BS 7799 was submitted to ISO for development as an international standard in 2000. ISO published the new standard, ISO 17799, in December 2000.

Guidelines

A *guideline* contains system-specific or procedural-specific suggestions for how to best accomplish a task. Guidelines are not requirements, but they should be followed. Guidelines often exist to streamline the implementation of security policy elements. Also, they are specific to a narrow set of circumstances and can be modified when necessary—with the proper approval. An example of a guideline is the installed software and services list when setting up a workstation. Although the basic list of software installed on a machine and services enabled should be largely the same across an organization, variations can exist based on individual needs.

Procedures

The last, and most specific, component of a security policy is the collection of procedures. A *procedure* is simply a list of steps that satisfy the desired guideline or standard. Although procedures are an integral part of a security policy structure, the actual procedure documents are often separate from the main policy documents. It is also common for procedure documents to be maintained by a different group from the policy documents. A procedure provides the step-by-step instructions on how to achieve a specific goal set forth in a higher level of the policy. For example, a policy element might state the need for secondary copies of data to be used for recovery, and the standard that supports such a policy might require that data be backed up on a periodic basis. The guideline would indicate the desired media, frequency, and storage method. And, finally, the procedure would outline the specific commands and hardware to use, along with physical labeling and handling of the backup media.

Security Policy

Understand the basic security concepts and use of security policy and procedures.

The Gartner Group expects that negligence suits and regulatory penalties that target careless security practices will begin to proliferate in the United States as early as 2003. The potential liability for organizations due to insufficient security precautions cannot currently be appreciated. The only way to protect your organization from such litigation is to plan ahead.

The CSI/FBI Computer Crime and Security Survey of March 2001, places the average loss per organization from security breaches at $2,031,337, with 186 organizations reporting $377,828,700 in financial losses. These organizations represented a cross section of industries and security planning capabilities. Even though the majority of the reporting organizations had security precautions in place, none were sufficient to completely protect the organizations from intrusions.

The management of an organization has an ethical and legal responsibility to provide security for all assets of that organization. The data stored in information systems is just as vital to many organizations as physical assets. In many cases, in today's organizations, the data is more valuable than any physical asset! It is imperative for an organization to ensure the availability, integrity, and confidentiality of information.

These three characteristics of secure data are often collectively referred to as the *security triad*. The three components of the security triad include

- **Confidentiality**—Ensures information is not intentionally or unintentionally disclosed
- **Integrity**—Protects from unauthorized modifications to data
- **Availability**—Ensures any needed data is available when it is needed

EXAM TIP

Security Triad Know the three components of the security triad.

An organization needs a vehicle to communicate its desires and methods to provide for each of the critical areas addressed in the security triad. This communication vehicle normally takes the form of a document, or collection of documents, called the *security policy*. The audience for the security policy is broad. This high-level policy statement speaks to employees, investors, legal personnel, auditors, regulatory agencies, and the media. It collectively states, "This is how we intend to protect ourselves."

All communication requires three components:

- **Sender**—The sender is the party who originates the message. It is the responsibility of the sender to initiate and set the tone of the communication process.
- **Message**—The message is the content and format the sender chooses to use to communicate with the receiver.
- **Receiver**—The receiver is the party who receives the message from the sender. The success of the communication process is entirely in the hands of the receiver. The impact of a message is at the discretion of the receiver.

So, when developing a security policy, you must ensure that the good intentions of the policy are accepted and embraced. Remember that a great security policy that everyone ignores is not really a great security policy. The first step in developing an effective security policy is to carefully select the sender(s) of the policy's message. The policy should come from someone in the company whose authority is respected. If the policy comes from someone who is not well-recognized in the company, it might not be taken seriously. The selection of an appropriate sender is important to the successful communication of the security policy's message.

WARNING

Management Support Without management support, you will quickly realize that your policy can't be enforced.

It is imperative that you have the full support of upper management in the security policy. When your organization's upper-level managers give their full support to the security policy, its contents automatically have more impact on both internal and external receivers of the policy. The first step in creating a sound security policy is to organize a policy committee with as many high-level managers and executives as possible. You will find many benefits to this strategy, and you'll find that having success without it is very difficult.

The second component of the security policy is the *message*, or actual content. As you develop your policy, consult policy samples and incorporate the parts that fit your organization. Many professional associations offer assistance in creating policies specific to your industry. Pay particular attention to the audience of each section of your policy. You will certainly write differently for the human resources section than for the new hire informational section. Ensure the message is targeted to the intended group and is pertinent. The easiest way to lose someone is to embed an important message in a mass of irrelevant information. Several content areas are covered in this chapter. Your security policy elements will differ from the list we provide because our presentation covers the most common and generic topics. Yours should be specific to address the security concerns of your organization.

The last component to consider in the development of your security policy document is the receiver. As stated in the previous discussion of the content of the message, the intended recipient is important when creating the message. Remember that the impact of any message is based on the interpretation of the receiver. Although the sender has a large responsibility in the creation of the message, the receiver's interpretation determines the message's level of success. Always remember that your security policy causes more work for nearly everyone involved, so it is imperative the affected people clearly understand the need for such a policy. This is where the involvement of upper-level management makes all the difference.

The next several sections look at the various parts of a security policy. These are the most common and generic areas the majority of security policies address. Your security policy will overlap with some of these areas, but it will certainly contain more content to address the specific needs of your organization. The sections of a security policy that we cover are

- Acceptable use
- Due care
- Privacy
- Separation of duties
- Need to know

- Password management
- SLA
- Disposal/destruction
- HR Policy

Acceptable Use

An acceptable use policy is one that defines proper use of an information system and the data it contains. You must specify what use is acceptable to an organization to inform users of your expectations. One of the most common responses when a user is confronted with a security violation is, "I didn't know that was against the rules." A sound acceptable use policy defines specific actions that are permitted and those that are not permitted.

After you create this policy, you must communicate its contents to existing, and new, end users. One common way to do this is through an access agreement with logon banner reminders. The reason for such perpetual reminders is twofold. First, you want to ensure users do not forget that they are being held responsible for their use of the organization's information system. Second, you might need to justify your level of preparation when confronted with a damaging intrusion.

EXAM TIP

Acceptable Use Policy Know what an acceptable use policy is.

Business Liability

Every organization bears some responsibility for the behavior of its employees. An acceptable use policy helps set limits to the organization's responsibility by defining actions that are prohibited. The extent to which an organization is held responsible for its employees' behavior is generally referred to as a *business liability.*

The responsibility of every organization is to conduct its business affairs in a manner that complies with all applicable laws and regulations. Further, the organization is responsible for ensuring its employees comply with these laws and regulations—failure to properly ensure compliance can result in substantial legal liabilities.

For example, suppose an employee of XYZ Corporation downloads a game from the Internet that contains a virus, which infects many computers in the organization and causes large losses of productivity and data.

The organization's response is to immediately fire the individual who downloaded the infected game. In response, the employee's union files a lawsuit against the organization for dismissal without sufficient grounds. The basis of the lawsuit is that there is no formal policy stating that downloading a game from the Internet constitutes unacceptable use of an information system. In this case, the lack of an acceptable use policy can open an organization to substantial liability.

The bottom line here for security is that some policies and steps, if followed, protect the organization from this type of liability. Due care, best practices, and awareness education are crucial steps necessary to protect against such liability issues.

Due Care

Due care is the knowledge and actions that a reasonably prudent person would possess or act on. An organization can be found negligent in its duties if it is shown to have failed to take common and necessary precautions to avoid a security threat. Likewise, an organization can be found negligent if actions taken by the organization contribute to an environment that allows a security threat to be realized. In either case, a court could find a lack of due care. One of the most compelling reasons to develop a security policy is to demonstrate due care in a formally documented policy. Your security policy, in this case, becomes your organization's best defense.

IN THE FIELD

DUE CARE

Our current legal environment has, in recent years, witnessed a dramatic increase in lawsuits citing due care, or actually, a lack thereof. In a recent high-profile case, a CIO lost his job, was charged with a felony, and was sentenced to jail time plus 250 hours of community service. All this occurred despite the fact that the CIO knew nothing about the crime—even the prosecution admitted the CIO didn't know about the embezzlement. The CIO did not commit the crime but was held accountable because the courts felt he should have known about it. Both criminal and civil laws are holding executives personally liable for events that occur during their service.

EXAM TIP

Due Care Know that due care is the knowledge and actions that a reasonably prudent person would possess or act on. Also know that a business exercises due care when it implements policies and procedures to protect its data, equipment, and customers.

An aggressive security policy, developed with intensive involvement of all levels of management, can provide the best deterrent to litigation involving "what you should or should not have done." Your security policy states your commitment to security and your plan for protecting your organization from threats.

Privacy

Privacy is a large concern in a security policy. Many laws exist in various countries that protect against the intentional or unintentional disclosure of private data. Your security policy must specify how your organization operates within applicable laws and regulations to ensure data privacy. At the same time, an organization needs to retain enough access to hardware and data to implement security procedures. Access to hardware and data can be necessary to conduct appropriate analysis to avoid security violations and conduct investigations into violations when they do occur.

A sound security policy should contain a privacy policy that defines the expectations of privacy with respect to issues such as monitoring of email, logging of keystrokes, and access to users' files. This statement of intent can be implemented as logon banners, periodic email notifications, and general security awareness training. The frequent notifications of your privacy policies provide advance warnings to internal and external computer users as to your organization's view of its data. You also need to notify users that any online activity can be viewed and will likely be reviewed from time to time to maintain the standards of the security policy.

Privacy alert messages can take many forms, but you should tell the end users the following:

- All online use is subject to examination.
- Acceptable use of this information system can be found at: (give location of acceptable use policy).
- There is no guarantee of privacy, unless specifically supported by data classification.

Users expect a measure of privacy that protects many of their interactions with information systems from disclosure, even to their employers.

For example, many users expect that private files and the contents of email messages are protected from disclosure, but this might not always be the case. Use your privacy policy alert messages to educate users on your policies.

Some organizations, such as those working with medical records, routinely handle sensitive data. In such organizations, privacy is a serious concern. The U.S. Congress passed the Health Insurance Portability and Accountability Act (HIPAA) of 1996 to require organizations with access to medical records to ensure personal privacy. Any organization that handles personal medical records must address HIPAA requirements in its security policy. This is one of many examples where legislation dictates security policy contents. Be aware of all the laws and regulations that govern your organization when developing your security policy.

Separation of Duties

Having access to too much power can lead to corruption. For this reason, most governments and other organizations implement some manner of a balance of power mechanism. In most organizations, this balance can be achieved through a separation of duties. The idea of separation of duties is based on the likelihood of multiple people conspiring to corrupt an information system being far less likely than a single person doing so. If a process can result in a security breach, divide the process among two or more people. Then, to violate the security controls of a system, all the participants of the process would have to agree to compromise the system. You should attempt to avoid having only one individual who has complete control or knowledge of a business process or transaction from inception to completion.

You can create a separation of duties policy in many ways. Here are three ways you can implement variations of the separation of duties principle:

- **Cross training**—Protects the organization by providing at least two people who can perform each task. This enhances security by removing the possibility that one person holds the sole ability to perform any task. It also increases the likelihood that a disaster could be successfully managed with multiple people trained for each task.

- **Job rotation**—Another way to ensure that one person does not abuse power. By moving each person from one job responsibility to another, you can contain the exposure for any one individual to a situation that could lead to security violations.
- **Mandatory vacations**—Removing a person from an environment for a specified period of time allows auditors time to examine the activities of an individual. This examination could be routine or specific in nature, based on suspicion of inappropriate activity.

A common guideline used in many organizations to implement a separation of duties is the strategy of least privilege. The *least privilege* principle states that an individual should be assigned only enough privilege to accomplish an assigned task, but no more. Adherence to this principle helps ensure no individual exceeds her intended authorization. Implementing the least privilege principle can be quite tedious for administrators; one way to lighten the load is to use groups and roles. A user is assigned to a specific security group based on the role she assumes, and each security group is then granted the minimal privilege to perform tasks associated with that role.

Need to Know

Another element of your security policy is the implementation of a *need to know* policy. This policy outlines the manner in which a user is associated with only the necessary information system resources she needs to perform her duties. The usual implementation of a need-to-know scenario is through the use of specific user IDs. Each person must have a unique ID and password to access any secure system. The privileges associated with each ID restrict activities based on job duties, responsibilities, and other business requirements.

Keep in mind that in general use, anonymous IDs are prohibited from logging in to systems or networks. Avoid all but the most necessary scenarios utilizing such anonymous IDs. However, exceptions to this stipulation do exist and must be part of your security policies and procedures. To make the exception process easier to implement, your security policy should also contain the procedures to add exceptions to the policy. Most major organizations now have an exception committee that meets to approve exceptions.

Most exceptions to a security policy are of a short duration and confined to a limited function. To ensure exceptions do not compromise the overall security of the system, additional controls are commonly implemented to limit the use of the stated exception.

Password Management

One of the most important areas of your security policy addresses *password management.* Your policy must clearly state that individuals are personally responsible for the usage of their IDs and passwords. They must choose passwords that are difficult to guess but easy to remember. You must educate users about the following common password pitfalls:

- **Do not use personal information**—Never choose a password based on your birth date, Social Security number, telephone number, or any other personal information.
- **Do not create passwords that are too easy to guess**—Short words or common acronyms are easy to crack and provide very little security.
- **Do not create passwords that are too hard to remember**—Very long or hard-to-remember passwords tempt users to write down the password and keep it handy. You would be surprised how many passwords are written on sticky notes and stuck on monitors or under keyboards. Intruders are aware, though.
- **Never store passwords in an unsecure location**—Continuing the previous point, never store a password in a location to which anyone but the user has access.

Also, as a general rule, longer passwords are more secure. For example, a password that is nine characters long and alphanumeric, with more than one special character in a string, currently can take three years to crack, whereas a password of only six characters takes less than 30 hours (based on a rate of 40,000 different attempts per second). Of course, as mentioned, passwords that are longer than users can remember can actually be less secure than shorter passwords because they tend to get written down. Pay attention to users' use of password cheats. A long password posted next to the keyboard has little real security value.

Password Rules

Classic password rules tell us passwords that are both easy to remember and hard to crack are good starting points. You also want a password that is acceptable to the end user. To make guessing more difficult, passwords should also be at least seven characters. Also, to ensure that a compromised password is not misused on a long-term basis, passwords should be changed every 35 days. When a staff member suspects that her password has become known to another person, the password must be immediately changed. You should also disable passwords of people who have left the company or were let go.

Table 8.1 provides a model that is easy for end users to understand and helps to build a win-win atmosphere between security personnel and end users. When a help desk or other technical support strategy is in place, you can use more stringent controls. Without a help desk, strict controls can result in too many access denials and raise end-user frustration.

TABLE 8.1

EFFECTIVE PASSWORD POLICIES FOR END USERS

Policy	*With the Help Desk*	*Without the Help Desk*
Maximum password at each (days)	Next logon	30
Minimum password age (days)	7	3
Minimum password length (characters)	7	7
Password uniqueness	12 cycles	6 cycles
Lockout	Yes	Yes
Number of bad attempts allowed	3	10
Duration of lockout	Permanent	30 minutes

This table is only a suggestion; you will need to tailor the suggestions for your own systems.

The following are some simple rules you should always keep in mind and educate your users on regarding passwords:

- Passwords must never be shared.
- Passwords should not be written in an unsecured manner.

- Passwords should be at least seven characters in length.
- Passwords should contain a combination of alphabetic, numeric, and special characters.
- Dictionary words should be avoided.
- Passwords should not be trivial, predictable, or obvious.
- Passwords such as secret, password, sex, computer, days of the week, months, names of persons, pet names, relatives names, cities, streets, ID, birth dates, car license plates, and so on should not be used.

Securing Removable Media with Disposal and Destruction

Information system procedures commonly use removable storage media. From time to time, you might need to remove media from use. After media has been removed from use, the media must be sanitized to remove all data from the media and prevent disclosure from retired media. Several methods of sanitizing data are available, the most common of which are *disposal* and *destruction.*

Disposal

Media *disposal* generally uses media-specific methods to remove all traces of the original data without disabling the media from storing new data. You can dispose of old data by overwriting the original data with specific characters and by degaussing.

Overwriting the data can remove traces of the original data if the file is overwritten multiple times. Many security practitioners use seven overwrites of standard character strings to cleanse a file. Remember that you also need to cleanse your free space to completely remove the data stored in a file.

Degaussing media simply uses a process of powerful magnets to remove the magnetic traces of data. Of course, this only works with magnetic media, such as floppy disks and hard disk drives.

Destruction

The other common alternative is *destruction.* Destroying media can also be used to remove data. If the media is totally destroyed, the data on the volume is also lost. Make sure you completely destroy the media if you use this option—it is surprising how much data can be retrieved from improperly destroyed media.

> EXAM TIP
>
> **Shredding Tips** You should use cross cut shredders or a service that comes to your office and shreds everything right there. Be sure to supervise the shredding company to ensure that all the papers are destroyed properly.

Before we leave the topic of disposal and destruction, remember that media on which you store data can be nonmagnetic or optical. In other words, paper is the most common media used to store information. Although you can dispose of the writing on paper by erasing it, the most popular method is destruction, and the most common method of paper destruction is shredding.

HR Policy

A security policy would be incomplete without a strong human resources policy section. This section of the security policy specifies how personnel should be handled with respect to system security. A human resources policy can be very detailed, but it generally covers the life of personnel from a prospective employee to the post-employment stage. Each step in the process has different security concerns. The human resources policy addresses each of the issues and states how security is maintained throughout the process.

Employee Termination Security Policy

Security has a special role as it relates to human resources through the security triad. All facets of the security policy must ensure the confidentiality, integrity, and availability of data.

Terminations can place undue risks on the organization, ranging from disgruntled individuals to a wide range of vulnerabilities. The terminated person, or others, might take advantage of the fact that the ID/access rights are still valid. An organization incurs the liability if there is no policy (and procedure to ensure it is followed) that specifically covers the removal of access for terminated persons.

Ensure the termination procedures are up-to-date and structured to address any security vulnerabilities before an attack can occur.

As soon as a person is terminated, all access to your information systems must immediately be revoked. Immediate revocation protects your system from grudge attacks and from other attackers piggybacking on the terminated person's user ID. This crucial part of a sound security policy is often overlooked, so pay attention to the termination policy.

Hiring and Security Policy

It is important to establish a known and accepted security policy that is to be implemented each time new staff is hired. Adherence to the policy ensures each new employee meets the organization's hiring standards. Most organizations have the Human Resources Department handle security-related tasks, such as

- Background checks
- References follow-up
- Educational record verification
- Ensuring staff signs employment agreements, nondisclosure agreements, security policies, and specific business ethics and usage agreements

These same organizations also typically have designated security personnel who handle setting up items such as ID management, access rights to buildings and physical grounds, remote devices (hardware and software), and necessary access to business systems. Larger organizations generally have multiple security departments that specialize in different types of security concerns. For example, access to business systems might be handled by the IT security department and physical access to buildings and grounds might be left to conventional security officers. Smaller businesses, however, might place all these responsibilities on one department. This ensures quarterly (or whatever the policy states) review by managers that their staff needs the access currently granted.

Code of Ethics

Another element that provides an overall set of basic rules for an employee's period of employment with a company or a group member's period of membership is the *code of ethics*.

Although most of the other policy sections are specific to a topic or functional area, a code of ethics serves to provide a cohesive set of general behavior rules under which the entire security policy operates. *Ethics* are rules that govern personal behavior, and a formal list of ethics that is adopted by a group of individuals or organizations is called a *code of ethics.*

Most professional organizations publish codes of ethics for their membership. Mandatory adherence to an organization's code of ethics is becoming a common condition of membership. Incorporating one or more codes of ethics as compulsory sections of your security policy demonstrates your organization's commitment to the overall security strategy. It also provides anyone associated with your organization an overall picture of your security vision.

An example of a code of ethics associated with a group membership can be seen in the security world. To be a member of the International Information Systems Security Certification Consortium, Inc.—(ISC)^2—formal acceptance of the code of ethics is required. It is a simple code with a preamble and four canons.

The (ISC)^2 code of ethics preamble is as follows: "Safety of the commonwealth, duty to our principals, and to each other requires that we adhere, and be seen to adhere, to the highest ethical standards of behavior. Therefore, strict adherence to this code is a condition of certification."

The code of ethics canons are as follows (as quoted by the (ISC)^2):

- Protect society, the commonwealth, and the infrastructure.
- Act honorably, honestly, justly, responsibly, and legally.
- Provide diligent and competent service to principals.
- Advance and protect the profession.

The (ISC)^2 code of ethics is only one example of a formal code of ethics. Contact any professional and trade organizations applicable to your organization for more information. You might choose to incorporate one or more of their codes of ethics into your security policy, or you could develop your own. Remember, though, that the code of ethics statements say a lot about your overall commitment to behavior standards, so ensure your code of ethics reflects your organization.

The next step is to ensure your organization reflects your code of ethics. After you have a solid code developed, frequent education is necessary to get the word out to your organization's personnel. More aggressive security education campaigns generally result in fewer security enforcement actions.

Incident Response Policy

The leading reason incidents are never reported is that many incidents are never recognized. Your incident response policy must begin with a definition of an incident and the criteria for identifying when one has occurred. The general definition of an *incident* is any violation, or threatened violation, of your security policy. Because every security policy is different, each organization has a different set of events it considers incidents.

For example, say company ABC prohibits any Internet access, whereas company DEF allows its employees to use the Internet for commerce transactions and research. Would checking the current news headlines be an incident? Well, without further input from the acceptable use policy, you could determine that it would be an incident from ABC's point of view. The policy states that Internet use is prohibited, and that policy was violated.

Because the definition of an incident depends on the interpretation of the rest of the security policy, it often helps to specifically identify the most important incidents in the policy. Your incident response policy should first define general incidents and then identify specific incidents that require the most attention. These would be incidents that indicate current, or impending, attacks. The purpose of identifying such incidents is to provide instructions on how to recognize and deal with each incident type.

The nature of an incident is that it puts your information system at risk. Here are some examples of what some organizations would consider incidents:

- You discover a virus in a file on your computer. Most security policies would require you to report the presence of a virus to stop it from spreading and to find out how it was introduced into the system.

- Customers report that your Web site is unavailable. Initial investigation reveals your organization's Web server is the victim of a denial-of-service (DoS) attack. Again, reporting this incident is important to both remove the problem and learn how to keep it from happening again.
- You notice a yellow sticky note on your manager's monitor with her passwords written on it. Whether this is just a bad security practice or a policy violation depends on how your security policy is written. If your policy allows you to disclose passwords, it is not very secure. However, you should report this incident for several reasons. First, passwords that are displayed in the open represent a tangible weakness to a system. This practice often means the password policy is too stringent. Either the passwords can be required to be so complex or changed so often that they are hard to remember. The security team should investigate why this incident occurred.

After you have identified an incident, you must decide whether to report the incident, to whom to report it, and how to report it. Some laws or agency regulations require incident reporting in certain circumstances. For example, any incident that threatens national security or involves hazardous materials must be reported to the appropriate authorities or agencies. Know your local laws and regulatory agency requirements in this area. Although reporting procedures vary for different environments and incident types, here is a general list of information you need to collect for your report:

- What is the nature of the incident?
- When was the incident detected?
- When did the incident actually occur?
- How was the incident detected?
- How was the incident initiated?
- What vulnerability was exploited?
- What type of information was the compromised system processing (classified or unclassified)?
- What service did the system provide (DNS, key asset servers, firewall, VPN gateways, IDS)?
- What level of access did the intruder gain?
- What hacking tools or techniques were used?

- What did the intruder delete, modify, or steal?
- Which unauthorized data collection programs, such as sniffers, were installed?
- What was the impact of the attack?
- Which preventative measures have been (are being) implemented?
- What is the responsible party's identification? (It's usually an IP address[es] or a hostname[s].)
- Does the compromise involve a country on the DOE Sensitive Country List?

Responding to an incident requires investigative skills. To do a good job, you must collect pertinent evidence and preserve the evidence for later use. Evidence is any hardware, software, or data you can use to prove the identity and actions of an intruder. The topic of evidence gathering and handling is the subject of many books. Do not underestimate the importance of understanding the needs of law enforcement and the court system when collecting evidence. If you are unsure, contact your local law enforcement agency for assistance.

It is of paramount importance that you preserve and protect any and all evidence you collect. The only way you can ensure evidence will be admissible in court is to properly handle it. This starts with your collection methods. After you have permission to collect evidence, you must ensure the evidence is preserved in an unaltered state. You must also document the location and custodian of the evidence from the moment it is collected. This documentation of the collection, storage, and custodian of evidence is called the *chain of custody*. The chain of custody can help show, in a court of law, that your evidence was handled in a proper fashion. (See Chapter 9, "Security Management," for more information on chain of custody.)

Your published security policy is the first place an attorney will look to see what your organization says about handling evidence. For a court to accept evidence, you must show that you followed your security policy by ensuring the following:

- All hardware, software, and data was obtained legally.
- All captured data was authenticated and proven to be unchanged.
- The chain of custody was maintained.

The best way to find evidence of an incident is to ensure the intruder leaves it for you, and one of the best places to collect evidence is from log files. You must ensure your systems are logging all pertinent activity and the log files are protected. The fact that log files can be so valuable when collecting evidence is not a secret to intruders. The more sophisticated intruders will undoubtedly attempt to cleanse the log files to cover their tracks. Most systems allow log files to be stored on remote systems. Logging activity can be sent to a central log server for storage, which is one tactic you can use to make log cleansing more difficult for an intruder. Remote log cleansing means attackers must successfully compromise at least two systems to cover their tracks. Know your system, and know its vulnerabilities and the current hacker tactics. Do your homework prior to an incident, and the investigation process might just yield the evidence you need.

Put as much information as possible about the incident reporting and investigation process into your security policy. The amount of planning you do up front can make the difference between a successful prosecution and a intruder who is never identified.

CASE STUDY: TIMBER NETWORK, INC.

ESSENCE OF THE CASE

Here are the essential elements in this case:

- Identify the members of the security policy development committee.
- Identify each element of the security policy necessary for this organization.
- Incorporate any legal or regulatory requirements applicable to this industry.
- Establish strategies for security policy approval, implementation, and maintenance.
- Implement the security policy.

SCENARIO

Timber Network, Inc., is a provider of secure business-to-business communication services focusing on the timber industry. Timber Network's clients use its services to conduct business electronically, cutting down paperwork and delays in order processing. The generic interface enables many providers and consumers to pass transaction messages to and from each other without the requirement that each vendor support all other interface types.

Case Study: Timber Network, Inc.

Timber Network's security staff is developing an updated security policy to address potential concerns related to the growth of the business and integration of federally regulated transactions. The Environmental Protection Agency (EPA) regulates transactions involving federally protected timber and requires standards of operation and reporting. Instead of modifying the existing policy, Timber Network has decided to create a new security policy to address all the current business needs.

Consider the elements Timber Network should address as it develops a security strategy.

ANALYSIS

The most important step in creating a security policy is to establish a policy committee that includes as many representatives from management and organization executives as possible. The only way a policy will have sufficient momentum to be effective is through the support from the top of an organization. After the policy team is selected, it will meet to decide on the major elements of the security policy. Timber Network decides to create a simple policy consisting of the following sections:

- Acceptable use policy
- Privacy policy
- Separation of duties policy
- Password policy
- Human resource policy
- Incident response policy
- Regulatory compliance policy
- Code of ethics
- Implementation and maintenance policy

Policy owners are assigned for each element of the policy, and each owner develops a section. For example, the Security Director develops the password policy and incident response policy. After the initial drafts are completed, the policy team reviews and amends the policies until the policy is adopted. After all policies are adopted, the overall security policy is published and the implementation phase begins.

Remember that the development of a security policy is an iterative process in which standards, guidelines, and procedures are also included in each element.

CHAPTER SUMMARY

KEY TERMS

- Availability
- Chain of custody
- Code of ethics
- Confidentiality
- Due care
- Evidence
- Guideline
- Incident
- Integrity
- Message
- Policy
- Procedure
- Receiver
- Sender
- Standard

In this chapter, we discussed the importance of a strong, cohesive security policy from a competitive business perspective and from the legal realities organizations find themselves dealing with in today's marketplace. The best first defense from security violations and related problems is a strong security policy. It documents the organization's vision and preparation in addressing various security threats.

A good security policy is really a collection of smaller, targeted policies. Each element of the overall security policy addresses concerns in a specific area. The following policy areas were covered in this chapter:

- Acceptable use policy
- Due care policy
- Privacy policy
- Separation of duties policy
- Need to know policy
- Disposal/destruction policy
- Human resource policy

Each policy area is usually developed with input from a representative of the affected department or group. In addition to high-level policies, the overall security policy is made up of standards, guidelines, and procedures. Each step in this progression specifies an increasingly detailed and specific list of steps to take to implement a security policy.

We finished the chapter with a discussion of incident response and reporting. The main purpose of a security policy is to avoid security violations through planning. However, we acknowledge that violations do occur, so another important function of a security policy is to indicate how to recognize and respond to violations. Together, these functions provide a heightened state of security readiness for an organization.

APPLY YOUR KNOWLEDGE

Exercises

8.1 Choosing Appropriate Security Policy Elements

In this exercise, you develop an awareness of the types of policies required for your own organization.

Estimated Time: 15 minutes

Think about the major operational groups of your organization. Create a short list of each of the groups (divisions, departments, and so on) that would need a specific security policy. One group we discussed in this chapter was the human resources group. See if you can identify any others.

Create a list of each group and the major features of a policy each might need when developing a comprehensive security policy. Remember, this is an exercise. It is not necessary for your list to be exhaustive. The point of the exercise is to begin the process of thinking about security needs from a high level.

8.2 Developing a Hiring Policy

In this exercise, you develop one of the policies discussed in the chapter. When a new employee is hired, certain tasks must be completed to ensure the overall security of your system.

Estimated Time: 10 minutes

Create a list of items that must be completed for each new employee. You can express this list as a set of guidelines (high-level tasks) or as a procedure (specific steps to take). Think of everything a new employee must have and know to access appropriate parts of your information system. Do not forget about any necessary training!

Review Questions

1. What is a security policy, and how does it affect the security of an organization?
2. Which element of a security policy (policies, guidelines, procedures, or standards) is the most detailed?
3. What are three methods used to implement separation of duties?
4. Are long passwords more secure than short passwords?
5. What is an incident?

Exam Questions

1. Who is responsible for security in an organization? (Choose the best answer.)

   A. Executives

   B. Everyone

   C. Management

   D. Staff

   E. Consultants

2. Which is the best definition of a procedure?

   A. Protection for unauthorized access

   B. Legally binding rules

   C. Step-by-step instructions

   D. Foundation for policies

   E. Shop standards

APPLY YOUR KNOWLEDGE

3. What is the leading reason many incidents are never reported? (Choose the best answer.)

   A. They result in less than $5,000 damage.

   B. They do not break laws or regulations.

   C. Many incidents are not identified.

   D. The reporting process is too tedious.

   E. No stringent punishment exists for failure to report.

4. Which might not ensure evidence will be admissible?

   A. Chain of custody

   B. Published security policy

   C. Separation of duties

   D. Authentication of captured data

5. Which of the following is usually considered the best method to keep a user from using current authorization to perform tasks outside his approved tasks? (Choose two.)

   A. Three factor identification

   B. Chain of custody

   C. Antivirus protection

   D. Role-based access

   E. Least privilege

6. Which of the following best describes due care?

   A. The knowledge and actions that satisfy all facets of your security policy

   B. The knowledge and actions that fulfill all facets of your security policy and all applicable laws and regulations

   C. The knowledge and actions that a reasonably prudent person would possess or act on

   D. The knowledge and actions that fulfill all chain of custody requirements

7. Which of the following would reduce the strength of a password? (Choose all that apply.)

   A. The password is too long.

   B. Change your password every 30 days.

   C. Use your birthday for your password.

   D. Change your password every 3 days.

8. What is the most important reason to secure backup media from disclosure?

   A. It is easy to intercept backed-up data as it is being dumped to a tape.

   B. Backup file formats are easy to read.

   C. Backup media are easy-to-carry copies of potentially sensitive data.

   D. Backup media can easily be damaged.

Answers to Review Questions

1. A security policy is a high-level document, or collection of documents, that provides instructions on how to conduct business and interact with an information system while maintaining an acceptable level of security. It provides a blueprint for implementing security and instructions on how to respond to security intrusions when they occur.

2. A procedure is the most detailed element of a security policy. A procedure is a step-by-step guide of how to implement a guideline, standard, or policy.

APPLY YOUR KNOWLEDGE

3. Three methods to implement separation of duties are
   - Cross-training
   - Job rotation
   - Mandatory vacations
4. Longer passwords are generally more secure than shorter passwords, until the passwords become so long that users start writing them down in obvious places.
5. An incident is any violation, or threatened violation, of your security policy.

Answers to Exam Questions

1. **B.** Although all answers are partially correct, the best answer is everyone because a chain is only as strong as its weakest link.
2. **C.** The answer is step-by-step instructions. The other answers address unrelated topics.
3. **C.** Many incidents are not identified as violations to the security policy. Although the other answers might indicate why a specific incident was not reported, the most common reason is lack of recognition.
4. **C.** The best answer is separation of duties. The others might play a part in admissibility, but generally this does not.
5. **D, E.** Role-based access and least privilege keep valid users from exceeding their authority. The other answers deal with stopping invalid users from accessing the system or stopping malicious code.
6. **C.** Answers A and B define the security goals but do not describe due care. Answer D addresses due care only as it relates to evidence.
7. **A, C, D.** Answers A and C would result in passwords that might be easy to guess. Answer D would require password changes so frequently that the users might resort to writing down copies of the passwords in an unsecure location.
8. **C.** A backup is a copy of part, or all, of your system that an intruder can carry to another system. Answer A is incorrect because intercepting backup data is possible but not generally easy. Answer B is incorrect because most backups have encryption options, making interpretation difficult. Answer D does not address disclosure. It addresses availability.

APPLY YOUR KNOWLEDGE

Suggested Readings and Resources

Publications

1. Amoroso, Edward G. *Fundamentals of Computer Security Technology*. Upper Saddle River, NJ: Prentice Hall, 1994.
2. Department of Defense. *Department of Defense Trusted Computer System Evaluation Criteria.* Darby, PA: Diane Publishing Co., 1985.
3. Krause, Micki and Harold F. Tipton, eds. *Information Security Management Handbook, Fourth Edition Volume I.* Boca Raton, FL: Auerbach Publications, 1999.
4. Smith, Martin R. *Commonsense Computer Security: Your Practical Guide to Information Protection, Second Edition.* New York: McGraw-Hill Companies, 1994.
5. Russell, Deborah and G. T. Gangemi, Sr. *Computer Security Basics.* Sebastapol, CA: O'Reilly & Associates, Inc., 1991.
6. Weckert, John and Douglas Adeney. *Computer and Information Ethics.* Westport, CT: Greenwood Publishing Group, 1997.

OBJECTIVES

This chapter covers the following CompTIA objectives for the Security+ exam.

Explain, implement, and configure privilege management.

- This objective looks at the process associated with managing privilege and access to resources. It includes user, group, and role management, single sign-on, auditing, and centralized and decentralized management configurations.

Understand and participate in forensics.

- No network is 100% secure. This objective examines the steps used to investigate and evaluate a network after an attack has occurred. If you don't learn from your mistakes, you are bound to be attacked again in the same way.

Understand, explain, and participate in risk identification.

- What needs to be protected? How much is a resource worth? What are you willing to spend to protect a resource? This objective answers each of these questions and many more. Proper risk identification and evaluation are critical to the entire security foundation.

Understand, explain, and participate in change management.

- Unauthorized changes in system configuration and software are a leading cause of security problems in today's networking environments. Who's allowed to make changes? When are changes implemented? What needs to be tested to ensure that security hasn't been compromised? This objective gives you the map to answer these questions.

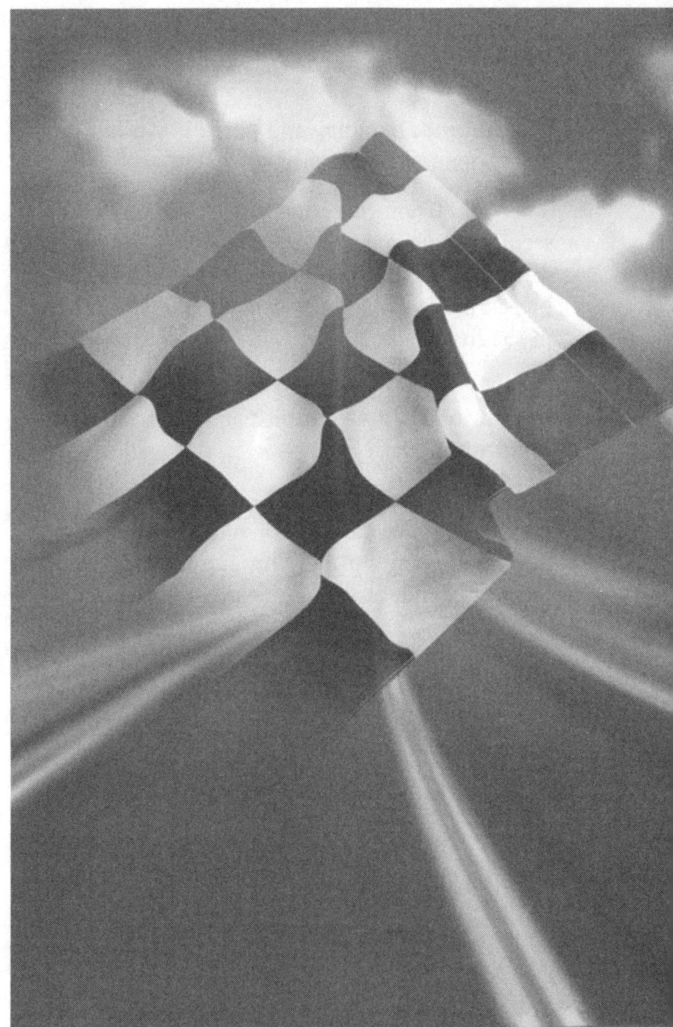

CHAPTER 9

Security Management

Objectives

Understand, explain, and participate in awareness.

- This objective focuses on the business process of security communications and training. It is unreasonable to expect someone to be responsible for a breech in security if he was never trained properly in the first place.

Understand, explain, and participate in documentation.

- Commonly overlooked, documentation is critical to the ongoing functionality of your network, business, and security plans. This objective sets the focus on standards and guidelines for documentation.

Outline

Outline

Study Strategies

- This chapter focuses on some areas covered in other chapters in the book. The focus for you here should be how to manage those areas of security and the security process.
- In this chapter, pay attention to the new concepts of computer forensics and investigation. You should understand the concepts and the mechanics of how to properly conduct an investigation.
- Where it applies, use the practical steps to help you work through the mechanics of the management of privileges. If you don't use the operating system shown in the step by steps, use the operating system that is most familiar to you and try to apply the concepts and mechanics of security management.
- Use the case study at the back of the chapter to help bring the broader picture into focus.

INTRODUCTION

The final chapter of this book focuses on the task of managing security. Different chapters have focused on different areas of the network. We have introduced and discussed hardware, software, protocols, and processes used to deploy and configure security for modern networks and facilities. This chapter strives to identify ways to make all these security components work together to achieve a long-term security configuration. Like any modern business process, security requires constant maintenance and management to work properly. Deploying security is really only half the battle, though. You also have to manage and adjust your security system on a constant basis.

Companies today often deploy systems and processes in a piecemeal fashion, with too little planning and too little follow-up to ensure success. It is our goal not only to get you through the Security+ exam, but also to ensure you have the skills necessary to deploy and maintain your security in the real world. By now, you should have a better understanding of the concepts of security, the various security pieces that can be deployed, when to deploy them, and how they work. This chapter revisits many of the areas already covered to highlight specific issues associated with the management of the technology.

Security is like putting on a Broadway play: Many pieces must be brought together, coordinated, and constantly monitored for change. Any one piece could not stand by itself—lighting, sets, actors, and music all have to be combined through the efforts of a director to make a play successful. In the same respect, the executives of a company direct and coordinate the many pieces of the security effort, set goals to be achieved, and make the decisions on which components to implement.

Time and again, companies deploy a firewall on their Internet connections and believe they have deployed security. The process is typically executed from the bottom up by the IT department with little long-term thought and very little long-term success. *Bottom-up deployment* refers to the decision and deployment process implemented at the user or worker level (in this case the IT department), instead of at an executive level. The situation can be worse if each department is left to implement, deploy, and manage security on its own with no coordination from upper management. It cannot be emphasized enough that this type of security and business practice is doomed to failure.

The key to good security is business-driven policies that are executed from the top down. There might be the odd success story out there, and you might even have an example, but for the vast majority of companies, bottom-up networking and bottom-up security will not work.

Therefore, the goal for you is to understand *top-down security management*. Top-down is a process in which the decisions are made by upper management and implemented at the interim and lower levels of the corporate structure. As you read through the rest of this chapter, keep this principle in mind. You might find yourself implementing security at the IT level today, manager level tomorrow, and executive level in the future. The first step of security management is the creation of goals. One of the first goals that we will look at is managing privilege.

PRIVILEGE MANAGEMENT

Explain, implement, and configure privilege management.

Privilege management is the process of controlling users and their abilities on the network. It is one of the first levels at which goals should be created and well understood. The modern network should be protected from its own users first. This might sound like an odd approach, but the internal user has access to the data and the opportunity to sabotage it. The goal of protecting data and defining the focus of privilege management sets the tone and effort for many of the other tasks we discuss.

Privilege management focuses on the following key areas:

- User, group, and role management
- Single sign-on
- Centralized versus decentralized management
- Auditing

User/Group/Role Management

The decision to implement privileges based on user, group, or role must be made early in the development of the security policy.

Users utilize information in their daily tasks, so the data must be protected. Also, some users and groups of users don't need access to certain data. For instance, general users do not need access to personal information of fellow workers found in the human resources department. This is where limiting access to data is a must for business integrity as well as the host of legal issues that could abound from such access. The days of centralized data being stored on mainframes and controlled by well-trained engineers are gone. Users now have access to huge volumes of critical business data and, in some cases, have little or no training at all on how to access, handle, or secure the critical data they are accessing.

Another factor that influences this process is the fact that few of us have the opportunity to deploy networks from scratch. The network security system must be developed and deployed on an existing network with resources already in use. So, developing security policies based on user-, group-, or role-based privileges must be carefully thought out and tested before implementation occurs. If not, you could easily open access to critical data to users who have no business seeing or using it simply by an oversight during policy development.

Changing an existing environment to include security or changing an existing security configuration should never be a task taken lightly. These changes can have serious consequences on the productivity of the users and the integrity of the company's data. If done improperly, the data can be exposed to corruption, deletion, or theft during the changes. Planning and testing eliminates the vast majority of these types of problems, and sufficient time must be spent to ensure that the transition and implementation go as smoothly as possible. Change management is covered later in this chapter, in the section titled "Change Management," and specifically addresses this issue.

The goal that needs to be set by management is where to set the focus of privilege. Management of privilege typically focuses on one of the following functional security objects:

- Users
- Groups
- Roles

Users

From a management standpoint, security that focuses on the user is primarily concerned with the activities and the level of privilege associated with each individual who will have access to resources. Privilege management that sets its focus on the user outlines proper procedures for assigning resource permissions and network rights based on an individual's need for them. This type of policy is time-consuming and difficult to handle from a management view and, in particular, does not scale well in large environments.

This doesn't mean that it is not useful. Later in the chapter, we discuss risk assessment and how to mitigate risk. If resources are particularly valuable or highly sensitive, a strict user privilege policy might be warranted as well as required. This is commonly found in government and military situations and in private companies that are protecting patented formulas or processes. User-based privilege management is normally used for very specific parts of the network or specific resource control.

Given a moderately sized network of 5,000 users, using a network with 30,000 distinct files and folders, it would be unreasonable to expect management to be able to handle the entire environment based on discrete, individual user-based privileges. If each user needed access to only 20% of the available resources, you'd need 30,000,000 separate privilege assignments for your network! That result is achieved by taking 20% of 30,000, which equals 6,000. Multiply the result by the total number of users (5,000), and you have an enormous management nightmare on your hands.

Given the same 5,000 users, however, and a single server that contains the formulas for a company's candy products, managing access to the resources on that single server by individual user privilege assignment would be not only attainable, but also might be advisable given the sensitive nature of the formulas. Looking at this situation, let's say that only 10 people in the entire company need access to the candy formulas. The single server has 100 formulas, so the resulting privilege assignments would be 1,000. That's still not a friendly number from the view of the IT department and the actual mechanics of assigning privilege, but it's a far better prospect than 30,000,000.

The mechanics of setting up user-based privileges must be understood as well because it will give you a sense of the effort involved and help you make better, more informed decisions. Step By Step 9.1 is a representation of how to set up user-based privilege on a Windows 2000 system.

STEP BY STEP

9.1 Assigning User-Based Privileges in Windows 2000 Professional

1. Create a user account by right-clicking My Computer and selecting Manage. This launches the Computer Management MMC interface.
2. Select the Local Users and Groups node in the left window pane, and select the Users folder (see Figure 9.1). Create a user named Bob.

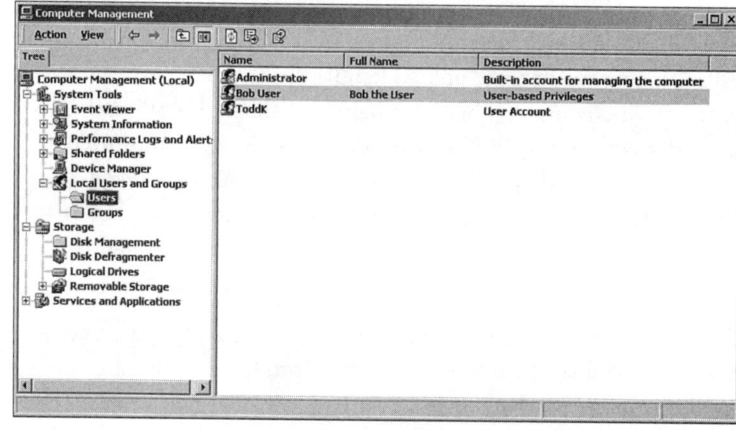

FIGURE 9.1
Creating a user in Windows 2000.

NOTE

Problems Viewing the Security Tab If the Security tab doesn't show, the volume is not formatted as an NTFS volume and this exercise won't work.

Remove Everyone To achieve true user-level privilege settings, you need to remove the default group Everyone.

3. Launch Windows Explorer and create a folder called Test, as shown in Figure 9.2.

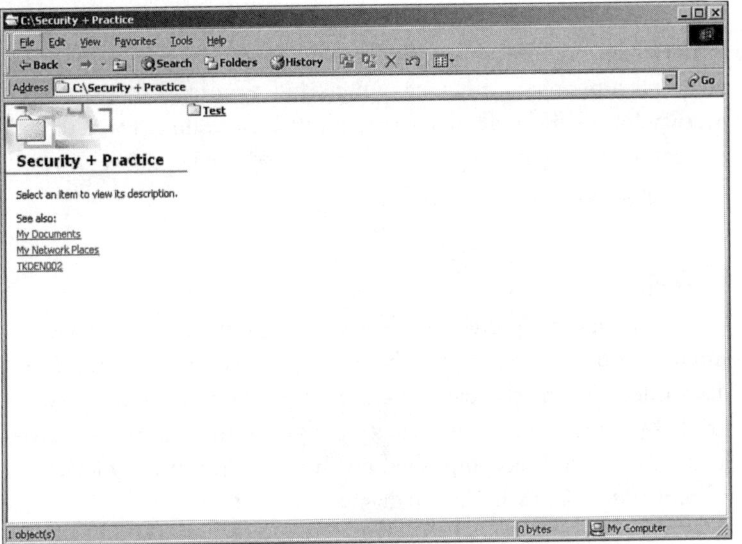

FIGURE 9.2
Creating a folder in Windows 2000.

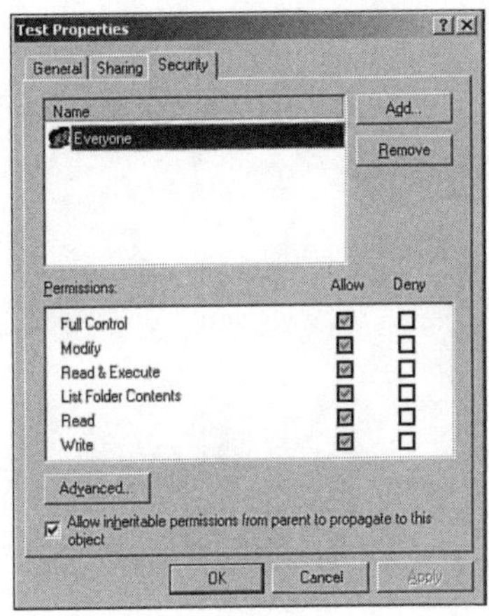

FIGURE 9.3
The Security tab.

4. Right-click the Test folder and select Properties. On the Properties folder, select the Security tab, as shown in Figure 9.3.

5. Click the Add button and add Bob's user account to the access list; then grant the account Read privilege, as shown in Figure 9.4.

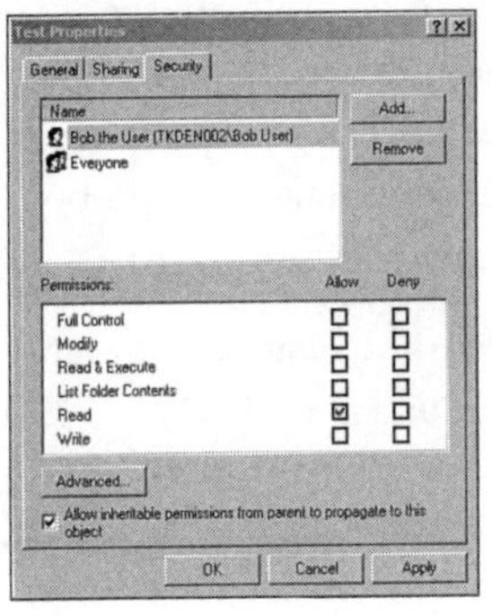

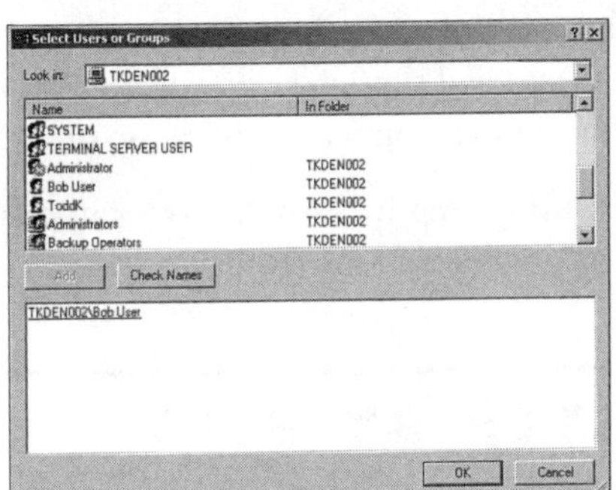

FIGURE 9.4
User-level privilege assignment.

The same steps are required for each user who needs read privilege to the folder. As you can see, the amount of work required to accomplish permissions for many users and resources can quickly overwhelm the most efficient IT administrative teams. A way to overcome the negative aspects of user-focused privilege assignment is by using groups.

Groups

Group privilege assignment enables you to group users who have similar resource access needs. These groups often reflect divisions or departments of the company, such as Accounting, Marketing, Sales, or IT. By using groups, the security goals of setting access and privilege control can be accomplished much more efficiently by fewer administrators and with less management overhead.

Reviewing the example of 5,000 users in a company, if they could all be grouped into 20 groups, the permissions assignments drop exponentially. Permissions could now be assigned to the 20 groups instead of each individual. If the users resource demands remained constant at 20% (or 6,000 objects), your tasks would drop from 30 million assignments to just 12,000. This is a far more reasonable number to manage and control.

The shift in focus when using group privilege management is away from the individual user and set on collections of users (departments) and their access requirements. Users still have to be placed in the appropriate groups to ensure that they are not granted rights and privileges inappropriately, but the burden of actual privilege assignment is reduced and simplified. This should also reduce mistakes and problems in the long-term application of the company's security goals.

By using Step By Step 9.2, you can clearly see the benefit of assigning privileges to groups instead of individual users.

STEP BY STEP

9.2 Assigning Group-Based Privileges in Windows 2000 Professional

1. Right-click My Computer and select Manage. This launches the Computer Management MMC interface.

2. Select the Local Users and Groups node on the left. Select the Groups folder and create a group named Accounting, as shown in Figure 9.5.

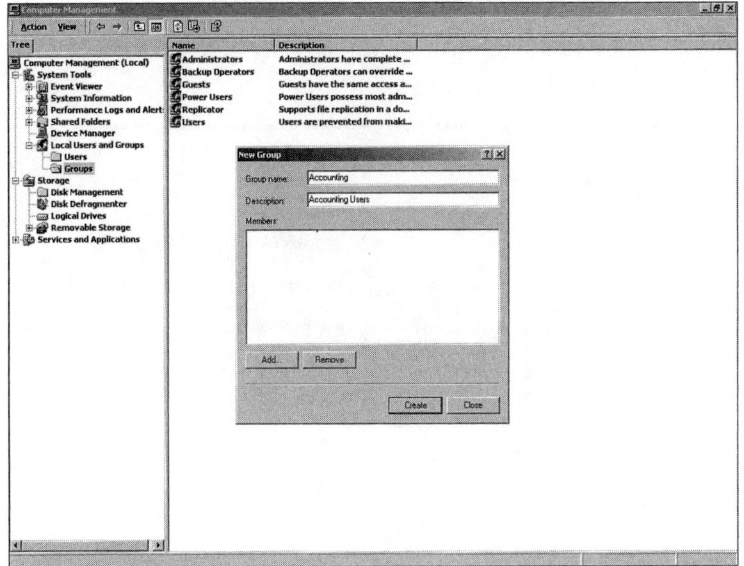

FIGURE 9.5
Creating a group in Windows 2000.

3. While still in the Computer Management MMC, select the Accounting group, right-click, and select Properties.

4. In the Properties dialog box, click the Add button (see Figure 9.6). Add the account Bob you created in the previous exercise.

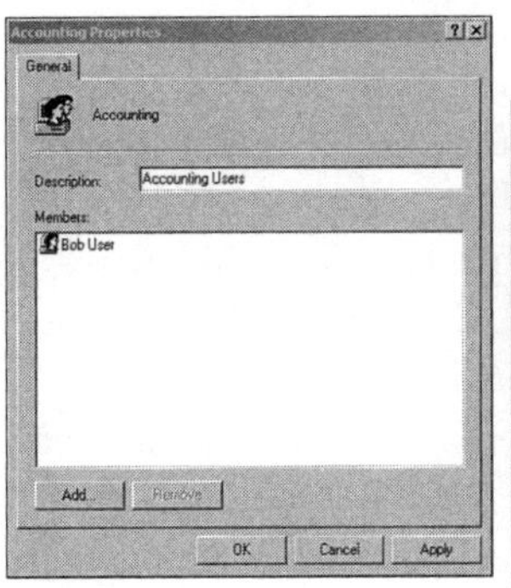

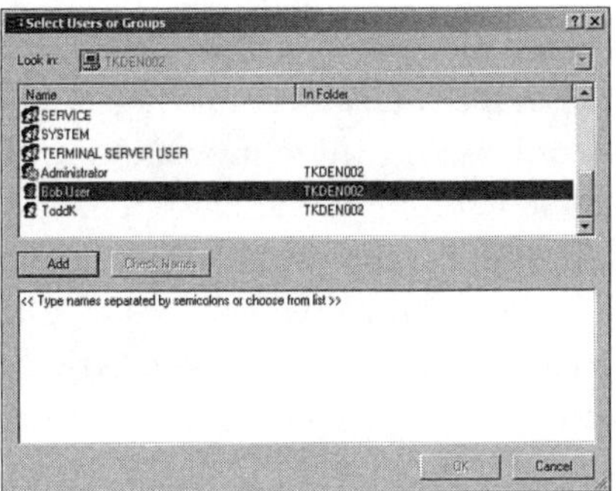

FIGURE 9.6
Adding users to groups.

> **NOTE**
>
> **Problems Viewing the Security Tab**
> If the Security tab doesn't appear, the volume is not formatted as an NTFS volume and this exercise won't work.

continues

continued

5. Right-click the Test folder and select Properties. Then, select the Security tab, as shown in Figure 9.7.
6. Click the Add button and add the Accounting group to the access list; then grant the group Read privilege (see Figure 9.8).

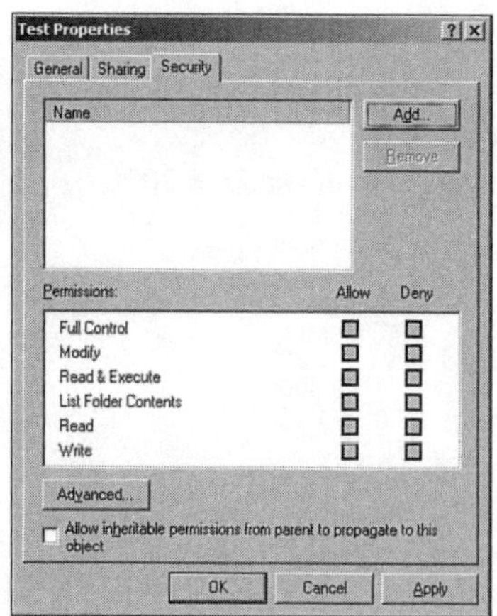

FIGURE 9.7▲
Security tab.

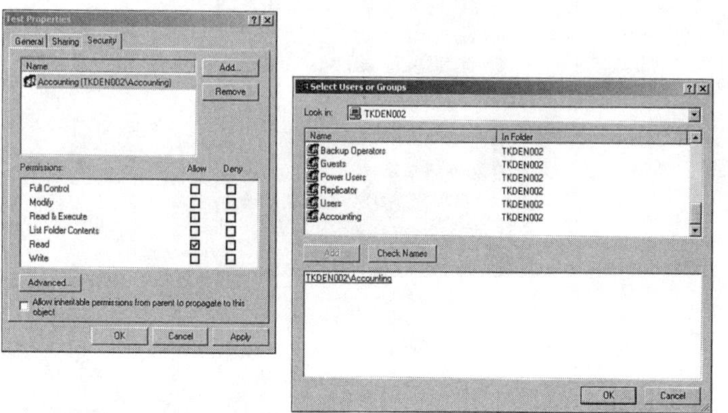

FIGURE 9.8▶
Group-level privilege assignment.

The process for granting a user read-level privileges to the Test folder is now a simple task of placing her user account in the Accounting group. Membership in the group grants the user the group's permission to the resource. This group privilege example organizes users based on the structure departments. However, you can also choose to organize your users based on the roles they have in the company.

Roles

The last method of setting privilege access is by identifying common roles in the company. A role is generally associated with a particular job or jobs assigned to people. An example of this would be backing up and restoring servers and applying service patches. A group (as defined in the preceding section) is created and given these rights and permissions. Users assigned to accomplish these tasks are then placed into these groups and inherit the group's capabilities. The mechanics of this approach differ only in how management chooses to focus on the users and their need for permissions.

Now that we have discussed all three possible types of privilege management for resources and rights, we should mention that most companies and even operating systems use all three. It is very uncommon to find a simple network that uses only one of these methods and excludes the others. In large networks, you will find group management common for file and print access. Special behaviors such as installing software, backing up and restoring information, running antivirus checks, and a host of other activities are best delegated by role assignments. As a last resort, you will undoubtedly be required to assign access and rights to specific users, such as the CEO, CFO, and internal auditors to name a few.

Security should be flexible; without flexibility, the strongest and tallest of structures break. Stand on a wide bridge or at the top of a tall building, and you will feel it sway in the wind. Security must be flexible, too, so it can survive the pace and diversity of the modern network environment; therefore, you must be flexible as well. No one solution is perfect for all situations, and even the best solution might last only weeks or months. Be ready and, more importantly, willing to adapt as your network and its users change and grow.

MAC/DAC/RBAC

The previous section discussed and demonstrated the process of assigning privileges using users, groups, or roles. Now that you know the mechanics of how to assign privileges, you need to determine who is allowed to do it through the setting of a policy. MAC, DAC, and RBAC were discussed in detail Chapter 1, "General Security Concepts," and are reviewed in Table 9.1.

TABLE 9.1

REVIEW OF ACCESS CONTROL POLICY

Access Control Method	*Control Description*
Mandatory Access Control (MAC)	Usually reserved for highly sensitive data, it requires a lot of administrative overhead to manage and maintain. Users have no control or influence over the data or the privilege assignments.

continues

TABLE 9.1 *continued*

REVIEW OF ACCESS CONTROL POLICY

Access Control Method	*Control Description*
Discretionary Access Control (DAC)	Users are typically grouped by department or similar administrative need and gain access and privilege by membership in a group instead of direct assignment to their user accounts. The users can set privileges and pass privileges to others at their discretion.
Role-based Access Control (RBAC)	Users are grouped by functional role within the company (backup operator, server manager, database administrator, and so on). These functional roles are translated into access and privilege requirements that fit the role the user has. The user has the ability to set privileges and pass privileges to others as needed.

Let's take, for example, a user Bob. An administrator has assigned Bob read privileges to a file called `protected.txt`. A MAC policy would not allow Bob to change or influence the decision surrounding the assignment of that privilege or allow Bob to transfer read privileges to any other users. This behavior would hold true under a MAC policy even if Bob owned the `protected.txt` file. So, a distinction exists between the privilege (read in this case) and the privilege management policy of MAC.

To sum up, you have two questions to answer:

- Who do I assign privileges to (where is the focus for permissions set): users, groups, or roles within my company?
- After the focus is set, who has the privilege of assigning, changing, and passing on those privileges to others?

Nothing, it seems, in networking is clear-cut for all situations all of the time. Keep in mind that one user could be a part of all three policies based on the need of a company and its overall security goal. Let's return to our sample user Bob. He might be under the influence of a MAC policy for the file (`protected.txt`) but might have a DAC policy for information that he is responsible for as a project manager. Bob also might be under a RBAC policy as the backup administrator for his department. This is just one example of the need within the security environment to adapt to the diversity of the network environment and needs of the company.

In the next section, we show you that the wide range of network operating systems and the needs of the company further influence security with the need for a single logon.

Single Sign-on

The idea of single sign-on (SSO) is simple: Using the principle of SSO, users sign on or log on to a network authority one time during the day and are able to gain access to any desired network resource regardless of the operating system managing it. Network administrators realize a benefit by being able to have a single set of users to track and grant privilege to. In addition, help desk calls are reduced because account lockouts and password resets don't occur as frequently. The SSO concept can integrate network operating systems, such as

- Novell
- Microsoft Windows
- Banyan Vines
- Mainframes
- Unix (and all its many flavors)

There was a long-held belief in the computer industry that for each server on the network to remain secure, users needed to maintain a different user account and password. Each server had its own accounts database and was not integrated with other systems on the network. The idea was that if a user's account was compromised, it would allow access to only a single server and its resources. This would reduce the impact of any one compromise and increase the apparent security on the network. This concept worked well in practice when networks were small and servers were few. There was, however, a quick breakdown of the application of this principle when users had not one or two servers to access but 10, 15, or even 100. In these situations, maintaining a separate username and password for every server system became tedious and problematic. The most common reaction from users was to write usernames and passwords down to remember them. As soon as this behavior developed, the concept of multiaccount/multipassword failed along with any security.

The behavior of using multiple accounts was not limited to large network environments with mainframes and PCs. Smaller companies often used this approach with servers from the same vendor, such as Microsoft and Novell. In fact, some vendors had no way for users to maintain a single password for multiple systems. Synchronization of accounts and passwords on multiple servers was done manually, was time-consuming, and didn't scale well as the network grew. This multiaccount business philosophy has been proven wrong over time and counter to the security of both single-vendor and multivendor network deployments. Users might have many servers to log on to each day to get resources, and the time and effort to do so when multiple accounts exist is counterproductive and prone to misconfiguration, error, and compromise (due to passwords being written down).

Implementing SSO with Software Solutions

SSO is easier said than done in many cases. Different operating systems and working environments require different solutions. Most solutions involve software and possibly hardware.

One type of software solution involves finding a solution provider that writes code for multiple operating systems. An example might be special software that integrates Kerberos authentication across Windows 2000, Unix, and an AS400 system. After the software is loaded, users can be authenticated by any one of the key distribution centers (KDCs) and all other KDCs will then trust resource requests submitted by those users. (See Chapter 1 for a more complete discussion on Kerberos.)

Another software solution might involve using certificate authentication and Web-deployed applications. Using this approach, a company can deploy its applications on Web servers running on any hardware or software platform they choose. After deployed, the users would be issued certificates and authenticated on any of the participating servers. This solution involves a shift in the standard method of application deployment, but it is becoming more and more popular every year.

In some cases in which the vendor software is the same (and simply configured differently), SSO is a simple process of configuring the operating system software to communicate. An example of this is getting two Windows 2000 domains in different forests to trust each other as shown in Step By Step 9.3.

STEP BY STEP

9.3 Establishing a Trust for SSO in a Windows 2000 Environment

1. On a Windows 2000 domain controller, select Start, Programs, Administrative Tools, Active Directory Domains and Trusts (see Figure 9.9).

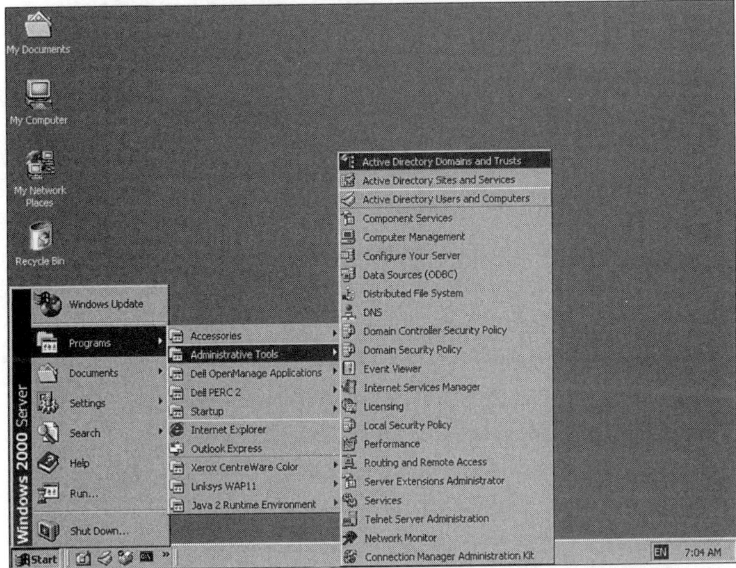

FIGURE 9.9
Administrative tools.

2. Right-click the domain that will use the trust and select Properties. The domain controller's Properties dialog box appears, as shown in Figure 9.10.

continues

continued

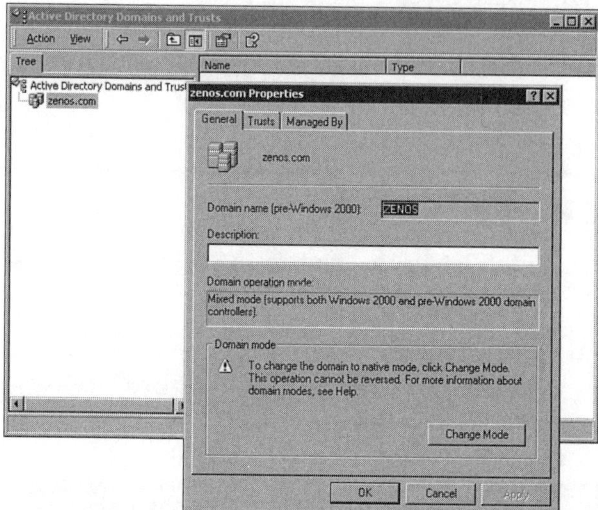

FIGURE 9.10▶
The domain controller's Properties dialog box.

3. Select the Trusts tab, click the Add button, and fill in the name of the domain to be trusted or trusting. We added the domain widgets.com to our list, as shown in Figure 9.11.

   The trusts will be verified and will allow users and resources to be shared between different domains in different forests.

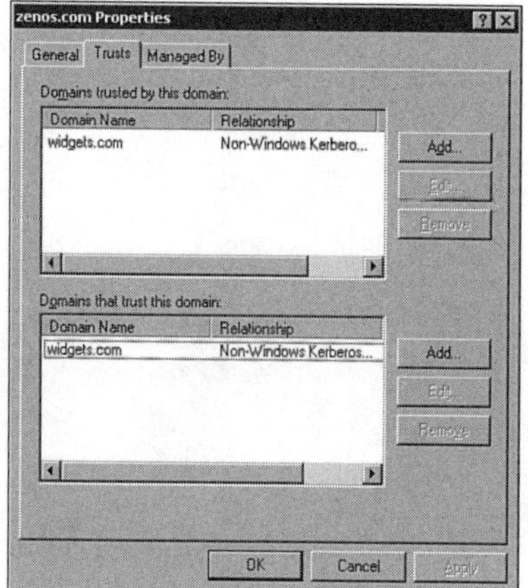

FIGURE 9.11▲
The Trusts tab of the Properties dialog box.

The trust allows users access to resources located in a different Kerberos domain without logging on again. Using this technique, someone in Zenos could access resources in Widgets without authenticating (logging in) twice. If the trusts are set up properly, and from both domains, Widgets users could access resources in Zenos the same way. This is an example of an internal SSO configuration. A complete explanation of trusts and more detailed instructions are available in the Windows 2000 online documentation.

Implementing SSO with Hardware Solutions

A hardware solution is actually a combination of hardware and software (as is normal). The concept of a universal smart card authentication system is viable now and is being deployed by some companies across a variety of network operating systems. Software for the smart card readers is deployed to each of the authentication systems, and users simply log on once and can be granted permissions to resources based on their smart card IDs.

The concept of SSO is not new, but this aspect of the computer industry is still in the early stages. SSO solutions are being developed and deployed rapidly to fill the need of simplifying the complexity of the modern network. SSO is desired because it lowers the total cost of owning a network and can improve the effectiveness and strength of security while easing the lives of the users as well as help desk and network administrative teams. Tying this back into the bigger picture of privilege management, you can see that administrators can track, assign, and change privileges on a smaller number of user objects, which reduces configuration errors, reduces response time when an error does occur, and allows for greater growth of the network. This centralization of user logon is only one approach to managing privileges, as you will see in the following section.

EXAM TIP

Make sure you know the concept of SSO and its benefits to security.

Centralized Management Versus Decentralized Management

Security management is based on one of two models: *centralized* or *decentralized*. There are merits and problems with both. The choice of which model to use must be a conscious decision made by the executive-level employees of a company. Too often, this choice is left to the IT department, and regardless of the decision, the IT department is forever blamed for the inefficiency of the model. This must be a top-down decision and be well defined in the corporate network documentation; then the IT department can develop and deploy the proper configuration. The following two sections define and detail these management models in further depth.

Centralized Privilege Management

Centralized privilege management has the greatest benefit of being more secure. Using this model, all new privilege assignments and changes made to existing privileges are funneled through one department or governing group. This group develops an expertise, efficiency, and familiarity with the systems and data, which reduces the number of security-related mistakes. In addition, a centralized system allows the managing administrators to become intimate with planning, controlling, and implementing access rights and privileges. Repetition and familiarity with the overall process allows the administrators a high level of efficiency.

The key drawback to the centralized model of privilege management is scalability. As the company and network grow, the administrators will find it more and more difficult to keep up with the daily and even weekly tasks of assigning and managing network resource access and privileges. If the company is confined to one geographic location, this problem might not develop for quite some time. When the problem does hit, though, it might be a minor issue for a considerable amount of time. If, however, the company is widely dispersed, the problem might occur much earlier in the company's growth cycle and be much more difficult to handle if not properly planned and supported.

Decentralized Privilege Management

Decentralized privilege management is the other side of the coin. It is less secure but more scalable. Security-related responsibilities are delegated among employees at different locations. These employees are trained and made responsible for managing privileges within their administrative areas. This model has its biggest advantage in large, geographically diverse companies. The burden of day-to-day tasks is offloaded to local administrators and allows the company's IT department to better handle large numbers of users.

However, decentralized management is less secure because more people are involved in the process and there is a greater possibility for errors. With a decentralized system, reaction times to problems can increase as well because of confusion created by decentralizing the responsibilities of management (the proverbial "I thought it was their job").

The truth is that, like most choices and methods in networking, there is no pure implementation. Most companies adopt a blended approach to accomplish the ever-increasing tasks of making the network work. Management might decide to centralize the creation of user accounts while decentralizing resource access and privilege assignment to the owners of the servers and data. There are many possibilities on what to centralize and what to decentralize, and covering them all is simply not necessary. As in so many other sections of this book, we have mentioned the key, which is *planning*. Setting goals and expectations at the upper management level enables the entire process to be tracked, adjusted, and ultimately implemented successfully. Thus far, we have looked at planning and implementing privilege management; now we need to keep our eyes on it. That process involves auditing.

Auditing

Auditing user privileges is generally a two-step process that involves turning auditing on within the operating system and then specifying the resources (files, folders, printers) to be audited. In addition to enabling auditing, you also need to monitor the logs that are generated. Auditing should include both privilege and usage.

Privilege

Privilege is a user's level of access to a given object or a right to change a process or object. Privileges can include the right to log on to a workstation, the ability to change the network configuration, or the level of permissions a user has to a file (such as read or write access). When auditing privileges, the main goal is to ensure that the users have the correct level of privilege within the networking environment. Although this is closely tied to usage auditing, it is a separate process. Usage auditing tracks resources that have been used, the user who used them, and the level at which they were accessed. Privilege auditing examines which rights a user has and when he has exercised those rights. This separation is key because certain rights are built into accounts, such as an administrator's account, and would not otherwise be a traceable security behavior. Periodic audits of users and their rights and permissions will help you identify errors in the current configurations and help you build procedures that reduce resource configuration errors.

One of the best ways to audit privilege is to monitor changes to the current security policy. The major operating systems on the market today include the capability to track administrative changes to the security policy. The addition of a user to the administrators group, the modification of the security on a critical folder, and a change in the password policy can all be tracked through auditing. In the big picture of your security policy and program, auditing falls under maintenance and management chores. Although it might seem time-consuming and tedious, it is a critical function in the ongoing security process. In addition to monitoring the current level of privilege, you also should monitor usage.

Usage

Closely related to the idea of monitoring privilege is that of monitoring actual *usage*. In highly secured environments, it is common to look at what people are using and how often. This is often your first indication that privileges are set incorrectly and that you need to fix access or rights of a single user or possibly even a group of users. Another function of auditing usage is monitoring for potential security breaches even when security is set properly.

When auditing, you should monitor the largest possible group, such as the Everyone group in Windows 2000. This might seem counterproductive at first, but it is necessary. Good thieves are not going to identify themselves on the network with a proper ID and then try to steal your corporate secrets. A good thief is going to sneak in anonymously and attempt to steal without proper access. By monitoring the Everyone group, you take into account all users and access both known and unknown.

When configuring auditing for your systems, you should monitor both successful and failed attempts to access resources and exercise privileges. If all you monitor is failed access from known users, you raise the potential to completely miss an attack by a skilled network hacker who slips in and takes important information.

By monitoring the largest group and looking at success and failures, you increase the chances of finding and logging illegal or unwanted activities. The basic process of auditing is covered in Step By Step 9.4.

STEP BY STEP

9.4 Configuring Auditing on Windows 2000

1. On a Windows 2000 system, select the Start, Programs, Administrative Tools, Local Security Policy.
2. Select Local Policies, Audit Policies in the left window of the policy console, as shown in Figure 9.12.

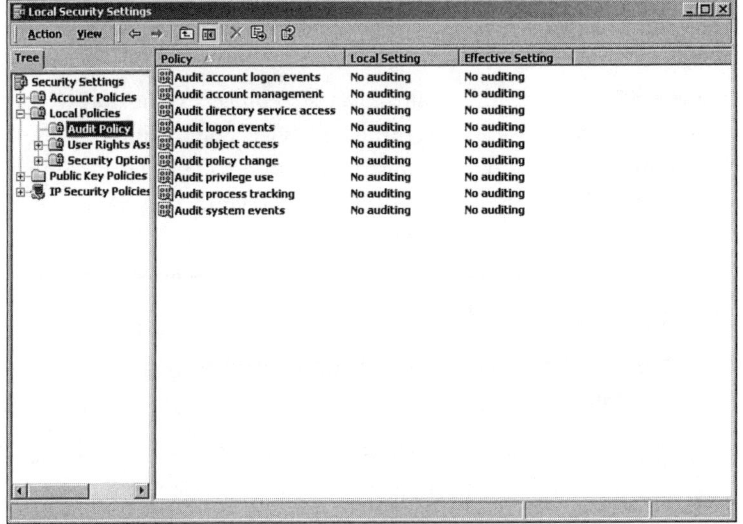

FIGURE 9.12
Local security settings.

3. Double-click the policy in the right pane you want to modify.
4. Select the desired options for auditing and enable them as shown in Figure 9.13.

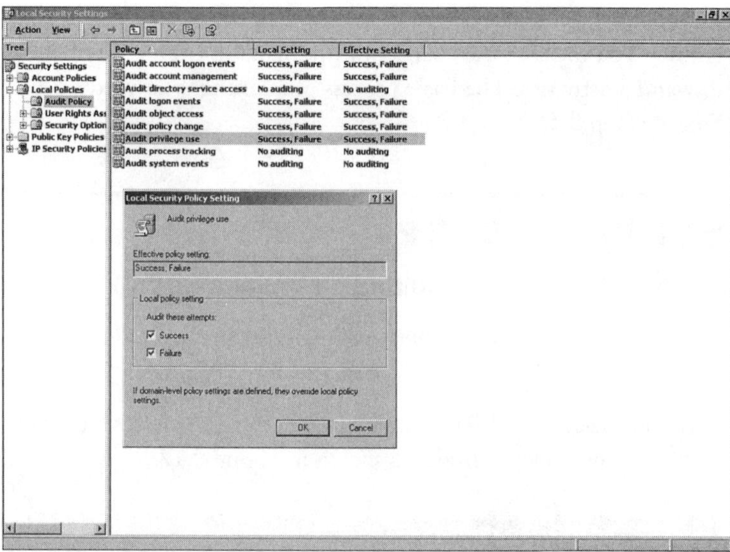

FIGURE 9.13
Configuring auditing in the Local Security Policy Setting dialog box.

Some aspects of auditing require a two-step process as previously mentioned. Object access was turned on (success and failure) in the last example, but will not log any activity until you set the auditing flag on specific resources to be tracked, as shown in Step By Step 9.5.

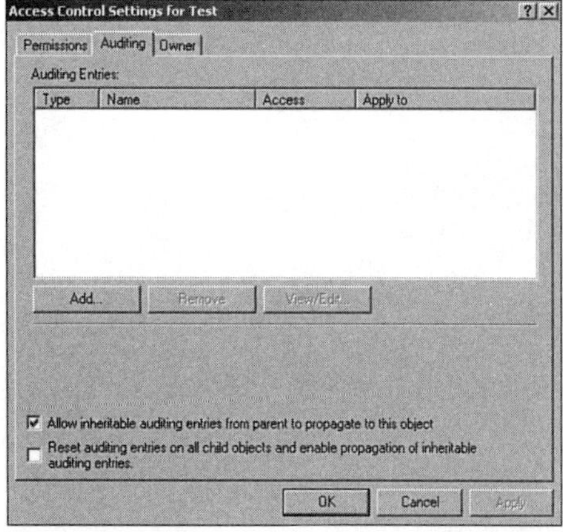

FIGURE 9.14
Configuring object auditing.

STEP BY STEP

9.5 Configuring Object Access Auditing on Windows 2000

1. On a Windows 2000 system, launch Explorer and select the folder for the object for which you want to set access auditing. Right-click the folder and select Properties. The object's Properties dialog box appears.

2. Select the Security tab and click the Advanced button in the lower-left corner. Then, click the Auditing tab, shown in Figure 9.14.

3. Add the Everyone group and select the actions to be audited. In very secure environments, success and failure of all actions are audited, as shown in Figure 9.15.

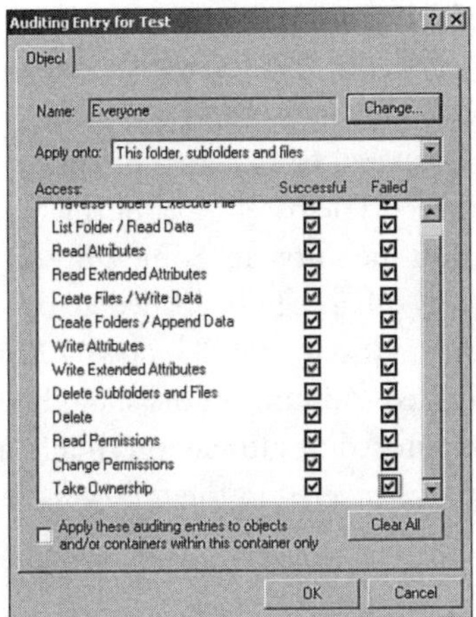

FIGURE 9.15
Setting auditing levels.

> **NOTE**
>
> **Problems Viewing the Security Tab**
> If the Security tab doesn't appear, the volume is not formatted as an NTFS volume and this exercise won't work.

The drawbacks to this process are the size of the log files and the time required to monitor them. If you collect all the data and never look at it, what is the point (other than filling up your hard drive with logs)? You need to have a set schedule and routine for reviewing your logs. To ease the workload, you can buy software that reviews your logs for you and flags data that falls outside normal parameters (as set by you). The system can then proactively notify you of problems and even attacks before a normal log review takes place.

Privilege Escalation

Privilege escalation occurs when a user changes or increases his level of access to a particular object. This can be done through virus code, the exploitation of known operating system vulnerabilities, or bugs in application code. Several ways exist to help protect your network and its equipment from such behavior. As part of your privilege management plan, you should check with the operating system and application manufacturers at regular intervals to find out whether any new problems or fixes are available for the systems you run on your network. One of the best ways to do this is through the Internet. Many software manufacturers now offer a notification service that sends you email if new patches are available or problems are reported.

Loading special software on your servers can also help you track and control privilege escalation. This software is designed to monitor your audit logs and system events and notify you via email or alert if a user or process has altered or escalated privileges on an object outside defined parameters. The baseline of normal behavior is set by you and configured in the software. Some software packages are platform specific, whereas others can be loaded across multiple types of systems (such as Unix, Novell, and Windows 2000) and centrally managed and controlled. Administrators should be trained on the software and proper procedures for action should an event occur. Many of these steps are covered in the following section.

FORENSICS

Understand and participate in forensics.

In physical crimes, such as robbery and murder, special investigative teams are trained in the science of collecting and analyzing crime-scene data. These teams include on-scene personnel as well as forensic scientists in labs. Computer forensics is no different in its practice. In fact, many people are shocked to find that computer attack forensics is more concerned with law and evidence gathering, handling, and preservation than with computers. Most companies today don't prepare or understand the forensics process until after an attack has occurred. It is our goal in this section to show you what is required and how to prepare before an attack occurs.

First things first—computer crime is increasing and our ability to cope with the complexity of the networks and software applications that are being created is decreasing. Now, this is most certainly a generalization, but it holds true for many of the clients and companies we see every year. Another truth is that given enough time, energy, and incentive, just about any network can be hacked. If you can accept these basic truths, the time you spend planning and training in areas such as computer forensics will seem less like a waste of time and more like an investment.

> NOTE
>
> **Incident Response Plans** Another unfortunate truth is that the majority of companies don't have incident response plans. Given that the network is likely to be hacked, this is a serious shortfall in planning.

Computer forensics is about collecting and analyzing data so it can be used and presented in court. Without proper forensic techniques, you are likely to destroy valuable data or render it inadmissible because it was improperly obtained, collected, or stored.

Without evidence, you can't prosecute offenders, properly terminate employees for inappropriate behavior, or seek damages when corporate espionage hits home. The next sections examine the following topics:

- Investigation techniques and tools
- Evidence collection
- Chain of custody and evidence preservation

EXAM TIP

Know the rules and the proper procedures for collecting and processing information, including the key rules surrounding the concept of the chain of custody.

Investigation Techniques and Tools

Computer crime, like any other crime, starts with an investigation of the crime scene and an analysis of the data and evidence collected. When an incident is discovered, it is important to have an incident response team and procedure already available. If this is overlooked, the severity of the incident can be increased because of improper reporting procedures or a failure to identify the systems affected (or worse, the attack could continue or be repeated). Keep in mind that the crime might still be in progress. With good software and proper incident response techniques, you might be able to collect data and identify the attacker while she is still in the process of illegally using your resources!

Investigative and response actions must address how to handle various situations and set up actions that are approved by management. Some of these situations might include

- If the attack is ongoing, maintain connectivity for continued data collection.
- If the attack is ongoing, immediately remove the affected systems to reduce the impact of the attack.
- If the attack is over, maintain connectivity for a possible return of the attacker.
- If the attack is over, remove the affected systems for immediate evidence collection and system recovery.

Eventually, the investigation team will be tasked with the process of evidence recovery and analysis. Procedures for this should also be well outlined and include the following basic behaviors:

- Analysis of the intrusion to identify the extent, severity, and type of attack, including the attacker's activity
- Containment of damage and deployment of a response plan for specific category of attack
- Collection and isolation of data evidence associated with the attack, including auditing and system logs
- Notification of proper personnel designated to handle publicity and internal corporate communications
- Interviewing appropriate personnel
- Post-attack analysis of collected data
- Post-attack report and analysis of investigative procedures

The investigation of computer attacks is generally focused on host-based evidence and information collected off the network. The collection process is detailed next.

Collection of Evidence

Collecting evidence can be done automatically or manually. The following two sections detail these methods of collecting evidence.

Automatic Data Collection

Automatic collection comes in the form of intrusion detection software and other applications, including network data analysis and monitoring tools. These tools are installed and configured by the security and networking teams and are set up to identify suspicious behaviors and activities.

Intrusion detection systems (IDSs) are built with many predefined attack behaviors and can be updated with definition files much like antivirus software is. A good example of a known attack behavior is a port scan. An IDS software or hardware solution looks for inbound packets pinging or attempting to connect to multiple ports either in or out of sequence. This behavior can be used to trigger advanced logging techniques and also to notify a management station of the incident. This type of automatic data collection and attack detection greatly increases the chance that an intruder can be stopped and prosecuted.

Another tool in use today is the network analyzer, or *sniffer*. The term *sniffer* was taken from an early version of the tool developed by Network General and has become synonymous with any tool that monitors and records network traffic. These applications can be deployed on sensitive network segments and configured to trigger alarms, email, and alerts if unwanted or suspicious traffic is captured. These tools can be set up to go into a verbose capture mode as well, pulling in all network traffic and storing it in a file for later analysis.

Automatic detection and notification can greatly improve the chances of catching attackers. By using software in this manner, you can reduce the number of administrators required to monitor the network and log files and improve response times and accuracy. In the event of an attack, manual data collection will likely also be used in retrieving clues and checking for traces of the intrusion.

Manual Data Collection

Software detection systems, though good, cannot think. Humans can identify behaviors and activity that software cannot. Add to this the fact that post-attack forensics almost always includes manual data collection and it highlights the need to know how to go about this process. Manual collection is accomplished by investigators and involves looking at the contents of the following components:

- Hard drives
- System and CPU caches
- Random access memory (RAM)
- System logs
- Audit logs
- Network data flow captures
- Virtual memory (swap, cache, or paging files)

Each of these areas can contain critical data that can be used as evidence or at least give clues as to the nature, duration, and target of a particular attack. Because of the impact of running monitoring software in these areas, it is unlikely to be automated. However, specialized software tools are used to retrieve data from these areas (particularly cache, RAM, and swap files). These tools are often platform specific and vary in capability and function. Most enable you to collect or harvest the data in a controlled fashion, allowing it to be used in a court of law or in an official capacity.

An administrator who is both intimate with the network and its systems and comfortable with the tools necessary to perform manual data collection should be in charge of data collection. Each of the suspect devices and areas should be inspected for remnants of the attack, including modified system files, virus-infected files, backdoor user accounts, the installation of backdoor applications, abandoned script files, and bogus log files. These represent a small sample of what to look for but should give you the basic idea. Each of these pieces of evidence should be properly collected and then analyzed for clues.

Preservation of Evidence

After the evidence has been identified, *it must be collected and preserved to maintain its usability in court.* Remember that the entire forensic process is built around that one concept. Computer evidence suffers from the same dangers as physical evidence: alteration, loss, or destruction. The task is made difficult in the computer world because the data is virtual, not physical. It resides on physical devices as magnetic encoding but is easily destroyed or altered. So, the software used in the field of computer forensics has a difficult task. How do you collect or image data and then ensure that it hasn't been changed since its retrieval? Many of the software programs used today have implemented a concept of digital evidence bags.

Similar in concept to what police use to gather and catalog physical data at a crime scene, forensic software enables you to collect and digitally sign a container that electronically stores evidence. After evidence is placed inside the digital bag, it is then signed with a certificate to prove that no tampering has occurred since collection.

The system enables investigators to look at the contents and analyze it for further discovery, and all access is logged along with any changes to the data. Evidence gathered properly in this manner has already withstood the rigors of court and been successful.

Another form of data collection is simple binary imaging of the system or systems that have been compromised. This can be accomplished with any number of public domain software packages (GHOST, Drive Copy, and so forth). Law enforcement and government agencies often have their own versions of this same type of software. If used, the affected system(s) should be immediately imaged before *any* other investigative tools are used. This ensures that data is preserved in its post-attack state. If this step is not followed, timestamps might be inadvertently changed, files might be modified, and viruses or logic bombs might be set off. After the image is captured, it should be written to nonerasable media and documented according to local evidence laws.

NOTE

Evaluating Memory and Cache If memory and cache are to be evaluated, the proper tools for capturing and reading these hardware devices should be used before imaging because imaging requires the computer to be rebooted. This process would destroy data located in RAM and cache devices.

Investigating Collected Data

After evidence is collected, the real investigation starts. Given the fact that 60GB hard drives are now common, this task alone can take considerable time. Understanding that 60GB of data, if printed, would produce a paper stack around 120 stories high should give you an idea of the kind of data volume involved. Software again comes to the rescue. Using software, investigators can input keywords and phrases and leave the software to do the actual searching. Evidence laws can be very specific about how data can be analyzed. If a hard drive is from a network server, users might have an expected right of privacy and evidence inspected improperly could result in details and data being thrown out in court proceedings.

You'll note that very few programs are mentioned by name in the previous paragraphs; this was done purposefully. Programs used in investigations need to meet the standards of evidence published in your state, country, or province. The tools you seek must work on the software and hardware platforms you run and maintain. As you work further into the planning process, research is required to find the products you will use when an attack hits. Training on the software is critical to ensure that you don't violate the rules of evidence during the investigation process. Training will also help you understand the concept of chain of custody.

Chain of Custody

When evidence is presented in court, the court wants to know how the evidence made it from the crime scene to the courtroom. The explanation that answers this question is known as the *chain of custody*. When data evidence is collected, stored, and eventually presented in court, the following must be true of the data itself:

- It must be relevant or admissible.
- It must be a complete copy.
- It cannot have been altered throughout the collection and storage procedure.
- It must have been copied with a reliable process.
- It must have been secured from the time it was collected until the time it was presented in court.

If any of these basic truths are violated, the collected data is likely to be inadmissible. Additionally, the company should be able to show a set of published procedures used to enforce each of the conditions presented; therefore, the court should have confidence that the data was collected properly. Remember that forensics is more about law and evidence than it is about computers.

Information obtained from a computer generally falls under the category of hearsay. *Hearsay* is a statement made outside of court by someone other than the person testifying at trial, and it is an attempt to prove a proposed truth. Hearsay is generally inadmissible and can be brought in only under an exception. Computer evidence can be admissible if it is shown to have been collected under defined procedures and as part of a regular or routine business practice. These procedures must be published *before* the incident and collection occur. Additionally, someone must testify that the data was collected under those circumstances to assure the court that the data is reliable and trustworthy on its own merits. This makes logging activities and strict adherence to procedure a critical step in evidence gathering and proving the chain of custody is reliable.

The copy process used must be shown to make a complete copy and not a subset or portion of the data that tells an incomplete or skewed story biased by a particular perspective. As discussed in previous sections, this can be done by copying an entire drive at the binary level or by copying data into a digital evidence bag.

After a complete copy is made, it should be sealed or rendered as read-only; burning the image to a write-once CD-ROM is a reliable method to accomplish this. The CD should be labeled with the date, the name of the machine from which the copied data was pulled, the contents (a brief description), and the collecting agent's signature. After a complete copy of the data is collected and stored, it must be secured from tampering or alteration to meet the necessary chain of custody rules. If the chain of custody is broken at any point, the court will simply throw out the evidence or bar it from being presented.

During each of the steps, logs should be kept of activity. If the data is accessed as a continuing part of the investigation, all such activity should be logged. Also, if the evidence is moved or relocated, the reason for the move and the procedures used should be documented. This might sound tedious, but it is critical to preserving the trustworthiness of the data so that it can be presented in court.

Risk Identification

Understand, explain, and participate in risk identification.

The idea behind security, any kind of security, is protecting something of value from loss, regardless of how that loss might occur. Previous chapters discussed the mechanics of such protection or the how-to aspect of protecting resources and assets. This chapter focuses on security management, and this section specifically focuses on the process of identifying the following:

- Assets
- Threats
- Vulnerabilities
- Risk

Asset Identification

One of the first steps in the entire security process and a task specifically before the security management team is the identification of assets.

The question that must be answered is, "What do we need to protect?" By focusing on this, you can quickly identify the assets of the company that need to be protected; at what level the protection should be set; and how much money, time, and energy should be spent in the protection process. Those who are disinterested in security always want to protect everything—this is the response of someone who has no concept of the security process or no interest. The money involved in protecting assets should be proportional to the assets' value.

The process of identifying assets and assigning value to them should be a team effort. It is time-consuming and can be a subjective process, so the more people involved, the more likely an accurate result will be derived. A sample of common assets used in business today include

- Servers
- Workstations
- Data
- Backup tapes
- Physical facilities

When evaluating assets and the cost, you can't simply take the value of the resource. Let's use the loss of a hard drive as an example. The base value would be the cost to replace the drive. But, additional costs that must be factored in are as follows:

- The loss of productivity while the drive is replaced
- The time it takes to install and recover the data to the drive
- The potential loss of data not on the current backup

After assets have been identified and valued, an appropriate level of money can be spent to help protect those assets from loss. The cost/benefit ratio should be an acceptable level. Following our hard drive example, if the drive costs $800 to replace, $1,000 in lost productivity, and $700 to recover data and re-create lost data, the total value of the hard drive asset would be $2,500. If you spent $8,000 protecting it, your cost of protection outweighs the cost of recovery and should not be implemented. If the $8,000 protects five hard drives as part of a protected disk configuration (RAID 5 set), your $8,000 now protects $12,500 (5 hard drives × $2,500) in assets and makes slightly more sense.

The cost of replacing the drive is fairly straightforward. The real skill (or work) is estimating the cost of the loss of productivity and recovery. Time and practice will make this process faster and more reliable. Each asset identified by the team should go through this evaluation process. After each asset has been identified and valued, additional discussion is required to identify the threats that might cause the actual loss of the resource.

Threat Identification

A *threat* or *threat agent* is anything that could cause the loss of an asset. Threats come in all shapes and sizes, as shown in the following list:

- Hacker
- Employee
- Virus
- Intruder/thief
- Fire
- Flood
- Power outage/power surge
- Equipment failure

Different assets are subject to different threats. A comprehensive security plan should seek to identify as many threats as possible for each asset. Each threat should then be evaluated and have an identified probability of occurrence assigned to it. Much like asset valuation, this process is sometimes easy and sometimes much more difficult. If we continue with our hard drive example, we can look at some of the threats that might cause the loss of the drive and then ultimately try to prevent that loss through planning.

A power outage/surge could cause the loss of the drive or the data on it. You would need to estimate the probability of that event occurring by looking at historical records, talking with onsite personnel, and talking with the local utility company. By researching, you can derive a fairly close estimate of the probability of a power surge or power outage happening at your facility.

Equipment failure is another threat that can unexpectedly rob you of your assets. Most drive manufacturers test their drives to produce a measurement called *mean time between failure (MTBF)*, which is usually measured in hours and based on statistical analysis. It must be carefully evaluated to come up with an accurate estimate of how long a drive can be in service before being replaced. The replacement should occur *before* failure to appropriately circumvent the threat of equipment failure. If a drive has an MTBF of 100,000 hours of use, it is important to check how that measurement or average was derived. If the manufacturer does its statistical analysis only to the first standard deviation, the drive has about a 68% chance of lasting 100,000 hours, which of course means it has a 32% chance of lasting shorter or longer than that (and you thought you'd never use statistics).

Other threats to your hard drive are more difficult to estimate. How often do fires occur? Do your estimates take into account the construction material of the building? How quickly can the fire department get there? When do floods occur? How often are they severe enough to flood the building based on its current location? These questions are much more difficult to answer based on probability, but they can still be estimated by doing research on historical occurrences of the events. So far, we have defined assets and threats; now we need to look at vulnerabilities.

Vulnerabilities

The word *vulnerability* is used to describe a weakness in an asset, its configuration, or its environment. We have identified your hard drive as an asset and identified some of the threats to it. Each threat exploits a vulnerability. A power outage is a threat that exploits the weakness of the hard drive's reliance on power; equipment failure exploits the hard drive's vulnerability to mechanical wear and tear. Other vulnerabilities might not be so obvious. Flooding has little to do with the actual hard drive itself and more to do with the environment in which the hard drive is placed. So, the vulnerability of the hard drive is that it can't safely be immersed in water, but it is really a vulnerability of the building or the facility and its location that most threatens the asset from flooding.

It is not just hardware that you need to be worried about when assessing vulnerabilities—you also need to consider software. Many of the operating systems and applications have well-known and not-so-well-known vulnerabilities. Often described as *exploits*, these are weaknesses in the software code or configuration that can result in a threat being able to take away access to the hard drive. Because of a misconfiguration in an operating system, it might become infected with a virus, and the virus can then attack the data on a drive and render it useless. A lesser-known virus might attack the hard drive directly by sending access requests continuously and cause the hard drive to spin at maximum speed indefinitely. This is a very indirect threat but no less real. The threat in this case is exploiting two vulnerabilities: the weakness in the software configuration and the hard drive's weakness of being a mechanical device.

Software vendors such as Microsoft, Novell, and IBM maintain Web sites where software vulnerabilities are posted. These sites also have configuration recommendations and software patches available to fix most of these problems. Other software configurations will be up to you, as a security manager, to fix. As our example illustrates, if you want to reduce the chances of infecting your systems with code viruses, you should invest in antivirus software on top of configuring the operating system properly. You can now combine your research, estimates, and best guesses into meaningful data for your security plan. We have looked at identifying assets, threats, and vulnerabilities and by combining them, we can arrive at risk.

Risk Assessment and Control

Risk can be described as the potential of a threat to exploit a vulnerability found in an asset. This combines all three of the previous points of discussion into a relevant and understandable principle. Table 9.2 further identifies the relationships between these concepts.

TABLE 9.2

THE RELATIONSHIPS OF ASSETS, THREATS, VULNERABILITIES, AND RISK

Asset	*Threat*	*Vulnerability*	*Risk*
Hard drive	Equipment failure	Mechanical wear and tear	Loss of drive, data, and productivity
Hard drive	Power outage	Reliance on constant power for proper operation	Loss of drive, data, and productivity
Data	User deleting files	Administrative mistake	Loss or corruption of data
Data	Virus	Nonexistent or outdated virus software	Loss or corruption of current data and possible loss of additional data
Web data	Hacker	Weak or misconfigured software	Company image, data corruption, loss of goodwill, loss of business
Corporate proprietary information	Corporate spy	Weak internal access policy	Loss of competitive edge in marketplace
Servers	Fire	Poor or nonexistent fire suppression system	Loss of a large volume of data and the possibility of enormous financial loss
Servers	Intruder	Poor facility security	Theft of servers
Database application	Administrator changing settings or configuration	Poor change policy or change control	Loss of data or access to the database, loss of productivity, and loss of functionality
Web-base database	Hacker	Poor or nonexistent firewall or Internet protection	Access, use, or release of confidential customer data, such as credit card numbers or personal information
IT manager	Being hit by a bus	Unique or key information known only to the IT manager	Loss of functionality of the IT department, loss of productivity, and loss of knowledge of configuration of mission-critical equipment and applications

This list could go on, but it is designed to give you an idea of the approach that should be taken during the process of identifying and assessing risk. Risk has one last piece of analysis: how likely it is that the scenarios listed might actually occur. To accurately gauge the probability of an event occurring, you can again use a combination of science and estimation.

Budgeting and Setting Probability Levels for Risk Management

To properly set probability and work out a budget to help control or manage risk (covered next), you should set a time window.

Most risk analysis utilizes the financial concept of a fiscal year. This sets a limit on the big picture of probability and confines the proposed expenditures, budget, and depreciation to a single 12-month period (not to mention the fact that the accountants will like you for it).

Let's use a specific event from Table 9.2 and analyze the probability of that event occurring. The table lists a virus as a possible threat to your data. Let's say that as a matter of procedure, you keep logs on all instances of virus attacks on your network. Using this historical data, you see that in the last two years of the life of your network, it was hit hard twice by viruses. Therefore, the likelihood that it will be hit is once per 12-month period. If the loss of each occurrence is estimated at $15,000 (a low estimate by most accounts), your annualized expectation is to lose $15,000 each year to virus attacks.

This example can illustrate the power of statistics. Because of the short time window used, your virus outlook is bad. If you went back a bit further, you might be able to identify that the viruses that hit the company were email based. Further analysis allows you to discover that, over the last ten years, your company was hit by viruses only five times. Now, your risk probability is cut in half to being infected only once every two years. Your annualized loss therefore drops to $7,500. This process would continue for each row of your risk table to produce a probability and cost outcome for each asset (see Table 9.3).

TABLE 9.3

RISK ASSOCIATED WITH PROBABILITY AND COST

Risk	*Value (includes loss of data, labor cost productivity, and replacement cost)*	*Probability (frequency in a 12-month period)*	*Annualized Cost*
Loss of hard drive due to mechanical failure	$4,000	100%	$4,000
Virus infection	$15,000	50%	$7,500
Hacker attack on Web site data resulting in lost credit card information	$500,000	30%	$150,000
Proprietary information loss	$2.5 million	10%	$250,000
Loss of key IT manager or IT personnel	$300,000	25%	$75,000

Now that you have a better understanding of how much you have at risk and the value of it, you can spend some money mitigating or reducing the probability.

If virus infections will cost $7,500/year, you can analyze the cost benefit of buying a $2,500 antivirus software package that needs to be upgraded only every two years (not the virus definition files but the actual application). If it is reasonable and the company executives see a benefit, the software should be purchased and deployed. If the loss of a key manager has an annualized cost of $75,000, several options exist to mitigate the loss of the data that person carries around in her head. Spending $10,000 to cross-train employees to be capable of doing each other's jobs would not be an unreasonable expenditure. It might even make sense to hire an additional employee to be an assistant to the IT manager and learn the necessary job skills to take over in the event of a bus accident.

The big conclusion to draw from this section is that no network is immune to risk, but by identifying assets, threats, and vulnerabilities, you will be able to make informed decisions on how to spend your money. Understanding the probabilities and costs will give you additional insight on what is likely and how to properly spend your money, reducing the most probable and expensive risks on your network. Not all risk can be mitigated to zero, however. Be as prepared as you can be and be comfortable with the levels of risk in your environment.

EXAM TIP

Know the differences between risks, vulnerabilities, and threats and their application to risk assessment and the overall security process.

CHANGE MANAGEMENT

Understand, explain, and participate in change management.

"Nothing is constant but change," and a modern network is no exception to the quote. The complexity of operating systems and networking hardware forces us to accept change as a constant. Unless you like being controlled by your network, you need to learn how to control the changes that must be deployed. Without change control, network, security, and software administrators (and managers) run the risk of undoing each other's changes or, worse, implementing changes that cause more problems than they solve.

An additional risk is that changes made will not be properly tested, documented, or thought out. If the change does cause problems, there will be no way back.

As a guideline, the following should be considered when creating a change management policy:

- Establish a schedule for changes.
- Utilize change notification.
- Conduct impact testing.

By following these three basic steps and the activities associated with them, you should be able to better control the changes made to your network and the equipment used on it. The first step is to schedule changes.

Scheduling Changes

Setting up a schedule for changes prevents the deployment of a change during key business times, such as a mission-critical process. We have been onsite at a client's facility when changes were made to a database application during end-of-month reporting. The changes caused the entire report process to fail, and it took several hours to get the system repaired and finally back online and available for the end users. Scheduling changes also ensures that multiple changes that could conflict or cause problems are not implemented on the same day or at the same time during the day.

Proper scheduling requires its own subprocess to be effective. Keep in mind that too much of a good thing can be counterproductive. If it takes three months to schedule a change, get it approved and finally implemented properly; you'll find that administrators and possibly even managers will bypass or subvert the process to get their jobs done. Long and bureaucratic processes have a tendency to worsen the situation, not help it. Scheduling changes should include the following:

- Change requests
- Change staging
- Change documentation

Change Requests

Change requests should involve some small amount of paperwork as a first step to scheduling and controlling change. The request should include the reasons the change is sought and both the potential benefits and possible downfalls. Also, the change request should be submitted a specific time prior to the requested change (say, two days or a week). This process relies on proper use by both management and administrators. If change requests are not answered promptly, administrators will be quick to abandon the process. On the other hand, if administrators submit too many change requests, managers are unlikely to have sufficient time to process all the requests submitted.

A hierarchy for the types of changes is necessary, and it should be relative to the potential impact and priority of the change. If established early and properly followed, the process can be fast and efficient. An example will help identify this behavior: A new driver for a network interface card (NIC) has been released by the manufacturer, and this particular card is widely used on your network. As a network administrator, you submit a request for changing the NIC drivers on your servers because of a key timing benefit that will improve network performance by 10%.

The benefit of this change relative to its impact should be taken into account and approved at the appropriate level in the management hierarchy. As you will see in the next section, an impact statement (along with the ability to undo the changes if they cause problems) should also be submitted. Generally, though, a driver upgrade should be processed quickly and at a low level in the IT department compared to a service pack installation or a major upgrade to a database application. This is primarily because drivers are small and the old driver can quickly be put back in place with minimal disruption in service if the new driver is found to be a problem.

Change Staging

In addition to a change request, *change staging* should be implemented to aid in the scheduling process. *Change staging* is a written plan that details the various deployment stages of a product, update, patch, and so on and the actions taken during these stages. For example, if a new version is released for your SQL database server and it solves a particular problem known to that database product, the change request should be submitted along with a staging statement outlining the proposed method for the deployment.

Staging enables large upgrades and changes to be gradually applied and efficiently undone (rolled back) if the change produces unexpected or undesirable results.

When upgrading our hypothetical SQL Server database systems, it would be foolish to upgrade all of them at the same time, unless the new software requires it. These types of changes should be staged one server at a time, and, if they're combined with other improvements (such as hardware upgrades), a complete staging schedule should be submitted and approved as part of the original change request. This procedure helps eliminate an upgrade to a database software package at the same time a new set of memory is installed. If the server stops functioning, the problem can easily be attributed to either the memory or the upgrade because they are not scheduled to take place at the same time.

NOTE

Change Staging Change staging, like change requests, should also be relative to the impact and type of the change and the priority and benefit of it.

Change Documentation

The preceding section implies that all this information is being written down: Documentation is critical. Meetings and discussions are not the same as actions, and documentation eliminates misunderstandings and misperceptions. Change documentation should include the following:

- Dates/times of proposed and approved changes
- Specific change details, such as files being replaced, configuration updates, software additions, and so on
- The approving agent
- The changing agent
- The immediate results of the change (good or bad)
- Long-term results of the change (good or bad)
- Specific change problems and issues that occur during the change process
- Recommendations and notes on this particular change event

After the change has been requested, documented, and approved, you should then send out notification.

Change Notification

Change notification can be done via email, or a copy of the change request can be circulated to those possibly affected by the change. The notification process should include a feedback option in case some detail was overlooked in the original submission and is identified by someone receiving the notification. At this point in the process, you still have not deployed the change but simply made others aware of your intent to do so. Before actually deploying the change, an impact assessment should be conducted.

Impact Assessment

What will the change do? Does it fix what you hope it will? Does it cause other problems? All these questions can be answered by an *impact assessment*, or *test phase*. This should be performed first on nonproduction equipment in a test lab and evaluated without affecting user productivity. The most effective way is to create a mock-up of the production environment and deploy changes there first. For example, if you are about to upgrade server software, you can accomplish your tasks by making a full backup of a production server and doing a restore on a server with a similar (or identical if necessary) hardware configuration in your lab. Deploying to test lab equipment first can uncover immediate problems and allow you time to adjust the deployment or the staging process to overcome the issues.

Impact testing should be well documented and involve simulated end user activity on the system. Using our database example, you would make a backup copy of the existing server and restore to your test server. Your next step would be to run scripts and execute stored procedures and queries to simulate what your end users would do. Hopefully, by testing, you can eliminate problems from the production deployment. In the real world, however, you never know the true impact of a change until you take the final step and upgrade your production systems. Things might go very smoothly on the test bench and fall apart when deployed on a production network with 4,000 users trying to query your newly upgraded SQL Server database.

Testing and impact analysis is still a critical step because it eliminates obvious errors and problems and lets you concentrate on the exceptions. Preparing for the exceptions leads us to our last discussion on changes: how you remove the changes if the result is not what you want.

Rollback Strategy

A *rollback strategy* should be part of every change operation. Although this might seem overly cautious, you need to remember that you are changing network components, software, and configurations that can impact productivity and the ability of the company to conduct business. Something as simple as upgrading a NIC driver can turn into a nightmare if you can't find a copy of the old driver when the new one fails to do its job. Events like this *do* happen, and you need to protect yourself and your company from such scenarios.

IN THE FIELD

IT'S JUST A NIC DRIVER!

While working on site at a factory, an administrator upgraded the driver for a server's NIC, believing all would go smoothly. Unfortunately, it didn't and the administrator spent almost an hour hunting for the original driver that had been overwritten in the upgrade process. In the meantime, an entire production line had to be shut down because the server was unavailable. That one simple change cost the company an estimated $22,000 for that one hour because of lost productivity and wages. ALWAYS have a path back to where you started!

As shown in the sidebar, even simple changes need to be tested and thought out and a rollback plan needs to be developed. If the administrator had simply spent an hour looking for the driver *before* upgrading the server, the upgrade would have been reversible within a minute or two.

Planning for a rollback should be part of the testing phase. After the system is deployed or upgraded or the network configuration is changed and tested, you must plan and practice your path back.

This is true even if the test upgrade goes smoothly. Changes do not always fail straight away; it might take a week before a particular error or problem is found. Documenting a path to return to a prechange state can make all the difference.

AWARENESS

Understand, explain, and participate in awareness.

You can't hold someone responsible for information or procedures you haven't made him aware of. This fact has been proven in court. Although there is a statement that "ignorance of the law is no excuse," ignorance of security policies because of lack of information or communication is an excuse. You must make the effort to inform employees of security and its importance to the company as well as tell them what is expected of them in terms of adherence to the policies.

Communication

Communication is the key to setting expectations. There are many ways to communicate your desires and expectations to your employees. User awareness starts when the employee is first hired and should continue throughout his career with the company. When first brought on board with the company, every employee should be briefed on the company security policies and expectations. These policies should be written in a language style that is easily understood, and the employee should be required to sign a paper that states that he has read and understood the policies and that he agrees to abide by the policies as stated. This signed document should then be placed in the employee's personnel file.

A word of caution is warranted here: Shoving a stack of documents under the nose of a newly hired employee and stating that he is required to sign them all on the first day of orientation is neither prudent nor will it hold up in court. An employee who is force-fed your security document is likely to make mistakes that could easily be avoided by taking the proper amount of time and explaining the documents fully. More importantly, in recent court cases, this behavior has been classified as aggressive and subjects the employee to a certain amount of fear of losing a new job.

This fear renders the signature invalid because of duress. If security is important, take the time to prove it by properly briefing all employees on expectations, policies, and procedures.

Employee awareness doesn't stop just because you briefed the employee when he was hired. Security and the network as a whole change constantly. At a minimum, employees should be reminded of their commitment to security once a year in a seminar or briefing or during their employee review. It is also a good time to have them re-sign a document stating that they have been briefed and updated on all the latest policy and procedural changes. By establishing this type of policy, good employees remain aware of security and the issues important to the company and bad employees are made aware of the possible punishments of being caught and effectively prosecuted.

Education and Resources

Awareness is not just the realm of the employees that you are in charge of. As a security administrator and engineer, you must constantly educate yourself by all means available. Taking classes, reading this and other books, and researching online will help you stay updated on all the latest security issues affecting corporate security environments.

The technology industry is still very young, and the security branch of it is younger still. Although viruses have been around for many years, the Internet and the idea of e-commerce are still in their infancy—along with many other aspects of the computer world. If security is something you have been put in charge of or volunteered for, then welcome to the challenging new science and art of computer security. It is, and will remain, a rapidly changing industry that requires constant education and awareness on the part of everyone involved.

DOCUMENTATION

Understand, explain, and participate in documentation.

What can we say but document, document, document? Document everything you do and be as detailed as necessary. It is a hard habit to get into but one worthy of the effort. Documenting security is particularly important because of the impact it can have on business and the potential impact if legal action is involved.

Without proper documentation, the time, energy, and money spent creating and deploying security on your network will become worthless in months or possibly even weeks. Most, if not all, of the documentation should be generated throughout the security process. From planning, to deployment, to ongoing management, documentation is the key to long-term success.

Some of the critical areas in which to build and maintain good documentation are

- Standards and guidelines
- Systems architecture and inventories
- Logs and auditing
- Classification

Creating good documentation in each of these areas establishes a solid foundation for building a security program that is both manageable and effective. Documentation gives users, managers, and executives a clear understanding of the intent and direction of the security program. Standards and guidelines should be the first set of documents created because they lay the foundation for the rest of security.

Standards and Guidelines

A *standard* outlines a desired outcome and is generally thought of as a rule. Rules enable a company to establish behaviors for everything from proper attire for work to how to send or store confidential information. Standards are particularly important in security because they set the ground rules for protecting the company's resources. Some examples of standards include the following:

- All email sent externally will have a corporate disclaimer at the bottom.
- Corporate ID badges will not be visible when off company property.
- When checking out highly sensitive or classified material, users must show a need for the material and have proper clearance.

- Anyone on company property who is not a direct employee or contractor must be identified with a red guest badge and be escorted at all times.

Each standard is designed to support a desired security outcome. The first item concerning email is used to protect the company if an employee misuses the corporate email system. Having users hide their ID badges when off company property at lunch or on appointments makes it more difficult for others to view and possibly copy the company ID and impersonate a legitimate user. Requiring users to prove a need to know as well as clearance prevents a user from accessing classified information just because she can. So, each standard is issued in support of a particular desired security outcome.

Guidelines are also rules, but they are more flexible than standards and often allow for use of personal and professional judgment when confronted with a situation. Examples of guidelines include the following:

- During the deployment of servers, all unnecessary services and applications should be disabled.
- Passwords should be created so they are difficult to guess.
- Audit and system logs should be archived in a consistent and well-organized manner.
- Server rooms shall be kept clean and free of dirt and debris.

Looking at the previous guidelines, you can see how they differ from standards. When you deploy your servers, you are guided to turn off unnecessary services and applications but have the flexibility to choose what those services will be. You are guided to make passwords difficult to guess but maintain the freedom to choose how that should be deployed. In the other two guidelines, users are told to archive properly and keep the server rooms clean but are again given the professional freedom to choose how to accomplish the requested actions.

When trying to choose between implementing a standard or guideline, ask yourself this question, "Do I want it done, or do I want it done in a specific way?" If you don't mind people using their own judgment, using a guideline is a flexible and effective way to accomplish a desired outcome. If consistency and reliability are more important, a standard is the best route. Documenting standards and guidelines enables you to build a framework for security and consistency.

Systems Architecture and Inventories

Consistency in the realm of security helps you at every turn. Early in the deployment of your security environment, you should document the architecture and configuration of your systems. This documentation should include

- **Network configuration**—This should include protocols, the system name, services installed (such as DNS, WINS, DHCP, and active ports), and special configurations that are specific to the system's networking configuration (such as access lists and specialized authentication mechanisms).
- **Operating system configuration**—This should include any special configurations not directly related to the network. If settings in configuration files (or the Registry) have been changed to enhance or improve performance or security, they should be documented.
- **Applications**—This part of the system documentation should include applications such as SQL, email services, and gateway functions and should include their configurations.
- **Hardware configuration**—This should include manufacturer information, current drivers, the date that item was put into service, and any other necessary hardware data.

When building documentation for systems architecture, the easiest way to develop it properly is to ask yourself what you would need to know if the system was stolen or what data would be required if the system had to be completely recovered due to a loss in a fire. This provides a good baseline for developing the details of the documentation.

Logs and Auditing

The log files themselves are documentation, but you need to know how to set up a log properly. If you have just deployed a Unix server or Windows 2000 Server, what are you supposed to log and audit? Standards should be developed for each platform, application, and server type to make this job more of a checklist function and less of a guessing game. A common storage location for all logs should be identified, and documentation should also state proper methods for archiving and reviewing logs.

Classification

The last area of documentation is classification of data. The standards for data classification can be taken directly from standards developed and published by the U.S. government or military, or you can come up with your own classification model. At a minimum, you should set standards for how information is evaluated and classified. After that is accomplished, you can then document how to store the data and ultimately destroy it.

Retention and storage documentation should outline the methods and standards for storing each classification level of data. If you choose the military levels of data classification, the documentation would include directions on handling and storage of data in each of the following categories:

- Unclassified
- Sensitive
- Confidential
- Secret
- Top secret

You can now look to your documentation for information on how to classify, handle, and store data. As a last event, the documentation should identify how to destroy your data when it's no longer needed. Several methods should be considered, including complete and assured erasure of information if the media (hard drive or floppy) is going to be reused and also complete destruction of the media when being decommissioned.

Military documentation outlines standards for the use of special programs to erase data off drives to allow them to be reused if still serviceable. The same documentation details how to *degauss* (demagnetize) the drive and disassemble and destroy each of the individual platters when destroying the drive after it is worn out. The important thing to remember here is to document your security desires and change and adjust that documentation when necessary.

CASE STUDY: Q-DRUGS

ESSENCE OF THE CASE

- How would you begin the investigation?
- Given the situation, would you continue to monitor the employee or stop her activity immediately?
- Which investigative techniques could be used to successfully prove or disprove the activities of the employee?

SCENARIO

You work in the IT department for a large pharmaceutical company and are the security investigator for computer incidents. You have received a call from a manager who suspects an employee of accessing highly sensitive documents and possibly copying them. You have been asked to investigate this possibility.

Several incidents have occurred recently to raise the suspicion of the manager of the suspected employee. On several occasions, the manager has observed the employee accessing protected areas of a key company server. The employee has also rushed to turn off the system or exit an application on the approach of other employees.

CHAPTER SUMMARY

KEY TERMS

- Asset
- Binary copy
- Chain of custody
- Change management
- Digital evidence bag
- Escalation
- Forensics
- Guideline
- Impact analysis
- Privilege management

This chapter examined the process of managing security. We discussed privilege management, focusing first on users, groups, and roles for maintaining and assigning privileges. We also discussed the concept of single sign-on and its benefits in the complexity of the modern network environment. Centralized and decentralized network management principles and concepts were also discussed, and we highlighted the fact that centralized networks tend to be more secure but less scalable and that decentralized networks are the opposite. Finally, we examined privilege management and the idea of auditing users and their use of privilege. In each case, where appropriate, we illustrated how to accomplish the tasks with step-by-step instructions.

We next looked into the legal world of computer forensics. We explained that this computer field is more about laws and rules of evidence and then proceeded to outline the steps necessary to accomplish a successful post-attack investigation, including collecting and preserving evidence and the chain of custody.

CHAPTER SUMMARY

Managing security is about managing risk and identifying and protecting assets. In risk assessment, we identified concepts of assets, threats, and vulnerabilities. Combining these three concepts gave us the foundation of risk assessment. We taught you how to evaluate risks and deploy solutions to mitigate and control risk exposure.

Change is constant, and you learned that change management will help you control your network and the inevitable changes that present themselves on a daily basis. We outlined procedures for change requests, staging, documentation, notification, testing, and rollback procedures. Documentation of changes was discussed and emphasized as an important aspect of the change process to ensure that people are aware of what has been changed and why. Other principles of awareness were covered next, highlighting the importance of communication in the network environment. Educating your users and yourself is a constant goal and should not be taken lightly.

Finally, we talked about documenting as part of security management. Without documentation, the security you struggle to implement won't last long. Specific areas that were highlighted as important included the following:

- Standards and guidelines
- Systems architecture and inventories
- Logs and auditing
- Classification

Security is a huge subject and security management is the key to controlling the situation. By following these guidelines and continuing to educate yourself, you'll find that it is a rewarding challenge.

- Probability
- Risk
- Role
- Rollback
- Single sign-on (SSO)
- Sniffer
- Staging
- Standard
- Threat
- Vulnerability

APPLY YOUR KNOWLEDGE

Exercises

9.1 Assigning Group-Based Privileges

This exercise demonstrates how to create a user and group relationship that allows you to assign privileges to the group and grant those privileges to a user through membership in a group.

Estimated Time: 10 minutes

1. On a Windows 2000 Professional computer, right-click My Computer and select Manage to open the Computer Management console.
2. Expand the Local Users and Groups node on the left side.
3. Right-click the Users folder and select New User. Create a new user account called `test1` with a password of `pass`. Fill in the rest of the data as necessary.
4. Right-click the Groups folder and select New Group. Create a new group called `testpriv` and add the `test1` user (created in step 3) to the group.
5. Open the Local Security Policy by selecting Start, Settings, Control Panel, Administrative Tools, Local Security Policy.
6. In the Local Security Policy MMC, expand the Local Policies node; then select the User Rights Assignment node.
7. In the Details pane (right side of window), select the right to Change System Time. Currently, only power users and administrators have the right to change the system time. Change this by double-clicking the text for the privilege and adding the `testpriv` group to the Local Policy setting.
8. Test your configuration by restarting the computer, logging on as the `test1` user and attempting to change the system time.

Review Questions

1. List three objects that can be the focus of privilege management and describe each.
2. What is the purpose of single sign-on?
3. What is risk?
4. Describe the principle of chain of custody.
5. What is the difference between a standard and a guideline?
6. What is the major drawback to deploying a network using only user-focused privilege management?
7. Why is it important to have a rollback plan?
8. Because computer evidence is hearsay, how can it be admitted into court?
9. What is the relationship between probability, risk, threat, asset, and vulnerability?
10. What is the primary purpose of auditing?

Exam Questions

1. Which of the following best describes group privilege management?

   A. Users get to decide who has access to files used and the level of permissions that will be set.

Apply Your Knowledge

B. Groups are built around business units, such as Marketing, and users are placed in appropriate groups. Privilege is then assigned to the group instead of individual users. Users are then placed in groups to grant privilege.

C. Groups are built around job function, such as server maintenance, and users are placed in appropriate groups. Privilege is then assigned to the group instead of individual users. Users are then placed in groups to grant privilege.

D. Users are directly assigned privilege based on job function or business need.

2. Which of the following best describes single sign-on?

   A. Users are required to log on only once to each operating system or platform throughout the day to gain access to network resources.

   B. Users maintain a single user account on each operating system or platform and manually synchronize their accounts so that multiple logons are not required.

   C. A single logon is required for access to all network resources with the exception of highly classified or sensitive data.

   D. Users are required to log on once to a single trusted authority for access to any needed network resources.

3. What best describes the process of tracking users and their use of privileges or permissions?

   A. Sniffing

   B. Single sign-on

   C. Auditing

   D. Forensics

4. Which of the following best describes the relationship between centralized and decentralized security?

   A. Centralized security is more scalable and less secure than decentralized.

   B. Decentralized security is more scalable and more secure than centralized.

   C. Centralized and decentralized security have the same scalability, but decentralized is more secure.

   D. Centralized and decentralized have about the same security, but centralized is more scalable.

   E. Centralized is more secure but less scalable, whereas decentralized security is less secure but more scalable.

5. A user using a known weakness in operating system code has made himself an administrator. This process is best known as what?

   A. Privilege escalation

   B. Single sign-on

   C. Virus

   D. Privilege management

   E. Rollback

6. Which of the following are activities associated with computer forensics? (Choose all that apply.)

   A. Collecting and analyzing data from hard drives

   B. Collecting and analyzing data from RAM and cache memory

   C. Dusting the computer case and equipment for possible fingerprints

APPLY YOUR KNOWLEDGE

D. Backing up drives and system files and analyzing them for changes or alterations

E. Analyzing phone logs for possible clues to the user's whereabouts

7. You are analyzing your network for possible clues during an attack. What tools would let you analyze, in real-time, the attack behavior on your systems and network equipment? (Choose two.)

   A. Auditing logs

   B. Defragmenter

   C. A network analyzer or sniffer

   D. Multimeter

   E. Network scope

8. You are conducting an investigation after a computer network has been attacked. You have dumped the contents of RAM and system cache on a victim server. What should be your next step?

   A. Run a disk checking utility to see whether files have been changed.

   B. Run a system file verifier to see whether files have been altered.

   C. Ensure that a backdoor has not been placed in the system.

   D. Image the system or back up the entire contents of the drives.

   E. Reboot the system.

9. Proving the integrity of evidence and its flow from crime scene to courtroom is best described as what?

   A. Digital signing

   B. Forensics

   C. Verification

   D. Imaging

   E. Evidence flow

   F. Chain of custody

10. Risk is made up of which of the following components? (Choose three.)

    A. Vulnerability

    B. Probability

    C. Annualized value

    D. Threat

    E. Value

11. Which of the following would be considered threats to a network? (Choose all that apply.)

    A. An end user accidentally deleting files

    B. An employee misusing her privilege on the network to steal company trade secrets

    C. A hard drive having a mechanical failure

    D. An unescorted guest stealing components from a computer

    E. Fire or flood

12. What is the first step in change control?

    A. Change staging

    B. Change testing

    C. Change request

    D. Change documentation

    E. Change notification

APPLY YOUR KNOWLEDGE

13. You are the system administrator for a small company and have just learned about a patch that is available for your servers. You download the patch, and several of the servers stop functioning properly. What should your next step be to return the servers to a functional state?

    A. Roll back the changes.

    B. Document the changes and troubleshoot.

    C. Call the manufacturer and see whether a fix is available.

    D. Reload the patch and see whether the problems stop.

    E. Issue a change notification and troubleshoot.

14. Which of the following statements is most accurate?

    A. Standards and guidelines are both sets of rules and are both flexible in their implementations.

    B. Standards and guidelines are both sets of rules and are both specific in their implementations.

    C. Guidelines are rules that have set methods for implementation, whereas standards are rules that are flexible in their implementation methods.

    D. Standards are rules that have set methods for implementation, whereas guidelines are rules that are flexible in their implementation methods.

15. Which of the following best describes a vulnerability?

    A. A vulnerability is any agent that could do harm to your network or its components.

    B. A vulnerability is a weakness in the configuration of software or hardware that could allow a threat to damage the network.

    C. A vulnerability measures the cost of a threat attacking your network.

    D. A vulnerability is the likelihood of a particular event happening given an asset and a threat.

16. What is the purpose of an impact assessment?

    A. It allows changes to be deployed and evaluated on a test network or nonproduction device to view possible effects.

    B. It allows a relationship to be built between vulnerability, asset, and probability.

    C. It sets a monetary value on a change so that financial impact can be evaluated.

    D. It identifies the impact that changes have after they've been deployed to a production network.

17. What is change staging?

    A. A process in which changes are tested before they are deployed

    B. A process of writing or scripting changes

    C. A process of applying changes in small phases so the change process can be controlled better and rolled back more quickly if necessary

    D. A process of documenting changes and then testing them

18. User awareness is best achieved by which of the following? (Choose two.)

    A. During employee orientation, briefing the employee on the standards and policies of the company

APPLY YOUR KNOWLEDGE

B. Wall posters

C. Email

D. A yearly briefing or seminar

19. What are the most common methods of data collection during a forensic investigation? (Choose two.)

A. Intrinsic

B. Automatic

C. Inferred

D. Manual

Answers to Review Questions

1. User, group, and role.

   User privilege management is focused on individual users and their needs. Privileges are assigned directly to a user's account.

   Group privilege management identifies the need of groups of people and assigns privilege to the group instead of the user's account. Users are placed into the groups to gain privilege, and groups are typically focused on business units or departments such as marketing, sales, IT, and so on.

   Role-based privileges are assigned and configured in the same way as group privileges. Roles focus on activities such as backup, restore, and application installation, whereas groups focus on business units.

2. Single sign-on attempts to simplify a user's ability to access resources by allowing him to log on once, authenticate against a single authority, and still be capable of gaining access to resources on any server regardless of operating system.

3. A risk is the probability that a threat will be capable of exploiting a vulnerability and causing damage to the network.

4. Chain of custody shows the path of evidence from the crime scene to the courtroom. If the chain of custody is broken (files are changed or deleted), data evidence is likely to be thrown out.

5. A standard is a well-defined rule of achieving a desired behavior. Methods of achieving the standard are spelled out in detail. A guideline is similar to a standard but has flexibility in its method of implementation.

6. A network deployed with user-focused privilege management is very hard to grow. User management is very administratively intensive.

7. A rollback plan enables you to undo network changes when those changes do more harm than good.

8. Hearsay evidence can be used in court when its trustworthiness can be proven. With regard to computer forensic evidence, it must be collected and stored in an appropriate manner so that the court trusts the reliability of the data presented.

9. Assets are items of value to the company, and a threat is any agent that can do harm to an asset. A vulnerability is a weakness in an asset that can be exploited by a threat; risk is the probability that a threat agent will damage an asset.

10. Auditing enables you to track which resources users have been using (files, services, servers, and so on) and helps you track activity on your network with regard to changes in privileges and privilege escalation.

APPLY YOUR KNOWLEDGE

Answers to Exam Questions

1. **B.** Group-based privilege management focuses on business units, such as marketing, to assign and control users. Functions such as server maintenance are role-based.

2. **D.** The goal of SSO is the use of a single user account on a single operating system. All other operating systems trust the authority of each other and allow a single account to be granted privilege to any network resource regardless of classification. Using multiple accounts defeats the purpose and idea of SSO.

3. **C.** Auditing is the process of tracking users. Sniffing looks at real-time data transfer on the network, and SSO is the use of a single logon account for access to all resources. Forensics is the practice of post-attack crime investigation.

4. **E.** Centralized security requires that a single group of administrators manages privileges and access. This makes the model more secure but less scalable than decentralized security, which is made up of teams of administrators trained to implement security for their areas.

5. **A.** The process of elevating privilege or access is referred to as privilege escalation.

6. **A, B, D.** Dusting for fingerprints is a law enforcement forensics function. Reviewing phone logs for a user's whereabouts is also a law enforcement function, not computer forensics. If the question had stated that you were reviewing phone logs to prove activity was occurring at a certain time, it would fall under computer forensic function.

7. **A, C.** Both auditing logs and network sniffing are activities that are updated in real-time and allow you to monitor user/network activity.

8. **D.** After dumping RAM and cache data, the next step is to preserve the contents of the hard drives so that any further evaluation doesn't corrupt or alter the data's state.

9. **F.** The description is of chain of custody.

10. **A, B, D.** Risk is comprised of the probability of a threat exploiting a vulnerability.

11. **A, B, C, D, E.** All the listed items have a potential to damage network resources. Intent is not measured, so even a user accidentally deleting files is a threat.

12. **C.** Requesting the change should be the first step because all other activity will be useless if the change is denied.

13. **A.** Rolling back changes should be the next step to recovering the servers and making them quickly available for users.

14. **C.** This answer correctly defines the differences between standards and guidelines.

15. **B.** A vulnerability is a weakness in hardware or software.

16. **A.** The purpose of an impact assessment is to view possible changes before they're deployed in a production environment.

17. **C.** This is the most correct description of staging changes.

18. **A, D.** Employee orientation and yearly briefings are the two most effective ways to maintain user awareness. Although the other answers listed would work, they are passive.

19. **B, D.** Manual and automatic are the two most common methods for data collection during a forensics process.

APPLY YOUR KNOWLEDGE

Suggested Readings and Resources

Online Material

1. Beta Systems. "Immediate Escalation of Security Related Events" (`http://www.betasystems.com`).
2. Brenner, Susan. "Private" Computing Security, Approaches to Computer Security: Practical and Legal Issues" (`http://www.cybercrimes.net`).
3. BS 7799 ""Security Standards" (`http://bsonline.techindex.co.uk`).
4. Collie, Byron S. "Computer Investigation and Post-Intrusion Computer Forensics Analysis" (`http://www.usyd.co.au/su/is/comms/security`).
5. Ernst and Young. "Computer" Forensics, Response Versus Reaction an Expert Paper" (`http://www.ey.com/au/itrma`).
6. Feldman, John, and Joseph V. Giordano. "Cyber Forensics" (`http://www.afrl.af.mil/techconn`).
7. ISO 17799 "Security Standards" (`http://www.iso.ch`).
8. Meta Security Group. " "Incident Response and Computer Forensic Services" (`http://www.metasecuritygroup.com`).
9. Noblett, Michael "G., Mark M. Pollitt, and Lawrence A. Presley. "Recovering and Examining Computer Forensic Evidence" (`http://www.fbi.gov/hq/lab/fsc/backissu/oct2000`).
10. Sans Institute. "Computer Security Incident Handling: Step by Step" (`http://www.sans.org`).
11. "What Is Computer" Forensics?" (`http://www.computer-forensics.com`).

PART II

Final Review

Fast Facts

Practice Exam

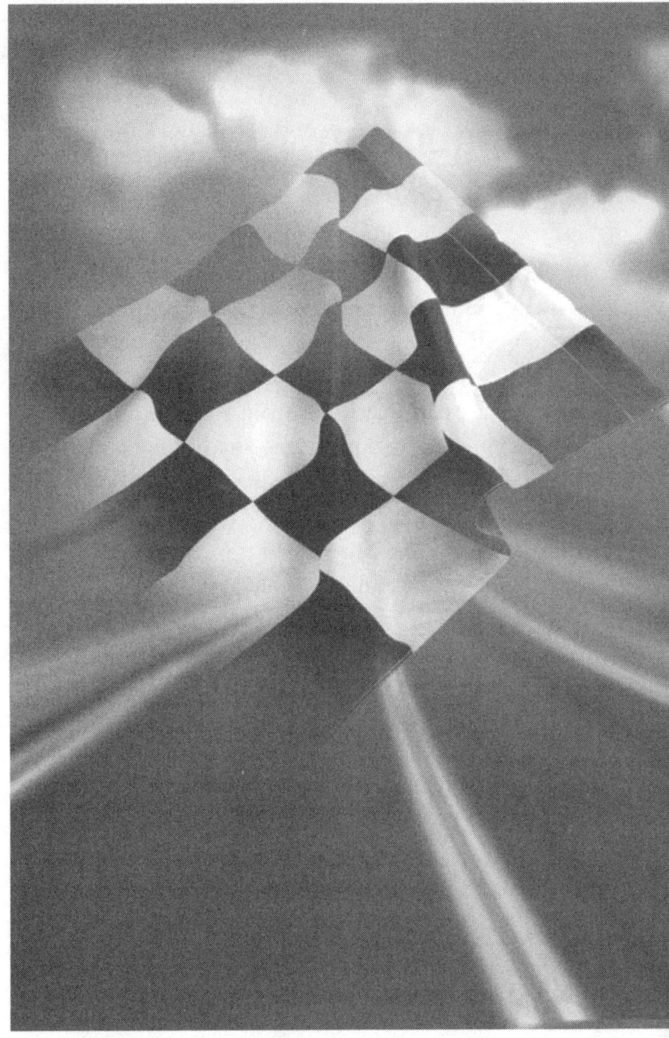

Fast Facts

The nine chapters of this book cover the objectives for the Security+ exam. After reading all of that, what are the important points that you really need to know? What should you review in that last hour prior to walking into the testing center to take the CompTIA Security+ certification exam?

In general, we recommend a regular, steady approach to exam preparation rather than cramming like crazy in the last few days or hours before taking the Security+ exam. In the weeks and months leading up to the exam, you should work your way through this book and various ancillary study materials as needed to become both familiar and comfortable with the information, terms, concepts, tools, and technologies covered in the Security+ exam. The day before the exam, spend some time reviewing your notes and read through these Fast Facts to get yourself as ready as possible. The day of the exam, get up early, have a good meal, and take your time driving to the exam site. Leave yourself plenty of time to drive to the test center, and try to get there at least 15 minutes early to give yourself time to prepare mentally. The last thing you want to do is to crank up your stress level by rushing to the test center at the last minute—or even worse, running late!

The following sections cover the most significant points of the previous nine chapters as well as provide some insight into what information makes particularly good exam prep material. There is no substitute for real-world, hands-on experience, and there is no substitute for reading the rest of this book. However, this material is a great review before heading for the testing center. Knowing what to expect on the exam goes a long way toward a passing score. The information that follows summarizes and calls attention to the material you must know to pass the exam. You needn't memorize these concepts; rather, if you seek to understand why and how they are as they are, you will have no difficulty passing the exam.

Introductory Note: Learn Key Terms!

In the sections that follow, we cover all five of the Security+ exam objectives, in detail, each under its own heading. But as you review this body of material, there is one general tip we can share with you about preparing for this exam that will do you a tremendous amount of good without giving any of the exam's confidential content away. That is, you should also review and attempt to master all the key terms in each of this book's nine chapters. Because the Security+ exam is primarily conceptual and terminological, it stands to reason that much of what you'll be tested on rests on a foundation of the terms and concepts that underlie information security. Become entirely familiar with the key terms in Chapters 1–9, and you'll be well on your way toward passing this exam. We review most of the other salient facts here (and you can find lots of details in related chapters).

General Security Concepts

- A mandatory access control (MAC) policy is characterized by information classification and user clearance levels.
- MAC policy dictates that a user cannot change the security permissions or configuration.
- MAC policy is layered and is also referenced as a "latticed" approach.
- A discretionary access control (DAC) policy is characterized by a user's ability to pass on permissions.
- A DAC policy also identifies the owner of information. The owner has control over who gets permissions to the object and what those permissions will be (hence, the owner's discretion).
- A role-based access control (RBAC) policy identifies users in the company based on a job function or logical business grouping. Permissions are granted to the group and not directly to the individual.
- Examples of RBAC groupings might include the help desk or a project team.
- Authentication is the process used to identify an agent on the system or network.
- Authorization is what your permissions and rights are based on a given authentication ID.
- Accounting/auditing is a system used to track what you have done (or tried to do) based on your authentication and authorization status.
- Authentication is based on something you know, something you have, or something you are.
- Something you know can be a simple PIN or a complex username and password.
- Something you have can be a software- or hardware-based token used during the logon process.
- Something you are is based on biology and can be a fingerprint, an iris profile, or a voiceprint.
- Passwords should use mixed case alpha characters, numbers, and special characters to make them resistant to brute-force and simple guessing attacks.
- Passwords should never be complete words. This makes them susceptible to dictionary attacks.
- To resist both brute-force and guessing attacks, a password should be at least eight characters long.

- A dictionary attack is software that uses a list of known words in an attempt to break a user's password.
- A brute-force attack is software designed to randomly guess a user's password.
- To help combat password guessing and dictionary attacks, an account lockout should be set to lock user accounts after a certain number of failed tries.
- Kerberos is a specific implementation of a username/password authentication scheme. It is available across a wide variety of operating system platforms.
- Kerberos is designed to allow mutual authentication (both parties are positively identified), secure the username and password during transmission, decrease the time it takes to access resources, and scale to large network environments.
- Kerberos components include an authentication server (AS), a ticket granting server (TGS or system manager), a security database, and a session ticket (ST).
- Challenge Handshake Authentication Protocol (CHAP) is a common username/password authentication scheme implemented on dial-up or remote access connections.
- CHAP was designed to replace schemes that are simpler and easier to hack, such as Password Authentication Protocol (PAP) and Shiva's Password Authentication Protocol (SPAP).
- CHAP sends its authentication challenge at the beginning of the session and at random intervals throughout to ensure a session hasn't been compromised.
- Certificates are used as another form of electronic identification.
- Certificates are operating system independent and can be used for encryption and digital signatures as well as electronic logon.
- Certificates rely on a trusted entity to issue certificates. The issuer is referred to as a certificate authority (CA).
- The CA can be self-signed (run within the company) or third party.
- A certificate is an authentication method based on something you have.
- Certificates include the following information: version, serial number, signature algorithm ID, issuer name, subject name, subject public key information, and issuer unique ID.
- There are two pieces to certificates: the public key and private key.
- The public key is usable by anyone; the private key is unique and must be protected from theft or damage. The private key should reside only with the owner of the key pair.
- Because a certificate uses two keys, it is an asymmetric cryptography system.
- If the private key is compromised, the CA should revoke the certificate and issue a new one. The CA should also publish the revocation in a certificate revocation list (CRL) so that other users know the original certificate is no longer valid.
- By using a portion of the private key, a digital signature can be produced (a unique hash). The digital signature can be verified using the public key of the same key pair (both keys are from the signer).
- Token authentication schemes rely on something you have, such as a hardware- or software-based token.

- The benefit of using tokens is that they cannot be readily shared (like passwords) and use a one-time password scheme.
- One-time passwords offer protection against password interception.
- Token systems can be complex to deploy, difficult to maintain, and expensive.
- Biometrics use an authentication scheme based on something you are (physical characteristic). See Table 1 for more details.

TABLE 1

BIOMETRIC REVIEW

Biometric	*Description*
Fingerprint	This involves the process of thumbprint or fingerprint scanning and matching.
Hand/Palm geometry	Identity is based on a person's palm or hand profile.
Voiceprint	A user identifies herself by speaking into a microphone.
Facial geometry	A user is identified on the profile and characteristics of her face.
Iris profile	The colored part of the eye is used to properly identify an individual.
Retina scan	The blood vessel pattern at the back of the eye is read to properly identify an individual.
Signature	An individual signs electronically, and the signature is matched to a database.

- Because they are based on physical characteristics, biometric authentication systems are very difficult to compromise.
- Biometrics can be complex, difficult to maintain, and expensive.
- To strengthen authentication security, more than one method can be used. This is called multi-factor authentication. Weaknesses of single-authentication methods are detailed further in Table 2.

TABLE 2

WEAKNESSES OF USING A SINGLE-AUTHENTICATION METHOD

Authentication Method	*Defeated by*
Username/Password; Kerberos; CHAP	Theft; disclosure (written down); dissemination (given out); guessing
Certificates; software tokens	Cloning; unsecured PC
Hardware tokens	Theft of token

- Mutual authentication is a process in which both agents are identified. IPSec, CHAP, and Kerberos can be configured to use mutual authentication.
- Plan and identify roles for servers in your network (that is, your Web server, file and print server, email server, and so on).
- Turn off unnecessary services and protocols to help reduce the risk of attacks against the servers, called *hardening*. Review some of the more common attacks in Table 3.

TABLE 3

ATTACK REVIEW

Attack Type	*Common Forms*	*Description*
Denial-of-service (DoS) and distributed denial-of-service (DDoS)	Smurf, fraggle, ping floods, land, teardrop, and SYN flooding	These attacks seek to deny legitimate users the use of network resources.
Back door	Back Orifice, NetBus, VNC, PC Anywhere, and SubSeven	This attack allows a system user to use a system outside normal procedures.
Spoofing	Network traffic that contains a different (and usually quite specific) source address from that of the machine actually generating the traffic	This allows a user to impersonate a valid source or destination of network traffic. It can also be used to impersonate entire network services such as DNS, Web, and email.
Man-in-the-middle	Use of network sniffing programs to collect and retransmit data	This attack allows an agent to be inserted between two communicating hosts generally for the purpose of intercepting sensitive data.
Replay	Use of network sniffing programs to collect and retransmit data	This form of attack involves capturing legitimate network traffic (possibly altering it) and then resending it at a later time.
Hijacking	Use of network-based programs to intercept, inject, and retransmit data	This results in an attacker stealing a session from a legitimate user. The attacker assumes the identity of the user whose session has been hijacked.
Software exploitation	N/A	This method uses a systematic approach to find security holes and weaknesses in published software.

- Malicious code is a form of attack that includes viruses, Trojan horses, logic bombs, and worms.
- A virus is a small chunk of code that generally attaches itself to executable program code and causes some form of damage when the program is executed.
- Viruses replicate each time the code is executed.
- Many of the common code viruses are now distributed through email and instant messaging.
- A Trojan horse is a program that has some apparent beneficial use and also has code hidden inside that allows the system to be attacked or infiltrated.
- A logic bomb is virus code that is built to do its damage when a particular event or condition is met. The virus code is triggered with the deletion of the programmer's user account or when a certain date is reached.
- A worm is just like a virus with the exception that it is self-replicating.
- Social engineering is a type of attack that attempts to exploit human behavior.
- Common social engineering attacks include piggybacking through doorways, physically impersonating legitimate clients or vendors, and impersonating through email and over the phone.

- The best defense against social engineering attacks is training and security awareness.
- Auditing gives security administrators the ability to track the use of corporate resources.
- Auditing can be used to track the use of entry systems, dial-up services, VPNs, files, and printers. Other behaviors, such as privilege escalation, can also be tracked.
- Privilege escalation occurs when a user changes or increases her level of access to a particular object. This can be done through virus code, exploiting known operating system vulnerabilities, or with bugs in application code.
- Auditing produces log files, and these log files must be reviewed on a regular basis to identify any inconsistencies. This behavior makes auditing a reactionary measure of security (as opposed to a preventative measure).

COMMUNICATIONS SECURITY

- 802.1x is an IEEE standard for wireless LANs. It relies on extensible authentication protocol (EAP) for authentication.
- Anyone with a proper receiver and proximity to the wireless network can receive a signal.
- The Wireless Equivalency Protocol (WEP) was designed to offer wireless networks a level of security equivalent to wired networks without encryption.
- Wireless access points (WAPs) are devices that allow users access to the wireless network and are the bridge between wired and wireless networks. These devices can be combined (daisy-chained) to provide extended service reach.
- Before deploying wireless networks, a site survey should be done to identify potential problems associated with use of the technology.
- Virtual private networking (VPN) gives users the ability to securely connect to a private network over a public network (usually the Internet).
- Remote access dial-in user service (RADIUS) is a centralized method of authentication, authorization, and accounting in dial-up and VPN services.
- Terminal access controller access control system (TACACS) is very similar to RADIUS in function and allows for centralization of authentication, authorization, and accounting services in a networking environment.
- RADIUS combines certain services, such as authentication and authorization, whereas TACACS keeps each of these components separate.
- The two most common VPN protocols are Point to Point Tunneling Protocol (PPTP) and Layer 2 Tunneling Protocol (L2TP).
- PPTP uses an embedded encryption system to protect data, and L2TP uses IP Security (IPSec) for its encryption.
- To further protect the systems, the tunnel is not established until both sides of the VPN are properly identified.
- PPTP uses TCP port 1723 and encapsulates (tunnels) encrypted packets inside clear-text IP packets.
- L2TP uses UDP port 1701 and encapsulates encrypted packets inside clear-text IP packets.
- Secure shell is a tool used primarily for remote administration. It uses TCP port 22 and can use IDEA, 3DES, DES, Blowfish, or RSA for its encryption.

- IPSec can be used independently of VPNs to secure network traffic between any two hosts that support the use of the IPSec protocol.
- IPSec works at the Network layer of the OSI model and uses authentication header (AH, `IP Protocol 51`), encapsulated secure payload (ESP, `IP Protocol 50`), and Internet key exchange (IKE, `UDP port 500`) as its three primary components.
- AH is used to ensure the data in transit has not been altered (data integrity) and was sent by the correct party. The data itself is not encrypted.
- ESP is used to encrypt the contents (confidentiality) and can establish data integrity as well.
- IKE is used to establish a secure key exchange when the two communicating sources do not have a preshared key.
- IPSec can use various encryption algorithms, including DES, 3DES, and SHA-1.
- Email is one of the most common applications deployed in business today. Some of the more common vulnerabilities include clear-text transfer of data, viruses, spam, hoaxes, and impersonation/social engineering.
- To protect email from clear-text exploits, S/MIME and PGP can be deployed.
- Secure Multipurpose Internet Mail Extensions (S/MIME) allows encryption of email and its attachments. A message being sent to a recipient is encrypted using the receiver's public key and decrypted with the receiver's private key.
- Pretty good privacy (PGP) is another method employed to protect email. It uses symmetric keys for message encryption and asymmetric keys for digital signatures and key distribution/management.
- Email systems can be protected from viruses using virus-checking applications and blocking attachments with certain extensions (usually extensions related to executable programs).
- Spam is unsolicited email that is generally credited with bogging down email systems and slowing network performance.
- Filters can be used to help eliminate many forms of spam, but no one method exists to eliminate all spam.
- Hoaxes are email messages sent with the intent of informing a recipient of a problem and providing instructions on how to fix the problem. The problem is usually a virus, and the fix is deleting a file from the local system.
- User awareness is the best form of prevention for hoaxes. Any email received stating that a virus is attacking the system should be investigated thoroughly before any action is taken on a local system.
- Impersonation is used to gain information or disrupt business and services to legitimate users. Email requesting passwords and other sensitive data should be treated as an attack. User awareness is the best protection from this type of attack.
- The Web and Web-based services are vulnerable to attack because of the use of clear-text transfer of data, Java, ActiveX, CGI, and cookies.
- Secure Socket Layer (SSL), Transport Layer Security (TLS), and Hypertext Transfer Protocol/Secure (HTTP/S) are protocols designed to protect clear-text, Web-based services from attack. These protocols work between the Application and Transport layers of the OSI model.

- Java, ActiveX, and GGI are all programming languages and must be properly controlled through the browser settings to prevent possible damage or exploitation of the system.
- Cookies are small bits of information placed on your system by Web servers that store data about you and your preferences. Browsers can be configured to disallow cookies.
- Lightweight Directory Access Protocol (LDAP) is a common protocol used in network operating systems for accessing information about users and services. LDAP can be secured using SSL, TLS, or IPSec.
- LDAP uses ports TCP 389 for regular information transfer and 636 for secure communication over SSL.
- FTP is a utility designed to transfer files. It uses port TCP 21 for the connection request and port TCP 20 for data transfer. It is a clear-text utility.
- S/FTP is a secure form of FTP based on SSH technology.
- It is common practice to allow anonymous connections to FTP servers. To better secure the server, you can turn off anonymous access and force users to supply a valid username/password to gain access.
- Instant messaging (IM) is an Internet service that provides real-time communication capabilities using text-based messaging.
- IM is clear text and subject to eavesdropping by use of programs such as network sniffers. (Note that some IM programs now have built-in transport encryption.)
- Instant messaging was built without security in mind, and it is therefore very difficult to use it securely.
- An IM user can be easily impersonated by theft or guessing of the IM user's password.
- Most IM clients are built with the capability to send and receive files, making them vulnerable to malicious code attacks.

INFRASTRUCTURE SECURITY

- A firewall is a hardware or software system designed to protect one network from another network. The various types of firewalls are covered in Table 4.

TABLE 4

REVIEW OF FIREWALL TYPES

Firewall Type	*Description*
Packet filtering	Uses lists to check the source/destination network address, source/destination port, and protocol.
Circuit-level gateway	Monitors at the Session layer of the OSI and checks relationships between hosts to ensure it is allowed traffic.
Application-level gateway	Known as a proxy, this device functions at the Application layer of the OSI. It has the most complex set of rules and can control access by user ID and policies.
Stateful inspection	Combination of all three of the other firewall types.

- A router is an OSI layer 3 device that connects two or more networks and routes traffic between them.
- Routers can generally act as packet filtering and circuit-level firewalls.

- A switch operates at the Data Link layer of the OSI model. It connects devices and operates using the MAC address of the network interface. Little security is associated with switches other than port blocking and MAC address filtering.
- Switches can be used to create virtual LANs, which helps reduce broadcast traffic and increase network performance.
- A switch, by design, does not forward all traffic out all ports as a hub does (with the exception of broadcast/multicast traffic). It forwards traffic out the destination port only (based on the MAC address of the recipient).
- Telcom and PBX equipment is a likely target of attack because it represents a centralization of communications lines. Eavesdropping and use of services such as long distance are common forms of attack.
- To reduce the likelihood of remote maintenance compromise on a PBX system, a strong authentication system should be used.
- Intrusion detection systems (IDSs) are designed to capture data off the network and notify administrators of attacks in progress.
- IDS can be active or passive. Passive IDS notifies administrators that the system is under attack and allows the security team to respond. Active IDS uses preconfigured actions and implements them as soon as the attack is registered.
- The IDS can be host based or network based. Host-based systems monitor all traffic on a host-by-host basis. Network IDS systems monitor data streams on a given network segment.
- IDSs can monitor for known attacks (pulled from a characteristics list) and trigger an alert. This is known as a misuse system. The IDS can look for traffic that is not in a defined list of good traffic, which is known as anomaly analysis.
- If an IDS triggers a response on traffic that is allowed, this is referred to as a false positive.
- A false negative is an acknowledgment of intrusion in an intrusion detection system, which means an intrusion has occurred but the IDS discarded related events or traces as false signals.
- Fault, configuration, accounting, performance, and configuration management are collectively known as FCAPS. It is a concept developed by the OSI to address issues associated with network management.
- Fault management focuses on detecting and fixing problems with equipment, media, and software faults.
- Configuration management focuses on managing device configuration and associated files.
- Accounting management looks at the physical composition of different network devices and their individual components.
- Performance management involves baselining and trend analysis of the network as a whole as well as individual components, such as routers, switches, and servers.
- Security management relates to data encryption and integrity, authentication, and managing the overall security processes.
- Current media types used in modern networking include coax, unshielded and shielded twisted pair (UTP/STP), fiber optic, and wireless.
- Coax, UTP, and STP are highly susceptible to electronic eavesdropping or tapping. Fiber is the least susceptible to tapping because it uses light instead of electronic signals.
- Wireless systems are prone to eavesdropping because of the wireless nature of the equipment. Encryption should be used to minimize this danger.

- Removable media represents a significant security risk to a company and its data resources because of the transportability of the media device. To achieve better security, such devices must be controlled and tracked when removed from the host system.
- Removable media devices include tape, writable/rewritable CD-ROMs, writable DVD-ROMs, hard drives, floppy disks, flash cards, and smart cards.
- There are three major types of security zones: *bastion host, screened-host gateway*, and *screened-subnet gateway*. These are detailed in Table 5.

TABLE 5

REVIEW OF SECURITY ZONES

Type	*Description*
Bastion host	Dual-homed device that allows only certain types of traffic to pass to the internal network. This is a single point of entry and exit between the protected (internal) network and the outside world.
Screened-host gateway	Also a packet-filtering device. It communicates only with a designated application gateway on the internal network. The host screens for approved traffic and then forwards the approved traffic to the application gateway, which then determines how to handle the traffic.
Screened-host subnet	This configuration includes two screened host gateways that are used to create an isolated LAN referred to as a screened subnet or DMZ. Key public resources such as WWW, FTP, email, and DNS can be placed in the DMZ, providing faster access for the public and reduced traffic on the internal corporate LAN.

- Network address translation (NAT) is a method of obscuring one network from another. This is usually done with private addressing on the inside (corporate network) to the outside network (Internet). It might or might not involve the use of private IP addressing defined in RFC 1918.
- The private IP addresses are 10.0.0.0–10.255.255.255, 172.16.0.0–172.31.255.255, and 192.168.0.0–192.168.255.255.
- A honeypot system is a computer configured with a lower level of security to act as a decoy and pull attacks away from other systems. The honeypot usually has an active IDS installed to notify the security team of attempted intrusion. It is designed to lure would-be attackers long enough for a trace to take place.
- An incident response team is responsible for reacting to successful attacks and performing the necessary actions to reduce the impact of the attack and increase the chances of identifying the hackers through computer forensic analysis.
- A security baseline is a model set of security-related modifications and settings that represent the technical implementation of security.
- Hardening an operating system (OS) is the act of tightening the security and maintaining functionality by turning off unnecessary services and protocols, installing and maintaining patches and hotfixes, and reconfiguring the basic OS parameters with more secure settings.
- Hardening a network works much the same as hardening an OS, but the focus is set on networking equipment and services. It involves installing the latest patches and firmware updates and maintaining physical security of networking media and devices.

- Hardening applications involves turning off unused subcomponents and applying hotfixes and configuration routines to reduce exposure of known exploits.

Table 6 lists some common port numbers and types.

TABLE 6

COMMON AND WELL-KNOWN PORT REVIEW

Application/Service	*Port*
FTP	20 and 21
SSH	22
Telnet	23
SMTP (Internet email)	25
DNS	53
TFTP	69
WWW	80
NetBIOS services	137, 138, and 139
SSL	443
LDAP	389 and 636
PPTP	1723
L2TP	1701

BASICS OF CRYPTOGRAPHY

- An algorithm is a set of steps that can be sequenced and repeated. The algorithm is used to define which encryption formula will be used when data is encrypted and unencrypted.
- Key pair encryption systems rely on a public and private key for encryption and decryption of data. The public key is freely distributed to any agent that needs secure communications with the holder of the matching private key.
- Hashing takes information and scrambles it into unreadable gibberish. Hashing strength is measured in bits with a longer value representing stronger (more difficult to break) encryption.
- Symmetric encryption uses the same key (private) on both sides of the encryption process. Symmetric encryption is fast but is easier to compromise relative to asymmetric.
- Asymmetric encryption is the use of different keys on either side of the encryption process (public and private keys). See Table 7 for more information on algorithms.

TABLE 7

REVIEW OF COMMON CRYPTOLOGY ALGORITHMS

Algorithm Name	*Algorithm Type*	*Algorithm Use*	*Key Bit Length*
Diffie-Hellman	Asymmetric	Crypt	Up to 8,192
RSA	Asymmetric	Crypt/Sign	Up to 16,384
DSA	Asymmetric	Sign	Up to 1,024
DSS	Asymmetric	Sign	Up to 1,024
IDEA	Symmetric	Crypt	128
CAST	Symmetric	Crypt	128, 256
DES	Symmetric	Crypt	56
3DES	Symmetric	Crypt	DESx3 = 168
AES	Symmetric	Crypt	128, 192, 256
TwoFish	Symmetric	Crypt	128, 192, 256
MD5	Hashing	Sign	128 digest
SHA	Hashing	Sign	160 digest

- Confidentiality is the process of hiding data from unintended viewing either in transit or in storage.

- Integrity refers to the ability to prove that data was not altered during transit or while in storage. The data might or might not also be encrypted for confidentiality purposes. One of the more popular ways to ensure data integrity is through the use of digital signatures.
- Authentication is the process of positively identifying an identity (in this case using a cryptographic process).
- Nonrepudiation is a cryptographic process designed to positively identify the origin of data. This term is commonly used in association with digital signatures and can extend to include proof of origin, submission, delivery, and receipt of data.
- Public key infrastructure (PKI) is the collection of resources necessary to properly deploy, use, and maintain public key cryptography.
- A certificate authority (CA) is responsible for issuing certificates and maintaining certificate policies governing the use of the issued certificates (email, data encryption, digital signatures, and so on).
- CAs also publish certificate revocation lists (CRLs) to notify users of certificates that are no longer valid for use. This might be necessary if a private key is electronically compromised (stolen).
- When deploying CAs within a large environment, a hierarchy typically exists with a root CA at the top and publishing CAs at various departments. This configuration distributes the certificate generation load and eliminates a single point of failure.
- The Public-Key Cryptography Standards (PKCS) were produced by RSA Laboratories, a division of the RSA Corporation, in an effort to create globally accepted specifications for the development of PKI solutions.
- PKI is governed by the Internet Engineering Task Force (IETF) X.509 specification. The X.509 standard defines a specific format of required data for digital certificates. Currently, this format requires the digital signature of the CA as well as the following fields to be compliant to the standard:
    - **Version**—Identifies to which version of the X.509 standard the certificate complies. Currently three versions are defined by the IETF.
    - **Serial number**—The CA that creates the certificate assigns a unique serial number for each certificate it issues. This information can then be used to identify specific certificates for activities such as revocation.
    - **Signature algorithm**—This identifies the cryptographic algorithm.
    - **Issuer**—This is the name of the CA that signed the certificate.
    - **Validity period**—This defines the period in which a certificate is valid. This period is noted with both a start and end time. It can be any duration—from a few seconds to any stated date. Typically, this period is set to one year for normal operations, but it can be different based on the security policy with which the certificate is associated.
    - **Subject name**—This is the name of the entity identified in the public key associated with the certificate. This is more often known as the distinguished name (DN). It uses the X.500 directory standard, which allows it to be queried accordingly. It is also meant to be unique across the entire Internet infrastructure.
    - **Subject public key information**—This is the public key of the entity being named in the certificate, cryptographic algorithm descriptor, and optional key parameters associated with the key.

- Keys can be stored in software or embedded in hardware. Hardware devices are considered to have higher security than software because they require special components. Hardware is also faster.
- Keys can be protected through backup mechanisms and key escrow. M of N control is a special mechanism used to back up key pairs across multiple systems so that no single system has the entire key pair in storage.
- Multiple key pairs can be issued to users to separate the process of encryption from digital signing.

Operational/ Organizational Security

- Physical security focuses on protecting equipment, people, and buildings that house company resources.
- Physical barriers act as deterrents and include
  - **No-man's land**—A wide expanse of clear, flat land that allows for easy view of anyone approaching the facility.
  - **Fences**—Fences can be made of a wide variety of materials, but they are all meant to do one thing: stop unwanted entry through nondesignated areas.
  - **Water/Moat**—Useful as both a physical barrier and an eye-pleasing addition to the landscape, it is very effective at stopping entry by vehicle.
  - **External lighting/cameras**—Lighting and cameras let would-be thieves know you are serious about security.
  - **External motion sensors**—These devices can see and hear where humans can't. They provide a wide variety of capabilities, including sound, heat, light, infrared, and ultrasonic.
  - **External doors/windows**—These external access points into your building should be strong and imposing without making the facility look like a prison.
  - **Mantraps**—Used as an internal physical barrier, a mantrap consists of two doors that can be locked to capture an unwanted individual.
  - **Internal motion sensors**—These function similarly to their outdoor counterparts but can be more sensitive and more reliable when properly deployed.
  - **Locks**—A wide range of locks exist to help you protect your facility both indoors and out. Deploying the correct locks in the right situation can make all the difference.
  - **Biometrics**—Discussed first in Chapter 1, "General Security Principles," biometrics offer some of the most secure forms of entry on the market.
- After physical barriers are in place, it is important to train users in security principles and procedures to avoid incidents such as piggybacking and eavesdropping of passwords and entry codes.
- Environment is a broad term used to describe the physical conditions that affect and influence growth, development, and survival. It can also be used to describe the physical conditions that affect security.
- Location, building materials, and ownership of the facility/property all have a significant influence on the deployment and use of physical security.

- All electronic equipment gives off electromagnetic emanations (EME). Unless shielding (such as TEMPEST) or a Faraday cage is used, data can be captured through electronic eavesdropping.
- TEMPEST is a shielding technique used to protect individual components from giving off EME. Monitors, keyboards, mice, and networking cables and equipment must all be protected.
- Faraday cages protect an entire area or section by placing a well-grounded wire mesh around the equipment or room. The mesh absorbs stray EME and grounds the signals before they can be captured.
- Fire suppression systems used around electronic equipment, such as server rooms, should be dry, chemical-based systems—not water-based. Other building areas can be protected with different types of fire suppression systems, including dry-pipe and wet-pipe sprinkler systems.
- A disaster recovery plan (DRP) is a set of procedures implemented when prevention doesn't work and a disaster takes out part or all of a facility. A DRP is an immediate action plan outlining steps to get the company back to a level of operational functionality.
- The first step in a DRP is analyzing which resources are business critical and what risk those resources are exposed to, such as fire, flood, theft, misuse, normal wear and tear, and so on.
- DRPs can include plans for use of hot, warm, and cold sites.
- A hot site is available 24/7 and is the most expensive but quickest solution for recovery.
- A warm site is generally configured with power, phone, network ports, and other base services. The site doesn't typically have computers and other specific resources. A warm site is less expensive, takes more time to set up than a hot site, and can be shared with other companies.
- A cold site is the least expensive solution but the most time-consuming to set up. Typically, a company has a prearranged request to use the facilities if necessary. The site might be a simple empty office or warehouse space with electricity and bathrooms.
- High availability of equipment and resources is usually deployed with redundant equipment and well-executed backup and restore plans.
- Backups should include offsite storage to protect against simultaneous destruction of the facility and the backups.
- When building a DRP, don't forget to include plans for utilities, WAN links (ISDN, Frame Relay, T1s, and so on), service level agreements (SLAs) for services, and equipment and code escrow.
- Business continuity plans (BCPs) are similar to DRPs except that a BCP is a longer-term look at recovery. The scope of a DRP might be 72 hours, whereas a BCP might be a year or longer.
- A security policy is a set of instructions on how to conduct business and interact with an information system while maintaining an acceptable level of security.
- A policy is a broad statement of views and position. It states high-level intent with respect to a specific area. It generally includes both statements of expected performance and consequences of noncompliance. Policies are made compulsory and reinforced by standards, guidelines, and procedures.
- A standard is usually best practices for specific platforms, implementations, operating system versions, and so on. Standards are usually mandatory and provide for uniform application of a technology across an organization.

- Guidelines are different from standards in that they are generally not mandatory and provide specific details on how standards should be implemented. Guidelines are more flexible than standards that allow for variations in specific applications, when necessary.
- A procedure is used to specify how the policies shall be put into practice in an environment. Procedures provide the steps required to carry out policy elements. Whereas policies state the intent, procedures provide the "how-to" instructions.
- The security policy is built around the security triad of confidentiality, integrity, and availability. Confidentiality is the process of ensuring information is not intentionally or unintentionally disclosed. Integrity is protecting data from unauthorized modifications. Availability is ensuring data is available when it is needed.
- An acceptable use policy is one that defines proper use of an information system and the data it contains.
- Due care is the knowledge and actions that a reasonably prudent person would possess or act upon. A business exercises due care when it implements policies and procedures to protect its data, equipment, and customers.
- Computer forensics is the science of collecting and analyzing computer crime-scene data. It is more about the law and evidence gathering, handling, and preservation than about computers.
- Collection of evidence can be done automatically or manually.
- Automatic data collection is usually accomplished through software applications such as IDS software and network sniffing utilities.
- Manual collection is accomplished by investigators and involves looking at the contents of hard drives, CPU caches, RAM, system logs, audit logs, network data captures, and virtual memory.
- Preservation of evidence should be accomplished with digital evidence bags or imaging of electronic material that is then written to read-only media (such as a CD-ROM).
- If memory and cache are going to be evaluated, ensure that you retrieve the contents *before* rebooting the system for imaging.
- When evidence is presented in court, the court will want to know how the evidence made it from the crime scene to the courtroom. The explanation that answers that question is known as the chain of custody.
- When data evidence is collected, stored, and eventually presented in court, the following must be true of the data. It must be relevant or admissible, a complete copy, not have been altered throughout the collection and storage procedure, have been copied with a reliable process, and have been secured from the time it was collected until the time it was presented in court.
- The process of risk identification and management centers around assets, threats, vulnerabilities, and risk.
- An asset is anything of value to the company.
- A threat or threat agent is anything that could cause the loss of an asset. Threats include hackers, employees, viruses, intruders, fire, flood, power outages, and equipment failures.
- A vulnerability is a weakness in an asset, its configuration, or its environment.
- Risk can be described as the potential of a threat to exploit a vulnerability found in an asset, causing its loss.

- Change management is the process of scheduling and controlling changes to the environment to help reduce security risks.
- Change management should include change requests, staging, documentation, notification, and impact analysis.
- The change process should always include a rollback procedure to reset changes that have unforeseen or undesirable effects.

This exam consists of 70 questions that reflect the material covered in the chapters and that are representative of the types of questions you should expect to see on the actual exam.

The answers to all the questions appear in their own section following the exam. It is strongly suggested that, when you take this exam, you treat it just as you would the actual exam at the test center. Time yourself, read carefully, and answer all the questions to the best of your ability.

The questions not only require you to recall facts but also might require deduction on your part to come up with the best answer. Run through the exam, and for any questions you miss, review the material associated with them.

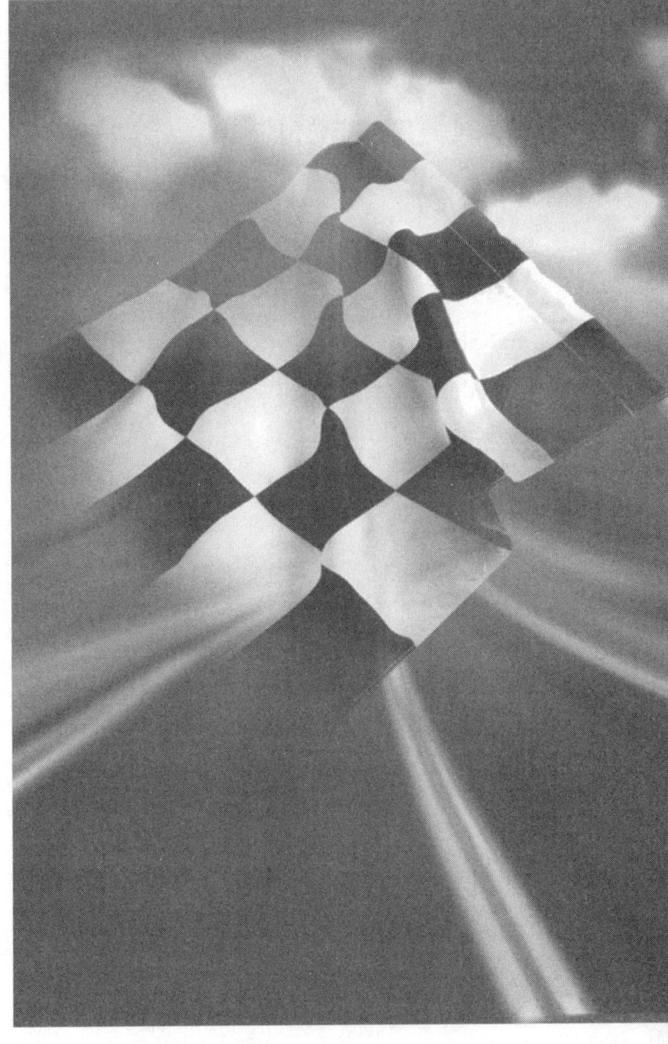

Practice Exam

Exam Questions

1. Which of the following are tunneling protocols used when setting up a VPN? (Choose two.)

   A. PPTP

   B. SSH

   C. FTP

   D. 3DES

   E. L2TP

   F. MD5

2. Which of the following are used with L2TP? (Choose two.)

   A. PPP

   B. L2F

   C. SSH

   D. PPTP

   E. IPSec

3. What is the difference between AH and ESP when configuring IPSec?

   A. AH verifies the integrity of the data and encrypts the data as well.

   B. AH only encrypts the data; it does not verify data integrity.

   C. ESP ensures data integrity but does not encrypt the payload.

   D. ESP encrypts the data payload and can also be used to verify data integrity.

4. What is the maximum key length in bits for RSA?

   A. 8,192

   B. 512

   C. 16,384

   D. 1,024

   E. 2,048

5. Which key type is used with the 3DES encryption algorithm?

   A. Asymmetric

   B. Symmetric

   C. Bidirectional

   D. Hashing

6. Which encryption system is used to protect email?

   A. MIME

   B. S/MIME

   C. IPSec

   D. L2TP

7. What is the purpose of RADIUS?

   A. It's a centralized user authentication, authorization, and accounting system used for dial-up access.

   B. It's centralized user authentication used for LANs.

   C. It's a centralized user authentication system used in LANs.

   D. It's a centralized accounting method used on dial-up systems.

8. Which of the following statements is correct?

   A. RSA is symmetric and supports up to 1024-bit encryption.

   B. DES is asymmetric and supports up to 168-bit encryption.

C. MD5 is asymmetric and supports up to 8192-bit encryption.

D. SHA is hashing and supports up to 160-bit encryption.

9. Which of the following best defines authentication?

A. The process of ensuring a user can only get to resources properly assigned to him

B. The process of electronically identifying a user or process

C. The process of tracking a user and the resources he has been using

D. All of the above

10. A DDoS attack is best described by which statement?

A. An attack that is a coordinated effort in which many machines attack a single victim or host.

B. An attack that installs software on machines that allows many users to connect to and view the contents of the hard drives.

C. An attack that is a coordinated effort in which many machines attack a single victim or host with the intent to disable services.

D. An attack that installs code that causes a system to fail if a particular event occurs.

11. When resources are designated with specific access labels and users are not allowed to change or influence permissions, this form of access control is best described as which of the following?

A. MAC

B. DAC

C. RBAC

D. LDAP

12. Which of the following are commonly associated with authentication? (Choose three.)

A. Something you know

B. Something you have

C. Something you do

D. Something you are

E. Something you make

13. What are some common uses of a certificate?

A. Encryption

B. Electronic ID

C. Data integrity

D. All of the above

14. Your company has decided to deploy a hardware token system along with usernames and passwords. The technique of using more than one system is known as what?

A. Mutual authentication

B. Factored authentication

C. Multifactor authentication

D. Parallel authentication

15. Which of the following best describes spoofing?

A. The process of sending information from multiple computers in an attempt to overload the victim

B. The process of capturing data, changing it, and then resending it

C. The process of inserting extra code that can be accessed later to gain entry into a network

D. The process of replacing the source address of a packet to impersonate a legitimate host

16. Which authentication method is almost immune to impersonation?

    A. Biometrics

    B. Username/Password

    C. Software token

    D. Certificates

17. What is the best word used to describe the process of tracking the use of resources on a network?

    A. Authentication

    B. Authorization

    C. Sniffing

    D. Accounting

18. The process by which users are grouped by function or need and are assigned permissions based on membership in a specific group is referred to as what?

    A. DAC

    B. RBAC

    C. MAC

    D. RAC

19. Which of the following objects enables a user to get multiple session IDs in the Kerberos authentication process?

    A. Ticket granting ticket (TGT)

    B. Session ticket (ST)

    C. Instance ticket (IT)

    D. Token

    E. Card granting ticket (CGT)

20. Which of the following statements best describes the behavior of a worm or virus?

    A. A worm is self-replicating, whereas a virus must be activated to replicate.

    B. A virus propagates itself and destroys data.

    C. A worm attacks only after triggered.

    D. A worm attacks only system files whereas a virus attacks email, system files, and data.

21. A hardware or software system that is designed to protect one network from another is described as what?

    A. Bastion host

    B. Honeypot

    C. Firewall

    D. Packet funnel

22. In general, when configuring a firewall, which of the following statements is most correct?

    A. All traffic from the outside network should be allowed in.

    B. All traffic from the outside network should be denied.

    C. All traffic going from an inside network to an outside network should be screened allowing only designated packets out.

    D. All traffic going from the outside network to the inside network should be screened allowing only designated packets in.

23. In which scenario is it favorable for a user to have two sets of private/public key pairs?

    A. When a user wants to have corporate and personal electronic credentials

    B. When an organization wants to separate encryption functions from signature functions for communications

C. When an organization wants to be able to revoke personal credentials without losing the ability to access data that has been encrypted by the user

D. All of the above

24. How does an IDS differ from a firewall?

    A. A firewall prevents attacks, whereas an IDS logs an attack.

    B. An IDS is the first line of defense, whereas a firewall is a safety net.

    C. A firewall generally filters packets and logs basic information, whereas an IDS can prevent application-specific attacks, actively notify administrators of attacks, and shut down network access.

    D. An IDS generally filters packets and logs basic information, whereas a firewall system can prevent application-specific attacks, actively notify administrators of attacks, and shut down network access.

25. Which protocol is commonly used on networks to manage devices?

    A. LDAP

    B. TCP/IP

    C. L2F

    D. SNMP

26. Which of the following would be considered the least secure access methodology? (Choose two.)

    A. Infrared

    B. Unshielded twisted pair (UTP)

    C. Coax

    D. Fiber

    E. RF

27. You have been asked to design a backup scheme for your company. The CIO wants to have the shortest recovery time possible using the fewest number of tapes during the recovery process. Which backup methods would you use? (Choose two.)

    A. Incremental

    B. Full

    C. Differential

    D. Copy

28. The network manager has asked you to deploy a security configuration for the company Internet connection that has built-in redundancy and a high degree of separation of services. Which configuration would you recommend?

    A. Bastion host

    B. Screened host

    C. Screened subnet

    D. Honeypot host

29. Which of the following is not a private IP address range?

    A. 192.168.0.0–192.168.255.255

    B. 168.254.0.0–168.254.255.255

    C. 10.0.0.0–10.255.255.255

    D. 172.16.0.0–172.31.255.255

30. Which of the following is not part of the standard network management approach?

    A. Fault

    B. Configuration

    C. Authorization

    D. Performance

    E. Security

31. Which of the following is a characteristic of a network-based intrusion detection system (NIDS)?

    A. Easy to alter the logs.

    B. Higher cost of ownership because of the centralization of resources.

    C. Can identify more complex attacks higher in the OSI model.

    D. NDIS is dependent on the operating system in use.

32. Your company has implemented an IDS solution that does simple signature comparison on a packet-by-packet basis. Which type of IDS solution has the company implemented?

    A. Stateful inspection

    B. Pattern matching

    C. Heuristic analysis

    D. Protocol decode

33. Stateful packet inspection differs from pattern matching in which of the following ways?

    A. Stateful inspection looks at each packet individually.

    B. Pattern matching looks at the entire session or data stream and compares it to known signatures.

    C. Stateful inspection is faster than pattern matching.

    D. Stateful inspection looks at the entire session or data stream and compares it to known signatures.

    E. Pattern matching is flexible.

34. When destroying a private key, when is it favorable to archive a copy of the private key prior to destruction?

    A. When a user forgets his password to access the key

    B. When the private key was used to encrypt data that might be needed in the future

    C. When you need the ability to re-create the digital signature of the user for verification

    D. When you need an auditable record of key available for review

35. Your company has asked you to deploy an IDS system that is operating system independent and will shut down the Internet connection if an attack is detected. Which type of solution will you recommend?

    A. Active host-based IDS

    B. Passive host-based IDS

    C. Active network-based IDS

    D. Passive network-based IDS

36. A system that has its security lowered and is designed to draw attacks is called a what?

    A. Firewall

    B. Honeypot

    C. Host-based IDS

    D. Network-based IDS

    E. Stateful packet system

37. You are the security administrator for a large company. You have been asked to design a security solution that will enable the detection of inappropriate activity as well as misuse of dial-up lines, VPNs, and extranet partners.

In addition, if an attack is detected, you want the system to react. Which of the following would help you accomplish your goal?

A. Network IDS

B. Host IDS

C. Active IDS

D. All of the above

38. Which of the following statements is most accurate?

A. A host-based intrusion detection system can detect activity against a single system, including file system access and logon and logoff. It is operating system dependent.

B. A network-based intrusion detection system can detect activity against a single system, including file system access and logon and logoff. It is operating system dependent.

C. A host-based IDS is commonly deployed to protect multiple network segments.

D. A network-based IDS does not require dedicated hardware.

39. A user on your network calls and notifies you of a misbehaving system. Upon further inspection, you suspect that the system and/or network is being attacked. What should be your next step?

A. Notify the security administrator.

B. Notify the security management team.

C. Notify the CEO of the company.

D. Initiate the incident response procedures.

E. Initiate the security response procedures.

40. Hardening systems and network components is best described as what?

A. Physically securing the devices

B. Altering the software and hardware configuration to maintain the highest possible security while still allowing functionality

C. Altering the software configuration to turn off unwanted components

D. Altering the hardware configuration to prevent unwanted individuals from gaining access to the system case or components

41. Which statement is true when using symmetric key encryption?

A. The public key is installed on both systems.

B. The private key is installed on both systems.

C. The same key is used to encrypt and decrypt data.

D. The sending system uses the private key to encrypt data.

E. The sending system uses the public key to encrypt data.

42. Which characteristic makes DES a weak algorithm?

A. It has been around for more than 25 years.

B. It uses symmetric encryption.

C. The bit strength is only 56.

D. All of the above.

43. Which algorithm was chosen to replace DES and 3DES?

A. MD5

B. SHA-1

C. RSA

D. MD2

E. AES

44. Asymmetric encryption ________________.
    A. Uses identical keys installed on two or more systems
    B. Uses a public key and private key configuration
    C. Is generally weaker than symmetric encryption
    D. Requires a private key to be distributed to the systems that want to encrypt data

45. Proof of origin, submission, delivery, and receipt are all provided by which of the following?
    A. Asymmetric encryption
    B. Symmetric encryption
    C. Nonrepudiation
    D. Confidentiality
    E. Integrity

46. What are the benefits of key escrow in a corporate PKI solution? (Choose two.)
    A. The ability to access data encrypted with the user's private key
    B. The ability to reissue keys for users who have forgotten their passwords to unlock the private key
    C. The ability to identify the user
    D. The ability to distribute private keys to other CAs

47. Which of the following best describes the process of using asymmetric encryption?
    A. The sending agent downloads the receiver's private key and encrypts the data. The receiver then decrypts the text using the private key.
    B. The sending agent downloads the receiver's public key and encrypts the data. The receiver then decrypts the text using its private key.
    C. The sending agent downloads the receiver's public key and encrypts the data. The receiver then decrypts the text using the sender's private key.
    D. The sending agent encrypts the data using its private key. The receiver then decrypts the text using the sender's public key.
    E. The sending agent encrypts the data using its private key. The receiver then decrypts the text using the sender's private key.

48. Advanced Encryption Standard (AES) supports which levels of bit strength? (Choose three.)
    A. 56
    B. 128
    C. 192
    D. 256
    E. 512
    F. 1024

49. Which of the following terms describes the process of scrambling data so only the intended recipient can read it?
    A. Data integrity
    B. Data security
    C. Data confidentiality
    D. Nonrepudiation

50. The Wired Equivalency Protocol (WEP) is used in which of the following situations? (Choose the most correct answer.)
    A. LAN - WAN egress point
    B. WAN - WAN interconnectivity
    C. Fiber-optic networks
    D. Wireless networks

51. Physical security is designed to protect networks from which of the following? (Choose all that apply.)

    A. Natural disasters

    B. Manmade disasters

    C. Theft of equipment

    D. Unauthorized users reading emails in transit

    E. Unauthorized users gaining access to a server

    F. Unauthorized users gaining access to a Web server from the Internet

52. What is the primary benefit of using M of N control to back up private keys?

    A. The ability to recover keys in a disaster recovery situation

    B. Offsite storage of keys

    C. The ability to prevent any one user from rebuilding the private keys

    D. All of the above

53. Which of the following are considered physical security components? (Choose all that apply.)

    A. VPN tunnel

    B. Man trap

    C. Closed circuit TV camera

    D. Network firewall

    E. Fence

    F. Faraday cage

    G. Public key certificate

    H. Lights

54. What is considered to be the most invasive biometric security device?

    A. Hand scanner

    B. Iris profiler

    C. Fingerprint scanner

    D. Retinal scanner

    E. Voiceprint

55. Which of the following will most influence the deployment of physical security?

    A. Building location

    B. Building ownership

    C. Sensitivity of the equipment and resources being protected

    D. Cost

    E. All of the above

56. What is the most common fire suppression system deployed in server/equipment rooms?

    A. Wet-pipe

    B. Dry-pipe

    C. Halon

    D. Dry chemical

57. What is the main difference between a disaster recovery plan (DRP) and a business continuity plan (BCP)?

    A. A DRP attempts to reduce the risks associated with a disaster, whereas a BCP attempts immediate recovery after a disaster has struck.

    B. A DRP is a long-term plan for recovering from a disaster, whereas a BCP is an immediate action plan.

    C. A DRP is an immediate plan, whereas a BCP is a long-term plan for disaster recovery.

    D. None of the above.

58. You are configuring a security policy for your company. Which of the following three components make up the security triad?

    A. Encryption

    B. Confidentiality

    C. Obscurity

    D. Integrity

    E. Authorization

    F. Accounting

    G. Availability

59. You have implemented a document that outlines specific activities for deploying new servers on your network, including steps on how to accomplish the desired result. This document would be considered a what?

    A. Procedure

    B. Guideline

    C. Policy

    D. Standard

60. Which of the following are characteristics that should be included in every password?

    A. Uppercase letters

    B. Lowercase letters

    C. Numbers

    D. Special characters

    E. All of the above

61. You are auditing your users' passwords and note that many users are using complete words when creating their passwords. Which common technique could be used against them?

    A. Manual attack

    B. Brute-force attack

    C. Dictionary attack

    D. Random binary decode (RBD)

62. In which mode of ESP is the source IP address of the packet hidden from view during transmission?

    A. Transport mode

    B. Authenticated header

    C. Tunnel mode

    D. Network Address Translation mode

63. A document or collection of documents designed to convey the security desires for each of the business's mission-critical areas is usually referred to as which of the following?

    A. Guideline

    B. Policy

    C. Standard

    D. Procedure

    E. Directive

64. You need to provide your users with the ability to log on once and retrieve any resource to which they have been granted access, regardless of where the resource is stored. Which configuration will you deploy?

    A. Multifactor

    B. Biometric

    C. Role-based access (RBAC)

    D. Single sign-on (SSO)

65. The process of collecting, processing, and storing evidence and analyzing systems after an attack is called what?

    A. Forensics

    B. Discovery

    C. Chaining

D. Due care

E. Due process

66. What is not a problem with using manual data collection techniques when investigating a computer incident?

A. It's easy to miss important information.

B. The data collection process is not standardized.

C. Too much information is typically gathered.

D. During the collection process evidence can be accidentally altered.

67. Which statement best describes a threat?

A. A threat is a weakness in the configuration of hardware or software that could allow damage to occur.

B. A threat is an agent that could do harm to your network intentionally.

C. A threat is an agent that could do harm to your network unintentionally.

D. A threat is the probability that an event will occur against a given asset.

E. B and C.

F. C and D.

G. A and D.

68. You are the primary investigator on a team that is investigating the theft of some important information from your network. You have collected and analyzed data and are preparing to present your information in court. What is the process called when presenting the path that the evidence took to the courtroom?

A. Chain of custody

B. Chain of evidence

C. Custodial path

D. Forensics

69. You are about to begin an investigation on a server that was compromised. What should be your first step in your investigation?

A. Physically dismantle the server and analyze each piece separately.

B. Image the hard drives.

C. Begin searching for clues in the system logs.

D. Search the system for files that have changed or files that have possibly been placed to aid further attacks.

E. Dump physical and virtual memory.

70. You are establishing a new change policy for your company. Which of the following best describes the steps of the change process? (Choose three.)

A. Change meetings

B. Change request

C. Change staging

D. Change flow

E. Change documentation

Answers to Exam Questions

1. **A, E.** PPTP and L2TP are both used for creating tunnels across the Internet. SSH and FTP are utilities, and 3DES and MD5 are encryption algorithms.

2. **B, E.** Layer 2 forwarding (L2F) establishes the tunnel, and IPSec encrypts the data. PPP is its own protocol; SSH is a shell program; and PPTP is the predecessor to L2TP.

3. **D.** Encapsulated secure payload (ESP) can encrypt data and verify data integrity. Authentication header (AH) can only verify data integrity.

4. **C.** RSA can support up to 16,384 as its key length.

5. **B.** 3DES is classified as a symmetric key cryptographic process.

6. **B.** S/MIME is specifically used to protect email. MIME is plain text; IPSec and L2TP are used for much broader data encryption.

7. **A.** Remote Dial-in User Service (RADIUS) is used to centralize authentication, authorization, and accounting in a dial-up or RAS environment.

8. **D.** SHA is properly matched with its encryption technique and key strength.

9. **B.** Authentication is the process of electronically identifying a user or process. Answer A describes authorization, and answer C describes accounting.

10. **C.** Distributed denial-of-service (DDoS) attacks aim to disable access to one or more services from a coordinated multihost attack. Answer A is a close answer but not as complete as answer C.

11. **A.** Mandatory access control (MAC) is best described as using labels and limiting users' abilities. DAC and RBAC are more flexible, and LDAP is a directory access protocol.

12. **A, B, D.** Something you know (password or PIN), something you have (swipe card or token), and something you are (fingerprint, voiceprint, retinal pattern) are commonly associated with authentication.

13. **D.** Certificates can be used for all three processes.

14. **C.** Multifactor authentication uses two or more authentication techniques. Mutual authentication is a process that authenticates both sides of a connection. The other answers are distracters.

15. **D.** Spoofing is specifically the process of altering the source address of a packet to impersonate a legitimate host. Answer A describes DDos; answer B describes replay; and answer C is a backdoor.

16. **A.** The physical attributes of a human (speech, fingerprints, retina, and so on) are the most difficult to impersonate.

17. **D.** Accounting is the specific process of tracking the use of resources. Authentication is proving identity; authorization is the process of granting rights or use of resources; and sniffing is a process of capturing network data traffic.

18. **B.** Role-based access control (RBAC) specifies that users are grouped by need or function and are assigned permissions through group membership. DAC and MAC focus on users, and RAC is a distracter.

19. **A.** The TGT is used to prove identity (as necessary) to any key distribution center (KDC) for access to session tickets. A session ticket is good for only one session. The rest of the options are distracters.

20. **A.** By definition, a worm replicates itself by exploiting known software problems. A virus must be executed to propagate.

21. **C.** A firewall is designed to protect one network from another. It is typically used to protect a corporate network from the Internet. A bastion host is a specific implementation of a firewall. A honeypot is a host designed to be attacked, and a packet funnel is a distracter.

22. **D.** The flow of data that is of greatest concern is from outside (Internet) to inside (corporate LAN).

23. **B.** Multiple key pairs are used when the corporation desires separation of the signature and encryption functions.

24. **C.** An IDS is more complex and capable than a firewall.

25. **D.** SNMP was developed specifically to manage devices.

26. **A, E.** Because these two technologies are wireless, the signals they produce can be received with little effort.

27. **B, C.** A full backup is required to periodically reset the archive bit. Differentials capture all changes between the last full and the current state of the file. Only two tapes are needed in this situation: the last full backup and the last differential.

28. **C.** Only a screened subnet has redundancy.

29. **B.** 168.254.0.0–168.254.255.255 is not a private IP address range. All the others are part of the private address class range.

30. **C.** Authorization deals with assigning permissions to users or groups. All the others are part of FCAPS. The missing management area is accounting.

31. **C.** NIDS can identify more complex attacks; it is cheaper to protect systems because of centralization; it is hard to alter the logs; and it is OS independent.

32. **B.** Stateful inspection, heuristic analysis, and protocol decode are complex and intelligent systems that can look at data flows.

33. **D.** Stateful inspection looks at data flows, whereas pattern matching is inflexible and looks at predefined packet signatures one packet at a time.

34. **B.** If data has been encrypted with the private key, it is common to have a backup of the key to facilitate recovery of data off of archives.

35. **C.** The requirement to shut down the Internet connection makes an active system a requirement, and the operating system-independent constraint makes an active NIDS solution the best choice.

36. **B.** This is the classic description of a honeypot.

37. **D.** The stated requirements would best be served by active host and network-based IDS components.

38. **A.** NIDS can't detect file system access. Host-based systems are usually designed to protect single hosts or single segments. NIDS does require dedicated hardware.

39. **D.** The proper first step is to implement the incident response procedures.

40. **B.** The other options are all partially correct; however, answer B is the most complete.

41. **C.** In symmetric encryption the same key is used to encrypt and decrypt the data. Answers A, B, D, and E all deal with asymmetric key issues.

42. **D.** All the listed options contribute to the weakness of DES.

43. **E.** AES was developed to overcome the weaknesses of the DES algorithm.

44. **B.** Asymmetric encryption functions on the public/private key pair concept. It is stronger than symmetric and distributes the public key to multiple systems.

45. **C.** The characteristics listed are all part of nonrepudiation.

46. **A, B.** Key escrow enables a company to gain access to data encrypted with the user's private key (protecting company owned intellectual property) as well as reissue a key if lost.

47. **B.** This answer lists the correct key and sequence.

48. **B, C, D.** AES supports 128-, 192-, and 256-bit strength.

49. **C.** Data confidentiality ensures that the data can be read only by the intended recipient. Integrity ensures that the data hasn't been altered; nonrepudiation tracks send and receive behaviors; and data security is a distracter.

50. **D.** WEP is used in wireless networking.

51. **A, B, C, E.** Unauthorized access to a Web server over the wire and email security are both part of data security, not physical security.

52. **C.** The primary purpose of using M of N technology is to prevent the duplication of keys by one individual.

53. **B, C, E, F, H.** VPN tunnels, firewalls, and public keys pertain to data security.

54. **D.** A retinal scan requires the participant to remove eyewear and place her head in a static device to be properly used.

55. **E.** All the listed options influence physical security.

56. **D.** Dry chemical is the most common fire suppression system deployed in server/equipment rooms. Wet and dry sprinkler systems both use water, and Halon is no longer legal to deploy.

57. **C.** A disaster recovery plan outlines immediate procedures following a disaster, whereas a business continuity plan defines long-term recovery steps.

58. **B, D, G.** Confidentiality, integrity, and availability make up the security triad.

59. **A.** A procedure usually includes steps and instructions on how to accomplish a specific task.

60. **E.** A good password includes all the listed components.

61. **C.** Dictionary attacks use a list of known words to guess a user's password.

62. **C.** Tunnel mode encrypts the entire packet inside a new IP packet.

63. **B.** The description given is that of a policy.

64. **D.** The ability to log on once and gain access to all necessary resources is referred to as single sign-on.

65. **A.** Forensics is the science of investigating a crime scene.

66. **C.** Using manual collection techniques, it is rare that too much information is collected.

67. **E.** A threat is an agent that could intentionally or unintentionally do harm to your network.

68. **A.** Verifying the path of evidence from the crime scene to the courtroom is called the chain of custody.

69. **E.** Because of the fragile nature of the information left in physical and virtual memory, the data in these locations should be collected first.

70. **B, C, E.** You should request, stage, and then document the change.

PART

APPENDIXES

A Security+ Resources

B Glossary

C Security+ Bibliography

D Overview of Certification Process

E What's on the CD-ROM

F Using the *PrepLogic Practice Tests, Preview Edition* Software

APPENDIX A

Security Resources

The following is a listing of online and published security resources that might be useful for exam preparation and further study and future reference:

- An extensive listing of security resources related to Web security, published by the W3 Consortium can be found at http://www.w3.org/Security/.
- The Microsoft Knowledge Base provides answers to very specific problems and issues and contains a broad range of how-to articles from very specific to quite general, including security in related products. Check out http://support.microsoft.com/.
- Network security primer from Computer Security Resource Center, a division of National Institute of Standards and Technology (NIST), at http://csrc.nist.gov/publications/nistpubs/800-10/node1.html.
- The Cisco Systems whitepaper titled "Internet Security for Small Businesses" is a good starting point on firewalls, their types, and their purposes. It can be found at http://www.cisco.com/warp/public/cc/pd/rt/800/prodlit/fire_wp.htm.
- AT&T features a War Dialing guide, detailing the practice and how to deal with it. It might not be very practical anymore, but it's something to be aware of. See http://www.att.com/isc/docs/war_dial_detection.pdf.
- The Cisco Systems whitepaper titled "The Science of Intrusion Detection System Attack Identification" is a good starting point on IDS and can be found at http://www.cisco.com/warp/public/cc/pd/sqsw/sqidsz/prodlit/idssa_wp.htm.
- The Modern Hacker's Desk Reference, fairly popular on the Internet, is a manual written by people who claim to be hackers. Regardless, it is a good collection of security-related information, configuration ideas, and the most popular vulnerabilities from recent history, all in one place. See http://www.leto.net/docs/mhd.html.
- The Encryption algorithms primer lists about 40 algorithms, features some vulnerability information where it applies, and has links to the sources of respective developers or patent holders for more authoritative information. See http://kremlinencrypt.com/crypto/algorithms.html.
- One of the headline associations battling spam has its rationale published at http://mail-abuse.org/rbl/rationale.html.
- The Institute of Electronics and Electric Engineers (IEEE) is a body of industry-leading companies and individuals working together to develop communication standards. The gateway to information on each of the 802 standards is located at http://grouper.ieee.org/groups/802/.

- SSL resource from Netscape is a good reference found at `http://developer.netscape.com/tech/security/ssl/howitworks.html`.
- SecurityFocus has established itself as one of the main sources of comprehensive vulnerability information. See `http://www.securityfocus.net`.
- The CERT Coordination Center (CERT/CC) is a center of Internet security expertise located at the Software Engineering Institute, a federally funded research and development center operated by Carnegie Mellon University. A listing of tools that aid in intrusion detection and reconnaissance is published at `http://www.cert.org/security-improvement/implementations/i042.07.html`.
- A database of intrusions detected by ISS's Network ICE system can be found at `http://www.iss.net/security_center/advice/Intrusions/default.htm`.
- The SANS Institute has a massive amount of security-related information available on its site. One of the articles of interest is a Honeypot primer, published at `http://www.sans.org/newlook/resources/IDFAQ/honeypot3.htm`.
- A network-based presentation outlining the main differences between, and advantages and disadvantages of, network-based intrusion versus host-based intrusion can be found at `http://secinf.net/info/ids/nvh_ids/`.
- Apache Web server-related information, including configuration and security materials, is available through `http://www.apache.org`.
- A headliner resource of security information related to Microsoft products, a must-read for administrators of networks running anything Microsoft, is published at `http://www.microsoft.com/security`.
- The *Microsoft Security Operations Guide for Windows 2000 Server*, by Microsoft, is one of the most comprehensive guides on security far beyond Microsoft products. It includes topics such as incident response and business continuity planning and is one of the must-read whitepapers; it's obtainable through `http://www.microsoft.com/security`.
- One of the best online resources for computer security is the U.S. National Security Agency's site. Declassified security manuals for Cisco, Microsoft, and related products are published on the site at `http://www.nsa.gov`.
- For any of the key terms used throughout the book and to discover more information on each topic, search `www.google.com`.
- One of the best hacker-run communities from Germany offers a wide range of guides, tools, and relevant security information. See `http://www.astalavista.com`.

APPENDIX **B**

Glossary

A

accounting Tracking users' access to resources primarily for billing purposes.

active detection Involves some action taken by the intrusion detection system in response to a suspicious activity or an intrusion (in essence, it is reactive detection).

algorithm A set of sequenced steps that are repeatable each time. In encryption, the algorithm is used to define how the encryption is applied to the data.

anomaly-based IDS Looks for traffic that is considered abnormal. To single out abnormal traffic patterns, the system has to be taught (or learn) what is considered normal in the first place.

asset A company resource that has value.

asymmetric algorithms A pair of key values, one public and the other private, used to encrypt and decrypt data. Only the holder of the private key can decrypt data encrypted with the public key, which means anyone who obtains a copy of the public key can send data to the private key holder in confidence. Only data encrypted with the private key can be decrypted with the public key; this provides proof of identity, ensures nonrepudiation, and provides the basis for digital signatures.

attribute certificate Digital certificate that binds data items to a user or system by using a name or public key certificate.

auditing Tracking users' access to resources primarily for security purposes.

authenticated header (AH) Component of the IPSec protocol that provides integrity, authentication, and anti-replay capabilities.

authentication The process of identifying users.

authorization The process of identifying what a given user is allowed to do.

availability Ensures any necessary data is available when it is requested.

B

back door A method of gaining access to a system or resource that bypasses normal authentication or access control methods.

binary copy A process of imaging a drive at the binary level (1s and 0s) to capture the contents and store them as evidence.

biometrics Authentication based on some part of the human anatomy (retina, fingerprint, voice, and so on).

block cipher Transforms a message from plaintext (unencrypted form) to ciphertext (encrypted form) one piece at a time, where the block size represents a standard chunk of data that is transformed in a single operation. Block ciphers also normally take prior encryption activity into account (called *block chaining* or *feedback modes*) to further strengthen the encryption they provide. (Adapted from `http://www.counterpane.com/crypto-gram-0001.html`.)

business continuity plan A plan that describes a long-term systems and services replacement and recovery strategy, designed for use when a complete loss of facilities occurs. Thus, a business continuity plan is similar to a disaster recovery plan, except that it assumes completely new facilities will be required going forward.

C

CA bridge A root CA that is at the top of a CA hierarchy that enables communication between two or more subordinate CAs.

centralized key management A certificate authority that generates both public and private key pairs for a user and then distributes them to the user.

certificate Also known as a *digital certificate*, it represents a unique way of establishing user identity and credentials to enable conducting business or other transactions online. Generally, digital certificates originate from a certificate authority (CA), which can be private (such as when a company or organization creates its own CAs) or public (such as when an individual, a company, or an organization obtains a digital certificate from a public CA like those operated by GE or Verisign). Typically, a digital certificate contains the holder's name, a serial number, expiration dates, a copy of the holder's public key (which can then be used to encrypt messages), and a digital certificate from the issuing authority to demonstrate its validity. Some digital certificates conform to the X.509 standard; numerous public registries of such certificates are maintained on the Internet and act as clearinghouses for such information.

certificate authority An online system that issues, distributes, and maintains currency information about digital certificates. Often abbreviated as CA, such authorities can be private (operated within a company or an organization for its own use) or public (operated on the Internet for general public access).

Certificate Enrollment Protocol (CEP) Proprietary Cisco protocol that allows Cisco IOS-based routers to communicate with certificate authorities.

Certificate Management Protocol (CMP) A protocol used for advanced management functions for a PKI. These functions include certificate issuance, exchange, invalidation, revocation, and key commission.

certificate policy A statement that governs the use of digital certificates.

Certificate practice statement A document that defines the practices and procedures a CA uses to manage the digital certificates it issues.

certificate revocation The act of invalidating a digital certificate.

certificate revocation list (CRL) A list generated by a CA that enumerates digital certificates that are no longer valid and the reasons they are no longer valid.

certificate suspension The act of temporarily invalidating a certificate while its validity is being verified.

chain of custody Documentation of all transfers of evidence from one person to another, showing the date, time, and reason for transfer, as well as the signatures of both parties involved in the transfer. Also refers to the process of tracking evidence from a crime scene to the courtroom.

change management A formal engineering discipline, change management describes the well-documented process for tracking and controlling changes to systems, as well as their design data and documentation, through agreed upon procedures and timelines. In security, this term indicates that a formal process to schedule, implement, track, and document changes to policies, configurations, systems, and software is employed in a company or organization.

Challenge Handshake Authentication Protocol (CHAP) A widely used authentication method in which a hashed version of a user's password is transmitted during the authentication process (instead of sending the password itself). Using CHAP, a remote access server transmits a challenge string, to which the client responds with a message digest (MD5) hash based on the challenge string and the user's password. Upon receipt, the remote access repeats the same calculation and compares the value sent to that value; if the values match, the client credentials are deemed authentic. CHAP was created for use with dial-up networking and is commonly used with PPP-encapsulated Windows remote access services. (Adapted from `http://www.microsoft.com/technet/prodtechnol/winxppro/proddocs/auth_chap.asp`.)

cipher A method for encrypting text, the term is also used to refer to an encrypted message (although the term *ciphertext* is preferred). The origin of the term lies in the Arabic word *sifr*, which means empty or zero. In a cipher, plaintext data (often of typically regular length, called a *block*, or otherwise, treating a message as a single stream of bits) is arbitrarily substituted or shifted according to some predetermined formula that includes all kinds of transforms. In addition, it often accepts previous ciphertext as well as plaintext as inputs.

cipher lock A door lock that uses a punch code or buttons to allow entry.

code escrow The process of placing application source code in the care of some trusted third party. In the event of a disagreement, dissolution of the development company, or failure to perform on the part of the software programmers, the code can be released to the purchasing company.

code of ethics A formal list of rules governing personal and professional behavior that is adopted by a group of individuals or organizations. Many security certifications, including Security+, require their holders to adhere to a code of ethics that's designed to foster ethical and legal behavior and discourage unethical or illegal behavior.

cold site A remote site that has electricity, plumbing, and heating installed, ready for use when enacting disaster recovery or business continuity plans. At a cold site, all other equipment, systems, and configurations are supplied by the company enacting the plan; thus, basic facilities that are ready to receive necessary systems and equipment are the hallmarks of a cold site.

confidentiality A rigorous set of controls and classifications associated with sensitive information to ensure that such information is neither intentionally nor unintentionally disclosed.

cross certification When two or more CAs choose to trust each other and issue credentials on each other's behalf.

cryptographic module Any combination of hardware, firmware, or software that implements cryptographic functions such as encryption, decryption, digital signatures, authentication techniques, and random number generation.

D

decentralized key management Key management that occurs when a user generates a public and private key pair and then submits the public key to a certificate authority for validation and signature.

degaussing A method of removing recorded magnetic fields from magnetic storage media by applying strong cyclic magnetic pulses, thereby erasing the content and making the media unreadable.

demilitarized zone (DMZ) Also called the *free-trade zone* or the *neutral zone*, this is an area in your network that allows a limited and controlled amount of access from the public Internet. The DMZ often hosts the corporation's Web and File Transfer Protocol (FTP) sites, email, external Domain Name Service (DNS), and the like. This network segment usually lies between the internal corporate network and the public Internet.

Denial-of-service and distributed denial-of-service (DoS/DDoS) A type of attack that denies legitimate users access to a server or services by consuming sufficient system resources or network bandwidth. The difference between a DoS and a DDoS attack is in its point(s) of origination: A DoS typically originates from a single system, whereas a DDoS originates from multiple systems simultaneously (thereby causing even more extreme consumption of bandwidth and other resources).

dictionary attack An attack in which software is used to compare the hashed data, such as a password, to a word in a hashed dictionary. This is repeated until matches are found in the hash, with the goal being to match the password exactly to determine the original password that was used as the basis of the hash.

digital certificate A formatted document that includes the user's public key as well as the digital signature of the certificate authority (CA) that has authenticated her. The digital certificate can also contain information about the user, the CA, and attributes that define what the user is allowed to do with systems she accesses using the digital certificate.

digital evidence bag A new tool in the form of an electronic container used to store computer evidence and prevent tampering.

digital signature A hash encrypted to a private key of the sender that proves user identity and authenticity of the message. Signatures do not encrypt the contents of an entire message. Also, in the context of certificates, a digital signature uses data to provide an electronic signature that authenticates the identity of the original sender of a message or data.

Disaster Recovery Plan (DRP) A plan outlining actions to be taken in case a business is hit with a natural or manmade disaster.

discretionary access control (DAC) A distributed security method that allows users to set permission on a per-object basis. The NTFS permissions used in Windows NT, 2000, and XP/.NET use DAC.

distributed computing A procedure in which multiple computers are networked and common sections of a larger task are distributed to the members of the group to process the larger task, presumably to complete that task more quickly.

dry-pipe fire suppression A sprinkler system with pressurized air in the pipes. If a fire starts, there is a slight delay as the pipes fill with water. Used in areas where wet-pipe systems might freeze.

due care Assurance that necessary steps are followed to satisfy a specific requirement. The requirement can be an internal or external requirement, as in an agency regulation.

E

electromagnetic emanations (EME) A condition of electronic equipment in which electrons leak from cables and the equipment itself. These emanations can possibly be picked up and reconstructed.

elliptic curve cryptography (ECC) A method in which elliptic curve equations are used to calculate encryption keys for use in general purpose encryption.

Encrypting File System (EFS) An integrated feature of Windows 2000 and XP/.NET that allows any file or folder stored on an NTFS partition to be encrypted or decrypted by the owner of the data or by the system's administrator.

encryption algorithms A mathematical formula or method used to scramble the information before transmitting it over insecure media. Examples include RSA, DH, IDEA, Blowfish, MD5, and DSS/DSA.

encryption hash A method in which a selection of data is mixed into a section of data based on an algorithm. The result is then called a *hash value.*

environment The physical conditions that affect and influence growth, development, and survival. Used in the security field to describe the surrounding conditions of an area to be protected.

escalation The upward movement of privileges when using network resources or exercising rights (that is, moving from read permissions to write).

evidence Any hardware, software, or data you can use to prove the identity and actions of an attacker.

Extensible Markup Language (XML) Like HTML, this flexible markup language is based on standards from the World Wide Web Consortium at `http://www.w3.org`. Unlike HTML, XML can be used to generate standard or fully customized content rich Web pages, documents, and applications. XML is used to provide widely accessible services and data to end users, exchange data among applications, and capture and represent data in a large variety of custom and standard formats. Numerous standard XML applications are security related, including the Security Assertion Markup Language (SAML), XML Signatures, XML Encryption, various XML key handling applications, and the Extensible Access Control Markup Language (XACML). See `http://www.coverpages.org` for more information on this topic and related standards.

extranet A special internetwork architecture wherein a company's or organization's external partners and customers are granted access to some parts of its intranet and the services it provides in a secure, controlled fashion.

F

false negative False negative acknowledgments of intrusion in an intrusion detection system, which means an intrusion has occurred but the IDS discarded related events or traces as false signals. *See also* false positive.

false positive False affirmative acknowledgment of intrusion, which means an intrusion detection has incorrectly identified certain events or traces as signaling an attack or intrusion when no such attack or intrusion is underway. Thus, a false positive is a false alarm.

Faraday cage A metal enclosure used to conduct stray EMEs to ground, thereby eliminating signal leakage and the ability of external monitors or detectors to "read" network or computer activity. A Faraday cage can be very small or encompass an entire building, and it is generally used only when security concerns are extremely high (as in national defense, classified areas, or highly sensitive commercial environments).

FCAPS An acronym that identifies the levels of a standard ISO model for network management, which can be expanded as fault, configuration, accounting, performance, and security management. For a more complete discussion of this model, please visit `http://www.searchnetworking.com` and search on "FCAPS."

Federal Information Processing Standard (FIPS) A standard created by the United States government for the evaluation of cryptographic modules. It consists of four levels that escalate in their requirement for higher security levels.

firewall A hardware device or software application designed to filter incoming or outgoing traffic based on predefined rules and patterns. Firewalls can filter traffic based on protocol uses, source or destination addresses, and port addresses and can even apply state-based rules to block unwanted activities or transactions. For an excellent source of information on this topic, see Matt Curtin and Marcus Ranum's Internet Firewalls FAQ at `http://www.interhack.net/pubs/fwfaq/`.

forensics As related to security, the process of analyzing and investigating a computer crime scene after an attack has occurred and of reconstructing the sequence of events and activities involved in such an attack.

G

guideline Specific information on how standards should be implemented. A guideline is generally not mandatory, thus it acts as a kind of flexible rule used to produce a desired behavior or action. A guideline allows freedom of choice on how to achieve the behavior.

H

hash value The resultant output or data generated from an encryption hash when applied to a specific set of data. If computed and passed as part of an incoming message and then recomputed upon message receipt, a hash value can be used to verify the authenticity of the received data if the two hash values match.

hashed message authentication code (HMAC) A mechanism for message authentication using cryptographic hash functions whose strength is dependent on the hash function used to create it.

hashing A methodology used to calculate a short, secret value from a data set of any size (usually for an entire message or for individual transmission units). This secret value is recalculated independently on the receiving end and compared to the submitted value to verify the sender's identity.

heuristics analysis A major improvement over the pattern-matching family of NIDS methodologies. Heuristics applies well-known analytic and rules-based techniques when interpreting network activity and traffic patterns; that is, it statistically analyzes the traffic coming over the network, as well as looking for specific patterns of activity. This method is sometimes referred to as *frequency*, *threshold*, or *excess* algorithm. When the pattern match count exceeds a threshold, an alarm is fired and action is taken.

honey pot A decoy system designed to attract hackers. A honey pot usually has all its logging and tracing enabled, and its security level is lowered on purpose. Likewise, such systems often include deliberate lures or bait, in hopes of attracting would-be attackers who think there are valuable items to be attained on the system.

host intrusion detection system Built around analysis of logs and activity on each individual host, rather than by observing and analyzing traffic on network cable segments, a host intrusion detection system looks for signs of system intrusion or compromise on specific systems and works in real-time or very close to real-time mode. Likewise, host intrusion detection systems often analyze events and conditions as they occur and monitor contents and activity related to key system, application, and data files, looking for signs of untoward activity.

hot site A site that is immediately available for occupation if an emergency arises. It typically has all the necessary hardware and software loaded and is available 24/7.

I–J

impact analysis Testing a proposed change to discover the impact on existing systems and software.

incident Any violation, or threatened violation, of a security policy.

incident response A clear action plan on what each response team member needs to do and when it has to be done in the event of an emergency or a security incident.

integrity A monitoring and management system that performs integrity checks and protects systems from unauthorized modifications to data, system, and application files. Normally, performing such checks requires access to a prior scan or original versions of the various files involved. When this term is applied to messages or data in transit, integrity checks rely on calculating hash or digest values before and after transmission to ensure nothing changed between the time it was sent and the time it was received.

Internet Key Exchange A method used in the IPSec protocol suite for public key exchange, security association parameter negotiation, identification, and authentication.

intranet A portion of the information technology infrastructure that belongs to and is controlled by the company in question.

intrusion detection system (IDS) A sophisticated network protection system designed to detect attacks in progress but not to prevent potential attacks from occurring (although many IDSs can trace attacks back to an apparent source and automatically notify all hosts through which attack traffic passes that they are forwarding such traffic). IDSs can be used to monitor network communication patterns network-wide (in which case, they're called *network intrusion detection systems [NIDS]*) or on a per-host basis (in which case, they're called *host intrusion detection systems [HIDS]*). IDSs are equally good at detecting internal intrusions or attacks as well as external ones.

IP Security (IPSec) Used for encryption of TCP/IP traffic, IP Security provides security extensions to the version of TCP/IP known as IPv4. IPSec defines mechanisms to negotiate encryption between pairs of hosts that want to communicate with one another at the Internet Protocol (IP) layer and can therefore handle all host-to-host traffic between pairs of machines. IPSec manages special relationships between pairs of machines, called *security associations*, and these govern which types of IPSec protocols are used, which types of keys are used, how they're exchanged, and how long such keys and security associations can last. For a good IPSec overview, please visit `http://www.networkmagazine.com/article/DCM20000509S0082`; for information about IPSec RFCs and standards, see `http://www.ietf.org/html.charters/ipsec-charter.html`.

ISO17799 International auditing standard for information security. The standard examines 10 major sections of information to ensure they conform with current best practices.

K–L

Kerberos A specific type of authentication developed at MIT, Kerberos takes its name from the three-headed beast that guards the gates of Hell in Greek mythology. Kerberos defines a set of authentication services, as defined in RFC 1510, and includes three protocols of particular importance: (1) the Authentication Service (AS) Exchange protocol, which enables a key distribution center (KDC) to grant clients a logon session key and the ticket granting ticket (TGT) used to access other services Kerberos controls; (2) the Ticket-Granting Service (TGS) Exchange protocol used to distribute service session keys and tickets for such services; and (3) the Client/Server (CS) Exchange protocol that clients use to send a ticket to request a ticket for access to some specific service. For a good overview of Kerberos and a description of how Kerberos works with Windows, look up Knowledge Base article Q217098 at `http://www.microsoft.com/technet/`.

key escrow Key escrow is a policy in which the certificate authority retains a copy of the private key it generates for the user for future use. This is most often used to allow an organization to access data that was encrypted by an employee using the private key.

key exchange A technique in which a pair of keys is generated and then exchanged between two systems (typically a client and server) over a network connection to allow a secure connection to be established between them.

Layer Two Tunneling Protocol (L2TP) A technology used with VPN to establish a communication tunnel between communicating parties over insecure media. L2TP permits a single logical connection to transport multiple protocols between a pair of hosts. L2TP is a member of the TCP/IP protocol suite and is defined in RFC 2661; a framework for creating virtual private networks that uses L2TP appears in RFC 2764.

Lightweight Directory Access Protocol (LDAP) A TCP/IP protocol that allows client systems to access directory services and related data. Examples of services that work with LDAP include the Windows 2000 Active Directory and Novell Directory Services (NDS), but LDAP works with any X.500-compliant directory service. In most cases, LDAP is used as part of management or other applications or in browsers to access directory services information. LDAP is defined in RFCs 1777 and 2559; numerous other RFCs address specific aspects of LDAP behavior or capabilities or define best practices for its use.

logic bomb A piece of software designed to do damage at a predetermined point in time or in response to some type of condition (for example, "disk is 95% full") or event (for example, some particular account logs in or some value the system tracks exceeds a certain threshold).

M

M of N Control Process of backing up private key material across multiple systems or devices.

magnetic overwrite A method of overwriting magnetic media several times with complimentary bit patterns to cause the loss of information. As degaussing, overwrite is used when discarding media with classified information.

man-in-the-middle An attack in which a hacker attempts to intercept data in a network stream and then inserts her own data into the communication with the goal of disrupting or taking over communications. Thus, the term itself is derived from the insertion of a third party—the proverbial "man in the middle"—between two parties engaged in communications.

Mandatory Access Control (MAC) A centralized security method that doesn't allow users to change permissions on objects.

mantrap A two-door configuration in a building or office that has the capability to lock unwanted individuals in a secured area, preventing them from entering other areas or even from exiting wherever it is that they're being held.

message The content and format a sender chooses to use to communicate with some receiver across a network, an intranet, an extranet, or the Internet.

message digest The output of an encryption hash that's applied to some fixed size chunk of data. A message digest provides a profound integrity check because even a change to one bit in the target data also changes the resulting digest value. This explains why digests are included so often in network transmissions.

moat The use of a water feature as a physical barrier to protect a building or office area. When designing medieval castles, architects often situated them on or near rivers or other bodies of water to make moat construction as easy as possible.

multifactor authentication An authentication process that uses more than one authentication method to establish user identity (for example, a multifactor system could combine a swipe card with a PIN or a voice scan with a pass phrase).

mutual authentication A situation in which a client provides authentication information to establish identity and related access permissions with a server and in which a server also provides authentication information to the client to ensure that illicit servers cannot masquerade as genuine servers.

N

network address translation (NAT) TCP/IP protocol technology that maps internal IP addresses to one or more external IP addresses through a NAT server of some type. NAT enables conservation of public IP address space by mapping private IP addresses used in an internal LAN to one or more external public IP addresses to communicate with the external world. NAT also provides address-hiding services (thereby denying outsiders access to "real" or private internal IP addresses), so that NAT adds both security and simplicity to network addressing.

network intrusion detection system (NIDS) An IDS system that monitors traffic and activity on one or more network segments. Thus, a NIDS has a complete picture of all the network segments it is configured to protect. Because such systems concentrate on the traffic and activity on the networks they monitor, NIDS are better able to recognize and document network-based attacks than are host-based IDSs.

no-man's land An area of clear land used as a buffer zone around a building or any other resource you are seeking to protect and secure. Such areas are typically monitored closely and can provide early warning of potential attacks or intrusion attempts.

nonrepudiation A service used with encryption to provide proof of the origin and integrity of data sent over a network. Nonrepudiation requires the use of private or secret keys that only a legitimate holder should be able to use. Later attempts to deny that a transaction occurred can be refuted owing to its use of such protected keys. Often, nonrepudiation involves some third party (such as a certificate authority that warrants the validity and currency of a key or digital signature); such parties log this activity, making them a witness to such transactions as well. For an excellent discussion of this topic, please visit `http://www.firstmonday.dk/issues/issue5_8/mccullagh/`.

nonrepudiation bit As defined in RFC 2459, this single bit of data is set when a public key is used to verify a digital signature that could only have been encrypted using the sender's or originator's private key.

O–P

Online Certificate Status Protocol (OCSP) A protocol defined by the IETF that is used to validate digital certificates issued by a CA.

padding Random data inserted after the payload in an IPSec ESP communication. It is designed to prevent attackers from using packet sniffers to estimate the amount of data being transmitted.

passive detection A method of intrusion detection that has an IDS present in the network in a silent fashion; it does not interfere with communications in progress.

pattern matching A network analysis method that uses a central box on the network. This approach compares each individual packet against a database of signatures (formats of packets known to be dangerous, offensive, or recognizable as parts of known attacks or vulnerability exploits). The weakness inherent in this method is that such patterns must be known (and definitions in place) before they can be used to recognize attacks or exploits. Thus, similar to virus signature files, attack pattern files (also called *signatures*) must be present to be useful.

plenum The space in a building between a false (drop) ceiling and the true ceiling or roof above. Typically used to run light fixtures and wiring, but also defined as a return air space in most building codes (which is why the coating on cables run through such space must be fire-retardant and nontoxic when burned).

Point-to-Point Tunneling Protocol (PPTP) A TCP/IP technology used to create virtual private network (VPN) or remote access links between sites (usually from one server to another) or for remote access (usually from a remote client to a local communications server). PPTP is the work of a vendor group that includes Microsoft, 3Com, and Copper Mountain Networks. It is generally regarded as less secure than L2TP and is used less frequently for that reason. PPTP is described in RFC 2637.

policy A broad statement of views and position. A policy states high-level intent with respect to a specific area of security and is more properly called a security policy. Security policies typically address how passwords are to be constructed and used, how various classes of data should be classified, which access controls apply, and which job roles can be granted remote access to a network. The formulation of security policy generally occurs after a risk analysis has been performed, represents an organization's formal attempts to describe how security works, and should be applied in its IT systems and services.

pretty good privacy (PGP) A shareware encryption technology for communications that utilizes both public and private encryption technologies to speed up encryption without compromising security. Also available in commercial product form, PGP products offer personal and enterprise-level encryption services of many kinds; visit `http://www.pgp.com` for more information.

private key A piece of data generated by an asymmetric algorithm that's used by the host to encrypt data. A matching public key can be used to decrypt data encrypted with the private key; this technique makes digital signatures and nonrepudiation possible. Likewise, anyone with access to the public key can encrypt data that only the private key holder can decrypt and read; this technique enables you to send information over public networks that only a designated recipient can read.

privilege management The process of controlling users and their capabilities on a network.

probability Used in risk assessment, probability measures the likelihood or chance that a threat will actually exploit some vulnerability.

procedure A procedure specifies how policies shall be put into practice in an environment. It defines the steps required to carry out policy elements and states intent (the "what" of security matters), whereas a procedure provides necessary "how-to" instructions.

protocol decode analysis A network analysis method that applies the rules specified for various network protocols (usually as prescribed in governing RFCs for TCP/IP) to interpret packet contents and search for suspicious traffic or related signs of attack or intrusion. This technique permits packets to be understood in the context of the protocols they use and often detects irregularities or outright illegal values in header field values and lengths. This technique also permits attack signatures to be used to analyze traffic by searching for related patterns in such traffic.

public branch exchange (PBX) A telephone switch used on a company's or organization's premises to create a local telephone network. Using a PBX obviates the need to order numerous individual phone lines from a telephone company and permits PBX owners to offer advanced telephony features and functions to their users.

public key A piece of data generated by an asymmetric algorithm distributed to the public for general use. Access to a public key provides tangible evidence of the identity of the corresponding private key holder because it can be used to decrypt information that only the private key holder can encrypt. Equally important, a public key can be used to encrypt information that only the private key holder can decrypt, thereby permitting messages to remain confidential and unreadable to any other user who does not possess a copy of the recipient's private key.

Public Key Infrastructure (PKI) A paradigm that encompasses certificate authorities and X.509 certificates used with public encryption algorithms to distribute, manage, issue, and revoke public keys. Of course, such a system also includes mechanisms to manage corresponding private keys for individual key holders. Public key infrastructures typically also include registration authorities to issue and validate requests for digital certificates, a certificate management system of some type, and a directory in which certificates are stored and can be accessed. Together, all these elements make up a PKI.

public switched telephone network (PSTN) Sometimes referred to as *plain old telephone service (POTS)*, this term describes the international telephone network that includes both analog and digital elements. Because the fundamental technology that underlies this infrastructure is a network based on telephone switching systems, it is identified as a switched network.

Finally, because this infrastructure is available to anyone with a dial tone and an account with dial-out capabilities, it's available to the public at large by its very nature. Because the PSTN is often used for dial-in remote access to private networks or the Internet, managing interconnections between the PSTN and such networks is an important security concern.

R

receiver The party that receives a message from its sender.

reconnaissance A general term to describe methods attackers use to gain insight and learn about the systems and networks they are targeting for potential attack or exploits.

Remote Authentication Dial-in User Services (RADIUS) An Internet protocol, described in RFC 2138, used for remote access services. It conveys user authentication and configuration data between a centralized authentication server (also called RADIUS server) and a remote access server (RADIUS client) to permit the remote access server to authenticate requests to use its network access ports. Users present the remote access server (RADIUS client) with credentials, which are in turn passed to the RADIUS server for authentication. If a user's access request is granted, the RADIUS server provides authorization and configuration information that the remote access server uses to establish a connection with that user; if a user's access request is denied, the connection with that user is terminated. In many ways, RADIUS offers a basic alternative to TACACS+, the Terminal Access Controller Access Control System described in RFC 1492.

remote monitoring (RMON) An Internet protocol that extends the Simple Network Monitoring Protocol (SNMP) functionality to include messages about and techniques for exchanging data between network systems and devices (managed nodes) and a network management application (management console). Because it allows managed nodes to report on events and conditions and allows management consoles to probe and request data from managed nodes, RMON presents a much richer set of data for network activity analysis. In its original designs, RMON did not provide security, however, so it can pose security threats as well as offer enhanced management and reporting capabilities.

replay An attack that involves capturing valid traffic from a network and then retransmitting that traffic at a later time to gain unauthorized access to systems and resources.

risk The potential that a threat might exploit some vulnerability.

role A defined behavior for a user or group of users based on some specific activity or responsibilities (that is, a tape backup administrator is usually permitted to back up all files on one or more systems; that person might or might not be allowed to restore such files, depending on the local security policies in effect).

Role-Based Access Control (RBAC) A security method that combines both MAC and DAC. Permissions are assigned based on a role or roles delegated to individual users or accounts in a company or an organization.

rollback A process used to undo changes or transactions when they do not complete, when they are suspected of being invalid or unwanted, or when they cause problems.

round A selection of encrypted data that is split into two or more blocks of data. Each block of data is then run through an encryption algorithm that applies an encryption key to each block of data individually, rather than applying encryption to the entire selection of data in a single operation.

router A device that connects multiple network segments and routes packets between them. Hardware routers run proprietary configurable software, and network operating systems often include routing functionality as well. Routers split broadcast domains.

S

Secure Hypertext Transfer Protocol (HTTPS or S-HTTP) An Internet protocol that encrypts individual messages used for Web communications rather than establishing a secure channel, like in SSL/TLS. S-HTTP supports choices among multiple security policies, various key management techniques, and encryption algorithms through a per-transaction negotiation mechanism.

Secure Multipurpose Internet Mail Extensions (S/MIME) An Internet protocol governed by RFC 2633 and used to secure email communications through encryption and digital signatures for authentication. It generally works with PKI to validate digital signatures and related digital certificates.

Secure Shell (SSH) A protocol designed to support secure remote login, along with secure access to other services across an insecure network (for example, inherently insecure services such as Telnet and FTP become secure when run with a secure shell session). SSH includes a secure Transport layer protocol that provides server authentication, confidentiality (encryption), and integrity (message digest functions), along with a user authentication protocol and a connection protocol that runs on top of the user authentication protocol.

Secure Sockets Layer (SSL) An Internet protocol originally created at Netscape Corporation that uses connection-oriented, end-to-end encryption to ensure that client/server communications are confidential (encrypted) and meet integrity constraints (message digests). SSL operates between the HTTP Application layer protocol and a reliable Transport layer protocol (usually TCP). Because SSL is independent of the Application layer, any application protocol can work with SSL transparently. SSL can also work with a secure Transport layer protocol, which is why the term *SSL/TLS* appears frequently. *See also* Transport Layer Security.

Security Association (SA) A method in IPSec that accounts for individual security settings for IPSec data transmission.

security baseline Defined in a company's or organization's security policy, a security baseline is a specific set of security-related modifications to and patches and settings for systems and services in use that underpins technical implementation of security.

security parameter index (SPI) A 32-bit pseudo-random number that specifies the security settings used by the transmitter to communicate with the receiver in an IPSec communication path.

sender The party that originates a message.

sequence number A counting mechanism in IPSec that increases incrementally each time a packet is transmitted in an IPSec communication path. It protects the receiver from replay attacks.

service level agreement (SLA) A contract between two companies that specifies, by contract, a level of service to be provided by one company to another. Supplying replacement equipment within 24 hours of loss of that equipment or related services is a simple example of an SLA.

shielded twisted pair (STP) A form of twisted pair cabling that incorporates a metallic braid or foil shield in its construction, thereby making it more resistant to magnetic and radio interference (and also more expensive) than unshielded twisted pair cabling (UTP).

signature-based IDS Any IDS, except anomaly (in a certain way), is signature based. A signature-based IDS looks for specific patterns of attack or intrusion, known as *intrusion signatures.* A signature is a set of specific conditions, packets, or activities that normally identifies an intrusion or other suspicious activity when matched.

Simple Network Management Protocol (SNMP) A UDP-based Application layer Internet protocol used for network management, SNMP is governed by RFCs 2570 and 2574. In converting management information between management consoles (managers) and managed nodes (agents), SNMP implements configuration and event databases on managed nodes that can be configured to respond to interesting events by notifying network managers.

single sign-on (SSO) The concept or process of using a single logon authority to grant users access to resources on a network regardless of what operating system or application is used to make or handle a request for access. The concept behind the term is that users need to authenticate only once but can then access any resources available on a network.

smart card A credit-card-sized device that contains an embedded chip. On this chip, varying and multiple types of data can be stored, such as a driver's license number, medical information, passwords or other authentication data, and even bank account data.

sniffer A hardware device or software program used to capture and analyze network data in real-time. Because such a device can typically read and interpret all unencrypted traffic on the cable segment to which it is attached, it can be a powerful tool in any competent hacker's arsenal.

social engineering The process of using human behavior to attack a network or gain access to resources that would otherwise be inaccessible. Social engineering is a term that emphasizes the well-known fact that poorly or improperly trained individuals can be persuaded, tricked, or coerced into giving up passwords, phone numbers, or other data that can lead to unauthorized system access, even when strong technical security measures can otherwise prevent such access. User education and well-documented policies (for example, stating that no passwords should ever be given by telephone under any circumstances) are the only remedy that can foil attacks based on this technique.

spoofing A technique for generating network traffic that contains a different (and usually quite specific) source address from that of the machine actually generating the traffic. Spoofing is used for many reasons in attacks: It foils easy identification of the true source; it permits attackers to take advantage of existing trust relationships; and it deflects responses to attacks against some (usually innocent) third party or parties.

staging The process of rolling out a change to network software or related configuration or policy data, in a carefully orchestrated phased manner, or through some type of step-by-step process through a software management or distribution environment.

standard This term is used in many ways. In some contexts, it refers to best practices for specific platforms, implementations, OS versions, and so forth. Some standards are mandatory and ensure uniform application of a technology across an organization. In other contexts, a standard might simply describe a well-defined rule used to produce a desired behavior or actions. In this case, a standard sets out specific actions for achieving desired behavior or results.

stateful matching Recognizes the need to match patterns beyond the scope of a single packet on a network and looks for signatures in data streams instead. Stateful inspection NIDSs can reassemble fragments of a single communication in order and compare such assembled communications against a signature database. Firewalls or other systems that perform stateful matching are sometimes said to be implementing *stateful inspection.*

switch A hardware device that manages multiple, simultaneous pairs of connections between communicating systems. In some cases, a switch is used as a network concentrator that splits traditionally flat network segments into dedicated communication links (microsegmentation). Likewise, switches split collision domains, but switches can also provide greater aggregate bandwidth between pairs or groups of communicating devices because each switched link normally gets exclusive access to available bandwidth. Thus, switches often improve overall performance, as well as providing logical network segmentation and collision domain management capabilities.

symmetric encryption An encryption technique in which a single encryption key is generated and used to encrypt data. This data is then passed across a network. After that data arrives at the recipient device, the same key used to encrypt that data is used to decrypt that data. This technique requires a secure way to share keys because both sender and receiver use the same key (also called a *shared secret* because that key should be unknown to third parties).

T

TACACS+ An enhanced version of Terminal Access Controller Access Control System. Whereas TACACS+ is TCP based, the original TACACS is a UDP-based authentication and access control Internet protocol governed by RFC 1492. In either implementation, TACACS recognizes three classes of devices: a network access server, an authentication server, and a remote terminal from which access requests originate. When a client requests access, a remote terminal passes an identifier and a password (or other authentication data that might originate from a smart card, a security token passing device, a biometric device, or even a multifactor authentication system) to the remote access server. In turn, the remote access server passes that information to an authentication server for validation. If the authentication server validates the credentials, the request is allowed to proceed; if not, the access request is denied.

TCP/IP hijacking A process used to steal an ongoing TCP/IP session for purposes of attacking a target computer. Essentially, hijacking works by spoofing network traffic so it appears to originate from a single computer, when in actuality, it originates elsewhere. Hijacking also depends on guessing or matching packet sequence numbers or other data so that the other party to communication doesn't realize another computer has taken over an active communications session.

TEMPEST A code word used by the United States government to describe a set of standards and specifications for reducing emanations from electronic equipment, thereby reducing vulnerability to eavesdropping. This term is sometimes (and incorrectly) expanded as an acronym for "test for electromagnetic propagation and evaluation for secure transmissions" or "telecommunications electronics material protected from emanating spurious transmissions," but this terminology is apocryphal or historical rather than real (visit `http://www.acronymfinder.com` for more information).

Although this term has military origins, it is now used mostly in civilian circles; in military nomenclature, the replacement term is EMSEC (an abbreviation for emissions security). Whatever source one might seek for this term, it always refers to limiting leakage of electronic signals from equipment to stop their unwanted monitoring.

threat A danger to a computer network or system (for example, a hacker or virus represents a threat).

threshold and excess analysis *See* heuristics analysis.

token Also known as a *security token*, this is a hardware- or software-based system used for authentication wherein two or more sets of matched devices or software generate matching random passwords with a high degree of complexity. Thus, a token-based security device presents a complex password or security token that is difficult to guess within a short period of time. Then, it enhances that security by changing the token on a regularly scheduled basis to limit the size of any data set encrypted with a single password or token. Finally, because token-based security systems also require their users to supply an additional password or personal identification number, such systems also qualify as two-factor authentication systems.

Transport Layer Security (TLS, sometimes TLSP) An end-to-end encryption protocol originally specified in ISO Standard 10736 that provides security services as part of the Transport layer in a protocol stack. More commonly, however, TLS refers to an Internet protocol defined in RFC 2246 that is also called TLSP. Because this TLS is based on and similar to SSL version 3.0, it is really misnamed because it operates at the Application layer, not the Transport layer.

Trojan horse Software that is hidden inside other software commonly used to infect systems with viruses, worms, or remote control software. As in the famous exploit that Odysseus perpetrated during the Trojan wars, a software Trojan horse represents itself as offering some type of capability or functionality when it also includes some means to destroy or take over systems on which it is installed.

U–V

unshielded twisted pair (UTP) A type of cabling in which pairs of wires are twisted around one another to improve transmission and interference susceptibility characteristics. UTP is used extensively in wiring LANs.

virtual local area network (VLAN) A software technology that allows grouping of network nodes connected to one or more network switches into a single logical network. By permitting logical aggregation of devices into virtual network segments, VLANs offer simplified user management and network resource access controls for switched networks.

virtual private network (VPN) A popular technology that supports reasonably secure logical private network links across some insecure public network infrastructure, such as the Internet. VPNs reduces PSTN costs by eliminating calls or requiring only local calls to be placed to an Internet service provider (ISP). VPNs are also more secure than traditional remote access because they can be encrypted. Finally, because VPNs support tunneling (the hiding of numerous types of protocols and sessions within a single host-to-host connection), they also support multiple connections that use the same wire.

virus A piece of (usually) malicious code that's normally disguised as something legitimate or innocuous (for example, an email attachment that purports to be a picture or a document file) that causes unexpected or unwanted events to occur. The defining characteristic of a virus is that it spreads to other computers by design; although some viruses also damage the systems on which they reside, not all viruses inflict damage. Viruses can spread immediately upon reception or implement other unwanted actions, or they can lie dormant until a trigger in their code causes them to become active. Viruses usually belong to one of three classes: file infectors, which attach themselves to executable files of some type; system or boot sector infectors, which infect key system files or boot areas on hard disks or removable media; and macro viruses, which infect applications such as Microsoft Word to implement their actions. The hidden code a virus executes is called its *payload.*

vulnerability A weakness in hardware or software that can be used to gain unauthorized or unwanted access to or information from a network or computer.

W

warm site A backup site that has some of the equipment and infrastructure necessary for a business to begin operating at that location. Typically, companies or organizations bring their own computer systems and hardware to a warm site, but that site usually already includes a ready-to-use networking infrastructure and also might include reliable power, climate controls, lighting, and Internet access points.

wet-pipe fire suppression A sprinkler system with pressurized water in its pipes. If a fire starts, the pipes release water immediately and offer the fastest and most effective means of water-based fire suppression.

Wired Equivalent Privacy (WEP) A security protocol used in IERR 802.11 wireless networking, WEP is designed to provide security equivalent to that found in regular wired networks. This is achieved by using basic symmetric encryption to protect data sent over wireless connections, so that sniffing of wireless transmissions doesn't produce readable data and so drive-by attackers cannot access a wireless LAN without additional effort and attacks.

Wireless Transport Layer Security (WTLS) WTLS defines a security level for applications based on the Wireless Application Protocol (WAP). As its acronym indicates, WTLS is based on Transport layer security (TLS) but has been modified to work with the low-bandwidth, high-latency, and limited processing capabilities found in many wireless networking implementations. WTLS also provides authentication, data integrity, and confidentiality mechanisms, all based on encryption methods using shared 56- or 128-bit symmetric keys.

worm A special type of virus designed primarily to reproduce and replicate itself on as many computer systems as possible, worms do not normally alter files but rather remain resident in a computer's memory. Worms typically rely on access to operating system capabilities that are invisible to users. Often worms are detected by their side effects (unwanted consumption of system resources, diminished system performance, or reprioritization of normal system tasks) rather than by overt behavior. Antivirus software is a key ingredient in preventing infection from worms, as it is with other types of viruses.

X–Y–Z

X.500 directory A standard that regulates global, distributed directory services databases, it's also known as a *white pages* directory (because lookup occurs by name, rather than by job role or other categorized information as in a yellow pages type of system). For a detailed overview of X.500, please search on that term at `http://searchnetworking.techtarget.com/`.

X.509 digital certificate A digital certificate that uniquely identifies a potential communications party or participant. Among other things, an X.509 digital certificate includes a party's name and public key, but it can also include organizational affiliation, service or access restrictions, and a host of other access- and security-related information.

XML Access Control Language (XACL) An XML application that allows granular access controls within XML-generated Web pages, documents, or other XML-generated applications. XACL is designed to browse and update XML documents securely on a per-element basis. For more information on this topic, visit `http://www.coverpages.org` and search on XACL.

APPENDIX C

General Security Resources and Bibliography

1. General Security Concepts

Online Material

1. Barkley, John. "Aspects of Security Policies" (`http://hissa.nist.gov`).
2. Coar, Ken. "Security and Apache: An Essential Primer Mandatory Versus Discretionary Access Control" (`http://www.linuxplanet.com`).
3. Gerck, E. "Overview of Certification Systems: X.509, CA, PGP and SKIP" (`http://www.mcg.org.br`).
4. Gibson, Steve. "The Strange Tale of Denial-of-Service Attacks Against GRC.COM" (`http://www.grc.com`).
5. Grand, Joe. "Authentication Tokens: Balancing the Security Risks with Business Requirements" (`http://www.atstake.com`).
6. Lynch, Clifford. "A White Paper on Authentication and Access Management Issues in Cross-organizational Use of Networked Information Resources" (`http://www.cni.org`).
7. Suares, Stuart. "Biometric Security Systems" (`http://www.biometricsecurity.com.au`).
8. Tung, Brian. "The Moron's Guide to Kerberos" (`http://www.isi.edu`).
9. "What is a digital. signature and what is authentication?" (`http://www.rsasecurity.com`).

Publications

1. *ALS Designing Microsoft Windows 2000 Network Security.* Redmond, WA: Microsoft Press, 2001.
2. Carter, Earl, and Rick Stiffler. *Cisco Secure Intrusion Detection System.* Indianapolis, IN: Cisco Press, 2002.
3. Feghhi, Jalal, and Peter Williams. *Digital Certificates Applied Internet Security.* Reading, MA: Addison-Wesley, 1999.
4. Harris, Shon. *All in One CISSP Certification Exam Guide.* New York: McGraw-Hill, 2002.
5. Maiwald, Eric. *Network Security: A Beginner's Guide.* New York: McGraw-Hill, 2001.
6. McClure, Stuart, Joel Scambray, and George Kurtz. *Hacking Exposed: Network Security Secrets and Solutions, Third Edition.* New York: McGraw-Hill, 2001.
7. *Managing Cisco Network Security.* Indianapolis, IN: Cisco Press, 2001.

8. *Microsoft Windows 2000 Server.* Redmond, WA: Microsoft Press, 2000.

9. Northcutt, Stephen, Donald McLachlan, and Judy Novak. *Network Intrusion Detection: An Analyst's Handbook, Second Edition.* Indianapolis, IN: New Riders, 2000.

2. Communication Security

Online Material

1. Cryptographic Algorithms (`http://kremlinencrypt.com/crypto/algorithms.html`).
2. "How SSL Works" (`http://developer.netscape.com/tech/security/ssl/howitworks.html`).
3. IEEE 802.11 WG "Hot Topics" (`http://grouper.ieee.org/groups/802/11/`).
4. The Mail Abuse Prevention System (MAPSSM) Realtime Blackhole List (RBLSM) (`http://mail-abuse.org/rbl/rationale.html`).
5. Modern Hacker's Desk Reference (`http://cyborg.virtualave.net/mhdr.htm`).
6. SecurityFocus (`http://www.securityfocus.net`).

Publications

1. McClure, Stuart, Joel Scambray, and George Kurtz. *Hacking Exposed Network Security Secrets and Solutions, Third Edition.* Berkeley, CA: McGraw-Hill Osborne Media, 2001.
2. Microsoft Corporation. *Windows 2000 Server TCP/IP Core Networking Guide.* Redmond, WA: Microsoft Press, 2002.

3. Devices, Media, and Topology Security

Online Material

1. HOW TO: Harden the TCP/IP Stack Against Denial of Service Attacks in Windows 2000 (`http://support.microsoft.com/default.aspx?scid=kb;en-us;q315669`).
2. Keeping Your Site Comfortably Secure: An Introduction to Internet Firewalls (`http://csrc.nist.gov/publications/nistpubs/800-10/node1.html`).
3. Local Area Detection of Incoming War Dial Activity (`http://www.att.com/isc/docs/war_dial_detection.pdf`).
4. White Paper: Internet Security for Small Businesses (`http://www.cisco.com/warp/public/cc/pd/rt/800/prodlit/fire_wp.htm`).
5. White Paper: The Science of Intrusion Detection System Attack Identification (`http://www.cisco.com/warp/public/cc/pd/sqsw/sqidsz/prodlit/idssa_wp.htm`).

Publications

1. Chappell, Laura. *Advanced Cisco Router Configuration.* Indianapolis, IN: Cisco Press, 1998.
2. Microsoft Corporation. *Windows 2000 Server TCP/IP Core Networking Guide.* Redmond, WA: Microsoft Press, 2002.

4. INTRUSION DETECTION, BASELINES, AND HARDENING

Online Material

1. The Apache Software Foundation (http://www.apache.org).
2. CERT Coordination Center. "Identifying tools that aid in detecting signs of intrusion" (http://www.cert.org/security-improvement/implementations/i042.07.html).
3. List of intrusions detected by Network ICE (http://www.iss.net/security_center/advice/Intrusions/default.htm).
4. Microsoft Security and Privacy Web site (http://www.microsoft.com/security).
5. Network Security Library. "Network- vs. Host-based Intrusion Detection" (http://secinf.net/info/ids/nvh_ids/).
6. SANs Institute "What Is a Honeypot?" (http://www.sans.org/newlook/resources/IDFAQ/honeypot3.htm).
7. "The Science of Intrusion Detection System Attack Identification" (http://www.cisco.com/warp/public/cc/pd/sqsw/sqidsz/prodlit/idssa_wp.htm).
8. "Security Operations Guide for Windows 2000 Server" (http://www.microsoft.com/technet/treeview/default.asp?url=/technet/security/prodtech/windows/windows2000/staysecure/default.asp).

Publications

1. *Windows 2000 Server TCP/IP Core Networking Guide.* Redmond, WA: Microsoft Press, 2002.

5. CRYPTOGRAPHY ALGORITHMS

Online Material

1. AES page at the NIST Web site (http://csrc.nist.gov/encryption/aes/).
2. El Gamal encryption discussion document on the RSA Web site (http://www.rsasecurity.com/rsalabs/staff/bios/mjakobsson/teaching/encryption_files/frame.htm).
3. How Encryption Works reference Web site (http://www.howstuffworks.com/encryption.htm).
4. Microsoft Kerberos deployment Web page (http://www.microsoft.com/technet/treeview/default.asp?url=/TechNet/prodtechnol/windows2000serv/deploy/kerberos.asp).
5. Microsoft Public Key Infrastructure introduction Web page (http://www.microsoft.com/technet/treeview/default.asp?url=/technet/prodtechnol/windows2000serv/evaluate/featfunc/pkiintro.asp).
6. National Institute of Standards and Technology Web site (http://www.nist.gov).
7. Request for Comment document for CAST-128 (http://www.faqs.org/rfcs/rfc2144.html).
8. Request for Comment document for CAST-256 (http://www.faqs.org/rfcs/rfc2612.html).
9. Rijndael Web site (http://www.esat.kuleuven.ac.be/~rijmen/rijndael/).
10. RSA-based Cryptographic Schemes Web site (http://www.rsasecurity.com/rsalabs/rsa_algorithm/).

11. Security books, journals, bibliographies, and publications listing Web site (http://www.cs.auckland.ac.nz/~pgut001/links/books.html).
12. W3C XML Encryption Working Group Web site (http://www.w3.org/Encryption/2001/).
13. XML Access Control Language (XACL) Web page at IBM (http://www.trl.ibm.com/projects/xml/xacl/).

Publications

1. Krutz, Ronald, and Russel Dean Vines. *The CISSP Prep Guide: Mastering the Ten Domains of Computer Security.* Indianapolis, IN: John Wiley and Sons, 2001.
2. Russel, Crawford. *Microsoft Windows 2000 Server Administrator's Companion.* Redmond, WA: Microsoft Press, 2000.

6. PKI AND KEY MANAGEMENT

Online Material

1. Internet Engineering Task Force. Request for Comment Document number 2401, "Security Architecture for the Internet Protocol" (http://www.ietf.org/rfc/rfc2401.txt?number=2401).
2. Internet Engineering Task Force. Request for Comment Document number 2459, "Internet X.509 Public Key Infrastructure Certificate and CRL Profile" (http://www.ietf.org/rfc/rfc2459.txt).
3. National Institute of Standards and Technology. "Security Requirements for Cryptographic Modules" (http://csrc.nist.gov/cryptval/140-1.htm).
4. RSA Corporation. "Public Key Cryptography Standards" (http://www.rsasecurity.com/rsalabs/pkcs/).

Publications

1. Housely, Russ, and Tim Polk. *Planning for PKI.* New York: John Wiley and Sons, 2001.

7. PHYSICAL SECURITY, DISASTER RECOVERY, AND BUSINESS CONTINUITY

Online Material

1. Davis, Warren, Ph.D. "How Does a Faraday Cage Work" (http://www.physlink.com).
2. Department of Defense Trusted Computer System Evaluation Criteria (http://www.radium.ncsc.mil).
3. McNamera, Joel. "The Complete, Unofficial TEMPEST Homepage" (http://www.eskimo.com/~joelm/tempest.html).
4. "Modern Protection: Elemental Faraday Cage" (http://www.boltlightningprotection.com).
5. Nelson, Michael. "Fire Suppression in Historic Places of Worship" (http://www.sacredplaces.org).

6. Pawliw, Borys. "TEMPEST" (`http://whatis.techtarget.com`).

Publications

1. Fennelly, Lawrence J. *Effective Physical Security.* Burlington, MA: Butterworth-Heinemann, 1996.
2. Garcia, Mary Lynn. *Design and Evaluation of Physical Protection Systems.* Burlington, MA: Butterworth-Heinemann, 2001.
3. Harris, Shon. *All in One CISSP Certification Exam Guide.* New York: McGraw-Hill Publishing, 2002.

8. Security Policy and Procedures

Publications

1. Amoroso, Edward G. *Fundamentals of Computer Security Technology.* Upper Saddle River, NJ: Prentice Hall, 1994.
2. Department of Defense. *Department of Defense Trusted Computer System Evaluation Criteria.* Darby, PA: Diane Publishing Co., 1985.
3. Krause, Micki, and Harold F. Tipton, eds. *Information Security Management Handbook, Fourth Edition Volume I.* Boca Raton, FL: Auerbach Publications, 1999.
4. Russell, Deborah, and G. T. Gangemi, Sr. *Computer Security Basics.* Sebastapol, CA: O'Reilly and Associates, Inc., 1991.
5. Smith, Martin R. *Commonsense Computer Security: Your Practical Guide to Information Protection, Second Edition.* New York: McGraw-Hill Companies, 1994.
6. Weckert, John, and Douglas Adeney. *Computer and Information Ethics.* Westport, CT: Greenwood Publishing Group, 1997.

9. Security Management

Online Material

1. Beta Systems. "Immediate Escalation of Security Related Events" (`http://www.betasystems.com`).
2. Brenner, Susan. "Private Computing Security, Approaches to Computer Security: Practical and Legal Issues" (`http://www.cybercrimes.net`).
3. BS 7799 "Security Standards" (`http://bsonline.techindex.co.uk`).
4. Collie, Byron S. "Computer Investigation and Post-Intrusion Computer Forensics Analysis" (`http://www.usyd.co.au/su/is/comms/security`).
5. Ernst and Young. "Computer Forensics, Response Versus Reaction an Expert Paper" (`http://www.ey.com/au/itrma`).
6. Feldman, John, and Joseph V. Giordano. "Cyber Forensics" (`http://www.afrl.af.mil/techconn`).
7. ISO 17799 "Security Standards" (`http://www.iso.ch`).
8. Meta Security Group. "Incident Response and Computer Forensic Services" (`http://www.metasecuritygroup.com`).
9. Noblett, Michael G., Mark M. Pollitt, and Lawrence A. Presley. "Recovering and Examining Computer Forensic Evidence" (`http://www.fbi.gov/hq/lab/fsc/backissu/oct2000`).
10. SANs Institute. "Computer Security Incident Handling: Step by Step" (`http://www.sans.org`).
11. "What Is Computer Forensics?" (`http://`

APPENDIX D

Overview of the Certification Process

Developed in consultation with IT security professionals, educators, vendors, and other industry experts, CompTIA certifications are knowledge based. They focus on a rather theoretical or academic approach to the subject matter. To obtain any CompTIA certification, you must meet the requirements of respective certification, prove your expertise by passing the respective exam, and accept an agreement.

Each direction of CompTIA's certification program is more specific to the area of practice and less specific to the product vendors. CompTIA exams have a tendency to be straightforward tests, in the form of rather short and clear questions and multiple-choice answers. On the Security+ exam, there are no "never-ending scenarios" as found in the latest designing series of Microsoft exams. There are no type-in-your-answer, drag-and-drop, mark-the-screenshot, multiple-choice answers with more than four options, or questions involving simulations or graphs; there's none of the stuff you are more than likely to face on the Cisco or Microsoft exams. The challenge is really to gain a broad understanding of the topic you are being tested on, not the very specific details of any product in particular.

At the time of this writing, in addition to Security+ certification, CompTIA association offers the following certificationprograms:

- A+
- CDIA+
- i-Net+
- Network+
- Server+
- Linux+
- IT Project+
- e-Biz+
- CTT+
- HTI+

Description of the Path to Certification

The Security+ exam is numbered SY0-101. The closed-book exam provides a valid and reliable measure of your technical proficiency and expertise. Developed in consultation with computer-industry professionals who have networking, TCP/IP, security, and cryptography experience in the workplace, the exams are conducted by Virtual University Enterprises (VUE), the electronic testing division of NCS Pearson as well as by Thomson Prometric.

VUE has more than 2,500 authorized testing centers serving more than 100 countries.

The exam prices vary depending on your CompTIA member status:

- CompTIA members: $175 each
- Non-CompTIA members: $225 each

To schedule an exam, call VUE at 877-551-7587 or 952-995-8758.

Thomson Prometric offers these exams at more than 2,000 Authorized Prometric Testing Centers worldwide. To schedule an exam, call Thomson Prometric at 1-800-755-EXAM (3926) or visit its Web page at `www.2test.com`.

Feel free to check the CompTIA Web page for more information at `http://www.comptia.org/certification/securityplus/index.htm`.

About the Security+ Certification Program

The Security+ certification is a certification designed to measure the competency of security professionals. The Security+ candidate should also have the skills and knowledge of individuals who have taken the CompTIA A+ and Network+ exams.

The Computing and Technology Industry Association (CompTIA) developed the Security+ certification in response to several factors, not the least of which was the growing need for computer security professionals.

You might be asking why this exam is for you, and why now. Aside from the fact that the certification brings certain obvious professional benefits to you, the Security+ program gives you access to the CompTIA organization and to the benefits this access affords.

CompTIA's Web site (`www.comptia.com`), for instance, identifies the following benefits for prospective CompTIA-certified individuals:

- **Recognized proof of professional achievement**—A level of competence commonly accepted and valued by the industry.
- **Enhanced job opportunities**—Many employers give preference in hiring to applicants with certification. They view this as proof that a new hire knows the procedures and technologies required.
- **Opportunity for advancement**—The certification can be a plus when an employer awards job advancements and promotions.
- **Training requirement**—Certification might be required as a prerequisite to attending a vendor's training course, so employers offer advance training to those employees who are already certified.
- **Customer confidence**—As the general public learns about certification, customers will require that only certified technicians be assigned to their accounts.

For any additional information or clarification of the CompTIA Security+ certification path and its history and benefits, consult the CompTIA home page at `www.comptia.com`.

APPENDIX E

What's on the CD-ROM

This appendix is a brief rundown of what you'll find on the CD-ROM that comes with this book. For a more detailed description of the *PrepLogic Practice Tests, Preview Edition* exam simulation software, see Appendix F, "Using the *PrepLogic Practice Tests, Preview Edition* Software." In addition to the *PrepLogic Practice Tests, Preview Edition,* the CD-ROM includes the electronic version of the book in Portable Document Format (PDF), several utility and application programs, and a complete listing of test objectives and where they are covered in the book.

PrepLogic Practice Tests, Preview Edition

PrepLogic is a leading provider of certification training tools. Trusted by certification students worldwide, we believe PrepLogic is the best practice exam software available. In addition to providing a means of evaluating your knowledge of the Training Guide material, *PrepLogic Practice Tests, Preview Edition* features several innovations that help you to improve your mastery of the subject matter.

For example, the practice tests allow you to check your score by exam area or domain to determine which topics you need to study more. Another feature enables you to obtain immediate feedback on your responses in the form of explanations for the correct and incorrect answers.

PrepLogic Practice Tests, Preview Edition exhibits most of the full functionality of the *Premium Edition* but offers only a fraction of the total questions. To get the complete set of practice questions and exam functionality, visit PrepLogic.com and order the *Premium Edition* for this and other challenging exam titles.

Again, for a more detailed description of the *PrepLogic Practice Tests, Preview Edition* features, see Appendix F.

APPENDIX F

Using the *PrepLogic Practice Tests, Preview Edition* Software

This Training Guide includes a special version of *PrepLogic Practice Tests*—a revolutionary test engine designed to give you the best in certification exam preparation. PrepLogic offers sample and practice exams for many of today's most in-demand and challenging technical certifications. This special Preview Edition is included with this book as a tool to use in assessing your knowledge of the Training Guide material, while also providing you with the experience of taking an electronic exam.

This appendix describes in detail what *PrepLogic Practice Tests, Preview Edition* is; how it works; and what it can do to help you prepare for the exam. Note that although the Preview Edition includes all the test simulation functions of the complete, retail version, it contains only a single practice test. The Premium Edition, available at PrepLogic.com, contains the complete set of challenging practice exams designed to optimize your learning experience.

EXAM SIMULATION

One of the main functions of *PrepLogic Practice Tests, Preview Edition* is exam simulation. To prepare you to take the actual vendor certification exam, PrepLogic is designed to offer the most effective exam simulation available.

QUESTION QUALITY

The questions provided in the *PrepLogic Practice Tests, Preview Edition* are written to highest standards of technical accuracy. The questions tap the content of the Training Guide chapters and help you review and assess your knowledge before you take the actual exam.

INTERFACE DESIGN

The *PrepLogic Practice Tests, Preview Edition* exam simulation interface provides you with the experience of taking an electronic exam. This enables you to effectively prepare for taking the actual exam by making the test experience a familiar one. Using this test simulation can help eliminate the sense of surprise or anxiety you might experience in the testing center because you will already be acquainted with computerized testing.

EFFECTIVE LEARNING ENVIRONMENT

The *PrepLogic Practice Tests, Preview Edition* interface provides a learning environment that not only tests you through the computer, but also teaches the material you need to know to pass the certification exam.

Each question comes with a detailed explanation of the correct answer and often provides reasons the other options are incorrect. This information helps to reinforce the knowledge you already have and also provides practical information you can use on the job.

SOFTWARE REQUIREMENTS

PrepLogic Practice Tests, Preview Edition requires a computer with the following:

- Microsoft Windows 98, Windows Me, Windows NT 4.0, Windows 2000, or Windows XP.
- A 166MHz or faster processor is recommended.
- A minimum of 32MB of RAM.
- As with any Windows application, the more memory, the better your performance.
- 10MB of hard drive space.

INSTALLING *PREPLOGIC PRACTICE TESTS, PREVIEW EDITION*

Install *PrepLogic Practice Tests, Preview Edition* by running the setup program on the *PrepLogic Practice Tests, Preview Edition* CD. Follow these instructions to install the software on your computer:

1. Insert the CD into your CD-ROM drive. The Autorun feature of Windows should launch the software. If you have Autorun disabled, click Start and select Run. Go to the root directory of the CD and select setup.exe. Click Open, and then click OK.
2. The Installation Wizard copies the *PrepLogic Practice Tests, Preview Edition* files to your hard drive; adds *PrepLogic Practice Tests, Preview Edition* to your desktop and Program menu; and installs test engine components to the appropriate system folders.

REMOVING *PREPLOGIC PRACTICE TESTS, PREVIEW EDITION* FROM YOUR COMPUTER

If you elect to remove the *PrepLogic Practice Tests, Preview Edition* product from your computer, an uninstall process has been included to ensure that it is removed from your system safely and completely. Follow these instructions to remove *PrepLogic Practice Tests, Preview Edition* from your computer:

1. Select Start, Settings, Control Panel.
2. Double-click the Add/Remove Programs icon.
3. You are presented with a list of software installed on your computer. Select the appropriate *PrepLogic Practice Tests, Preview Edition* title you want to remove. Click the Add/Remove button. The software is then removed from your computer.

USING *PREPLOGIC PRACTICE TESTS, PREVIEW EDITION*

PrepLogic is designed to be user friendly and intuitive. Because the software has a smooth learning curve, your time is maximized because you start practicing almost immediately. *PrepLogic Practice Tests, Preview Edition* has two major modes of study: Practice Test and Flash Review.

Using Practice Test mode, you can develop your test-taking abilities as well as your knowledge through the use of the Show Answer option. While you are taking the test, you can expose the answers along with a detailed explanation of why the given answers are right or wrong. This gives you the ability to better understand the material presented.

Flash Review mode is designed to reinforce exam topics rather than quiz you. In this mode, you are shown a series of questions but no answer choices. Instead, you are given a button that reveals the correct answer to the question and a full explanation for that answer.

Starting a Practice Test Mode Session

Practice Test mode enables you to control the exam experience in ways that actual certification exams do not allow. You have the following options:

- **Enable Show Answer Button**—Activates the Show Answer button, allowing you to view the correct answer(s) and full explanation for each question during the exam. When not enabled, you must wait until after your exam has been graded to view the correct answer(s) and explanation.
- **Enable Item Review Button**—Activates the Item Review button, allowing you to view your answer choices and marked questions and facilitating navigation between questions.
- **Randomize Choices**—Randomizes answer choices from one exam session to the next. Makes memorizing question choices more difficult, therefore keeping questions fresh and challenging longer.

To begin studying in Practice Test mode, click the Practice Test radio button from the main exam customization screen. This enables the options detailed previously.

To your left, you are presented with the option of selecting the preconfigured Practice Test or creating your own Custom Test. The preconfigured test has a fixed time limit and number of questions. Custom Tests enable you to configure the time limit and the number of questions in your exam.

The Preview Edition included with this book includes a single preconfigured Practice Test. Get the compete set of challenging PrepLogic Practice Tests at PrepLogic.com and make certain you're ready for the big exam.

Click the Begin Exam button to begin your exam.

Starting a Flash Review Mode Session

Flash Review mode provides you with an easy way to reinforce topics covered in the practice questions. To begin studying in Flash Review mode, click the Flash Review radio button from the main exam customization screen. Either select the preconfigured Practice Test or create your own Custom Test.

Click the Best Exam button to begin your Flash Review of the exam questions.

Standard *PrepLogic Practice Tests, Preview Edition* Options

The following list describes the function of each of the buttons you see. Depending on the options, some of the buttons will be grayed out and inaccessible or missing completely. Buttons that are appropriate are active. The buttons are as follows:

- **Exhibit**—This button is visible if an exhibit is provided to support the question. An exhibit is an image that provides supplemental information necessary to answer the question.
- **Item Review**—This button leaves the question window and opens the Item Review screen. From this screen you will see all the questions, your answers, and your marked items. You will also see the correct answers listed here when appropriate.
- **Show Answer**—This option displays the correct answer with an explanation of why it is correct. If you select this option, the current question is not scored.
- **Mark Item**—Check this box to tag a question you need to review further. You can view and navigate your Marked Items by clicking the Item Review button (if enabled). When grading your exam, you will be notified if you have marked items remaining.
- **Previous Item**—View the previous question.
- **Next Item**—View the next question.
- **Grade Exam**—When you have completed your exam, click this to end your exam and view your detailed score report. If you have unanswered or marked items remaining, you will be asked whether you would like to continue taking your exam or view your exam report.

Time Remaining

If the test is timed, the time remaining is displayed in the upper-right corner of the application screen. It counts down the minutes and seconds remaining to complete the test. If you run out of time, you will be asked whether you want to continue taking the test or whether you want to end your exam.

Your Examination Score Report

The Examination Score Report screen appears when the Practice Test mode ends—as the result of time expiration, completion of all questions, or your decision to terminate early.

This screen provides you with a graphical display of your test score with a breakdown of scores by topic domain. The graphical display at the top of the screen compares your overall score with the PrepLogic Exam Competency Score.

The PrepLogic Exam Competency Score reflects the level of subject competency required to pass this vendor's exam. Although this score does not directly translate to a passing score, consistently matching or exceeding this score does suggest you possess the knowledge to pass the actual vendor exam.

Reviewing Your Exam

From Your Score Report screen, you can review the exam you just completed by clicking the View Items button. Navigate through the items viewing the questions, your answers, the correct answers, and the explanations for those questions. You can return to your score report by clicking the View Items button.

Getting More Exams

Each *PrepLogic Practice Tests, Preview Edition* that accompanies your Training Guide contains a single PrepLogic Practice Test. Certification students worldwide trust PrepLogic Practice Tests to help them pass their IT certification exams the first time. Purchase the Premium Edition of PrepLogic Practice Tests and get the entire set of all-new challenging Practice Tests for this exam. PrepLogic Practice Tests – Because You Want to Pass the First Time.

Contacting PrepLogic

If you would like to contact PrepLogic for any reason, including information about our extensive line of certification practice tests, we invite you to do so. Please contact us online at `www.preplogic.com`.

Customer Service

If you have a damaged product and need a replacement or refund, please call the following phone number:

800-858-7674

Product Suggestions and Comments

We value your input! Please email your suggestions and comments to the following address:

`feedback@preplogic.com`

License Agreement

YOU MUST AGREE TO THE TERMS AND CONDITIONS OUTLINED IN THE END USER LICENSE AGREEMENT ("EULA") PRESENTED TO YOU DURING THE INSTALLATION PROCESS. IF YOU DO NOT AGREE TO THESE TERMS DO NOT INSTALL THE SOFTWARE.

Index

SYMBOLS

A

B

D

F

G - H

I

J- K

L

M

N

O

P

Q - R

S

T

W

X - Y - Z